Native American Autobiography

Wisconsin Studies in American Autobiography

William L. Andrews
General Editor

Edited by Arnold Krupat

Native American Autobiography

An Anthology

The University of Wisconsin Press

The University of Wisconsin Press
1930 Monroe Street, 3rd floor
Madison, Wisconsin 53711-2059

3 Henrietta Street
London WC2E 8LU, England

www.wisc.edu\wisconsinpress

Printed in the United States of America

Library of Congress Cataloging-in-Publication Data
Native American autobiography: an anthology / edited by Arnold Krupat.
560 p.   cm. — (Wisconsin studies in American autobiography)
Includes index.
ISBN 0-299-14020-2   ISBN 0-299-14024-5 (pbk.)
1. Indians of North America—Biography—History and criticism.
2. Autobiography—Indian authors. 3. Indians of North America—History.
4. American literature—Indian authors. I. Krupat, Arnold.
II. Series.
E89.N37   1994
970.004'970092—dc20
[B]   93-39068

Contents

Illustrations

Acknowledgments

I would like to thank William L. Andrews, H. David Brumble III, Paul John Eakin, and, in particular, Sylvan Esh, for his careful attention throughout the preparation of this book.

Native American Autobiography

Introduction

The genre of writing referred to in the West as *autobiography* had no close parallel in the traditional cultures of the indigenous inhabitants of the Americas, misnamed "Indians." Like people the world over, the tribes recorded various kinds of personal experience, but the western notion of representing the whole of any one person's life—from childhood through adolescence to adulthood and old age—was, in the most literal way, foreign to the cultures of the present-day United States. The high regard in which the modern West holds egocentric, autonomous individualism—the "auto" part of "autobiography"—found almost no parallel whatever in the communally oriented cultures of Native America.

Just as the "auto" part of "autobiography" was alien to Native understanding, so, too, was the "graph" part, for alphabetic writing was not present among the cultures of Native America. Tribal people were oral people who represented personal experience performatively and dramatically to an audience. Personal exploits might be presented pictographically (i.e., in tipi decorations or other types of drawing), but never in alphabetic writing. When, after considerable contact with the Euramerican invader-settlers, some Native people did attempt to offer extensive life histories, these made their way into writing in two distinct but related forms. One of these I refer to as "autobiographies by Indians," and the other as "Indian autobiographies."

Autobiographies by Indians are individually composed texts, and, like western autobiographies, they are indeed written by those whose lives they chronicle. For the Native American to become author of such a text requires that he—and later also she—must have become "educated" and "civilized" and, in the vast majority of cases, also Christianized. Indian autobiographies, as I have detailed the matter elsewhere, are not actually self-written, but are, rather, texts marked by the principle of original, bicultural composite composition. That is to say, these texts are the end-products of a rather complex process involving a three-part collaboration between a white editor-amanuensis who edits, polishes, revises, or otherwise fixes the "form" of the text in writing, a Native "subject" whose orally presented life story serves as the "content" of the autobiographical narrative, and, in almost all cases, a mixedblood interpreter/translator whose exact contribution to the autobiographical project remains one of the least un-

3

derstood aspects of Indian autobiography. Historically, Indian autobiographies have been produced under the sign of history and (social) science, while, with certain exceptions, autobiographies by Indians have been produced under the sign of religion, non-scientific cultural commentary, and art.

Both Indian autobiographies and autobiographies by Indians may be seen as the textual equivalent of the "frontier," as the discursive ground on which two extremely different cultures met and interacted. In this regard, Native American autobiography may usefully be studied for what it tells us about Native culture, Euramerican culture, the view each had of the other, and the shifting relations, i.e., the discursive/textual relations but also material relations of power, between them. In the multicultural age we all inhabit, self-life-writing by Indians—Native American autobiography—is important not only for its intrinsic interest, but also because it can provide a different, alternate, or, indeed, radically *other* perspective on the meaning of the terms ("self-life-writing") one cannot help but use in referring to it.

For example, Native American conceptions of the self tend toward integrative rather than oppositional relations with others. Whereas the modern West has tended to define personal identity as involving the successful mediation of an opposition between the individual and society, Native Americans have instead tended to define themselves as persons by successfully integrating themselves into the relevant social groupings—kin, clan, band, etc.—of their respective societies. On the Plains, to be sure, glory and honor were intensely sought by male warriors who wanted, individually, to be "great men," but even on the Plains, any personal greatness was important primarily for the good of "the people." These conceptions of the self may be viewed as "synecdochic," i.e., based on part-to-whole relations, rather than "metonymic," i.e., as in the part-to-part relations that most frequently dominate Euramerican autobiography.

In the same way that Native American autobiography can put the western concept of the self in perspective by making us see that what we have taken as only natural is, instead, a matter of cultural convention, so, too, can it offer a critical perspective on the western conception of the importance of writing. This is a subject that has occupied the attention of a great many theorists of late, perhaps because we are currently in a stage of transition to what Walter Ong has called a "secondary orality," a condition in which print media and writing certainly exist but do not occupy the social-functional position they held before the computer revolution.

Let me turn here to a brief historical sketch of Native American autobiography.

1

The earliest Native American autobiography I know is an autobiography by an Indian, by the Reverend Samson Occom, a Mohegan, who produced a short narrative of his life in 1768. In 1791, Hendrik Aupaumut, referred to as a "Mahican," included a good deal of what might be taken as autobiographical material in his *Journal of a Mission to the Western Tribes of Indians*. Neither of these texts was published in its author's lifetime, Occom's reposing for many years in the Dartmouth College Library before finally appearing in 1982, Aupaumut's seeing print—somewhat obscurely—in 1827. This latter date is perhaps not strictly an accident, for it was in the second quarter of the nineteenth century that American interest in the first-person life history (only recently, in 1808, named autobiography by the British poet Robert Southey) began to grow. Just two years after Aupaumut's work, the Reverend William Apess, a Pequot and a Methodist minister, published the first extended autobiography by an Indian to attract a relatively wide readership. Apess's *A Son of the Forest: The Experience of William Apess a Native of the Forest, Written by Himself*, appeared in 1829, and went through several editions in its author's lifetime. It is the christianized Indian's relation to Euramerican religion that thematically dominates the early period of autobiographies by Indians.

Only a few years after Apess's autobiography was published, there appeared in the West (Cincinnati) the first of those compositely produced texts I call Indian autobiographies. This was the *Life of Ma-ka-tai-she-me-kia-kiak, or Black Hawk*, the autobiography not of a Christian Indian but, rather, of a resisting Indian who came to public attention as a result of his military opposition to the encroachment of whites onto Indian lands. After being defeated in the Black Hawk War of 1832, the last Indian war to be fought (for the most part) east of the Mississippi, Black Hawk endured imprisonment and a public tour of the East before being allowed to return home. Once back on his ancestral lands on the Rock River in Illinois, he narrated the story of his life. Black Hawk was a traditionally-raised Sac and Fox person who did not speak English and did not write any language—nor is it clear, in the distinction proposed by Watson and Watson-Franke, whether his autobiography was "elicited or prompted by another person" or whether it was, instead, "self-initiated."[1] Indeed, this distinction itself, while logically tenable, is empirically almost impossible to apply. Black Hawk's editor, the young journalist J. B. Patterson, claimed that Black Hawk himself initiated the autobiographical project, but we also know that Black Hawk was much solicited by various Euramericans for the story of his life, and he may have been urged in this direction by Native people, too. In any case, even if the Native subject of an Indian autobiography was pressed to the task by a journalist, historian, or anthropologist, we now understand that only those Native persons who found such a task consistent with their own needs and desires eventually complied. This would be the case as well for autobiographies by Indians, for even these ostensibly "self-initiated" texts were not "initiated" in a vacuum, but in a cultural and historical context which "prompted" some Indians who could write about themselves to do so while others simply did not.

Although I believe that we can rarely know with any assurance the full motivation behind a given Indian autobiography, we can in many cases know something about what may be called its mode of production. Here, again, Black Hawk's autobiography is exemplary, for the text is one that comes into being through the collaborative labor of Black Hawk, who is its subject and the person to whom the "I" of the text refers; of Antoine LeClair, a mixedblood person who served as official government interpreter to the Sac and Fox Indians, and who transcribed and translated the old war chief's words into written English; and of J. B. Patterson, who ultimately "edits"—inscribes and fixes in writing—the text we read as "Black Hawk's autobiography." What kind of transcription LeClair must have made, in that age before the tape recorder, we do not know, nor do we know what kind of English LeClair would have written by way of translation, inasmuch as no notes or transcripts seem to have survived.

It is reasonable to imagine, however, that LeClair presented Patterson with a text in what has since been called "Red English," the English that Native people with little or no formal schooling speak and sometimes write. In the absence of a text from LeClair, it may be useful to cite an autobiographical text roughly contemporary with his—one which, like Black Hawk's story, is more a military memoir (in this case, of the American Revolution and the War of 1812) than a personal narrative. I quote here a brief passage from the autobiography of

1. Lawrence Watson and Maria Barbara Watson-Franke, *Interpreting Life Histories* (New Brunswick, NJ: Rutgers Univ. Press, 1985), p. 2.

Chainbreaker, also known to the whites as Governor Blacksnake. Somewhere between the years 1833 and 1843, when he was ninety or a hundred years old, Chainbreaker told his story to Benjamin Williams, who was nearly fifty years his junior and, like Chainbreaker, a Seneca. Williams' manuscript was not taken up by an editor until very recently (1989), when Thomas Abler prepared it for print. Abler's editing, however, is very different from that of J. B. Patterson, in that he has not transformed Williams' text into standard English, as Patterson almost surely did for LeClair's text. In the quotation below, the square brackets are Abler's additions:

> The year [1799] Certifies that from a personal Acquanted called good lake—that year he was Sick Confined on his bed he was not able to Rise from the bed and it hapen one morning He was called to Rise and go to Door. He Did So—Saw three [or four?—both have been written] person Standing by the Door And Take hands with him all—and comminced That he felt Vend [faint] and fall down on the ground By theirs feets and lost his Senses. . . .[2]

What I would have the reader consider is that there are, broadly speaking, two ways to read this sort of text. One way is to take it as a rather pathetic approximation of the conventional standard of educated authors. The other is to take it not so much as *failed* English but as an invention, a hybrid or creolized language *based on* English. Standard English provides a vocabulary and a set of grammatical rules, which, on the one hand, may have been imperfectly mastered but which, on the other, may simply have been adapted, creatively manipulated for the purposes at hand, and, of course, manipulated in relation to the writer's prior familiarity with another language (Seneca).

I do not for a moment suggest that Benjamin Williams was consciously engaged in inventive experimentation, nor does it seem likely to me that, if we did have a manuscript from Antoine LeClair, we would necessarily find it a shining example of the creative transformation of English. I do, however, suggest that the reader worry less about the formal "errors" of this English and try to imagine more the Indian linguistic modes that it may convey. Like Black Hawk's autobiography, many of the Indian autobiographies we read in "good" English have some intermediate version—intermediate between

2. *Chainbreaker: The Revolutionary War Memoirs of Governor Blacksnake*, as told to Benjamin Williams (Lincoln: Univ. of Nebraska Press, 1989), p. 210.

speech in a Native language and *writing* in standard English—that exists, or once existed, in some variant of this written "Red English," or "Reservation English."

One version or another of the triangulated textual generation of Black Hawk's autobiography—Indian subject, mixedblood interpreter/translator, Euramerican editor/amanuensis—became standard for the texts I call Indian autobiographies; and it is important to keep in mind the very particular mode of production of these texts, because it bears, among other things, upon the virtually irresistible question of whether or to what degree Indian autobiographies give us the "real" or "authentic" Indian.

To open this question is potentially to lead the reader into a patch of theoretical thorns. One line of thought urges that we give up entirely the desire for "reference," the desire to encounter the "real" Black Hawk and other persons we know to have existed outside of and beyond the words of their autobiographical texts, but whom we can only know through the words of those and other texts. Another, oppositional, line of thought insists upon the referentiality of the autobiographical text, admitting that, while the language of the text inevitably mediates our encounter with the real, historical subject of the autobiography, still, the abiding appeal of autobiography is exactly the sense we have of an encounter with lives other than and apart from our own. If the former view insists that any feel for the real is only a produced effect of language, the latter tends to insist upon the autobiographical "pact" between writer and reader involving a conventionally-prescribed commitment to tell the "truth," albeit in words. I incline to the latter view while taking very seriously the warnings of the former as to the inevitable disparities between—in the terms of Michel Foucault—the order of words and the order of things.

As I have noted above, the Indian autobiography in its first manifestations appears as a historical document of the nineteenth century, as whites urge Indians who had resisted the "advance" of "civilization" to tell their story and explain their resistance. Interest in the resisting Indian, the world-historical chief or warrior, would persist well into the twentieth century, no longer as a "dominant" societal concern, in Raymond Williams' sense, but as a "residual" one. From early in the twentieth century, Native persons were approached for their life stories not because they had uniquely distinguished themselves in war or diplomacy or any other public or historical activity, but because they were considered "representative" of their culture, persons who might be attended to precisely because they were *not* extraordinary, because they were *not* among those great men whose biographies, as Thomas Carlyle had put it, comprised what we call history. Rather, as Paul Radin said of the informant he named "Crashing Thunder," the appropriate subject of the anthropological life history would more nearly be "a representative middle-aged individual of moderate ability," one who could "describe his life in relation to the social group in which he had grown up."[3]

In an approximately parallel fashion, autobiographies by Indians in the late nineteenth and early twentieth century may be said to shift their emphasis from a relation to Euramerican religion to a relation to Euramerican culture and society, as in the texts of Charles Alexander Eastman, Gertrude Bonnin, and Luther Standing Bear, among others. These Native writers spoke for the ongoing value of traditional tribal ways, while generally accepting many of the values of the dominant "civilization."

It is clearly social science, in the form of an anthropological interest in the professionally and academically defined categories of culture and culture-and-personality that dominates the production of Indian autobiographies from about 1913 (the date of Paul Radin's first Winnebago autobiography) into at least the early 1940s, when Franz Boas, the dominant figure in American anthropology for half a century, called life histories of use only for illustrating the "perversion of truth by the play of memory with the past."[4] Parallel to the work of the professional anthropologists in this period, however, are the efforts of "amateurs" — journalists, westerners, and devotees of things Indian — in obtaining the life stories of warriors like Wooden Leg, who participated in the Custer fight (1876), Yellow Wolf, who was part of the "flight" of the Nez Perces (1877), and Plenty-Coups, chief of the Crow, among other aged Natives who saw and made "history."

Although non-Natives continue to this day to produce Indian autobiographies in collaboration with Native people, the most noted Native American autobiographies of late have been autobiographies by Indians, the self-written texts of Native people who first came to public notice as artists, as writers of poetry and fiction. I am thinking foremost of N. Scott Momaday, whose 1969 Pulitzer Prize for the novel *House Made of Dawn* ushered in the contemporary "Native American Renaissance" in written literature. Momaday's two autobi-

3. *The Autobiography of a Winnebago Indian* (New York: Dover, 1963), p. 2.
4. Franz Boas, "Recent Anthropology II," *Science* 98 (1943): 335.

ographies, *The Way to Rainy Mountain* (1969), in which oral and tribal histories are combined with the author's personal history, and *The Names* (1976), in which reflections on this personal history are combined with passages of modernist prose-poetry and family photographs, are widely known and have been widely influential. They have, for example, influenced Leslie Marmon Silko, whose novel *Ceremony* (1977) first brought her to the attention of the dominant culture, and whose loosely autobiographical text, *Storyteller* (1981), includes not only photographs of the author and her family, but short stories and poems as well. At least one anthology of autobiographical statements by Native-American writers currently exists, and there are several collections of interviews with Native American artists which provide a good deal of autobiographical reflection. Most recently, the mixedblood Chippewa novelist and poet Gerald Vizenor has produced a substantial body of autobiographical writing.

2

I have already, in passing, referred to several of the terms that structure this anthology, and I will now try to comment on them in a more detailed fashion. It has often been said that any anthology is an act of criticism, that an editor, by her or his selection of writers and by the arrangement of these selections, asserts not merely personal taste but a set of critical principles. This is most certainly the case for the present anthology—as indeed, it must acutely be the case for any anthology of non-canonical texts. This matter of the canon has been much discussed of late, so I will only remark here that the term refers to those texts which are taken by general consensus to be the texts of major importance. This general consensus is asserted and affirmed pedagogically, so that typical reading lists of "American literature" in the schools, colleges, and universities of the United States overlap to a very great degree. Whether one speaks of the "best" or the most "relevant" books—and these terms are not complementary or interchangeable—the canonical texts are the ones that publishers, reviewers, teachers, "educated people," and government agencies (e.g., the National Endowment for the Humanities) presume to be those that count most. While various canons are currently in the process of being challenged, almost any "educated person" (the kind of education one undergoes to become an "educated person" virtually assures this) will come up with a fairly predictable set of authors and titles when asked for the canon of say, nineteenth-century American literature, or British romanticism. But this is not yet the case when one is asked to name the authors and titles of the canon of Native American literature, or, our particular concern here, of Native American autobiography.

Inasmuch as the verbal expression of indigenous people is in the first full stages of development, a general consensus, even an embattled one, does not exist regarding which examples of that expression are the most "important." The exception to this statement, of course, is the case of contemporary Native American fiction, where, since N. Scott Momaday's Pulitzer Prize for *House Made of Dawn* (1968), Momaday, Leslie Marmon Silko, James Welch, and, most recently, Louise Erdrich have become the canonical Indian novelists, with attention to Gerald Vizenor growing day by day. But so far as our subject, Native American autobiography, is concerned, there is no broadly agreed-upon body of major or canonical texts. Of course, it is quite possible to note, as I shall below, that *Black Elk Speaks* is probably the most widely known of Native American autobiographies, as, in a somewhat more specialized context, it is possible to say that a good number of anthropologists probably know or at least know of Paul Radin's *Crashing Thunder: The Autobiography of an American Indian.* In the same way, the autobiographies edited by Walter Dyk, Ruth Underhill, and Leo Simmons are more or less well-known among social scientists. Among contemporary autobiographies, Momaday's *The Way to Rainy Mountain* and *The Names*, as I have noted, are probably a good deal more familiar to the "general reading public" than any number of other autobiographical texts by Native writers. But beyond these few titles, the "necessary" texts, i.e., the *canon* of Native American autobiography, simply has not been established.

Thus, my choices for this anthology, and my ordering of them, cannot be justified by an appeal to common consensus. To be sure, some of my choices are fairly "safe"—"no common consensus" does not signify a complete absence of agreement—but other choices, including my organization of the whole, need to be explained and, so far as possible, justified. Although I agree with the Native historian and poet Jack Forbes that *"Native American literature is an international body of literature,"* one that is *"hemispheric in dimension,"*[5] I have not been

---

5. Jack Forbes, "Colonialism and Native American Literature: Analysis," *Wicazo Sa Review* 3 (1987): 17–23.

11

able to reflect the hemispheric/international range of Native American autobiography in this volume. The Spanish Americas are completely missing and there is very little from north of the border. I plead practical considerations for these omissions. This is already a large volume and it would have had to be double its present size to include Mexico, South and Central America, etc. Perhaps a second volume will fill this gap.

With respect to the material I have selected and my arrangement of the volume as a whole, let me say the following. With the exception of Part One, I have generally followed a chronological order from the eighteenth century to the present. In parts Two and Three, which present Native American autobiographies of the eighteenth and nineteenth centuries, I have taken Native "response" to the white invaders—i.e., the decisions to become Christian or resisting Indians—as a useful ordering principle. My decision here may be criticized for ethnocentrism, since, even though the response is *Indian*, it is the Euramerican invaders who are represented as acting, with Native peoples re-acting. The only answer to such a charge is that history did, in fact, happen this way. From perhaps the sixteenth century in the Southwest, and from early in the seventeenth century on the East Coast, in the Mid-Atlantic and the Southeast, Native Americans had to factor into their lives the presence and pressures of an increasingly numerous, highly aggressive group of new arrivals. This is not to say that Native people stopped doing most of what they had always done, or that they adopted a new center to their lives. It is to say that for many of the Native persons who came to the autobiographical project, their lives could not be recounted independently of some relation-reaction to the encroaching whites. (The exceptions to this generalization have their life stories grouped in Part One, "Traditional Lives," about which I shall have more to say below.) In the excerpts both from the converts' and the combatants' life histories, I have tried to present, in whatever measure possible, some sense of both the ongoing, uninterrupted quality of these lives and the temporally specific, new, and unprecedented reactiveness of these lives.

For all that I have taken acceptance or rejection of Christianity and Euramerican "civilization" as providing useful distinctions among eighteenth- and nineteenth-century Native American autobiographies, it is hardly the case that these categories account for all the Indian lives written during this period. Paul Cuffe's brief autobiography (1839), for example, tells the story of a part-black, part-Indian seaman who shows no particular interest in Christianity, and active resistance to white dominance in Cuffe's New York of the 1830s was altogether a thing of the past. Something similar would be true for the Seneca Chainbreaker, also known as Governor Blacksnake, whom I have mentioned above: his life could not, no more than Paul Cuffe's, easily be thematized in terms of a resistance to or acceptance of Christianity and "civilization." We could also say much the same sort of thing of Okah Tubbee, part black and part Choctaw, whose extraordinary story of his life in Mississippi was published in 1848.

With regard to those many Native American autobiographers for whom my Christian/resisting distinction accounts relatively well, it should not be thought that either acceptance or resistance can directly be translated into some version of treason or heroism. While an older climate of opinion would have approved the converts and scorned or pitied the traditionalists, it is more likely, these days, that the reader's sympathies will lie with the resisters rather than with the Christian Indians. Such good/bad or hero/traitor judgments will do no service to the particular persons and texts involved, regardless of the criteria for "goodness," "heroism," or their presumed antitheses.

William Apess, for example, while a passionate convert to Methodism, was equally passionate as an activist for Native American rights, and in his denunciation of racism in all its forms. Along with his autobiographical texts, he published a "Eulogy on King Philip," which named this warrior chief of the Pequots the greatest man that America ever produced. In a later day, Charles Alexander Eastman, a university and medical school graduate and youthful practicioner ministering to the Lakota at Wounded Knee, for all his movement "from the deep woods to civilization," fought tirelessly for the recognition of the worth of traditional Native American values. His autobiographies are structured in a manner easily recognizable to Euramericans as rags-to-riches success stories of the type frequently associated with the name of Horatio Alger, but they are equally structured (if perhaps more loosely and less recognizably) according to a fairly widespread Native use of what Robin McGrath, in her comments on Inuit Eskimo autobiography, refers to as "a sort of male Cinderella."[6] This figure is represented by "the orphan boy Kaujjarkuk" among the Inuit and by other traditionally known protagonists among other Native peoples. Eastman's "baby name" in Lakota (Sioux) was Hakada, "the pitiful

---

6. Robin McGrath, "Oral Influences in Contemporary Inuit Literature," in *The Native in Literature: Canadian and Comparative Perspectives*, ed. Thomas King, Cheryl Calver, and Helen Hoy (Oakville, Ontario: ECW Press, 1987), p. 161.

last [of five children]." From the victory at lacrosse that won him the name of Ohiyesa, "the winner," to his success as a kind of young warrior in the white man's world, Eastman's narrative of his rise to prominence has traditional Native as well as Euramerican models.

This may also be the place to say that the reader should not assume that persons named "Wooden Leg" or "Black Elk" are somehow "more Indian" or "authentic" than persons named "William Apess," "Charles Alexander Eastman," or "Maria Chona." Eastman, as I have just noted, was also known as "Ohiyesa," although he did not publish under that name — as Zitkala Ša was also Gertrude Bonnin, or, indeed, the great Sequoyah, inventor of the Cherokee syllabary, was also George Guess, and as the Paiute Wovoka, initiator of the Ghost Dance religion, was also Jack Wilson. We need to recall that the Spanish in the Southwest tended to bestow names familiar to them, names, for example, like Maria Chona, rather than — as the English did at least sometimes — to translate names from the Indian, e.g., "Chainbreaker" or "Black Hawk."

Once the West was "won," and the "frontier" closed, Indian acceptance or rejection of "civilization" was no longer an issue of historical concern for Americans; rather, the only issue seemed to be whether the Indian would "vanish" or survive. For the American Indian to survive, it was assumed that he or she would have to become the Indian-American, and, like other hyphenate Americans (Italian-American, Chinese-American, etc.), be melted into general Christian, bourgeois, capitalist citizenship. Government policy toward Native people in this period was founded on the Dawes or General Allotment Act of 1887, which sought to destroy tribal culture by an attack on the tribally (e.g., communally, "communistically") held landbase. The project was, in many ways, a continuation of the effort, in a phrase of Captain Richard Pratt, founder of the Carlisle Indian school, to "Kill the Indian and Save the Man." The autobiographical texts in Part Four of the anthology, "The Closed Frontier," provide personal responses to this exceedingly difficult — some have called it "transitional" — time for Native American people.

One response to the generally accepted notion that the Indian as Indian could not survive was what came to be called "salvage anthropology," a determined effort on the part of professional anthropologists to document the record of cultures presumably slated for oblivion. This led to those Indian autobiographies I have grouped under the heading for Part Five, "The Anthropologists' Indians." Here, again, it needs to be said that such a phrase is not meant to imply in any way that the Native people who complied with the anthropologists' request to "tell the story of their life" somehow betrayed themselves or their culture, yielding themselves up to alien purposes. To the contrary, the more these matters have been studied of late, the more it has become apparent that the Native subjects of the anthropologists' life histories had their own purposes for engaging in the autobiographical project; they "used" the anthropologists to the same or even greater extent than the anthropologists "used" them.

While the professional anthropologists were interested in Indians as the embodiment of a particular culture, there remained, as I have said, a number of amateurs who were still interested in those surviving Native people who had, indeed, made "history." Their labors resulted in the composite composition of such Indian autobiographies as those of Yellow Wolf, Wooden Leg, and Geronimo, among many others. Although the "resisting Indians" had resisted somewhere between 1832 and 1890, many accounts of their resistance did not appear until the 1930s, a period marked by intense concern to overturn the materially and culturally destructive Dawes Act. The Merriam Report of 1928 severely criticized federal Indian policy, and, upon Franklin Roosevelt's election to the presidency, major changes were instituted. Roosevelt's appointment of John Collier, a strong and knowledgeable admirer of Native American cultures, led to the passage in 1934 of the Wheeler-Howard Act, (also called the Indian Reorganization Act), which gave Native Americans an opportunity to decide for themselves how they would live. Their decision, unfortunately, had to be made known to the federal government by parliamentary means that were untraditional, and, indeed, to many Native people repugnant; nonetheless, for all its defects, Wheeler-Howard was a clear admission on the part of the federal government of the worth and potential viability of Native cultures.

Since Wheeler-Howard, government policy toward the Indians has steered an uneven course, so uneven as not at all to have resolved, but, rather, to have exacerbated some of the deep-seated confusions and ambiguities the dominant American society has long felt toward the Indian. In the 1950s, "termination"—an ominous word—was the guiding policy, enunciating the de-termination of the federal government to end its treaty-bound relations and obligations to the tribes. Like most federal Indian policy, this had the encouragement both of those who wished to see the Indian "independent" and strong in the modern world and of those who wished to be done with an inconvenient burden. More recently, at least since 1968, the watchwords have been "self-determination" and "civil rights," although for all the positive connotations of these terms, their operative meaning has been somewhat ambiguous.

Whatever the Native person on the "rez"—the reservation—may have felt or experienced as a result of the shifts and changes in government policy, the talented Native writer living mostly off the "rez" has been able to find the resources to produce some very extraordinary work. Momaday's Pulitzer in 1969 does indeed seem to have initiated or perhaps only highlighted a "Native American Renaissance" in the writing of fiction and poetry. Thus the autobiographies of mixed-blood Native American writers appear in Part Six of the anthology.

Part Seven, the final section of the anthology, is called "Traditional Lives Today," a title which refers back, of course, to Part One, "Traditional Lives." In the same way as the texts that appear in Part One are out of chronological order, so, too, is my explanation of the rationale for beginning this anthology in the way I have.

To have stuck to strict chronology from beginning to end would have meant beginning with some eighteenth-century autobiographies by Christian Indians, for these are the earliest Native American autobiographies in existence. But for any reader opening the book in the hope of discovering a distinctively Native life-experience, first encounters with Samson Occom, Catharine Brown, and their contemporaries was certain to be off-putting. Inasmuch as earlier texts of Native lives simply do not exist, any attempt to convey a sense of traditional lives—Native lives not governed by Christian belief and western "civilization"—was bound to be a risky business. Still, to try to imagine what those lives might have been like seemed a risk worth taking, and it is a risk that involves the attempt to infer from later texts what the earlier texts by traditional people that we do not have might have told us. I develop the issues involved in such inferences more fully in the introduction to Part One of the anthology.

Part Seven, "Traditional Lives Today," the concluding section of the anthology, offers life histories of tribal people who are intimately acquainted with the ways of the dominant, non-Indian culture but whose lives are nonetheless guided by traditional values. It seemed particularly important to conclude with such a section, because of the testimony it provides that Native people and Native lifeways have not only not vanished but are, locally and particularly, flourishing. (This is also true of a number of Native languages.) Angela Sidney and Peter Kalifornsky are not, to be sure, as well known to the general American public as N. Scott Momaday and Leslie Marmon Silko, but any consideration of Native American autobiography today must include them also.

Finally, let me alert the reader to what she or he will quickly enough notice. Although this is an anthology that is intended for use in the schools, it is nonetheless a *critical* anthology. This is to say that I have not tried to be all things to all people, and I have not suppressed my own judgments and evaluations of the materials under consideration. These are *informed* judgments and evaluations, but they are not necessarily consensual or authoritative judgments and evaluations. Whereas the usual school anthology tries to put the best face on everything, pretending to objectivity, I have allowed myself to be *opinionated*. Nothing would please me more than to have students and teachers argue and disagree with me. In an area that is relatively undeveloped critically, i.e., the area of Indian literatures generally and of Native American autobiography in particular, there is a great need for honest debate. This anthology, if it inevitably leaves much out, also brings to the reader a wealth of materials that have never before been gathered all in one place. I invite teachers and students to consider these rich accounts of the lives of indigenous people.

New York, 1992

Part 1
Traditional Lives

We simply do not know what Native peoples' stories of their lives would "really" have been like in the distant past, before the arrival of the Europeans. To make that point, I half-seriously suggested to the publisher that the first section of this volume should consist of blank pages—a tough rather than an easy reading assignment for students who may use the book! But, of course, there is no need to be so absolute about the matter. Indigenous cultures, because they were *oral* cultures, were always conservative, emphasizing continuity even as they adaptively changed. Thus, we can with some justification attempt informed guesses, from the records we do have, about what we do not have.

With regard to this matter, H. David Brumble describes what he calls "Preliterate Traditions of American Indian Autobiography,"[1] and Hertha Wong writes of "Pre-Contact Oral and Pictographic Autobiographical Narratives."[2] I am unhappy with both these terms because "pre-literate" privileges literacy as the positive entity, while "pre-contact" privileges contact as the defining event. I have, therefore, opted for the rather bland "traditional" in referring to the lives represented in this section; still, both Brumble and Wong point usefully to existing forms of self-reference that probably have important connections to earlier forms. Wong singles out "coup tales, vision stories, and naming practices," while Brumble has elaborated six categories which he calls the coup tales, "informal autobiographical tales" (usually of "war and the hunt"), self-examinations, self-vindications, educational narratives, and stories of the acquisition of powers. As Brumble himself notes, these categories overlap; in any case, as he remarks in commenting on the life of the Crow warrior Two Leggings, we don't really have "the story of his life, but rather the stories of his life."[3]

Stories, it should be said, are extremely important to the autobiographical accounts of traditional people. In an oral culture, as Walter Ong has written, "Categories are mnemonically unstable. Stories you

1. H. David Brumble, *American Indian Autobiography* (Berkeley: Univ. of California Press, 1988).
2. Hertha Wong, *Sending My Heart Back Across the Years: Tradition and Innovation in Native American Autobiography* (New York: Oxford Univ. Press, 1992).
3. Brumble, *Autobiography*, p. 37.

can remember."[4] On the one hand, this means that Native autobiographers will typically cast their personal experience into the form of a story (i.e., they won't offer abstract interpretations or evaluations but present a continuous narrative), and, on the other, it means that they may tell a traditional story—about a bear or hummingbird or a set of twins—as a way of conveying an experience of their own. The story may not seem to be *about* them—in fact, it is actually about someone else—but it nonetheless speaks *of* them.

Chronology, we should note, is a "category," and as such it does not, in traditional narrative, play anything like the important part it plays in western personal narrative. If childhood, or, as in Aua's account, prenatal experience is narrated, this is not in order "to begin at the beginning" as we would say; rather, it is because something important *happened* at that period. Although many editors have adopted what Brumble calls the Chronological Imperative to make the narrative more accessible to non-Indian readers, a great many autobiographical accounts by Native people were not actually told in chronological order.

The stories of Indian lives that the reader will find in this section, had they actually been presented to a Native audience, would have been *public* and *occasional*. They would have been public in that oral or spoken narrative is always oral-aural, from someone's mouth to someone's ear—or, in regard to the recitation of important matters, the ears of many. Speech, then, is directed to a specific audience, or public. And it is directed to this public on specific, culturally prescribed occasions when members of the community would gather to celebrate brave deeds in battle, to learn of dreams or visions that promised specific powers, or to judge the value of self-examinations or vindications, in Brumble's terms. The speaker would narrate his experience and the audience would carefully attend to it because the achievements or, indeed, failures of any given individual were important to the survival and good fortune of the community as a whole. Thus, for example, in the case of the formal recitation of a warrior's coups—his striking or touching of the enemy in battle—persons who had witnessed the deeds in question were expected to be present and to confirm or deny the account given. Self-examinations would be offered to explain failure in battle (as, for example, in the case of Two Leggings, below) or illness; self-vindications would be occasioned by

4. Walter Ong, "Writing Is a Technology that Restructures Thought," in *The Written Word: Literacy in Transition*, ed. Gerd Bauman (New York: Oxford Univ. Press, 1986), p. 25.

charges raised, such as witchcraft. In all of these cases, one's kin and one's acquaintances—almost everyone, that is—would have a stake in the "autobiographical" narration. As for dreams and visions, because these were for the people as a whole, not only for the individual dreamer, they might need to be publicly enacted and performed, as in the well-known case of Black Elk's great vision (see below, Part Three).

Finally, we need to remember that the effective power and meaning of oral narration, and so of these personal accounts, are not a matter of words alone. Words were often accompanied by physical movements, on the part of the audience as well as the speaker. People gestured as they spoke, or they danced; drumming might take place; and wives of the warriors sometimes helped them re-enact their coups. Powerful as the words on the page may be, they give us only a part of what any full performance would have presented.

We begin this section with the story of the Mandan warrior Crows Heart, who tells in striking fashion of the self-torture he underwent to gain power. Two Leggings, a Crow, also fasted, sacrificed his flesh, and otherwise endured difficult conditions to acquire the powerful songs or visions that promised success in warfare or raiding. Two Leggings' account is most extraordinary, perhaps, for its admission of relative failure; for all his ambition, Two Leggings did not become the great man he desired to be. Then, Aua's brief account puts us for a moment in touch with the shamanic world, of the ability to see and to heal beyond the ability of other men. Finally, we have the account of the Tubatulabal woman FP, Frances Philips. No warrior or shaman, FP nonetheless appears to see the world very nearly as her ancestors might have seen it. Hers is at once a twentieth-century autobiography —all of these texts were produced in the twentieth century—and yet, so it seems to me, one with a much older feel, very much an account of a "traditional life."

1
Crows Heart's Reminiscences and Personal Experiences

Edited by

ALFRED E. BOWERS

Crows Heart, born about 1858, was a Mandan warrior who served as one of Alfred E. Bowers' principal informants during Bowers' fieldwork among the Mandan in 1930 and 1931. Crows Heart's short autobiography, "Crows Heart's Reminiscences and Personal Experiences," appears as pages 169–73 in Part II, "Introduction to Mandan Ceremonialism," of Bowers' Mandan Social and Ceremonial Organization.[1] *Inasmuch as Crows Heart's life story came into being at the request of an anthropologist, it could well appear in Part Five of this book, "The Anthropologists' Indians" rather than in this opening section, something that is true of the other selections in this section as well.*

I offer it here because it seems to me to present a worldview and a set of actions that, in spite of Bowers' presence among the Mandan, have very little to do with the Euramerican world. The hunting, eagle trapping, fasting, vision seeking, self-torture, and the warfare with the Sioux that Crows Heart tells of, so far as one can judge these things—and in spite of the references to Custer that mark the year as 1876—are all very traditionally Mandan. Or to be more ethnographically accurate, they are Mandan with an admixture of Hidatsa, Arikara, and Crow, all peoples who shared friendship and a number of similar cultural traits with the Mandan.

The Mandan were (there are Mandan today, although eighty percent of the population was wiped out by a smallpox epidemic in 1837, and although, in 1910, the Mandan numbered only 197 persons) a sedentary tribe of the Upper Missouri Valley who lived in permanent dwellings inside large fortified villages. Originating in the Southeast, and with many of the agricultural habits of the southeastern tribes, they also adopted, as they moved north and west, traits of the Woodlands and, especially, the Plains tribes. The subjects that Crows Heart covers are the traditional matters of importance to Mandan males. The phrase to "kick the stone" in his narrative means to lose a warrior

1. *Mandan Social and Ceremonial Organization,* by Alfred E. Bowers (Chicago: Univ. of Chicago Press, 1950). The selection here is reprinted by permission of the University of Chicago Press. Copyright 1950 by the University of Chicago.

in battle. For the "Old Wolf," or raid leader, to "kick the stone" once was a serious matter; to do so twice, however, disqualified him from ever leading a war party again.

Alfred E. Bowers, from whose account Crows Heart's story is taken, was born in Canada in 1901. He became a naturalized American citizen and completed a Ph.D. in anthropology at the University of Chicago in 1948. Along with his interests in the Mandan and Hidatsa, Bowers worked with the Mimbres people of Mexico. He concluded his distinguished career with a long tenure at the University of Idaho. Bracketed and parenthetical materials are from Bowers.

When a man has a real dream, everything that is going to happen comes to him in his dream. Hairy Coat [owner of a People Above bundle], fasted nine days and everything he did came to him in his dreams. An animal came to him in his dream and said, "You have suffered long enough, and I am going to send you home now. I will give you one enemy, and you can go out and bring in his scalp." The Mandan did all this fasting to get scalps just as you white men are always working to get money.

I was twenty-three years old when I first went out to trap eagles. When the lodge was ready, the men went in. That night I knew the leader would suggest that someone should suffer for the birds. That day I looked around and found a sharp bank. On top of the bank I drove a sharp stake and tied a long lariat to it as securely as I could. I knew that the Old Male Black Bear [leader of eagle-trapping party] would suggest that I go out on the top of the hills to cry as long as I could, so I did this to be ready. When I finished driving the stake, I came back and got two men of my father's clan, one being the Good Shot, to go out with me to cut holes through the skin of my chest with an arrow and insert two sticks each two inches long through the holes. After they did it, they said the bank was too high to get down alone and that they would put the rope around my breast to let me down. I told them to leave me alone and go back to camp.

When they left, the lariat [30–35 feet long] was coiled up by the stake. I crawled over the edge and fell to the end of the rope. I got such a jerk that I lost my senses. When I came to, I found myself still hanging down. I cried and ran until I made a trail along the sharp edge. Then the weight became less painful.

That night there was a heavy frost. I cried all the time. I kept running, and it was very cold. I began at dark and suffered until about ten o'clock, when two of the hunters came after me. When they got there, they caught the rope and pulled me up to the top. They tried to take the sticks out, but the swellings were so great that they could not get them loose. I had to carry the rope and sticks in my arms to camp.

When we got there, the head man laid me up where the buffalo skull was. He used a big bunch of buffalo hair to thaw out the swelling, and then the sticks came out. After the sticks were out, I went back to bed, but the swelling extended from my navel to my chin. I rolled without sleeping until nearly daybreak. I could not sleep, so I got up early to see the flag on the hill. I wanted to see if we had the right kind of wind to go to the pits.

I found that we had the right kind of wind, came back to camp, wakened the others, and told them the wind was in the west, the right direction for trapping. My breast was so swollen I had to put the rope for carrying the bait around my forehead when walking to the pit. I put my bait where it was supposed to be and sat there in the pit looking up through the covering. Soon I heard a noise and looked up. There was a large eagle coming down. He sat on top of my bait, and I stuck my right hand out and caught him. He was a big beautiful eagle, and that was the result I got for my suffering the night before. Before I finished killing him, another big one came down on top of my pit and walked over to the bait. I caught him as I had the other one and pulled him into the pit where I killed him, and there was never a happier person than I. I forgot all about my pains. I was happy as I thought of what I had done the night before. I did not have to go very far to get results for the suffering I did the night before. After that the leader said, since I was lucky, I should get up mornings and look at the flag to see if the winds were right.

If a man goes out on the hills to fast and suffer and some holy person or animal comes to him and tells him that he will be lucky and kill an enemy, but when he goes out as leader, the enemy kills one of his party instead, he will come home crying because the people will think that he didn't fast right or that his dream wasn't real. Brave men will start fasting again and seek an even stronger god by fasting longer and offering their flesh to the Sun. The older men watch one who has lost a warrior when he fasts. If the suffering is too severe, men of his father's clan pay him to stop for fear that he will kill himself. After he has suffered a while, the parents of the warrior who was killed in battle will give a feast to the man and ask him to stop. When a leader goes out to war as a result of the promise of a certain animal and loses one of his men, he will reject that animal's vision instructions if sent to

25

Bird's-eye view of a Mandan Village, 1800 miles above St. Louis, ca. 1837–1839. Painting by George Catlin. Courtesy of the National Museum of American Art, Smithsonian Institution. Gift of Mrs. Joseph Harrison, Jr.

him again in a dream. He will keep on fasting until another god comes to him. It is often hard to get men to follow an unlucky leader. If he goes out a second time and kills or strikes an enemy, the people will say, "You have a real protector now, one that is going to be a great help to you."

My god is the horse. When I was a young man, I led a horse around the sacred cedar standing in the center of Like-a-Fishhook Village by means of thongs in my flesh until I fell down unconscious. As I lay there, a horse came to me and promised me success in hunting and warfare. I killed two enemies a long ways from home because of this dream. The horse sang me his sacred songs, but I am not allowed to sing them for you. I have done all the things the horse asked of me, and the horse has done everything he promised me he would. The doctoring you saw me do did not come from the instructions the horse gave me. The sharp stick I used for letting out matter came from my rights in the Big Bird ceremony my sisters and I bought of Big Black, my father's brother.

I can illustrate by a story how a man organizes a war party to go out for the enemy that his god has promised him. The leader is careful to do just as he was instructed.

The party was to leave from Fishhook Village. The leaders were Old Bear (Tamisik clan), Crows Breast (Tamisik clan), and Porcupine Head (Speckled Eagle clan). I joined the party because of a suggestion by Afraid To Be Chief [his mother's brother and head of the lodge at that time] that he had no horses. If we got horses, we would be pretty well fixed. When a party of this kind is made up, they do not announce it but act quietly in preparation for the trip. A night was set to leave. Those planning to join got together a supply of moccasins and food. A lodge was designated as our meeting place. The party met this time in Two Chiefs' lodge. Others came to look on and wish us luck so that the lodge was packed full of people.

In addition to the leaders mentioned already, there were these warriors in the party: Big Steal (Tamisik clan), Long Tail (Prairie Chicken clan), Afraid To Be Chief (Prairie Chicken clan), Raven Turns (WaxikEna clan), Bear Chief (Prairie Chicken clan), Short Bears Teeth (Tamisik clan), Crows Heart (Prairie Chicken clan), Tree Bark (Tamisik clan), and Crow (Prairie Chicken clan).

We met at Two Chiefs' lodge, since he was a brother-in-law of Crows Breast, one of the Old Wolves. We had enough bullboats in readiness to carry the party down the river. It was planned that the party should sing the songs belonging to the whole group before leaving. All of us wore a white piece of cloth for a headgear and a white cloak reaching to the knees. While singing the songs, we made a noise by "hitting the mouth"; this brought a great crowd of onlookers. While we were singing, a heavy shower of rain fell, and water ran everywhere in small torrents. The leaders decided not to go that night; they would wait until the next evening just at sunset.

When the schedule was changed, each of us took up his medicine bundle and equipment and left the lodge. Upon reaching our earth lodge, I lay aside my medicine bag and moccasins and went out of the village to attend to my horses. While there I met an Hidatsa named Puts Away His Hair, who said he was organizing a war party of his own and wanted me to go along as a Young Wolf [scout].

He said, "When I was making the ceremony, my gods gave me one tepee at a place called Cedars Facing Each Other [southwest of the present town of Dickinson, North Dakota]."

When he said that, I was undecided what to do. I thought it over for a long time and finally decided to go with him as a Young Wolf. I had already left a bullboat with the other party. I prepared to leave immediately with the newly organized party. It did not take me long to get ready, since I had only to fetch my horse. My medicine bundle and moccasins were already packed for the other expedition I had planned accompanying. In a short time I plunged my horse into the muddy waters of the Missouri at a point just below the village and swam him to the opposite shore where we were to meet. It was late spring, and the river was quite high. Big Steal also changed over to this party.

We went to a sand bar to wait for the party. We were told that we would wait for him there, but we did not know who he meant. We later learned that they meant Four Bears, whom you are named after.

The leaders or Old Wolves were Puts Away His Hair (Water-buster clan, Hidatsa), Sitting Elk (Water-buster clan, Hidatsa), Four Bears (Prairie Chicken clan, Hidatsa), and Shaved Forehead (Water-buster clan, Hidatsa). The others of the party were Yellow Robe (Prairie Chicken clan, Hidatsa), Foolish Man (Tamisik clan, Louie Baker's brother, Mandan), Rattlesnake (Tamisik clan, Mandan), No Arm (Tamisik clan, Mandan), and Crows Heart (Prairie Chicken clan, nineteen years old, Mandan).

The route we took was a little east of the present post office of Defiance by Lake Gap [Mandan name]. There were plenty of antelope, and we had enough meat. Our route took us by Red Bank, where we made our first camp. From there we went directly toward the present site of the town of Dickinson and on the second night stopped on the river bottoms there. Next day we went on to Rose Bud Ground to the southwest. From our camp there, we climbed the grass-covered buttes from which we saw the hill called Home-of-the-Buffalo, the place where the animals were believed to come out. Some of the party decided to go there to look at the place. On reaching Home-of-Buffalo Hill some of us looked around for the blue clay used for painting our faces and known to be plentiful there. On top of the hill there was a deep crack in the ground, and we could see the buffalo spirits' tracks in there, for it was well packed down. On the west side we came to a great cavity half-full of bones. There were so many bones there I think the animals must have been killed by lightning.

This was the same summer that Custer's party went through the country [1876]. Their army went just a little to the west of the hill and made a regular road. We went there to see their trail. When we came to where it went down to the Little Missouri River, we found skeletons of mules, wrecked and abandoned wagons, and much other material discarded by the army. Their trail was plain, so we followed it all the way to the Little Missouri. Just before crossing the Little Missouri, we went through rough country. There we found oats, clothing, and harness; it looked as though the men had spent a long time there making the road. We found good bridles, reins, and tents which we took. All of us were well supplied. From there we rode to Like-a-Chicken-Tail Butte. This was one of the places where we usually got red paint. All in the party said they would need it when they captured the one lodge. From there we followed the west bank of the Little Missouri River a ways, then crossed and camped on the bank, all the time going up the river. The country abounded with elk, antelope, and blacktail deer. We were never short of meat.

Soon we could see Cedars Facing Each Other Buttes. There we killed two elk, for we were afraid we might not find the tepee at once and might need meat while we were scouting around for it. There we built a sweat lodge and dried our meat in it with heated stones, for we did not dare shoot game when in the vicinity of the enemy. The scouts constantly traveled ahead of us, headed by Yellow Robe and assisted by Foolish Man and Rattlesnake. On the third day after drying the elk meat, they came back running to inform us that they had found where a tepee had been and that the coals were still hot. They said they could still see the place where the horses had been picketed.

When Puts Away His Hair reached the site of the tepee, he went to the west side of the tepee ring to fast and cry. He cried until the next noon.

Then he pointed to the Sun and said, "Old Man, what you have given me, you have also taken away." Then he turned to the Young Wolves and said, "Now, my Young Wolves, this is the place designated by my medicine. It would not be good policy to follow this enemy. We could catch him at his next stop but that would be beyond the authority given me by my medicine. I might be harmed and some of you Young Wolves might be killed. Young Wolves, I am going to turn back, but you may go on if you wish. Old Man gave me this lodge (one family), but now he has taken it back again."

When he made that decision, Sitting Elk decided to go on as leader and took with him Yellow Robe, Foolish Man, and No Arm. They went on for one day when they found the camp fire again burning. Sitting Elk was leader, but he decided that in view of the fact that another had been given the lodge, it would be dangerous to them.

He said, "By the looks of things, the enemy is wise to us. I don't want to lose any Young Wolves. It would be a blur to my record to 'kick the stone' so I am going back." The others returned with him.

When we came back, there was nothing of importance until we reached the Killdeer Mountains, where a Sioux war party saw us. We

29

took the middle of the flat east of the Killdeer Mountains, and one of the party killed an antelope. We wasted no time pulling the hide off, and went right on to Red Paint Creek. I laid the hide out to dry to use on my horse that had a sore back. While we were roasting the meat, a whirlwind took the hide up into the air and whirled it, all the time with the flat side down.

When it happened, we said as a joke, "The enemy is upon us," but each of us jumped onto his horse and followed the creek down to the Little Missouri. We did not stop until we reached Cedar Butte, four miles above Hans Creek, when we went into an elm thicket to rest the horses. While there, an owl came and hooted. The enemy had outnumbered us ten to one and had been watching us from the Killdeer Mountains. They thought they had us, but it was the whirlwind that saved us. It was almost a miracle that we escaped the enemy. [The enemy was never seen but was merely suspected by the signs.] From our camp in Hans Creek we left at dawn without food and rode until we reached Manure Creek, where we grazed our horses in a clearing in the woods and cooked meat. We reached Like-a-Fishhook Village at sunset.

Puts Away His Hair got no credit for the lodge even though he found it just where his medicine said it would be.

2
Two Leggings: The Making of a Crow Warrior

Edited by

PETER NABOKOV

Two Leggings was probably born in 1847 or 1848 (Crow Indian Agency files, however, give 1851 as his birthdate), and he died in 1923. Although the Crow had most likely encountered white men (French fur traders) for the first time in 1742, had seen trading posts established on their lands early in the nineteenth century, and had signed their first friendship treaty with the American government in 1825, nonetheless, Two Leggings' early years seem to have been almost entirely devoted to, as the subtitle of his autobiography suggests, "the making of a Crow Warrior." There are very few references in his story to the presence of whites.

The Crow, or Absaroke—"children of the large beaked bird," mistranslated by the French as corbeau or Crow—are a Siouan speaking tribe of the middle Yellowstone Valley closely related to the Hidatsa and the Mandans. Their chief enemies to the east were the Sioux, and, to the northwest, the Blackfeet. They sometimes traded with, sometimes raided the Flatheads, Nez Perces, and Shoshoni. Like other tribes of their region, they lived for the most part by hunting, and were especially dependent on the buffalo.

Crow men sought renown as raiders and warriors, engaging in rituals of fasting and isolation in the hope of attracting the medicine powers of one or another animal or supernatural being. Two Leggings seems extraordinary in his efforts in these regards—and extraordinary, too, it must be said, in the relative ineffectiveness of these efforts. In the end, his dreams and visions were not considered particularly strong, and he "bought" his medicine from Sees the Living Bull. Even that never quite brought him the success he had always longed for; in comparison to the widely acclaimed Plenty-Coups, his exact contemporary (they may well have been born in the same year), Two Leggings was never considered a particularly important person among the Crow. Although he was occasionally referred to by the whites as "chief," he seems never to have risen above the status of pipe-holder—an important status, but not one of the first rank. Nonetheless, everything about Two Leggings' life as we can know it seems exemplary of the expectations and efforts of a traditional Crow male.

Two Leggings met William Wildschut, a Dutch-born field researcher for

31

the Museum of the American Indian, in the summer of 1919. Wildschut carried on the interviews with Two Leggings from which the autobiography was written until the old warrior's death in 1923. Wildschut worked through a Crow interpreter, Jasper Long, and possibly, as well, with Thomas Leforge, a "White Crow Indian." Their labors resulted in a 480-page manuscript which, however, was never published as produced. It appeared only in 1967, after extensive editing and some rearrangement by Peter Nabokov. What we have, then, as Two Leggings: The Making of a Crow Warrior, *is a fairly familiar sort of composite, the outcome of Two Leggings' narration in Crow, Jasper Long's English version, Wildschut's written version, and, finally, Nabokov's edited version, the only one that has been published, and the one that appears below, minus Nabokov's notes.[1] To Nabokov's credit, he provides, in an appendix, some examples of the original for comparison with his edited version. The examples are not many, and, to my eye, the originals are often more satisfying than Nabokov's versions.*

Be that as it may, I have placed Two Leggings' life story in this section because it does seem to present an account of a man totally shaped by the traditional ethos of his culture. I have included selections from chapters 5, 10, 11, 21, and 24. The first of these offers an intense and detailed account of fasts, sacrifices, dreams, and visions, while the latter speak to the practice of buying medicine and, finally, the warrior society rivalries involved in wife-stealing practices. It is worth noting that Two Leggings' autobiography concludes with his last war experience. As John C. Ewers notes in his foreword to the autobiography, "For [Two Leggings] it was not the extermination of the buffalo but the end of intertribal warfare that marked the demise of the traditional Crow way of life."

5

Now I must tell you some sacred stories which were told to me by our chiefs and medicine men and came from their many winters. So I will begin at the time when there was no earth, when there was nothing but water.

We have always believed in one creator of everything and call him

1. *Two Leggings: The Making of a Crow Warrior*, ed. Peter Nabokov (New York: Thomas Crowell, 1967). The selections included here are reprinted by permission of HarperCollins Publishers, Inc. © 1967 by Peter Nabokov.

First Worker. One day First Worker was looking over the world and did not like all this water. He made a duck dive down and bring him some mud. After rubbing this between his palms he blew it everywhere, creating the land and mountains and rivers. First Worker wanted to make human beings and formed the mud into many groups of clay people. To test them he made arrows and stuck them into the ground pointing east. When he ordered the first group of clay people to charge the arrows, they fell back. The next group also stopped when they met the arrows. Although the last group were pierced by the arrows, they ran on through. These different clay peoples became the different Indian tribes, and the bravest, who had charged through, became the Crows.

First Worker was proud of them because they were not afraid to die. He told the other groups to spread out and live in different places but he placed the Crows in the center so that whatever direction they traveled they would always meet other tribes.

First Worker also created two boys and ordered them to teach the Crows how to live and to give them their religion. These boys were First Worker's servants and that is why when we dream and have visions we receive both a medicine and a sacred helper to guide us through life. Except for important ceremonial occasions and when we fast for visions, we address our prayers to our sacred helper, who will pray for us to First Worker. These helpers are different for each of us as we all have different dreams.

Our medicine men, the chiefs, and our parents wanted us to fast for a medicine when we felt the need. Sometimes powerful dreams were seen by a child who did not understand them until years later. But the stories we heard in the winter tipis and around the summer campfires were usually enough to make us want power and protection in our future lives and war trails.

Once I remember a leading medicine man asking through the camp for our young men to fast in the mountains. Our enemies had been repeatedly successful. He hoped one of us would receive a medicine and take revenge.

Many of our women fasted and some obtained powerful medicines. But usually they did not fast until they had married or were old enough to be married, and then it was because they were mourning someone's death or because of an unhappy love affair.

The sweat bath was the first medicine First Worker and his two boy servants gave us. In the old days it was our most sacred medicine and

Two Leggings, photographed in 1919 by William Wildschut, wearing his pipeholder's war shirt. Reprinted by permission of the National Museum of the American Indian, Smithsonian Institution (#13762).

came before all fasts and important ceremonies. It cleansed our bodies, and when we burned incense inside the sweat lodge while praying to First Worker, it cleansed our souls.

The two boys told us that the sweat lodge represented First Worker's body. The steam from the heated stones, or the smoke from the incense, was his image. It used to be taken as a cure for an illness, but now it is used at any time, like a bath. They still pour the four, seven, ten, and countless number of cupfuls on the red-hot stones, but many do not know what this means. The first four cupfuls are First Worker's arms and legs. They are also the four main supporting willows of the sweat lodge. The next seven are the pipe-pointer star [the Big Dipper]. The ten cupfuls represent the cluster stars, and the countless number means the Other Side Camp, where we live after we die.

If we were preparing for a fast we followed the sweat bath by carefully washing our bodies in a stream and scrubbing our nails. Then we purified ourselves in a sacred smudge of burning pine needles. After that we took no food or water. This also cleansed our minds and took away as much as possible our human smell. The Without Fires do not like the smell of men, and we fasted for them to favor us.

The two boy servants taught us to weep and pray as we fasted for our own medicine. If there was no reason to weep we were to torture ourselves and sprinkle the earth with our tears and blood. We were told that First Worker's birds like to eat, and when we cut a piece of our flesh it softens their hearts so they will help us and perhaps become our medicine.

If we fasted on a mountaintop we built a small bed of rocks running east and west, spread it with pine branches, and faced east as we lay down. Then we covered ourselves with a freshly tanned buffalo robe rubbed with white clay to show cleanliness. For four days we lay there, sleeping and watching the sun until we saw our vision.

The two boys sent by First Worker taught us how to make medicine bundles after we had received our vision. The bundles contained the skins of animals we had seen in our dreams. If the sun, the moon, clouds, or other things appeared in those dreams, the boys showed us how to represent them in different ways.

The two boy servants taught us that there is another world like our earth, the Other Side Camp. The same animals, birds, fishes, and plants live there. The same rivers flow and the same mountains rise to the sky.

The Other Side Camp is divided into two clans and together they are called the Without Fires. One contains the animals, the sun and the moon and the stars, except for the star with a tail which sometimes appears during the summer months, and the souls of the dead—the little whirlwinds which dance over the plains. All the water animals of both our world and this Other Side Camp world belong to this clan, and so do the birds, the thunder, and the dwarfs. Old Man Coyote is its chief.

The other Without Fires clan is made up of everything that comes from the earth: the plants, flowers, trees, and rocks. This earth clan has four chief spirits: the wind, the fire, the water, and the earth itself.

The earth is our mother; our body is born from it and returns to it after we die. Our breath is wind and it is also our soul. Our words are our breath and they are sacred.

Each of the two clans is divided into many clans represented by different Without Fires. When we receive a medicine we join the Other Side Camp clan of our helper. Sometimes we fasted many times, dreaming of different helpers. Then all these and the dreamer made one personal medicine clan.

The Without Fires chiefs also have their servants. The sun is the chief of all the sky beings and its most important servant is the eagle. The moon is a lesser chief and has the owl for its servant. The lightning, wind, and rain also have birds as their helpers.

The chief helpers of the most powerful Without Fires can choose who among the lesser Without Fires will belong to the dreamer's medicine bundle. He will be told this in his vision. The objects within a medicine bundle are the actual dwelling places of the members of the dreamer's medicine clan. Many different things are found in each bundle because every item represents one of the Without Fires or something the dreamer was promised; only he can explain them.

I have seen a shield on which there were pictures of the sun, rain, clouds, and an eagle with lightning striking from its claws. The dreamer who was told in his vision to make that medicine may have only had a vision of an eagle. But the sun, lightning, wind, and rain belonged to the eagle's Other Side Camp clan and he pictured them also.

Certain things in a medicine bundle always mean the same: Horsehair represents the hope for horses, elk teeth or beads mean wealth, and a strip of otter skin means water because the otter is the chief of all water animals.

All Crows have a sacred helper from the time of their birth, but some do not know him because they never receive their own medicine or because their dreams are not powerful. In that case they can buy a duplicate medicine bundle from a well-known medicine man or warrior. Some of us bought powerful medicine bundles from well-known medicine men even if we had a vision of our own because we wanted their power and their sacred helpers. But the owner would rarely duplicate all of his bundle. He would hold a little power over his copies, as was right.

We are fond of gambling and the two boys taught us this. The two Without Fires clans like to gamble against each other and their stakes are the lives of the Indians they have adopted through the medicine dreams. When a clan member loses, his adopted child is "eaten" by the winning clan.

The man who dies fighting is lucky. He was looked after with special care by some Without Fire father who had won his life in the gambling. After he dies his soul is dressed with all the honors of a warrior. He becomes one with the helper who won him and will live an honored life in the Other Side Camp.

We did not want to receive a vision of the sun because he is a bad gambler. Although the dreamer usually became a powerful medicine man, he almost always died young. We preferred the moon which gambles often but rarely loses; its adopted children lead long lives.

The clans of the Without Fires also have a servant. He looks like an Indian but has pine trees growing out of his lower eyelids. He arranges war parties, brings enemies together, and leads the souls of the dead to be adopted by the winning members. If no one is killed in these battles he is disappointed and tired as he returns home.

Old age is not as honorable as death, but most people want it. It proves that a sacred helper was powerful and fond of his child. It also shows that he was a good gambler and never lost a game during his child's earlier life. When the time comes and we old men go to the Other Side Camp to live in peace and happiness, we are one with our sacred helper.

Many men die young on the battlefield. This shows that their sacred helper was not very powerful and lost his game early in the life of his adopted child. Or perhaps the adopted man did not obey his sacred father. When we receive a medicine our sacred helper gives us certain instructions. Sometimes we must not do certain things, like eating certain foods. If we disobey we may have bad luck or sickness or suffer a wound in battle. If we keep disobeying our sacred helper he will grow angry and place the life of his child as a stake against some powerful opponent who always wins. The souls of people who die this way are of a lower kind, but they are allowed to enter the Other Side Camp. However, the souls of suicides and murderers must roam the earth as ghosts.

When the Black Robes came to us they talked about the devil but we could not find him in the things we knew. We think that everything is good and bad and that no person or thing is all good or all bad. I have known many men who had the ghosts as their medicine.

But we are afraid of ghosts because they may have a grudge against someone and plant a cactus needle in his body, making him sick. This can only be pulled by a medicine man and that costs many presents.

Rock medicines were also given to us by First Worker's two boy helpers. Before First Worker created people there were only himself, Old Man Coyote, and a man who was the spirit of all rocks. This man wandered over the earth looking for a mate, but without any luck. Then he met Old Man Coyote and told him about his search. Old Man Coyote advised him to go to the tobacco plant. Inside its husk were seeds, and Old Man Coyote said that these were the female people. The spirit of all rocks went to the tobacco plant and entered the husk. There he found a mate and took her to his home. They were the origin of life.

When the two boy helpers gave the Crows the sweat lodge and the Sun Dance they also gave us the tobacco-planting ceremony and the rock medicines. Four is our sacred number and that is why they gave us four medicines.

Rock medicines are both male and female because they began with the marriage of the male rock and the female tobacco plant. Sometimes we place a male rock medicine with a female one and do not disturb them for a year. By that time a little rock will have come into the medicine bundle.

If we pass a strangely shaped rock we will often stop and pray to it, asking it for good luck and health and happiness. Sometimes we will carry that rock home, hoping it may appear in a dream. If we do not dream about it, we forget it. But if we do, we believe it is a medicine rock. We make it into a bundle and pray to it.

Our bundles, the songs belonging to them, and the ceremony for using them were all taught to us in our dreams. Together they made our medicine. A man who ordered his life with this help was a good and happy man and lived for a long time.

10

Toward leaf-falling season we moved from the Musselshell River to Elk River and then to the Bighorn River, camping near the present town of Hardin. The valley seemed covered with buffalo and we hunted for our winter supply. Then we broke camp again, forded the river, and traveled down the valley, stopping in the cottonwood grove where our dance hall now stands—a few miles above the present Mission of St. Xavier.

The leaves were turning yellow and we expected the first snow any day, but when we reached this place it was still hot. As we passed the flat before the grove, I noticed thousands of prairie dogs sitting on their haunches and barking at us.

The next morning the men were parading around on their finest horses, singing love songs and joyful songs. The girls, whom I was just beginning to notice, were dressed in their best clothes. Someone told me that a big dance would be held that night.

It was a day to make anyone happy, but I was still disappointed over my failure to receive a vision during the Sun Dance. Without it I could never hope for success on the warpath. So I decided to go on a fast. This time I would stay and torture myself, trusting that the Great Above Person would help me.

In my tipi I wrapped an elkskin shield cover around my shoulders because it was strong medicine. Picking up a newly tanned elk robe, I went to the river, took a sweat bath, bathed, and went to the prairie-dog town.

As I walked among the barking and staring prairie dogs I thought that maybe these earth creatures who live underground as the birds live in the sky could help me receive a powerful medicine.

I found the biggest hill in the dog town and dug away some earth with my knife to make a more comfortable resting place. Then I lay down, facing the east. The next morning I awoke to prairie dogs barking all around me. As I walked around I found a root-digger's stick. I turned toward the sun and drew out my long knife. On the ground I crossed the knife and the stick and then raised my left index finger.

I called the sun my grandfather and said that I was about to sacrifice my finger end to him. I prayed that some bird of the sky or animal of the earth would eat it and give me good medicine because I wanted to be a great chief some day and have many horses. I said that I did not want to stay poor.

Kneeling, I placed my finger on the stick and hacked off the end. Then I held the finger end up to the sun with my right hand and said my prayer again. Finally I left the finger end on a buffalo chip where it would be eaten by some bird or animal.

For three days and nights I lay in that dog town, without eating or drinking. In the dark-face time of the fourth night I heard a voice calling from somewhere. Lying very still, I heard it again, but could not locate it. The next time I heard the words of my first medicine song and I never forgot them: "Anywhere you go, anywhere you go, you will be pleased."

I saw the face of a man who was singing and shaking a buffalo-hide rattle. I also heard a woman's voice but could see only her eyes and the beautiful hair on top of her head. They filled me with joy and I thought that if I ever saw a woman with those eyes I would marry her. Then the voices sang: "You. I am coming. There is another one coming."

Many people seemed to be talking and I became confused. My vision people seemed to be coming from behind a hill. First I saw the man's head and then I saw him from the waist up. After his song he faced east and shouted. Then he shouted to the north and finally to the west. The singing grew faster and I fell back as if drunk. When he shook his rattle I saw a face painted on it. The man was painted with red stripes across his chest and face and other stripes running up and down under his eyes and nose. A mouth opened in a face painted on the rattle, and I began to faint. The woman did not show any more of her face or body but kept singing, and I learned the words to her other song: "I am doing it now. I am doing it now. Discovered Plant. I am making his lodge. I am doing it now."

A voice told me that if Comes Out Of The Water came to me I would have much property. The woman kept telling me that what I was wishing for had come true. I noticed the parting in her hair was painted yellow. Then someone seemed to be driving horses toward me. As they drew closer I recognized Shot In The Face walking behind them. The horses were real and I had woken. Shot In The Face said that he had watched me staggering around but did not realize that I had been fasting. He was sorry to have disturbed me and asked where my blanket was. I saw it was some distance away and then noticed my swollen finger. Although it hurt badly I was more unhappy not to have dreamt all my dream. I had intended to stay another night but felt too weak and returned to camp. My finger was bandaged in my tipi. After eating a little food I slept.

I did not think my dream was powerful, but at least I had some medicine songs I had dreamt myself. These were much more powerful and valuable than the ones I had sung before in battle, which had been bought or given to me. I did not tell my friends or the medicine men about my dream. As soon as possible I would fast again for a stronger vision.

In the meantime I did not want to remain in camp. When I heard that Crazy Sister In Law was going out I found him. He said that he had noticed me in the Sun Dance and wanted such brave men.

Now it was late in leaf-falling moon and the nights were cold. One morning at dawn we gathered on the outskirts of our village. I carried my flintlock, the powder horn and bullet bag were on a strap at my side, and my bow case and quiver hung on my back. But I was not warmly dressed and the men called me Belly Robe because of the old wrinkled buffalo robe wrapped around my waist.

The pipeholder often selected younger men for his scouts so I was not surprised when Crazy Sister In Law chose me. It was a good sign when he gave me the coyote skin to carry. In my last dream my spirit man had carried a coyote skin over his arm. Now I was a scout, soon I would be a pipeholder, and then I would be a chief. But I still said nothing to my friends.

The other scouts, Woman Does Not Know Anything, Spotted Horse, and Medicine Father, picked me as leader because I was the only sun dancer. As soon as we left, Woman Does Not Know Anything and I rode ahead to cover the country for game or enemy signs, arranging with Crazy Sister In Law to meet at a place on the Musselshell River.

The two of us rode all that day without seeing any signs, while the other two scouts kept us in contact with our men. At dusk we headed for the meeting place. Crazy Sister In Law was inside the brush shelter which his helpers had built and he invited me to sit next to him across from the entrance. It was the first time in my life that I sat there and for a while I could not speak. Crazy Sister In Law filled his pipe and after we had smoked I gave my report. No one else had any luck locating meat and we went to sleep hungry.

At daybreak the four of us set out again. I carried my coyote skin and we all painted our faces red. The older men taught us to carry red paint ground from rocks, explaining that it is part of the everlasting earth and would protect us.

For a long time we rode without seeing any animals. Finally we came to a bluff giving us a wide view. Since I had not slept well the night before I told my companions to wake me if they saw anything. The wind was blowing hard and I lay down in the shelter of a little knoll, folding my coyote skin next to me.

I dreamt the coyote skin stood up and began howling. It faced east and then north and finally sang this song: "I am going far. I shall bring some bones."

41

It howled again, still facing east while it sang another song: "I shall have a good time."

Then it threw a bone into the air which came down covered with meat. I noticed that the coyote's paws and face were painted red. It howled and sang a third song: "My partner. I am going. He is lying still."

This meant that the coyote saw an enemy's body lying on the ground. Then it howled a fourth time, faced south, and sang a fourth song: "This is the land where I used to live. Look that way. I want that over there."

I looked in that direction and a black horse was galloping away. My foot was kicked and Woman Does Not Know Anything was standing over me, saying that the other scouts had already left. That coyote had shown me where to find meat, where I would kill an enemy, and where I would capture a beautiful black horse. But I was sorry I had been woken. I might have learned more. I carefully picked up the coyote skin and followed my friends. On the way I told them to say thank you. After saying it they asked what it meant and I told them of my dream and pointed out a high ridge to the west. On the other side, I said, would be buffalo.

Spotted Horse was on the fastest horse and reached the ridge top before we were at the foot. We saw him looking, and then he took the blanket from his shoulders and waved it at us. We thought he meant enemies and made signs back. But he held up the robe's points, which meant buffalo. Joining him we saw three animals grazing down the slope. Someone said we should pray and sacrifice to the Great Above Person, so we all prayed that we would like to eat some of this meat. If we killed a buffalo we vowed to sacrifice skin from our hands.

The dream had been mine so I did the shooting. Hanging the coyote skin over my shoulders with the head piece over my forehead, I began to crawl on my hands and knees while two scouts circled to drive the buffalo toward me.

At last a buffalo walked close, thinking I was a coyote. As it pawed the ground I killed it with one shot in the left side.

Each of us pinched the skin on the left hand between two fingers, stuck in an awl to hold the skin up, and cut off a small piece with a knife. We made a prayer of thanks as we sacrificed this skin to the Great Above Person. Then we roasted some of the meat for ourselves. The other three butchered the rest and carried the pieces to our starving companions not far behind. I did not carry any because I was the leader. We met no enemies on that trip and soon returned to our village.

11

I had hoped for better luck on that war party when I was leader of the scouts, and still felt I did not have a strong medicine. After our return I went deer-hunting for skins for moccasins, and then camp moved from the Musselshell River to the Elk River where I killed several buffalo for robes. Traveling slowly up Elk River, we finally camped close to the present town of Livingston, at the foot of a place we called Bad Mountain.

After those hunts I was more unhappy and took only a small part in the dances and celebrations. My brother noticed this and one night in his tipi asked what was wrong. When I explained he said that no one should go out as often as I did without some protection. I told him that I had fasted and received a vision, but he said I had never told him about it and would be killed if I kept on.

The next morning Medicine Crow, Young Mountain, Blue Handle, Walking Mouse, Bull Does Not Fall Down, and others whose names I have forgotten joined me in a ceremonial sweat bath. That afternoon we started to climb Bad Mountain, each of us carrying a newly tanned buffalo hide painted all over with white clay.

On our climb we passed a spring and stopped to take off our clothing, wash, and clean our fingernails and toenails. Then we built a fire, dropping in some pine needles to purify our bodies with their smoke.

It was a long climb and although leaf-falling moon had just arrived the weather was hot. We were tired as each man selected his spot, built a rock bed, and covered it with fresh pine branches. Then we prayed and slept under our buffalo robes.

That night none of us received a vision, but we continued our fast, praying and weeping through the following day. The second night I dreamt of a man telling me that a bird sitting on top of Bad Mountain would see me the next night. The dream ended as the man disappeared. The following morning I woke to find the others preparing a meal down the mountainside. When I joined them, Medicine Crow said that they had not dreamt and he thought we should break our fast.

I told them that they could return home but I was wanted on the mountaintop that night. Then Medicine Crow decided to stay on, but Little Fire, Young Mountain, Blue Handle, and the others said that they would wait at the foot of the mountain. They lacked the courage to fast one more day.

I chose a new resting place and fasted for three more days and nights, growing very hungry and thirsty. All the time I prayed and my heart pounded like a drum.

After dark-face time of the third night, rain fell, and I crawled from my place underneath an overhanging rock to lie on my back and catch drops. I must have fallen asleep because a voice on my right told me to look at a man over there who was well known all over the world. The voice said that he was Sits Down and that he was sitting on the mountaintop.

Looking up I saw a person with clouds floating in front of his mouth. A ring of clouds hung above his head, but then I saw that it was really a hoop with many kinds of birds flying around it. An old eagle flew and perched on this hoop.

When a voice asked if I knew that I was known all over the earth I did not answer.

The person's face was painted with pink stripes down his cheeks which meant the clouds. Then clouds rolled in front of him, and when they separated, his face was painted with a wide red stripe across his forehead. This meant I would get what I wanted. His eyebrows were painted yellow and this meant sight. He sang this song: "I am going to make the wind come. I am going to make the rain come."

A different voice said that all the birds of the air were going to show their feeling toward me and that it would come true. After some silence this second voice said that it had been told to sing. Now I understood that the second voice was the cloud person's servant who had been instructed to give me a medicine song: "Come. Long ago. Thanks. You will be a chief."

I followed the man-in-the-cloud's pointing arm and saw a large number of horses appear above the horizon.

The words "come" and "long ago" referred to a time years before when I had joined some boys on a fast on this mountain. Although we had tortured ourselves we had been too young and had given up when we became hungry.

The dream was over and I woke to the rising sun. Soon Medicine Crow walked over and pointed down the mountainside to our people breaking camp.

After joining our friends down the mountainside we all walked to the valley. Medicine Crow told me that he was afraid he would never live to be an old man. (But his life disproved this. When he died in the summer of 1920, he was over seventy years old.) He did not tell what he had seen but he felt miserable and was so weak he could hardly walk.

Three other young men who had come signalled with a blanket for us to join them on a ridge top. Before reaching them we came upon some antelope, killed one, and built a cooking fire. We finally walked into camp just as it was pulling out for the Musselshell River.

During the time we camped along that river an old man named Four Dance visited our tipi and told us the story of his medicine dream. It made a great impression on me. This was his story.

I had three older brothers, Passes All The Women, Does Not Care For Women, and Women Leggings. Now they are all in the Other Side Camp.

When I was about seventeen I wanted to make a name for myself. But my older brothers would never let me join a raid. We were living with our grandmother, Holds By The Gun, because our parents had died long before.

Once my brothers were gathering their weapons for a raid. When my grandmother asked them to pity me they said I was too fat to run. She told Does Not Care For Women that they were wrong not to take me and that she would help me.

The next day, after they had left, she called for me. Holding a big bundle, she explained that this powerful medicine had belonged to her grandfather and contained a Sun Dance doll and a skunkskin. If I took it to a high ridge and fasted and prayed she was sure the Great Above Person would pity me because the bundle had brought powerful dreams the few times it had been used.

We were camped along Elk River near the present town of Billings. Some young men and I climbed the rimrocks along the southern shore. My grandmother had loaned me a white-painted buffalo robe and had given me a stick hung with two eagle feathers and painted with white clay. After building my rock pile on the highest place I planted this stick at the head and fasted for four days.

On the morning of the fifth day I woke and thought about going home. Everyone else had left. But I fell asleep again and saw seven men and one woman far off to the west. At first they seemed to be standing on Bad Mountain in the Crazy Mountains north of the present town of Livingston—which we also call the Bird Home Mountains. As I watched they sang a song. The second time they appeared on Snow Mountain in the Crazy Mountains. One man was dancing and wore feathers tied like a fan behind his head. His face was painted with lines across his cheeks and forehead. Then they disappeared, and the third time I saw them standing on Bear Head, one of the bluffs between the present towns of Park City and Columbus.

The men held up drums but I could see their painted faces through the drumheads. A skunk inside one drum had fire burning in both ears. The seven men and the woman were singing and dancing but I could not hear the words. They disappeared again, returning a fourth time on the rimrocks north of the present town of Billings, singing: "Buffalo are coming toward me."

Then they stood in front of my rock pile. When they threw off my blanket I lay still. They hid their eyes with eagle feathers and sang again: "Your poles are bulrushes."

Beating their drums, they tried to prevent me from seeing what they held. I thought it was my grandmother's doll but then I saw it was a screech owl. When the owl sat on my chest they sang again: "Beat the drums."

A man stood on my right, his face covered with a large elk robe. Suddenly he threw it off, pulled out his flintlock, and shot the owl. It hooted and I think went inside my body. The man picked up some dirt and put it in his gun, saying that rocks all over the earth are hard but that even if all the guns were aimed at me I would not be hurt.

The he shot at me, and the owl, which had returned to my chest, jumped aside. I felt myself bouncing up and down. A big black owl flew up from the valley and sat beside me. The man holding the gun told the other people that I was poor and that they might help me.

The black owl sang this song: "I shall run all over the earth."

When he had finished I noticed the trees had turned into people who were all shooting at the owl. A few feathers dropped as it flew away and returned again. Some tree people gave me small pieces of meat. Some of my own horses appeared and I noticed one dead on the ground. I thought it meant bad luck.

When I first woke I thought I had been shot and that my dream had been given by some bad spirit.

After returning to camp I gave my medicine back to my grandmother, but it was not time to tell her about my dream. She seemed worried since the bundle had always brought powerful visions before.

Some of our best-known medicine men thought my dream was very strong and that I would never be killed in battle. Then I told my grandmother.

One day after I had married I was camped close to the Arrowhead Mountains near a good spring. A man rode up to my tipi and, pointing to some willows near the spring, said that enemies had built trenches there. They could not be chased away since the best warriors were hunting. He had heard of my dream and asked me to do something.

I told him to wait and went inside. After painting yellow stripes across my eyes and zigzag lines from my forehead down across my cheeks, I put on a fringed buckskin shirt decorated with large quillwork circles on front and back. I also hung two red sashes under each arm and wore a scalp-lock necklace. When I walked toward the enemies my wife came behind holding one sash. After stopping four times I told her to go back.

They had covered their trench with buckskins and dirt and now raised the cover to fire, but I continued walking. A few feet away one man shot at me but missed. Another jumped out and held his gun muzzle against my chest. But when the gun went off I was not shot. As I walked I made a noise like a hooting owl and sang my medicine song. Behind me our men began firing. The enemies tried to escape from their trenches but then they were in the open and all were killed.

I was never wounded and only once had a horse killed under me. My dream was powerful and though I had been a poor boy I grew to be a chief and a medicine man.

I was excited by this story and hoped to make a name for myself the same way. But I needed a strong medicine to protect me and decided to fast again soon.

21

That hunt was not very successful and everyone was hungry for fresh meat after the long winter of eating only dried meat. Our chief decided to move east and meet the herds that roamed south each spring season. After crossing the Bighorn River we camped near the Wolf Mountains where we got most of the robes and fresh meat we needed. Then we left for the joining of the Little Bighorn and Bighorn rivers where Two Belly wanted to camp briefly before moving into the Arrowhead Mountains. When I told him of large herds which I had heard were grazing in the Pine Ridge Hills he announced camp would head there after some more hunting along the Elk River bottom lands.

Two days later we left and at dusk arrived at a camping place. We hunted again for several days and then one morning left for Elk River, spending the first night at the Mountain Lion's Lodge. That night I had a dream. My medicine bird flew to earth with a man in its claws, dropping the body near the Musselshell River on a ridge in the Bull Mountains. Then four enemies heading toward this same ridge fell dead, and a beautiful buckskin horse came to me.

When I woke up I lay still, wondering what it meant. I remembered my dream during my escape from the Cheyennes and the Wise Ones' advice not to go out. But they could not know how clear and strong my dreams had been. I would go out this coming snow season for the things my medicine fathers had promised.

That day I built a sweat lodge for the Great Above Person and said prayers for success, gave thanks for my dream, and offered red feathers instead of the usual red blanket. People heard that I was preparing for a raid. Young Mountain rode over from the Many Lodges and several other warriors asked to join.

Two Belly and Crooked Arm invited Young Mountain and me to Crooked Arm's tipi. After our smoke Two Belly said that if I took those other men with me camp would be unprotected. He said Crooked Arm had dreamt that if I left now someone would be killed. Two Belly wanted to move camp to the mouth of Arrow Creek and from there through Hits With The Arrows to the Buffalo Heart Mountain. Enemy signs had been found and he thought we would be safe there. He said we had killed enough buffalo and now the women needed new tipi poles which we could cut in the mountains. Two Belly asked why I wanted to bring sorrow to the people.

I promised to tell him the next day whether I was going. But I described the four bodies and the beautiful horse which had come to me. A successful raid, I said, would give our people more reason to be happy and to dance.

I lied when I said I might give up my trip. I could not forget what my medicine bird had given me. When we were outside I told Young Mountain that we would remain with the camp through the next day but would leave early the following morning.

On one of his last hunts north of the Elk River and close to the Bull Mountains Young Mountain had seen enemies, but being alone he had turned back. That was my dream's direction, and I told him of the bodies and the beautiful buckskin.

Early the next morning the tipis were taken down, the pack horses and travois loaded, and our camp leader led us to the mouth of the Arrow Creek. From the Mountain Lion's Lodge to here was not far and our tipis were up long before sunset. The chief wanted to stay for a few days while our people traded at the new white man's store built by Long Beard [Thomas McGirl].

Telling Young Mountain and the others to keep their horses in camp that night, I also warned them not to mention our plans. But someone must have talked because late in the evening I was called to Two Belly's tipi. On the way I met Young Mountain and said that whatever happened we would leave as soon as I left the tipi.

After we smoked I was given a good meal and then Two Belly said that he had heard I was taking away many of his best warriors. He told me it was not safe to leave camp without protection and to remember Crooked Arm's advice.

As I was promising not to go a horse galloped up to the tipi and One Blue Bead ran in, covered with sweat. We had been raided during the night and all of his and Shot In The Arm's horses were gone along with many more. He had found one of the thieves' ropes and they were Sioux.

Outside I joined Young Mountain and we ran for the horses. Camp was wide awake with most men jumping on the first horse they found. The women and children were crying over their stolen horses; the men were singing war songs.

Riding up to my tipi I dashed inside for my gun and medicine and ran out. When I jumped on my horse to catch up with the others, Young Mountain was close behind. Everyone seemed to be spreading out. I noticed someone near the river bank calling to us. It was Black Head, who had discovered where the Sioux had crossed.

He told me to lead since I had been planning a raid and had said my dream was good. But he said that the earth does not move and by traveling steadily we could overtake them. He wanted to be sure our horses would not lose their strength.

After fording the river and picking up their tracks on the other side I made them stop so I could make medicine. Kneeling on the Sioux tracks which headed north over a group of ridges toward the Bull Mountains, I drew a straight line across their trail with my finger. Then I formed a dirt bank along the line's far side and made a smudge of white pine needles. Sitting on the trail I faced where the Sioux had gone and smoked my pipe. I pointed the stem and told the Sioux to smoke this and wait until I caught up with them. Now their trail would be rough and they would grow sleepy.

After I stood up I unwrapped my medicine and prayed to the Great Above Person through whom I had received it, saying that I had acted as he had said and asking him to have pity on the women and children crying over their horses.

As I finished a stolen horse walked out of brush toward us. Here I said was the sign of my medicine's power. We were eight but Black

Head asked me to wait for others. Whenever we were about to leave, men would call to us from the opposite bank.

About the middle of the day we finally left. It grew very hot and I prayed this would make the Sioux sleepy. Their trail led east and north, directly toward the spot where I had seen the four bodies. Now I knew that everything would come true.

Late that afternoon we came to where they had killed a buffalo and made a fire. I would never have stopped for a meal the first day out; already they were growing careless.

Young Mountain, Hawk High Up, and I rode ahead to a nearby hill. If we saw anything we were to ride our horses back and forth. But when we searched through my telescope there was no sign of Sioux, and we signaled for the others to join us. After doing the same thing on the next ridge my men killed a deer and cooked some meat. We rode to a third hill, picketed our horses near the top, and crawled to the cover of some tall bushes. A big basin lay before us and at the far end I could see the Bull Mountains covered with pine trees. By the time the rest had caught up the shadows were long. But we had ridden slowly during the day and our horses were still fresh. I told my friends we would travel the shortest route to the pine-covered ridge in my dream, close to the Musselshell River.

The moon shone brightly enough for us to ride apart from the Sioux tracks. I did not want to come upon them in the night. Soon after the first streaks of dawn showed in the east we reached the ridge. Black Head had noticed a big buffalo herd to the east. The Sioux had not yet passed.

After picketing our horses we took off our saddles and rested. Young Mountain, One Blue Bead, Paints His Body Red, and I kept a careful lookout from behind the trees on top.

Noticing movement on the hills several rifle-shot distances to the south, I picked up my telescope. Horses broke out of some timber with men riding behind, all heading for us. I counted five Sioux and recognized our horses.

I left One Blue Bead and ran down to the others. We painted our faces and unwrapped our medicines, tying them where we had been told in our dreams. Bobtail Wolf painted seven red spots on his face running from one side of his jawbone over his forehead to the other and representing the dipper. He tied his foretop with a piece of otter skin, fastened some feathers to the back of his head, and sang a medicine song: "My son is coming."

Boils His Leggings sang a medicine song for Young Mountain, painted a red bar over his mouth, and fastened a red-painted eagle feather in his hair. Making him face the Sioux, he pointed to the sun and said that he wanted Young Mountain to do some brave thing so the people would know him. He called him his son and told him to look into the sky.

Bobtail Wolf sang a medicine song for his brother Goes First. Then he fastened an otter-skin strip to his brother's forehead and gave him a shield painted with the thunderbird. He sang another medicine song, repeating it until Black Head and Few warned him to stop.

Black Head asked me to sing a medicine song for the whole party. Seeing that the Sioux were still far away, I sang one. Bobtail Wolf was singing another medicine song for his brother: "My child, I am coming toward you."

He told his brother that it was strong medicine and would protect him. He sang again: "I am coming toward you today."

Telling my men to stand close together, I rode around them four times, praying for the Great Above Person to help us recover our horses and kill some Sioux. Then I sang my medicine song: "Anywhere I go I will always thank you. Thank long ago. I will be a chief."

Bobtail Wolf was still singing for his brother. When we tried to stop him he said we meant nothing to him. We felt sorry for his brother.

Taking my eagle-tail medicine out of its wrappings, I whistled seven times and looked under the hoop. Four enemies lay on the ground and a number of horses ran toward me. Black Head had watched and asked what would happen. I told him not to be afraid, that I had seen my true dream again.

One Blue Bead ran down to say they were getting close. When he had first looked through my telescope he had recognized a pinto, a roan, a baldface, and a black horse. These were among our fastest horses; it would have been difficult to catch them. A Sioux was leading the pinto as if he meant to ride it and another man was on the black. But just before One Blue Bead had left, this man on the black had changed mounts to chase a small buffalo herd to the north.

I sent Young Mountain up the ridge, telling him to signal when they were within rifle shot. I told my men to shoot straight because One Blue Bead had reported that they all carried good guns and one also had a bow. The younger men were very excited and I had trouble holding them back.

Then Young Mountain made signs and jumped on his horse. Yelling our war cries, we whipped our horses over the ridge. When the Sioux heard us they dropped the stolen horses and raced to a nearby hill, dismounting and shooting from behind rocks.

Some of us rounded up our horses while the rest surrounded the

Sioux. When we had driven them a safe distance I left some younger men as guards and rode back. Our men were riding in fast circles around the Sioux, hanging over their horses' sides and shooting from under their necks.

One of their horses broke loose and galloped in front of me. When I caught its reins I saw the beautiful buckskin of my dream. Now I was sure we would kill the four men. We had seen the fifth Sioux return from his hunting and run off when he saw his friends surrounded.

We were not hitting anyone so I told my men to dismount and crawl up. A Sioux called to us, waving his knife over his head. Loud Hawk said that he was calling us women and asking us to come near so he could stab us. I told my men to close in and not let the yelling make them nervous.

Big Lake was lying in front behind a boulder. As he lifted his rifle he fell back. We thought he was dead but his forehead had only been grazed. We dragged him out of the shooting. After a quick council we decided to charge. The first time we were thrown back but then we drove them out of the rocks and into a coulee. The one who had called us women had run first. Big Lake recovered and now crawled to the coulee's edge and shot into it. A Sioux stumbled out with blood pouring from his forehead, threw out his arms, and fell on his back.

As Goes First ran to join Big Lake, singing his medicine song, he was shot through the heart. This was because his brother had sung too many songs over him.

We were all angry and charged the three remaining men. One was killed immediately but we did not know who did it, he was hit so many times. Young Mountain was in front of me running down the coulee with his head bent forward. A bullet struck him in the neck, coming out his spine. Another bullet cut a hole in my shirt but I kept running and shot into the head of the man who had killed Young Mountain. Pulling out my knife, I slashed at his scalp. Then I began crying and shot him again and again. I forgot everything until I heard sounds like animals growling and turned to see Old Tobacco holding the last Sioux's rifle barrel. We could not aim because they were jumping around so much. Old Tobacco gave a wrench and the Sioux slipped on a stone. As he fell he pulled the trigger and the bullet hit Old Tobacco in the forearm, coming out the middle of his upper arm. Before the Sioux could get to his feet two bullets knocked him on his back. He was still trying to stand when Bobtail Wolf ran up and stabbed him twice in the neck. Blood poured out and he fell dead.

We scalped only three because the last man's hair was short and dirty. We let that fifth man get away. After carrying my partner and Goes First to the top of a high bluff we covered their bodies with rocks.

My dream had come true, but our homecoming was sad. Crooked Arm's dream had also come true. Young Mountain's death was a great sorrow for me. I could not be content with our success and made up my mind to take revenge.

When we returned Two Belly called me to his tipi and reminded me that he had wanted to go to the Arrowhead Mountains. Now I had lost my best friend and another man also. He said that my dream might have been true but that if I had listened to the older men's advice I could have found another opportunity. Their dreams, he said, had more truth than those of young men.

He was right and I kept silent. Immediately we broke camp and moved to Arrow Creek, traveling through Hits With The Arrows towards the Buffalo Heart Mountain. As our camp moved from place to place, following the buffalo, I would often walk into the hills to weep over Young Mountain.

24

The melting snow came, followed by the grass-growing season. My wife and I packed our belongings and traveled to the Mountain Crows where Sees The Living Bull had moved. After waiting one day I picketed my white horse, loaded with presents, by my tipi door. Then I invited my medicine father for a smoke. When he came I told him that the presents and horse were his. I asked him to adopt me during a Tobacco Dance which I had heard would be held in three days. Calling him father, I said that although he had showed me many things I still had not received what I wanted most. I asked him to give me or make me one of his medicines so I could bring back more horses and scalps.

For a long time he would not answer. Finally he said that if I had patience he would give me a pipe so I could be a pipeholder. He reminded me that he was not medicine himself, that it was the Great Above Person who gave all medicines. But he promised to give me some of the Great Above Person's medicine and to teach me many things. In seven days there would be a full moon. I was to visit him then and he would build a sweat lodge and do something for me.

The next morning the Mountain Crows broke camp and went down Elk River to meet the River Crows for the planting of the tobacco. On the way Sees The Living Bull and I struck camp with them in the mountains. We traveled no farther because the River Crows joined us there. During the celebration of the tobacco planting Sees The Living Bull adopted me. I was very happy. Now he could not refuse me.

On the sixth day I brought Sees The Living Bull a beautiful Hudson Bay blanket, a buckskin shirt, leggings, moccasins, and a buckskin-colored horse. I was poor, I said, and asked him to have pity on me. I promised him everything I owned if only he would give me his powerful medicine.

He answered that since I wanted this so badly he would give me all he had. The following morning I was to cut one hundred and four willows and he would teach me how to make a sweat lodge. Then I was to bring twenty-four more for a separate sweat lodge. He also wanted seven stones, a long cottonwood pole, seven buffalo chips, red paint, charcoal, sweet grass, bear root, and a red blanket. He told me to begin the sweat lodge by digging a hole elbow-deep for the hot stones. Then I was to plant the first willow in the ground one full step from this hole and continue the other hundred and three in a circle around the hole. Finally he told me its location.

By dawn I had cut all the willows and had collected the other things at the lodge site. I dug the center hole and piled dirt around the edge so it looked like a prairie-dog mound. With my fingers I traced little trails in the pile to represent prairie-dog paths and covered them with powdered charcoal which meant success in war. Sees The Living Bull arrived in time to help me plant the willows in the ground. Then I intertwined their branches to form the roof frame and left a door space facing east. We covered the entire frame with buffalo hides, the last being a large robe with the head on, which faced the east. Finally I dug a hole west of the lodge for the long cottonwood pole.

Sees The Living Bull had me invite seven medicine men to assist in the ceremony: Little Face, Burns Himself, Face Turned Round, Bird Has A Shirt, Tobacco, Neck Bone, and Little Belt, because they had dreamt many dreams. After I had visited their tipis they walked up to our sweat lodge. Neck Bone was just about to enter when Cuts The Turnip arrived and told Sees The Living Bull that if he loved his children he would let him enter this sweat lodge.

Sees The Living Bull gave his consent but told me later that he had invited seven men because the number represented the dipper, one of his medicines. He had hoped that while they were inside he would receive a vision. By spoiling that number Cuts The Turnip had disturbed his medicine spirit. Cuts The Turnip should have known better but Sees The Living Bull could not turn him away.

As I raised the door a fourth time for Neck Bone he called me his child and said that he had seen a snow-covered ground showing many tracks. He hoped I would live until then and bring home many horses.

When I raised the door for Burns Himself he called me his child and said he had seen the leaves turn yellow and hoped I would live until then.

Then Face Turned Round said he had seen a returning war party driving four captured horses. One was a fine bay and he wished me to have it before the leaf-turning season.

Bird Has A Shirt was last and his dream showed a war party returning from the Sioux country. Leading it was a fine warrior carrying a scalp from the end of a long pole. This man was singing and rode a beautiful captured roan horse. Bird Has A Shirt called me his son and hoped I would be that warrior.

The other three men and Cuts The Turnip entered without a word. During their sweat bath Sees The Living Bull and I waited outside. After a while I filled a pipe and passed it in. As each man smoked he pointed the stem to the sky and then to the ground, asking the Great Above Person to give me success on the warpath, plenty of game, good health, and a long life. When they came out some younger men took baths in the same lodge.

I had already given Sees The Living Bull the red blanket. Now he spread it on the ground and with charcoal painted a black circle in the middle and a disc above that, representing the sun and moon. Holding the blanket up to the sun he told the White Man Above In The Sky, the moon, and all the stars that I was giving them this red blanket. Again he called to the sun, his father, and said that he was giving me this sweat lodge and asked him to help me if I needed anything.

After his prayers he had it announced in camp that he wished to see all the children. When they arrived each child rubbed himself with the blanket. Then it was tied to the top of the pole I had planted on the west side of the lodge. Sees The Living Bull told the sun that now the blanket belonged to him.

Sees The Living Bull invited me to his tipi early the next morning to receive a medicine he would make. The other sweat lodge of twenty-four willows which I had built close to the larger one was left for the following day.

In the morning some medicine men were already in his tipi: Two Belly, Crazy Wolf, Sees Under, Crooked Arm, Scar On The Mouth, Face Turned Round, Burns Himself, Hesitates, and Neck Bone.

When I sat down Sees The Living Bull began to tell us about his own medicine dream and his first raid. This was his story.

I fasted in the same place four times, staying four days each time. But it was not until the last of these fasts that I met my medicine father. Early the fifth morning a person rose above the horizon until I saw his entire body. As he walked toward me, fires burst out where he stepped. At last he stood next to me and delivered the message that Bird Going Up was coming to me.

He was wearing strange moccasins, the left upper made from a silver fox's head, the right from a coyote's head. The ears had been left and scalp locks were tied around the moccasins' edges. The right heel was painted black and the left red. The man wore a beautiful war shirt trimmed with scalp locks along the arms, and his leggings were decorated with horsehair scalp locks from the manes of different colored horses.

A little rain woke me and my dream became a real vision. My dream person was standing next to me when I heard the little coyote head on his moccasin howling. When the fox on the other moccasin barked, flames blew from its mouth. I kept trying to see if this man's face was painted but it was hidden. He carried a coup stick with a raven sitting on it. This raven tried to teach me the language of the birds but the man stopped it. Suddenly I heard a loud thunderclap. I seemed to be picked up and dropped while my blanket was thrown in the opposite direction. Landing unhurt on the mountain slope with my head downhill, I saw a bird's big tail and large claws, but could not see the body. Red streaks of lightning shot from each claw, leaving trails on the rocks. I noticed hailstones on the bird's spread-out tail. As the rain turned into fog I tried to see the bird's head but lightning flashes crossed in front of it. My dream person told me that this bird was great, that the noise from its throat sounded like thunder. The raven on the coup stick said that I was to have had many visions but that the messenger prevented him from giving them. It meant my dream person, the real messenger from Bird Going Up who was giving me all these visions. Then the raven disappeared and I looked again at my dream person. A large red circle was painted on his face, broken by two other circles scratched into the red paint. The raven returned to its perch on the coup stick and my dream person told me that Bird Going Up had told him not to let the raven teach me the language of the birds. Instead, he said, he would teach me some of his medicine songs and sang the first one: "The bird is saying this: Wherever we are, nothing may be in our way."

After each song he blew several times on an eagle-bone whistle. The second song was: "The bird is gone. I will let him return and watch over you."

The third song went: "I am letting him stay. I am letting him stay."

He sang the fourth song: "I am going toward human beings and they are weak."

His fifth song was: "The bird from the sky will take care of you."

He sang his sixth song: "Wherever I am going, I say this: I am the Bird of the world."

His last song went: "My child, I am living among the clouds and there is nothing impossible for me."

When my dream man finished the seven songs he pointed east, saying that people there would make me suffer. Whatever direction I looked he said he could tell me what was there.

Pointing west he asked if I saw a burning mountain. I saw it but did not understand its meaning. My dream person told me never to go to the Flathead or Shoshoni country.

A strong wind came up and I watched my blanket blow away. When I turned back my dream man was gone. I was wide awake and the sun was already high in the sky. As I started home my feet were very sore and I felt weak. More than two days later I came upon White Mouth near the village. He said many people thought I had been killed by a bear and were mourning my death. He was my relative and as we walked back together asked why I tortured myself so much. He said I knew I would not live forever. There were many like myself who were poor and had large families, but he said they did not torture themselves. He kept talking that way but I made no answer. The hunters had just returned with fresh meat and he told me to eat some in my grandmother's tipi.

The news spread that I was back and many came to visit. After talking to them I greased the soles of my feet and slept. The following morning White Mouth invited me to eat in his tipi. After our meal he told me again not to starve or torture myself. Still I did not answer. He agreed to pass on my request that everyone bring a willow branch until I had forty-four and that they should also collect firewood. He went outside and soon I could hear the camp crier speaking to the people. When I had the willows and firewood I was asked if I had any further instructions. I told the people to build four sweat lodges in a row with openings to the east and west. In front of the first lodge they were to pile firewood because we would take our bath there. I had them plant a long pole near the lodge's eastern opening.

Everyone helped me build those sweat lodges. When they were

made I told the people to follow me and led the men, women, and children into the eastern opening of the first lodge and out the western opening. As I led them through the second, third, and fourth lodges the people laid presents on the sweat lodge frames and also tied a piece of cloth and other presents to the long pole. Coming out of the fourth lodge I turned right, walked back to the eastern entrance of the first lodge, and announced for anyone wanting a sweat bath to prepare himself.

Has A Red Feather On The Side Of His Head, our chief, told me that he had been watching over our people for many years and now was growing old. He said he had seen these lodges and believed I had received a powerful vision. I did not tell him what I had seen. He hoped that sometime I would be able to look after our people but advised me to marry and make a home for myself.

I still did not reply but thought I should do as he said. A few days later we broke camp and moved down Powder River where we pitched our tipis again. There I heard that Not Dangerous was going on a raid and decided to try out my medicine. It was the moon when the leaves turn yellow and I had seen my vision in the moon when the chokecherries ripen. Not Dangerous asked if I had made my medicine bundle and I told him no. But I also told him that before my last fast I had dreamt of a gray horse near Red River (in the Black Hills country) and the time had been when the leaves turn yellow.

He had seen me build the four sweat lodges and make the ceremony for the whole camp to share. He had faith in my medicine and said that we would travel toward the horse in my dream.

He appointed me chief scout. After traveling for several days I had a dream. Before sunrise the next morning I told the five other scouts that we would bring good news to our leader. By the time the sun was a man's height above the horizon we had discovered some Sioux chasing buffalo in a valley. We knew they could not move before their animals had been skinned so we raced back to Not Dangerous. He was so pleased he offered me his title as pipeholder, but I could not accept. While we waited for the sun to rise higher our men prepared their medicines and sang their medicine songs. I was the only one without medicine and just carried a buffalo-hide rope. When Not Dangerous asked what I was going to do with it I answered that I was going to capture many horses. His expression showed he thought I was a powerful man. Everyone was ready but we traveled slowly and did not reach the hilltop until after sunset. In the distance we could see their fires.

Saying I was looking for my horse, I began to follow a coulee not far from their camp, keeping in the shadows. Around a bend I saw a dark shape and thought first it was a guard. But it was a horse and I tied my rope around its mouth.

As I led it up the coulee I discovered another horse which I mounted, leading the gray closer to the Sioux camp. Soon I came upon a large bunch, grazing quietly and unguarded. Riding around until I was between them and the campfires I began to walk them out. When I was far enough away I drove them into a run. As I met our men I told Not Dangerous to divide the bunch up, but that I would keep the gray.

We left immediately and arrived safely in our village above the present Crow Agency.

Everyone believed I had some great medicine. But in dreams later on I was given an even greater medicine. It is the rock with many faces which my wife found and which has given me powerful visions.

Sees The Living Bull then taught me those seven songs and I never forgot them. When he finished he said he wanted me to take his horse and ride east until I had reached the top of Bushy Pine Hill. If I did not find a dead eagle there I should turn right and ride to the top of Red Top Hill south of camp. If I found nothing there I was to ride to West Hill west of camp. If I still had no luck I should ride north to Cherry Hill. If my entire search was unsuccessful he said I would not become a pipeholder or a medicine man.

It was a beautiful day. When I reached the top of Bushy Pine Hill I looked into the valley with our tipis and lines of smoke rising to the sky. Soon I would do things to make me a great warrior and a chief. My medicine father had also said that I might become a medicine man. I made a prayer for success to the Great Above Person and to the sun. Somehow I never thought I might fail. Galloping down the slope I rode through a little stream and into the valley. As I searched the ground for the eagle I saw six men sitting and smoking on the side of West Hill, Yellow Crane, Three Wolves, Shot In The Hand, Nursing, Chicken Hawk Cap, and Bucket Leg. I rode up and noticed a spotted eagle dead on the ground and immediately told them that I had come for it. When Three Wolves asked if I had left it there I explained that Sees The Living Bull was going to make me a medicine and had sent me for an eagle. I asked if they had shot it or touched it, but they had just arrived. When they allowed me to take whatever part I needed I was very happy. I dismounted, pulled out the two middle feathers of the tail, and rode to my medicine father's tipi.

When I handed them to him he said he had expected the whole

bird. I described the six men sitting nearby and said that I was glad they let me have a part.

Sees The Living Bull said he would make a great medicine that would permit me to go out as a war leader. He told me to walk around camp and bring him a raven, or a small red fox, or a coyote. He gave me my choice, saying that a raven medicine would mean any bird could tell me where to find the enemy. A red fox medicine would not be very powerful but would give me that animal's cunning. A coyote medicine would bark and bite, and those noises would become a human voice leading me to horses. But if I wanted to a powerful chief he advised me to take the eagle-tail medicine.

Another man asked Sees The Living Bull what medicine he had made for Red Bear and he answered an eagle medicine. They all agreed I had been going on raids without much luck and that if I continued without a proper medicine I might lose some men. If I took this eagletail medicine which my medicine father was willing to make, they would feel I was going to be successful.

Sees The Living Bull asked if I wanted a red circle on my face or a half circle painted over my forehead with the ends reaching from jawbone to jawbone. He also asked if I wanted my eyelids and lips painted red. When I narrowed my eyes the red lids would mean lightning, the power to see the enemy before they saw me. The red lips meant that my medicine songs would be more powerful. I wanted the red circle for the sun and also a red eyelids and red lips.

Then Sees The Living Bull lit a sweet-grass smudge and purified his hands and face. After painting them he reached for his medicine and opened it. On one side of the rock was a human head and under it a buffalo head. On the other side were the heads of an eagle and a horse. When it was completely opened he told me that he was my father but that this rock was my grandfather to whom I should pray.

When I finished praying he took a small rock from the bundle and said it was the large rock's child. He picked up a small tobacco medicine bag and told his wife to tie a small buckskin wrapper around the rock child. After tying it to the medicine bag he placed the bag on different-colored pieces of cloth which he said were the clouds. He sewed a weasel skin and a horse tail to the eagle tail and laid this before him together with an eagle claw.

Sees The Living Bull said that I thought I was now a chief but I was not. However, he said he would give me something to make me a chief. When he had finished he said I could go anywhere and not be afraid.

Laying each medicine down, he sang the song belonging to it. Then he painted a red circle on his face and a red streak on his eyelids and lips. He said if I chose the eagle medicine I must paint a red streak over my eyes. For the rock medicine I was to paint my mouth red and for the tobacco medicine I must paint a red circle on my face. The streak over my eyes meant I could always see the enemy; the red over my mouth, good luck and plenty to eat. The red circle on my face was the red clouds. If I saw a ring around the sun or moon or stars I should paint myself like that because it represented all three. The paint had been given to him by the star which always stands close to the moon. After I had my medicine, he said, I would never fear bad dreams. I could go my way and bring back horses and give him his share.

He wrapped some red paint in a paint bag. He told me that the earth was everlasting but that things on this earth do not last long. However, I would live to be an old man. Then he painted the rest of his face and body with red paint.

He promised to give me the eagle tail for a medicine and also an eagle head. Whenever I saw this kind of eagle flying high in the sky I would notice smaller birds flying around it. He promised to include one in my medicine.

After showing me a blackbird, a redheaded woodpecker, and a sparrow, he asked which I wanted on top of my medicine. I chose the blackbird since these birds are usually found with horses. A man with their medicine always takes the lead on a horse raid.

I walked to a place where blackbirds were swarming and killed one with a stone. When I returned Face Turned Round took the bird, skinned it, and gave the skin to Sees The Living Bull, who then told me to bring him three hairs from a horse's tail or mane. Again I walked out and when I met Fox driving some horses I asked for a few mane hairs. He told me to come with him to the river and there I recognized a mouse-colored horse, one of the fastest of the tribally owned horses. Fox gave me permission to cut a few mane and tail hairs. In the tipi Sees The Living Bull asked if they had been taken from a mare or a stallion. After I described the horse he approved and sent me out for different-colored beads. When I returned he asked if I wanted my wife to string them. But I said that I would do it since she might not always be mine, while this medicine would stay with me always.

Stuffing the blackbird's head with bighorn sheep hair, he mixed in some sweet grass and a little horsehair. He placed the rest of the horsehair in the beak, painting two pink spots on each end to represent different-colored horses. Between two strips of weasel skin

61

which he had tied to the eagle-tail feathers, he wrapped my string of black, white, and yellow beads, representing the clouds.

When Sees The Living Bull finished these preparations he undressed to his breechcloth and moccasins and told me to do likewise. We knelt facing east in the middle of the tipi, I on his right and the old men sitting around us. Handing me his famous rock medicine, he told me to press it to my heart. He mixed some pink paint with water and sweet grass and rubbed it all over his body and smeared it on my hair. Then he painted a red circle on my face and painted my eyes and lips red. Finally he fastened the eagle tail to my hair and gave me an eagle-bone whistle.

When he had fasted on that high mountain peak he said his vision person had been painted as he had painted me now. What he had seen was better than my vision which had caused my bad luck. But though my dreams had not been powerful, he said now they would change. Before I had only seen shadows, but now I would see real things. He said that when a spirit person appeared in my dream I would notice how he had painted himself. He said he was almost finished. After singing me a song he was going to raise the eagle tail to my eyes and under it I might see a horse or a body.

After blowing his eagle-bone whistle he asked how many times he had blown it and I answered seven. He told me to remember that number. On the warpath I was to blow my whistle seven times before singing. Then he sang: "Whenever I go, I shall see them."

Whistling four times he raised the eagle tail and looked under it. He held it before my eyes and I saw hair hanging down which disappeared when I looked closer.

When I told him this he said I should go to Musselshell River when the leaves turn yellow and continue to Where The Lightning Strikes on the other side of Big River. There I would kill an enemy and would see another lying on his back whom I was also to kill.

Giving me some dried pine needles, he taught me more songs to sing during my raid. He also gave me his pipe and told me to put away my own. Whenever I went on a raid he said one of my men should carry this pipe before me. Then the enemy would think it was night and not see us.

My medicine father said he had shown me real things. I was to fast again, leaving my medicine behind and waiting on a high hill for my spirit man. My first war party would be to the Musselshell River and there I would find the scalps he had described. Before I left he promised to tell me where to camp each night. If I wanted to be successful and justify his trust, he said, I must follow all this.

Finally he taught me one more song which gave the power to make rain. While I escaped ahead of the downpour an enemy would be slowed down.

It was dark when I returned to my tipi. At last I had received a medicine. At last I was a real pipeholder, known to everyone. Now I had to show I could hold the respect of these sacred men. Although it would be awhile before I could test my powers, this time the waiting was not so hard.

3
How Aua Became a Shaman

Edited by

KNUD RASMUSSEN

Aua was an Iglulik Eskimo who was born about 1870 and interviewed by the Danish explorer Knud Rasmussen about 1922. An angakoq, *or shaman, Aua speaks of the curious circumstances of his birth, and of his acquisition of special powers, particularly those of the* aua, *"a little spirit, a woman, that lives down by the sea shore," from which he takes his name.*

Rasmussen, the son of a Danish pastor, had some Eskimo blood in his distant background, although he was not, as is sometimes said, a recently acculturated Eskimo himself. He seems to have known the languages of several of the peoples he visited quite well, and to have achieved an unusually good rapport and ease with them. He died in 1933.

Found originally in Rasmussen's Intellectual Culture of the Iglulik Eskimos *as "Aua is Consecrated to the Spirits" and published somewhat obscurely in 1930 as the seventh volume of the* Report of the Fifth Thule Expedition, 1921–24,[1] *Aua's brief narrative has been reprinted more recently in Joan Halifax's* Shamanic Voices: A Survey of Visionary Narratives *and in Penny Petrone's* Northern Voices: Inuit Writing in English.[2] *The first of these is dedicated to Joseph Campbell, and, in the Campbell-Jungian mode of seeing all spiritual things as largely the same thing, is full of generalizations that tend not to be particularly accurate. The second, from which the text below is taken, is a wide-ranging, modestly edited, and quite useful text worthy of further examination.*

I was yet but a tiny unborn infant in my mother's womb when anxious folk began to enquire sympathetically about me; all the children my mother had had before had lain crosswise and been stillborn. As soon as my mother now perceived that she was with child, the

1. Knud Rasmussen, *Intellectual Culture of the Iglulik Eskimos* (Copenhagen: Gyldendalske Boghandel, 1930).

2. *Shamanic Voices: A Survey of Visionary Narratives*, ed. Joan Halifax (New York: Dutton, 1979); *Northern Voices: Inuit Writing in English*, ed. Penny Petrone (Toronto: Univ. of Toronto Press, 1988).

child that one day was to be me, she spoke thus to her house-
fellows:

Now I have again that within me which will turn out no real human
being.

All were very sorry for her and a woman named Ârdjuaq, who was
a shaman herself, called up her spirits that same evening to help my
mother. And the very next morning it could be felt that I had grown,
but it did me no good at the time, for Ârdjuaq had forgotten that she
must do no work the day after a spirit-calling, and had mended a hole
in a mitten. This breach of taboo at once had its effect upon me; my
mother felt the birth-pangs coming on before the time, and I kicked
and struggled as if trying to work my way out through her side. A
new spirit-calling then took place, and as all precepts were duly observed this time, it helped both my mother and myself.

But then one day it happened that my father, who was going out on
a journey to hunt, was angry and impatient, and in order to calm him,
my mother went to help him harness the dogs to the sledge. She forgot that in her condition, all work was taboo. And so, hardly had she
picked up the traces and lifted one dog's paw before I began again
kicking and struggling and trying to get out through her navel; and
again we had to have a shaman to help us.

Old people now assured my mother that my great sensitiveness to
any breach of taboo was a sign that I should live to become a great
shaman; but at the same time, many dangers and misfortunes would
pursue me before I was born.

My father had got a walrus with its unborn young one, and when
he began cutting it out, without reflecting that my mother was with
child, I again fell to struggling within the womb, and this time in ear-
nest. But the moment I was born, all life left me, and I lay there dead
as a stone. The cord was twisted round my neck and had strangled
me. Ârdjuaq, who lived in another village, was at once sent for, and
a special hut was built for my mother. When Ârdjuaq came and saw
me with my eyes sticking right out of my head, she wiped my mother's blood from my body with the skin of a raven, and made a little
jacket for me of the same skin.

He is born to die, but he shall live, she said.

And so Ârdjuaq stayed with my mother, until I showed signs of
life. Mother was put on very strict diet, and had to observe difficult
rules of taboo. If she had eaten part of a walrus, for instance, then that
walrus was taboo to all others; the same with seal and caribou. She
had to have special pots, from which no one else was allowed to eat.
No woman was allowed to visit her, but men might do so. My clothes

were made after a particular fashion; the hair of the skins must never lie pointing upwards or down, but fall athwart the body. Thus I lived in the birth-hut, unconscious of all the care that was being taken with me.

For a whole year my mother and I had to live entirely alone, only visited now and again by my father. He was a great hunter, and always out after game, but in spite of this he was never allowed to sharpen his own knives; as soon as he did so, his hand began to swell and I fell ill. A year after my birth, we were allowed to have another person in the house with us; it was a woman, and she had to be very careful herself; whenever she went out she must throw her hood over her head, wear boots without stockings, and hold the tail of her fur coat lifted high in one hand.

I was already a big boy when my mother was first allowed to go visiting; all were anxious to be kind, and she was invited to all the other families. But she stayed out too long; the spirits do not like women with little children to stay too long away from their house, and they took vengeance in this wise; the skin of her head peeled off, and I, who had no understanding of anything at that time, beat her about the body with my little fists as she went home, and made water down her back.

No one who is to become a skilful hunter or a good shaman must remain out too long when visiting strange houses; and the same holds good for a woman with a child in her amaut.

At last I was big enough to go out with the grown up men to the blowholes after seal. The day I harpooned my first seal, my father had to lie down on the ice with the upper part of his body naked, and the seal I had caught was dragged across his back while it was still alive. Only men were allowed to eat of my first catch, and nothing must be left. The skin and the head were set on the ice, in order that I might be able later on to catch the same seal again. For three days and nights, none of the men who had eaten of it might go out hunting or do any kind of work.

The next animal I killed was a caribou. I was strictly forbidden to use a gun, and had to kill it with bow and arrows; this animal also only men were allowed to eat; no woman might touch it.

Some time passed, and I grew up and was strong enough to go out hunting walrus. The day I harpooned my first walrus my father shouted at the top of his voice the names of all the villages he knew, and cried: Now there is food for all!

The walrus was towed in to land, while it was still alive, and not until we reached the shore was it finally killed. My mother, who was to cut it up, had the harpoon line made fast to her body before the harpoon head was withdrawn. After having killed this walrus, I was allowed to eat all those delicacies which had formerly been forbidden, yes, even entrails, and women were now allowed to eat of my catch, as long as they were not with child or recently delivered. Only my own mother had still to observe great caution, and whenever she had any sewing to do, a special hut had to be built for her. I had been named after a little spirit, Aua, and it was said that it was in order to avoid offending this spirit that my mother had to be so particular about everything she did. It was my guardian spirit, and took great care that I should not do anything that was forbidden. I was never allowed, for instance, to remain in a snow hut where young women were undressing for the night; nor might any woman comb her hair while I was present.

Even after I had been married a long time, my catch was still subject to strict taboo. If there but lived women with infants near us, my own wife was only allowed to eat meat of my killing, and no other woman was allowed to satisfy her hunger with the meat of any animal of which my wife had eaten. Any walrus I killed was further subject to the rule that no woman might eat of its entrails, which are reckoned a great delicacy, and this prohibition was maintained until I had four children of my own. And it is really only since I had grown old that the obligations laid on me by Ârdjuaq in order that I might live have ceased to be needful.

Everything was thus made ready for me beforehand, even from the time when I was yet unborn; nevertheless, I endeavoured to become a shaman by the help of others; but in this I did not succeed. I visited many famous shamans, and gave them great gifts, which they at once gave away to others; for if they had kept the things for themselves, they or their children would have died. This they believed because my own life had been so threatened from birth. Then I sought solitude, and here I soon became very melancholy. I would sometimes fall to weeping, and feel unhappy without knowing why. Then, for no reason, all would suddenly be changed, and I felt a great, inexplicable joy, a joy so powerful that I could not restrain it, but had to break into song, a mighty song, with only room for the one word: joy, joy! And I had to use the full strength of my voice. And then in the midst of such a fit of mysterious and overwhelming delight I became a shaman, not knowing myself how it came about. But I was a shaman. I could see and hear in a totally different way. I had gained my qaumaneq, my enlightenment, the shaman-light of brain and body, and this in such a manner that it was not only I who could see through the darkness of life, but the same light also shone out from me, imperceptible to human beings, but visible to all the spirits of earth and sky and sea, and these now came to me and became my helping spirits.

My first helping spirit was my namesake, a little aua. When it came to me, it was as if the passage and roof of the house were lifted up, and I felt such a power of vision, that I could see right through the house, in through the earth and up into the sky; it was the little Aua that brought me all this inward light, hovering over me as long as I was singing. Then it placed itself in a corner of the passage, invisible to others, but always ready if I should call it.

An aua is a little spirit, a woman, that lives down by the sea shore. There are many of these shore spirits, who run about with a pointed skin hood on their heads; their breeches are queerly short, and made of bearskin; they wear long boots with a black pattern, and coats of sealskin. Their feet are twisted upward, and they seem to walk only on their heels. They hold their hands in such a fashion that the thumb is always bent in over the palm; their arms are held raised up on high with the hands together, and incessantly stroking the head. They are bright and cheerful when one calls them, and resemble most of all sweet little live dolls; they are no taller than the length of a man's arm.

My second helping spirit was a shark. One day when I was out in my kayak, it came swimming up to me, lay alongside quite silently and whispered my name. I was greatly astonished, for I had never seen a shark before; they are very rare in these waters. Afterwards it helped me with my hunting, and was always near me when I had need of it. These two, the shore spirit and the shark, were my principal helpers, and they could aid me in everything I wished. The song I generally sang when calling them was of few words, as follows:

> Joy, joy,
> Joy, joy!
> I see a little shore spirit,
> A little aua,
> I myself am also aua,
> The shore spirit's namesake,
> Joy, joy!

These words I would keep on repeating, until I burst into tears, overwhelmed by a great dread; than I would tremble all over, crying only: "Ah-a-a-a-a, joy, joy! Now I will go home, joy, joy!"

Once I lost a son, and felt that I could never again leave the spot where I had laid his body. I was like a mountain spirit, afraid of human kind. We stayed for a long time up inland, and my helping spirits forsook me, for they do not like live human beings to dwell upon any sorrow. But one day the song about joy came to me all of itself and quite unexpectedly. I felt once more a longing for my fellow men, my helping spirits returned to me, and I was myself once more.

4
Autobiography of FP

Edited by

ERMINIE WHEELER-VOEGELIN

Frances Philips (c. 1863–1933), the Tubatulabal woman identified in her autobiography as FP, was interviewed by the anthropologist Erminie Wheeler-Voegelin in 1933. Philips' daughter served as interpreter. Voegelin's headnote to the autobiography says that Philips was at first sceptical about telling the story of her life, commenting that she "had never been anywhere, just stayed in the South Fork Valley [southeastern California] all her life." Nonetheless, she began to narrate, and she completed the account given below in two weeks. This, Voegelin says, "is little more than an outline, which she was beginning to fill in with increasing amounts of detail." Sadly, however, "a day or so after our last session together she went to Bakersfield for shamanistic treatment; on the return trip she was run over by a car and killed."

The Tubatulabal are one of the many California tribes virtually destroyed by the Anglos. First visited by the Spanish in 1776, it was the California Gold Rush of the late 1850s that proved most destructive to them in their traditional Kern Valley home. The 1972 census listed only twenty-nine fullbloods, with just six persons, all over fifty years old, speaking the (Uto-Aztecan) Tubatulabal language.

"Tubatulabal" means "pine nut eaters;" acorns, small seeds, berries, and roots were also part of the traditional Tubatulabal diet, which was supplemented by hunting and fishing. Today, most of the people identifying themselves as Tubatulabal follow occupations in the Anglo society, although the use of jimsonweed in religious and medicinal practices persists, and many of the old stories continue to be told — in winter only, lest one succumb to snakebite.

FP's life story is very much of the twentieth century, although, as I have noted in the introduction to this part of the anthology, it seems to me to offer a worldview deeply rooted in an earlier time.

Erminie Wheeler-Voegelin (1903–88) was raised in California, where, with her anthropologist husband, Charles (Carl) F. Voegelin, she studied under the distinguished Alfred Kroeber. The Voegelins made the acquaintance of Eli Lilly, who had made a fortune in pharmaceuticals, and, in large part as a result of

Lilly's influence, Erminie Wheeler-Voegelin became the holder of the Yale Indiana Fellowship, and the first woman to take a doctoral degree in anthropology at Yale in 1939. She went on to be the editor of Ethnohistory, *the journal of the organization that was to call itself The American Society for Ethnohistory, until 1964. Frances Philips' story was one of Erminie Wheeler-Voegelin's earlier projects; for all that, it remains an important one. The text below reprints in its entirety "The Autobiography of FP."*[1]

I was born about 2 yrs. after the soldiers killed all those Indians over at Kernville (1863); my older brother was still being kept in a cradle then and I was born about 2 yrs. later.

My mother used to tell me about the massacre; Jose Chico pulled my father out from those men and the soldiers didn't kill him; he ran away. There was one man who was shot in the eye, but he had power and recovered. Lots of men were killed. The fight started over the Indians' killing other people's cattle; Jose Chico interpreted for the white men and the Indians; he was the man who took my father out. There were 3 men saved when the soldiers shot at the Indians.

One man had an amulet, a bearclaw with beads on it. He was running and he got out of breath and dropped that claw; then he was killed. The people found it afterward. If he hadn't lost his power he would have escaped all right. Another man had rattlesnake for his pet. He was badly hurt; his insides were all cut up; when the people saw him after the massacre there was a rattlesnake lying on top of him, and that snake made that man get all right. Rattlesnake was his pet and took care of him. That man's name was hi·ay·ši·l; he was a Monilabal (Yokuts). He got all right again; my father saw him when he was helping bury those dead Indians; he saw that rattlesnake come and help him. PN has a rattlesnake for her pet, too; perhaps she got it from dreaming. She never took jimsonweed, I know.

I was born at omomïp. My mother had 8 children; most of them died before they grew up. Three of my brothers died; all of them are dead now except myself; I am just left, one.

When I was a little girl I used to go with my mother to pack wood. She tied a rope over her chest and packed wood on her back; not too heavy loads. I liked to go with her to haul wood all the time. And I

1. "The Autobiography of FP," ed. by Erminie Wheeler Voegelin, *University of California Publications in Anthropological Records* 2 (1938–40): 72–80.

went with my mother over to the pit mortars and helped her grind acorns; that's what I knew how to do. All my other sisters stayed home; I only went. The boys would be playing at hunting rats, and the 2 girls cooked for them. Some girls didn't want to grind seeds or haul wood; they used to call me "old woman" because I did that. We would get up early in the morning, about daylight, and build a fire, and then my mother and I would go out. My father would be around the house working; he would go out and get a lot of quail.

There was one time when we were living over at cuhka·yl in a mud and brush house. That's the way the Indians used to do, they just moved all around; they'd camp under some willows, anywhere; they'd keep moving around all the time. A big earthquake came and frightened everybody. I was a little girl then, about 7 yrs. old; afterward my father used to tell me about that earthquake. I remember only a little bit; the springs got white, like milk, when that earthquake came. Everybody cried and went around shouting; there were lots of people living at cuhka·yl. PN was living there then. We had to get water to drink from the river at Kernville; the water in the springs was hot and white, just like milk, for about 3 days. Nobody would drink it. I just remember a little bit about it; I know all the children were frightened and cried when the earth quaked.

After we left cuhka·yl we moved up where SM lives now, at yïtiya-mup. There were lots of people living there; 5 families. We just camped there in a brush house, and we had a ramada (shade) made from willows. Nobody owned that land then; we just moved around. We children used to play on the big boulders up there; my sister and I pushed a little boy down on one of the boulders; he fell down and hurt himself, and his mother was angry and quarreled with my mother. Then my father and mother got mad and moved up to the pit mortar bed near there; they stayed there 2 days; then we moved up to omomïp again. They all moved up to omomïp, all those people living that time at yïtiyamup; that woman who got angry came along, too. That's the way the Indians did; they moved all around, camping; they should have gotten land. And that woman camped at omomïp, too. We made a mud and brush house there, different from the ramada.

One brother of mine had died while we were staying down at yï-tiyamup. We stayed at omomïp for 2 yrs. I was rather sickly; weak; I didn't feel good, all the time; my father told me to take jimsonweed. Everybody had supper over at our house; I didn't eat anything that whole day. After they had had supper everybody left, and about sundown, when it was getting dark my father said, "I'm going to give you this medicine. You'll be all right."

He gave me a big basket half full of the drink. I drank it all; it was bitter, o-o-o-oh! My father blew on a (quill) whistle, after he gave me that medicine. One old woman and 2 old men could hear him blowing, away off on the other side of the world.

After I had taken that medicine a white man came to see us. He said, "What's the matter with her?" I was outside there, walking around; I didn't eat anything. People walk around like that, heavy-footed, when they drink jimsonweed. I didn't know anything; I was "drunk." They told that white man they had given me medicine, Indian medicine.

"What are you giving her that for? You're going to kill her," the white man told my father.

"No," they said, "that's good medicine."

For about 3 days I didn't know anything; I just walked around drunk; they watched me, but I didn't know anything. I didn't see anything, except for everything running past me. Some people get power when they take jimsonweed, but I didn't. After 3 days I woke up; I was much better after that.

Just for fun, after we had stayed at omomïp for 2 yrs., we moved from there up to u·u·pu·lap; all the people at omomïp did. We had gardens at u·u·pu·lap; we planted onions and potatoes. We put a long rope down and then planted the onions in a long straight line.

I became sick at u·u·pu·lap; my arm was bent and I couldn't straighten it. So I didn't eat meat for a month, then my aunt gave me red ants. She gave me half a baking-powder can full of little balls of cotton with live red ants wrapped up inside them. I hadn't eaten anything the day before my aunt gave me those ants. One time a man ate pinole, and then took ants and he died that night, because he had eaten that pinole. I took the ants in the morning and slept all day; then I woke up and everything was clear and bright. The red ants that are all around here now are the ones I took. I didn't eat any meat for a month; if I had, then when I took the ants, they would have killed me.

Those ants are good to take for a bad cold too, wrapped up in eagle down. When you take them you burn inside in your stomach, just like fire; you get hot inside; they bite you there, I guess. I slept all day the time I took ants; I was unconscious and I slept outside on the ground and rolled over and over in the dirt. My hair got all full of dirt; I didn't know anything. They gave me warm water to drink when I woke up that evening; then I vomited, but nothing came up except water. The cotton and ants had disappeared. I could straighten out my arm again. After that I just ate acorn gravy and a little bread; no meat or grease for a month.

One time when I was visiting my aunt up at Canebrake Piñon Joe's mother (a Koso) tattooed me. I was about Esther's age (FP's grand-daughter, aged 12); we were playing out some place and the old woman took a spine from a bush that grows all over up there and made the marks on me. My mother didn't know about it until after-ward, because she wasn't there. At first I ran away from the old woman; I didn't want her to do it, but she said those marks would look pretty on me. Then I said, "All right," and she made them. It hurt a lot. And then she rubbed in charcoal made from the wood of some sort of a bush. I tried to rub the marks off; I grabbed dirt and rubbed it all over my face and arm, but the marks wouldn't come off. They used to show on my face for a long time, when I was younger. Indians used to do that to make themselves look pretty. PN and Petra Miranda have those marks on their faces, too.

Two of my brothers died while we were at u·u·pu·lap. The bad doc-tor, Old Bill Chico, killed them. He said when he got drunk one time that he was going to kill all the children, so later they burned him over at Kernville; they tied him with a hair rope and threw him into the fire.

When my brothers died my parents made a fiesta to have their faces washed; my mother cut off her hair down to her shoulders, too, when they died.

We lived at omomïp for awhile after that. Then some men went over on the desert and saw lots of ku·l over there, so lots of people from here went to get it. That was when I was a young girl, about 16. I went over on the desert with my grandma (mother's mother), to a place this side of Randsburg, on a hill. A lot of people went. There were 4 camps of people over there. We all went afoot, men and women. One little girl went with her grandma; the little girl was maybe 9 or 10 yrs. old. There weren't any babies taken; the women couldn't carry them. It was in the early summer, maybe in June. We took flour from omomïp; Bill Scodie had a store near omomïp where he sold flour and coffee and sugar and whiskey. But we ate all that flour up when we got over on the desert, so then we just had ku·l seeds and Mariposa lily bulbs and chia seeds to eat; we ate all those. There were lots of boxthorn berries over there, too; we gathered those. And lots of Mariposa lily bulbs, big ones that we peeled a little and then boiled. We'd get half a sackful. The Mariposa lily bulbs over here are little and sweet, but those over on the desert are big.

That little girl who went over there used to grind ku·l seeds on a grinding slab. She was little, and everybody stood around watching her, all the people; she cried then, because she was ashamed, I guess. Her grandma told her it was all right, and not to cry.

We ate rabbits and ku·l and chia seeds. There was nice water there, cold. We made a shade from greasewood brush; not a ramada, but a shade with a single pole sticking up out of the ground and another pole leaning against the first one in the fork at the top; then we piled greasewood on both sides against that slanting pole. There were 4 camps over there that time, each a little distant from the other. We used to work early, before sunup, grinding that ku·l. One man killed doves, lots of them, at a spring. He made a little brush house and sat inside that house; when the doves came to get a drink at the spring they couldn't see him inside the house and he shot them with bow and arrow. In the evening he would bring half a sackful to camp; those doves were good and fat. He'd give 5, maybe 6, to all the people camping there.

I got tired of camping over there; we had no white flour to eat. Another girl, younger than I was, and I started home afoot. We just came alone; there was no one else with us. We traveled all night on that desert; it was moonlight. There are lots of doglike animals on the desert, lots of yu·mu·gi·wal but we didn't see any; maybe they would eat you up.

We packed water in a pitched water jar, and we took along a little lunch of ku·l meal. When we got to Coyote Hole where there is a spring, we wanted to drink that water there. So we stopped at the spring. Then we saw a camp on a hill above the spring a little way off; we ran the other way, up into the hills, when we saw that camp. We were afraid that the people at the spring were Frenchmen and that they would kill us. The people in the camp were all asleep; they didn't see us. There were Frenchmen up here then, lots of them; they chase women, right away when they see them. We were afraid of Frenchmen.

When we arrived at the other side of the summit (Walker pass) we got water at a spring a little way down; then we ate our lunch and rested a little, because we were tired. It was sunup when we got to the summit. Then we came down to Canebrake from the summit. By Canebrake we saw 2 men coming up the canyon, but we were afraid and ran over on a little hill where we watched them. They were trappers, I think; white men.

We got to u·u·pu·lap; there were some people living there. We were going home to omomïp from there, but they told us my mother had left omomïp to gather chia seeds and that nobody was home. The people at u·u·pu·lap said everybody from omomïp was over at Scodie's mt., so that same day we went over there. We were very tired, but we couldn't stay over at omomïp all alone, with nobody in the house. We found my mother all right.

My grandmother came back from over on the desert a week after we got back. That girl who came home with me that time is still living; she lives over at Paiute all by herself; her husband is dead; she lives in a house near a white lady. She looks young yet; the Indians never used to get old-looking for a long time in the old days; these young people do now though because they eat everything hot, with too much salt. Indians used to eat salt too, but only a little bit.

I was growing up then. When wišimlït (SM's mother) came back from Tejon ranch she made a fiesta over at cuhka·yl. She was living over there then. Her son's (Steban's) daughter had died, his eldest daughter. So wišimlït was making a fiesta; then Steban could eat meat again. They killed a big steer. The men cooked the meat; they boiled and fried it. I met wišimlït's youngest son, Pete, over there then; I had never seen him before, because after wišimlït's man was killed in the massacre she had taken Steban and Pete to Tejon ranch. There she married a Tejon man and lived at Tejon about 20 yrs.; then she came back here with her husband and Steban and Pete.

Pete was about the same age that I was. He saw me over there at the fiesta.

"Oh," he said, "I want to live with you."

But my mother didn't want me to go with him; he was mean when he was drunk. I wanted to stay with Pete that time, but my mother said, "No."

Over at cuhka·yl where they had that fiesta there was a man who used to get eagles from Nichols peak. He used to raise them; he had one eagle for a long time. When that eagle grew big the man set him free; the eagle lived over in the mts. near the man's place for a long time. The man would go to Kernville to buy meat; when that man came back Eagle would be sitting up on top of a hill, watching for him. He could see a long way off, that eagle. When Eagle saw that man coming he would fly close to him, knock him down with his wings; then he would cut that man's load all to pieces and eat the meat. He would scratch that man, too, sometimes. One day that eagle flew away; he never came back any more. That old man raised him; anyone who wanted to could raise eagles.

There was another man, a bad doctor, whom my father told me about. It happened a long time ago. The people told that bad doctor, "Go get eagles on Nichols peak." "All right," he said, "I'll go."

Four men went with him, away up on the S side of Nichols peak, behind the cliffs. When they got up on top of the cliffs, they tied a rope around the doctor's waist. Then they lowered him down over the cliff. When he was halfway down they let go of that rope. That's how they killed that bad doctor.

A long time after the fiesta at cuhka·yl we were picking piñons up at Long valley. And Pete came to our camp and he asked for me again. That time my mother said to him, "You're all right." Then Pete stayed over there, picking piñons and helping us. His mother, wišim-lït, didn't pay anything for me; she had paid for a wife for Pete's brother, Steban (SM), though. She liked a Monilabal woman she knew; that Monilabal woman was a good worker, not lazy at all, so wišimlït paid for her and brought her to yïtiyamup to be Steban's wife. Steban wasn't home at the time; he was working down around Bakersfield I think; he didn't know anything about it. When he came home there was a wife for him, sitting there in the house.

After we left that piñon camp in the hills we came down to u·u·pu·lap again. We moved around too much. An Indian agent had come, Anderson; he used to live at Tule River reservation. All the Indians had gotten land; Steban and everybody (in 1893). The Indian agent gave my father and mother land at Canebrake. My parents went to Canebrake to live and Pete and I moved up there with them.

There was a witch at Canebrake and she made me sick all the time, like I am now. My husband and my mother took me to a doctor at Paiute; he was a good Indian doctor. He said, "Don't you live up there at Canebrake any more; you stay some other place." So we all moved down to yïtiyamup; Steban and his wife owned yïtiyamup by that time.

Steban's mother was living with Steban and his wife up there. I used to quarrel with my mother-in-law; she was mean, that woman. My sister-in-law was a nice woman and for her sake sometimes I wouldn't say anything to our mother-in-law. Sometimes my mother-in-law would scold me and then cry afterward; she would feel bad about it, I suppose.

Sometimes they made fiestas there at Steban's. They played handgames all night; everybody stayed up all night. Two doctors were over there at a fiesta once; one, Old Bill Chico, got drunk and got mad at an old woman. "I'm going to kill all the people," he said, and one woman came and hit him over the ear. They had built a fire in the middle between 3 houses that were there, on some level ground. When Bill Viejo was hit he went over to his wife by the fire; his wife told him to keep still and not to talk like that.

My husband used to get drunk sometimes. He began going with a woman up at Onyx when he was drunk; he brought that woman home with him to our house at yïtiyamup. I left there then and went back to my parents' home. They were living at u·u·pu·lap then. Pete took that woman to yïtiyamup with him, but his mother didn't like her because she drank too much and went around with many men. That woman stayed a long time at the rancheria and Pete went to work cattle at Kelso valley. Pete was mean when he was drunk; I guess he was jealous; that's why that woman left him and went to Tule River reservation. She married over there and died there.

I didn't go back to Pete for a yr.; I didn't want him any more. Then a priest came traveling around here; first he went down to the Jesus ranch, then up to Onyx. He talked to us; he prayed and we did, too; we prayed in Spanish. All the Indians went there where he was; I went; my parents didn't go. We all prayed and sang loudly; every day for a week he talked to us. I was baptized that time.

That priest said Pete and I had to be married. "You'd better get your man back; if you don't you aren't going to live any longer," he told me. The priest had a ramada made, up at Onyx, and told everybody to come there for a week; he told everybody to pray there, morning and afternoon. And all the people were married there; šumukat married wïsok, and my younger sister was married, too.

Pete and I went home to u·u·pu·lap after we were married; my people were living up there, making gardens. It was nice up there by the river. My grandmother (mother's mother) didn't like Pete; she kept scolding me for taking him again. She didn't like him because when he got drunk he was mean and chased around with other women. My parents and sisters and my grandmother and my husband and I were living in one big house. My sister's husband was a good man; he bought everything for her. We all got on well together; my family had lots of gardens there, with lots of onions. We sold some onions and beans, long black and white beans. The men and women both worked in the gardens; they helped each other; they worked early in the morning. Pete and I didn't have any garden of our own; we were just staying there with my parents. That was the way the Indians used to do; the man lived with his wife's family a long time.

My sister died at u·u·pu·lap, so we left the house where we had all been living; we moved away from there. Only my half brother stayed up there; he had alfalfa growing there; he stayed there until a white man came and told him to get out of there. All the rest of us moved.

Pete and I moved down to yïtiyamup. We stayed there all winter; we built a wattle house with a tule roof down there. My husband had wanted me to have a baby for a long time, and my mother-in-law gave me some medicine; I didn't know what it was for, and I drank it; after that I didn't menstruate any more, and then I had Legora. When she was born I got sick and pretty nearly died; I was in labor all night and all day; my mother took care of me. My husband's stepfather had power; I was lying around, unconscious, weak; the baby didn't want to come out. Pete's stepfather touched me all over with his amulet. My father had power, too, but he couldn't do anything for me; I don't know why. I was old, about 25 yrs. old; my bones were getting hard, I think. When my son Pete was born it was easier, but Legora very nearly killed me. Each time I had a baby I didn't eat meat or grease for one month afterward; just flour and beans. After my first baby was born my mother made a fire in the ground with hot rocks on top, for me to lie on. The rocks stayed hot all night; it was a good bed. I only had the 2 children.

When we were up there at yïtiyamup my sister-in-law and I used to get chia seeds on that little hill near Steban's house. My 2 children would stay home and go visiting over at another woman's house; they played marbles and made rag dolls to play with. We used to cut barley down here in the valley, too; we didn't make any tobacco; my mother made that, though. Little Bill Chico's second wife made it, too, and we used to buy it from her. One other woman, mapali·p, used to make it, too; only those 2 made it.

My husband used to haul water and wood for me; he was a good man when he wasn't drunk. My children were good, too; I never whipped them. Legora learned to make baskets; she made a pretty one. My husband took it to a lady at Weldon; she paid him $5 for it.

One time an old woman from omomïp was visiting my grandmother at yïtiyamup. They went out to get ku·l seeds this side (E) of the Goat ranch on the flats there. They were carrying their baskets on their backs; they had little blankets with them. When it got late they slept down by the river, under some willows. And they heard something flying above the tops of the willows, going "wo, wowo, wo, wo" all night; first the noise would seem to be above their heads, then it would grow fainter, then louder again. They left that place; they took their blankets and they went over toward the flat. They slept on the flat; it was dark. Anangayat came out of his cave up there on the Goat ranch; they heard him say, "Aha, aha, ha, ha!" so grandmother's friend said, "You better get up; hurry up!" They were frightened. They left that place and they went up the valley to omomïp, where grandmother's friend lived.

When Legora was little, one time my nose started bleeding, one day in summer. It wouldn't stop. My father took me over to Paiute Ramon (Kawaiisu shaman) in a little buggy; I left Legora home with my sister-in-law. We traveled all night; my nose bled all the time, unceasingly. The blood filled a big bucket we carried along in the buggy. We got to Ramon's place about 3 o'clock the next afternoon. That doctor was standing on the other side of a little hill watching us; he knew we were coming. Doctors know lots. When we got to the house we heard somebody crying, making a noise, behind us. The witch (a Tübatulabal woman) who had made me sick was doing that crying. That doctor knew all that; he said she had followed me there. And he worked over me all night; we paid him $20. The next day my nosebleed stopped. Then the next day we returned home; the doctor said that mapali·p (a witch), had put a cat inside my nose and that it was scratching all the time inside there; that's what made my nose bleed like that.

I was well for one year after that. Then a big whirlwind came, oh!, a big one, carrying sticks and straw in it; it came close to me; it touched me. Then right away my knee swelled up; I could hardly sleep at night. My knee looked as though it were going to burst. I dreamt bad dreams, about that woman, mapali·p. I told my husband about my dream. He got mad and went over to Kernville where mapali·p was staying. He said to her,

"I know you're witching my wife; that doctor over at Paiute told me. I want you to cure her."

Mapali·p didn't say anything for a long time. Then she said, "Well, what's the matter with her?"

"She's sick all the time. You made her nose bleed, her knee swell up; she's pretty sick. You'd better see about that; if she dies, I'm going to kill you." He was half-drunk; that's why he talked like that.

I guess mapali·p went out in the daylight after that and talked to her pet; I guess she was scared after that time when my husband talked to her, because I got better again.

All that time my mother and father were living at Canebrake most of the time; my mother was making tobacco and baskets all the time. She was making a living for herself. My mother used to visit me down at yïtiyamup for a week or so sometimes; then she'd go back to Canebrake. My husband and I used to go up there to see my parents, too, on horseback. It took all day to ride up there. All the Indians here had horses; they used to make saddles out of tule and bridles from milkweed twine.

When my 2 children were about 9 and 5 yrs. old, Old Bill Chico witched me; I don't know why. My father gave him a horse and 3 sacks of flour to make him stop, but he didn't want to stop; he wanted to kill me, I guess. Then my mother took me to Jose Chico; my father was working at Weldon that time. Jose was living on Bull Run creek. He worked 2 nights on me; he danced and sang; he sucked me in lots of places, on my throat and chest. I didn't see what he sucked out. Jose didn't want to tell us who was making me sick, because it was his own brother doing that; he just told us to move from the house we were living in. "There is a devil (ghost) living there," he said. It was a tule house and we burnt it; Jose said, "If you live there again, you'll be sick again." So we burnt the house and our baskets; everything. And my father built another house, of adobe, up at yïtiyamup, a little this side of Steban's house; we lived in it after that.

That man from Tejon (Francesco Sasterray, a Chumash) whom wišimlït married could make rain; he used to make rain all the time when he lived over at Tejon ranch; the people paid him to. He made rain over here, too, but we never paid him for doing it. He used to make lots of rain; there was deep grass up at yïtiyamup all the time and lots of flowers and seeds. It was pretty up at the rancheria then.

He had 3 different rain machines; one for snow, one for rain, and one to make waterspouts. He could stop the rain, too. A man living up at yïtiyamup stole the rain machine though. One day everybody was away; my sister-in-law was up at the spring washing clothes, and that man stole the rain machines. He was mean, that man; he couldn't use the rain machine, because he didn't know how to; I don't know why he stole it. Then one time after that the Tejon man got sick. He was in bed; he told wišimlït, "Give me that thing; I want to see it." She went and got the basket where he kept it; there was nothing there; it was all gone. The Tejon man felt bad; he cried and cried.

After that he died. The mother of those 2 witches up at Onyx had put poison in his coffee. He coughed, coughed, coughed all night; he got thin and died after awhile. A long time after that wišimlït's daughter-in-law, Tumasa, got sick; someone went and got Paiute Ramon. Ramon's friend came over here with him that time; he was a doctor, too. They were both Kawaiisu. Ramon worked on Tumasa and she got better. They told him about the rain machine. Doctors can tell where everything is; they see everything. Ramon told SM who had stolen his stepfather's machine. The thief had been watching Ramon doctor; Ramon pointed to him and said, "There he is; he's the one who stole your rain machine." The other doctor said, "He's right; he knows." Those doctors know everything; who is making you sick, or if you are a doctor, too, or if you have poison; everything.

Ramon started to lead that man over to the place where the thief had hidden the rain outfit. "Come on, show us where it is," the doctor told him. The man didn't want to go very much; he just stopped every little while. My husband was there. He got mad seeing that man take one or 2 steps and then stop, and he hit him over the head with a shovel. The man didn't say anything; he just walked away; he wouldn't go with that doctor at all then.

A long time afterward another man found that outfit; he said he would give it to Steban if he would pay him $10 for it. But Steban wouldn't. He should have though, then he could make rain now. The man who found it buried it somewhere else, in a dry place; it's there now. Bob Rabbit (a Kawaiisu) can make rain, too, but he says he doesn't want to make it any more. The people won't pay him anything for doing it. He says, "Let the country go dry."

But when they had those rain machines there were lots of plants here then. And my husband killed deer all the time; we always had deermeat. He was a good shot; he had a good rifle. The Indians used to use everything in a deer; they'd put the heart, liver, blood, all the guts inside the stomach lining and tie it up good and boil that up; it was fine. We never did that; just the oldtime Indians, but my mother's brother (a Koso) used to.

When my husband or my mother's brother hunted deer they always gave the mts. beads and tobacco and eagle down; they did that first, then they could kill all the deer they wanted. They gave the mts. little pieces of tobacco broken off the ball.

When Legora was about 11 yrs. old, one time my father went over to Jose Chico's. He and Jose got drunk; Jose talked badly to my father. "You're going on a good road (going to die)," Jose told my father. He was drunk when he said it.

My father came home. About a month later he started working in the tobacco patch with my mother; they came down from Canebrake to work in a patch near Weldon. They were camping at Tom Cook's place that time they were working the tobacco. One night my father returned to camp, sick; he could hardly walk. And then he was sick in bed for one week; he didn't get up any more. Somebody came and told me, "Your father's sick over there," so I went and stayed with him for a week. Then he died. Two white men came and made a coffin and they buried him in back of the Onyx rancheria, in the cemetery there. Lots of Indians are buried there. They put away his feather headdress in the coffin with him; he had been a dancer and always danced at fiestas.

I took my mother over to my house at yïtiyamup in the evening after we had buried my father. My mother lived with me for a long time after that; my husband used to work all the time, on ranches, or going to the mts. with cattle; my son, too, when he got big. After awhile my mother went over to her cousin's at Canebrake to get her face washed by her ta·gin; she didn't make any fiesta then, she just had her face washed. She gave that ta·gin $30 and some calico for washing her face. Finally my mother went back to Canebrake to live there. She lived with her brother and his daughter and a grandson of hers. She made lots of baskets up there to sell to a peddler who came around.

Then one day in July that grandson came down to SM's rancheria and told me my mother was dead. There had been a cloudburst up at Canebrake; my mother had been fixing a basket under a ramada when it began to rain. She had some tobacco drying down below in the canyon, and she got up and went down to take it in. Her brother and his daughter were standing watching. "Don't you go there," they said, but my mother didn't heed them. The water came down the canyon awfully quickly: it was all muddy and running strong. It caught my mother where she was, in the canyon.

I went up to Canebrake right away, on horseback, with my son and daughter and Mike Miranda; we looked all over in that canyon, but we never found my mother's body. Maybe it was buried in the sand. The others were looking for the body, too, but they couldn't find it. We stayed there one night and I burned her clothes. She had lots of clothes; Petra Miranda used to give her lots of them every time she went down to the Jesus ranch. I burned my mother's trunk with all her clothes in it, but I brought all her baskets home with me. I couldn't find her money. I asked my cousin where it was, but she didn't know where she kept it either. My mother must have had money, because she sold baskets all the time when the peddler went over to Canebrake. Maybe she had it buried good, some place.

After we had searched for my mother's body, the next day we returned to SM's rancheria, all of us, Mike and my children and I. We stayed there all the time then. Legora used to work for white people on the ranches over here, over there. I moved close to Steban's house. We didn't go to Poso Flat any more for acorns then; it was too far; no one goes over there now for acorns from here. We'd just gather about half a sackful right near home. Those acorns that grow up at Steban's aren't much good; they are too bitter. You have to work with them a long time to get them sweet. The acorns down by Isabella are all right; they're pretty sweet. But the best ones come from Poso Flat; you don't have to work with them hardly at all to get them sweet.

Sometimes I'd go down to see Petra Miranda at the Jesus ranch; we'd go in the morning and return in the afternoon, about 3 o'clock.

We'd just talk together, Petra and I; we'd tell each other what we had been doing all the time. I'd gather seeds, too; we bought flour instead of using acorn meal, but the children all liked chia and ku·l and pacist[?] gruel. That peddler used to come around all the time to trade baskets for clothes; I bought Legora a cape once, from him. It was pretty, with fur around it; it cost me $4 in trade.

One time my husband rode a bronco, all alone in a field over here, and Hawk came down when he was riding that horse and hit him on the side of his head with his wing. Six months after that my husband died; he was killed. He went over to Kernville one day; he got drunk over there with a white man. Nobody else was with them; no one saw what happened. My husband had $20 in gold in his pocket. He was shot in 3 places; somebody killed him and then took that money off him, because the pocket he had it in was cut off with a knife. Steban was cutting wood, camping with his wife down here, working for the Brown company; a white man came and told him about Pete's being killed. Then they all left that camp and came up and told me. Legora was working at Mrs. Nichols'; Estefana and another girl went up and got her, then we waited here all day. They were going to bring my husband's body over here and bury it down here, but they kept it over in Kernville all day. My son had no money to pay a man for bringing it over here in a wagon. One white man said, "Have you money?" My son said, "No." Then that white man gave my son $7. The white men at Kernville wanted to bury my husband over there at Kernville, but my son paid a man at Kernville and that man brought the body over here.

When they brought Pete's body back from Kernville everybody came and stayed at our place that night; they prayed for Pete. Steban prayed (in Spanish). We all cried; one person would start crying, then everybody would cry, all night long. The next morning we buried the body. I burned all Pete's clothes, then, right away; the mattresses, pillows, quilts, blankets; I didn't save anything of his. The plates I broke and threw away. He had a good rifle; I buried that well. If I hadn't done all that his ghost would have walked around inside the house, bothering us. Pete had 3 horses that time; I got one and my son and daughter each got one. SM wanted to get one, but the judge at Kernville told him he couldn't because Pete had children and the horses belonged to them. That's the way the old-timers always wanted to do; if a man died his brothers or parents took away the man's possessions instead of letting the widow have any of them. Not the dead man's clothes, because they were burned, but his horses, wagon, or anything like that. Now they can't do that way.

My husband was killed in November and I didn't eat meat after that until the next March. I cut my hair right after he was killed; I cut it off so that it came down a little way over my shoulders. And Legora and I wore black dresses for one yr. It gives you bad luck if you wear black too long; one yr. is enough. The old-timers never used to wash their faces after a relative had died, until they ate meat again; they bathed, but they never washed their faces. I washed mine though, before I ate meat. Legora and my son helped me get that money to eat meat again; I paid my ta·gin $50 for washing my face. I had a cousin for a ta·gin; she moved over to Visalia and died there.

Nobody saw that white man kill my husband; a long time afterward Legora heard that man tell somebody, "I killed my good friend, but he talked bad to me; I couldn't stand it." One time after that Legora saw that white man when he was drunk; she went up to him and she said, "You killed my father; now I'm going to kill you." He was frightened; it made us all laugh, how frightened he was. "Oh, no, Legora; don't do that! Don't kill me," he said. He looked funny when he said that, so frightened. Legora and all of us laughed and laughed at him.

Two yrs. after my husband died Willie Andreas started living with Legora. She was 17 yrs. old then. We lived up at yïtiyamup; Legora and Willie and I lived in the same house. I used to sit down all the time and make baskets. Not very many women made baskets then; Petra Nichols made them, too. Legora had a boy born to her.

One time my son had a fight with a Tule River reservation man living up here. They got into a quarrel; my son hit the Tule man on the head with a spur. After that fight the Tule man wouldn't ever talk to my son again. That man had poison; something, I don't know what; all those Tule reservation people have poison and they all know about it, men, women, young boys. It's Indian poison. The Tübatulabal don't have that poison up here, but one of those witches living up at the Onyx rancheria has some; they say she got it when she lived at Tule, and that she has it up here now. They put it in your food, in your cigarettes, in your drinks; in anything like that.

After that fight, one time my son got drunk and slept outside on the ground all night. It was cold; it was in November and there was frost on the ground. November was the same month my husband was killed in, 4 yrs. before.

My son used to do that; it was bad. He'd get drunk and then lie down, outside, but he had never gotten sick before from doing that. But when we went outside that morning we found him lying there with his mouth all blue, and he was dead. There were tracks around there; they said the Tule man had been there, but we hadn't heard anything that night. But they tracked the Tule man on horseback, down to the canyon. He had told somebody before that, "I'm going to kill that boy." That's how we knew he had done it.

When the Tule man saw Legora one time after that he told her not to tell her son Lloyd about it when Lloyd grew up; he said, "Don't tell that boy when he gets big, anything about that." He was afraid, you see.

Legora had another boy 3 yrs. after her first child. Then she had a daughter 3 yrs. after that. When her second son was a baby, just crawling around, I got a telegram. We were at yïtiyamup; Steban brought the telegram up there with him when he went to Weldon one day. It had stayed in the postoffice at Weldon for 2 days. My brother, ku·pal, had died over at Paiute and his relations had sent for me and for his 2 sons. They were both working on ranches around here at that time.

I started for Paiute that afternoon; Tony Pablo's father went with me and took his oldest son along. We went in a buggy; my nephews went ahead, on horseback. We stayed all night at Havilah; we camped out alongside the road. It was cold; we had to keep a fire going all night long. At sunup we started off again; it was too cold to start before the sun was up. We had to go over 2 big mts.; the road was steep; it takes a long time to get there in a buggy. But we arrived that afternoon about 3 o'clock.

"Oh, we buried him yesterday," they told us. They took me over there where they had buried him. They were just staying around the house waiting for us to get there; there were 2 houses; my brother's wife was living in one with 3 children and her married daughter lived in the other one with her children.

We stayed over there 2 nights. The day after we got there they burned my brother's clothes. I had bought $2 worth of calico at a store, to burn with his clothes. We cried for him when we burned his clothes. I could eat meat after that without having my face washed, but my sister-in-law couldn't; if my parents had been alive they wouldn't have either.

The next day after the burning we returned home. It only took us one day to get home; we left there early in the morning and arrived at the rancheria about sundown.

Then my mother's brother told me to come and live up at Canebrake. "Pretty soon I'm going to die, then you can have this land," he said. He was living at Canebrake; when we moved up there he stayed with us. We all went up there; Irene (LT's daughter) was little then and Legora was married to John Tungate (a white man). We had a tent up there; Mike Miranda made us a tent to live in all winter. There was no road to Canebrake then, when we first moved up there. The children grew old enough to go to school, so every winter we would move down to Sweet's ranch; Legora's children used to go to school from there in a buggy. In summer we'd move back to Canebrake again. Finally they built a road and the bus came up there for the children; then we stayed there all the time and didn't move back and forth.

When we were down at Sweet's one winter an old man rode down from Canebrake and told us my uncle had been burnt up in his house up there. My uncle had a little tule house and he used to build a big fire all the time in the middle of the house, on the ground. There were big dry logs all around outside the house. We went up there; everybody went up to see the corpse. There was just a little bit of it left; the house was all burnt up.

I got my uncle's land after he died; I already owned some my mother and father had.

Two yrs. after Irene was born, Legora had Annie; then 2 yrs. after that, Esther; then Johnnie 2 yrs. after Esther. Legora's husband, John Tungate, kept living with us at Canebrake. One time when Irene was about 11 or 12 yrs. old, we were sitting outside the house one evening in summer, around sundown. Mike was up there that time, too. Fred (a grandson) was playing his guitar. We saw a hummingbird coming straight toward Irene; he was hitting that little girl. None of us could catch him. The next day Irene felt sick; that night she had convulsions and foam was coming out of her mouth. She didn't talk, she didn't eat anything. That night, about midnight, we asked Mike, "Have you money?" "Yes, I have $10," he said. "All right," we said. He gave us that money and we harnessed a horse up to the buggy. We were going to take Irene to a (Kawaiisu) doctor at Kelso valley.

Passing by Onyx we heard a chicken crow; it was about 3 a.m. We got to Kelso valley at 2 o'clock that afternoon. Irene's face was swollen; she wouldn't eat or drink anything.

We arrived at the doctor's house about 8 o'clock. He worked with Irene all night; he sang; he danced, hopping all around inside his house; near daylight he went outside and looked toward the E. He sang, "All my animals are coming here now." Then elk came to that doctor. We couldn't see that elk, but the doctor could. Elk told the doctor, "I'm looking all over; I see 2 witches, those 2 women at the Onyx rancheria. Those are the only 2 witches there are in this country; there are no others," Elk told that doctor.

After awhile, after the doctor had sucked Irene, that devil inside her went out. The doctor asked Legora if she had heard the devil leaving Irene's body. "No," Legora said. But the doctor had heard it, when it went out; he sucked it out. That morning Irene was glad, happy; she was all right again. Two months ago she came up here to see us from Riverside. She didn't want us to tell anyone at the Onyx rancheria that she was up here visiting. "Those witches might make me sick again," she said. She's still frightened because those witches made her sick that time. They're mean, those women. They killed Barney's wife because she ate meat right after her husband died, without having her face washed. They got mad at Legora because she and John Tungate went down to Bakersfield and testified about a horse one of the witches wanted to get after a son died. I guess maybe that's why they made Irene sick that time.

When Johnnie was a little baby, just crawling around, John Tungate got work in Inyo county. We all went up there; we stayed at Bishop and then at Lone Pine. I like to camp around; so does Legora. But after awhile I like to return home again. We stayed at Lone Pine for a yr.; I didn't like it up there. The Indians there (Owens Valley Paiute) said, "Why don't you take up land here, and stay here?" But I wanted to get home; we all did, the children, too. They liked Canebrake; they always liked to live up there. So we returned to Canebrake. Then John Tungate left; he and Legora separated. After he left we used to go over to Visalia in the summertime to pick fruit; Legora and I both worked and Esther and Annie took care of the house and of Johnnie. We used to camp at Tule River reservation on the way home; there was a man there who loaned us a house. He told us, "Don't go visiting around here, because all these people are bad; they all have poison they use." They are queer people over there at Tule; they don't visit each other any over there, because they are afraid they will be poisoned.

We made 3 trips to Visalia to work in the fruit. The second time we went with Steban and his daughter. Then we heard, "There's no money over there at all; they're not picking the fruit, they're letting it go." That's why we stopped going over; everybody here stopped going. The last time we went to Visalia we left Annie and Irene up at Onyx and then they went to Riverside, to school down there.

I was feeling good all that time. We always used to go live at Canebrake in the summer, and then we'd come down to the Mack ranch in winter, so that Esther and Johnnie could go to school at Weldon. At the Mack ranch though I began to dream bad again; I'd see one woman whom I don't know, holding my head. That's why my ear hurts now; I have been sick like that for 4 yrs.

Then we had to leave our house at the Mack ranch. A white man wanted to live in that house. We moved up to Rafael Chico's place; they kept asking us at the Onyx rancheria, "Why don't you move up here, to Rafael's?" But there were too many drunken men around up there; they would come and fight inside the houses. We didn't like that. And those witches live too close to Rafael's. I was sick all the time up there. We lived there 2 months; I coughed, coughed all the time. So 2 yrs. ago last April we moved down here (near Weldon) from there. When we moved down here I got well. But last summer I got this cough again, only not so bad as I have it now. I can't do much now; I can't make tobacco this year; because I'm too sick. We got lots last year; enough to last this year too, I think. I got some chia seeds last year too, over by the little hill in Charley Andress' meadow. But it's too hot to go cut the tobacco this year, and kneeling hurts me. I'd like to go to that Indian doctor they have over at Bishop; there's a good one over there. Maybe Legora and I will go over this fall. If I could see that doctor I think I'd be all right again.

Part 2
The Christian Indians, from the Eighteenth
Century to Indian Removal, 1830

The dissenting English, pilgrims and Puritans, who established and then fortified their settlement in the New World, had some strongly-held if not very accurate ideas about the manner of person they would encounter here. They were unsure about the origin of the misnamed Indians, because—and these were people who looked to their Bibles for all things—Noah had had but three sons, progenitors of the white, the yellow, and the black peoples of the earth. Except for Esau, a red man and a hunter (but *hairy*, it was written, and so, quite unlike the Indian!), there was no biblical figure who seemed a likely ancestor of these people indigenous to America.

Whatever the Indian's origin might be, there was little doubt as to his present condition. In 1625, Samuel Purchas called the indigenous population (which he did not in the least know), "more brutish than the beasts they hunt, more wild and unmanly than that unmanned wild country which they range rather than inhabit." William Bradford, constructing the authoritative account *Of Plymouth Plantation*, affirms that his fellow *Mayflower* pilgrims expected to find "only savage and brutish men which range up and down, little otherwise than the wild beasts. . . . " Roger Williams, interested in Indians and Indian languages, listed as the names the English used for the Natives "Salvages [savages], Indians, Wild-men . . . Abergeny men [aborigine], Pagans, Barbarians, Heathens" none of which could be considered very positive.[1]

Although they were considered "savage," the Indians were at least acknowledged to be men (the Puritans did not, in this regard, re-enact the debates on this subject of their Spanish predecessors a century earlier), and so were held to be in possession of immortal souls. As the Reverend Solomon Stoddard would write in the eighteenth century, "It is an act of Love to our own nature to seek their Salvation."[2] This, men like Richard Bourne of Plymouth, the Mayhews of Martha's

1. The passages by Purchas, Bradford, and Williams are quoted in Roy Harvey Pearce, *Savagism and Civilization: A Study of the Indian and the American Mind* (Berkeley: Univ. of California Press, 1988), p. 7.
2. Pearce, *Savagism*, p. 32.

Vineyard, and, perhaps most importantly, John Eliot had begun to do from the 1640s on, for "Love" or for more complex reasons. Eliot, who translated the Bible into an Indian language, established the First Indian Church at Natick (Massachusetts) in 1660, and, by the time of the Wampanoag attempt under Metacom ("King Philip") to repel the colonists (1675–76), there were a number of so-called "praying towns" of Christian Indians. (For all their prayers, the Christian Indians were not spared the murderous wrath of their Puritan "friends" during King Philip's War.) Daniel Gookin in the seventeenth century and Cotton Mather very early in the eighteenth century offered some brief biographical accounts of Indian lives, but it took another half century before the first autobiographies by Indians began to appear.

These are the stories of Native men and women who were sufficiently impressed by what the missionaries offered to accept Christ. Along with the acceptance of "the Word" came the acceptance of training in the rudiments of literacy; they learned to read the Bible (with what understanding we will never know), and to write—letters, accounts, and, in some cases, the stories of their lives. Although these are indeed self-written lives, autobiographies in the western sense, they are inevitably bicultural; this is to say that, while, on the one hand, we have Native American versions of Christian "exemplary" lives, or "spiritual autobiographies," we also have, on the other hand, cases of self-presentations that consciously or not are influenced by traditional Indian thought about the appropriate way to speak of oneself. This latter dimension of the early autobiographies by Christian Indians has only just begun to be studied, so that I would here only urge the reader who is tempted to see these texts as dry, goody-goody, or even traitorous, to keep open the possibility that they are more complicated than that. If they explicitly reject a traditional Native worldview (and they do), that same worldview may, nevertheless, be residually active in the text. And, in any case, in the writing of the Reverends Samson Occom and William Apess, if not of Catharine Brown, we have strong defenses of Indian "morals" and strong attacks against the hypocrisy and (in Apess) the racism (although he did not use that word) of the whites.

The eighteenth century was, of course, the century in which the American colonies became the United States of America, a development that did not bode well for the tribes who had, for the most part, backed the British in the Revolutionary War. (This was the case because, among other reasons, the British offered valuable trade goods and they were not, unlike the colonists, particularly interested in permanent settlement on Indian lands.) Apess fought on the American side in the War of 1812, but Black Hawk, whose autobiography we shall encounter in Part Three of this book, along with many other Native leaders, did not. It was after the Louisiana Purchase by President Thomas Jefferson in 1802, and after the departure of the Spanish from Florida and Louisiana, that the entire eastern seaboard, north to south, became part of the United States—with important and negative consequences for the Native inhabitants of those lands.

It was in Indian warfare, for example, that Andrew Jackson, whose ascendancy to the presidency in 1828 was to prove so disastrous for the eastern Indians, achieved his reputation. It was Jackson who supported the movement to relocate the eastern Indians to areas west of the Mississippi, a position that was consistent, most particularly, with the wishes of the state of Georgia. It is with the Indian Removal Act of 1830, passed by Congress by only five votes, that the section immediately following this one begins.

It should be noted here, however, that the autobiographies by Christian Indians in this section are the life writings of persons who were converted by Protestants in the eighteenth and early nineteenth centuries. So far as I am aware, there is very little in the way of Native autobiographical records of similar attempts in the Southwest and California, where Catholic priests had aggressively missionized and converted many tribal peoples for almost two hundred years. The southwestern Indian autobiographies of which I am aware all date from the twentieth century.

David Fowler, Samson Occom, Catharine Brown, and William Apess all left records that I consider autobiographical. In the case of Fowler, there exist a number of letters documenting an important stage of his life; while these do not amount to an autobiography as such, they do convey a strong sense of his experience. Brown was a letter writer, too, and a journal keeper; what we know of her life is the result of a compilation by a Methodist cleric. Occom, surely the best-known Indian preacher of the eighteenth century, wrote his own life, explaining, justifying, and representing himself. Apess also was a convert to Methodism and a man whose life and work are only beginning to become widely known.

5
The Letters of Eleazar Wheelock's Indians

Edited by

JAMES D. McCALLUM

David Fowler, a Montauk and the brother-in-law of the better known Samson Occom, entered Reverend Eleazar Wheelock's Moor's Charity School in 1759, at the age of twenty-four. He worked among various tribes during the 1760s, and, in the 1770s, along with Occom and other Christian Indians from New England, helped form the Brothertown Settlement among the Oneidas in New York.

Although he courted Amy Johnson and Hannah Poquantiup, whom he mentions in his letters, Fowler eventually married Hannah Garret, a Pequot. Also mentioned in his letters are two other Moor's students, Joseph Woolley, who taught at Onohquaga, and Samuel Kirkland, one of the most important Protestant missionaries to the Six Nations in the eighteenth century.

Fowler's letters to his teacher and benefactor Eleazar Wheelock are not in any sense what we usually think of as constituting an autobiography, but I have included them because I believe they do present a good sense of a life. This life is, of course, one that the eighteenth century regarded more or less favorably, for David Fowler was regarded as an appropriately educated, more or less civilized, Christian Indian—one engaged in a strenuous, often painful attempt to extend the benefits of his own enlightened condition to his fellow Indians. I have also included one of Wheelock's letters to Fowler among our selections, to provide a reference point for the reader with regard to "proper" eighteenth-century spelling, syntax, and diction.

It should be noted that although Fowler's commitment to Christianity, civilization, and his mentor Wheelock is surely sincere, still, he is hardly so docile or acquiescent as Catharine Brown, whom we shall consider next. Indeed, recent work by Laura Murray[1] suggests that there is a good deal of "resistance" in Fowler's "subordination."

Fowler's letters are from The Letters of Eleazar Wheelock's Indians,

---

1. Laura Murray, " 'Pray Sir, Consider a Little': Rituals of Subordination and Strategies of Resistance in the Letters of Hezekiah Calvin and David Fowler to Eleazar Wheelock, 1764–1768," *Studies in American Indian Literatures* 4 (1992): 48–74.

edited by James Dow McCallum and published as part of the Dartmouth College Manuscripts Series.[2] *Variants in the text, e.g.,* $_{\text{I cant keep}}^{\text{it is difficult}}$ *, represent McCallum's best guesses for blurred, illegible, or otherwise unclear portions of Fowler's manuscript.*

List of David Fowler's Books

"Books that David Fowler Carried into the Mohawk Count^{ry}" from the Libery to destribute among the Boys that are keeping School there & found for himself" —

20 New Spelling book, Auther Gilleo Ker
10 Smaller Intitleed the British Instructor first Ser
2 Small catacism by John Watts
2 Second Ser. do by John Watts
1 Book. I. Divine Breathing by John Beart. A.
1 Book Con^{g} twenty five Discourses Sutable to the Lords Supper
—by John Owen
1 School Masters Assistant

David Fowler to Eleazar Wheelock

Conawarohare in Oneida June 15th 1765

REV.^{d} AND HON.^{d} SIR,

THIS is the twelfth Day since I began to keep this School, and I have put eight of my Scholars into third Page of the Spelling book: some almost got down to the Bottom of the same third: —I never saw Children exceed these in learing. The Number of my Scholars are twenty six when they are all present togather: but $_{\text{I cant keep}}^{\text{it is difficult}}$ them togather: they are $_{\text{always}}^{\text{often}}$ roving about from Place to Place to get something to live upon. Provision is very scarace with them. —

I am also teaching a singing School: they take great pleasure in learning to sing: We can already carry three Parts of several Tunes.

My Friends are always looking for the Ministers there is scarce a Day passes over but that some Body will ask me when will the Ministers come: all $_{\text{what}}^{\text{that}}$ I can tell them, is, I expect they will come middle

2. *The Letters of Eleazar Wheelock's Indians,* ed. James Dow McCallum, Dartmouth College Manuscripts Series, I (Hanover, NH, 1932). Reprinted by permission of the Dartmouth College Library.

of this Month. I have been treated very kindly since I came to this Place, — I believe I should want for nothing if they had wherewith to bestow it.

I find it very hard to live there without the other Rib, for I am oblig'd to eat with Dogs, I say, with Dogs because they are continually liking Water out off their Pales and Kettles; yea, I have often seen Dogs eating their Victuals when they set their Dishes down, they'll ony make a little Noise to show their Displeasure to Dogs and take up the Dish. finish of what was left. My Cooks are nasty as Hogs; their Cloaths are black and greasy as my Shoes. their Hands are dirty as my Feet, but they cleanse them by kneading Bread; their Hands will be very clean after they have kneaded three of four Loaves of Brad. I am oblig'd to eat whatsoever they give me for fear they will be displeas'd with me; after this Month I shall try to clean some of them. for I must move along by Degrees, if the once get out with me it is all over with me.

I shall have a House built me next Week, then I shall have my Victuals cleaner.

I think 30 lawful money per Annum as the least that will be necessary will not be too much for my Support for the ^{first Year or two} _{three first Years:} It is very costly ^{living} _{to live} here, ^{being} _{because} it is so far from an English Settlement; and I determine to live better than a Hog, for my Food now is not fit for any Man, that has been used to have his Victuals drest clean: I am almost sick now for want of some Refreshment that is nourishing. I wish I had some of Mrs. Wheelock's Bread & Milk, little sweet Cake and good boild Meat. I could eat those things gready as a Hog that has been kept in a Pen two Days without it's Swill. —

I now & then drink some   which I carried with me

My Daily Meat is Tea   and dry Bread,

which I bought

little Fish which I cetch out of a small River and their Pottage which is made of pounded Corn.

If you ^{could obtain the Favair to} _{can get me Writing} that will draw Provision ^{now & then out of the} _{from Kings} Stores I wish you would do it: for I am obliged to go forty Miles to buy my Provision. —

I heard from Mr Kirtland a few Days ago. he is well and teaching Children to read. "Please to give my kind Respects to Madam." Master and Love to all the rest of your Family, especialy to "your Children." I ask the continuance of your Prayers, that God would give me Grace and fill my Heart with the Love of God and Compassion to perishing Souls and that God would make me an Instrument of wining many Souls to Christ before I leave this World. — Please to accept much Love & Respects from,

> *your affectionate.*
>> *though unworthy Pupil,*
>>> David Fowler.

Onoyda June 24, 1765

Hon.^d & Rev^d, Sir

I now write you a few Lines just to inform you that I am well at present, and have been so ever since I left your House, blessed be God for his goodness to me. —I am well contented here as long as I am in such great Business. My Scholars learn very well; I have put eleven in a, b, abs: I have three more that will go to that Place this week; and some have got to the sixth Page. —It is ten thousand Pities they cante keep togather, they are _often always_ going about to get their Provision. My Father _one of the Chiefs at in whose House I keep_ told me, be beleived some of the Indians would starve to Death this Summer; some of them have almost consum'd all their Corn already.

I came too late this Spring, I could not put anything in the Ground, I hope I shall next Year. —I beleive I shall _perswade the get all these_ Men in this Castle at least the most of them to labour next Year: They begin to see now that they would live better if they cultivate their Lands than they do now by Hunting & fishing: These men are the laziest Crew I ever Saw in all my Days: their Women _will would_ get up early in the Morning and be pounding corn for Breakfast _the men and they lie_ Sleeping till the Victuals is almost ready and as soon as the Breakfast is over the Women take up their Axes and Hoes and way to the Fields and leave their Children with the Men to tend; you _may would_ see half a Dozen walking about with Children upon their Backs: a lazy and sordid Wretches, but they are to be pitied not frown'd.

I have been miserably of for an Interpreter I _can cant_ say but very little to them; I hope by next Spring I shall be my own Interpreter. It is very hard to live here without the other Boon; I now am oblig'd to wash, mend my Clothes, cook all my Victuals and wash all the things I use, which is exceeding hard; I can't go into a Feild as I should do if I had a Cook here. I shant be able to employ my vacant Hours in improving ye Lands as I should do. . . .

I beleive, I shall come down latter end of August but I shall tarry a little while with you. I design to hasten up here again; I shall make this Place my Home as long as I live. —Give my kind Respects to Mrs. Wheelock, Love to your Children and to all the scholars."

And may the Blessings of Heaven rest on you &c &c and continue you a long & rich Blessing in the World, may the Heathen in the Wilderness feel the goodness of thy Labours. —May you have Double Measure of the Spirit of God, and fill your Heart with Love of God and Compassion to poor perishing Souls, and may the Giver of all things, give Strength and Health, Wisdom and Authority to rule govern and theach those who are commited to your Care in Fear of the Lord: which is the sincere Prayer of him who desires the Continuance of your Prayers.

> *your affectionate.*
> *tho: unworthy Pupil,*
> DAVID FOWLER.

Canawarohare Janr^y 21 1766

REV.^d AND HON.^d SIR

After much Warry and Fatigue about my House and Journeys after also hungry Belly I began to keep my School steadily sometime in November. My Scholars learn very well: I find it is impossible to keep the Children steadily to School, lett Men labour and work as English do: They are lazy and inhuman pack of Creatures as I ever saw in the World; They have seen me working and tuging Day after Day and never offerd to help me in the least thing I had to do in my House only finish'd covering it and left me. I was oblig'd to eat with Dogs near two Months—I say with Dogs because they are always licking Water out off the Pails and Kettles we use: Now I live like a Gentleman, I have a planty of Corn, Flour, Meat and rotten Fish. —I applied to Sir William for Provision; accordingly, he order the Commanding Officer at the Royal Block House to give me out Privision as long as I should want.

I am exceeding sorry as well as my poor Friends that Mr Chamberlain does not return to us this Winter. —The Indians cannot conceive what can be the Reason why he don't return. But I told them three Reason, why he dont, return: and after they heard them they were easy.

I never saw such general Disposition of hearing the Word of God amongst these poor People as I do now: most every one of the adults of this Place, have openly renounc'd their Liquor and said that they will devote themselves in hearing the Word of God. Now is the time for Ministers to come up whilst they, are in such Disposition. —O for a Minister whose Heart is full of Love to God and Compassion to poor Sinners, one who is meak and lowly and crafty in wining Souls to Christ. who has a real Sence and worth of Immortal Souls would greatly weaken the Strong Holds of Satan in this Place. —Dear Sir, do all that is in your Power to get up a Minister early in the Spring. for the poor Creatures are rearly desirous to hear the Word of God, we have no Minister and yet we have a full Assembly every Sabbath. I have nothing New to acquaint you; I enjoyy a good State of Health and am contented.

I cant come down till some of ye Scholars come up and take my School. If Jacob is to come up; do let him take a School near me so that I may take care of him. —I want all my Cloaths in readiness. for I shall be in a very great Hast when I do come. I determine to see my poor Parents before I return; for I serv'd them basely last Fall. If they suffer I cant tell how I can come up. Joseph dertermines to come down and pay you Visit also Thomas who has done me more Service than all the Town. He tells me; that he designs to go down with me and set my Rib on his Horse and he will come up with own his Horses or Legs, that is if I shall find one.

I rejoie greatly because I could not get one last year, espicially for Wooley. I hear he has no House.

I just now heard of Mr Kirtland he is poor forsaken Man. The Indians have drove him out off their Houses and now he lives in a poor House in the Woods my friends cant conceive what he keeps them for: the Indians dont want him there; for they all hat him. It seems to me by what Mr Gray has wrote to him that he is uneasy. Capt Butler received a Letter from him whilst I was at his House, and immediately ask'd me how many Letters I brought for Mr Kirtland I told him one. &c Tell y^r oldest Boy who went down the last that both his Parents left off geting Drunk.

I forgot to tell you what sort of Cloth I would have for my Cloaths. I want blue Broadcloth and that which is good. Give my kind Regards to Madam, also to Sir Wheelock, and Master, and Love to the rest of the Family also to all the Scholars. —That the Lord would prolong your worthy Live, and make you a rich Blessing in the World, also an Instrument of spreading the Gospel amongst the poor Heathen in this Continent and after well spent Life here receive your in the Mansions Joy and there to shine as the Stars in the Firmament forever and ever is the Desire and Prayer,

Revd Sir,

Of your affecionte
and obedient Servant

DAVID FOWLER

P.S. I hope you will overlook all my imperfections in this Letter for I wrote the bigest Part of it in Darkness.

Lebanon Aug.^st 26 1766

REV.^d AND HON.^d SIR,

I think it very hard that I must be blam'd so much as I have been since my Return from home, and all for taking up those things at Mr Breeds, when I have Orders from Mr Wheelock to get them, for which I am now accounted a Devil or Proude as the Devil. After you have repeatedly and manifestly told me that I should have whatsoever I wanted; If you denied me when I came to ask for them; I should not feel half so bad as I do now, or if you told me in a mild Manner when I got home: those things which you got were too good and too costly, you must not have them, I should not resist you—. You know, Sir, I have always been governd and advis'd by you with all ease imaginable.

This brings into my mind what Treatment I met since I came here. yea it is shameful, when I have been so faithful to you as if I was your Negro, yea I have almost kill'd my self in Labouring.—I have done hither to all what laid in my Power to help you; I think I can say and beleive you too that I have done more Service to you than all the rest of the Indian Boys. and now I am too bad to live in the House for one of my misstepes, therefore I must leave you and your School this very Day and go weeping in the Road homeward

I am greiv'd that I have troubled you so much as I have. I am sorry those things were not denied me at first and then it would been allwell and easy before now.—But asure you, Sir, you shall receive Payment from me yearly till every Fathing be paid, it shall not be said all that Money and Pains which was spent for David Fowler on Indian was for nought. I can get Payment as well as white Man. O Dear me! I cant say no more,

I am
your unworthy Servant

DAVID FOWLER

101

Eleazar Wheelock to David Fowler

Lebanon 26th Augt 1766

DAVID FOWLER

I this Minute received Yours and Sorry to find that you are not yet come to your right Temper of Mind. Who has calld You a Devil, or Said you are as proud as the Devil Since You came here?[3] Who has ever said that you have not behaved well in the Main since you lived with me, or that I have not sat as much by You and expected as much benefit to ye grand Design as by any Indian I ever Educated or there has there been any Indian y^t I ha' been mo. friend^y to y^n to y^o & y^r Charact^r.—ha' I ev^r S^d y^o ha' not done mo. for my Benefit y^n all ye Indians I ever had &c. and now y^o say I am too bad to live in Y^e House for one of my mySteps y^{re}fore I must leave y^o & y^r School y^s very day & go weep^g in y^s Road Homeward—Now David cons^r a little. Is this Just comely and reasonable Treatment of me. ha' I s^d worse of y^o or to y^o y^n y^t I was afraid y^t ye Prid of y^r ①* aspird aft^r such Grand^r as was not for ye Gl^y of G. & cod not consist with ye good of ye gen^l Design in view. y^t w^n I had given y^o leave to get every thing y^t y^o wanted for ye Design & told y^o I begrutchd y^o noth^g y^t was necess^{ry} for y^o.—y^t y^o shod affect to cloath yslf & Hannah like Courtiers & w^n y^o knew y^t I had been already reproachd thro' ye Country, as I ha' been only for lett^g y^o Wear an old velvet Coat y^t was given to y^o—I told y^o y^t ye Eyes of all Europe & America w^{re} Upon y^o & me too. & ye Eyes of thousands w^o are unfriendly & will not fail to Catch at any occasion to reproach me & ye Design—I told y^o it was no Interest of mine but only y^r Hon^r & Interest of X y^t I was plead^g for, & ye Success of y^t Cause w^c has been so long an [—?] & in w^c I ha' So much labourd & Worn out myself—& w^c certainly so nearly concerns y^o as me to Lab^r to promote—did y^o not w^n I was only Enquir^g w^t it was prud^t & best for y^o to ha' so many as 4 p^r of shoes at once rise up & wth a very unbecom^g air go out of ye Room & Say I w^{ll} ha' no shoes I'll wear Indian shoes—& how y^o & Hannah ha' Spent y^r prec. Hours yesterday & t'day I know not—Or how y^o will live or w^n y^o will serve tog^r I know not I wish y^r Sett^g out we^{re} mo. in ye Meekness & Humility of X—as for my own p^t great as ye prospects of y^r Usefulness are, (and y^e are

3. Wheelock makes frequent use of abbreviation. In particular, he uses the *y* to stand for both *y* and *the*, so that its meaning in the following lines runs both as "[the] grand Design" and "[w]here has there been any Indian that I have been more friendly to than to you and your character" (6, 7). The symbol in line 13 signifies "heart," according to James D. McCallum (p. 104).

very great if y° will take G. with You) I don't at all des^r you shod return to Onoida wth y^r present Tempers—nor am I at all afraid but I can fully vindicate my own Reputation, take w^t Course y° Will—I suppose y° cant reasonably think it unjust if ye Whole & plain Truth comes to ye Light of ye World, if I am put upon my own Vindication—nor do I think y° can feal very Easie if y° sho^d go 'till y° return to me again. w^c I promise myself y° will do as Soon as y° return to God. my Heart is ye Same and as full of Kindness & Good Will tow^{ds} You as ever it has been. and I am as ready to do any thing y^t will Hon^r Christ && promote ye Salv^n of ye Souls of ye poor Indians as ever I was—but I ha' no notion of Send^g any Man w° is aiming to set up himself instead of XJ. as ye obj^t of y^r W^P & w^n y° will app^r ye Same as y° ha' heretofore done y° will find me ye same

I am

Y^r Sincere Well wisher
ELEAZR WHEELOCK

David Fowler to Eleazar Wheelock

Mohegan May 25 1768

REV^d SIR

I must write again for that Money I sent for last year. I think you did not deal justly with me. For these things which Mr Kirtland had of me were my own procureing, Some I got by the Money which Mr Whelock gave me. Now I always thought whatsoever you gave me were never to be recalld again; because I have heard you say many times to give Gifts is like casting them into the Sea; But my things came to me a little harder, for I sufferd Hunger, Cold, Heat, and Weariness for them.

Pray Sir, consider a little what I have done for Mr Kirtland. I helpd to build his House and cleared two Fields, all this work I give him freely, as you would give a meal of Victuals to a perishing man. It would be a grand Imposition indeed for me to come to you for Money when I am imployed by others. But now I call for my own propety.

Reverend Sir, Dont fail of geting Money and send it down to Sister Occom. if you dont allow me but three Pound I shall be glad of it because I shall be troubled if I dont get the Money. I should not feal so distessd if I had not been sick so long. I was confind ten Weeks by Sickness, and after I got about a little, Fathers Wigwam was burnt into ashes and all their household stuff were consumed in it also—all our things save only our best Cloathing.

I have nothing new to acquaint you with. I shall be glad to hear of your School (also of you and your Family, I write in utmost hast for my company are waiting.

DAVID FOWLER

6
A Short Narrative of My Life

SAMSON OCCOM

Samson Occom was certainly not the last of the Mohegans, but, in 1725, two years after his birth, the Mohegans numbered no more than 351 persons—and they were unfortunately divided, just then, over who ought to be their sachem, or leader. Born in New London, Connecticut, Occom eventually found his way to Eleazar Wheelock, who began to teach him before actually founding his Indian Charity School. Occom returned to New London where he taught for two years before moving on to teach the Montauk of Long Island. It was there that he was licensed to preach and that he met and married Mary Fowler, a Montauk, and David Fowler's sister.

In 1765, Occom went to England, together with the Reverend Nathaniel Whitaker, with the purpose of raising funds for Wheelock's school. Occom delivered about three hundred sermons in England and Scotland, collecting some twelve thousand pounds; this money allowed Wheelock to move his school from Lebanon, Connecticut, to New Hampshire, where it would, without any particular benefit to the Indians, soon become Dartmouth College.

Occom's first "autobiography," actually a letter he wrote in Boston on November 28, 1765, before he set off for England, detailed his education in a single page. He then composed an autobiographical text of ten pages, dated September 17, 1768, that remained unpublished in the Dartmouth archives until 1982. The document is, in David Brumble's sense, one of self-vindication, and so, for all of Occom's Christian acculturation, it perhaps also exhibits elements of traditional Mohegan narrative modes. This is, in any case, an area for further study.

In his lifetime, Occom was perhaps best known for his Sermon at the Execution of Moses Paul *(Moses Paul was an Indian convicted of murder), which was published in 1772 and was popular enough to run through some nineteen editions, extending into the nineteenth century. Occom was the minister of New Stockbridge and an occasional teacher to the Tuscarora at the time of his death in 1792.*

Our text comes from Bernd Peyer's first publication of it in The Elders Wrote: An Anthology of Early Prose by North American Indians, 1768–1931 *(1982).[1] All material in parentheses has been added by Peyer.*

1. *The Elders Wrote: An Anthology of Early Prose by North American Indians, 1768–1931,* ed. Bernd Peyer (Berlin: Dietrich Reimer Verlag, 1982).

David Murray, in Forked Tongues: Speech, Writing and Representation in North American Indian Texts,[2] *offers a chapter called "Christian Indians: Samson Occom and William Apes" that is useful for further study.*

From my Birth till I received the Christian Religion

I was Born a Heathen and Brought up In Heathenism, till I was between 16 & 17 years of age, at a Place Calld Mohegan, in New London, Connecticut, in New England. My Parents Livd a wandering life, for did all the Indians at Mohegan, they Chiefly Depended upon Hunting, Fishing, & Fowling for their Living and had no Connection with the English, excepting to Traffic with them in their small Trifles; and they Strictly maintained and followed their Heathenish Ways, Customs & Religion, though there was Some Preaching among them. Once a Fortnight, in ye Summer Season, a Minister from New London used to come up, and the Indians to attend; not that they regarded the Christian Religion, but they had Blankets given to them every Fall of the Year and for these things they would attend and there was a Sort of School kept, when I was quite young, but I believe there never was one that ever Learnt to read any thing, — and when I was about 10 Years of age there was a man who went about among the Indian Wigwams, and wherever he Could find the Indian Children, would make them read; but the Children Used to take Care to keep out of his way; — and he used to Catch me Some times and make me Say over my Letters; and I believe I learnt Some of them. But this was Soon over too; and all this Time there was not one amongst us, that made a Profession of Christianity — Neither did we Cultivate our Land, nor kept any Sort of Creatures except Dogs, which we used in Hunting; and we Dwelt in wigwams. These are a Sort of Tents, Covered with Matts, made of Flags. And to this Time we were unacquainted with the English Tongue in general though there were a few, who understood a little of it.

2. David Murray, *Forked Tongues: Speech, Writing, and Representation in North American Indian Texts* (Bloomington: Indiana Univ. Press, 1991).

From the Time of our Reformation till I left Mr. Wheelocks

When I was 16 years of age, we heard a Strange Rumor among the English, that there were Extraordinary Ministers Preaching from Place to Place and a Strange Concern among the White People. This was in the Spring of the Year. But we Saw nothing of these things, till Some Time in the Summer, when Some Ministers began to visit us and Preach the Word of God; and the Common People all Came frequently and exhorted us to the things of God, which it pleased the Lord, as I humbly hope, to Bless and accompany with Divine Influence to the Conviction and Saving Conversion of a Number of us; amongst whom I was one that was Imprest with the things we had heard. These Preachers did not only come to us, but we frequently went to their meetings and Churches. After I was awakened & converted, I went to all the meetings, I could come at; & Continued under Trouble of Mind about 6 months; at which time I began to Learn the English Letters; got me a Primer, and used to go to my English Neighbours frequently for Assistance in Reading, but went to no School. And when I was 17 years of age, I had, as I trust, a Discovery of the way of Salvation through Jesus Christ, and was enabl'd to put my trust in him alone for Life & Salvation. From this Time the Distress and Burden of my mind was removed, and I found Serenity and Pleasure of Soul, in Serving God. By this time I just began to Read in the New Testament without Spelling, — and I had a Stronger Desire Still to Learn to read the Word of God, and at the Same Time had an uncommon Pity and Compassion to my Poor Brethren According to the Flesh. I used to wish I was capable of Instructing my poor Kindred. I used to think, if I Could once Learn to Read I would Instruct the poor Children in Reading, — and used frequently to talk with our Indians Concerning Religion. This continued till I was in my 19th year: by this Time I Could Read a little in the Bible. At this Time my Poor Mother was going to Lebanon, and having had Some Knowledge of Mr. Wheelock and hearing he had a Number of English youth under his Tuition, I had a great Inclination to go to him and be with him a week or a Fortnight, and Desired by Mother to Ask Mr. Wheelock whether he would take me a little while to Instruct me in Reading. Mother did so; and when She Came Back, She Said Mr. Wheelock wanted to See me as Soon as possible. So I went up, thinking I Should be back again in a few Days; when I got up there, he received me With kindness and Compassion and in Stead of Staying a Fortnight or 3 Weeks, I Spent 4 Years with him. — After I had been with him Some Time, he began

The Reverend Sampson Occom. Courtesy of the Dartmouth College Library.

to acquaint his Friends of my being with him, and of his Intentions of Educating me, and my Circumstances. And the good People began to give Some Assistance to Mr. Wheelock, and gave me Some old and Some New Clothes. Then he represented the Case to the Honorable Commissioners at Boston, who were Commission'd by the Honorable Society in London for Propagating the gospel among the Indians in New England and parts adjacent, and they allowed him 60 £ in old Tender, which was about 6 £ Sterling, and they Continu'd it 2 or 3 years, I cant't tell exactly. —While I was at Mr. Wheelock's, I was very weakly and my Health much impaired, and at the End of 4 Years, I over Strained my Eyes to such a Degree, I Could not persue my Studies any Longer; and out of these 4 years I Lost Just about one year; — And was obliged to quit my Studies.

From the Time I left Mr. Wheelock till I went to Europe

As soon as I left Mr. Wheelock, I endeavored to find Some Employ among the Indians; went to Nahantuck, thinking they may want a School Master, but they had one; then went to Narraganset, and they were Indifferent about a School, and went back to Mohegan, and heard a number of our Indians were going to Montauk, on Long Island, and I went with them, and the Indians there were very desirous to have me keep a School amongst them, and I Consented, and went back a while to Mohegan and Some time in November I went on the Island, I think it is 17 years ago last November. I agreed to keep School with them Half a Year, and left it with them to give me what they Pleased; and they took turns to Provide Food for me. I had near 30 Scholars this winter; I had an evening School too for those that could not attend the Day School—and began to Carry on their meetings, they had a Minister, one Mr. Horton, the Scotch Society's Missionary; but he Spent, I think two thirds of his Time at Sheenecock, 30 Miles from Montauk. We met together 3 times for Divine Worship every Sabbath and once on every Wednesday evening. I (used) to read the Scriptures to them and used to expound upon Some particular Passages in my own Tongue. Visited the Sick and attended their Burials. —When the half year expired, they Desired me to Continue with them, which I complied with, for another half year, when I had fulfilled that, they were urgent to have me Stay Longer. So I continued amongst them till I was Married, which was about 2 years after I went there. And Continued to Instruct them in the Same manner as I did before. After I was married a while, I found there was need of a Support more than I needed while I was Single, —and made my Case Known to Mr. Buell and to Mr. Wheelock, and also the Needy Circumstances and the Desires of these Indians of my Continuing amongst them, and the Commissioners were so good as to grant £ 15 a year Sterling— —And I kept on in my Service as usual, yea I had additional Service; I kept School as I did before and Carried on the Religious Meetings as often as ever, and attended the Sick and their

Funerals, and did what Writings they wanted, and often Sat as a Judge to reconcile and Decide their Matters Between them, and had visitors of Indians from all Quarters; and, as our Custom is, we freely Entertain all Visitors. And was fetched often from my Tribe and from others to see into their Affairs Both Religious, Temporal, — Besides my Domestic Concerns. And it Pleased the Lord to Increase my Family fast — and Soon after I was Married, Mr. Horton left these Indians and the Shenecock & after this I was (alone) and then I had the whole care of these Indians at Montauk, and visited the Shenecock Indians often. Used to set out Saturdays towards Night and come back again Mondays. I have been obliged to Set out from Home after Sun Set, and Ride 30 Miles in the Night, to Preach to these Indians. And Some Indians at Shenecock Sent their Children to my School at Montauk, I kept one of them Some Time, and had a Young Man a half year from Mohegan, a Lad from Nahantuck, who was with me almost a year; and had little or nothing for keeping them.

My Method in the School was, as Soon as the Children got together, and took their proper Seats, I Prayed with them, then began to hear them. I generally began (after some of them Could Spell and Read,) With those that were yet in their Alphabets, So around, as they were properly Seated till I got through and I obliged them to Study their Books, and to help one another. When they could not make out a hard word they Brought it to me — and I usually heard them, in the Summer Season 8 Times a Day 4 in the morning, and in ye after Noon. — In the Winter Season 6 Times a Day, As Soon as they could Spell, they were obliged to Spell when ever they wanted to go out. I concluded with Prayer; I generally heard my Evening Scholars 3 Times Round, And as they go out the School, every one, that Can Spell, is obliged to Spell a Word, and to go out Leisurely one after another. I Catechised 3 or 4 Times a Week according to the Assembly's Shout or Catechism, and many Times Proposed Questions of my own, and in my own Tongue. I found Difficulty with Some Children, who were Some what Dull, most of these can soon learn to Say over their Letters, they Distinguish the Sounds by the Ear, but their Eyes can't Distinguish the Letters, and the way I took to cure them was by making an Alphabet on Small bits of paper, and glued them on Small Chips of Cedar after this manner A B & C. I put these on Letters in order on a Bench then point to one Letter and bid a Child to take notice of it, and then I order the Child to fetch me the Letter from the Bench; if he Brings the Letter, it is well, if not he must go again and again till he brings ye right Letter. When they can bring any Letters this way, then I just Jumble them together, and bid them to set them in Alphabetical order, and it is a Pleasure to them; and they soon Learn their Letters this way. —I frequently Discussed or Exhorted my Scholars, in Religious matters. —My Method in our Religious Meetings was this; Sabbath Morning we Assemble together about 10 o'C and begin with Singing; we generally Sung Dr. Watt's Psalms or Hymns. I distinctly read the Psalm or Hymn first, and then gave the meaning of it to them, after that Sing, then Pray, and Sing again after Prayer. Then proceed to Read from Suitable portion of Scripture, and so Just give the plain Sense of it in Familiar Discourse and apply it to them. So continued with Prayer and Singing. In the after Noon and Evening we Proceed in the Same Manner, and so in Wednesday Evening. Some Time after Mr. Horton left these Indians, there was a remarkable revival of religion among these Indians and many were hopefully converted to the Saving knowledge of God in Jesus. It is to be observed before Mr. Horton left these Indians they had Some Prejudices infused in their minds, by Some Enthusiastical Exhorters from New England, against Mr. Horton, and many of them had left him; by this means he was Discouraged, and was disposed from these Indians. And being acquainted with the Enthusiasts in New England & the make and the Disposition of the Indians I took a mild way to reclaim them. I opposed them not openly but let them go on in their way, and whenever I had an opportunity, I would read Such pages of the Scriptures, and I thought would confound their Notions, and I would come to them with all Authority, Saying "these Saith the Lord"; and by this means, the Lord was pleased to Bless my poor Endeavours, and they were reclaimed, and Brought to hear almost any of the ministers. — —I am now to give an Account of my Circumstances and manner of Living. I Dwelt in a Wigwam, a Small Hut with Small Poles and Covered with Matts made of Flags, and I was obligd to remove twice a Year, about 2 miles Distance, by reason of the Scarcity of wood, for in one Neck of Land they Planted their Corn, and in another, they had their wood, and I was obligd to have my Corn carted and my Hay also, —and I got my Ground Plow'd every year, which Cost me about 12 shillings an acre; and I kept a Cow and a Horse, for which I paid 21 shillings every year York currency, and went 18 miles to Mill for every Dust of meal we used in my family. I Hired or Joined with my Neighbours to go to Mill, with a Horse or ox Cart, or on Horse Back, and Some time went myself. My Family Increasing fast, and my Visitors also. I was obligd to contrive every way to Support my Family; I took all opportunities, to get Some thing to feed my Family Daily. I Planted my own Corn, Potatoes, and Beans; I used to be out hoeing my Corn Some times before Sun Rise and after my School is Dismist, and by this means I was able to raise my own Pork, for I was allowed to keep 5 Swine. Some mornings & Evenings I would be out with my Hook and Line to Catch fish and in the Fall of Year and in the Spring, I used my gun, and fed my Family with Fowls. I Could more than pay for my Powder & Shot with Feathers. At other Times I Bound old Books for Easthampton People, made wooden Spoons and Ladles, Stocked Guns, & worked on Cedar to make Pails, (Piggins), and Churns & C. Besides all these Difficulties I met with advers Providence, I bought a Mare, had it but a little while, and she fell into the Quick Sand and Died. After a while Bought another, I kept her about half year, and she was gone, and I never have heard of nor seen her from that Day to this; it was Supposed Some Rogue Stole her. I got another and Died with a Distemper, and last of all I Bought a Young Mare. and kept her till She had one Colt, and She broke her Leg and Died, and Presently after the Cold Died also. In the whole I Lost 5 Horse Kind; all these Losses helped to pull me down; and by this Time I got greatly in Debt and acquainted my Circumstances to Some of my Friends, and they Represented my Case to the Commissioners of Boston, and Interceded with them for me, and they were pleased to vote 15 £ for my Help, and Soon after Sent a Letter to my good Friend at New London, acquainting him that they had Superseded their Vote; and my Friends were so good as to represent my Needy Circumstances Still to them, and they were so good at Last, as to Vote £ 15 and Sent it, for which I am very thankful; and the Revd Mr. Buell was so kind as to write in my behalf to the gentlemen of Boston; and he told me they were much Displeased with him, and heard also once again that they blamed me for being Extravagant; I Can't Conceive how these gentlemen would have me Live. I am ready to (forgive) their Ignorance, and I would wish they had Changed Circumstances with me but one month, that they may know, by experience what my Case really was; but I am now fully convinced, that it was not Ignorance, For I believe it can be proved to the world that these Same Gentlemen gave a young Missionary a Single man, *one Hundred Pounds* for one year, and fifty Pounds for an Interpreter, and thirty Pounds for an Introducer; so it Cost them one Hundred & Eighty Pounds in one Single Year, and they Sent too where there was no Need of a Missionary.

Now you See what difference they made between me and other missionaries; they gave me 180 Pounds for 12 years Service, which they gave for one years Services in another Mission. — In my Service (I speak like a fool, but I am Constrained) I was my own Interpreter. I was both a School master and Minister to the Indians, yea I was their Ear, Eye & Hand, as Well as Mouth. I leave it with the World, as wicked as it is, to Judge whether I ought not to have had half as much, they gave a young man Just mentioned which would have been but £ 50 a year; and if they ought to have given me that, I am not under obligations to them, I owe them nothing at all; what can be the Reason that they used me after this manner? I can't think of any thing, but this as a Poor Indian Boy Said, Who was Bound out to an English Family, and he used to Drive Plow for a young man, and he whipt and Beat him allmost every Day, and the young man found fault with him, and Complained of him to his master and the poor Boy was Called to answer for himself before his master, and he was asked, what it was he did, that he was So Complained of and beat almost every Day. He Said, he did not know, but he Supposed it was because he could not drive any better; but says he, I Drive as well as I know how; and at other Times he Beats me, because he is of a mind to beat me; but says he believes he Beats me for the most of the Time "because I am an Indian."

So I am *ready* to Say, they have used me thus, because I Can't Influence the Indians so well as other missionaries; but I can assure them I have endeavoured to teach them as well as I know how;—but I *must Say*, "I believe it is because I am a poor Indian." I Can't help that God has made me So; I did not make my self so. —

7

Memoir of Catharine Brown, a Christian Indian of the Cherokee Nation

Edited by

RUFUS B. ANDERSON

Catharine Brown was born about the year 1800 in what is now Alabama, of mixed white and Cherokee background. In 1817, she entered the missionary school at Brainerd, where she was soon baptized and admitted to the Church. Although her piety was remarked by the missionaries almost from the first, Catharine nonetheless accompanied her parents when they decided to move westward. She very soon returned to the religious community she loved, and, consistent with the sort of work regularly assigned to David Fowler and other Indian converts, she was sent to oversee a school for Cherokee girls at Creek-Path in 1820. Young as she was, Catharine Brown had already manifested symptoms of a lung disorder, and, as she worked at her new task, her health continued to deteriorate. The best medical attention of the time could do nothing to help her, and Catharine Brown died, a very young woman, in 1823.

Rufus B. Anderson, Assistant Secretary of the American Board of Commissioners for Foreign Missions, produced the book of Catharine Brown's life, Memoir of Catharine Brown, a Christian Indian of the Cherokee Nation, *in which he collected her letters and diary entries and included as well the personal testimony of some of the people who knew her best.[1] Anderson's book of Catharine's life presents this Cherokee woman as a model of Christian faith, one who was actively committed to God's service even as she acquiesced in her death as a manifestation of God's will. Anderson's purpose in producing this volume, was, as he wrote, "to augment the courage, animate the zeal, and invigorate the efforts of the friends of missions in their benevolent attempts to send the Gospel of Jesus Christ to all nations."*

Although today we readily question the "benevolence" of missionary pressures on the Indians, we need also to recognize that, for a number of people of Native American descent, the teaching of the missionaries was extremely welcome. The various selections from Anderson's record of Catharine Brown's

---

1. *Memoir of Catharine Brown, a Christian Indian of the Cherokee Nation*, ed. Rufus B. Anderson (Philadelphia: American Sunday School Union, 1832).

life—and these do not, any more than David Fowler's letters, constitute an autobiography in our usual understanding of the term—include letters from her to friends and to her brother David (who also died young), commentary by Rufus B. Anderson, and, finally, the account given by Doctor Campbell, the attending physician at her death.

We will not learn of Cherokee lifeways in the early nineteenth century from Catharine Brown. But hers, too, is a Native American life, one that needs to be taken into account in any generalizations we would make about Native people in the Americas.

Her History Until She Entered the Mission School at Brainerd

Her nativity.—Notice of her parents.—Condition of her people.—Her triumph over temptation.—A missionary station commenced at Chickamaugah, and named Brainerd.—She becomes a member of the school.

Catharine Brown was born about the year 1800. The place of her nativity was a beautiful plain, covered with tall forest trees, in a part of the country belonging to the Cherokee Indians, which is now called Wills-Valley, and is within the chartered limits of the State of Alabama. It is between the Raccoon and Lookout mountains, twenty-five miles southeast of the Tennessee river. David, the brother of Catharine, says, that the name, by which the place is known among his countrymen, is *Tsu-sau-ya-sah*, or *the ruins of a great city*. But, if such ruins ever existed, all traces of them have long since disappeared.

The Indian name of Catharine's father, is *Yau-nu-gung-yah-ski*, which signifies *the drowned by a bear*. He is, however, known among the whites by the name of *John Brown*. The Cherokee name of her mother is *Tsa-luh*. The whites call her *Sarah*.—Neither of Catharine's parents understand the English language. They are now about sixty years of age. Since the decease of the daughter, whose history and character are to form the subject of this memoir, they have removed beyond the Mississippi river, to the Arkansas Territory, whither a part of the Cherokee nation of Indians have emigrated, within the last fifteen or twenty years. . . .

Letters of Catharine Brown

To Mrs. Williams, at Elliot.

Brainerd, Nov. 1, 1818.

My dearly beloved Sister,

I have been wishing to write to you ever since you left us. You can hardly tell how my heart ached when I parted with you, expecting never to see you again in this world; but when I remembered that you were in the hands of the Lord, and that he would dispose of you as he pleased, it gave me joy equal to my sorrow.

O how I rejoiced, to think that you were going to carry the glad tidings of salvation to a people who had never heard of the dear Saviour. I do hope and pray that the Lord will bless your labours among them, as he has here.

We were very lonesome when you left us, especially at our prayer meeting; but I hope our hearts were united in love. I was very sorry to hear that you were sick; but it rejoiced me to hear that you were recovering, O, my dear sister, I will join with you in praising the Lord for his goodness in restoring you to health. I shall never forget you, or your kind endeavours to bring me to a knowledge of the Saviour. Sometimes I feel the love of God shed abroad in my heart, and feel as if I should be willing to give up every thing in this world to Christ. O how good is it to enjoy the presence of God; O that I might always enjoy it: but my heart is so bad and so prone to leave the God I love, that I am afraid he will leave me. O my dear sister, do pray for me.

All the Cherokee brothers and sisters are well. Three of the scholars, viz. Lydia Lowry, Alice, and Peggy Wilson, we hope have obtained an interest in the Saviour. Mr. Wilson came here, and wished to take his daughters on a visit to Mr. Brown's. Nearly a week after, he sent word that he was not going to send them back to school again. We felt very much grieved to hear it.

I expect my father here every day. I do not know whether I shall go to the Arkansas, or not. I feel grieved when I think of leaving my Christian friends, and of going far from all religious people, into a wild howling wilderness, where no star shines to guide my wandering feet to the Babe of Bethlehem; where no warning voice is heard to keep me in the straight path that leads to heaven. When I look to that dark region, I start back; but when I think of my two brothers there, and my dear parents, who are soon to go, I feel reluctant to stay behind, and leave them to perish alone.

Tell Mr. Williams and Mr. Kingsbury, that I remember them most affectionately, and also all the dear brothers and sisters at Yello Busha.

From your loving sister,

Catharine Brown.

To Mr. and Mrs. Chamberlain, at Brainerd.

Fort Deposit, Dec. 12, 1818.

My dearly beloved Brother and Sister Chamberlain,

I just sit down to address you with my pen. But is this all? Am I so soon called to bid you adieu, and see your faces no more in this world? O my beloved friends, you know not the love I bear to that blessed spot, where I have spent so many happy hours with you; but it is past never to return.

Dear friends, I weep; my heart is full; tears flow from my eyes while I write; and why is it so? Do I murmur? God forbid. Ought I not to praise the Lord for what I have received, and trust Him for every thing? O yes, his ways are best, and he has graciously promised, that "all things shall work together for good to them that love him." But do I love him? Have I that love to him, which will enable me to keep all his commandments? Do I love him with all my heart? O that the Lord would search me, and lead me in the way of eternal life.

Since I left you, I have led a very lonesome life, and not heard the Gospel preached but once; that is, when father Hoyt was here, and Milo. They came here on Tuesday evening. I was sitting in my room, and heard a knocking at the door. I bid them come in; and who but Milo appeared. I inquired if any body was with him. He said his father was at the door. That rejoiced me very much, and I enjoyed very much while they were here. Blessed be God for sending them here to instruct us.

I am here amongst a wicked set of people, and never hear prayers, nor any godly conversation. O my dear friends, pray for me: I hope you do. There is not a day passes but I think of you, and the kindness I received during the time I staid with you. It is not my wish to go to the Arkansas; but God only knows what is best for me. I shall not attempt to tell you what I have felt since I left you, and the tears I have shed when I called to mind the happy moments we passed in singing the praises of God. However, I bear it as well as I possibly can, trusting in our dear Saviour, who will never leave nor forsake them, that put their trust in him.

It may be possible, that I may see you once more; it would be a great happiness to me if I don't go to the Arkansas; perhaps I may;

but if I should go, it is not likely we shall meet in this world again: — but you will excuse me, for my heart feels what I cannot express with my pen. When I think and see the poor thoughtless Cherokees going on in sin, I cannot help blessing God, that he has led me in the right path to serve him.

Commentary by Rufus B. Anderson

We now enter upon the last three, and the most interesting years of Catharine's life, in which we shall behold her in new circumstances; her character more fully developed; and her graces shining with greater lustre.

In order that she may speak for herself as much as possible, that part of her private diary will be inserted, which was saved from the destruction, to which many of her papers were devoted, a little before her sickness. It was obtained from Mrs. Gilbreth, a sister of Catharine, and a faithful copy was transmitted by Mrs. Potter, the wife of the Rev. William Potter, missionary at Creek-Path. It commences the day before her departure from Brainerd.

Extracts from Her Diary

"*Brainerd, May 30, 1820.* To-morrow morning I shall leave this school, perhaps never to return. It is truly painful to part with my dear Christian friends, those, with whom I have spent many happy hours in the house of worship. I must bid them farewell. This is the place, where I first became acquainted with the dear Saviour. He now calls me to work in his vineyard, and shall I, for the sake of my Christian friends and of my own pleasures, refuse to go, while many of my poor red brothers and sisters are perishing for lack of knowledge? O no. I *will not* refuse to go. I will go wherever the Saviour calls me. I know he will be on my right hand, to grant me all the blessings, that I shall need, and he will direct me how to instruct the dear children, who shall be committed to my care.

"31. This morning I set out from Brainerd, with my dear father. Travelled about twenty miles. Thought much of my beloved Christian friends. Whether I shall ever see them again, is uncertain. The Lord only knows.

Letters of Catharine Brown

To Her Brother David.

Huntsville, Aug. 30, 1822.

My dear Brother,

I am sorry to tell you, that I have but a few moments of time to write this evening. I came here the 13th inst. and expect to return in a few weeks.

I left our friends all very well, and walking in the fear of God. I should have written long before this, had I not been sick; but my health is now much better than it was when I left home. Brother David, remember that your sister Catharine loves you much, and prays for you every day. I trust you will not return before you are prepared to preach the Gospel. Let me know your feelings in this respect when you write again, and I shall know how to pray for you. I do not expect you to go through all the studies, that ministers generally do in New England, but wish you to be qualified enough to withstand the enemies of God, and teach the truths of Christianity. If your health does not permit you to study, and your hesitation of speech still continues, I should not think it was your duty to pursue your studies.

However, I know the Lord will make every path of duty plain before you Do not think we are unhappy. It is true we were greatly tried, last winter, in losing our dear brother. But, blessed be God, it was not more than we are able to bear.

We feel it was good for us to be afflicted, knowing that the Lord is good, and will always do what is right. I have not time to write all I wish to send you. When I return home, you shall have a long letter from your affectionate sister

Catharine.

Limestone, June 13, 1823.

My dear Brother,

Mrs. Potter has told you the particulars of my illness. I will only tell you what I have experienced on my sick-bed.

I have found that it is good for me to be afflicted. The Saviour is very precious to me. I often enjoy his presence, and I long to be where I can enjoy it without sin. I have indeed been brought very low, and did not expect to live until this time. But I have had joy, such as I never experienced before. I longed to be gone; was ready to die at any moment.

I love you very much, and it would be a great happiness to me to see you again in this world. Yet I don't know that I shall. God only knows. We must submit to his will. We know, that if we never meet again in this world, the Lord has prepared a place in his heavenly kingdom, where I trust we shall meet, never to part. We ought to be thankful for what he has done for us. If he had not sent us the Gospel, we should have died without any knowledge of the Saviour.

You must not be grieved, when you hear of my illness. You must remember, that this world is not our home, that we must all die soon.

I am here under the care of Dr. Campbell, and his very kind family. My mother, and sister Susan are with me. Since I came here, I have been a great deal better, and the doctor sometimes gives encouragement of my getting well. But we cannot tell. I am willing to submit myself to the will of God. I am willing to die, or live, as he sees best.

I know I am his. He has bought me with his blood, and I do not wish to have any will but his. He is good, and can do nothing wrong. I trust if he spares my life, he will enable me to be faithful to his cause. I have no desire to live in this world, but to be engaged in his service.

It was my intention to instruct the people more than I had done, when I returned from Brainerd; but when I got home, I was not able to do it.

It was a great trial to me not to be able to visit our neighbours, and instruct them. But I feel that it is all right. It is my prayer that you may be useful, and I hope the Lord *will* make you useful to our poor people.

From your affectionate sister

Catharine.

Dr. Campbell's account of her death

"As death advanced, and the powers of nature gave way, she frequently offered her hand to the friends around her bed. Her mother and sister weeping over her, she looked steadily at the former, for a short time, filial love beaming from her eyes; and then, — she closed them in the sleep of death.

"She expired without a groan, or a struggle. Even those around the bed scarcely knew, that the last breath had left her, until I informed them she was gone.

"Thus fell asleep this lovely saint, in the arms of her Saviour, a little past 6 o'clock, on the morning of July 18th, 1823."

8

The Experiences of Five Christian Indians of the Pequot Tribe

WILLIAM APESS

Very little is known of William Apess' life other than what he tells us in A Son of the Forest, *the first extensive autobiography to be published by a Native American (1829). His grandfather, says Apess, was a white man who married the granddaughter of King Philip, or Metacomet, a Pequot leader, and the loser, in 1637, of what has been called the first deliberately genocidal war conducted by the English in North America. Philip was a figure who was increasingly to occupy Apess' thought, serving as the subject of his last published work. Apess' father was of mixed blood, but made the decision to join the Pequot tribe, and to marry a fullblood Indian woman. Apess was born in Colrain, Massachusetts, in 1798, and drops from the public record after 1838; only recently have obituaries in the New York* Sun *and the New York* Observer *been found recording his death, as the result of alcoholism, in New York, in the spring of 1839.*

A Son of the Forest was published, apparently at the author's expense, in 1829. In this text, Apess details the pains of his early life, his attraction to evangelical Methodism, his backsliding, eventual participation in the abortive American attack on Montreal in the War of 1812, and finally, his return to the Church, in whose service he eventually was granted an "exhorter's"—a sort of preacher's— license. At the conclusion of A Son of the Forest, *Apess had not yet been granted what he ultimately desired, full admission to the Methodist ministry.*

A fervent Christian, Apess increasingly focused his life work on his perception of the incompatibility of Christianity with any and all forms of racism, in his terms, color prejudice. In his "Eulogy on King Philip," for example, delivered in 1836 at the Odeon in Boston, one of the city's largest public lecture halls, Apess called Philip the foremost man that America had produced, and he excoriated his audience, descendants of the Pilgrims, for the crimes of their forefathers, offering a vision of the kingdom not only in Heaven but on earth of what I have elsewhere called "the community of the colorblind saved."[1]

The text that follows comes from Apess's The Experiences of Five Chris-

---

1. Arnold Krupat, *The Voice in the Margin: Native American Literature and the Canon* (Berkeley: Univ. of California Press, 1989), chap. 4.

tian Indians of the Pequot Tribe,[2] *a book which Apess begins with a short autobiography of his own. This opening section constitutes, for the most part, an extreme condensation of* A Son of the Forest.

Although Apess was long ignored as an unfortunately acquiescent Christian convert, his life and work have recently been re-appraised by Kim McQuaid, who calls him a "Christian reformer of the Pequot tribe," and his complete works have just appeared in an edition superbly edited by Barry O'Connell, On Our Own Ground: The Complete Writings of William Apess, A Pequot *(1992). I have studied Apess in "Monologue and Dialogue in Native American Autobiography," in* The Voice in the Margin: Native American Literature and the Canon, *and in "Native American Autobiography and the Synecdochic Self," in* Ethnocriticism: Ethnography, History, Literature. *David Murray also includes an important study of Apess in his* Forked Tongues: Speech, Writing and Representation in North American Indian Texts.[3]

It is not my intention to descend to particulars in this pamphlet, any farther than to notice the origin of my life for the purpose of giving the youth a transient view between their condition and mine; or those poor children of the forest, who have had taken from them their once delightful plains and homes of their peaceful habitations; their fathers and mothers torn from their dwellings, and they left to mourn, and drop a tear, and die, over the ruins of their ancient sires. Perhaps you may ask, Why is this? I answer, because of deception and power, assisted with the fiery waters of the earth—rum. Such, my young friends, was the case of this poor self-taught Indian youth, whose experiences you are about to read.

My parentage, according to the custom of the country, was none of the least—being the descendant of a chief, or the head officer of the nation. But this availed nothing with me; the land of my fathers was

2. William Apess, *The Experiences of Five Christian Indians of the Pequot Tribe* (Boston: James B. Dow, 1833). Other editions, as well as other copies of Apess's first edition, give slightly different titles.

3. *On Our Own Ground: The Complete Writings of William Apess, a Pequot,* ed. Barry O'Connell (Amherst: Univ. of Massachusetts Press, 1992); Arnold Krupat, *The Voice in the Margin,* especially "Monologue and Dialogue in Native American Autobiography"; Arnold Krupat, *Ethnocriticism: Ethnography, History, Literature* (Berkeley: Univ. of California Press, 1992), especially "Native American Autobiography and the Synecdochic Self"; and David Murray, *Forked Tongues: Speech, Writing and Representation in North American Indian Texts* (Bloomington: Indiana Univ. Press, 1991).

gone; and their characters were not known as human beings but as beasts of prey. We were represented as having no souls to save, or to lose, but as partridges upon the mountains. All these degrading titles were heaped upon us. Thus, you see, we had to bear all this tide of degradation, while prejudice stung every white man, from the oldest to the youngest, to the very center of the heart.

It was thought no crime for old and young to hiss at the poor Indians, the noblest work of God, who had met with great misfortunes, and lost everything they had, by those very persons who despised them; yea, look which way they would, they could see no friends, nor even hear a pleasant sound from the lips of the white. Yea, there was but little help for them.

When you read this, ask yourselves if ever you had such trials. If not, begin now to prize your privileges and show pity to those whose fates are wretched and cruel. I shall now enter more fully upon my experience in childhood. It will be well to speak to the point; I shall make but few remarks here, as I intend publishing, should the Lord spare my life, a book of 300 pages, 18 mo. in size; and there the reader will find particulars respecting my life.

My parents were of the same disposition of the Indians, that is, to wander to and fro. And, although my father was partly white, yet he had so much of the native blood that he fashioned after them in traveling from river to river, and from mountain to mountain, and plain to plain, on their journey.

I was born at Colrain, Massachusetts, A.D. 1798, on the 30th day of January. We lived here but a few months and then removed to Colchester, Connecticut, within about twelve miles of our native tribe; and there, to my sad misfortune, my father and mother parted, I being at this time but a babe, being not more than three years old, and I saw my mother's face no more for twenty years. I was then placed with my grandparents on my mother's side, who, my readers, were not the best people in the world: for they would at times drink New England rum, and then I was neglected. How awful it is to have parents who will drink spirituous liquors or alcohol and, by that, to neglect their dear little children and leave them to suffer. You will see how much I had to suffer on the account of rum.

During my stay with the old folks our fare was hard, there being five children of us, and our fare was about equal as to earthly comforts. Sometimes we had something to eat, and at other times nothing. Many are the times in which we have gone to bed supperless, to rest our little weary limbs, stretched upon a bundle of straw, and how thankful we were for this comfort; and in the morning we were thankful to get a

William Apess. Courtesy, American Antiquarian Society.

cold potato for our breakfasts. We thought it good fare. There was a
white man who lived about a mile off, and he would, at times, bring
us some frozen milk, which for a time supplied the calls of nature. We
suffered thus from the cold; the calls of nature, as with almost nakedness; and calumny heaped upon us by the whites to an intense degree.

Little children, how thankful you ought to be that you are not in the
same condition that we were, that you have not a nation to hiss at
you, merely because your skins are white. I am sure that I rejoice for
you, that it is not the case. But to proceed: At a certain time, when my
grandmother had been out among the whites, with her baskets and
brooms, and had fomented herself with the fiery waters of the earth,
so that she had lost her reason and judgment and, in this fit of intoxication, raged most bitterly and in the meantime fell to beating me
most cruelly; calling for whips, at the same time, of unnatural size, to
beat me with; and asking me, at the same time, question after question, if I hated her. And I would say yes at every question; and the

reason why was because I knew no other form of words. Thus I was beaten, until my poor little body was mangled and my little arm broken into three pieces, and in this horrible situation left for a while. And had it not been for an uncle of mine, who lived in the other part of the old hut, I think that she would have finished my days; but through the goodness of God, I was snatched from an untimely grave.

The white man will say, "What cruel creatures, to use children so!" If I could see that this blame was attached to the poor degraded Indians, I should not have one word to say. But when not a whit of it belongs to them, I have the more to say. My sufferings certainly were through the white man's measure; for they most certainly brought spirituous liquors first among my people. For surely no such sufferings were heard of, or known among our people, until the burning curse and demon of despair came among us: Surely it came through the hands of the whites. Surely the red man had never sought to destroy one another as this bane of hell would! And we little babes of the forest had to suffer much on its account. Oh white man! How can you account to God for this? Are you not afraid that the children of the forest will rise up in judgment and condemn you?

Little children, if you have parents that drink the fiery waters, do all you can, both by your tears and prayers and friendly admonitions, to persuade them to stop; for it will most certainly ruin them, if they persist in it. But to proceed: I did not long continue in this situation but was relieved from it by my uncle making his complaint to the selectmen of the town, who took up my case and placed me for a while among some of the white neighbors, until I was healed of my wounds, although it was a year before I was able to help myself much without aid. Being now about five or six years old, it was agreed upon that I should live with this white family until I had arrived at the age of twenty-one. They, being Baptist people and having no children of their own, became more fond of me than is usual for people to be of adopted children and treated me with the utmost kindness, and particularly Mrs. Furman, who was very kind and generous. And as they had agreed to send me to school, accordingly, when I had arrived at the age of six years, they sent me to school. And this they continued to do for six successive winters, which was about all the education that I received. The amount of benefit which I have received from this, none can tell. To God be all the praise.

Things began now to wear a different aspect; and my little heart began again to be expanded, and I began to be inquisitive about many things. At times, the children of God would assemble around me, to worship the Great Spirit, something new to me. Of course I listened with great attention. Their songs were sweet, and as the oil of joy no doubt was in their hearts to indite their petitions, to nerve their admonitions, to send home the word to the hearts of those who heard it, doubtless made it the more interesting. And so it caught my youthful heart, being a constant hearer of these things. And my mind became more knitted together with them. And I would question Mrs. Furman respecting these things. She would give me a great many good, wholesome admonitions and tell me the young must die as well the old, and often point me to the graveyard and cite me to small graves and warn me to prepare to die. It would leave a powerful effect upon my mind, which was not easily effaced. I recollect the first time I visited a chapel for the worship of God. It being a new place, and look-- ing to me somewhat fine to the eye, I took great liberties, was something like a country clown passing through populous villages and cities, staring all the while upon those fine piles of buildings which he saw, or like a rabble of boys and girls going to church to hear the Indian preach: something so indeed, and so much so that I lost my balance of behavior. And when I returned I received a short address, accompanied with a handsome present, that I have not yet forgotten; it weighed well with me, so that forever afterward I was enabled to keep my balance well. It would be well for heads of families to supply their children with such presents, when needed; it would save the country from much disgrace. But to proceed: When I was about eight years old, the preaching of the Gospel powerfully affected my mind, although I was ignorant of the plan of salvation through Jesus Christ; but I had no doubt but the word was spoken with divine authority, which not only drew tears of contrition from *me* but from many others. But being small, and of little note in the world, no one supposed that I wanted religion.

In those days, the aged thought the youth were not subjects of grace; such is the fact, although it may be surprising to many; so there was none to comfort the little Indian boy. How different now! Lord, help the youth who are exalted to heaven in point of privileges so to prize them, that they might not be thrust down to hell.

I would remark here that many rise up against this doctrine; but why not rise up against, or in opposition to, the state's prison and house of correction and even the gallows itself? These are places to punish the people for their crimes. Some say their crimes are punished here; indeed, this is a new doctrine. Whoever saw a crime in the state's prison, locked up to hard labor; or whoever saw a crime hung up by the neck? How absurd, then, to delineate such doctrine. Crime is crime and stands for what is, let scoffers say what they will; may grace be imparted to enlighten our eyes. But to return: For the profiting of the youth, I would speak a little further of the exercises of my mind. Although they could not believe that I wanted religion, yet the Spirit of the Lord followed me daily; and my mind was so overwhelmed that I could hardly contain myself to rest without giving vent to my feelings. But little did the people with whom I lived think that I was serious about a future state; and although I could weep to be at church, yet they would deny me at times, saying I only wanted to look at the boys and play with them. Those sudden rebuffs would dampen my serious thoughts, and I would turn away to wicked paths of vice and unite with wicked boys and break the Sabbath, by wandering to and fro about the swamps, hedges, ponds, and brooks, sporting with whatever came in our way. But when I came home at night and retired to rest, the darkness itself was a terror to me, as I would picture to my imagination that the fiends of night stood around me, ready to devour me. Then I would cry to the Lord to have mercy upon my poor soul and promise him, if he would spare me, I would do better. But, when the darkness was past, I, like Pharaoh, forgot my promise: Thus I was led on by wicked youths until I was almost ruined, until I was persuaded to leave my home and wander to and fro to seek by bread. This displeased Mr. Furman; he, supposing I had become discontented, had sought me out another place, without my consent, which displeased me and made me more discontented than ever, I being at this time about ten years of age, entirely unfit to choose for myself. But so it was; I was alone in the world, fatherless, motherless, and helpless, as it were, and none to speak for the poor little Indian boy. Had my skin been white, with the same abilities and the same parentage, there could not have been found a place good enough for me. But such is the case with depraved nature, that their judgment for fancy only sets upon the eye, skin, nose, lips, cheeks, chin, or teeth and, sometimes, the forehead and hair; without any further examination, the mind is made up and the price set. This is something like buying chaff for wheat, or twigs of wood for solid substance.

But to proceed with our story: The place that he had procured for me was with a people professing religion that belonged to the Presbyterian church, and withal very strict. They also thought much of themselves, he being formerly a judge, likewise a member of Congress, in the House of Representatives, and had sufficient to supply all the common calls of life, for all his household. I went to try my new home; and while there on trial, they used me pretty fairly, made

me a few presents suited to please children, etc. They had now secured my favor, as they thought; the agreement was now made that I
should have clothing and schooling, so as to read and write, and
plenty of work. Now this man is what is generally called an enlightened Christian.

But let us look at his proceedings and see if he was actuated by the
spirit of Christ or the custom of the day: Hear, and then decide. And
there was work enough. This part of the bargain was completely fulfilled on his part, and that was all. As to my fare, it was none of the
best, though middling: It was not so bad as I have seen—I mean my
table fare and lodging—but when we came to the clothing part, it was
mean enough, I can assure you. I was not fit to be seen anywhere
among decent folks, and of course there was no meeting for me to
attend, although I had a desire. But this good man did not care much
about the Indian boy. He wished to hear me read: I could make out to
spell a few words, and the judge said, "You are a good reader." I
hope he was a better judge at law. Now, some may think me hard,
but truth will stand.

Now, the judge had family prayers and was exact in having all his
family to hear him pray; so he would always have a repetition of
words, and I soon could pray as well as he; and of course I did not
care for his prayers any longer. I would remark, however, that a colored woman, who had lived with the judge for many years, told me
that he once prayed, though previous to it there was one of the most
powerful thunderstorms that ever was known in these parts; and after he had made that prayer he forgot to pray again.[4] I expect there are
many such in the world. But to proceed: The poor little Indian boy,
when the Sabbath came, had nowhere to go to worship God, and so,
like all other little boys who are left alone in the world, would stroll
about the lots and meditate upon past times and listen to the little
songsters of the forest, which would chaunt the praise of God for me,
while there was none to take me by the hand and lead me to the holy
place or to the fountain of blessedness. Now, if my face had been
white, it would have been a town talk. But as it was an Indian face, no
matter whether it was dirty or poor or whether I had clothing or not.
But the judge has gone to the great Judge above, who will do right. I
would not live with him, and he sold me, as a farmer would sell his
sheep for the slaughter, without any of my knowledge whatever, to

4. Barry O'Connell, in *On Our Own Ground: The Complete Writings of William Apess, a
Pequot* (Amherst: Univ. of Massachusetts Press, 1992), p. 124, suggests that Apess dis-
tinguishes here between rote and spontaneous prayer, the latter being the only kind
evangelicals would consider real prayer.

Mr. Williams, of New London; and through hypocrisy alone they carried me along to my place of destination. I had now arrived at the age of about eleven years and a half, and now I found that I had a new home; and in fact, I was not so much displeased with it as some might suppose, for now I found myself in a comfortable situation—enough to eat and drink, and things comfortable to wear—whereas before I was quite destitute of many things. This improvement somewhat settled my mind, and I became more contented. But soon I found that all his household wished me to become their servant, from the cook to the clerk. This I did not stomach well; it was too much for one to bear, to call every man "master." I thought it beneath my dignity; of course, there was war in the wigwam—who should be master. But Mr. Williams settled with us all, and with me in particular, as he said he meant to make me a good boy, but at the same time told me that I must obey the heads of his family, and all this was perfectly right; and some good, I think, was accomplished. However, I never cried out like the poor African, "Massa, Massa—Mister, Mister," but called them by their regular names.

Things now went on smoothly for some time. The general and his family generally attended the Congregational church or society on the Sabbath, to hear the word of God dispensed; though neither he nor his family were religious, yet they used to be often there; and their example was good so far as it went; and so I had an opportunity to attend with them. My mind was much occupied about those who preach the Gospel, there being a difference between those who preach and those who read. I could discover this; the preaching that I formerly attended was with divine power, which made the language of the speaker eloquent and sublime, and withal called the attention of those who heard it to seek the salvation of their souls; while that of the latter, being a selection of fine sentences, and read off in an elegant style, which only seemed to please the ear and lull the people to sleep. How much better, then, to study and trust in God than to study and trust to head and pen; for a curse is pronounced upon all such: "Cursed is he that putteth his trust in an arm of flesh." And what is the difference whether a preacher puts it in his own arm or the arm of his neighbor? Now, I have not said this because I am biased by any sectarian principle whatever; I should condemn it in one sect as much as in another. But what said our Lord? He said to his servants, "Go and preach the Gospel to every creature." Why did he not say, "Go, read my Gospel to every creature?" Therefore, no man who reads his sermon can be justified in so doing; for Jesus has said, "Now are ye my disciples, if ye do whatsoever I have commanded you." And if they who are the servants of God go astray, and do wrong continually, and place things where they ought not to be, no wonder the churches are all the time in commotion. But to proceed:

After I had attended the meeting a while, I had a desire to attend Methodist meeting, in the same neighborhood. This was altogether new to me; but it was interesting to attend them, and so much so that I desired to be a constant attendant of them. By these meetings I was led to look more into the plan of salvation, that it was free for all: "Whosoever would, let him come and take of the waters of life freely,"

It was now that the Lord began to revive his work. The powers of darkness began to gather round, that the light of the Gospel might be shut out. Beelzebub was busy, both day and night, to prevent good. He employed all that would work for him, from the pharisee to the educated scholar in the desk, even down to the peasant and drunkard that reeled around in gutters and mud puddles in the street. It was now that these people had to suffer much; they were openly called the scum and filth of the earth, deceivers, and, in a word, all the calumny that could be heaped upon them, by those who ought to have known better. It was said that it was a disgrace for any character of respectability to attend these meetings. But I can say this much about it; I believe it arose from sectarian bigots. Not that I could suppose that they (the Methodists) were free from it, but have as much as their neighbors; and it is the case with all sects, that they are more or less bigoted. And if they are, they need not join with the devil's crew, to do all the hurt they can to one another. This, to me, does not look much like religion.

But the work of God rolled on, like an overwhelming flood. Persecution seemed to cement the hearts of the brethren and sisters together, and their songs were sweet. Their prayers and exhortations were like arrows sticking in the heart of their King's enemy, while the preachers poured the thunders of the law upon them, as if God himself had spoken to them, as he did to the children of Israel from Mount Sinai, that they should fear and tremble at his word.

My heart now became much troubled, and I felt determined to seek the salvation of my soul, for their sayings did not affect me much (although they did not want me to attend their meetings), though I had neither respectability nor character to lose but was like the partridge upon the mountain, a mark for them all to shoot at, and hiss at, and quack at—which often put me in mind of the geese and crows.

But, notwithstanding, this sectarian nonsense raged most bitterly, and I do suppose that they who could help it would not be willing for their dogs to go there to meeting, for fear of bringing disgrace upon themselves. I would to God that people were more consistent than what they are. Say, would you like to lose everything that was near and dear to you, merely because your skin is white? I had to do it, merely because I had a red one. Judge ye, if this is right; and if not, stop where you are, and cease to do evil and learn to do well. But again, as I had no character to lose, I became a constant attendant on these meetings, and although a sinner before God, yet I had no disposition to make sport of the people of God or his word. Why I mention this is because so many go on purpose to sport with one another and make derision of the people of God, and those, too, who call themselves gentlemen and ladies. Such, however, disgrace themselves and are, in the judgment of good men, and their Maker, below the beasts of the field. Shame! shame! shame! to be so indecent, who boast of so much correctness and purity! But, notwithstanding the people would be so bad, yet the "Lord had respect unto his people, and his ears were open to the cries of his servants, and his ears were open to their supplication"; and in answer to prayer, he was pleased to revive his work; the Holy Ghost moved upon the face of the congregation; and his children were built up, and gathered strength at every meeting, and were built up in the most holy faith of the Gospel, and soon the power of the Holy Ghost fell powerfully among the people, so that the cries of the wounded were distinctly heard at every part of the house. The great Physician of souls was present, to heal all that would come to him and seek his favor. Thus the work of God went on most powerfully, so much so that Satan and his army retreated, at times, before it; and then would gather around it like a thick cloud of darkness, and mimic the catamount, or owls of the forest, or the young lion, which had lost its mother, and roaring to be answered. But the Lord assisted his servants to overcome them, through the word of his testimony.

It was now that conviction settled upon my mind, more and more; and I was more serious than usual. But being young, only about fourteen years of age, was somewhat flighty; though when I considered how great a sinner I was before God, and how often I had grieved the good Spirit of the Lord, my distress for mercy was very great.

At one of these meetings I was induced to laugh, not because I wanted to but to hide my distress from those around me. Being among the young people, I did not wish for them to know it; but such was my seriousness that it could not be hid, and I became affected,

131

even unto tears, until they coursed down my cheeks like rain. And when the bold persecutors saw it, they inquired if I was one of the Lamb's people.

Brother Hill was at this time preaching from these words: "Behold the Lamb of God, who taketh away the sins of the world." He spoke feelingly of his (Christ's) sufferings on the cross; of his precious blood, that flowed like a purifying river from his side; of his sustaining the accumulated weight of the sins of the whole world; and dying to satisfy the demands of justice, which could only be appeased by an infinite atonement. I felt convinced that Christ had died for all mankind; that age, sect, color, country, or situation made no difference. I felt assured that I was included in the plan of redemption, with all my brethren. No one can conceive with what joy I hailed this new doctrine, as it was called. It removed all my excuses, and I freely believed that all I had to do was to look in faith upon the Lamb of God, who made himself a free-will offering for unregenerated and wicked souls, upon the cross. My spirits were depressed; my crimes were arrayed before me; and no tongue can tell the anguish of soul I felt. After meeting, I returned home with a heavy heart, determined to seek the salvation of my soul.

This night I slept but little; at times I would be melted down into tenderness and tears; and then again, my heart would seem as hard as adamant. I was awfully tempted; the evil one would try to persuade me that I was not in the pale of mercy. I fancied that evil spirits stood around my bed; my condition was deplorable, and awful; and I longed for day to break, as much as the tempest-tossed mariner, who expected every moment to be washed from the wreck he fondly clings to; so it was with me, upon the wreck of the world, buffeted by Satan, assailed by the world; sometimes in despair; then believing against hope; my heart, at times, seemed almost broke, while the tears of contrition coursed down my cheeks like rain.

But sin was the cause of all this, and no wonder; I groaned and wept; I had often sinned, and my accumulated transgressions had piled themselves as a rocky mountain upon my heart; and how could I endure it? The weight thereof seemed to crush me down; in the night seasons, I had fearful visions, and would often start from my sleep and gaze around the room, as I was ever in dread of seeing the evil one ready to carry me off. I continued in this frame of mind for more than seven weeks. My distress, finally, became so acute that the family took notice of it; some of them persecuted me because I was serious and fond of attending meetings. Now persecution raged on every hand, within and without; and I had none to take me by the hand and say, "Go with us and we will do you good." But in the midst of difficulties, so great to one only little more than fourteen years of age, I ceased not to pray for the salvation of my soul: Very often my exercises were so great that sleep departed from me. I was fearful that I should wake up in hell. And one night I was in bed mourning, like the dove for her absent mate, I fell into a doze. I thought I saw the world on fire; it resembled a large bed of coals, red, and glowing with heat; I shall never forget the impression it made upon my mind. No tongue can tell or possibly describe the agony of my soul; for now I was greatly in fear of dropping into hell, that awful place, where the smoke of their torments ascendeth up forever and ever. I cried earnestly for mercy; then I was carried to another place where perfect happiness seemed to pervade every part, and the inhabitants thereof. Oh, how I longed to be among them and partake of their happiness. I sighed to be freed from pain and misery; I knew that nothing but the attenuated thread of life kept me from sinking into the awful lake which I beheld. I cannot think it is in the power of human language to describe the feelings that rushed upon my mind at that moment, or thrilled through my veins; everything seemed to bear the signet of reality. When I awoke, I was glad to find it was a vision and not a reality. I went on from day to day, with my head bowed down, seeking the Savior of sinners, but without success. The heavens appeared to be brass; my prayers wanted the wings of faith to waft them to the skies. The disease of my heart increased; the heavenly Physician had not stretched forth his hand and poured upon my soul the panacea of the Gospel; the scales had not fallen from my eyes; and no ray of celestial light had dispelled the darkness that had gathered around my soul; the cheering sound of sincere friendship fell not upon my ear. It seemed as if I was friendless, unpitied, and unknown; and at times I wished to become a dweller in the wilderness. Who can wonder, then, that I was almost in despair, surrounded by difficulties and apparent dangers? But I was resolved to seek the salvation of my soul with all my heart; to trust entirely to the Lord and, if I failed, to perish pleading for mercy at the foot of the throne. I now hung all my hopes upon the Redeemer, and clung with indescribable tenacity to the cross, on which he purchased salvation for my soul, "the vilest of the vile." The result was such as is always to be expected, when a lost and ruined sinner throws himself entirely on the Lord—*perfect freedom*. On the 15th day of *March*, in the year of our Lord, 1813, I heard a voice saying unto me, in soft and soothing accents, *"Arise, thy sins that are many are all forgiven thee; go in peace and sin no more."* There was nothing very singular, save that the Lord stooped to lift me up, in my conversion.

133

I had been sent into the garden to work, and while there, I lifted up my heart to God, when, all at once, my burden and fears left me; my soul was filled with love; love to God, and love to all mankind. Oh, how my poor heart swelled with joy! And I would cry, "Glory to God in the highest." There was not only a change in my heart but everything around me. The scene was entirely changed; the works of God praised him, and I saw in everything that he had made his glory shine. My love now embraced the whole human family; the children of God, I loved most dearly. Oh, how I longed to be with them; and when any of them passed me, I would gaze at them until they were lost in the distance. I could have pressed them to my bosom, as they were more precious to me than gold, and I was always loath to part with them whenever we met together. The change, too, was visible in my very countenance. I enjoyed great peace of mind, and that peace was like a river, full, deep, and wide, and flowing continually. My mind was employed in contemplating the works of God and in praising his holy name. I dwelt so particularly upon his mercy and goodness that I could praise him aloud, even in my sleep, and when I awoke, it was glory to God and the Lamb, and my heart burnt continually with the love of God. Well might the poet say,

> O for such love, let rocks and hills
> Their lasting silence break;
> And all harmonious human tongues
> The Savior's praises speak.

I continued in this happy frame of mind for some time; it was very pleasant to live in the enjoyment of pure and undefiled religion, and naught could I see but seas of rest and waves of glory before me. I wanted only the wings of angels to waft me to Paradise, that I might dwell around the throne of God forever. But alas! I dwelt in a tent below, that held me fast and would not let me go, and here to resist the fiend, the Christian's foe—to war, and tug, and toil at the oar of prayer, till time with me no more should be; and then, if faithful to my Lord, with all the faithful saints should be.

But here I can say, I had none to make me the object of their care, to encourage me to press forward in the ways of well doing. But, on the other hand, persecution raged most bitterly, and soon I was deprived of that privilege that was near and dear to me: such as the privilege of class meetings, and other means of grace, that are usually among the Methodists; and being young, I was again led astray. How hard it is to be robbed of all our earthly rights and deprived of the means of grace, merely because the skin is of a different color; such had been the case with me. I would ask the white man if he thinks that he can be justified in making just such a being as I am, or any other person in the world, unhappy; and although the white man finds so much fault because God has made us thus, yet if I have any vanity about it, I choose to remain as I am, and praise my Maker while I live that an Indian he has made.

But again: The burden that was heaped upon me, at this time, was more than I could bear, being only about fifteen years old, and I now began to relapse back again into my former state. I now became acquainted with wicked and silly youths, and one of them whose name was *Miner* and myself agreed to try some other parts of the world. Children as we were, we made the best arrangements for our journey that we could; and so off we started and steered our course for New York. With difficulties and fears, we arrived there. Many of the people thought that we were sailor boys, as we informed them that we had been privateering and had been taken and set on a shore near New London and were going home to New York, to our parents; and it being wartime, we informed the people all we knew about it. When we had arrived at New York City, and almost alone in the world, and but little economy to take care of ourselves, we thought best to engage in the war. So I became a musician in the army, while my comrade went on board of a privateer.

We now parted, and I went with the soldiers to Canada, where I experienced all the horrors of war; fought in the great Battle of Lake Champlain, with General McComb, with Hampton and Wilkinson, at the Mills. After the war was over, I went to Montreal and from thence to upper Canada, Fort Niagara; from thence to Kingston, and through the wilderness, and saw many of my brethren, who ornamented the wood with their camps and chanted the wild beasts of prey with their songs. Being now satisfied with these regions and their curiosities, I now began to think of home and those kindred friends who had long before buried me beneath the sods of the forest, to behold my face no more forever here, being gone so long, nearly five years.

This journey was not instructing to the paths of virtue but of vice—though I did not forget the past, and often recollected those happy moments, and sighed on account of my condition, but had no heart to pray, no pious parents to instruct me, no minister of God's holy word to notice me and pour into my ear the blessed truths of God, but a poor, destitute, helpless child of the forest, all alone in the world, as it were. I now made the best of my way home to my kindred in the flesh, and when I arrived there, I found them surprised and rejoiced to see me on this side of the grave. After a while I became more steady and began once more to attend the worship of God, and had a desire to return for my backsliding state to the worship of God, that I might enjoy his smiles again. For it was now that I had become wretched and miserable through the deceitfulness of sin, and bad examples of the white soldiers, and nothing but thick darkness gathered around me; and, apparently, my situation was worse than before. It was now harder to seek the Lord than it was when I was young, for now my sins were redoubled; and it appeared indeed that there was no mercy for me. And when I went to pray and call upon God for mercy, I was met by the enemy of souls, who very readily thrusted a dart at me filled with a message of despair, that there was nothing but eternal death for me; that I had committed the unpardonable sin, by having sinned against the Holy Ghost, and it was all in vain for me to try again for help in God; that he was sure that I should make up his host in hell.

My distress became more acute than ever; but I attended the meetings where God's children meet and at last I made known my distress to them; and they, the dear children of God, comforted me, by saying that Christ would have mercy upon the worst of sinners, and encouraged me to pray; and then prayed with and for me.

I sought the Lord for weeks and months, and at last I began to see that I had received some of his divine approbation: To say that I immediately had as clear an evidence as I had before, I cannot. But when I acknowledged myself a sinner before the people and confessed what a sinner I had been, then the light of God's countenance broke into my soul, and I felt as if I were on the wings of angels and ready to leave this world. I united with the Methodists, and was baptized by immersion, and strove to walk with them in the way to heaven, and can say that I spent many happy hours with them in the worship of God; and to this day, I most heartily rejoice that I was brought again from the dead to praise God. After a while, I began to exercise my gift in the way of prayer and exhortation and was blest in so doing. I began to be exercised more abundantly about the salvation of precious souls and began to have a desire to call sinners to repentance in a public way; and it appeared I could not rest in any other way. But I knew that I was weak and ignorant as to the letter; and not only so, I was already a hissing-stock and a byword in the world, merely because I was a child of the forest; and to add any more occasion to the weak and scornful family of the whites was more than I wished to do; but there was no peace for me, either by day or night. Go I must, and expose my ignorance to the world, and strive to preach, or exhort sinners to repentance. I soon found men like adders, with poison under their tongues, hissing around me; and to this day, I find now and then one hissing at me. My trials again were many, and apparently more than I could bear; but I entreated of God to show me my duty and prayed to him for a token of his grace, when I went to call sinners to repentance. The Lord heard my prayer, and sent down his awakening power, and convinced sinners of the error of their ways; but I was too unbelieving, believing that I was not the character that God should take to thresh the mountains of sin. The angel of the Lord appeared to me in the visions of the night and read some extracts of John's Gospel. It appeared that before me there was a plain, and upon that the sun shone delightfully; but it was a difficult place for me to reach, being a dark and winding way, through mire, but I reached it; here I was encouraged by the angel to persevere. It was now, when I awoke, that I was troubled still the more; and night and day it was preach, preach, though many thought it would be a miracle for such an ignorant creature as I to preach the Gospel. But it is a fact that I had a difficult road to travel before I really got to preaching; but I can say that I have seen the salvation of the Lord in so doing, and God has made me, the unworthiest of all his servants, the humble, happy instrument in bringing many to bow at his scepter. To him be all the glory forever.

I would now say that I have been a regular member in the Methodist Episcopal and Protestant Methodist church for about nine years; in the Methodist Episcopal church I was an exhorter for eighteen months. I left them in good standing, and with good credentials on April 11, 1829, and united with the Protestant Methodists, not because I had anything very special against the former, any further than their government was not republican. Their religion is as good as it ever was. I have been in the Protestant church something like four years, as a preacher of the Gospel; and in that time have received holy orders as an authorized minister of Christ, to attend to the duties of a pastor; and I am no sectarian whatever, but boldly declare that I have preached for all that would open their doors; and all sects have bid me welcome; and this is as it should be. May God pour his Spirit upon them all, and all the world. Amen.

William Apess

Part 3
The Resisting Indians, from Indian Removal to Wounded Knee, 1830–90

In 1829 gold was discovered at Dahlonega, Georgia, on the western boundary of the lands of the Cherokee Nation, and whites flocked—as they would flock to the Black Hills of the Dakotas in the 1870s—to mine it. This movement was illegal, for the lands belonged to the Cherokee; nonetheless, neither the government of the state of Georgia nor the federal government under the Indian fighter President Andrew Jackson was much interested in protecting Cherokee rights.

The Cherokee were the most "advanced" of the so-called five "civilized" tribes (the other four were the Chickasaw, Creek, Choctaw, and Seminole). Using the syllabary invented by the legendary Sequoyah (George Guess) in 1821, many of the Cherokee could read and write in their own language, and a considerable number could also read and write English. In 1827, with much national attention, the Cherokee had adopted a written constitution based upon the Constitution of the United States. Many of them had extensive agricultural holdings, and capacious permanent dwellings; indeed, so "civilized" were the Cherokee that they even, like their white southern compatriots, held slaves.

But Georgians wanted land as well as gold, and invoked what Brian Dippie has called "the embarassment of 1802 when the federal government, in exchange for Georgia's western lands, bound itself by compact to extinguish existing Indian title in the state"[1] in spite of all sorts of solemn vows to the tribes in one treaty after another to respect their rights. Eventually, in 1830, Congress passed, and Jackson signed into law the Indian Removal Act which gave the President the right to "remove" the eastern Indians to areas west of the Mississippi. This the President did in 1838 when some twelve thousand Cherokee were forced by federal troops under the command of General Winfield Scott to head westward on the infamous "Trail of Tears." Fully one third, some four thousand people, died on this westward march.

Even before the removal of the Cherokee, the Black Hawk War of 1832, the last Indian war to be fought east of the Mississippi, had pitted

1. Brian Dippie, *The Vanishing American: White Attitudes and United States Relations* (Middletown, CT: Wesleyan Univ. Press, 1982), p. 56.

the Sac and Fox nations against the state militias of Illinois and federal troops. The young Abraham Lincoln and his future adversary, Jefferson Davis, among other soon-to-be-famous Americans, participated in the action. The results for the Indians were disastrous, as they would be disastrous again and again in the years that followed, with the famous exception of the Custer fight in 1876.

The nineteenth century is the age of the Indian war, as an expanding American nation of settlers and fortune-seekers again and again invades territory that was legally off-limits to non-Indians. When this, predictably, led to defensive violence on the part of the Indians, the invaders claimed the protection of the federal government, whose laws they had flouted, with strong encouragement on the part of state or territorial governors. For all its promises to the Indians, the federal government repeatedly backed its citizens, forcing the Indians on to increasingly smaller and more barren tracts of land. Although a loose coalition of Cheyenne and Lakota (Sioux) did manage to defeat the ambitious and careless George Armstrong Custer on the Little Big-horn (with news of the disaster of 25 June 1876 reaching the East just as the first celebrations of the centennial of the American Revolution were getting underway), this Native victory was the exception rather than the rule.

Soon after the adventures of Custer, the nation avidly followed the "flight of the Nez Perces," as this small group of people from the Wallowa Valley of what is now eastern Oregon, rather than exchange the million or so acres of their ancestral lands for some twelve hundred acres of reservation land, undertook a journey for freedom to "Grandmother's Land," i.e., Canada, under the rule of Queen Victoria. After four months and thirteen hundred miles of relentless pursuit by federal troops, the Nez Perces were forced to surrender to General Nelson Miles, in October of 1877, just thirty miles short of the Canadian border. By flatboats and boxcars, they were shipped to what Yellow Wolf calls Eeikish Pah, the Hot Place, Indian Territory, west of Arkansas and Mississippi, where those who did not sicken and die languished until 1885. At that point, Joseph and his band were returned, not to the Wallowa country, but to the Colville reservation at Nespelem, Washington.

And so it went. In 1886, Geronimo and his small Apache band, the "last of the wild Indians," surrendered to General Crook and were immediately sent to a hotter place still, to Fort Marion, Florida where, after eight years of captivity, some twenty-five percent of the Apache had died of disease and despair. But even then the Apache were not returned home; rather, they were sent to Fort Sill, Oklahoma, far from their Arizona homes. Geronimo died, a prisoner of war, in the military hospital at Fort Sill.

We close this section with the events of 1890. This is the year of the massacre of Big Foot's band at Wounded Knee, but there is another event of that year which also deserves mention. I refer to the report of the Superintendent of the Census in 1890, which announced what historians have referred to as the "close" of the western "frontier." "At present," the report stated, "the unsettled [!] area has been so broken into by isolated bodies of settlement that there can hardly be said to be a frontier line." The concept of the "frontier," highlighted no doubt by its apparent closure, gave rise to the influential explanation of the nature of American culture by Frederick Jackson Turner, at the World's Columbian Exposition in 1893. Indians, in Turner's thesis, appeared not as human agents so much as natural facts, like trees, rivers, or valleys; lands inhabited by the Indians were, as the Superintendent of the Census seems to have believed, "unsettled." Turner's thesis, intentionally or not, treated the Indian as largely an annoying footnote to the progress of "civilization," and this thesis has been influential until fairly recently, when the concept of the frontier has been redefined to suggest not so much a line marking the point to which "civilization" had extended itself, but, rather, in the words of the anthropologist James Clifton, a "social setting . . . a culturally defined place where peoples with different culturally expressed identities meet and deal with each other."[2]

And Wounded Knee. The events at Wounded Knee are bound up with the messianic movement known as the Ghost Dance religion. Originating in the vision on New Year's Day of 1889 of a Nevada Paiute named Wovoka, or Jack Wilson, the Ghost Dancers worked toward a world made new, when the buffalo and the Indian dead would return, and all the land would be free again. To hasten this happy day, adherents of the new religion were to perform an extended dance which took five nights to complete; special songs and decorated shirts—Ghost Dance shirts—also played a part in the ceremony. Wovoka's teachings had a strongly Christian tinge; Indians were to put aside war and love one another. They were even to love the whites—who would, nonetheless, disappear once the Messiah came to usher in the new age.

In the fall of 1889, the Sioux sent eleven men from the Pine Ridge,

2. *Being and Becoming Indian*, ed. James Clifton (Chicago: Dorsey Press, 1989), p. 24.

Wovoka in Yerington, circa 1915. Courtesy of the Nevada Historical Society.

Rosebud, and Cheyenne River agencies to discover the truth about this new religion. When they returned, it was the report of Kicking Bear, an Oglala, married to the niece of Chief Big Foot of the Minne-conjou, that seemed to have the most influence. And Kicking Bear's account made of the Ghost Dance a decidedly militant and potentially violent business. In desperate straits, squeezed onto smaller and smaller reservations and accorded only half the rations they had been promised by the government, the Sioux began to perform the Ghost Dance. The government and its representatives, as had happened so often before, reacted with confusion, contradiction, and in the end, deadly force.

By November of 1890, troops had arrived at the Pine Ridge and Rosebud agencies, along with reporters avid for war stories. In mid-December, as General Nelson Miles headed westward to take command of the situation, Indian police at the Standing Rock agency came with orders to arrest Sitting Bull, most notable of the resisting chiefs and a supporter of the Ghost Dancers. (Gall, leader of the Hunkpapa against Custer, and a formidable warrior, had finally decided the only way for his people to survive was to follow the way of the whites.) At first the old Chief agreed to come along peaceably; then, chided by Catch-the-Bear and by his own son, Crow Foot, he resisted the officers. Catch-the-Bear shot the Indian policeman Bull Head, who, as he fell, shot Sitting Bull.

But let us now shift attention to the Cheyenne River Camp of Big Foot, who had first welcomed but subsequently shunned the Ghost Dance. Severely ill of pneumonia, and expecting his arrest, Big Foot decided to take his people, all of them cold and hungry, south to surrender to the Army at Wounded Knee. Major Samuel Whitside was to be in charge of Big Foot's surrender with the troops already in place there, but his superior, General John Brooke, decided that reinforcements were needed. Most prominent among the reinforcements called in by Brooke were four troops of the Seventh Cavalry, among them soldiers who had fought with Reno and Benteen's commands not far from Custer on the Little Big Horn.

On the morning of 29 December 1890, the men of Big Foot's band assembled at Wounded Knee, where they were ordered to hand over their weapons. When they produced only a few old rifles, soldiers entered their tipis to search for more. There, they knocked things about and frightened the women. But many rifles were indeed hidden in the tipis, while others were held concealed by the men under their blankets. The Sioux medicine man Yellow Beard circled the

Sitting Bull, as photographed by D. F. Barry shortly after his surrender in
1881. Courtesy of the Library of Congress.

assembled warriors, urging them to fight, and reminding them that they could not, with their magic Ghost Dance shirts, be pierced by the soldiers' bullets. Finally, it was a man named Black Coyote or Black Fox who, refusing to surrender his rifle, discharged it, perhaps accidentally, leading to other of the warriors firing. The old Winchesters of the Indians went against the much more efficient Springfields of the soldiers—until the big shells of the Army's Hotchkiss guns rained down, and quickly all was over.

A blizzard swept the area. The dead could not be buried until New Year's Day, when civilian entrepeneurs, charging the Army two dollars a body, threw the dead Sioux into a mass grave. By the time the long-awaited fighting had actually come to pass, only three intrepid news reporters remained at Wounded Knee; it was from their reports that tabloids across the nation reported either an Army triumph over the last savage hostiles (this mostly in the West)—or a massacre of the helpless red men by soldiers still concerned to avenge Custer (this mostly in the East).

Thus, what Ralph Andrist has called "the long death" of the Indian in the nineteenth century seemed finally to have been achieved. From sea to shining sea, America had now affirmed its manifest destiny, subduing the "wild men" and "savages," the continent's original inhabitants. As the American nation, come to the Pacific, still "faced west," in Richard Drinnon's phrase, preparing for new "frontier" encounters with the yellow-skinned peoples of the earth, the question was whether, in time, Native people might rise from the ashes.

What does all of this mean for Native American autobiography? I will hardly pretend to be comprehensive, but a few things can be said. Whereas the Christian autobiographies of the early nineteenth century were indeed autobiographies, self-written personal testaments to the benefits and, often, the shortfalls of Christian civilization, the autobiographies of the present section are all texts that are collaborations, and they are texts whose Indian subjects resisted christianization and civilization. As I have noted in the Introduction, these are also texts solicited or at least encouraged by non-Indians, who typically considered themselves to be contributing to "history," or historical explanation. J. B. Patterson with Black Hawk, Thomas Marquis with Wooden Leg, L. V. McWhorter with Yellow Wolf, and (although the situation becomes more complicated here) even S. M. Barrett with Geronimo, all see themselves as producing accounts that will amplify and balance the historical record by permitting a Native person to explain his resistance to "progress" or to the march of "civ-

American Horse and Red Cloud at the Pine Ridge Agency in January 1891.
Courtesy of the Library of Congress.

ilization" from his own point of view. (Frank Linderman's work with Plenty-Coups does not appear in this part of the anthology because the Crow, fierce warriors of great repute, did *not* resist the whites; they served, rather, as scouts with Custer, and against the Nez Perces, a subject we shall consider below.) More than any of these editors, perhaps, John Neihardt, recorder of Black Elk's story, was a firm partisan of Christian "civilization," for all that he—and the others—are quite sympathetic to and generally admiring of Native peoples.

Although these Indian autobiographies probably do give us a fairly accurate rendition of what these nineteenth-century warriors "said," what we have is in a language and an order chosen by the editor. As the mixedblood Pomo scholar Greg Sarris has recently insisted, the "real" or "authentic" Indian voice remains to be restored to these texts. To the extent that this is possible, it is a task that Native American critics today are particularly well-positioned to undertake. Still, that these Indian autobiographies of the nineteenth century do claim to offer an Indian subject speaking in his own voice, however mediated—*as an Indian*—is an important fact to note, for never before, not in some two hundred years of American "history," was the Indian *as* Indian considered worthy to be heard.

My selections from these book-length autobiographies reflect the point made in the Introduction, that in this period Native people continued to live, for the most part, in the way they had traditionally lived. But they also had to cope with an aggressive and increasingly numerous invading white population. Living traditionally for the Plains warrior involved a life in which a long nursing period was followed by "vision quests" in early adolescence, when the young man would spend four days, or a part thereof, alone, fasting and praying for dreams, visions, or visitations by animals or spirits who would bestow upon him "power" or medicine. It also involved training in horsemanship, hunting, and warfare, and a strong commitment to kin and community, all joined to an intense desire to excel and be "a great man." Sioux, Cheyenne, and Crow shared many aspects of this Plains culture, although the Sioux and Cheyenne were traditionally close friends, while both were enemies to the Crow.

The autobiographical selections in this section are from texts that are relatively well-known. Many more of these have been written, in large part to meet the persistent interest of many Americans in military history and in the life stories of generals—or, in this case, of famous "chiefs." For those interested in additional Native American autobiographies of resistance, e.g., the different Sioux divisions, the Cheyenne, etc., the best beginning point is probably the index of tribes in H. David Brumble's *Annotated Bibliography of American Indian and Eskimo Autobiographies*.[3]

3. H. David Brumble, *Annotated Bibliography of American Indian and Eskimo Autobiographies* (Lincoln: Univ. of Nebraska Press, 1981).

9
Life of Ma-ka-tai-me-she-kia-kiak, or Black Hawk

Edited by

J. B. PATTERSON

After his defeat in the Black Hawk War of 1832, Black Hawk, an elderly traditional war chief of the Sac and Fox, endured brief imprisonment at Jefferson Barracks, south of St. Louis, confinement at Fort Monroe in Virginia, and, finally, a tour of the East before being allowed to return to the Rock River country of present-day Illinois where he had been born and raised. It was there that Black Hawk apparently told Antoine LeClair, the government interpreter for the Sac and Fox, that he wished to narrate the story of his life.

Although he was highly regarded by both Indians and whites as an interpreter, and reputed to be competent in some dozen Native languages, LeClair's English was sufficiently uncertain for him to recruit the services of young John B. Patterson, editor of the Galena, Illinois, Galenian *to aid him in the process of producing Black Hawk's life story. It was Patterson who actually wrote the version we have, working from LeClair's transcription and translation of what Black Hawk said. For this first Indian autobiography, as for a good many that follow it, we have no original manuscript, not even rough notes, to consult for the purpose of making some nearer approximation to what Black Hawk may actually have said.*

Published in 1833 in Cincinnati, i.e., in the "West," the Life of Black Hawk *was sufficiently popular to justify no fewer than four more editions the following year in the East, and, after many years, an elaborately revised edition by Patterson himself in 1882. In the latter edition, Patterson referred to himself as the "editor and sole proprietor" of Black Hawk's* Life, *which was now for the first time called* The Autobiography of Ma-ka-tai-me-she-kia-kiak. *In the 1882 edition, Patterson expanded a number of the descriptions in the original 1833 text, and he elaborated the diction in several places. Although Black Hawk had supposedly approved the 1833 text, he could not be held responsible for the 1882 version of his story, having died in 1838.*

Shortly after Black Hawk's death, his grave was robbed by persons unknown and his bones placed on display in Iowa. Keokuk, an accomodationist rival of Black Hawk, died ten years later, and was commemorated by a bronze bust in the nation's capital, in Washington, D.C.

149

The selections which follow are from the 1833 edition of the Life, *to which section heads (in brackets) have been added. The relatively recent* Black Hawk: An Autobiography, *edited by Donald Jackson, contains an excellent and detailed introduction, as well as comprehensive and illuminating notes.*[1]

Few, if any, events of note, transpired within my recollection, until about my fifteenth year. I was not allowed to paint, or wear feathers; but distinguished myself, at that early age, by wounding an enemy; consequently, I was placed in the ranks of the Braves!

Soon after this, a leading chief of the Muscow nation, came to our village for recruits to go to war against the Osages, our common enemy. I volunteered my services to go, as my father had joined them; and was proud to have an opportunity to prove to him that I was not an unworthy son, and that I had courage and bravery. It was not long before we met the enemy, when a battle immediately ensued. Standing by my father's side, I saw him kill his antagonist, and tear the scalp from his head. Fired with valor and ambition, I rushed furiously upon another, smote him to the earth with my tomahawk—run my lance through his body—took off his scalp, and returned in triumph to my father! He said nothing, but looked pleased. This was the first man I killed! The enemy's loss in this engagement having been great, they immediately retreated, which put an end to the war for the present. Our party then returned to our village, and danced over the scalps we had taken. This was the first time that I was permitted to join in a scalp-dance.

After a few moons had passed (having acquired considerable fame as a *brave*), I led a party of seven, and attacked *one hundred Osages!* I killed one man, and left him for my comrades to scalp, whilst I was taking an observation of the strength and preparations of the enemy; and finding that they were all equally well armed with ourselves, I ordered a retreat, and came off without losing a man! This excursion gained for me great applause, and enabled me, before a great while, to raise a party of one hundred and eighty, to go against the Osages. We left our village in high spirits, and marched over a rugged country, until we reached that of the Osages, on the Missouri. We followed their trail until we arrived at their village, which we approached with great caution, expecting that they were all there; but

---

1. *Black Hawk: An Autobiography*, ed. Donald Jackson (Urbana, IL: Univ. of Illinois Press, 1964).

found, to our sorrow, that they had deserted it! The party became dissatisfied, in consequence of this disappointment,—and all, with the exception of *five*, dispersed and returned home. I then placed myself at the head of this brave little band, and thanked the Great Spirit, that *so many* remained,—and took up the trail of our enemies, with a full determination never to return without some trophy of victory! We followed on for several days—killed one man and a boy, and then returned with their scalps.

In consequence of this mutiny in my camp, I was not again enabled to raise a sufficient party to go against the Osages, until about my nineteenth year. During this interim, they committed many outrages on our nation and people. I succeeded at length, in recruiting two hundred efficient warriors, and took up the line of march early in the morning. In a few days we were in the enemy's country, and had not travelled far before we met an equal force to contend with. A general battle immediately commenced, although my braves were considerably fatigued by forced marches. Each party fought desperately. The enemy seemed unwilling to yield the ground, and we were determined to conquer or die! A large number of the Osages were killed, and many wounded, before they commenced retreating. A band of warriors more brave, skilful, and efficient than mine, could not be found. In this engagement I killed five men and one squaw, and had the good fortune to take the scalps of all I struck, except one. The enemy's loss in this engagement was about one hundred men. Ours nineteen. We now returned to our village, well pleased with our success, and danced over the scalps we had taken.

The Osages, in consequence of their great loss in this battle, became satisfied to remain on their own lands; and ceased, for awhile, their depredations on our nation. Our attention, therefore, was directed towards an ancient enemy, who had decoyed and murdered some of our helpless women and children. I started, with my father, who took command of a small party, and proceeded against the enemy. We met near Merimack, and an action ensued; the Cherokees having greatly the advantage in numbers. Early in this engagement my father was wounded in the thigh—but had the pleasure of killing his antagonist before he fell. Seeing that he had fallen, I assumed command, and fought desperately, until the enemy commenced retreating before us. I returned to my father to administer to his necessities, but nothing could be done for him. The *medicine man* said the wound was *mortal!* from which he soon after *died!* In this battle I killed three men, and wounded several. The enemy's loss being twenty-eight, and ours seven.

Muk-a-tah-mish-o-kah-kiak, Black Hawk, prominent Sauk Chief, 1832. Painting by George Caitlin. Courtesy of the National Museum of American Art, Smithsonian Institution. Gift of Mrs. Joseph Harrison, Jr.

I now fell heir to the great *medicine bag* of my forefathers, which had belonged to my father. I took it, buried our dead, and returned with my party, all sad and sorrowful, to our village, in consequence of the loss of my father. Owing to this misfortune, I blacked my face, fasted, and prayed to the Great Spirit for five years—during which time I remained in a civil capacity, hunting and fishing.

The Osages having commenced aggressions on our people, and the

Great Spirit having taken pity on me, I took a small party and went against the enemy, but could only find *six* men! Their forces being so weak, I thought it cowardly to kill them,—but took them prisoners, and carried them to our Spanish father at St. Louis, and gave them up to him; and then returned to our village. Determined on the final extermination of the Osages, for the injuries our nation and people had received from them, I commenced recruiting a strong force, immediately on my return, and started, in the third moon, with five hundred Sacs and Foxes, and one hundred Ioways, and marched against the enemy. We continued our march for several days before we came upon their trail, which was discovered late in the day. We encamped for the night; made an early start next morning, and before sun down, fell upon *forty lodges*, and killed all their inhabitants, except *two squaws!* whom I captured and made prisoners. During this attack I killed seven men and two boys, with my own hand.

In this engagement many of the bravest warriors among the Osages were killed, which caused the balance of their nation to remain on their own lands, and cease their aggressions upon our hunting grounds.

The loss of my father, by the Cherokees, made me anxious to avenge his death, by the annihilation, if possible, of all their race. I accordingly commenced recruiting another party to go against them. Having succeeded in this, I started, with my party, and went into their country, but only found five of their people, whom I took prisoners. I afterwards released four men—the other, a young *squaw*, we brought home. Great as was my hatred for this people, I could not kill so small a party.

During the close of the ninth moon, I led a large party against the Chippewas, Kaskaskias and Osages. This was the commencement of a long and arduous campaign, which terminated in my thirty-fifth year: Having had seven regular engagements, and a number of small skirmishes. During this campaign, several hundred of the enemy were slain. I killed *thirteen* of their bravest warriors, with my own hand.

Our enemies having now been driven from our hunting grounds, with so great a loss as they sustained, we returned, in peace, to our villages; and after the seasons of mourning and burying our dead relations, and of feast-dancing had passed, we commenced preparations for our winter's hunt, in which we were very successful. . . .

When our national dance is over—our corn-fields hoed, and every weed dug up, and our corn about knee-high, all our young men would start in a direction towards sun-down, to hunt deer and buffalo—being prepared, also, to kill Sioux, if any are found on our hunting grounds—a part of our old men and women to the lead mines to made lead—and the remainder of our people start to fish, and get mat stuff. Every one leaves the village, and remains about forty days. They then return: the hunting party bringing in dried buffalo and deer meat, and sometimes *Sioux scalps*, when they are found trespassing on our hunting grounds. At other times they are met by a party of Sioux too strong for them, and are driven in. If the Sioux have killed the Sacs last, they expect to be retaliated upon, and will fly before them, and vice versa. Each party knows that the other has a right to retaliate, which induces those who have killed last, to give way before their enemy—as neither wish to strike, except to avenge the death of their relatives. All our wars are predicated by the relatives of those killed; or by aggressions upon our hunting grounds.

The party from the lead mines bring lead, and the others dried fish, and mats for our winter lodges. Presents are now made by each party; the first, giving to the others dried buffalo and deer, and they, in exchange, presenting them with lead, dried fish and mats.

This is a happy season of the year—having plenty of provisions, such as beans, squashes, and other produce, with our dried meat and fish, we continue to make feasts and visit each other, until our corn is ripe. Some lodge in the village makes a feast daily, to the Great Spirit. I cannot explain this so that the white people would comprehend me, as we have no regular standard among us. Every one makes his feast as he thinks best, to please the Great Spirit, who has the care of all beings created. Others believe in two Spirits: one good and one bad, and make feasts for the Bad Spirit, *to keep him quiet!* If they can make peace with him, the Good Spirit will not hurt them! For my part, I am of opinion, that so far as we have *reason*, we have a right to use it, in determining what is right or wrong; and should pursue that path which we believe to be right—believing, that "whatever is, is right." If the Great and Good Spirit wished us to believe and do as the whites, he could easily change our opinions, so that we would see, and think, and act as they do. We are *nothing* compared to His power, and we feel and know it. We have men among us, like the whites, who pretend to know the right path, but will not consent to show it without *pay!* I have no faith in their paths—but believe that every man must make his own path!

When our corn is getting ripe, our young people watch with anxiety for the signal to pull roasting-ears—as none dare touch them until the proper time. When the corn is fit to use, another great ceremony takes place, with feasting, and returning thanks to the Great Spirit for giving us corn.

I will here relate the manner in which corn first came. According to tradition, handed down to our people, a beautiful woman was seen to descend from the clouds, and alight upon the earth, by two of our ancestors, who had killed a deer, and were sitting by a fire, roasting a part of it to eat. They were astonished at seeing her, and concluded that she must be hungry, and had smelt the meat—and immediately went to her, taking with them a piece of the roasted venison. They presented it to her, and she eat—and told them to return to the spot where she was sitting, at the end of one year, and they would find a reward for their kindness and generosity. She then ascended to the clouds, and disappeared. The two men returned to their village, and explained to the nation what they had seen, done, and heard—but were laughed at by their people. When the period arrived, for them to visit this consecrated ground, where they were to find a reward for their attention to the beautiful woman of the clouds, they went with a large party, and found, where her right hand had rested on the ground, *corn* growing—and where the left hand had rested, *beans*—and immediately where she had been seated, *tobacco.*

The two first have, ever since, been cultivated by our people, as our principal provisions—and the last used for smoking. The white people have since found out the latter, and seem to relish it as much as we do—as they use it in different ways, viz. smoking, snuffing and eating!

We thank the Great Spirit for all the benefits he has conferred upon us. For myself, I never take a drink of water from a spring, without being mindful of his goodness.

We next have our great ball play—from three to five hundred on a side, play this game. We play for horses, guns, blankets, or any other kind of property we have. The successful party take the stakes, and all retire to our lodges in peace and friendship.

We next commence horse-racing, and continue our sport and feasting, until the corn is all secured. We then prepare to leave our village for our hunting grounds. The traders arrive, and give us credit for such articles as we want to clothe our families, and enable us to hunt. We first, however, hold a council with them, to ascertain the price they will give us for our skins, and what they will charge us for goods. We inform them where we intend hunting—and tell them where to build their houses. At this place, we deposit part of our corn, and leave our old people. The traders have always been kind to them, and relieved them when in want. They were always much respected by our people—and never since we have been a nation, has one of them been killed by any of our people.

We disperse, in small parties, to make our hunt, and as soon as it is over, we return to our traders' establishment, with our skins, and remain feasting, playing cards and other pastimes, until near the close of winter. Our young men then start on the beaver hunt; others to hunt raccoons and muskrats—and the remainder of our people go to the sugar camps to make sugar. All leave our encampment, and appoint a place to meet on the Mississippi, so that we may return to our village together, in the spring. We always spent our time pleasantly at the sugar camp. It being the season for wild fowl, we lived well, and always had plenty, when the hunters came in, that we might make a feast for them. After this is over, we return to our village, accompanied, sometimes, by our traders. In this way, the year rolled round happily. But these are times that were!

On returning, in the spring, from our hunting ground, I had the pleasure of meeting our old friend, the trader of Peoria, at Rock Island. He came up in a boat from St. Louis, not as a trader, as in times past, but as our *agent*. We were all pleased to see him. He told us, that he narrowly escaped falling into the hands of Dixon. He remained with us a short time, gave us good advice, and then returned to St. Louis.

The Sioux having committed depredations on our people, we sent out war parties that summer, who succeeded in killing *fourteen*. I paid several visits to fort Armstrong during the summer, and was always well treated. We were not as happy then in our village as formerly. Our people got more liquor than customary. I used all my influence to prevent drunkenness, but without effect. As the settlements progressed towards us, we became worse off, and more unhappy. Many of our people, instead of going to their old hunting grounds, where game was plenty, would go near to the settlements to hunt—and, instead of saving their skins to pay the trader for goods furnished them in the fall, would sell them to the settlers for whisky! and return in the spring with their families, almost naked, and without the means of getting any thing for them.

About this time my eldest son was taken sick and died. He had always been a dutiful child, and had just grown to manhood. Soon after, my youngest daughter, an interesting and affectionate child, died also. This was a hard stroke, because I loved my children. In my distress, I left the noise of the village, and built my lodge on a mound in my corn-field, and enclosed it with a fence, around which I planted corn and beans. Here I was with my family alone. I gave every thing

I had away, and reduced myself to poverty. The only covering I retained, was a piece of buffalo robe. I resolved on blacking my face and fasting, for two years, for the loss of my two children—drinking only of water in the middle of the day, and eating sparingly of boiled corn at sunset. I fulfilled my promise, hoping that the Great Spirit would take pity on me.

My nation had now some difficulty with the Ioways, with whom we wished to be at peace. Our young men had repeatedly killed some of the Ioways; and these breaches had always been made up by giving presents to the relations of those killed. But the last council we had with them, we promised that, in case any more of their people were killed by ours, instead of presents, we would give up the person, or persons, that had done the injury. We made this determination known to our people; but, notwithstanding, one of our young men killed an Ioway the following winter.

A party of our people were about starting for the Ioway village to give the young man up. I agreed to accompany them. When we were ready to start, I called at the lodge for the young man to go with us. He was sick, but willing to go. His brother, however, prevented him, and insisted on going to die in his place, as he was unable to travel. We started, and on the seventh day arrived in sight of the Ioway village, and when within a short distance of it, halted and dismounted. We all bid farewell to our young brave, who entered the village alone, singing his *death-song*, and sat down in the square in the middle of the village. One of the Ioway chiefs came out to us. We told him that we had fulfilled our promise—that we had brought the brother of the young man who had killed one of their people—that he had volunteered to come in his place, in consequence of his brother being unable to travel from sickness. We had no further conversation, but mounted our horses and rode off. As we started, I cast my eye towards the village, and observed the Ioways coming out of their lodges with spears and war clubs. We took our trail back, and travelled until dark—then encamped and made a fire. We had not been here long, before we heard the sound of horses coming towards us. We seized our arms; but instead of an enemy, it was our young brave with two horses. He told me that after we had left him, they menaced him with death for some time—then gave him something to eat—smoked the pipe with him—and made him a present of the two horses and some goods, and started him after us. When we arrived at our village, our people were much pleased; and for the noble and generous conduct of the Ioways, on this occasion, not one of their people has been killed since by any of our nation.

That fall I visited Malden with several of my band, and were well treated by our British father, who gave us a variety of presents. He also gave me a medal, and told me there never would be war between England and America again; but, for my fidelity to the British during the war that had terminated sometime before, requested me to come with my band every year and get presents, as Col. Dixon had promised me.

I returned, and hunted that winter on the Two-Rivers. The whites were now settling the country fast. I was out one day hunting in a bottom, and met three white men. They accused me of killing their hogs; I denied it; but they would not listen to me. One of them took my gun out of my hand and fired it off—then took out the flint, gave back my gun, and commenced beating me with sticks, and ordered me off. I was so much bruised that I could not sleep for several nights.

Some time after this occurrence, one of my camp cut a bee-tree, and carried the honey to his lodge. A party of white men soon followed, and told him that the bee-tree was theirs, and that he had no right to cut it. He pointed to the honey, and told them to take it; they were not satisfied with this, but took all the packs of skins that he had collected during the winter, to pay his trader and clothe his family with in the spring, and carried them off!

How could we like such people, who treated us so unjustly? We determined to break up our camp, for fear that they would do worse—and when we joined our people in the spring, a great many of them complained of similar treatment.

This summer our agent came to live at Rock Island. He treated us well, and gave us good advice. I visited him and the trader very often during the summer, and, for the first time, heard talk of our having to leave my village. The trader explained to me the terms of the treaty that had been made, and said we would be obliged to leave the Illinois side of the Mississippi, and advised us to select a good place for our village, and remove to it in the spring. He pointed out the difficulties we would have to encounter, if we remained at our village on Rock river. He had great influence with the principal Fox chief (his adopted brother), and persuaded him to leave his village, and go to the west side of the Mississippi river, and build another—which he did the spring following.

Nothing was now talked of but leaving our village. Ke-o-kuck had been persuaded to consent to go; and was using all his influence, backed by the war chief at fort Armstrong, and our agent and trader at Rock Island, to induce others to go with him. He sent the crier through the village to inform our people that it was the wish of our

Great Father that we should remove to the west side of the Mississippi—and recommended the Ioway river as a good place for the new village—and wished his party to make such arrangements, before they started out on their winter's hunt, as to preclude the necessity of their returning to the village in the spring.

The party opposed to removing, called upon me for my opinion. I gave it freely—and after questioning Quàsh-quà-me about the sale of the lands, he assured me that he "never had consented to the sale of our village." I now promised this party to be their leader, and raised the standard of opposition to Ke-o-kuck, with a full determination not to leave my village. I had an interview with Ke-o-kuck, to see if this difficulty could not be settled with our Great Father—and told him to propose to give other land (any that our Great Father might choose, even our *lead mines*), to be peaceably permitted to keep the small point of land on which our village and fields were situate. I was of opinion that the white people had plenty of land, and would never take our village from us. Ke-o-kuck promised to make an exchange if possible; and applied to our agent, and the great chief at St. Louis (who has charge of all the agents), for permission to go to Washington to see our Great Father for that purpose. This satisfied us for some time. We started to our hunting grounds, in good hopes that something would be done for us. During the winter, I received information that three families of whites had arrived at our village, and destroyed some of our lodges, and were making fences and dividing our corn-fields for their own use—*and were quarreling among themselves about their lines, in the division!* I immediately started for Rock river, a distance of ten day's travel, and on my arrival, found the report to be true. I went to my lodge, and saw a family occupying it. I wished to talk with them, but they could not understand me. I then went to Rock Island, and (the agent being absent), told the interpreter what I wanted to say to those people, viz: "Not to settle on our land—nor trouble our lodges or fences—that there was plenty of land in the country for them to settle upon—and they must leave our village, as we were coming back to it in the spring." The interpreter wrote me a paper, and I went back to the village, and showed it to the intruders, but could not understand their reply. I expected, however, that they would remove, as I requested them. I returned to Rock Island, passed the night there, and had a long conversation with the trader. He again advised me to give up, and make my village with Ke-o-kuck, on the Ioway river. I told him that I would not. The next morning I crossed the Mississippi, on very bad ice—but the Great Spirit made it strong, that I might pass over safe. I travelled three days farther to see the Winnebago sub-agent, and converse with him on the subject of our difficulties. He gave me no better news than the trader had done. I started then, by way of Rock river, to see the prophet, believing that he was a man of great knowledge. When we met, I explained to him every thing as it was. He at once agreed that I was right, and advised me never to give up our village, for the whites to plough up the bones of our people. He said, that if we remained at our village, the whites would not trouble us—and advised me to get Ke-o-kuck, and the party that had consented to go with him to the Ioway in the spring, to return, and remain at our village.

I returned to my hunting ground, after an absence of one moon, and related what I had done. In a short time we came up to our village, and found that the whites had not left it—but that others had come, and that the greater part of our corn-fields had been enclosed. When we landed, the whites appeared displeased because we had come back. We repaired the lodges that had been left standing, and built others. Ke-o-kuck came to the village; but his object was to persuade others to follow him to the Ioway. He had accomplished nothing towards making arrangements for us to remain, or to exchange other lands for our village. There was no more friendship existing between us. I looked upon him as a coward, and no brave, to abandon his village to be occupied by strangers. What *right* had these people to our village, and our fields, which the Great Spirit had given us to live upon?

My reason teaches me that *land cannot be sold*. The Great Spirit gave it to his children to live upon, and cultivate, as far as is necessary for their subsistence; and so long as they occupy and cultivate it, they have the right to the soil—but if they voluntarily leave it, then any other people have a right to settle upon it. Nothing can be sold, but such things as can be carried away.

In consequence of the improvements of the intruders on our fields, we found considerable difficulty to get ground to plant a little corn. Some of the whites permitted us to plant small patches in the fields they had fenced, keeping all the best ground for themselves. Our women had great difficulty in climbing their fences (being unaccustomed to the kind), and were ill-treated if they left a rail down.

One of my old friends thought he was safe. His corn-field was on a small island of Rock river. He planted his corn; it came up well—but the white man saw it!—he wanted the island, and took his team over, ploughed up the corn, and re-planted it for himself! The old man shed tears; not for himself, but the distress his family would be in if they raised no corn.

The white people brought whisky into our village, made our people drunk, and cheated them out of their horses, guns, and traps! This fraudulent system was carried to such an extent that I apprehended serious difficulties might take place, unless a stop was put to it. Consequently, I visited all the whites and begged them not to sell whisky to my people. One of them continued the practice openly. I took a party of my young men, went to his house, and took out his barrel and broke in the head and turned out the whisky. I did this for fear some of the whites might be killed by my people when drunk.

Our people were treated badly by the whites on many occasions. At one time, a white man beat one of our women cruelly, for pulling a few suckers of corn out of his field, to suck, when hungry! At another time, one of our young men was beat with clubs by two white men for opening a fence which crossed our road, to take his horse through. His shoulder blade was broken, and his body badly bruised, from which he soon after *died!*

Bad, and cruel, as our people were treated by the whites, not one of them was hurt or molested by any of my band. I hope this will prove that we are a peaceable people—having permitted ten men to take possession of our corn-fields; prevent us from planting corn; burn and destroy our lodges; ill-treat our women; and *beat to death* our men, without offering resistance to their barbarous cruelties. This is a lesson worthy for the white man to learn: to use forbearance when injured.

We acquainted our agent daily with our situation, and through him, the great chief at St. Louis—and hoped that something would be done for us. The whites were *complaining* at the same time that *we* were *intruding* upon *their rights!* THEY made themselves out the *injured* party, and *we* the *intruders!* and called loudly to the great war chief to protect *their* property!

How smooth must be the language of the whites, when they can make right look like wrong, and wrong like right.

During this summer, I happened at Rock Island, when a great chief arrived (whom I had known as the great chief of Illinois), in company with another chief, who, I have been told, is a great writer.[2] I called upon them and begged to explain to them the grievances under which me and my people were laboring, hoping that they could do something for us. The great chief, however, did not seem disposed to

___

2. Jackson's notes identify these two men as Governor Cole and Judge James Hall, respectively.

council with me. He said he was no longer the great chief of Illinois—that his children had selected another father in his stead, and that he now only ranked as they did. I was surprised at this talk, as I had always heard that he was a good, brave, and great chief. But the white people never appear to be satisfied. When they get a good father, they hold councils (at the suggestion of some bad, ambitious man, who wants the place himself), and conclude, among themselves, that this man, or some other equally ambitious, would make a better father than they have, and nine times out of ten they don't get as good a one again.

I insisted on explaining to these two chiefs the true situation of my people. They gave their assent: I rose and made a speech, in which I explained to them the treaty made by Quàsh-quà-me, and three of our braves, according to the manner the trader and others had explained it to me. I then told them that Quàsh-quà-me and his party *denied*, positively, having ever sold my village; and that, as I had never known them to *lie*, I was determined to keep it in possession.

I told them that the white people had already entered our village, *burnt our lodges, destroyed our fences, ploughed up our corn, and beat our people*: that they had brought *whisky* into our country, *made our people drunk*, and taken from them their *horses, guns*, and *traps*; and that I had borne all this injury, without suffering any of my braves to raise a hand against the whites.

My object in holding this council, was to get the opinion of these two chiefs, as to the best course for me to pursue. I had appealed in vain, time after time, to our agent, who regularly represented our situation to the great chief at St. Louis, whose duty it was to call upon our Great Father to have justice done to us; but instead of this, we are told *that the white people want our country, and we must leave it to them!*

I did not think it possible that our Great Father wished us to leave our village, where we had lived so long, and where the bones of so many of our people had been laid. The great chief said that, as he was no longer a chief, he could do nothing for us; and felt sorry that it was not in his power to aid us—nor did he know how to advise us. Neither of them could do anything for us; but both evidently appeared very sorry. It would give me great pleasure, at all times, to take these two chiefs by the hand.

That fall I paid a visit to the agent, before we started to our hunting grounds, to hear if he had any good news for me. He had news! He said that the land on which our village stood was now ordered to be sold to individuals; and that, when sold, *our right* to remain, by treaty, would be at an end, and that if we returned next spring, we would be *forced* to remove!

We learned during the winter, that *part* of the lands where our village stood had been sold to individuals, and that the *trader* at Rock Island had bought the greater part that had been sold. The reason was now plain to me, why *he* urged us to remove. His object, we thought, was to get our lands. We held several councils that winter to determine what we should do, and resolved, in one of them, to return to our village in the spring, as usual; and concluded, that if we were removed by force, that the *trader*, agent, and others, must be the cause; and that, if found guilty of having us driven from our village, they should be *killed!* The trader stood foremost on this list. He had purchased the land on which my lodge stood, and that of our *graveyard* also! Ne-a-pope promised to kill him, the agent, interpreter, the great chief at St. Louis, the war chief at fort Armstrong, Rock Island, and Ke-o-kuck—these being the principal persons to blame for endeavoring to remove us.

Our women received bad accounts from the women that had been raising corn at the new village—the difficulty of breaking the new prairie with hoes—and the small quantity of corn raised. We were nearly in the same situation in regard to the latter, it being the first time I ever knew our people to be in want of provision.

I prevailed upon some of Ke-o-kuck's band to return this spring to the Rock river village. Ke-o-kuck would not return with us. I hoped that we would get permission to go to Washington to settle our affairs with our Great Father. I visited the agent at Rock Island. He was displeased because we had returned to our village, and told me that we *must* remove to the west of the Mississippi. I told him plainly that we *would not!* I visited the interpreter at his house, who advised me to do as the agent had directed me. I then went to see the trader, and upbraided him for buying our lands. He said that if he had not purchased them, some person else would, and that if our Great Father would make an exchange with us, he would willingly give up the land he had purchased to the government. This I thought was fair, and began to think that he had not acted as badly as I had suspected. We again repaired our lodges, and built others, as most of our village had been burnt and destroyed. Our women selected small patches to plant corn (where the whites had not taken them within their fences), and worked hard to raise something for our children to subsist upon.

I was told that, according to the treaty, we had no *right* to remain upon the lands *sold*, and that the government would *force* us to leave them. There was but a small portion, however, that *had been sold*; the balance remaining in the hands of the government, we claimed the right (if we had no other) to "live and hunt upon, as long as it remained the property of the government," by a stipulation in the same treaty that required us to evacuate it *after* it had been sold. This was the land that we wished to inhabit, and thought we had the best right to occupy.

I heard that there was a great chief on the Wabash, and sent a party to get his advice. They informed him that we had not sold our village. He assured them then, that if we had not sold the land on which our village stood, our Great Father would not take it from us. . . .

[The war begins]

I arranged war parties to send out in different directions, before I proceeded further. The Winnebagoes went alone. The war parties having all been fitted out and started, we commenced moving to the *Four Lakes*, the place where our guides were to conduct us. We had not gone far, before six Winnebagoes came in with *one scalp!* They said they had killed a man at a grove, on the road from Dixon's to the lead mines. Four days after, the party of Winnebagoes who had gone out from the head of Kish-wá-co-kee, overtook us, and told me that they had killed four men, and taken their scalps; and that one of them was Ke-o-kuck's father (the agent). They proposed to have a dance over their scalps! I told them that I could have no dancing in my camp, in consequence of my having lost three young braves; but they might dance in their own camp—which they did.

Two days after, we arrived in safety at the place where the Winnebagoes had directed us. In a few days a great number of our warriors came in. I called them all around me, and addressed them. I told them, "Now is the time, if any of you wish to come into distinction, and be honored with the medicine bag! Now is the time to show your courage and bravery, and avenge the murder of our three braves!"

Several small parties went out, and returned again in a few days, with success—bringing in provision for our people. In the mean time, some *spies* came in, and reported that the army had fallen back to Dixon's ferry; and others brought news that the horsemen had broken up their camp, disbanded, and returned home.

Finding that all was safe, I made a *dog feast*, preparatory to leaving my camp with a large party (as the enemy were stationed so far off).

Before my braves commenced feasting, I took my *medicine bags*, and addressed them in the following language:

"*Braves and Warriors*:—These are the medicine bags of our forefather, Muk-a-tà-quet, who was the father of the Sac nation. They were handed down to the great war chief of our nation, Na-nà-ma-kee, who has been at war with all the nations of the lakes and all the nations of the plains, and have never yet been disgraced! I expect you all to protect them!"

After the ceremony was over, and our feasting done, I started with about two hundred warriors, following my great medicine bags! I directed my course towards sunset, and dreamed, the second night after we started, that there was a great feast for us after one day's travel! I told my warriors my dream in the morning, and we all started for Mos-co-ho-co-y-nak. When we arrived in the vicinity of a fort the white people had built there, we saw four men on horseback. One of my braves fired and wounded a man, when the others set up a yell, as if a large force were near and ready to come against us. We concealed ourselves, and remained in this position for some time, watching to see the enemy approach—but none came. The four men, in the mean time, ran to the fort and gave the alarm. We followed them, and attacked their fort! One of their braves, who seemed more valiant than the rest, raised his head above the picketing to fire at us, when one of my braves, with a well-directed shot, put an end to his bravery! Finding that these people could not all be killed, without setting fire to their houses and fort, I thought it more prudent to be content with what flour, provisions, cattle and horses we could find, than to set fire to their buildings, as the light would be seen at a distance, and the army might suppose that we were in the neighborhood, and come upon us with a force too strong. Accordingly, we opened a house and filled our bags with flour and provisions—took several horses, and drove off some of their cattle.

We started in a direction towards sunrise. After marching a considerable time, I discovered some white men coming towards us. I told my braves that we would get into the woods and kill them when they approached. We concealed ourselves until they came near enough, and then commenced yelling and firing, and made a rush upon them. About this time, their chief, with a party of men, rushed up to rescue the men we had fired upon. In a little while they commenced retreating, and left their chief and a few braves, who seemed willing and anxious to fight! They acted like *braves*, but were forced to give way when I rushed upon them with my braves. In a short time the chief returned with a larger party. He seemed determined to fight, and anxious for a battle. When he came near enough, I raised the yell, and firing commenced from both sides. The chief (who seemed to be a small man) addressed his warriors in a loud voice; but they soon retreated, leaving him and a few braves on the battle-field. A great number of my warriors pursued the retreating party, and killed a number of their horses as they ran. The chief and his few braves were unwilling to leave the field. I ordered my braves to rush upon them, and had the mortification of seeing two of my *chiefs* killed, before the enemy retreated.

This young chief deserves great praise for his courage and bravery; but, fortunately for us, his army was not all composed of such brave men!

During this attack, we killed several men and about forty horses, and lost two young chiefs and seven warriors. My braves were anxious to pursue them to the fort, attack, and burn it. But I told them that it was useless to waste our powder, as there was no possible chance of success if we did attack them—and that, as we had run the bear into his hole, we would there leave him, and return to our camp.

On arriving at our encampment, we found that several parties of our *spies* had returned, bringing intelligence that the army had commenced moving. Another party of *five* came in and said they had been pursued for several hours, and were attacked by twenty-five or thirty whites in the woods; that the whites rushed in upon them, as they lay concealed, and received their fire, without seeing them. They immediately retreated, whilst we reloaded. They entered the thicket again, and as soon as they came near enough, we fired! Again they retreated, and again they rushed into the thicket and fired! We returned their fire, and a skirmish ensued between two of their men and one of ours, who was killed by having his throat cut! This was the only man we lost. The enemy having had three killed, they again retreated. . . .

[In dire straits, near war's end]

Myself and band having no means to descend the Ouisconsin, I started, over a rugged country, to go to the Mississippi, intending to cross it, and return to my nation. Many of our people were compelled to go on foot, for want of horses, which, in consequence of their having had nothing to eat for a long time, caused our march to be very slow. At length we arrived at the Mississippi, having lost some of our old men and little children, who perished on the way with hunger.[3]

We had been here but a little while, before we saw a steam boat (the "Warrior") coming. I told my braves not to shoot, as I intended going on board, so that we might save our women and children. I knew the captain, and was determined to give myself up to him. I then sent for my *white flag*. While the messenger was gone, I took a small piece of white cotton, and put it on a pole, and called to the captain of the boat, and told him to send his little canoe ashore, and let me come on board. The people on the boat asked whether we were Sacs or Winnebagoes. I told a Winnebago to tell them that we were Sacs, and wanted to give ourselves up! A Winnebago on the boat called to us *"to run and hide, that the whites were going to shoot!"* About this time one of my braves had jumped into the river, bearing a white flag to the boat—when another sprang in after him, and brought him to shore. The firing then commenced from the boat, which was returned by my braves, and continued for some time. Very few of my people were hurt after the first fire, having succeeded in getting behind old logs and trees, which shielded them from the enemy's fire.

The Winnebago, on the steam boat, must either have misunderstood what was told, or did not tell it to the captain correctly; because I am confident that he would not have fired upon us, if he had known my wishes. I have always considered him a good man, and too great a brave to fire upon an enemy when sueing for quarters.

After the boat left us, I told my people to cross, if they could, and wished: that I intended going into the Chippewa country. Some commenced crossing, and such as had determined to follow them, remained—only three lodges going with me. Next morning, at daybreak, a young man overtook me, and said that all my party had determined to cross the Mississippi—that a number had already got over safe, and that he had heard the white army last night within a few miles of them. I now began to fear that the whites would come up with my people, and kill them, before they could get across. I had determined to go and join the Chippewas; but reflecting that by this I could only save myself, I concluded to return, and die with my peo-

3. Jackson's notes (p. 136) include the following citation describing the condition of Black Hawk's band at a point very near the end of their resistance: "The prisoners are the most miserable looking poor creatures you can imagine. Wasted to mere skeletons, clothed in rags scarcely sufficient to hid their nakedness, some of the children look as if they had starved so long they could not be restored."

ple, if the Great Spirit would not give us another victory! During our stay in the thicket, a party of whites came close by us, but passed on without discovering us!

Early in the morning a party of whites, being in advance of the army, came upon our people, who were attempting to cross the Mississippi. They tried to give themselves up—the whites paid no attention to their entreaties—but commenced *slaughtering* them! In a little while the whole army arrived. Our braves, but few in number, finding that the enemy paid no regard to age or sex, and seeing that they were murdering helpless women and little children, determined to *fight until they were killed!* As many women as could, commenced swimming the Mississippi, with their children on their backs. A number of them were drowned, and some shot, before they could reach the opposite shore.

One of my braves, who gave me this information, piled up some saddles before him (when the fight commenced), to shield himself from the enemy's fire, and killed three white men! But seeing that the whites were coming too close to him, he crawled to the bank of the river, without being perceived, and hid himself under it, until the enemy retired. He then came to me and told me what had been done. After hearing this sorrowful news, I started, with my little party, to the Winnebago village at Prairie La Cross. On my arrival there, I entered the lodge of one of the chiefs, and told him that I wished him to go with me to his father—that I intended to give myself up to the American war chief, and *die,* if the Great Spirit saw proper! He said he would go with me. I then took my *medicine bag,* and addressed the chief. I told him that it was "the soul of the Sac nation—that it never had been dishonored in any battle—take it, it is my life—dearer than life—and give it to the American chief!" He said he would keep it, and take care of it, and if I was suffered to live, he would send it to me.

During my stay at the village, the squaws made me a white dress of deer skin. I then started, with several Winnebagoes, and went to their agent, at Prairie du Chien, and gave myself up.

On my arrival there, I found to my sorrow, that a large body of Sioux had pursued, and killed, a number of our women and children, who had got safely across the Mississippi. The whites ought not to have permitted such conduct—and none but *cowards* would ever have been guilty of such cruelty—which has always been practised on our nation by the Sioux.

The massacre, which terminated the war, lasted about two hours. Our loss in killed, was about sixty, besides a number that were drowned. The loss of the enemy could not be ascertained by my braves, exactly; but they think that they killed about *sixteen*, during the action. . . .

[Black Hawk in defeat]

On our way down, I surveyed the country that had cost us so much trouble, anxiety, and blood, and that now caused me to be a prisoner of war. I reflected upon the ingratitude of the whites, when I saw their fine houses, rich harvests, and every thing desirable around them; and recollected that all this land had been ours, for which me and my people had never received a dollar, and that the whites were not satisfied until they took our village and our grave-yards from us, and removed us across the Mississippi.

On our arrival at Jefferson barracks, we met the great war chief, who had commanded the American army against my little band. I felt the humiliation of my situation: a little while before, I had been the leader of my braves, now I was a prisoner of war! but had surrendered myself. He received us kindly, and treated us well.

We were now confined to the barracks, and forced to wear the *ball and chain!* This was extremely mortifying, and altogether useless. Was the White Beaver afraid that I would break out of his barracks, and run away? Or was he ordered to inflict this punishment upon me? If I had taken him prisoner on the field of battle, I would not have wounded his feelings so much, by such treatment—knowing that a brave war chief would prefer *death* to *dishonor!* But I do not blame the White Beaver for the course he pursued—it is the custom among white soldiers, and, I suppose, was a part of his duty.

The time dragged heavily and gloomy along throughout the winter, although the White Beaver done every thing in his power to render us comfortable. Having been accustomed, throughout a long life, to roam the forests o'er—to go and come at liberty—confinement, and under such circumstances, could not be less than torture! . . .

Before I take leave of the public, I must contradict the story of some *village criers*, who (I have been told), accuse me of "having murdered women and children among the whites!" This assertion is *false!* I never did, nor have I any knowledge that any of my nation ever killed a white woman or child. I make this statement of truth, to satisfy the white people among whom I have been travelling (and by whom I have been treated with great kindness), that, when they shook me by the hand so cordially, they did not shake the hand that had ever been raised against any but warriors.

It has always been our custom to receive all strangers that come to our village or camps, in time of peace, to share with them the best provisions we have, and give them all the assistance in our power. If on a journey, or lost, to put them on the right trail—and if in want of mocasins, to supply them. I feel grateful to the whites for the kind manner they treated me and my party, whilst travelling among them—and from my heart I assure them, that the white man will always be welcome in our village or camps, as a brother. The tomahawk is buried forever! We will forget what has past—and may the watchword between the Americans and Sacs and Foxes, ever be— *"Friendship!"*

I am now done. A few more moons, and I must follow my fathers to the shades! May the Great Spirit keep our people and the whites always at peace—is the sincere wish of

Black Hawk.

10

Wooden Leg, a Warrior Who Fought Custer

Edited by

THOMAS B. MARQUIS

Wooden Leg was born a northern Cheyenne in 1858. His "baby name" was Eats From the Hand, a name which was changed to Wooden Leg in honor of an uncle whose ability to walk prodigious distances he was supposed to have inherited. Wooden Leg grew up in the traditional horse culture of the western Plains, learning to ride, to hunt buffalo, and to prepare for the life of a warrior. This preparation stood him in good stead with "The Coming of Custer," as he calls it in his autobiography. And indeed, whether as a result of hindsight and/or of his editor's influence, Wooden Leg would seem to recognize the Custer fight as the beginning of the end for the Plains way of life.

After the Custer fight, Wooden Leg went with the Cheyenne camp up the Powder River, where the Cheyenne joined their friends, the Oglala Sioux. By the first of January, 1877, the Cheyenne had been engaged in battle by Colonel Nelson Miles on the Tongue River, and, after sporadic fighting and skirmishing, most of the Cheyenne of Wooden Leg's band decided to surrender. Eventually Wooden Leg was shipped off to Oklahoma, where, as happened to so many violently displaced Native people, he found his relatives sickening and dying. He was allowed to return home to the Plains six years later, and, in 1889, he enlisted, as other Cheyenne before him had done, as a scout for the U.S. Army at Fort Keogh. Rather than an alliance with the enemy, the Indians who signed up for scouting duty more likely saw themselves as engaging, in the only way available to them, in the horsemanship and warfare for which they had culturally been prepared.

Unfortunately, Wooden Leg's time at Fort Keogh also included an apprenticeship in whiskey drinking—although in 1906, he most soberly attended a ceremony to commemorate the 30th anniversary of the Custer fight. Even at that late date, many Indians were fearful of the invitations that had been extended to them, believing that the whites, their desire for vengeance still unsatisfied even by the massacre at Wounded Knee, would seek further revenge. As things turned out, the only friction was with Crow warriors, traditional enemies of the Cheyenne, who had served as scouts for Custer. Before his death in 1940, Wooden Leg paid visits east to Washington, D.C., and to New York, and served as a judge in the Indian court.

171

Thomas Marquis was a Missouri newspaperman who obtained a medical degree and then went west to serve as government doctor for the northern Cheyenne on the Tongue River Reservation. After retirement from government service, he moved still further west to Hardin, Montana, where he became the friend and historian of a number of Native Americans. A Warrior Who Fought Custer, originally published in 1931, was Marquis' major contribution to Indian autobiography and the history of Indian-white relations in the last quarter of the nineteenth century, although he also published valuable accounts of Rain-in-the-Face, Gall, and Sitting Bull.

Our selections, taken from the University of Nebraska Press edition of Wooden Leg: A Warrior Who Fought Custer, are from Chapter 4, "Worshiping the Great Medicine," which provides some sense of the quest undertaken by the typical young man of the Plains for vision and power, and from Chapter 9, "The Coming of Custer." These two chapters have been chosen specifically to dramatize the point made in the general introduction to this volume: that in the nineteenth century, Native people both lived their lives in the old ways of their ancestors, and, as well, adapted to changing conditions resulting from the aggressive advance of the whites.

Worshiping the Great Medicine

I made medicine the first time when I was seventeen years old (1875). It was during the month of May, I believe, although we did not divide the years into months or weeks as the white people later taught us to divide them. Our family was in a camp of fourteen or fifteen lodges of Cheyennes in the hills at the head of Otter creek, a stream flowing into the eastern side of Tongue river. The main camp of the tribe was on Powder river, east of our location.

To "make medicine" is to engage upon a special period of fasting, thanksgiving, prayer and self denial, even of self torture. The procedure is entirely a devotional exercise. The purpose is to subdue the passions of the flesh and to improve the spiritual self. The bodily abstinence and the mental concentration upon lofty thoughts cleanses both the body and the soul and puts them into or keeps them in health. Then the individual mind gets closer toward conformity with the mind of the Great Medicine above us.

I said to my father: "All during my boyhood and youth the Great Medicine has been good to me. I have fond parents and kind brothers and sisters. I have had plenty of food and have had no bad sickness. No bullet nor arrow has hit me. No serious injury of any kind has fallen upon me. I ought to do something to show my gratitude for all of these favors."

"Yes, my son, you owe a debt for them," my father agreed.

Red Haired Bear, a good medicine man or spiritual adviser, was in our small camp. His wife was my mother's sister. I went to him.

"I want to make medicine," I told him. "I think I have lived in a way good enough to render me worthy. I want to become still better. I want to thank the Great Medicine and ask His continued favor. I want to become able to kill all enemies I may meet and to be shielded from their assaults upon me. I do not want to die in any manner until I reach old age. I wish you would help me."

"How," he responded encouragingly. "What number of days do you think you can endure?"

"The whole four days," I replied confidently.

"How," he glowed. "I will help you."

He warned me it was a difficult undertaking for any young man. He urged me to be brave. He said the bravest ones always got the greatest spiritual benefit. I asserted myself as feeling equal to any distress that might come to me.

"That is good," he cheered me on. "You shall have the strongest of trials. You shall stay out one night without any shelter, the next night you may have a little cone tepee, the third night you may build for yourself a willow dome lodge."

This proposition put a check upon my eagerness. I had not thought of being unprotected from bad weather during any part of the time. It occurred to my mind that a rainstorm might interfere with the devotions. Even with a little cone tepee over me, a strong wind might upset the entire programme. My medicine might be broken by accidents like these. I asked if a willow dome lodge could be used during the entire procedure.

"How. It shall be as you desire."

He started me out to cut willow wands for making the medicine lodge. He told me I must get seventeen of them, each a clean and strong and long piece of pliable green wood. I carefully gathered them, selecting and rejecting. I tied them into a pack bundle. Throwing the bundle upon my back and taking a crowbar in my hands, I carried the burden far up a gulch and into the timber at the hilltop. I chose a spot for the lodge and put down my load. With the crowbar I punched in the ground sixteen holes around a circle about eight feet in diameter. Into these holes I set upright sixteen of the wands. I then bent their tops across, pairing them and tying together the pairs. The skeleton dome was completed by weaving through the coupled tops the seventeenth strand, this running from east to west. I returned then to Red Haired Bear for further instructions.

"Get a buffalo head," he ordered me.

I searched the neighborhood until I found one. Under his directions I heaped up dirt into a low mound about eight feet due east from where was to be the eastern entrance opening of the lodge. Upon this mound was placed the buffalo head, it being set to face toward the lodge. I cleared off all grass and twigs to make a clean path between the buffalo head and the lodge opening. I gathered armfuls of sweet sagegrass and spread it as a carpet upon the floor of the enclosed circle. The two of us returned then to Red Haired Bear's lodge.

The medicine man painted my whole body. Red clay mixed into water, in a dish, was used for most of the painting. Four times he took portions of the powdered red earth, each separate time casting the portion upon the water's surface and uttering low prayers as he stirred it into solution. After having put the red coloring upon the entire surface of my skin he got out from his medicine bag a package of pulverized black earth. Four different casts and four separate stirrings into water were made likewise with this coloring material. With the black paint he made first a circle about my face, including the forehead, the chin and the cheeks. Black wristlets and black anklets were next formed. On the middle of my breast he painted a black sun. On my left shoulderblade he put a black moon.

My director then offered a prayer:

"Great Medicine Above: You see Wooden Leg. He wants to be a good man. Look upon him and favor him. Make him brave and wise and kind. Make him generous to his people, to all Indians, even to his enemies if they come peaceably and in need. Help him to defeat all enemies who may beset him, and shield him from their efforts to take his life. Guide him so that he may be rich in food and skins and horses. Help him to find a good wife. Give to them many children. Keep them all in good health and make them live a long time."

He prayed also to the ground spirits. As he prayed to the Great Medicine he looked upward, and as he addressed the spirits below he looked down toward the ground. When the prayers were ended we walked together to the medicine lodge I had built in the hilltop forest. We sat down there beside the slender path I had made to connect the buffalo head and the entrance to the lodge. He talked to me:

"This is going to be a hard trial for you, the hardest trial you ever have had. Throughout four days you will have neither food nor water. Your desires will distress you. Other distresses may be piled upon these. You may retreat now and postpone it to another time if you want to do so. What say you?"

"I dread it," I confessed, "but I know it will not kill me. I do not want to wait. I want to go on right now. I shall keep my courage from failing by fixing my thoughts upon being a good man."

"That is good," he cheered me. Then he added: "Be brave."

The medicine man prayed again for me. He looked again upward and again downward, going through the same prayer for the spirits as he had made to the Above Spirit. The praying was the same kind as he had uttered just after the painting preparations, but he added some other solicitations for my welfare.

After this prayer had ended I crept in upon the sagegrass floor of the skeleton willow dome. He covered the frame all over with many buffalo robes we had brought. Not even a faint ray of light could get inside. He then went away to our camp.

I now was alone. For a little while I just sat there in the darkness—complete darkness, although it was about the middle of the afternoon. I was naked, except for the breechcloth and a buffalo robe. I had a supply of kinnikinick, some matches, and my medicine pipe that had been given to me by my father. I loaded and lit the pipe for a thoughtful smoke. The flash of the match dazzled my eyes. Time dragged along. I could not smoke continuously, so I just sat there and meditated, or tried to do so. I did not know when the sun went down nor when darkness came. It began to seem rather lonely. I grew sleepy, so I stretched myself out with the robe about me and drifted into a doze. But every little sound startled me. I sat up and had another smoke. Soon I had another, and then another. I slept again, this time more soundly. I had not the least notion as to how long I remained asleep. It seemed I had been there more than a day and night, that the medicine man had forgotten me. I listened intently to every slight rustle in the surrounding forest. My prayers all had been in thoughts, not in spoken words. I almost wished for some disturbing intrusion to break up the entire proceeding. Noise of a horse's footsteps fell into my ears. Closer, closer, very close.

"Hey, Wooden Leg!" It was the voice of Red Haired Bear. "One day has passed. It now is noon."

He dismounted and opened slightly the entrance covering. The light blinded me for a moment. Gradually he opened it wider, finally throwing it altogether aside. He allowed me to go outside for a few minutes, then I had to return to the interior.

"Let us smoke together," he invited.

He sat just outside and I sat just inside. My smoking equipment was brought into use. He pointed the stem and sent a puff to each of the four principal directions, then to the above, to the below and to the buffalo head. We passed the pipe back and forth in many exchanges, until one loading of it was exhausted. He prayed again for me. Then he admonished me:

"The next day will be more difficult. But, be not afraid. The Great Medicine sees you."

He shut up the lodge, mounted his horse and went away.

Fitful slumbers, prayers, smoking, efforts at meditation, these alternated in my quiet activities. I was hungry and thirsty, especially thirsty. My body was hot. My heart was heavy. My ears constantly were listening, listening, to every faint whisper of Nature. All of the time appeared to be night, the blackest of nights. Suddenly there came a stamp—stamp—stamp. Then:

"Boo-o-o-o! Boo-o-o-o!"

A buffalo bull! The animal snorted, stamped and bellowed again. It surely would charge upon my lodge and tear it to pieces, I thought. I did not move, but I prayed earnestly: "Great Medicine, shield me. I have tried to be a good young man. You have been kind to me in past times. Be kind to me now." I heard the threatening beast move away. It did not return.

Hours, hours, hours. I did not know whether it was day or night. I heard a horse coming. That was a welcome sound. I was all attention.

"Hey, Wooden Leg!"

"Hey!"

"Two days have passed," Red Haired Bear informed me. "The sun now is far toward the west on your third day."

Again he opened my dark retreat, gradually letting in more and more light. Again we smoked together. I told him of the buffalo bull. He listened with evident great interest.

"That is a good sign," he comforted me. "No buffalo ever will harm you. You and all other Cheyennes will get plenty of meat and skins from them. The bull was our friend, telling you all this."

Another prayer went from the medicine man to the Above and to the below. After a short allowance of time for me outside, he put me again into the enclosure and shut tightly the small hole.

"Be brave," were his parting words.

"Yes," I replied. But I was not sure.

Hot, thirsty, yet more hot and more thirsty. I prayed particularly for strength of body and firmness of heart to carry me through to the end of the trial. I loaded my pipe for a solacing smoke. But it was not a solace. The heat burned my already parching tongue. I tried to sleep. Maybe I did sleep. I do not know. I made attempts to meditate quietly. I do not know whether I actually was thinking or was following dreams racing through my mind. All I could be sure about was that I either was sitting down or lying down all the time. I heard something that cleared my mind at once. My mother brought wood and stones and placed them out by the buffalo head. She did not speak nor make any sign of recognition, but I knew it was my mother. It seemed I could look right through the robes and see her there. After she had deposited her burden she went away.

Oh, how lonely I was! I loaded and lit my pipe. No, it was not good. My mouth and throat were burning. Water! Water! But: "The Great Medicine sees me," I kept thinking. My thoughts whirled and chased each other rapidly in circles. I dreamt that I heard the footsteps of a horse.

"Hey, Wooden Leg!"

"Hey!"

"This is the day."

Happiness almost filled my heart. The only hindrance was in the thirst and the hot body. After I had been let out we smoked together. It was a torture to my tongue, but I did not complain. We went then to my father's lodge in the camp. My father called out invitations to old men friends. They came and sat in a circle upon the robes spread over the lodge's floor. I sat with them, by the side of my father. My mother brought a bucketful of water and set it off a little distance in front of me. I suppressed a strong desire to plunge my face into it, but I could not keep my eyes from staring at it. The medicine man sprinkled red powder upon the surface of the water, four small scatterings in four separate places. He passed his hands to and fro over it and prayed. It seemed I never in my life had heard so long a prayer. When it was ended he said to me:

"Wooden Leg, you have been four days without water. Now you may drink four sups."

I seized the sides of the bucket. The four sups were four long-drawn mouthfuls. The water rumbled through my bowels. After a few minutes I was told, "Now you may have more, but do not take all you want." I drank slowly, but I drew in big mouthfuls and took many of them. Not long afterward I was allowed to apply myself a third time at the bucket.

My mother brought a potful of buffalo meat she had been boiling. All of the guests were given portions of it. A piece was put upon a tin plate and set before me. It looked good enough to grab and swallow immediately. But I waited for advice. My adviser did not long detain me.

"Wooden Leg, you have been four days without meat. Take four sliced-off bites, one for each day of the fast."

I selected a long chunk from the plate. I stuck the end of it far into my mouth, and with a sheathknife I cut it off. The chewing was vigorous, and I soon had it swallowed. The chunk was pushed a second time into my mouth and its end cut off there. A third and a fourth mouthful were taken in the same manner. After a few minutes, more meat was allowed to me. Then still more, all I cared to eat. It was the best meat I ever tasted.

The old men joined in asking me:

"Tell us of your experience."

I told them—told them particularly of the coming of the buffalo bull. They complimented me, said I was brave, said the Great Medicine was my friend, assured me that no buffalo ever would harm me. Their approval and their assurances made me glad. My heart was like the sun coming up on a summer morning.

All of these old men, some of their wives, my father and mother and the medicine man went with me to my medicine lodge. We were to have a sweat bath worship together. My mother carried a bucketful of water for sprinkling upon the hot stones inside the lodge. The medicine man piled the stones into a cone heap. He leaned sticks of wood up the sides of this stone structure and set a fire to going among them. The other men stripped themselves to breech-cloth and crept into the lodge. When the stones had become well heated by the wood fire over them the medicine man passed them to one of the men inside. They were handled with forked sticks and were piled into a pit some of the men had made in the center of the lodge's earth floor. When the pit was filled with the hot stones the medicine man set inside the bucketful of water. He himself then crept in, on hands and knees as we all had done. One man remained outside to close the opening, to ventilate temporarily when we might require, to wait upon us in whatever way our needs might demand. Not any of the women went into the lodge. Twelve men were in there.

At the left inside of the entrance sat the medicine man. I was next at his left side. My father was third, at my left. The other men were seated on beyond, the row extending around the circle. All had backs to the wall. We had smoked together while the stones were being heated, but the pipe now had been placed outside. Its bowl rested on the ground beside the buffalo head and its stem projected upward past the nose and eyes of the hallowed object. A good spirit influence was coming from the nostrils of the head straight along the clean path and into the lodge. No knowing and worshipful Indian ever crossed that path. Such act would cut off the steady flow of healing virtue.

The medicine man opened the interior proceedings with another prayer for my welfare. Once more he pleaded with the Great Medicine to make me good and generous, to give me success in hunting, to protect me from enemies and to enable me to kill them. Once more he asked that I might get a good wife, might have many children, and that myself and all of my family might keep good health and live to advanced years. He beseeched again that I might gather together many horses and not lose any of them. I believed his prayers would be heard. My hopes were high. My trust in the Being Above was strong.

Water was squirted upon the hot stones in the central pit. The medicine man first gave each one in the lodge a drink of water. He took into his own mouth a chew of herb. After its mastication he supped and squirted four successive mouthfuls of water. Between the acts were short prayers. Thus he released from the stones the vitality put into them by the burning wood that had got it from the sun, the material representative of the Great Medicine. The stones hissed their protests as the water compelled them to release into the air the spiritual curative forces. Our bodies were enveloped by the steam wherein floated the vital energy. The vivifying and purifying influence soaked into our skins. Bad spirits were driven out of us and drowned in the water that dripped from us. The medicine man repeated from time to time the sprinkling of water upon the protesting stones.

The soft whisperings of an eagle wing bone flute came into my ears. The sound seemed to come from the roof and from other points in the utterly dark interior of the lodge. After a few of the gentle blasts, I felt the instrument being placed in my hands. My father put it there. It now was mine, to keep. It was to be worn about my neck, suspended at the midbreast by a buckskin thong, during all times of danger. If I were threatened with imminent harm I had but to put it to my lips and cause it to send out its soothing notes. That would ward off every evil design upon me. It was my mystic protector. It was my medicine.

After an hour or more together in the devotional dome, all of us went to our respective lodge homes. There my father presented me also with a shield of rawhide taken from the rump of a buffalo bull. The hair had been removed and the piece of skin had been dried rapidly before a fire, to make it extremely tough. It was covered with antelope buckskin sewed in place. The cover had medicine designs drawn in color upon its surface. This shield would turn off any bullet or arrow or other missile coming toward me. My father made it. He delivered it into my left hand. . . .

The Coming of Custer

In my sleep I dreamed that a great crowd of people were making lots of noise. Something in the noise startled me. I found myself wide awake, sitting up and listening. My brother too awakened, and we both jumped to our feet. A great commotion was going on among the camps. We heard shooting. We hurried out from the trees so we might see as well as hear. The shooting was somewhere at the upper part of the camp circles. It looked as if all of the Indians were running away toward the hills to the westward or down toward our end of the village. Women were screaming and men were letting out war cries. Through it all we could hear old men calling:

"Soldiers are here! Young men, go out and fight them."

We ran to our camp and to our home lodge. Everybody there was excited. Women were hurriedly making up little packs for flight. Some were going off northward or across the river without any packs. Children were hunting for their mothers. Mothers were anxiously trying to find their children. I got my lariat and my six shooter. I hastened on down toward where had been our horse herd. I came across three of our herder boys. One of them was catching grasshoppers. The other two were cooking fish in the blaze of a little fire. I told them what was going on and asked them where were the horses. They jumped on their picketed ponies and dashed for the camp, without answering me. Just then I heard Bald Eagle calling out to hurry with the horses. Two other boys were driving them toward the camp circle. I was utterly winded from the running. I never was much for running. I could walk all day, but I could not run fast nor far. I walked on back to the home lodge.

My father had caught my favorite horse from the herd brought in by the boys and Bald Eagle. I quickly emptied out my war bag and set myself at getting ready to go into battle. I jerked off my ordinary clothing. I jerked on a pair of new breeches that had been given to me by an Uncpapa Sioux. I had a good cloth shirt, and I put it on. My old moccasins were kicked off and a pair of beaded moccasins substituted for them. My father strapped a blanket upon my horse and arranged the rawhide lariat into a bridle. He stood holding my mount.

"Hurry," he urged me.

I was hurrying, but I was not yet ready. I got my paints and my little mirror. The blue-black circle soon appeared around my face. The red and yellow colorings were applied on all of the skin inside the circle. I combed my hair. It properly should have been oiled and braided neatly, but my father again was saying, "Hurry," so I just looped a buckskin thong about it and tied it close up against the back of my head, to float loose from there. My bullets, caps and powder horn put me into full readiness. In a moment afterward I was on my horse and was going as fast as it could run toward where all of the rest of the young men were going. My brother already had gone. He got his horse before I got mine, and his dressing was only a long buckskin shirt fringed with Crow Indian hair. The hair had been taken from a Crow at a past battle with them.

The air was so full of dust I could not see where to go. But it was not needful that I see that far. I kept my horse headed in the direction of movement by the crowd of Indians on horseback. I was led out around and far beyond the Uncpapa camp circle. Many hundreds of Indians on horseback were dashing to and fro in front of a body of soldiers. The soldiers were on the level valley ground and were shooting with rifles. Not many bullets were being sent back at them, but thousands of arrows were falling among them. I went on with a throng of Sioux until we got beyond and behind the white men. By this time, though, they had mounted their horses and were hiding themselves in the timber. A band of Indians were with the soldiers. It appeared they were Crows or Shoshones. Most of these Indians had fled back up the valley. Some were across east of the river and were riding away over the hills beyond.

Our Indians crowded down toward the timber where were the soldiers. More and more of our people kept coming. Almost all of them were Sioux. There were only a few Cheyennes. Arrows were showered into the timber. Bullets whistled out toward the Sioux and Cheyennes. But we stayed far back while we extended our curved line farther and farther around the big grove of trees. Some dead soldiers had been left among the grass and sagebrush where first they had fought us. It seemed to me the remainder of them would not live many hours longer. Sioux were creeping forward to set fire to the timber.

Suddenly the hidden soldiers came tearing out on horseback, from the woods. I was around on that side where they came out. I whirled my horse and lashed it into a dash to escape from them. All others of my companions did the same. But soon we discovered they were not following us. They were running away from us. They were going as fast their tired horses could carry them across an open valley space and toward the river. We stopped, looked a moment, and then we whipped our ponies into swift pursuit. A great throng of Sioux also were coming after them. My distant position put me among the leaders in the chase. The soldier horses moved slowly, as if they were very tired. Ours were lively. We gained rapidly on them.

I fired four shots with my six shooter. I do not know whether or not any of my bullets did harm. I saw a Sioux put an arrow into the back of a soldier's head. Another arrow went into his shoulder. He tumbled from his horse to the ground. Others fell dead either from arrows or from stabbings or jabbings or from blows by the stone war clubs of the Sioux. Horses limped or staggered or sprawled out dead or dying. Our war cries and war songs were mingled with many jeering calls, such as:

"You are only boys. You ought not to be fighting. We whipped you on the Rosebud. You should have brought more Crows or Shoshones with you to do your fighting."

Little Bird and I were after one certain soldier. Little Bird was wearing a trailing warbonnet. He was at the right and I was at the left of the fleeing man. We were lashing him and his horse with our pony whips. It seemed not brave to shoot him. Besides, I did not want to waste my bullets. He pointed back his revolver, though, and sent a bullet into Little Bird's thigh. Immediately I whacked the white man fighter on his head with the heavy elk-horn handle of my pony whip. The blow dazed him. I seized the rifle strapped on his back. I wrenched it and dragged the looping strap over his head. As I was getting possession of this weapon he fell to the ground. I did not harm him further. I do not know what became of him. The jam of oncoming Indians swept me on. But I had now a good soldier rifle. Yet, I had not any cartridges for it. . . .

I had remained on my horse during most of the long time of the fighting at a distance. I rode from place to place around the soldiers, keeping myself back, as my father had urged me to do, while my older brother crept close with the other warriors. I got off and crept with them, though, for a little while at the place where the band of soldiers rode down toward the river. After they were dead I got my horse and mounted again. I stayed mounted until I got around into the gulch north from the west end of the soldier ridge. By this time all of the soldiers were gone except a band of them at the west end of the ridge. They were hidden behind dead horses. Hundreds or thousands of warriors were all around them, creeping closer all the time. From the gulch where I was I could see the north slope of the ridge covered by the hidden Indians. But the soldiers, from where they were, could not see the warriors, except as some Indian might jump up to shoot quickly and then duck down again. We could get only glimpses of the soldiers, but we knew all the time right where they were, because we could see their dead horses.

I got down afoot in the gulch. I let out my long lariat rope for leading my horse while I joined the warriors creeping up the slope toward the soldiers. During all of the earlier fighting, when I had been most of the time going from place to place on horseback, I had fired several shots with my rifle captured from the soldier when we chased them across the river. I also had used my six-shooter. I had replaced the four bullets expended during the chase of the first soldiers in the valley. In this second battle I used up the six, reloaded the six-shooter, and fired all of these additional six shots at the soldiers. But it is hard to shoot straight when on horseback, especially when there is much noise and much shooting and excitement, as the horse will not stand still. When I went crawling up the slope I could lie down and shoot. I could not see any particular soldier to shoot at, but I could see their dead horses, where the men were hiding. So I just sent my bullets in that direction.

A Sioux wearing a warbonnet was lying down behind a clump of sagebrush on the hillside only a short distance north of where now is the big stone having the iron fence around it. He was about half the length of my lariat rope up ahead of me. Many other Indians were near him. Some boys were mingled among them, to get in quickly for making coup blows on any dead soldiers they might find. A Cheyenne boy was lying down right behind the warbonnet Sioux. The Sioux was peeping up and firing a rifle from time to time. At one of these times a soldier bullet hit him exactly in the middle of the forehead. His arms and legs jumped in spasms for a few moments, then he died. The boy quickly slid back down into a gully, jumped to his feet and ran away.

A soldier on a horse suddenly appeared in view back behind the warriors who were coming from the eastward along the ridge. He was riding away to the eastward, as fast as he could make his horse go. It seemed he must have been hidden somewhere back there until the Indians had passed him. A band of the Indians, all of them Sioux, I believe, got after him. I lost sight of them when they went beyond a curve of the hilltop. I suppose, though, they caught him and killed him.

The shots quit coming from the soldiers. Warriors who had crept close to them began to call out that all of the white men were dead. All of the Indians then jumped up and rushed forward. All of the boys and old men on their horses came tearing into the crowd. The air was full of dust and smoke. Everybody was greatly excited. It looked like thousands of dogs might look if all of them were mixed together in a fight. All of the Indians were saying these soldiers also went crazy and killed themselves. I do not know. I could not see them. But I believe they did so.

Seven of these last soldiers broke away and went running down the coulee sloping toward the river from the west end of the ridge. I was on the side opposite from them, and there was much smoke and dust, and many Indians were in front of me, so I did not see these men running, but I learned of them from the talk afterward. They did not get far, because many Indians were all around them. It was said that these seven men, or some of them, killed themselves. I do not know, as I did not see them.

After the great throng of Indians had crowded upon the little space where had been the last band of fighting soldiers, a strange incident happened: It appeared that all of the white men were dead. But there was one of them who raised himself to a support on his left elbow. He turned and looked over his left shoulder, and then I got a good view of him. His expression was wild, as if his mind was all tangled up and he was wondering what was going on here. In his right hand he held his six-shooter. Many of the Indians near him were scared by what seemed to have been a return from death to life. But a Sioux warrior jumped forward, grabbed the six-shooter and wrenched it from the soldier's grasp. The gun was turned upon the white man, and he was shot through the head. Other Indians struck him or stabbed him. I think he must have been the last man killed in this great battle where not one of the enemy got away.

This last man had a big and strong body. His cheeks were plump. All over his face was a stubby black beard. His mustache was much longer than his other beard, and it was curled up at the ends. The spot where he was killed is just above the middle of the big group of white stone slabs now standing on the slope southwest from the big stone. I do not know whether he was a soldier chief or an ordinary soldier. I did not notice any metal piece nor any special marks on the shoulders of his clothing, but it may be they were there. Some of the Cheyennes say now that he wore two white metal bars. But at that time we knew nothing about such things.

One of the dead soldier bodies attracted special attention. This was one who was said to have been wearing a buckskin suit. I had not seen any such soldier during the fighting. When I saw the body it had been stripped and the head was cut off and gone. Across the breast was some writing made by blue and red coloring into the skin. On each arm was a picture drawn with the same kind of blue and red paint. One of the pictures was of an eagle having its wings spread out. Indians told me that on the left arm had been strapped a leather packet having in it some white paper and lots of the same kind of green picture-paper found on all of the soldier bodies. Some of the Indians guessed that he must have been the big chief of the soldiers, because of the buckskin clothing and because of the paint markings on his breast and arms. But none of the Indians knew then who had been the big chief. They were only guessing at it.

11
Yellow Wolf: His Own Story

Edited by

L. V. MCWHORTER

Heinmot Hihhih, White Thunder, as he called himself, or Hemene Moxmox, Yellow Wolf, as he was more frequently known, was born about 1856. A nephew of the celebrated Chief Joseph, he early excelled as a breaker and trainer of horses. While with the Nez Perces during their flight in 1877, he participated both as a warrior and a scout. As Yellow Wolf tells us in his autobiography, he did not surrender with Joseph's band to Colonel Miles at the Bear Paw, but escaped to Canada, where he remained for a year before returning and giving himself up to the Americans at Lapwai. Sent to Indian Territory, he remained for six years, until, with the other Nez Perces, he was allowed to return to the Northwest. They were not sent to their home in the Wallowa Valley, however, but to Colville Reservation, at Nespelem, Washington, where his Uncle, Chief Joseph, also resided. Yellow Wolf died at Nespelem in August of 1935.

Home for the Nez Perces was the area where the present-day states of Washington, Oregon, and Idaho converge. The Nez Perces obtained horses sometime after 1730 from raids on their traditional enemies the Shoshoni (who had obtained them from Apaches and Utes, who in turn had taken them from the Spanish, the horse having become extinct in America), and soon became famous as breeders of the desirable Appaloosa ponies ("a Palouse," from the name of a part of the original Nez Perce territory). Although they did at one time wear small pieces of shell in their noses, a custom they adopted along with some of the fishing practices of the Columbia River tribes, they had largely abandoned the practice by the time they came into regular contact with French trappers and traders; nonetheless, the name "Nez Perces" remained with them. Although President Grant in 1873 had set aside the Wallowa Valley as a reservation for the Nez Perces and ordered white intruders to withdraw, the Governor of Oregon supported the settlers in their refusal, and, in the words of Alvin Josephy, "a new and confusing presidential edict reopened the Wallowa to white homesteaders."[1] Events unrolled in what had already become a familiar fashion, and, in 1877, rather than limit themselves to the

1. Alvin Josephy, *The Patriot Chiefs: A Chronicle of American Indian Resistance* (New York: Penguin, 1977), p. 321.

territory the government would permit, the Nez Perces began their famous flight.

Yellow Wolf met Lucullus Virgil McWhorter in 1908, and their work on the warrior's story proceeded irregularly for a great many years, Yellow Wolf appearing as a book only in 1940. McWhorter was a passionate partisan of the Indians, as the "Dedication" to Yellow Wolf's story, given below, indicates. He also did important work with Mourning Dove, the Okanagan author of Cogewea, *one of the earliest Native American novels, and with Two Moons and other Nez Perces.[2]*

The selections from Yellow Wolf: His Own Story[3] *are, like others in this section, of two sorts. First, we have Yellow Wolf's account of an encounter with spirit powers, and of the hunts of his youth and early manhood. Next, we have his narrative of the last days of the historical flight from the whites. Unlike other editors of Indian autobiographies, McWhorter did not try to erase his presence from the text. That is, for better or for worse, he provides a running commentary, indicating questions he has asked, responses to them, his own reactions, and so on. (These appear in smaller type, with brief explanatory notes, also by McWhorter, appearing in brackets.) Frank Linderman, whose work with Plenty Coups we shall consider in the next part of the anthology, also worked this way some ten years before McWhorter published.*

Dedication by L. V. McWhorter

To the shades of patriotic warriors, heroic women, feeble age, and helpless infancy—sacrificed on the gold-weighted altars of Mammon and political chicanery, 1863–77, are these pages most fervently inscribed.

Youth of the Warrior

Hoping to incorporate something of Yellow Wolf's earlier life as a prelude to his war career, I broached the subject to him at our last interview at his home in May, 1935. The effort was futile. His native pride and modesty proved aversive to the measure. "I am now getting old," he protested. "I had seen twenty-one snows when the war was fought. It is not right for me to tell of

2. See especially *Hear Me My Chiefs: Nez Perce History and Legend*, ed. Ruth Bordin (Caldwell, ID: Caxton, 1952).

3. *Yellow Wolf: His Own Story*, ed. L. V. McWhorter (Caldwell, ID: Caxton, 1940). Reprinted by permission of Caxton Printers, Ltd.

my own growing-up life. That does not belong to history. Would not look well in this history we are writing. I do not want to hurt, to spoil what I did in the war. Only that should go in my story of the war. The other would not be well placed."

Insistence was not to be thought of. It was only by an assemblage of items gleaned from our previous interviews, covering more than a quarter of a century, that a meager glimpse of his early career as set forth in this chapter could be constructed.

I was born in the Wallowa Valley, Oregon, long the home of Nez Perces. Our name for that river is Kahmuenem, named for a trailing vine growing at places along its banks and sands. There is where I grew up.

My father, Seekumses Kunnin [Horse Blanket], was rich in horses and cattle. A true horseman himself, he raised me among horses. Lived part of time east of Lapwai, Idaho, but mostly in the Wallowa Valley.

I was with my father until well grown. Hunting, sporting of all kinds known to Indians. We would go to Wallowa in spring for salmon. Stay there all summer and until late fall. Plenty of game. It was easy to get our winter's food.

We often wintered in the Imnaha Valley, and most Indians wintered there always. The Imnaha was warmer than the Wallowa.

I was told that in early days my father was in battle near Walla Walla, fighting for the soldiers. With another man whose wife was with him, they were chased for their lives by Chief Kamiakun's warriors. They saw, and fled to a bunch of soldiers who received them kindly. The two joined the soldiers in a fight against the enemies.

Kamiakun's warriors rode swift circles about the camp, shooting arrows and bullets from horseback. But they were stood off and night drew on. In the darkness my father and companion guided the soldiers out from there. All escaped. It may have been other Indians than those of Chief Kamiakun, the Yakima. I do not know.

My name as a boy can not be translated. Too deep! You can not write it down. One inherited name was Inneecheekoostin.

My mother Yiyik Wasumwah [Swan Woman; Swans Lighting on Water] was a sister [first cousin] to Chief Joseph. It was this way. The mother of "Old" Chief Joseph, and my grandfather on my mother's side were full brother and sister. This was why I belonged to Young Joseph's band. Joseph's people held strong to blood kinship.

My great grandfather [maternal], Seeloo Wahyakt [Eye Necklace], was a great war chief. He was killed in battle with the Pokatellas, fighting for possession of Wallowa Valley. Became separated from his band and outnumbered. His arrows exhausted, he was captured. His arms and legs were cut off before he was killed.

My grandfather [maternal], Homas, son of Seeloo Wahyakt, died on a buffalo hunt in Yellowstone Park. I am not mistaken! It was at Sokolinim [Antelope] where he was buried. This is north of some hot springs. Not over or beyond any big mountain, but is above where two rivers meet. Names of larger river Pahniah Koos [Tongue Water]. A smaller river above there is Wiyukea Koos [Elk Water]. There were Indians living around there somewhere. We hunted there, for the Sioux [Assiniboins] attacked us if we went on south side of the big mountain.

We knew that park country, no difference what white people say! And when retreating from soldiers we went up the river and crossed where are two big rocks. The trail there is called Pitou Kisnit, meaning Narrow Solid Rock Pass. This is on south side of Pahniah Koos. We did not enter the Park by our old trail when on war retreat.

I grew up among warriors, and since old enough to take notice, I made defending myself a study. The whites call me Yellow Wolf, but I take that as a nickname. My true name is different, and is after the Spirit which gave me promise of its power as a warrior.

I am Heinmot Hihhih, which means White Thunder. Yellow Wolf is not my own chosen name.

Upon being asked how he came by the designation of Yellow Wolf, the warrior discoursed earnestly for some moments with interpreter Hart, and then gave this explanation:

I was a boy of about thirteen snows when my parents sent me away into the hills. It was to find my *Wyakin*. I saw something—not on the ground, but about four feet up in the air.

I took my bow and shot an arrow.

It was in moon you call May when my parents again sent me out. This time it was to the wildest part of the mountains. To a place beyond Kemei Koois. Gave me one blanket, but no food. I might go fifteen, maybe twenty, suns with nothing to eat. But could drink water aplenty. Only trees for shelter, and fir brush to sleep on. I might stay in one place three nights, maybe five nights, then go somewhere else. Nobody around, just myself. No weapons, for nothing would hurt me. No children ever get hurt when out on such business.

After going so many suns without food I was sleeping. It was just like dreaming, what I saw. A form stood in the air fronting me. It talked to me in plain language, telling me:

"My boy, look at me! You do as I am telling you, and you will be as I am. Take a good look at me! I will give you my power; what I have got. You may think I am nothing! You may think I am only bones! But I am alive! You can see me! I am talking to you! I am Hemene Moxmox [Yellow Wolf]."

It was a Spirit of a wolf that appeared to me. Yellowlike in color, it sort of floated in the air. Like a human being it talked to me, and gave me its power.

I did not say anything back to the Spirit talking to me. I was asleep [in a trance]! I was not scared. Was just as I am now. Nothing was there to hurt me.

After I saw this wolf-thing, after I heard the Spirit-voice, I awoke and started for home. When near to maybe quarter mile of home, I dropped down, supposed dead. Someone, man or woman, came and brought me to the tepee. They had seen me, had watched for me. It was good for the one finding me.

That was how I got named Yellow Wolf. Named for that vision-wolf appearing to me. It was yellow-colored, and gave me the power of the wolf.

The name of thunder is to kill as it strikes and rolls along. My *kopluts* [war club] I made when a boy, by directions of the Spirit that gave me promise of warrior power. It has the same killing strength as thunder.

I have had different spirit guidance. I was not full-grown when we were hunting, moving into Montana, near falls in the river. It was dark night and freezing cold. The chiefs told me to watch the horses. So cold I did not know all the time what I was doing. Horseback, I was doubled over, eyes closed. I went sound asleep. Did not know anything. I must have been near death. I felt something lightly touch and shake my thigh. Felt it about three times. Then I heard a voice speaking, "What are you doing? Wake up! You are dead! Go home!"

I awoke, numb with cold. I could see no one. But the way that Spirit directed, I drove the horses. I moved them the direction that Spirit guided. I was afraid enemy Indians would take the herd. I was scared. About two miles I must have gone when I heard a voice calling, "Where are you going? Come this way!"

I awoke again, came to myself. I turned that way where my people were calling. I was freezing! A wild northeast wind was blowing. Coldest of all winds, it kills quickly!

I would have died had not that Spirit guided me where I could hear my people calling. They heard the horses passing.

Always after that night I could smell an enemy anywhere for a long distance away. This Spirit at that time gave me such power. I could then tell if enemies were around watching to take our horses or attack our camp.

This Spirit told me never to be mean. Never hurt a dog without cause. To do nothing violent only as had to be done. When in war, this Spirit wanted me to be alone. For this reason did I scout mostly alone on our retreat. Sometimes I never ate for three or four days. Only drank water. Water is medicine for everything.

What I am giving you is from my heart. I could have been dead many times only for this Spirit protection. For all this I am thankful. Happy for it all.

Another way I feel now. All my people are dead. I am alone. My heart is heavy because of way I am treated by whites. In early days my parents were to the whites as brothers. Why should I be badly treated by whites? Why is it they do not want to pay me for my land? They robbed us of all our country, our homes. We got nothing but bullets. I am now old. I feel worried about my grandchildren, what may become of them. It can not be for them as with me, when growing up hunting buffaloes.

In Montana my uncle traded a yearling horse to some miners for a magazine rifle. It was like one I carried through the war [1866 repeating Winchester]. With it I hunted buffaloes until somebody stole it. I killed yearlings mostly. It was robes we were after more than meat.

You had to be a good horseman when running buffaloes. Sometimes they chased you, horned your horse. If a man was thrown to the ground, best that he lie still. The buffalo would then lick his face raw, but he could thereby escape.

At times the Nez Perces hunted goats, bighorns, deer, and elk. All kinds of game in that country. We knew that country well before passing through there in 1877. The hot smoking springs and the high-shooting water were nothing new to us.

Once I returned from hunting in the Yellowstone country, to Idaho. From there I went to Wallowa by stage. One snow from that time war broke out.

My age was then twenty-one snows. A strong young man, I was never sickly.

One time I was out hunting with other Indians. We separated. Snow was about ankle-deep. I came onto a bear's trail, and tracked him to his home in a rock cliff. I jumped off my horse, went to the door, and looked in. I saw two eyes just like fire. If you see animal eyes in darkness, they always shine as coals of fire. I leveled my gun and fired, aiming at center between those eyes.

I stood in the doorway, listening. I heard him knocking against the walls of his house. Soon the knocks stopped. Then I knew that bear was dead.

I got the lariat from my saddle and crawled in where the bear lay. Slipped the loop over his head, drawing it tight. Then I backed out and tried to pull him from his house. Only got him part way. I brought my horse, and fastening the rope to saddlehorn, soon had that bear outside.

I now went to top of a ridge and gave the signal yell. The other hunters not too far away understood. They came and helped skin and get the meat to camp. I always had good luck hunting bears.

One other time I met a bear at his home. There were three of us horseback. I dismounted and went to the opening in the rocks. I peeked in. Yes, that bear was there, all right. I called in to the bear, "Come out! I want you!"

My partners were afraid, and stayed off a distance. I told them to come closer, but they would not mind me at all. One was afraid the bear might get hold of him. He stayed on his horse about thirty steps away. The other man was maybe forty steps from the bear's ground lodge. He dismounted and stood behind a big pine tree. His name was Jesse. I told them again to come closer, but they said "No!"

Those two Indians were scared at nothing.

I now put my head in at the bear's doorway and told him, "I want you! I have come for you. You must come out!"

But that bear would not come. He only growled and talked to himself. I now yelled a sharp command and struck him with a stone. That bear made a bad noise with his mouth, and started out. I took three steps back. That bear came out of his doorway, mad. Just as he made to jump, I shot him through the head. I now called to my partners, "Come over!" They said, "No!" Told me to examine if the bear was dead.

I laughed at them. I put my rifle down and gripped the bear's head. They now said, "We were afraid to come close. We thought that bear might put up a bad fight."

They laughed, seeing the bear dead. I told them, "The bear is nothing to me. He is just like a dog to me. I can kill him with a club."

I was hunting deer in the mountains. I was alone. I heard a voice coming from the east. From some place among the big rocks. I thought it was a true voice of a person. I listened good! Yes, it was there all right.

I ran, and came near where the voice had sounded. No human voice whatever. Only the voice of *itsiyiyi* [coyote]. That *itsiyiyi* was crying, "Quit that! Quit that!" A bear was trying to catch that *itsiyiyi*, and I thought to shoot him. I shot just as he reared up, and the bullet struck his right paw.

I ran to get closer to that bear, but he saw and came at me. Getting close, I shot him in the head.

After killing that bear, I discovered a dead deer. A fresh-killed deer. That bear had been fighting *itsiyiyi* from eating the deer.

It is a strange story I am now telling you. I had hunted two suns and seen nothing. In camp all morning, I went out in the afternoon. There was a good snow. I found no tracks. I wondered what was wrong. I have never felt as I did that time. I sat down to think. Sun shining, nice day. The way I was looking, I saw a deer about fifty steps away. It was reaching up, eating the long moss from lower limbs of a tree. It was the kind of moss we cook in the ground ovens for food. The same kind you liked at our camp dinner. Yes, it was a deer standing broadside to me. I raised my rifle and fired.

That deer continued to eat the hanging moss. I thought, "What is wrong?" I fired again, aiming good. *Eeh!* That deer did not move. Just kept eating moss. I did not hurry as I fired a third time.

That deer remained in same place, still filling on moss. Paid no attention to what was being done to it. I thought, "Maybe gun sight not good?" I put my eye to rifle sight and back again quickly. *Eeh!* That deer was gone. My rifle sight was nothing wrong.

I went over where that deer had stood. No tracks whatever. I looked up. A long lodgepole could not reach that moss—that high it was above the ground! I must have been shooting *atemis* [dead] deer. A spirit deer, maybe from out the ground. I never saw such any other time. I thought about it for many long snows. I have never forgotten it. I returned to camp, hunting no more that sun.

The Last Stand: Bear's Paw Battlefield

Evening came, and the battle grew less. Darkness settled and mostly the guns died away. Only occasional shots. I went up toward our camp. I did not hurry. Soldiers guarding, sitting down, two and two.

Soldiers all about the camp, so that none could escape from there. A long time I watched. It was snowing. The wind was cold! Stripped for battle, I had no blanket. I lay close to the ground, crawling nearer the guard line.

It was past middle of night when I went between those guards. I was now back within the camp circle. I went first and drank some water. I did not look for food.

On the bluffs Indians with knives were digging rifle pits. Some had those broad-bladed knives [trowel bayonets] taken from soldiers at the Big Hole. Down in the main camp women with camas hooks were digging shelter pits. All this for tomorrow's coming.

Shelter pits for the old, the women, the children.

Rifle pits for the warriors, the fighters.

You have seen hail, sometimes, leveling the grass. Indians were so leveled by the bullet hail. Most of our few warriors left from the Big Hole had been swept as leaves before the storm. Chief Ollokot, Lone Bird, and Lean Elk were gone.

Outside the camp I had seen men killed. Soldiers ten, Indians ten. That was not so bad. But now, when I saw our remaining warriors gone, my heart grew choked and heavy. Yet the warriors and no-fighting men killed were not all. I looked around.

Some were burying their dead.

A young warrior, wounded, lay on a buffalo robe dying without complaint. Children crying with cold. No fire. There could be no light. Everywhere the crying, the death wail.

My heart became fire. I joined the warriors digging rifle pits. All the rest of night we worked. Just before dawn, I went down among the shelter pits. I looked around. Children no longer crying. In deep shelter pits they were sleeping. Wrapped in a blanket, a still form lay on the buffalo robe. The young warrior was dead. I went back to my rifle pit, my blood hot for war. I felt not the cold.

Morning came, bringing the battle anew. Bullets from everywhere! A big gun throwing bursting shells. From rifle pits, warriors returned shot for shot. Wild and stormy, the cold wind was thick with snow. Air filled with smoke of powder. Flash of guns through it all. As the hidden sun traveled upward, the war did not weaken.

I felt the coming end. All for which we had suffered lost!

Frequent pauses had marked Yellow Wolf's description of the battle thus far, and at this point came a break of several minutes. With no visible emotion, warrior and interpreter sat silent, gazing toward the desert hills beyond the Nez Perce camp at the river's side. When at last Yellow Wolf resumed his story, it was in the same low, evenly modulated tone—generally tinged with sadness, but with an unusual degree of rhetoric.

Thoughts came of the Wallowa where I grew up. Of my own country when only Indians were there. Of tepees along the bending river. Of the blue, clear lake, wide meadows with horse and cattle herds. From the mountain forests, voices seemed calling. I felt as dreaming. Not my living self.

The war deepened. Grew louder with gun reports. I raised up and looked around. Everything was against us. No hope! Only bondage or death! Something screamed in my ear. A blaze flashed before me. I felt as burning! Then with rifle I stood forth, saying to my heart, "Here I will die, fighting for my people and our homes!"

Soldiers could see me. Bullets hummed by me, but I was untouched. The warriors called, "Heinmot! Come back to this pit. You will be killed!"

I did not listen. I did not know if I killed any soldiers. To do well in battle you must see what you want to shoot. You glimpse an enemy in hiding and shoot. If no more shots from there, you know you have succeeded.

I felt not afraid. Soldier rifles from shelters kept popping fast. Their big gun boomed often but not dangerous. The warriors lying close in dugout pits could not be hit. I know not why the shells never struck our rifle pits on the bluffs.

The sun drew on, and about noon the soldiers put up the white flag. The Indians said, "That is good! That means, 'Quit the war.'"

But in short minutes we could see no soldiers. Then we understood.

Soldiers quit the fight to eat dinner!

No Indian warrior thought to eat that noon. He never thinks to eat when in battle or dangerous places. But not so the soldier. Those soldiers could not stand the hunger pain. After dinner they pulled down their white flag.

That flag did not count for peace.

The fight was started again by the soldiers after stopping their hunger. There was shooting all the rest of that second sun's battle. Stronger cold, thicker snow came with darkness. No sleeping in warm tepees. No eating warm food. Only at times was there shooting during the night.

It came morning, third sun of battle. The rifle shooting went on just like play. Nobody being hurt. But soon Chief Looking Glass was killed. Some warriors in same pit with him saw at a distance a horseback Indian. Thinking he must be a Sioux from Sitting Bull, one pointed and called to Looking Glass: "Look! A Sioux!"

Looking Glass stepped quickly from the pit. Stood on the bluff unprotected. It must have been a sharpshooter killed him. A bullet struck his left forehead, and he fell back dead.

That horseback Indian was a Nez Perce.

In the afternoon of this sun we saw the white flag again go up in the soldier camp. Then was heard a voice calling in a strange language, "General [Colonel] Miles would like to see Chief Joseph!"

The chiefs held council and Chief Joseph said, "Yes, I would like to see General Miles."

Tom Hill, interpreter, went to see what General Miles wanted, to tell General Miles, "Yes, Joseph would like to see you!" After some time, we saw Tom Hill with General Miles and a few men come halfway. They stopped and Tom Hill called to Chief Joseph. Chief Joseph with two or three warriors went to meet them.

I did not go where they met. I looked around. There was a hollow place off a distance in the ground. I went there and lay down. I could see General Miles where Chief Joseph met him. I could see all plainly where they stood. I was saying to myself, "Whenever they shoot Chief Joseph, *I* will shoot from here!"

There was talk for a while, and Chief Joseph and General Miles made peace. Some guns were given up. Then there was a trick. I saw Chief Joseph taken to the soldier camp a prisoner!

The white flag was pulled down!

The white flag was a lie!

The warriors came back, and right away a soldier officer [Lieutenant Lovell H. Jerome] rode into our camp. Chief Yellow Bull yelled a warning and grabbed him. I could see them take the officer to the main shelter pit. When I saw all this—Chief Joseph taken away—I ran to where the captured soldier was being held. Held that Chief Joseph might not be hurt. He had on a yellowcolored outside coat to keep off the wet. A stronglooking young man, he did not say much. Looked around, but seemed not much afraid. I do not think he was bad scared.

The chiefs instructed the warriors to guard him. Ordered: "Treat him right! He is one of the commanders."

One man, Chuslum Hihhih [White Bull] got mad at this officer and tried to get the best of him. He said, "I want to kill this soldier!"

The Indians told him, "No, we do not want you to kill him!"

Chuslum Hihhih was mean-minded, had a bad heart. He did no great fighting. Stayed behind where bullets could not reach him.

Espowyes, my relation, kept telling him, "Do not hurt the prisoner." Scolding, he said, "Don't you know Chief Joseph is prisoner on other side? We have this officer prisoner here on our side. When they turn Chief Joseph loose, we will turn our prisoner loose at the same time. For this we are holding him, to make the trade. We do not want to kill him. He might be headman of the soldiers. Don't you see soldiers on other side with guns? Why do you not shoot them? Not shoot one who is caught! You see all the warriors who do fighting are not mad at him. Why do you, who do little fighting, want to kill him?"

Chuslum Hihhih made no reply. He walked away.

We all thought Chief Joseph was not killed on the other side, so we let this officer soldier keep his own life. You know we were resting a little. Not after the soldiers, nor soldiers after us. We wanted to remain quiet a few moments.

Two men you already have names of, Wottolen and Yellow Bull, took good care of the prisoner officer. Night drew on, and he was given food. We gave him water and a safe place to sleep in. He was given plenty of blankets.

A buffalo robe for a bed to keep him warm. Nothing was taken from him. Guards watched his shelter pit all night. This, that he might not escape nor be hurt by mad Indians.

But we did not know how our Chief Joseph was being treated over there. He might be alive, or he might be killed.

When morning broke, we did not wake that officer. We let him sleep if he wanted. When he woke, he was brought water to wash hands and face. He was given breakfast and water to drink. As far as that [indicating two hundred feet], that officer could go if he liked. Walk there and back often as he pleased. The chiefs gave strong words that he must not be harmed.

It was about noon of the fourth sun when the officer took paper from his pocket and wrote. I know what he wrote. One Nez Perce understood English very well, and the officer said to him, "You must take my letter to the soldier chief!"

The officer read what he wrote on the paper, and when the Indian interpreted it to the chiefs, they said, "All right!"

This is what the interpreter said the paper told: "I had good supper, good bed. I had plenty of blankets. This morning I had good breakfast. I am treated like I was at home. I hope you officers are treating Chief Joseph as I am treated. I would like to see him treated as I am treated."

But Chief Joseph was not treated right. Chief Joseph was hobbled hands and feet. They took a double blanket. Soldiers rolled him in it like you roll papoose on cradle board. Chief Joseph could not use arms, could not walk about. He was put where there were mules, and not in soldier tent. That was how Chief Joseph was treated all night.

When soldier officers received that letter, they took hobbles off Chief Joseph. He could then walk around a little where they let him. Those officers wrote a letter to our prisoner officer. When he read it, he said, "I have not been treated like Chief Joseph!"

The officer then read from the letter, "You come across to us. When you get here, then Chief Joseph can go."

The chiefs and warriors replied to the officer, "No! If General Miles is speaking true, he will bring Chief Joseph halfway. To same ground we did that other time. It will be that, if he is speaking true words."

This letter was carried to the soldiers by the same interpreter. The soldier officers must have read it, for soon a white flag went up. Then those officers sent a letter to the Indian chiefs. It said, "Yes, we will bring Chief Joseph halfway. You bring the officer to that same place."

The chiefs said, "That is fair enough!"

Then we looked across and saw officers and Chief Joseph. They were coming to halfway ground. A buffalo robe was spread there. The chiefs and a few older warriors took our prisoner to meet them. He shook hands with Joseph and those officers. Then each party returned to its own side, Chief Joseph coming back to our camp.

The soldiers now pulled down their white flag. When the warriors saw that flag come down, they laughed. They said to each other, "Three times those soldiers lie with the white flag. We can not believe them." We younger warriors had not gone to the meeting place marked by buffalo robe.

Chief Joseph now spoke to all headmen: "I was hobbled in the soldier camp. We must fight more. The war is not quit!"

Then the fighting began again. Shot for shot whenever a soldier was seen. All that day we had the war. Those soldiers stayed at long distance. They did not try mixing us up. They did not charge against our rifle pits.

Some warriors talked to charge the soldiers and fight it out. If we whipped them, we would be free. If we could not whip, we would all be killed, and no more trouble. But others said, "No! The soldiers are too strong. There are the big guns, the cannon guns. If we are killed, we leave women and children, old people, and many wounded. We can not charge the soldiers."

It was slowed-up fighting. Cloudy, snowy, we did not see the sun set. Full darkness coming, the fighting mostly stopped. Some shooting in darkness by soldiers, but less by Indians. The gun sounds died down as night went on.

All night we remained in those pits. The cold grew stronger. The wind was filled with snow. Only a little sleep. There might be a charge by the soldiers. The warriors watched by turns. A long night.

The Last Day: The Surrender

Finally the fifth morning of the battle drew on, but no sun could be seen. With first light, the battle began again. It was bad that cannon guns should be turned on the shelter pits where were no fighters. Only women and children, old and wounded men in those pits. General Miles and his men handling the big gun surely knew no warriors were in that part of camp. The officer we had held prisoner well knew no fighting warriors were where he sheltered. Of course his business was to carry back all news he could spy out in our camp.

It was towards noon that a bursting shell struck and broke in a shelter pit, burying four women, a little boy, and a girl of about twelve snows. This girl, Atsipeeten, and her grandmother, Intetah, were both killed. The other three women and the boy were rescued. The two dead were left in the caved-in pit.

When a few Indians, mad and wild on white man's whisky, killed mean settlers on Indian lands on the Salmon River, along with one or two women and maybe one child, that was very bad.

Soldiers did not need whisky to kill a great many women and children throughout this war.

This woman and child, and Chief Looking Glass, were only ones killed in this battle after the first sun's fighting. None even wounded. All those not fighting were in the shelter pits. The warriors in rifle pits could not be seen by the soldiers. Indians are not seen in the fighting. They are hid.

The fight went on, but we did not fire continually. We thought the soldiers would get tired, maybe freeze out and charge us. We wanted plenty of ammunition for them if they did.

Darkness again settled down, and only occasional shots were heard. These came mostly from soldiers, as if afraid we might slip up on them in their dugout forts.

That night, General Howard arrived with two of his scouts, men of our tribe. He did not see much fighting of this battle, and I think maybe he put it wrong in history. Towards noon next day we saw those two Indians coming with a white flag. Heard them calling and I understood. One of them said, "All my brothers, I am glad to see you alive this sun!"

Then the same bad man, Chuslum Hihhih, came and wanted to shoot this Indian messenger from General Howard. Chuslum Hahlap Kanoot [Naked-footed Bull] took his gun from him. Another fellow said, "Let him alone! Let him kill him!"

Hahlap Kanoot asked Chuslum Hihhih, "Why are you mad! While we were warring, fighting, you lay on the ground, afraid! You are mean! I will take a whip after you!"

Chuslum Hihhih was again ordered to leave. He walked away.

The two Indians he was trying to kill, now speaking again, said "We have traveled a long ways trying to catch you folks. We are glad to hear you want no more war, do not want to fight. We are all glad. I am glad because all my sons are glad to be alive. Not to go in battle any more." This speaker's name was Chojykies [Lazy]. He had a daughter with Chief Joseph's warriors, was why he followed us.

The other man said, "We have come far from home. You now see many soldiers lying down side by side. We see Indians too, lying dead. I am glad today we are shaking hands. We are all not mad. We all think of Chief Joseph and these others as brothers. We see your sons and relations lying dead, but we are glad to shake hands with you today. I am glad to catch up with you and find my daughter, too, alive.

"You, my brothers, have your ears open to me. General Miles and Chief Joseph will make friends and not let each other go today. General Miles is honest-looking man. I have been with General Howard. I was afraid myself. I have been in wars and am no longer a warrior.

"Listen well what I say. I heard General Howard telling, 'When I catch Chief Joseph, I will bring him back to his own home.'

"Do not be afraid! General Miles said, 'Tell Joseph we do not have any more war!' "

Chief Joseph sent those two Indians back where they belonged. Then there was a council. Some of us said to Chief Joseph, "We are afraid if you go with General Howard he will hang you. You know how he destroyed our property, our homes."

Then Espowyes spoke, "I understand every word. If General Howard tries to take us, we will not go with him. All you farmers who had property destroyed feel bad over it. Feel bad because the whites may talk to General Howard, and he will hang us. We should get something out of our destroyed property. Get pay for our homes and lands taken from us."

We heard and believed the words of Espowyes to be true. It must be that we get some pay for our property lost and destroyed.

All feared to trust General Howard and his soldiers.

General Howard we now saw standing, calling loud to know why the Indians were not coming.

All Indians said, "General Howard does not look good. He is mean acting!"

Then came again those two Indians from the soldier camp. They carried a white flag, and General Miles had told them to say to us: "I want to speak to Chief Joseph."

I heard this message, and I heard Chief Joseph make reply, "We will have council over this. We will decide what to do!"

There was a council, and the main messenger talked this way: "Those generals said tell you: 'We will have no more fighting. Your chiefs and some of you warriors are not seeing the truth. We sent our officer to appear before your Indians—sent all our messengers to say to them, "We will have no more war!" ' "

Then our man, Chief Joseph, spoke, "You see, it is true. I did not say 'Let's quit!'

"General Miles said, 'Let's quit.'

"And now General Howard says, 'Let's quit!'

"You see, it is true enough! I did not say 'Let's quit!' "

When the warriors heard those words from Chief Joseph, they answered, "Yes, we believe you now."

So when General Miles's messengers reported back to him, the answer was, "Yes."

Then Chief Joseph and other chiefs met General Miles on halfway ground. Chief Joseph and General Miles were talking good and friendly when General Howard came speaking loud, commanding words. When General Miles saw this, he held the Indians back from him a little. He said, "I think soon General Howard will forget all this. I will take you to a place for this winter; then you can go to your old home."

Chief Joseph said, "Now we all understand these words, and we will go with General Miles. He is a headman, and we will go with him."

General Miles spoke to Chief Joseph, "No more battles and blood! From this sun, we will have good time on both sides, your band and mine. We will have plenty time for sleep, for good rest. We will drink good water from this time on where the war is stopped."

"Same is here," General Howard said. "I will have time from now on, like you, to rest. The war is all quit." He was in a better humor. General Howard spoke to Chief Joseph, "You have your life. I am living. I have lost my brothers. Many of you have lost brothers, maybe

201

more than on our side. I do not know. Do not worry any more. While you see this many soldiers living from the war, you think of them as your brothers. Many brothers of yours—they are my brothers—living from the war.

"Do not worry about starving. It is plenty of food we have left from this war. Any one who needs a sack of flour, anything the people want, come get it. All is yours."

The chiefs and officers crossed among themselves and shook hands all around. The Indians lifted their hands towards the sky, where the sun was then standing. This said: "No more battles! No more war!"

That was all I saw and heard of chiefs' and generals' ending the war.

General Miles was good to the surrendered Indians with food. The little boys and girls loved him for that. They could now have hot food and fires to warm by.

What I heard those generals and chiefs say, I have always remembered. But those generals soon forgot their promises. Chief Joseph and his people were not permitted to return to their own homes.

We were not captured. It was a draw battle. We did not expect being sent to Eeikish Pah [Hot Place]. Had we known this we never would have surrendered. We expected to be returned to our own homes. This was promised us by General Miles. That was how he got our rifles from us. It was the only way he could get them.

The fighting was done. All who wanted to surrender took their guns to General Miles and gave them up. Those who did not want to surrender, kept their guns. The surrender was just for those who did not longer want to fight. Joseph spoke only for his own band, what they wanted to do. Of the other bands, they surrendered who wanted to.

Chief White Bird did not surrender.

When Chief Joseph surrendered, war was quit, everything was quit, for those who surrendered their guns.

One side of war story is that told by the white man.

The story I have given you is the Indian side. You now have it all, as concerned the war.

I did not surrender my rifle. . . .

This is all for me to tell of the war, and of our after hardships. The story will be for people who come after us. For them to see, to know what was done here. Reasons for the war, never before told. Nobody to help us tell our side—the whites told only one side. Told it to please themselves. Told much that is not true. Only his own best deeds, only the worst deeds of the Indians, has the white man told.

12
Geronimo's Story of His Life

Edited by

S. M. BARRETT

It was only a year before the passage of the Dawes Act of 1887, presumably intended to "civilize" the Indian, that Geronimo and his band of some thirty warriors surrendered to the twenty-five-hundred-man army of General Nelson Miles. Geronimo's Chiricahua Apache band, along with other Apache, were put aboard trains and sent from their dry southwestern homelands to the malarial environs of Florida. Like the Nez Perces and others who were sent long distances from their traditional homes, Apache people sickened and died in great numbers. Eight years later, the survivors were shipped as prisoners to Fort Sill, Oklahoma. Geronimo never did get back home to the Southwest; he died, still a "prisoner of war" as he called himself in his autobiography, in 1909.

It was in Oklahoma, in 1904, that Geronimo met Stephen Melvil Barrett, newly appointed superintendent of schools at Lawton. Barrett was no stranger to Indians or the "frontier." His father had been a wagon-train boss, and his grandfather had settled the family in Indian Territory in the 1830s. Barrett's interest in Indians was lifelong; his last book, published in 1946 when he was eighty-one, was called Indian Sociology.

Barrett got Geronimo to agree to tell him the story of his life for a fee—but first he had to get the permission of the officers at Fort Sill. They objected, and it was only after Barrett wrote to President Theodore Roosevelt, who had often shown concern for things Indian, that the project could go forward. At the President's suggestion, whenever Geronimo leveled criticism at some American soldier or official, Barrett appended a footnote disclaiming all responsibility for the negative remarks. (I have deleted those footnotes, although they are many.) Geronimo narrated whatever seemed of importance to him and in whatever way he chose, and he did so in the Apache language, to Asa Daklugie, son of a Nedni Apache chief, who translated for Barrett. No manuscript of the collaboration exists, so that we do not know, for example, whether the chapter "Origin of the Apache Indians," which opens the book, represents Geronimo's quite traditional desire to begin his story with the story of his people—or whether it represents Barrett's desire to offer the reader some "anthropological" background in myth (or both).

Born in 1829 and raised around the headwaters of the Gila River in what is now Arizona, Geronimo and the Apache were of little interest to the United States government until, in 1848, as a provision of the Treaty of Guadalupe Hidalgo ending the Mexican War, the Americans got not only much of the southwest from Mexico, but also responsibility for the Apache. An Athabaskan-speaking people (the Athabaskans extend from the sub-Arctic to Mexico), the Apache were relative newcomers to the Southwest, arriving probably no more than five hundred years ago. A people who lived by raiding—whether their Pueblo neighbors, the Mexicans, or, in time, the Americans—Apache bands were always on the move. Young Apache males were trained to run, to wrestle, to hunt, and to shoot (although a girl's puberty ceremony was the most important ritual occasion of Apache culture). With the increased movement into Apacheria by the ever-advancing whites, a series of "wars" broke out sometime around 1860. In the complicated history of the Southwest during the Civil War, at least Confederate and Union troops were united on one thing, both paid bounties for Apache scalps.

Ten years after the end of the Civil War, the reservation system was extended to the Apache. Following a series of skirmishes with American troops, Geronimo agreed to bring his band in to the San Carlos reservation. He fled the reservation in 1881, only to be forced to return by General Crook. In 1885, Geronimo was off once more and once more was successfully tracked and cornered by Crook and a vastly superior force that included Apache scouts. Yet one more time did Geronimo elude the Army (this is alluded to briefly in the chapter entitled "The Final Struggle," included below), at which point Crook resigned and Nelson Miles, successful pursuer of the Nez Perces, took over. Within five months, outnumbered almost a hundredfold, Geronimo made his last surrender, in 1886.

The selections below begin with the first chapter of the book, entitled the "Origin of the Apache Indians." This is followed by Geronimo's "Early Life," which, once more, is as much about the early life of any Apache male as it is about his "personal" life—although it should be emphasized that frequently an Indian autobiographer is talking "personally" by offering what seems to us impersonal information about culture: these are the things that have formed his sense of self. Consistent with the procedure adopted above with regard to selections from the autobiographies of other "resisting Indians," the selection here also includes Geronimo's account of "The Final Struggle," which ends with his surrender to Miles. The reader will note that he presents it as much more a matter of choice than most Anglo histories have—and that he considers himself to have been outrageously lied to by Miles (and Crook before him); Barrett has, in the original, added footnotes assuring the reader that these are the views only of Geronimo. Finally, we have the book's last chapter, "Hopes for the Future," which concludes with Geronimo's strong wish that his people be returned to their homeland. *At least in some degree, this wish was finally granted in 1913, when Geronimo's Chiricahua people were sent to the Mescalero Apache reservation in New Mexico. They were not sent home to Arizona, the governor of Arizona having warned that any train carrying Apache back into his state would be dynamited.*

The selections are from Barrett's original edition of 1906, which was reprinted by Corner House Publishers of Williamstown, Massachusetts, in 1973. There is a more readily available (and less expensive) edition by Frederick W. Turner, but it has some deletions and alterations of Barrett's text. For anyone who would read Geronimo's story in full, I recommend the original. Other Apache who participated in the culture and history of the Apache in this period have also published autobiographies. See, for example, Jason Betzinez (with Wilbur S. Nye), I Fought With Geronimo, James Kaywaykla (with Eve Ball), In the Days of Victorio: Recollections of a Warm Springs Apache, *and H. David Brumble,* An Annotated Bibliography of American Indian and Eskimo Autobiographies *for other Apache accounts.[1]*

Origin of the Apache Indians

In the beginning the world was covered with darkness. There was no sun, no day. The perpetual night had no moon or stars.

There were, however, all manner of beasts and birds. Among the beasts were many hideous, nameless monsters, as well as dragons, lions, tigers, wolves, foxes, beavers, rabbits, squirrels, rats, mice, and all manner of creeping things such as lizards and serpents. Mankind could not prosper under such conditions, for the beasts and serpents destroyed all human offspring.

All creatures had the power of speech and were gifted with reason.

There were two tribes of creatures: the birds or the feathered tribe and the beasts. The former were organized under their chief, the eagle.

These tribes often held councils, and the birds wanted light admit-

1. Jason Betzinez, with Wilbur S. Nye, *I Fought with Geronimo* (New York: Bonanza Books, 1959); James Kaywaykla, with Eve Ball, *In the Days of Victorio: Recollections of a Warm Springs Apache* (Tucson: Univ. of Arizona Press, 1970); and H. David Brumble, *An Annotated Bibliography of American Indian and Eskimo Autobiographies* (Lincoln: Univ. of Nebraska Press, 1981).

ted. This the beasts repeatedly refused to do. Finally the birds made war against the beasts.

The beasts were armed with clubs, but the eagle had taught his tribe to use bows and arrows. The serpents were so wise that they could not all be killed. One took refuge in a perpendicular cliff of a mountain in Arizona, and his eye (changed into a brilliant stone) may be seen in that rock to this day. The bears, when killed, would each be changed into several other bears, so that the more bears the feathered tribe killed, the more there were. The dragon could not be killed, either, for he was covered with four coats of horny scales, and the arrows would not penetrate these. One of the most hideous, vile monsters (nameless) was proof against arrows, so the eagle flew high up in the air with a round, white stone, and let it fall on this monster's head, killing him instantly. This was such a good service that the stone was called sacred. (A symbol of this stone is used in the tribal game of Kah.) They fought for many days, but at last the birds won the victory.

After this war was over, although some evil beasts remained, the birds were able to control the councils, and light was admitted. Then mankind could live and prosper. The eagle was chief in this good fight: therefore, his feathers were worn by man as emblems of wisdom, justice, and power.

Among the few human beings that were yet alive was a woman who had been blessed with many children, but these had always been destroyed by the beasts. If by any means she succeeded in eluding the others, the dragon, who was very wise and very evil, would come himself and eat her babes.

After many years a son of the rainstorm was born to her and she dug for him a deep cave. The entrance to this cave she closed and over the spot built a camp fire. This concealed the babe's hiding place and kept him warm. Every day she would remove the fire and descend into the cave, where the child's bed was, to nurse him; then she would return and rebuild the camp fire.

Frequently the dragon would come and question her, but she would say, "I have no more children; you have eaten all of them."

When the child was larger he would not always stay in the cave, for he sometimes wanted to run and play. Once the dragon saw his tracks. Now this perplexed and enraged the old dragon, for he could not find the hiding place of the boy; but he said that he would destroy the mother if she did not reveal the child's hiding place. The poor mother was very much troubled; she could not give up her child, but she knew the power and cunning of the dragon, therefore she lived in constant fear.

Soon after this the boy said that he wished to go hunting. The mother would not give her consent. She told him of the dragon, the wolves, and the serpents; but he said, "To-morrow I go."

At the boy's request his uncle (who was the only man then living) made a little bow and some arrows for him, and the two went hunting the next day. They trailed the deer far up the mountain and finally the boy killed a buck. His uncle showed him how to dress the deer and broil the meat. They broiled two hind quarters, one for the child and one for his uncle. When the meat was done they placed it on some bushes to cool. Just then the huge form of the dragon appeared. The child was not afraid, but his uncle was so dumb with fright that he did not speak or move.

The dragon took the boy's parcel of meat and went aside with it. He placed the meat on another bush and seated himself beside it. Then he said, "This is the child I have been seeking. Boy, you are nice and fat, so when I have eaten this venison I shall eat you." The boy said, "No, you shall not eat me, and you shall not eat that meat." So he walked over to where the dragon sat and took the meat back to his own seat. The dragon said, "I like your courage, but you are foolish; what do you think you could do?" "Well," said the boy, "I can do enough to protect myself, as you may find out." Then the dragon took the meat again, and then the boy retook it. Four times in all the dragon took the meat, and after the fourth time the boy replaced the meat he said, "Dragon, will you fight me?" The dragon said, "Yes, in whatever way you like." The boy said, "I will stand one hundred paces distant from you and you may have four shots at me with your bow and arrows, provided that you will then exchange places with me and give me four shots." "Good," said the dragon. "Stand up."

Then the dragon took his bow, which was made of a large pine tree. He took four arrows from his quiver; they were made of young pine tree saplings, and each arrow was twenty feet in length. He took deliberate aim, but just as the arrow left the bow the boy made a peculiar sound and leaped into the air. Immediately the arrow was shivered into a thousand splinters, and the boy was seen standing on the top of a bright rainbow over the spot where the dragon's aim had been directed. Soon the rainbow was gone and the boy was standing on the ground again. Four times this was repeated, then the boy said, "Dragon, stand here; it is my time to shoot." The dragon said, "All right; your little arrows cannot pierce my first coat of horn, and I have three other coats—shoot away." The boy shot an arrow, striking the dragon just over the heart, and one coat of the great horny scales fell to the ground. The next shot another coat, and then another, and the dragon's heart was exposed. Then the dragon trembled, but could not move. Before the fourth arrow was shot the boy said, "Uncle, you are dumb with fear; you have not moved; come here or the dragon will fall on you." His uncle ran toward him. Then he sped the fourth arrow with true aim, and it pierced the dragon's heart. With a tremendous roar the dragon rolled down the mountain side—down four precipices into a cañon below.

Immediately storm clouds swept the mountains, lightning flashed, thunder rolled, and the rain poured. When the rainstorm had passed, far down in the cañon below, they could see fragments of the huge body of the dragon lying among the rocks, and the bones of this dragon may still be found there.

This boy's name was Apache. Usen taught him how to prepare herbs for medicine, how to hunt, and how to fight. He was the first chief of the Indians and wore the eagle's feathers as the sign of justice, wisdom, and power. To him, and to his people, as they were created, Usen gave homes in the land of the west.

Early Life

I was born in No-doyohn Cañon, Arizona, June, 1829.

In that country which lies around the headwaters of the Gila River I was reared. This range was our fatherland; among these mountains our wigwams were hidden; the scattered valleys contained our fields; the boundless prairies, stretching away on every side, were our pastures; the rocky caverns were our burying places.

I was fourth in a family of eight children—four boys and four girls. Of that family, only myself, my brother, Porico (White Horse), and my sister, Nah-da-ste, are yet alive. We are held as prisoners of war in this Military Reservation (Fort Sill).

As a babe I rolled on the dirt floor of my father's tepee, hung in my tsoch (Apache name for cradle) at my mother's back, or suspended from the bough of a tree. I was warmed by the sun, rocked by the winds, and sheltered by the trees as other Indian babes.

When a child my mother taught me the legends of our people; taught me of the sun and sky, the moon and stars, the clouds and storms. She also taught me to kneel and pray to Usen for strength, health, wisdom, and protection. We never prayed against any person, but if we had aught against any individual we ourselves took vengeance. We were taught that Usen does not care for the petty quarrels of men.

My father had often told me of the brave deeds of our warriors, of the pleasures of the chase, and the glories of the warpath.

With my brothers and sisters I played about my father's home. Sometimes we played at hide-and-seek among the rocks and pines; sometimes we loitered in the shade of the cottonwood trees or sought the shudock (a kind of wild cherry) while our parents worked in the field. Sometimes we played that we were warriors. We would practice stealing upon some object that represented an enemy, and in our childish imitation often perform the feats of war. Sometimes we would hide away from our mother to see if she could find us, and often when thus concealed go to sleep and perhaps remain hidden for many hours.

When we were old enough to be of real service we went to the field with our parents: not to play, but to toil. When the crops were to be planted we broke the ground with wooden hoes. We planted the corn in straight rows, the beans among the corn, and the melons and pumpkins in irregular order over the field. We cultivated these crops as there was need.

Our field usually contained about two acres of ground. The fields were never fenced. It was common for many families to cultivate land in the same valley and share the burden of protecting the growing crops from destruction by the ponies of the tribe, or by deer and other wild animals.

Melons were gathered as they were consumed. In the autumn pumpkins and beans were gathered and placed in bags or baskets; ears of corn were tied together by the husks, and then the harvest was carried on the backs of ponies up to our homes. Here the corn was shelled, and all the harvest stored away in caves or other secluded places to be used in winter.

We never fed corn to our ponies, but if we kept them up in the winter time we gave them fodder to eat. We had no cattle or other domestic animals except our dogs and ponies.

We did not cultivate tobacco, but found it growing wild. This we cut and cured in autumn, but if the supply ran out the leaves from the stalks left standing served our purpose. All Indians smoked—men and women. No boy was allowed to smoke until he had hunted alone

Geronimo, 1829–1909. Photo by A. Frank Randall, 1896. Courtesy of the Arizona Historical Society/Tucson, 20602.

and killed large game—wolves and bears. Unmarried women were not prohibited from smoking, but were considered immodest if they did so. Nearly all matrons smoked.

Besides grinding the corn (by hand with stone mortars and pestles) for bread, we sometimes crushed it and soaked it, and after it had fermented made from this juice a "tis-win," which had the power of intoxication, and was very highly prized by the Indians. This work was done by the squaws and children. When berries or nuts were to be gathered the small children and the squaws would go in parties to hunt them, and sometimes stay all day. When they went any great distance from camp they took ponies to carry the baskets.

I frequently went with these parties, and upon one of these excursions a woman named Cho-ko-le got lost from the party and was riding her pony through a thicket in search of her friends. Her little dog was following as she slowly made her way through the thick underbrush and pine trees. All at once a grizzly bear rose in her path and attacked the pony. She jumped off and her pony escaped, but the bear attacked her, so she fought him the best she could with her knife. Her little dog, by snapping at the bear's heels and detracting his attention from the woman, enabled her for some time to keep pretty well out of his reach. Finally the grizzly struck her over the head, tearing off almost her whole scalp. She fell, but did not lose consciousness, and while prostrate struck him four good licks with her knife, and he retreated. After he had gone she replaced her torn scalp and bound it up as best she could, then she turned deathly sick and had to lie down. That night her pony came into camp with his load of nuts and berries, but no rider. The Indians hunted for her, but did not find her until the second day. They carried her home, and under the treatment of their medicine men all her wounds were healed.

The Indians knew what herbs to use for medicine, how to prepare them, and how to give the medicine. This they had been taught by Usen in the beginning, and each succeeding generation had men who were skilled in the art of healing.

In gathering the herbs, in preparing them, and in administering the medicine, as much faith was held in prayer as in the actual effect of the medicine. Usually about eight persons worked together in making medicine, and there were forms of prayer and incantations to attend each stage of the process. Four attended to the incantations and four to the preparation of the herbs.

Some of the Indians were skilled in cutting out bullets, arrow heads, and other missiles with which warriors were wounded. I myself have done much of this, using a common dirk or butcher knife.

Small children wore very little clothing in winter and none in the summer. Women usually wore a primitive skirt, which consisted of a piece of cotton cloth fastened about the waist, and extending to the knees. Men wore breech cloths and moccasins. In winter they had shirts and leggings in addition.

"How the Book Was Made." From the left, S. M. Barrett, Geronimo, and interpreter Asa Daklugie, second cousin of Geronimo.

Frequently when the tribe was in camp a number of boys and girls, by agreement, would steal away and meet at a place several miles distant, where they could play all day free from tasks. They were never punished for these frolics; but if their hiding places were discovered they were ridiculed.

The Final Struggle

We started with all our tribe to go with General Crook back to the United States, but I feared treachery and decided to remain in Mexico. We were not under any guard at this time. The United States troops marched in front and the Indians followed, and when we became suspicious, we turned back. I do not know how far the United States army went after myself, and some warriors turned back before we were missed, and I do not care.

I have suffered much from such unjust orders as those of General Crook. Such acts have caused much distress to my people. I think that General Crook's death was sent by the Almighty as a punishment for the many evil deeds he committed.

Soon General Miles was made commander of all the western posts, and troops trailed us continually. They were led by Captain Lawton, who had good scouts. The Mexican soldiers also became more active and more numerous. We had skirmishes almost every day, and so we finally decided to break up into small bands. With six men and four women I made for the range of mountains near Hot Springs, New Mexico. We passed many cattle ranches, but had no trouble with the cowboys. We killed cattle to eat whenever we were in need of food, but we frequently suffered greatly for water. At one time we had no water for two days and nights and our horses almost died from thirst. We ranged in the mountains of New Mexico for some time, then thinking that perhaps the troops had left Mexico, we returned. On our return through Old Mexico we attacked every Mexican found, even if for no other reason than to kill. We believed they had asked the United States troops to come down to Mexico to fight us.

South of Casa Grande, near a place called by the Indians Gosoda, there was a road leading out from the town. There was much freighting carried on by the Mexicans over this road. Where the road ran through a mountain pass we stayed in hiding, and whenever Mexican freighters passed we killed them, took what supplies we wanted, and destroyed the remainder. We were reckless of our lives, because we felt that every man's hand was against us. If we returned to the reservation we would be put in prison and killed; if we stayed in Mexico they would continue to send soldiers to fight us; so we gave no quarter to anyone and asked no favors.

After some time we left Gosoda and soon were reunited with our tribe in the Sierra de Antunez Mountains.

Contrary to our expectations the United States soldiers had not left the mountains in Mexico, and were soon trailing us and skirmishing with us almost every day. Four or five times they surprised our camp. One time they surprised us about nine o'clock in the morning, and captured all our horses (nineteen in number) and secured our store of dried meats. We also lost three Indians in this encounter. About the middle of the afternoon of the same day we attacked them from the rear as they were passing through a prairie—killed one soldier, but lost none ourselves. In this skirmish we recovered all our horses except three that belonged to me. The three horses that we did not recover were the best riding horses we had.

Soon after this we made a treaty with the Mexican troops. They told us that the United States troops were the real cause of these wars, and agreed not to fight any more with us provided we would return to the United States. This we agreed to do, and resumed our march, expecting to try to make a treaty with the United States soldiers and return to Arizona. There seemed to be no other course to pursue.

Soon after this scouts from Captain Lawton's troops told us that he wished to make a treaty with us; but I knew that General Miles was the chief of the American troops, and I decided to treat with him.

We continued to move our camp northward, and the American troops also moved northward, keeping at no great distance from us, but not attacking us.

I sent my brother Porico (White Horse) with Mr. George Wratton on to Fort Bowie to see General Miles, and to tell him that we wished to return to Arizona; but before these messengers returned I met two Indian scouts—Kayitah, a Chokonen Apache, and Marteen, a Nedni Apache. They were serving as scouts for Captain Lawton's troops. They told me that General Miles had come and had sent them to ask me to meet him. So I went to the camp of the United States troops to meet General Miles.

When I arrived at their camp I went directly to General Miles and told him how I had been wronged, and that I wanted to return to the United States with my people, as we wished to see our families, who had been captured and taken away from us.

General Miles said to me: "The President of the United States has sent me to speak to you. He has heard of your trouble with the white men, and says that if you will agree to a few words of treaty we need have no more trouble. Geronimo, if you will agree to a few words of treaty all will be satisfactorily arranged."

So General Miles told me how we could be brothers to each other. We raised our hands to heaven and said that the treaty was not to be broken. We took an oath not to do any wrong to each other or to scheme against each other.

Then he talked with me for a long time and told me what he would do for me in the future if I would agree to the treaty. I did not greatly believe General Miles, but because the President of the United States had sent me word I agreed to make the treaty, and to keep it. Then General Miles said to me: "I will take you under Government protection; I will build you a house; I will fence you much land; I will give you cattle, horses, mules, and farming implements. You will be furnished with men to work the farm, for you yourself will not have to work. In the fall I will send you blankets and clothing so that you will not suffer from cold in the winter time.

"There is plenty of timber, water, and grass in the land to which I will send you. You will live with your tribe and with your family. If you agree to this treaty you shall see your family within five days."

I said to General Miles: "All the officers that have been in charge of the Indians have talked that way, and it sounds like a story to me; I hardly believe you."

He said: "This time it is the truth."

I said: "General Miles, I do not know the laws of the white man, nor of this new country where you are to send me, and I might break their laws."

He said: "While I live you will not be arrested."

Then I agreed to make the treaty. (Since I have been a prisoner of war I have been arrested and placed in the guardhouse twice for drinking whisky.)

We stood between his troopers and my warriors. We placed a large stone on the blanket before us. Our treaty was made by this stone, and it was to last until the stone should crumble to dust; so we made the treaty, and bound each other with an oath.

I do not believe that I have ever violated that treaty; but General Miles never fulfilled his promises.

When we had made the treaty General Miles said to me: "My brother, you have in your mind how you are going to kill men, and other thoughts of war; I want you to put that out of your mind, and change your thoughts to peace."

Then I agreed and gave up my arms. I said: "I will quit the warpath and live at peace hereafter."

Then General Miles swept a spot of ground clear with his hand, and said: "Your past deeds shall be wiped out like this and you will start a new life."

Hopes for the Future

I am thankful that the President of the United States has given me permission to tell my story. I hope that he and those in authority under him will read my story and judge whether my people have been rightly treated.

There is a great question between the Apaches and the Government. For twenty years we have been held prisoners of war under a treaty which was made with General Miles, on the part of the United States Government, and myself as the representative of the Apaches. That treaty has not at all times been properly observed by the Government, although at the present time it is being more nearly fulfilled on their part than heretofore. In the treaty with General Miles we agreed to go to a place outside of Arizona and learn to live as the white people do. I think that my people are now capable of living in accordance with the laws of the United States, and we would, of course, like to have the liberty to return to that land which is ours by divine right. We are reduced in numbers, and having learned how to cultivate the soil would not require so much ground as was formerly necessary. We do not ask all of the land which the Almighty gave us in the beginning, but that we may have sufficient lands there to cultivate. What we do not need we are glad for the white men to cultivate.

We are now held on Comanche and Kiowa lands, which are not suited to our needs — these lands and this climate are suited to the Indians who originally inhabited this country, of course, but our people are decreasing in numbers here, and will continue to decrease unless they are allowed to return to their native land. Such a result is inevitable.

There is no climate or soil which, to my mind, is equal to that of Arizona. We could have plenty of good cultivating land, plenty of grass, plenty of timber and plenty of minerals in that land which the Almighty created for the Apaches. It is my land, my home, my fathers' land, to which I now ask to be allowed to return. I want to spend my last days there, and be buried among those mountains. If this could be I might die in peace, feeling that my people, placed in their native homes, would increase in numbers, rather than diminish as at present, and that our name would not become extinct.

I know that if my people were placed in that mountainous region lying around the headwaters of the Gila River they would live in peace and act according to the will of the President. They would be prosperous and happy in tilling the soil and learning the civilization of the white men, whom they now respect. Could I but see this accomplished, I think I could forget all the wrongs that I have ever received, and die a contented and happy old man. But we can do nothing in this matter ourselves—we must wait until those in authority choose to act. If this cannot be done during my lifetime—if I must die in bondage—I hope that the remnant of the Apache tribe may, when I am gone, be granted the one privilege which they request—to return to Arizona.

13
Black Elk Speaks

Edited by

J O H N   G .   N E I H A R D T

When Black Elk speaks, in William Powers' phrase, everybody listens! Black Elk Speaks *is probably the best known of Native American autobiographies, having been translated into German, French, Portuguese, Italian, Russian, and Hungarian. Although Powers considers the text to be Indian religion for the white man, "obscur[ing] Lakota religion rather than explain[ing] it," the Lakota scholar Vine Deloria, Jr., calls it a "religious classic," a book that has become a "North American bible of all tribes," especially for the younger generation of Native people today. Certainly there is a sufficient number of studies of* Black Elk Speaks, *of Black Elk himself, of John Neihardt, his collaborator, and of the transcripts of the interviews between Neihardt and Black Elk (meticulously edited by Raymond DeMallie, and the object of numerous studies) for the reader to decide for him- or herself whether this may be true. Hertha Wong's recent short study of Black Elk[1] refers to him regularly as Nicholas Black Elk, the name he was known by for at least the second half of his life. Julian Rice's booklength study of 1991,* "Black Elk Speaks": Discerning Its Lakota Purpose,[2] *is the most detailed and comprehensive account of all these matters.*

Black Elk was an Oglala born in 1863 (his tombstone says 1858, and other dates have also been given) on what is now the Pine Ridge Reservation. At the age of five he received an important vision, and then at the age of nine a more powerful and detailed vision, which was publicly performed. He was present at the Custer fight of 1876, and ten years later joined Buffalo Bill's Wild West Show. The show required that all Indians employed be Christian, but this seems not to have been a problem, for Black Elk readily converted—if he had not earlier converted—to Episcopalianism. He spent three years with the show touring Europe, and returned to South Dakota in time to join the Ghost Dance. Many years after Wounded Knee, Black Elk was baptized as a Catholic at

---

1. Hertha Wong, *Sending My Heart Back Across the Years: Tradition and Innovation in Native American Autobiography* (New York: Oxford Univ. Press, 1992).

2. Julian Rice, *"Black Elk Speaks": Discerning Its Lakota Purpose* (Albuquerque: Univ. of New Mexico Press, 1991).

Holy Rosary Mission, on December 6, 1904, the feast of Saint Nicholas, at which time he was given the saint's name. (Upon his confirmation in 1905, he received the name of William, although he continued to be known as Nick.)

In 1930, Nicholas Black Elk met John Neihardt, poet laureate of Nebraska, a Christian of a rather mystical temper, and participated in an extended set of interviews in May of 1931 that were eventually edited, by Neihardt, into the book, Black Elk Speaks *(1932). Black Elk's two visions, his performance of the Horse Dance, his recollections of the Custer fight, and his accounts of the years with Buffalo Bill and of the Ghost Dance all appear in the book; there is no mention, however, of his long and intense activity (from 1907–30) as a Catholic catechist. These were the last years of the Dawes disdain for Native cultures and the book received wide critical acclaim, although it was not, apparently, a financial success. (Neihardt proposed at least the Horse Dance as suitable for a movie.) In 1934, the year the Indian Reorganization Act initiated a federal Indian policy more sympathetic to traditional ways, Black Elk made public a long letter[3] affirming his Catholic beliefs, and concluding "I want to go straight in the righteous way that the Catholics teach us so my soul will reach heaven. This is the way I wish it to be. With a good heart I shake hands with all of you." He reaffirmed his Christian faith to Joseph Epes Brown, author of the popular* The Sacred Pipe, *in 1947. Black Hawk died in 1950 and was buried in St. Agnes Cemetery, Manderson, South Dakota.*

This is quite a complicated situation. It seems likely that Black Elk adjusted his account of his own experience and of Lakota religious experience generally so that they might be comprehensible to the dominant society. But it is hard to know whether or to what extent this is the case because Black Elk Speaks, *to a degree far greater than what we find in other Indian autobiographies, is very much Neihardt's creation. For all of Black Elk's commitment to Catholicism, it is nonetheless the case that, as Clyde Holler[4] has shown, he probably was using this opportunity to speak of his life experience ritually, as a means to renew the Lakota way. Despite his many years as a Catholic, for example, Black Elk narrated in the presence of Fire Thunder, Standing Bear, and Iron Hawk, just as though he were narrating a traditional coup tale. In the same way, Black Elk has produced the story of his life as a kind of "self-examination," one of David Brumble's categories for traditional (Brumble calls it preliterate) autobiography, considering why things went wrong (and, again,*

3. Black Elk's letter appears in Raymond DeMallie, ed. *The Sixth Grandfather: Black Elk's Teaching Given to John G. Neihardt* (Lincoln: University of Nebraska Press, 1984), pp. 60–61.

4. Clyde Holler, "Lakota Religion and Tragedy: The Theology of 'Black Elk Speaks,'" *Journal of American Academy of Religion* 52 (1984): 19–43.

perhaps very much in the interest of setting them right). We know that the western insistence that things be either this way or that—that Black Elk "really" be Lakota or Christian—tends to falsify the kinds of dual, syncretistic, or situational modes in which Native people operate, and so, I believe, we must try to read Black Elk Speaks *as a deeply-felt Lakota testimony by a Lakota who nonetheless wishes his soul to go to the Catholic Heaven. Rather than a "North American bible of all tribes" (my emphasis), as Vine Deloria, Jr., has called the book (that is, rather than one we simply should take on faith), we may better take* Black Elk Speaks *as a challenge to our usual ways of understanding a life—and its religious faith.*

The selection from Black Elk Speaks *included here features Black Elk's account of his great vision in 1872, from Chapter 3, pp. 20–47, of the current University of Nebraska Press edition.*[5]

The Great Vision

What happened after that until the summer I was nine years old is not a story. There were winters and summers, and they were good; for the Wasichus had made their iron road along the Platte and traveled there. This had cut the bison herd in two, but those that stayed in our country with us were more than could be counted, and we wandered without trouble in our land.

Now and then the voices would come back when I was out alone, like someone calling me, but what they wanted me to do I did not know. This did not happen very often, and when it did not happen, I forgot about it; for I was growing taller and was riding horses now and could shoot prairie chickens and rabbits with my bow. The boys of my people began very young to learn the ways of men, and no one taught us; we just learned by doing what we saw, and we were warriors at a time when boys now are like girls.

It was the summer when I was nine years old, and our people were moving slowly towards the Rocky Mountains. We camped one evening in a valley beside a little creek just before it ran into the Greasy Grass, and there was a man by the name of Man Hip who liked me and asked me to eat with him in his tepee.

5. Reprinted from *Black Elk Speaks*, by John G. Neihardt, by permission of the University of Nebraska Press. Copyright 1932, 1959, 1972, by John Neihardt. Copyright © 1961 by the John G. Neihardt Trust.

While I was eating, a voice came and said: "It is time; now they are calling you." The voice was so loud and clear that I believed it, and I thought I would just go where it wanted me to go. So I got right up and started. As I came out of the tepee, both my thighs began to hurt me, and suddenly it was like waking from a dream, and there wasn't any voice. So I went back into the tepee, but I didn't want to eat. Man Hip looked at me in a strange way and asked me what was wrong. I told him that my legs were hurting me.

The next morning the camp moved again, and I was riding with some boys. We stopped to get a drink from a creek, and when I got off my horse, my legs crumpled under me and I could not walk. So the boys helped me up and put me on my horse; and when we camped again that evening, I was sick. The next day the camp moved on to where the different bands of our people were coming together, and I rode in a pony drag, for I was very sick. Both my legs and both my arms were swollen badly and my face was all puffed up.

When we had camped again, I was lying in our tepee and my mother and father were sitting beside me. I could see out through the opening, and there two men were coming from the clouds, headfirst like arrows slanting down, and I knew they were the same that I had seen before. Each now carried a long spear, and from the points of these a jagged lightning flashed. They came clear down to the ground this time and stood a little way off and looked at me and said: "Hurry! Come! Your Grandfathers are calling you!"

Then they turned and left the ground like arrows slanting upward from the bow. When I got up to follow, my legs did not hurt me any more and I was very light. I went outside the tepee, and yonder where the men with flaming spears were going, a little cloud was coming very fast. It came and stooped and took me and turned back to where it came from, flying fast. And when I looked down I could see my mother and my father yonder, and I felt sorry to be leaving them.

Then there was nothing but the air and the swiftness of the little cloud that bore me and those two men still leading up to where white clouds were piled like mountains on a wide blue plain, and in them thunder beings lived and leaped and flashed.

Now suddenly there was nothing but a world of cloud, and we three were there alone in the middle of a great white plain with snowy hills and mountains staring at us; and it was very still; but there were whispers.

Then the two men spoke together and they said: "Behold him, the being with four legs!"

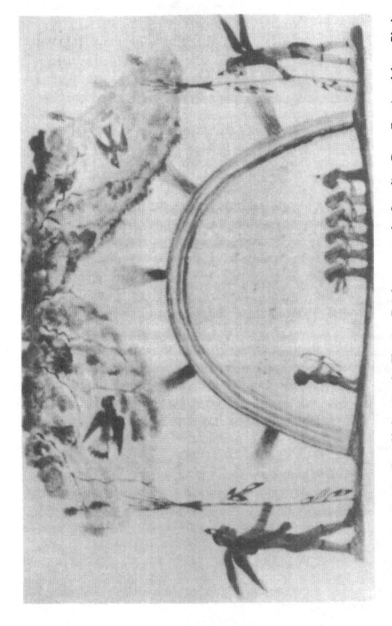

Black Elk before the Six Grandfathers in the Flaming Rainbow tepee, by Standing Bear. Reprinted from *Black Elk Speaks*, by permission of the University of Nebraska Press.

I looked and saw a bay horse standing there, and he began to speak: "Behold me!" he said, "My lifehistory you shall see." Then he wheeled about to where the sun goes down, and said: "Behold them! Their history you shall know."

I looked, and there were twelve black horses yonder all abreast with necklaces of bison hoofs, and they were beautiful, but I was frightened, because their manes were lightning and there was thunder in their nostrils.

Then the bay horse wheeled to where the great white giant lives (the north) and said: "Behold!" And yonder there were twelve white horses all abreast. Their manes were flowing like a blizzard wind and from their noses came a roaring, and all about them white geese soared and circled.

Then the bay wheeled round to where the sun shines continually (the east) and bade me look; and there twelve sorrel horses, with necklaces of elk's teeth, stood abreast with eyes that glimmered like the day-break star and manes of morning light.

Then the bay wheeled once again to look upon the place where you are always facing (the south), and yonder stood twelve buckskins all abreast with horns upon their heads and manes that lived and grew like trees and grasses.

And when I had seen all these, the bay horse said: "Your Grandfathers are having a council. These shall take you; so have courage."

Then all the horses went into formation, four abreast—the blacks, the whites, the sorrels, and the buckskins—and stood behind the bay, who turned now to the west and neighed; and yonder suddenly the sky was terrible with a storm of plunging horses in all colors that shook the world with thunder, neighing back.

Now turning to the north the bay horse whinnied, and yonder all the sky roared with a mighty wind of running horses in all colors, neighing back.

And when he whinnied to the east, there too the sky was filled with glowing clouds of manes and tails of horses in all colors singing back. Then to the south he called, and it was crowded with many colored, happy horses, nickering.

Then the bay horse spoke to me again and said: "See how your horses all come dancing!" I looked, and there were horses, horses everywhere—a whole skyful of horses dancing round me.

"Make haste!" the bay horse said; and we walked together side by side, while the blacks, the whites, the sorrels, and the buckskins followed, marching four by four.

I looked about me once again, and suddenly the dancing horses without number changed into animals of every kind and into all the fowls that are, and these fled back to the four quarters of the world from whence the horses came, and vanished.

Then as we walked, there was a heaped up cloud ahead that changed into a tepee, and a rainbow was the open door of it; and through the door I saw six old men sitting in a row.

The two men with the spears now stood beside me, one on either hand, and the horses took their places in their quarters, looking inward, four by four. And the oldest of the Grandfathers spoke with a kind voice and said: "Come right in and do not fear." And as he spoke, all the horses of the four quarters neighed to cheer me. So I went in and stood before the six, and they looked older than men can ever be—old like hills, like stars.

The oldest spoke again: "Your Grandfathers all over the world are having a council, and they have called you here to teach you." His voice was very kind, but I shook all over with fear now, for I knew that these were not old men, but the Powers of the World. And the first was the Power of the West; the second, of the North; the third, of the East; the fourth, of the South; the fifth, of the Sky; the sixth, of the Earth. I knew this, and was afraid, until the first Grandfather spoke again: "Behold them yonder where the sun goes down, the thunder beings! You shall see, and have from them my power; and they shall take you to the high and lonely center of the earth that you may see; even to the place where the sun continually shines, they shall take you there to understand."

And as he spoke of understanding, I looked up and saw the rainbow leap with flames of many colors over me.

Now there was a wooden cup in his hand and it was full of water and in the water was the sky.

"Take this," he said. "It is the power to make live, and it is yours."

Now he had a bow in his hands. "Take this," he said. "It is the power to destroy, and it is yours."

Then he pointed to himself and said: "Look close at him who is your spirit now, for you are his body and his name is Eagle Wing Stretches."

And saying this, he got up very tall and started running toward where the sun goes down; and suddenly he was a black horse that stopped and turned and looked at me, and the horse was very poor and sick; his ribs stood out.

Then the second Grandfather, he of the North, arose with a herb of power in his hand, and said: "Take this and hurry." I took and held it toward the black horse yonder. He fattened and was happy and came prancing to his place again and was the first Grandfather sitting there.

The second Grandfather, he of the North, spoke again: "Take courage, younger brother," he said; "on earth a nation you shall make live, for yours shall be the power of the white giant's wing, the cleansing wind." Then he got up very tall and started running toward the north; and when he turned toward me, it was a white goose wheeling. I looked about me now, and the horses in the west were thunders and the horses of the north were geese. And the second Grandfather sang two songs that were like this:

> They are appearing, may you behold!
> They are appearing, may you behold!
> The thunder nation is appearing, behold!
>
> They are appearing, may you behold!
> They are appearing, may you behold!
> The white geese nation is appearing, behold!

And now it was the third Grandfather who spoke, he of where the sun shines continually. "Take courage, younger brother," he said, "for across the earth they shall take you!" Then he pointed to where the daybreak star was shining, and beneath the star two men were flying. "From them you shall have power," he said, "from them who have awakened all the beings of the earth with roots and legs and wings." And as he said this, he held in his hand a peace pipe which had a spotted eagle outstretched upon the stem; and this eagle seemed alive, for it was poised there, fluttering, and its eyes were looking at me. "With this pipe," the Grandfather said, "you shall walk upon the earth, and whatever sickens there you shall make well." Then he pointed to a man who was bright red all over, the color of good and of plenty, and as he pointed, the red man lay down and rolled and changed into a bison that got up and galloped toward the sorrel horses of the east, and they too turned to bison, fat and many.

And now the fourth Grandfather spoke, he of the place where you are always facing (the south), whence comes the power to grow. "Younger brother," he said, "with the powers of the four quarters you shall walk, a relative. Behold, the living center of a nation I shall give you, and with it many you shall save." And I saw that he was holding in his hand a bright red stick that was alive, and as I looked it sprouted at the top and sent forth branches, and on the branches many leaves came out and murmured and in the leaves the birds began to sing. And then for just a little while I thought I saw beneath it in the shade the circled villages of people and every living thing with roots or legs or wings, and all were happy. "It shall stand in the center of the nation's circle," said the Grandfather, "a cane to walk with and a people's heart; and by your powers you shall make it blossom."

Then when he had been still a little while to hear the birds sing, he spoke again: "Behold the earth!" So I looked down and saw it lying yonder like a hoop of peoples, and in the center bloomed the holy stick that was a tree, and where it stood there crossed two roads, a red one and a black. "From where the giant lives (the north) to where you always face (the south) the red road goes, the road of good," the Grandfather said, "and on it shall your nation walk. The black road goes from where the thunder beings live (the west) to where the sun continually shines (the east), a fearful road, a road of troubles and of war. On this also you shall walk, and from it you shall have the power to destroy a people's foes. In four ascents you shall walk the earth with power."

I think he meant that I should see four generations, counting me, and now I am seeing the third.

Then he rose very tall and started running toward the south, and was an elk; and as he stood among the buckskins yonder, they too were elks.

Now the fifth Grandfather spoke, the oldest of them all, the Spirit of the Sky. "My boy," he said, "I have sent for you and you have come. My power you shall see!" He stretched his arms and turned into a spotted eagle hovering. "Behold," he said, "all the wings of the air shall come to you, and they and the winds and the stars shall be like relatives. You shall go across the earth with my power." Then the eagle soared above my head and fluttered there; and suddenly the sky was full of friendly wings all coming toward me.

Now I knew the sixth Grandfather was about to speak, he who was the Spirit of the Earth, and I saw that he was very old, but more as men are old. His hair was long and white, his face was all in wrinkles and his eyes were deep and dim. I stared at him, for it seemed I knew him somehow; and as I stared, he slowly changed, for he was growing backwards into youth, and when he had become a boy, I knew that he was myself with all the years that would be mine at last. When he was old again, he said: "My boy, have courage, for my power shall be yours, and you shall need it, for your nation on the earth will have great troubles. Come."

He rose and tottered out through the rainbow door, and as I followed I was riding on the bay horse who had talked to me at first and led me to that place.

Then the bay horse stopped and faced the black horses of the west, and a voice said: "They have given you the cup of water to make live the greening day, and also the bow and arrow to destroy." The bay neighed, and the twelve black horses came and stood behind me, four abreast.

The bay faced the sorrels of the east, and I saw that they had morning stars upon their foreheads and they were very bright. And the voice said: "They have given you the sacred pipe and the power that is peace, and the good red day." The bay neighed, and the twelve sorrels stood behind me, four abreast.

My horse now faced the buckskins of the south, and a voice said: "They have given you the sacred stick and your nation's hoop, and the yellow day; and in the center of the hoop you shall set the stick and make it grow into a shielding tree, and bloom." The bay neighed, and the twelve buckskins came and stood behind me, four abreast.

Then I knew that there were riders on all the horses there behind me, and a voice said: "Now you shall walk the black road with these; and as you walk, all the nations that have roots or legs or wings shall fear you."

So I started, riding toward the east down the fearful road, and behind me came the horsebacks four abreast—the blacks, the whites, the sorrels, and the buckskins—and far away above the fearful road the daybreak star was rising very dim.

I looked below me where the earth was silent in a sick green light, and saw the hills look up afraid and the grasses on the hills and all the animals; and everywhere about me were the cries of frightened birds and sounds of fleeing wings. I was the chief of all the heavens riding there, and when I looked behind me, all the twelve black horses reared and plunged and thundered and their manes and tails were whirling hail and their nostrils snorted lightning. And when I looked below again, I saw the slant hail falling and the long, sharp rain, and where we passed, the trees bowed low and all the hills were dim.

Now the earth was bright again as we rode. I could see the hills and valleys and the creeks and rivers passing under. We came above a place where three streams made a big one—a source of mighty waters—and something terrible was there. Flames were rising from the waters and in the flames a blue man lived. The dust was floating all about him in the air, the grass was short and withered, the trees were wilting, two-legged and four-legged beings lay there thin and panting, and wings too weak to fly.

Then the black horse riders shouted "Hoka hey!" and charged down upon the blue man, but were driven back. And the white troop shouted, charging, and was beaten; then the red troop and the yellow.

And when each had failed, they all cried together: "Eagle Wing Stretches, hurry!" And all the world was filled with voices of all kinds that cheered me, so I charged. I had the cup of water in one hand and in the other was the bow that turned into a spear as the bay and I swooped down, and the spear's head was sharp lightning. It stabbed the blue man's heart, and as it struck I could hear the thunder rolling and many voices that cried "Un-hee!" meaning I had killed. The flames died. The trees and grasses were not withered any more and murmured happily together, and every living being cried in gladness with whatever voice it had. Then the four troops of horsemen charged down and struck the dead body of the blue man, counting coup; and suddenly it was only a harmless turtle.

You see, I had been riding with the storm clouds, and had come to earth as rain, and it was drouth that I had killed with the power that the Six Grandfathers gave me. So we were riding on the earth now down along the river flowing full from the source of waters, and soon I saw ahead the circled village of a people in the valley. And a Voice said: "Behold a nation; it is yours. Make haste, Eagle Wing Stretches!"

I entered the village, riding, with the four horse troops behind me—the blacks, the whites, the sorrels, and the buckskins; and the place was filled with moaning and with mourning for the dead. The wind was blowing from the south like fever, and when I looked around I saw that in nearly every tepee the women and the children and the men lay dying with the dead.

So I rode around the circle of the village, looking in upon the sick and dead, and I felt like crying as I rode. But when I looked behind me, all the women and the children and the men were getting up and coming forth with happy faces.

And a Voice said: "Behold, they have given you the center of the nation's hoop to make it live."

So I rode to the center of the village, with the horse troops in their quarters round about me, and there the people gathered. And the Voice said: "Give them now the flowering stick that they may flourish, and the sacred pipe that they may know the power that is peace, and the wing of the white giant that they may have endurance and face all winds with courage."

So I took the bright red stick and at the center of the nation's hoop I thrust it in the earth. As it touched the earth it leaped mightily in my hand and was a waga chun, the rustling tree, very tall and full of leafy branches and of all birds singing. And beneath it all the animals were mingling with the people like relatives and making happy cries. The women raised their tremolo of joy, and the men shouted all together: "Here we shall raise our children and be as little chickens under the mother sheo's wing."

Then I heard the white wind blowing gently through the tree and singing there, and from the east the sacred pipe came flying on its eagle wings, and stopped before me there beneath the tree, spreading deep peace around it.

Then the daybreak star was rising, and a Voice said: "It shall be a relative to them; and who shall see it, shall see much more, for thence comes wisdom; and those who do not see it shall be dark." And all the people raised their faces to the east, and the star's light fell upon them, and all the dogs barked loudly and the horses whinnied.

Then when the many little voices ceased, the great Voice said: "Behold the circle of the nation's hoop, for it is holy, being endless, and thus all powers shall be one power in the people without end. Now they shall break camp and go forth upon the red road, and your Grandfathers shall walk with them." So the people broke camp and took the good road with the white wing on their faces, and the order of their going was like this:

First, the black horse riders with the cup of water; and the white horse riders with the white wing and the sacred herb; and the sorrel riders with the holy pipe; and the buckskins with the flowering stick. And after these the little children and the youths and maidens followed in a band.

Second, came the tribe's four chieftains, and their band was all young men and women.

Third, the nation's four advisers leading men and women neither young nor old.

Fourth, the old men hobbling with their canes and looking to the earth.

Fifth, old women hobbling with their canes and looking to the earth.

Sixth, myself all alone upon the bay with the bow and arrows that the First Grandfather gave me. But I was not the last; for when I looked behind me there were ghosts of people like a trailing fog as far as I could see—grandfathers of grandfathers and grandmothers of grandmothers without number. And over these a great Voice—the Voice that was the South—lived, and I could feel it silent.

And as we went the Voice behind me said: "Behold a good nation walking in a sacred manner in a good land!"

Then I looked up and saw that there were four ascents ahead, and these were generations I should know. Now we were on the first ascent, and all the land was green. And as the long line climbed, all the old men and women raised their hands, palms forward, to the far sky yonder and began to croon a song together, and the sky ahead was filled with clouds of baby faces.

When we came to the end of the first ascent we camped in the sacred circle as before, and in the center stood the holy tree, and still the land about us was all green.

Then we started on the second ascent, marching as before, and still the land was green, but it was getting steeper. And as I looked ahead, the people changed into elks and bison and all four-footed beings and even into fowls, all walking in a sacred manner on the good red road together. And I myself was a spotted eagle soaring over them. But just before we stopped to camp at the end of that ascent, all the marching animals grew restless and afraid that they were not what they had been, and began sending forth voices of trouble, calling to their chiefs. And when they camped at the end of that ascent, I looked down and saw that leaves were falling from the holy tree.

And the Voice said: "Behold your nation, and remember what your Six Grandfathers gave you, for thenceforth your people walk in difficulties."

Then the people broke camp again, and saw the black road before them towards where the sun goes down, and black clouds coming yonder; and they did not want to go but could not stay. And as they walked the third ascent, all the animals and fowls that were the people ran here and there, for each one seemed to have his own little vision that he followed and his own rules; and all over the universe I could hear the winds at war like wild beasts fighting.

And when we reached the summit of the third ascent and camped, the nation's hoop was broken like a ring of smoke that spreads and scatters and the holy tree seemed dying and all its birds were gone. And when I looked ahead I saw that the fourth ascent would be terrible.

Then when the people were getting ready to begin the fourth ascent, the Voice spoke like some one weeping, and it said: "Look there upon your nation." And when I looked down, the people were all changed back to human, and they were thin, their faces sharp, for they were starving. Their ponies were only hide and bones, and the holy tree was gone.

And as I looked and wept, I saw that there stood on the north side of the starving camp a sacred man who was painted red all over his body, and he held a spear as he walked into the center of the people, and there he lay down and rolled. And when he got up, it was a fat bison standing there, and where the bison stood a sacred herb sprang up right where the tree had been in the center of the nation's hoop. The herb grew and bore four blossoms on a single stem while I was looking—a blue, a white, a scarlet, and a yellow—and the bright rays of these flashed to the heavens.

I know now what this meant, that the bison were the gift of a good spirit and were our strength, but we should lose them, and from the same good spirit we must find another strength. For the people all seemed better when the herb had grown and bloomed, and the horses raised their tails and neighed and pranced around, and I could see a light breeze going from the north among the people like a ghost; and suddenly the flowering tree was there again at the center of the nation's hoop where the four-rayed herb had blossomed.

I was still the spotted eagle floating, and I could see that I was already in the fourth ascent and the people were camping yonder at the top of the third long rise. It was dark and terrible about me, for all the winds of the world were fighting. It was like rapid gun-fire and like whirling smoke, and like women and children wailing and like horses screaming all over the world.

I could see my people yonder running about, setting the smoke-flap poles and fastening down their tepees against the wind, for the storm cloud was coming on them very fast and black, and there were frightened swallows without number fleeing before the cloud.

Then a song of power came to me and I sang it there in the midst of that terrible place where I was. It went like this:

> A good nation I will make live.
> This the nation above has said.
> They have given me the power to make over.

And when I had sung this, a Voice said: "To the four quarters you shall run for help, and nothing shall be strong before you. Behold him!"

Now I was on my bay horse again, because the horse is of the earth, and it was there my power would be used. And as I obeyed the Voice and looked, there was a horse all skin and bones yonder in the west, a faded brownish black. And a Voice there said: "Take this and make him over; and it was the four-rayed herb that I was holding in my hand. So I rode above the poor horse in a circle, and as I did this I could hear the people yonder calling for spirit power, "A-hey! a-hey!

a-hey! a-hey!" Then the poor horse neighed and rolled and got up, and he was a big, shiny, black stallion with dapples all over him and his mane about him like a cloud. He was the chief of all the horses; and when he snorted, it was a flash of lightning and his eyes were like the sunset star. He dashed to the west and neighed, and the west was filled with a dust of hoofs, and horses without number, shiny black, came plunging from the dust. Then he dashed toward the north and neighed, and to the east and to the south, and the dust clouds answered, giving forth their plunging horses without number—whites and sorrels and buckskins, fat, shiny, rejoicing in their fleetness and their strength. It was beautiful, but it was also terrible.

Then they all stopped short, rearing, and were standing in a great hoop about their black chief at the center, and were still. And as they stood, four virgins, more beautiful than women of the earth can be, came through the circle, dressed in scarlet, one from each of the four quarters, and stood about the great black stallion in their places; and one held the wooden cup of water, and one the white wing, and one the pipe, and one the nation's hoop. All the universe was silent, listening; and then the great black stallion raised his voice and sang. The song he sang was this:

> My horses, prancing they are coming.
> My horses, neighing they are coming;
> Prancing, they are coming.
> All over the universe they come.
> They will dance; may you behold them.   (4 times)
> A horse nation, they will dance. May you behold them.   (4 times)

His voice was not loud, but it went all over the universe and filled it. There was nothing that did not hear, and it was more beautiful than anything can be. It was so beautiful that nothing anywhere could keep from dancing. The virgins danced, and all the circled horses. The leaves on the trees, the grasses on the hills and in the valleys, the waters in the creeks and in the rivers and the lakes, the four-legged and the two-legged and the wings of the air—all danced together to the music of the stallion's song.

And when I looked down upon my people yonder, the cloud passed over, blessing them with friendly rain, and stood in the east with a flaming rainbow over it.

Then all the horses went singing back to their places beyond the summit of the fourth ascent, and all things sang along with them as they walked.

And a Voice said: "All over the universe they have finished a day of happiness." And looking down I saw that the whole wide circle of the day was beautiful and green, with all fruits growing and all things kind and happy.

Then a Voice said: "Behold this day, for it is yours to make. Now you shall stand upon the center of the earth to see, for there they are taking you."

I was still on my bay horse, and once more I felt the riders of the west, the north, the east, the south, behind me in formation, as before, and we were going east. I looked ahead and saw the mountains there with rocks and forests on them, and from the mountains flashed all colors upward to the heavens. Then I was standing on the highest mountain of them all, and round about beneath me was the whole hoop of the world. And while I stood there I saw more than I can tell and I understood more than I saw; for I was seeing in a sacred manner the shapes of all things in the spirit, and the shape of all shapes as they must live together like one being. And I saw that the sacred hoop of my people was one of many hoops that made one circle, wide as daylight and as starlight, and in the center grew one mighty flowering tree to shelter all the children of one mother and one father. And I saw that it was holy.

Then as I stood there, two men were coming from the east, head first like arrows flying, and between them rose the day-break star. They came and gave a herb to me and said: "With this on earth you shall undertake anything and do it." It was the day-break-star herb, the herb of understanding, and they told me to drop it on the earth. I saw it falling far, and when it struck the earth it rooted and grew and flowered, four blossoms on one stem, a blue, a white, a scarlet, and a yellow; and the rays from these streamed upward to the heavens so that all creatures saw it and in no place was there darkness.

Then the Voice said: "Your Six Grandfathers—now you shall go back to them."

I had not noticed how I was dressed until now, and I saw that I was painted red all over, and my joints were painted black, with white stripes between the joints. My bay had lightning stripes all over him, and his mane was cloud. And when I breathed, my breath was lightning.

Now two men were leading me, head first like arrows slanting upward—the two that brought me from the earth. And as I followed on the bay, they turned into four flocks of geese that flew in circles, one above each quarter, sending forth a sacred voice as they flew: Br-r-r-p, br-r-r-p, br-r-r-p, br-r-r-p!

Then I saw ahead the rainbow flaming above the tepee of the Six

Grandfathers, built and roofed with cloud and sewed with thongs of lightning; and underneath it were all the wings of the air and under them the animals and men. All these were rejoicing, and thunder was like happy laughter.

As I rode in through the rainbow door, there were cheering voices from all over the universe, and I saw the Six Grandfathers sitting in a row, with their arms held toward me and their hands, palms out; and behind them in the cloud were faces thronging, without number, of the people yet to be.

"He has triumphed!" cried the six together, making thunder. And as I passed before them there, each gave again the gift that he had given me before—the cup of water and the bow and arrows, the power to make live and to destroy; the white wing of cleansing and the healing herb; the sacred pipe; the flowering stick. And each one spoke in turn from west to south, explaining what he gave as he had done before, and as each one spoke he melted down into the earth and rose again; and as each did this, I felt nearer to the earth.

Then the oldest of them all said: "Grandson, all over the universe you have seen. Now you shall go back with power to the place from whence you came, and it shall happen yonder that hundreds shall be sacred, hundreds shall be flames! Behold!"

I looked below and saw my people there, and all were well and happy except one, and he was lying like the dead—and that one was myself. Then the oldest Grandfather sang, and his song was like this:

> There is someone lying on earth in a sacred manner.
> There is someone—on earth he lies.
> In a sacred manner I have made him to walk.

Now the tepee, built and roofed with cloud, began to sway back and forth as in a wind, and the flaming rainbow door was growing dimmer. I could hear voices of all kinds crying from outside: "Eagle Wing Stretches is coming forth! Behold him!"

When I went through the door, the face of the day of earth was appearing with the day-break star upon its forehead; and the sun leaped up and looked upon me, and I was going forth alone.

And as I walked alone, I heard the sun singing as it arose, and it sang like this:

With visible face I am appearing.
In a sacred manner I appear.
For the greening earth a pleasantness I make.
The center of the nation's hoop I have made pleasant.
With visible face, behold me!
The four-leggeds and two-leggeds, I have made them to walk;
The wings of the air, I have made them to fly.
With visible face I appear.
My day, I have made it holy.

When the singing stopped, I was feeling lost and very lonely. Then a Voice above me said: "Look back!" It was a spotted eagle that was hovering over me and spoke. I looked, and where the flaming rainbow tepee, built and roofed with cloud, had been, I saw only the tall rock mountain at the center of the world.

I was all alone on a broad plain now with my feet upon the earth, alone but for the spotted eagle guarding me. I could see my people's village far ahead, and I walked very fast, for I was homesick now. Then I saw my own tepee, and inside I saw my mother and my father bending over a sick boy that was myself. And as I entered the tepee, some one was saying: "The boy is coming to; you had better give him some water."

Then I was sitting up; and I was sad because my mother and my father didn't seem to know I had been so far away.

Part 4
The Closed Frontier, 1890–

After Wounded Knee, it was as if the Indian had dropped out of American history. With the end of military resistance (excepting the Ute War in 1911), the period of domestic colonization seemed at an end. But what was to become of the survivors? The prevailing social darwinism of the period suggested that the Indian must either step up to the next rung of the evolutionary ladder and become "civilized" or, quite simply, go the way of the dinosaur and die. As Commissioner of Indian Affairs T. J. Morgan wrote in his Annual Report for 1890, "The American Indian was to become the Indian American." And well before 1890, those who had given thought to the matter generally agreed that for Native people to survive, both instruction in the Christian religion and, even more, instruction in the benefits of competitive capitalism (whose cornerstone was the private ownership of property) were necessary. To destroy Indian reliance on tribal and communal ways, it was now thought necessary to destroy the Indian reservations, those lands that had been set aside not for individuals but for whole peoples.

This was the purpose of the General Allotment Act of 1887, known as the Dawes Act, after its sponsor Senator Henry Dawes of Massachusetts. As William Hagan explains,

> The law provided that at his discretion the President could allot reservation land to the Indians, the title to be held in trust by the United States for twenty-five years. Full citizenship for the Indian would accompany the allotment. Heads of families were to receive 160 acres with smaller amounts going to other Indians. The surplus, after the Indians had been taken care of, was to go on the market.[1]

"[A]fter the Indians had been taken care of": the phrase rings with unintended irony. For Dawes took such "care of" the Indians that, between 1887 and 1934 (when the Indian Reorganization Act instituted a new federal Indian policy), of the 138,000 acres of land held by

1. William T. Hagan, *American Indians* (Chicago: Univ. of Chicago Press, 1979), p. 141.

Native people, no more than 48,000 to 55,000 remained, and at least half of that was desert or semidesert, too poor for the whites to covet.

If it appears, with hindsight, that this was robbery akin to murder, such a charge would not have bothered even some of those who considered themselves friends of the Indian. The motto of Captain Richard Pratt, the founder of the Carlisle Indian School, for example, was precisely "Kill the Indian and save the man!" Pratt's Carlisle was only the best-known of the several institutions that set out to do exactly that. Run by various church denominations or by the Bureau of Indian Affairs, the practices of many of the Indian boarding schools have become familiar—or, more precisely, notorious—in a great number of autobiographies. Whether come to school willingly or virtually abducted (some Klamath people Andrea Lerner recently worked with felt that these were the real "captivity narratives" of America), Indian children were stripped of their clothing, had their hair cut, and, dressed as little ladies and gentlemen, forbidden to speak their Native languages at any time or any place. Infractions of any rules were punished by beatings; the Phoenix Indian School was not the only one to use a ball and chain.

Students ran away regularly, and suicides were not infrequent. Mary Crow Dog, in a chapter of her recent autobiography called "Civilize Them with a Stick,"[2] talks of having attended such a school in the sixties—the 1960s. Crow Dog writes, "I think such children were like the victims of Nazi concentration camps trying to tell average, middle-class Americans what their experience had been like." Before her, her mother and grandmother had been forced to attend the same school, always in the interest of "civilizing the Indian."

And yet, not all of the schools were quite so bad as I have described. The Santee Indian school, run by the Reverend Alfred Riggs, for example, taught in both Lakota and English. And not all the young Native people who passed through even some of the more extreme Indian schools felt themselves at all times to be oppressed victims. Indeed, the number of Native graduates of the Indian schools who thought their experience a positive one is large enough for H. David Brumble to speak of a virtual subgenre of Native American autobiography he calls "the Carlisle Success Story."[3] If many Native people found their residence at Carlisle, Haskell, or any other of the Indian boarding schools painful, many of these also, nonetheless,

2. Mary Crow Dog, *Lakota Woman* (New York: Harper, 1990).

3. H. David Brumble, *American Indian Autobiography* (Berkeley: Univ. of California Press, 1988), p. 141.

found it ultimately valuable. Thus, for example, Jason Betzinez, a cousin of Geronimo's and a Carlisle graduate, opposed the Apache return to the Southwest. Having established a life as a farmer in Indian country and having married a white missionary of Dutch descent, Betzinez, in his autobiography *I Fought with Geronimo*,[4] is distinctly disapproving of the old Apache ways. For him, the "closed frontier," as I have called it, represents an opening of an important kind. This is also the case with the most famous of those whom Hazel Hertzberg calls "The Red Progressives"[5]: the Yavapai Dr. Carlos Montezuma, the Sioux Dr. Charles Alexander Eastman, and Mrs. Gertrude Bonnin, the full-blood Arapaho Reverend Sherman Coolidge, and the Seneca Arthur Parker. They and other well-educated Native people joined together in 1911 to form the Society of American Indians, for the purpose of lifting up the Indian and preparing him to compete in the modern world.

Yet in the autobiographies written by some of these progressives (and others, like Joseph Griffis [Chief Tahan], Thomas Wildcat Alford, and Luther Standing Bear), the situation is not so simple. For all the conviction of these highly "civilized" Indians that the way to go is forward and upward, still there is a strong pride in traditional Native moral (if not strictly cultural) values, and a passionate refusal— which, to be sure, expressed itself in a variety of ways—to admit that the Indian past has nothing to offer to the future. Particularly as these Indian doctors, clergymen, social scientists, and writers became disillusioned with one or another aspect of American civilization— broken promises, exploitation, and prejudice—many revived a sense of their identity as Indians. Or, as Charles Alexander Eastman concluded his autobiography, *From the Deep Woods to Civilization* (1916): "I am an Indian. . . . I am an American."[6] But the questions for Eastman, as for others, remained: could one be both in twentieth-century America? and if so, how?

The observations offered above should serve to provide a context for the selections from Eastman, Bonnin, and Luther Standing Bear. This part of the anthology begins, however, with Plenty-Coups, and a word of explanation is in order regarding this. Born in 1847, Plenty-Coups, as we shall see, grew up in traditional Crow fashion; no white

4. Jason Betzinez, with Wilbur S. Nye, *I Fought with Geronimo* (New York: Bonanza Books, 1959).
5. Hazel Hertzberg, *The Search for an American Indian Identity: Modern PanIndian Movements* (Syracuse: Syracuse Univ. Press, 1971).
6. Charles Alexander Eastman, *From the Deep Woods to Civilization* (Lincoln: Univ. of Nebraska Press, 1977), p. 195.

ever cut his hair, nor did he toil at school. He is the contemporary of the five warriors whose life stories were included in the preceding section of this book, "The Resisting Indians," and in these regards Plenty-Coup's life story is out of place here. But the Crow did not resist the advancing whites; when the soldiers went against the Lakota and Cheyenne, traditional enemies of the Crow, the Crow chose the side of the enemy of their enemy. So I have put Plenty-Coups in this section as a kind of bridge from the nineteenth to the twentieth century. His is a traditional life—but one that tried to maintain its traditionalism through accommodation rather than resistance to Euro-American expansion.

14
Plenty-Coups, Chief of the Crows

Edited by

FRANK B. LINDERMAN

Plenty-Coups was a Crow warrior, member of a Siouan tribe of the Upper Missouri which lives today, for the most part, in Montana. In the nineteenth century, the Crow were full participants in the horse culture of the open plains, a culture they largely shared with their Lakota and Cheyenne neighbors. But the Lakota and Cheyenne were the traditional enemies of the Crow, and it was Crow antipathy toward these neighboring tribes that in substantial regard led them to alliances with the invading whites. Crow scouts served with Custer, as they had served earlier with Crook, and as they would serve again in battles against the Sioux and Cheyenne.

Born in 1847, very likely the same year as Two Leggings, Plenty-Coups achieved a major vision when he was only nine years old. This vision, or "medicine-dream," as the old warrior Coyote-runs commented to Plenty-Coups in the hearing of Frank Linderman, the editor of his autobiography, "pointed the way of your life, and you have followed it."[1] Because this vision assured Plenty-Coups of the coming dominance of the whites, and because the Crow already, in his lifetime, had at least a brief tradition of cooperation with the whites, his character, to cite Lynne Woods O'Brien, "was not broken during the transition period [sic], because his vision had prepared him with a pattern which organized his life and made his experience understandable. . . . [It] showed him how to live with the white man."[2] Thus, as O'Brien further notes, and as our selections confirm, the story of Plenty-Coups' life has a very different tonality than that of Black Elk, for example, who also guided his life by an early, powerful vision.

Plenty-Coups' story includes buffalo hunts, war with the Sioux, and horse-stealing raids. But "after the passing of the buffalo," as Frank Linderman writes, "Plenty-Coups refused to speak of his life. . . . In Plenty-Coups' words, 'when the buffalo went away, the hearts of my people fell to the

1. *Plenty-Coups, Chief of the Crows*, ed. Frank B. Linderman (Lincoln: Univ. of Nebraska Press, 1962), p. 5. Subsequent references appear in text. The excerpts below are reprinted from this text. Copyright 1930 Frank B. Linderman. Copyright renewed 1957. Reprinted by permission of HarperCollins Publishers, Inc.

2. Lynne Woods O'Brien, *Plains Indian Autobiographies* (Boise, ID: Western Writers Series, 1973), p. 23.

ground, and they could not lift them up again. After this nothing happened. There was little singing anywhere' " (311).

Plenty-Coups followed his vision to the end, encouraging his people to learn the ways of the whites. It should not be thought, however, that he was an uncritical adherent of "civilization." In his own words, "we know that with all his wonderful powers, the white man is not wise: He is smart, but not wise, and fools only himself" (94). Plenty-Coups died in 1932.

Frank Bird Linderman was born in 1869 and went west at the age of sixteen to follow the life of the cowboy, trapper, and hunter. Intimately acquainted with the Cree and Chippewa, as well as the Crow—who knew him as Sign-talker—he published widely on western and Indian subjects, and also wrote fiction and poetry. Plenty-Coups, Chief of the Crow, from which the following selections are taken, is a cross between biography and autobiography. Although Plenty-Coups' book is an autobiography, Linderman also writes of him in the third-person, and he also, quite unself-consciously, dramatizes his own presence—and his part in the making of the book. As noted earlier, it may be that L. V. McWhorter, who also followed this practice, was influenced by Linderman's work; in any case, both Linderman and McWhorter procede in a manner very different from their anthropologist contemporaries, who tended to obscure their role in the production of Indian lives. Here, as in the McWhorter edited chapter, Linderman's commentary, both as main text and bracketed information, is retained. The downside, as it were, of Linderman's openness is that Plenty-Coups' story, in print, has a rather meandering feel.

Recent interest in Linderman and his work with Native people and subjects has given rise to SIGN-TALKER, a newsletter for the Frank Bird Linderman Society. Readers may contact Celeste River, 309 McLeod Avenue, Missoula, MT 59801. River's study of Linderman appears in New Voices in Native American Literary Criticism. Another Native American autobiography by Linderman is Pretty Shield: Medicine Woman of the Crow. For coup tales and other traditional "autobiographical" narrative modes, see Lynne Woods O'Brien, Plains Indian Autobiography, and H. David Brumble, American Indian Autobiography.[3]

Our selections from the 1962 University of Nebraska edition document Plenty-Coups' acquisition of the visions that would guide his life. As the reader will note, Linderman offers his own brief interpolations, and we have,

---

3. Celeste River's "The Great Stillness: Visions and Native Wisdom in the Writings of Frank Bird Linderman," appears in *New Voices in Native American Literary Criticism*, ed. Arnold Krupat (Washington, DC: Smithsonian Institution Press, 1993); Frank B. Linderman's *Pretty Shield: Medicine Woman of the Crow*, first published in 1932, has been republished by the Univ. of Nebraska Press (1974); Lynne Wood O'Brien's *Plains Indian Autobiography*, cited above, is a Western Writers Series pamphlet; H. David Brumble's *American Indian Autobiography* is published by the Univ. of California Press (1988).

as well, in traditional fashion, the commentary of other Crow elders who were attendant to the narration.

I

Plenty-Coups' thoughts now turned to those very days when mimic battles were fought with snowballs in winter, mud in summer. . . .

"I hoped to become a chief, even then, and in my actions while playing games never permitted myself to be unjust to my companions. I tried hard to excel them in everything, and yet was very careful to let them see that I was fair. I soon became a leader among them, and they spoke my name with respect.

"My grandfather, who had given me my name, had told my mother that I should live to count many coups and be old. His dream had also told him that I should be a chief. 'I name him Aleek-chea-ahoosh [Many Achievements],' he told my mother, 'because in my dream I saw him count many coups.' Of course all the people knew this, and even as a boy I felt obliged to excel my companions, to be a leader among those of my own age. I must live up to my name, you see; and now I was beginning to think of dreaming. . . ."

II

"When the village was set up on the Big River [Missouri], news reached us that my brother was gone—killed by Sioux on Powder River.

"My heart fell to the ground and stayed there. I mourned with my father and mother, and alone. I cut my flesh and bled myself weak. I knew now that I must dream if I hoped to avenge my brother, and I at once began to fast in preparation, first taking a sweat-bath to cleanse my body.

"Nobody saw me leave the village. I slipped away and climbed The-buffalo's-heart, where I fasted two more days and nights, without success. I saw nothing at all and gave up to travel back to my father's lodge, where I rested.

"The fourth night, while I was asleep, a voice said to me, 'You did

243

not go to the right mountain, Plenty-coups.' I knew then that I should sometime succeed in dreaming.

"The village was preparing to move to the Little Rockies, a good place for me, and before the women began to take down the lodges I started out alone. Besides extra moccasins, I had a good buffalo robe, and as soon as I reached the mountains I covered a sweat-lodge with the robe and again cleansed my body. I was near the Two Buttes and chose the south one, which I climbed, and there I made a bed of sweet-sage and groundcedar. I was determined that no smell of man should be on me and burned some *e-say* [a root that grows in the mountains] and sweet-sage, standing in their smoke and rubbing my body with the sage.

"The day was hot; and naked I began walking about the top of the mountain crying for Helpers, but got no answer, no offer of assistance. I grew more tired as the sun began to go toward the west, and finally I went to my bed, lying down so my feet would face the rising sun when he came again. Weakened by my walking and the days of fasting, I slept, remembering only the last rays of the sun as he went to his lodge. When I wakened, looking into the sky, I saw that The-seven-stars [the Big Dipper] had turned round The-star-that-does-not move [North Star]. The night was westward. Morning was not far away, and wolves were howling on the plains far below me. I wondered if the village would reach the Little Rockies before night came again.

" 'Plenty-coups.'

"My name was spoken! The voice came from behind me, back of my head. My heart leaped like a deer struck by an arrow. 'Yes,' I answered, without moving.

" 'They want you, Plenty-coups. I have been sent to fetch you,' said the voice yet behind me, back of my head.

" 'I am ready,' I answered, and stood up, my head clear and light as air.

"The night had grown darker, and I felt rather than saw some Person go by me on my right side. I could not tell what Person it was, but thought he beckoned me.

" 'I am coming,' I said, but the Person made no answer and slipped away in a queer light that told me where he was. I followed over the same places I had traveled in the afternoon, not once feeling my feet touch a stone. They touched nothing at all where the way was rough, and without moccasins I walked in the Person's tracks as though the mountain were as smooth as the plains. My body was naked, and the winds cool and very pleasant, but I looked to see which way I was traveling. The stars told me that I was going east, and I could see that I was following the Person downhill. I could not actually see him, but I knew I was on his trail by the queer light ahead. His feet stirred no stone, nothing on the way, made no sound of walking, nor did mine.

"A coyote yelped on my right, and then another answered on my left. A little farther on I heard many coyotes yelping in a circle around us, and as we traveled they moved their circle along with us, as though they were all going to the same place as we. When the coyotes ahead stopped on a flat and sat down to help together, the ones behind closed in to make their circle smaller, all yelping loudly, as though they wished to tell the Person something. I knew now that our destination was not far off.

"The Person stopped, and I saw a lodge by his side. It seemed to rise up out of the ground. I saw that he came to it at its back, that it faced east, and that the Person reached its door by going around it to the right. But I did not know him, even when he coughed to let someone inside the lodge know he was there. He spoke no word to me but lifted the lodge door and stepped inside. 'Come, Plenty-coups,' he said gently. And I too stepped into the lodge.

"There was no fire burning, and yet there was light in the lodge. I saw that it was filled with Persons I did not know. There were four rows of them in half-circles, two rows on each side of the center, and each Person was an old warrior. I could tell this by their faces and bearing. They had been counting coup. I knew this because before each, sticking in the ground, was a white coup-stick bearing the breath-feathers of a wareagle. Some, however, used no stick at all, but only heavy first-feathers whose quills were strong enough to stick in the ground. These first-feathers were very fine, the handsomest I had ever seen, and I could not count them, they were so many.

" 'Why have you brought this young man into our lodge? We do not want him. He is not our kind and therefore has no place among us.' The words came from the south side, and my heart began to fall down.

"I looked to see what Persons sat on the south side, and my eyes made me afraid. They were the Winds, the Bad Storms, the Thunders, the Moon, and many Stars, all powerful, and each of them braver and much stronger than men."

I believe the Persons on the south side of the lodge, the Winds, Bad Storms, the Moon, and many Stars, were recognized by Plenty-coups as the great forces of nature, and that this is what he wished to convey to me.

" 'Come, Plenty-coups, and sit with *us*.' This voice was kind. It came from the north side.

" 'Sit,' said the Person who had brought me there, and then he was gone. I saw him no more.

"They, on the north side of the lodge, made a place for me. It was third from the head on the left, and I sat down there. The two parties of Persons were separated at the door, which faced the east, and again in the west, which was the head of the lodge, so that the Spirit-trail from east to west was open, if any wished to travel that way. On neither side were the Persons the same as I. All were different, but I knew now that they had rights in the world, as I had, that Ah-badt-dadt-deah had created them, as He had me and other men. Nobody there told me this, but I felt it in the lodge as I felt the presence of the Persons. I knew that to live on the world I must concede that those Persons across the lodge who had not wished me to sit with them had work to do, and that I could not prevent them from doing it. I felt a little afraid but was glad I was there.

" 'Take these, Plenty-coups.' The Person at the head of the lodge on the north side handed me several beautiful first-feathers of a war-eagle.

"I looked into his eyes. He was a Dwarf-person, chief of the Little-people who live in the Medicine-rock, which you can almost see from here, and who made the stone arrow points. I now saw that all on my side were the same as he, that all were Dwarfs not tall as my knee. . . ."

" 'Stick one of your feathers in the ground before you and count coup,' said the Dwarf-chief.

"I hesitated. I had never yet counted coup, and here in this lodge with old warriors was no place to lie.

" 'Count coup!' commanded the Dwarf-chief.

"I stuck a first-feather into the ground before me, fearing a dispute.

" 'That,' said the Dwarf-chief, 'is the rider of the *white* horse! I first struck him with my coup-stick, and then, while he was unharmed and fighting, I took his bow from him.'

"The Thunders, who sat at the head of the lodge on the south side, said, 'Nothing can be better than that.'

" 'Stick another feather before you, Plenty-coups,' said the Dwarf-chief.

"I stuck another first-feather in the ground, wondering what the Dwarf-chief would say for it. But this time I was not afraid.

" 'That,' he said, 'is the rider of the *black* horse. I first struck him with my bow. Then, while he was armed with a knife and fighting me, I took his bow from him, also his shield.'

246

" 'Enough!' said the Persons on the south side. 'No Person can do better than that.'

" 'Let us leave off counting coups. We are glad you have admitted this young man to our lodge,' said the Bad Storms, 'and we think you should give him something to take back with him, some strong medicine that will help him.' "

Plenty-coups had been speaking rapidly, his hands followed his spoken words with signs, acting parts, while his facial expressions gave tremendous emphasis to his story. He was perspiring and stopped to brush his face with his hand.

"I had not spoken," he went on, "and could not understand why the Dwarf-chief had ordered me to stick the feathers, nor why he had counted coups in my name before such powerful Persons.

" 'He will be a Chief,' said the Dwarf-chief. 'I can give him nothing. He already possesses the power to become great if he will use it. Let him cultivate his senses, let him use the powers which Ah-badt-dadt-deah has given him, and he will go far. The difference between men grows out of the use, or non-use, of what was given them by Ah-badt-dadt-deah in the first place.'

"Then he said to me, 'Plenty-coups, we, the Dwarfs, the Little-people, have adopted you and will be your Helpers throughout your life on this world. We have no medicine-bundle to give you. They are cumbersome things at best and are often in a warrior's way. Instead, we will offer you advice. Listen!

" 'In you, as in all men, are natural powers. You have a will. Learn to use it. Make it work for you. Sharpen your senses as you sharpen your knife. Remember the wolf smells better than you do because he has learned to depend on his nose. It tells him every secret the winds carry because he uses it all the time, makes it work for him. We can give you nothing. You already possess everything necessary to become great. Use your powers. Make them work for you, and you will become a Chief. . . .' "

"When I wakened, I was perspiring. Looking into the early morning sky that was growing light in the north, I went over it all in my mind. I saw and understood that whatever I accomplished must be by my own efforts, that I must myself do the things I wished to do. And I knew I could accomplish them if I used the powers that Ah-badt-dadt-deah had given me. I *had* a will and I would use it, make it work for me, as the Dwarf-chief had advised. I became very happy, lying there looking up into the sky. My heart began to sing like a bird, and I went back to the village, needing no man to tell me the meaning of my dream. I took a sweat-bath and rested in my father's lodge. I *knew* myself now.''

III

''We feasted there,'' said Plenty-coups. ''Fat meat of bighorn, deer, and elk was plentiful. The hunters had killed many of these animals because they knew there would soon be a very large village to feed. Besides, light skins were always needed for shirts and leggings. Even the dogs found more than they could eat near that village, and our horses, nearly always feasting on rich grass, enjoyed the change the mountains gave them. All night the drums were beating, and in the light of fires that smelled sweet the people danced until they were tired.

''I was wakened by a crier. He was riding through the village with some message from the council of the night before. I sat up to listen. ''There are high peaks in these mountains, O young men! Go to them and dream!' the crier said. 'Are you men, or women? Are you afraid of a little suffering? Go into these mountains and find Helpers for yourselves and your people who have so many enemies!'

''I sat there in my robe, listening till his voice was far off. How I wished to count coup, to wear an eagle's feather in my hair, to sit in the council with my chiefs, holding an eagle's wing in my hand. . . .''

''I got up from my robe. The air was cool and smelled of the trees outside. Ought I to go again and try to dream?

'' 'Go, young man!'

''Another crier had started through the village. His first words answered my unspoken question. I walked out of the lodge, only half hearing the rest of his message. The sun was just coming, and the wind was in the treetops. Women were kindling their fires, and hunters were leaving the camp when I started out alone.

''I decided to go afoot to the Crazy Mountains, two long days' journey from the village. The traveling without food or drink was good for me, and as soon as I reached the Crazies I took a sweat-bath and climbed the highest peak. There is a lake at its base, and the winds are always stirring about it. But even though I fasted two more days and nights, walking over the mountain top, no Person came to me, nothing was offered. I saw several grizzly bears that were nearly white in the moonlight, and one of them came very near to me, but he did not speak. Even when I slept on that peak in the Crazies, no bird or animal or Person spoke a word to me, and I grew discouraged. I could not dream.

"Back in the village I told my closest friends about the high peaks I had seen, about the white grizzly bears, and the lake. They were interested and said they would go back with me and that we would all try to dream.

"There were three besides myself who set out, with extra moccasins and a robe to cover our sweat-lodge. We camped on good water just below the peak where I had tried to dream, quickly took our sweat-baths, and started up the mountains. It was already dark when we separated, but I found no difficulty in reaching my old bed on the tall peak that looked down on the little lake, or in making a new bed with ground-cedar and sweet-sage. Owls were hooting under the stars while I rubbed my body with the sweet-smelling herbs before starting out to walk myself weak.

"When I could scarcely stand, I made my way back to my bed and slept with my feet toward the east. But no Person came to me, nothing was offered; and when the day came I got up to walk again over the mountain top, calling for Helpers as I had done the night before.

"All day the sun was hot, and my tongue was swollen for want of water; but I saw nothing, heard nothing, even when night came again to cool the mountain. No sound had reached my ears, except my own voice and the howling of wolves down on the plains.

"I knew that our great Crow warriors of other days sacrificed their flesh and blood to dream, and just when the night was leaving to let the morning come I stopped at a fallen tree, and, laying the first finger of my left hand upon the log, I cut part of it off with my knife. [The end of the left index finger on the Chief's hand is missing]. But no blood came. The stump of my finger was white as the finger of a dead man, and to make it bleed I struck it against the log until blood flowed freely. Then I began to walk and call for Helpers, hoping that some Person would smell my blood and come to aid me.

"Near the middle of that day my head grew dizzy, and I sat down. I had eaten nothing, taken no water, for nearly four days and nights, and my mind must have left me while I sat there under the hot sun on the mountain top. It must have traveled far away, because the sun was nearly down when it returned and found me lying on my face. As soon as it came back to me I sat up and looked about, at first not knowing where I was. Four war-eagles were sitting in a row along a trail of my blood just above me. But they did not speak to me, offered nothing at all.

"I thought I would try to reach my bed, and when I stood up I saw my three friends. They had seen the eagles flying over my peak and had become frightened, believing me dead. They carried me to my bed and stayed long enough to smoke with me before going back to their own places. While we smoked, the four war-eagles did not fly away. They sat there by my blood on the rocks, even after the night came on and chilled everything living on the mountain."

Again the Chief whispered aside to the Little-people, asking them if he might go on. When he finally resumed, I felt that somehow he had been reassured. His voice was very low, yet strained, as though he were tiring.

"I dreamed. I heard a voice at midnight and saw a Person standing at my feet, in the east. He said, 'Plenty-coups, the Person down there wants you now.'

"He pointed, and from the peak in the Crazy Mountains I saw a Buffalo-bull standing *where we are sitting now*. I got up and started to go to the Bull, because I knew he was the Person who wanted me. The other Person was gone. Where he had stood when he spoke to me there was nothing at all.

"The way is very long from the Crazies to this place where we are sitting today, but I came here quickly in my dream. On that hill over yonder was where I stopped to look at the Bull. He had changed into a Man-person wearing a buffalo robe with the hair outside. Later I picked up the buffalo skull that you see over there, on the very spot where the Person had stood. I have kept that skull for more than seventy years.

"The Man-person beckoned me from the hill over yonder where I had stopped, and I walked to where he stood. When I reached his side he began to sink slowly into the ground, right over there [pointing]. Just as the Man-person was disappearing he spoke. 'Follow me,' he said.

"But I was afraid. 'Come,' he said from the darkness. And I got down into the hole in the ground to follow him, walking bent-over for ten steps. Then I stood straight and saw a small light far off. It was like a window in a white man's house of today, and I knew the hole was leading us toward the Arrow Creek Mountains [the Pryors].

"In the way of the light, between it and me, I could see countless buffalo, see their sharp horns thick as the grass grows. I could smell their bodies and hear them snorting, ahead and on both sides of me. Their eyes, without number, were like little fires in the darkness of the hole in the ground, and I felt afraid among so many big bulls. The Man-person must have known this, because he said, 'Be not afraid,

Plenty-coups. It was these Persons who sent for you. They will not do you harm.'

"My body was naked. I feared walking among them in such a narrow place. The burrs that are always in their hair would scratch my skin, even if their hoofs and horns did not wound me more deeply. I did not like the way the Man-person went among them. 'Fear nothing! Follow me, Plenty-coups,' he said.

"I felt their warm bodies against my own, but went on after the Man-person, edging around them or going between them all that night and all the next day, with my eyes always looking ahead at the hole of light. But none harmed me, none even spoke to me, and at last we came out of the hole in the ground and saw the Square White Butte at the mouth of Arrow Creek Canyon. It was on our right. White men call it Castle Rock, but our name for it is The-fasting-place.

"Now, out in the light of the sun, I saw that the Man-person who had led me had a rattle in his hand. It was large and painted red. [The rattle is used in ceremonials. It is sometimes made of the bladder of an animal, dried, with small pebbles inside, so that when shaken it gives a rattling sound.] When he reached the top of a knoll he turned and said to me, 'Sit here!'

"Then he shook his red rattle and sang a queer song four times. 'Look!' he pointed.

"Out of the hole in the ground came the buffalo, bulls and cows and calves without number. They spread wide and blackened the plains. Everywhere I looked great herds of buffalo were going in every direction, and still others without number were pouring out of the hole in the ground to travel on the wide plains. When at last they ceased coming out of the hole in the ground, all were gone, *all!* There was not one in sight anywhere, even out on the plains. I saw a few antelope on a hillside, but no buffalo—not a bull, not a cow, not one calf, was anywhere on the plains.

"I turned to look at the Man-person beside me. He shook his red rattle again. 'Look!' he pointed.

"Out of the hole in the ground came bulls and cows and calves past counting. These, like the others, scattered and spread on the plains. But they stopped in small bands and began to eat the grass. Many lay down, not as a buffalo does but differently, and many were spotted. Hardly any two were alike in color or size. And the bulls bellowed differently too, not deep and far-sounding like the bulls of the buffalo but sharper and yet weaker in my ears. Their tails were different, longer, and nearly brushed the ground. They were not buffalo. These were strange animals from another world.

251

"I was frightened and turned to the Man-person, who only shook his red rattle but did not sing. He did not even tell me to look, but I did look and saw all the Spotted-buffalo go back into the hole in the ground, until there was nothing except a few antelope anywhere in sight.

" 'Do you understand this which I have shown you, Plenty-coups?' he asked me.

" 'No!' I answered. How could he expect me to understand such a thing when I was not yet ten years old?

"During all the time the Spotted-buffalo were going back into the hole in the ground the Man-person had not once looked at me. He stood facing the south as though the Spotted-buffalo belonged there. 'Come, Plenty-coups,' he said finally, when the last had disappeared.

"I followed him back through the hole in the ground without seeing anything until we came out *right over there* [pointing] where we had first entered the hole in the ground. Then I saw the spring down by those trees, this very house just as it is, these trees which comfort us today, and a very old man sitting in the shade, alone. I felt pity for him because he was so old and feeble.

" 'Look well upon this old man,' said the Man-person. 'Do you know him, Plenty-coups?' he asked me.

" 'No,' I said, looking closely at the old man's face in the shade of *this* tree.

" 'This old man is yourself, Plenty-coups,' he told me. And then I could see the Man-person no more. He was gone, and so too was the old man.

"Instead I saw only a dark forest. A fierce storm was coming fast. The sky was black with streaks of mad color through it. I saw the Four Winds gathering to strike the forest, and held my breath. Pity was hot in my heart for the beautiful trees. I felt pity for all things that lived in that forest, but was powerless to stand with them against the Four Winds that together were making war. I shielded my own face with my arm when they charged! I heard the Thunders calling out in the storm, saw beautiful trees twist like blades of grass and fall in tangled piles where the forest had been. Bending low, I heard the Four Winds rush past me as though they were not yet satisfied, and then I looked at the destruction they had left behind them.

"Only one tree, tall and straight, was left standing where the great forest had stood. The Four Winds that always make war alone had this time struck together, riding down every tree in the forest but *one*. Standing there alone among its dead tribesmen, I thought it looked sad. 'What does this mean?' I whispered in my dream.

252

" 'Listen, Plenty-coups,' said a voice. 'In that tree is the lodge of the Chickadee. He is least in strength but strongest of mind among his kind. He is willing to work for wisdom. The Chickadee-person is a good listener. Nothing escapes his ears, which he has sharpened by constant use. Whenever others are talking together of their successes or failures, there you will find the Chickadee-person listening to their words. But in all his listening he tends to his own business. He never intrudes, never speaks in strange company, and yet never misses a chance to learn from others. He gains success and avoids failure by learning how others succeeded or failed, and without great trouble to himself. There is scarcely a lodge he does not visit, hardly a Person he does not know, and yet everybody likes him, because he minds his own business, or pretends to.

" 'The lodges of countless Bird-people were in that forest when the Four Winds charged it. Only one is left unharmed, the lodge of the Chickadee-person. Develop your body, but do not neglect your mind, Plenty-coups. It is the mind that leads a man to power, not strength of body.'

IV

"I wakened then. My three friends were standing at my feet in the sunshine. They helped me stand. I was very weak, but my heart was singing, even as my friends half carried me to the foot of the mountain and kindled a fire. One killed a deer, and I ate a little of the meat. It is not well to eat heartily after so long a time of fasting. But the meat helped me to recover my strength a little. Of course we had all taken sweat-baths before touching the meat, or even killing the deer, and I was happy there beside the clear water with my friends. Toward night two of them went back to the village to bring horses for me and the man who stayed with me at the foot of the mountains. I was yet too weak to travel so far afoot.

"Lying by the side of the clear water, looking up into the blue sky, I kept thinking of my dream, but could understand little of it except that my medicine was the Chickadee. I should have a small medicine-bundle, indeed. And I would call upon the Wise Ones [medicine-men] of the tribe to interpret the rest. Perhaps they could tell the meaning of my dream from beginning to end.

"In the middle of the third day my ears told me that horses were coming. My friend and I walked a little way to meet them, and very soon I heard the voices of my uncles, White-horse and Cuts-the-turnip. They were singing the Crow Praise Song with several others who were leading extra horses for my friend and me.

"I was stronger now and could ride alone, but the way seemed very far indeed. Of course I had spoken to nobody of my dream, but when I came in sight of the village my uncles began again to sing the Praise Song, and many people came out to meet us. They were all very happy, because they knew I now had Helpers and would use my power to aid my people.

"None spoke to me, not because he did not wish to be kind but because the people knew I must first cleanse myself in a sweat-lodge before going about the village with my friends. I saw my young sweetheart by her father's lodge, and although she did not speak to me I thought she looked happier than ever before.

"While I was in the sweat-lodge my uncles rode through the village telling the Wise Ones that I had come, that I had dreamed and wished interpretation of my vision in council. I heard them calling this message to those who had distinguished themselves by feats of daring or acts of wisdom, and I wondered what my dream could mean, what the Wise Ones would say to me after I had told them all I had seen and heard on the peak in the Crazy Mountains. I respected them so highly that rather than have them speak lightly of my dream I would willingly have died."

Plenty-coups hesitated, his dimmed eyes staring over my head into the past. His last words, spoken in a whisper, had lifted him away. He had forgotten me and even the two old men who, like himself, appeared to be under a spell and scarcely breathed.

"My father was gone," the Chief went on, brushing his forehead with his hand, "so that I had only my uncles to speak for me before the Wise Ones. But my uncles were both good men. Both loved me and both belonged to the tribal council, whose members had all counted coup and were leaders. No man can love children more than my people do, and while I missed my father this day more than ever, I knew my uncles looked on me as a son and that they would help me now.

"Both of them were waiting, and when I was ready they led me to the lodge of Yellow-bear, where our chiefs sat with the Wise Ones. When I entered and sat down, Yellow-bear passed the pipe round the lodge, as the sun goes, from east to west. Each man took it as it came, and smoked, first offering the stem to the Sun, the father, and then to the Earth, the mother of all things on this world. But no one spoke. All in that lodge had been over the hard trail and each knew well what was in my heart by my eyes. The eyes of living men speak words which the tongue cannot pronounce. The dead do not see out of their bodies' eyes, because there is no spirit there. It has gone away forever. In the lodge of Yellow-bear that day seventy years ago I saw the spirits [souls] of my leaders in their eyes, and my heart sang loudly because I had dreamed.

"When the pipe was finished, my uncle, White-horse, laid his hand on my shoulder. 'Speak, Plenty-coups,' he said. 'Tell us your dream. Forget nothing that happened. You are too young to understand, but here are men who can help you.' "

At this point a rolling hoop bumped violently against the Chief's chair and fell flat beside it. The old man did not start or show the least displeasure, even when a little bright-eyed girl ran among us to recover it. He did not reprove her with so much as a look. Instead, he smiled. "I have adopted many children," he said softly. Then he went on.

"I told my dream, all of it. Even a part I forgot to tell you, about trying to enter a lodge on my way back from this place to the Crazies. A Voice had spoken. 'Do not go inside,' it said. 'This lodge contains the clothes of small babies, and if you touch them or they touch you, you will not be successful.' Of course I did not enter that lodge, but went on to my bed in the mountains. This I told in the order it came in my dream.

"When I had finished, Yellow-bear, who sat at the head of the lodge which faced the east, lighted the pipe and passed it to his left, as the sun goes. Four times he lit the pipe, and four times it went round the lodge, without a word being spoken by anybody who took it. I grew uneasy. Was there no meaning in my dream?

" 'White-horse,' the voice of Yellow-bear said softly, 'your nephew has dreamed a great dream.'

"My heart began to sing again. Yellow-bear was the wisest man in the lodge. My ears were listening.

" 'He has been told that in his lifetime the buffalo will go away forever,' said Yellow-bear, 'and that in their place on the plains will come the bulls and the cows and the calves of the white men. I have myself seen these Spotted-buffalo drawing loads of the white man's goods. And once at the big fort above the mouth of the Elk River [Fort Union, above the mouth of the Yellowstone] on the Big River [Missouri] I saw cows and calves of the same tribe as the bulls that drew the loads.

" 'The dream of Plenty-coups means that the white men will take and hold this country and that their Spotted-buffalo will cover the plains. He was told to think for himself, to listen, to learn to avoid disaster by the experiences of others. He was advised to develop his body but not to forget his mind. The meaning of his dream is plain to me. I see its warning. The tribes who have fought the white man have all been beaten, wiped out. By listening as the Chickadee listens we may escape this and keep our lands.

" 'The Four Winds represent the white man and those who will help him in his wars. The forest of trees is the tribes of these wide plains. And the one tree that the Four Winds left standing after the fearful battle represents our own people, the Absarokees, the one tribe of the plains that has never made war against the white man.

" 'The Chickadee's lodge in that standing tree is the lodges of this tribe pitched in the safety of peaceful relations with white men, whom we could not stop even though we would. The Chickadee is small, so are we against our many enemies, white and red. But he was wise in his selection of a place to pitch his lodge. After the battle of the Four Winds he still held his home, his country, because he had gained wisdom by listening to the mistakes of others and knew there was safety for himself and his family. The Chickadee is the medicine of Plenty-coups from this day. He will not be obliged to carry a heavy medicine-bundle, but his medicine will be powerful both in peace time and in war.

" 'He will live to be old and he will be a Chief. He will some day live differently from the way we do now and will sit in the shade of great trees on Arrow Creek, where the Man-person took him in his dream. The old man he saw there was himself, as he was told. He will live to be old and be known for his brave deeds, but I can see that he will have no children of his own blood. This was told him when he tried to enter that lodge on his way from Arrow Creek to the peak in the Crazy Mountains where he dreamed. When the Voice told him not to enter, that the lodge was filled with the clothes of babes, that if he touched them he would not succeed, it meant he would have no children. I have finished.' "

" 'Your dream was a great dream. Its meaning is plain,' said the others, and the pipe was passed so that I might smoke with them in the lodge of Yellow-bear.

"Ho!" said Plenty-coups, making the sign for "finished." "And here I am, an old man, sitting under this tree just where that old man sat seventy years ago when this was a different world."

Coyote-runs and Plain-bull began a conversation between themselves when Plenty-coups left off talking. Both said that the dream of the Chief was well known to all the tribe, even the day after he had returned from his dreaming. "We traveled by that dream," said Coyote-runs. "The men who sat in that lodge when Plenty-coups told what he had seen and heard knew a heap better than he did that it was time the Crows turned their faces another way. They saw it was best to do something to prove their friendship to white men, and they began to watch for a chance, too. When they found it, the Crows pointed their guns with the white man's, and some of us died and we lost many horses. . . ."

15
From the Deep Woods to Civilization

CHARLES A. EASTMAN (OHIYESA)

*Born in Minnesota in 1858, the youngest of five children, Charles A. East-
man was named Hakadah, meaning "the pitiful last." This "humiliating
name," as he calls it in his first book,* Indian Boyhood *(1902), was changed
to Ohiyesa, "the winner," as a result of a victory in a lacrosse game. His
father was a Wahpeton Sioux known as Many Lightnings, and his mother,
who died soon after his birth, was Mary Eastman, daughter of the artist Seth
Eastman. With the Minnesota Sioux uprising of 1862, Eastman's history becomes complex. His father was imprisoned and the family fled north to Canada, where, until his fifteenth year, as Ohiyesa, he apparently led a traditional
Lakota life.*

*But in 1873, Many Lightnings, now a Christian convert who had taken the
name Jacob Eastman, came for his son, named him Charles Alexander Eastman, and set the boy on the white man's road. Charles Eastman attended a
great many schools, continuing his formal education by way of a scholarship
to Dartmouth before taking his M.D. at the Boston University School of Medicine. In the same year that he received his degree, Eastman took a post as
physician at the Pine Ridge Agency. The year was 1890, and the acculturated
doctor soon found himself ministering to wounded Ghost Dancers, his fellow
Sioux.*

Writing about Indians in 1902, Eastman could say:

> the Indian no longer exists as a natural and free man. Those remnants that
> dwell upon the reservations present only a sort of tableau—a fictional copy of
> the past.[1]

*H. David Brumble has pointed to this passage as indicative of Eastman's ac-
ceptance of so-called "scientific" racialism and social darwinism—the belief
that "races" exist, that they are inevitably in competition (e.g., Herbert
Spencer's phrase, "the survival of the fittest"), and that the "higher" must
always win out. For the Indian to survive required the end of the reservation
system (Eastman wholeheartedly supported the Dawes Act), and the adoption*

1. Quoted in H. David Brumble, *American Indian Autobiography* (Berkeley: Univ. of
California Press, 1988), p. 147. Subsequent references are given in text.

of a competitive individualist perspective. To this end, Eastman devoted mighty efforts to "Red Progressive" causes. And yet, to leave the matter here would be too simple.

If from 1903 to 1908 he carried out a government project to assign the Sioux anglicized names, in 1923 he was a member of the Committee of One Hundred instructed to investigate Indian policies; this work led to the Merriam Report of 1928, a report intensely critical of what the Dawes/ assimilationist policies had achieved (or failed to achieve), and a prime mover in the change in federal Indian policy that would occur in the thirties. Eastman was a founder and a strong supporter of the Boy Scout movement, in which American youth were to have "Indian" outdoor experiences, but he came increasingly to believe that Native values and knowledge might also have a place in adult Americans' experience. In the 1930s, Eastman spent most of his time living simply in a forest cabin in Ontario, a move, as Hertha Wong has noted, from "civilization" to the "deep woods," and a reversal of the title of his autobiography of 1916, From the Deep Woods to Civilization.[2] *Most recently, Erik Peterson has argued that, for all the "assimilationist" content of this text, it has a structure that very much parallels that of traditional Lakota oral narratives.[3]*

The selections included here are chapters 1, 3, and 6, "The Way Opens," "On the White Man's Trail," and "A Doctor Among the Indians." The source of the text is From the Deep Woods to Civilization: Chapters in the Autobiography of an Indian, *which was first published in 1916 and is now available in a Bison Paperback from the University of Nebraska Press.*

The Way Opens

One can never be sure of what a day may bring to pass. At the age of fifteen years, the deepening current of my life swung upon such a pivotal day, and in the twinkling of an eye its whole course was utterly changed; as if a little mountain brook should pause and turn upon itself to gather strength for the long journey toward an unknown ocean.

From childhood I was consciously trained to be a man; that was,

2. Hertha Wong, *Sending My Heart Back Across the Years: Tradition and Innovation in Native American Autobiography* (New York: Oxford Univ. Press, 1992).

3. Erik Peterson, "An Indian, An American: Ethnicity, Assimilation, and Balance in Charles Eastman's 'From the Deep Woods to Civilization,' " *Studies in American Indian Literatures* 4 (1992): 145–60.

after all, the basic thing; but after this I was trained to be a warrior and a hunter, and not to care for money or possessions, but to be in the broadest sense a public servant. After arriving at a reverent sense of the pervading presence of the Spirit and Giver of Life, and a deep consciousness of the brotherhood of man, the first thing for me to accomplish was to adapt myself perfectly to natural things—in other words, to harmonize myself with nature. To this end I was made to build a body both symmetrical and enduring—a house for the soul to live in—a sturdy house, defying the elements. I must have faith and patience; I must learn self-control and be able to maintain silence. I must do with as little as possible and start with nothing most of the time, because a true Indian always shares whatever he may possess.

I felt no hatred for our tribal foes. I looked upon them more as the college athlete regards his rivals from another college. There was no thought of destroying a nation, taking away their country or reducing the people to servitude, for my race rather honored and bestowed gifts upon their enemies at the next peaceful meeting, until they had adopted the usages of the white man's warfare for spoliation and conquest.

There was one unfortunate thing about my early training, however; that is, I was taught never to spare a citizen of the United States, although we were on friendly terms with the Canadian white men. The explanation is simple. My people had been turned out of some of the finest country in the world, now forming the great states of Minnesota and Iowa. The Americans pretended to buy the land at ten cents an acre, but never paid the price; the debt stands unpaid to this day. Because they did not pay, the Sioux protested; finally came the outbreak of 1862 in Minnesota, when many settlers were killed, and forthwith our people, such as were left alive, were driven by the troops into exile.

My father, who was among the fugitives in Canada, had been betrayed by a half-breed across the United States line, near what is now the city of Winnipeg. Some of the party were hanged at Fort Snelling, near St. Paul. We supposed, and, in fact, we were informed that all were hanged. This was why my uncle, in whose family I lived, had taught me never to spare a white man from the United States.

During the summer and winter of 1871, the band of Sioux to which I belonged—a clan of the Wah petons, or "Dwellers among the Leaves"—roamed in the upper Missouri region and along the Yellowstone River. In that year I tasted to the full the joy and plenty of wild existence. I saw buffalo, elk, and antelope in herds numbering thousands. The forests teemed with deer, and in the "Bad Lands" dwelt the Big Horns or Rocky Mountain sheep. At this period, grizzly bears were numerous and were brought into camp quite commonly, like any other game.

We frequently met and camped with the Hudson Bay half-breeds in their summer hunt of the buffalo, and we were on terms of friendship with the Assiniboines and the Crees, but in frequent collision with the Blackfeet, the Gros Ventres, and the Crows. However, there were times of truce when all met in peace for a great midsummer festival and exchange of gifts. The Sioux roamed over an area nearly a thousand miles in extent. In the summer we gathered together in large numbers, but towards fall we would divide into small groups or bands and scatter for the trapping and the winter hunt. Most of us hugged the wooded river bottoms; some depended entirely upon the buffalo for food, while others, and among these my immediate kindred, hunted all kinds of game, and trapped and fished as well.

Thus I was trained thoroughly for an all-round out-door life and for all natural emergencies. I was a good rider and a good shot with the bow and arrow, alert and alive to everything that came within my ken. I had never known nor ever expected to know any life but this.

In the winter and summer of 1872, we drifted toward the southern part of what is now Manitoba. In this wild, rolling country I rapidly matured, and laid, as I supposed, the foundations of my life career, never dreaming of anything beyond this manful and honest, unhampered existence. My horse and my dog were my closest companions. I regarded them as brothers, and if there was a hereafter, I expected to meet them there. With them I went out daily into the wilderness to seek inspiration and store up strength for coming manhood. My teachers dreamed no more than I of any change in my prospects. I had now taken part in all our tribal activities except that of war, and was nearly old enough to be initiated into the ritual of the war-path. The world was full of natural rivalry; I was eager for the day.

I had attained the age of fifteen years and was about to enter into and realize a man's life, as we Indians understood it, when the change came. One fine September morning as I returned from the daily hunt, there seemed to be an unusual stir and excitement as I approached our camp. My faithful grandmother was on the watch and met me to break the news. "Your father has come—he whom we thought dead at the hands of the white men," she said.

It was a day of miracle in the deep Canadian wilderness, before the Canadian Pacific had been even dreamed of, while the Indian and the buffalo still held sway over the vast plains of Manitoba east of the Rocky Mountains. It was, perhaps, because he was my honored father that I lent my bewildered ear to his eloquent exposition of the so-called civilized life, or the way of the white man. I could not doubt my own father, so mysteriously come back to us, as it were, from the spirit land; yet there was a voice within saying to me, "A false life! a treacherous life!"

In accordance with my training, I asked few questions, although many arose in my mind. I simply tried silently to fit the new ideas like so many blocks into the pattern of my philosophy, while according to my untutored logic some did not seem to have straight sides or square corners to fit in with the cardinal principles of eternal justice. My father had been converted by Protestant missionaries, and he gave me a totally new vision of the white man, as a religious man and a kindly. But when he related how he had set apart every seventh day for religious duties and the worship of God, laying aside every other occupation on that day, I could not forbear exclaiming, "Father! and does he then forget God during the six days and do as he pleases?"

"Our own life, I will admit, is the best in a world of our own, such as we have enjoyed for ages," said my father. "But here is a race which has learned to weigh and measure everything, time and labor and the results of labor, and has learned to accumulate and preserve both wealth and the records of experience for future generations. You yourselves know and use some of the wonderful inventions of the white man, such as guns and gunpowder, knives and hatchets, garments of every description, and there are thousands of other things both beautiful and useful.

"Above all, they have their Great Teacher, whom they call Jesus, and he taught them to pass on their wisdom and knowledge to all other races. It is true that they have subdued and taught many peoples, and our own must eventually bow to this law; the sooner we accept their mode of life and follow their teaching, the better it will be for us all. I have thought much on this matter and such is my conclusion."

There was a mingling of admiration and indignation in my mind as I listened. My father's two brothers were still far from being convinced; but filial duty and affection overweighed all my prejudices. I was bound to go back with him as he desired me to do, and my grandmother and her only daughter accompanied us on the perilous journey.

The line between Canada and the United States was closely watched at this time by hostile Indians, therefore my father thought it best to make a dash for Devil's Lake, in North Dakota, where he could get assistance if necessary. He knew Major Forbes, who was in command of the military post and the agency. Our guide we knew to be an unscrupulous man, who could easily betray us for a kettle of whisky or a pony. One of the first things I observed was my father's reading aloud from a book every morning and evening, followed by a very strange song and a prayer. Although all he said was in Indian, I did not understand it fully. He apparently talked aloud to the "Great Mystery," asking for our safe guidance back to his home in the States. The first reading of this book of which I have any recollection was the twenty-third Psalm, and the first hymn he sang in my presence was to the old tune of Ortonville. It was his Christian faith and devotion which was perhaps the strongest influence toward my change of heart and complete change of my purpose in life.

I think it was at our second encampment that we met a large caravan of Canadian half-breeds accompanied by a band of Northern Ojibways. As was usual with the former, they had plenty of whisky. They were friendly enough with us, at least while sober, but the Indians were not. Father showed them his papers as a United States citizen and a letter from Major Forbes, telling of his peaceful mission, but we could not trust our ancestral enemies, the Ojibways, especially when excited with strong drink. My father was calm and diplomatic throughout, but thus privately instructed me:

"My son, conceal yourself in the woods; and if the worst comes you must flee on your swift pony. Before daylight you can pass the deep woods and cross the Assiniboine River." He handed me a letter to Major Forbes. I said, "I will try," and as soon as it was dark, I hid myself, to be in readiness. Meanwhile, my father called the leading half-breeds together and told them again that he was under the protection of his government, also that the Sioux would hold them responsible if anything happened to us. Just then they discovered that another young brave and I were not to be found, which made them think that father had dispatched us to the nearest military post for help. They immediately led away their drunken comrades and made a big talk to their Ojibway friends, so that we remained undisturbed until morning.

Some days later, at the south end of Devil's Lake, I left our camp early to shoot some ducks when the morning flight should begin. Suddenly, when out of sight of the others, my eye caught a slight movement in the rank grass. Instinctively I dropped and flattened myself upon the ground, but soon a quick glance behind me showed plainly the head of a brave hidden behind a bush. I waited, trying to figure out some plan of escape, yet facing the probability that I was already surrounded, until I caught sight of another head almost in front and still another to my left.

In the moments that elapsed after I fully realized my situation, I thought of almost everything that had happened to me up to that day; of a remarkable escape from the Ojibways, of the wild pets I had had, and of my playmates in the Canadian camps whom I should never see again. I also thought with more curiosity than fear of the "Great Mystery" that I was so soon to enter. As these thoughts were passing through my mind, I carelessly moved and showed myself plainly to the enemy.

Suddenly, from behind the nearest bush, came the sound of my own Sioux tongue and the words, "Are you a Sioux?" Possibly my countenance may not have changed much, but certainly I grew weak with surprise and relief. As soon as I answered "Yes!" I was surrounded by a group of warriors of my tribe, who chuckled at the joke that had come so near to costing me my life, for one of them explained that he had been on the point of firing when I exposed myself so plainly that he saw I was not an Ojibway in war paint but probably a Sioux like himself.

After a variety of adventures, we arrived at the canvas city of Jamestown, then the terminal point of the Northern Pacific railroad. I was out watering the ponies when a terrific peal of thunder burst from a spotless blue sky, and indeed seemed to me to be running along the surface of the ground. The terrified ponies instantly stampeded, and I confess I was not far behind them, when a monster with one fiery eye poked his head around a corner of the hill. When we reached camp, my father kindly explained, and I was greatly relieved.

It was a peaceful Indian summer day when we reached Flandreau, in Dakota Territory, the citizen Indian settlement, and found the whole community gathered together to congratulate and welcome us home.

On the White Man's Trail

It was in the fall of 1874 that I started from Flandreau, then only an Indian settlement, with a good neighbor of ours on his way to Santee. There were only a dozen houses or so at Sioux Falls, and the whole country was practically uninhabited, when we embarked in a homemade prairie schooner, on that bright September morning.

I had still my Hudson Bay flintlock gun, which I had brought down with me from Canada the year before. I took that old companion, with my shot-pouch and a well-filled powder-horn. All I had besides was a blanket, and an extra shirt. I wore my hunting suit, which was a compromise between Indian attire and a frontiersman's outfit. I was about sixteen years old and small of my age.

"Remember, my boy, it is the same as if I sent you on your first war-path. I shall expect you to conquer," was my father's farewell. My good grandmother, who had brought me up as a motherless child, bestowed upon me her blessing. "Always remember," said she, "that the Great Mystery is good; evil can come only from ourselves!" Thus I parted with my first teacher—the woman who taught me to pray!

Our first night out was at Hole-in-the-Hill, one of the most picturesque spots in the valley. Here I brought in a doe, which I had come upon in the tall grass of the river bottom. Peter shot several ducks, and we had a good supper. It seemed to me more like one of our regular fall hunts than like going away to school.

After supper I said, "I am going to set some of your traps, uncle."

"And I will go with you, " replied Peter. "But before we go, we must have our prayer," and he took out his Bible and hymn-book printed in the Indian tongue.

It was all odd enough to me, for although my father did the same, I had not yet become thoroughly used to such things. Nevertheless, it was the new era for the Indian; and while we were still seated on the ground around the central fire of the Sioux teepee, and had just finished our repast of wild game, Peter read from the good book, and performed the devotional exercises of his teepee home, with quite as much zeal as if he were within four walls and surrounded by civilized things. I was very much impressed when this primitive Christian prayed that I might succeed in my new undertaking.

The next morning was frosty, and after an early breakfast we hurried to our traps. I got two fine minks and a beaver for my trouble, while Peter came home smiling with two otters and three beaver. I saw that he had something on his mind, but, like a true Indian, I held my peace. At last he broke the news to me—he had changed his mind about going to Santee agency!

I did not blame him—it was hard to leave such a trapper's paradise as this, alive with signs of otter, mink, and beaver. I said nothing, but thought swiftly. The temptation was strong to remain and trap too. That would please my grandmother; and I will confess here that no lover is more keen to do the right thing for the loved one than I was at that time to please my old grandmother.

Charles Alexander Eastman at Knox College, 1880.

The thought of my father's wish kept me on my true course. Leaving my gun with Peter, I took my blanket on my back and started for the Missouri on foot.

"Tell my father," I said, "that I shall not return until I finish my war-path."

But the voice of the waterfall, near what is now the city of Sioux Falls, sounded like the spirits of woods and water crying for their lost playmate, and I thought for a moment of turning back to Canada, there to regain my freedom and wild life. Still, I had sent word to my father that this war-path should be completed, and I remembered how he had said that if I did not return, he would shed proud tears.

About this time I did some of the hardest thinking that I have ever done in my life. All day I traveled, and did not see any one until, late in the afternoon, descending into the valley of a stream, I came suddenly upon a solitary farm-house of sod, and was met by a white man—a man with much hair on his face.

I was hungry and thirsty as a moose in burned timber. I had some money that my father had given me—I hardly knew the different denominations; so I showed the man all of it, and told him by signs that he might take what he pleased if only he would let me have something to eat, and a little food to carry with me. As for lodging, I would not have slept in his house if he had promised me a war-bonnet!

While he was cordial—at any rate, after I exhibited my money— there was something about his manner that did not put me at my ease, and my wild instincts told me to keep an eye on him. But I was not alone in this policy, for his flock of four daughters and a son nearly put their necks out of joint in following my modest, shy movements.

When they invited me to sit down with them at the table, I felt uncomfortable, but hunger was stronger than my fears and modesty. The climax came when I took my seat on a rickety stool between the big, hairy man and one of his well-grown daughters. I felt not unlike a young blue heron just leaving the nest to partake of his first meal on an unsafe, swinging branch. I was entirely uncertain of my perch.

All at once, without warning, the man struck the table with the butt of his knife with such force that I jumped and was within an ace of giving a war-whoop. In spite of their taking a firm hold of the home-made table to keep it steady, the dishes were quivering, and the young ladies no longer able to maintain their composure. Severe glances from mother and father soon brought us calm, when it appeared that the blow on the table was merely a signal for quiet before saying grace. I pulled myself in, much as a turtle would do, and possibly it should be credited to the stoicism of my race that I scarcely ever ate a heartier meal.

After supper I got up and held out to the farmer nearly all the money I had. I did not care whether he took it all or not. I was grateful for the food, and money had no such hold on my mind as it has gained since. To my astonishment, he simply smiled, shook his head, and stroked his shaggy beard.

I was invited to join the family in the sod-house parlor, but owing to the severe nerve-shocks that I had experienced at the supper-table, I respectfully declined, and betook myself to the bank of the stream near by, where I sat down to meditate. Presently there pealed forth a peculiar, weird music, and the words of a strange song. It was music from a melodeon, but I did not then know what that was; and the tune was "Nearer, my God, to Thee." Strange as it sounded to me, I felt that there was something soothing and gentle about the music and the voices.

After a while curiosity led me back to the sod house, and I saw for the first time how the white woman pumps so much air into a box that when she presses on the top boards it howls convulsively. I forgot my bashfulness so far as to listen openly and enjoy the operation, wondering much how the white man puts a pair of lungs into a box, which is furnished with a whole set of black and white teeth, and when he sings to it, it appears to answer him.

Presently I walked over to a shed where the farmer seemed to be very busy with his son, earnestly hammering something with all their might in the midst of glowing fire and sparks. He had an old breaking-plow which he was putting into shape on his rude forge. With sleeves rolled up, face and hands blackened and streaming with sweat, I thought he looked not unlike a successful warrior just returned from the field of battle. His powerful muscles and the manly way in which he handled the iron impressed me tremendously. "I shall learn that profession if ever I reach the school and learn the white man's way," I thought.

I thanked the good man for his kind invitation to sleep within the sod walls with all his family, but signed to him that I preferred to sleep out-of-doors. I could see some distrust in his eyes, for his horses were in the open stable; and at that my temper rose, but I managed to control it. He had been kind to me, and no Indian will break the law of hospitality unless he has lost all the trails of his people. The man looked me over again carefully, and appeared satisfied; and I rolled myself up in my blanket among the willows, but every star that night seemed to be bent upon telling the story of the white man.

I slept little, and early the next morning I was awakened by the barking of the farmer's collie and the laughter of his daughters. I got up and came to the house. Breakfast was nearly ready, and every member of the family was on hand. After breakfast I once more offered my money, but was refused. I was glad. Then and there I loved civilization and renounced my wild life.

I took up my blanket and continued on my journey, which for three days was a lonely one. I had nothing with which to kill any game, so I stopped now and then at a sod house for food. When I reached the back hills of the Missouri, there lay before me a long slope leading to the river bottom, and upon the broad flat, as far as my eyes could reach, lay farm-houses and farms. Ah! I thought, this is the way of civilization, the basis upon which it rests! I desired to know that life.

Thirty miles from the school I met Dr. Riggs on the road, coming to the town of Yankton, and received some encouraging words from him, for he spoke the Sioux language very well. A little further on I met the Indian agent, Major Sears, a Quaker, and he, too, gave me a word of encouragement when he learned that I had walked a hundred and fifty miles to school. My older brother John, who was then assistant teacher and studying under Dr. Riggs, met me at the school and introduced me to my new life.

The bell of the old chapel at Santee summoned the pupils to class. Our principal read aloud from a large book and offered prayer. Although he conducted devotional exercises in the Sioux language, the subject matter was still strange, and the names he used were unintelligible to me. "Jesus" and "Jehovah" fell upon my ears as mere meaningless sounds.

I understood that he was praying to the "Great Mystery" that the work of the day might be blessed and their labor be fruitful. A cold sweat came out upon me as I heard him ask the "Great Mystery" to be with us in that day's work in that school building. I thought it was too much to ask of Him. I had been taught that the Supreme Being is only concerned with spirits, and that when one wishes to commune with Him in nature he must be in a spiritual attitude, and must retire from human sound or influence, alone in the wilderness. Here for the first time I heard Him addressed openly in the presence of a house full of young men and young girls!

All the scholars were ordered to various rooms under different instructors, and I was left in the chapel with another long-haired young man. He was a Mandan from Fort Berthold—one of our ancient enemies. Not more than two years before that time my uncle had been on the war-path against this tribe and had brought home two Mandan scalps. He, too, was a new scholar, and looked as if he were about to come before the judge to receive his sentence. My heart at once went out to him, although the other pupils were all of my own tribe, the Sioux. I noticed that he had beautiful long hair arranged in two plaits, and in spite of his sad face he was noble-looking and appeared to great advantage, I thought, in contrast with the other pupils, whose hair was cut short and their garments not becoming to them at all. This boy, Alfred Mandan, became a very good friend of mine.

Dr. Riggs took me in hand and told me the rules of the school and what was expected of us. There was the chapel, which was used as a church every Sunday and as a schoolhouse on week days. There was the Dakota Home for the girls' dormitory—a small, square frame building—and for the boys a long log house some two hundred yards from the chapel under the large cottonwood-trees.

Dr. Riggs said that I need not study that first day, but could fill up the big bag he brought me with straw from the straw pile back of his barn. I carried it over to the log cabin, where the Doctor was before me and had provided a bunk or framework for my bed. I filled a smaller bag for a pillow, and, having received the sheets and blankets, I made my first white man's bed under his supervision. When it was done it looked clean and dignified enough for any one, I thought.

He said that I must make it every morning like that before going to school. "And for your wash, there is a tin basin or two on a bench just outside of the door, by the water-barrels." And so it was. We had three barrels of Missouri River water, which we ourselves filled up every week, for we boys had to furnish our own water and wood, and were detailed in pairs for this work.

Dr. Riggs supplied axes for the wood-choppers, and barrels and pails for the water-carriers, also a yoke of large and gentle white oxen and a lumber-wagon. It seems to me that I never was better acquainted with two animals than with these two! I have done some of my solemnest thinking behind them. The Missouri River was about two miles from our log house, with a wide stretch of bottom land intervening, partly cottonwood timber and partly open meadow with tall grass. I could take a nap, or dance a war-dance, if I cared to do so, while they were carrying me to wood or to water.

Dr. Riggs gave me a little English primer to study, also one or two books in the Dakota language, which I had learned to read in the day-school. There was a translation of the Psalms, and of the Pilgrim's Progress. I must confess that at that time I would have preferred one of grandmother's evening stories, or my uncle's account of his day's experiences in the chase. I thought it was the dullest hunting I had ever known!

Toward evening a company of three young men arrived from up the river—to all appearance full-fledged warriors. Ah, it was good to see the handsome white, blue, and red blankets worn by these stately Sioux youths! I had not worn one since my return from Canada. My brother got me a suit of clothes, and had some one cut my hair, which was already over my ears, as it had not been touched since the year before. I felt like a wild goose with its wings clipped.

Next morning the day pupils emerged in every direction from the woods and deep ravines where the Indians had made their temporary homes, while we, the log-cabin boarders, came out in Indian file. The chapel bell was tolling as we reached the yard, when my attention was attracted to a pretty lass standing with her parents and Dr. Riggs near the Dakota Home. Then they separated and the father and mother came toward us, leaving the Doctor and the pretty Dakota maiden standing still. All at once the girl began to run toward her parents, screaming pitifully.

"Oh, I cannot, I cannot stay in the white man's house! I'll die, I'll die! Mamma! Mamma!"

The parents stopped and reasoned with the girl, but it was of no use. Then I saw them leading her back to the Dakota Home, in spite of her pleading and begging. The scene made my blood boil, and I suppressed with difficulty a strong desire to go to her aid.

How well I remember the first time we were called upon to recite! In the same primer class were Eagle-Crane, Kite, and their compatriot from up the river. For a whole week we youthful warriors were held up and harassed with words of three letters. Like raspberry bushes in the path, they tore, bled, and sweated us—those little words rat, cat, and so forth—until not a semblance of our native dignity and self-respect was left. And we were of just the age when the Indian youth is most on his dignity! Imagine the same fellows turned loose against Custer or Harney with anything like equal numbers and weapons, and those tried generals would feel like boys! We had been bred and trained to those things; but when we found ourselves within four walls and set to pick out words of three letters we were like novices upon snow-shoes—often flat on the ground.

I hardly think I was ever tired in my life until those first days of boarding-school. All day things seemed to come and pass with a wearisome regularity, like walking railway ties—the step was too short for me. At times I felt something of the fascination of the new life, and again there would arise in me a dogged resistance, and a voice seemed to be saying, "It is cowardly to depart from the old things!"

Aside from repeating and spelling words, we had to count and add imaginary amounts. We never had had any money to count, nor potatoes, nor turnips, nor bricks. Why, we valued nothing except honor; that cannot be purchased! It seemed now that everything must be measured in time or money or distance. And when the teacher placed before us a painted globe, and said that our world was like that—that upon such a thing our forefathers had roamed and hunted for untold ages, as it whirled and danced around the sun in space—I felt that my foothold was deserting me. All my savage training and philosophy was in the air, if these things were true.

Later on, when Dr. Riggs explained to us the industries of the white man, his thrift and forethought, we could see the reasonableness of it all. Economy is the able assistant of labor, and the two together produce great results. The systems and methods of business were of great interest to us, and especially the adoption of a medium of exchange.

The Doctor's own personality impressed us deeply, and his words of counsel and daily prayers, strange to us at first, in time found root in our minds. Next to my own father, this man did more than perhaps any other to make it possible for me to grasp the principles of true civilization. He also strengthened and developed in me that native strong ambition to win out, by sticking to whatever I might undertake. Associated with him was another man who influenced me powerfully toward Christian living. This was the Rev. Dr. John P. Williamson, the pioneer Presbyterian missionary. The world seemed gradually to unfold before me, and the desire to know all that the white man knows was the tremendous and prevailing thought in me, and was constantly growing upon me more and more.

My father wrote to me in the Dakota language for my encouragement. Dr. Riggs had told him that I was not afraid of books or of work, but rather determined to profit by them. "My son," he wrote, "I believe that an Indian can learn all that is in the books of the white man, so that he may be equal to them in the ways of the mind!"

I studied harder than most of the boys. Missionaries were poor, and the Government policy of education for the Indian had not then been developed. The white man in general had no use for the Indian. Sitting Bull and the Northern Cheyennes were still fighting in Wyoming and Montana, so that the outlook was not bright for me to pursue my studies among the whites, yet it was now my secret dream and ambition.

It was at Santee that I sawed my first cord of wood. Before long I had a little money of my own, for I sawed most of Dr. Riggs's own wood and some at the Dakota Home, besides other work for which I was paid. Although I could not understand or speak much English, at the end of my second year I could translate every word of my English studies into the native tongue, besides having read all that was then published in the Sioux. I had caught up with boys who had two or three years the start of me, and was now studying elementary algebra and geometry.

One day Dr. Riggs came to me and said that he had a way by which he could send me to Beloit, Wisconsin, to enter the preparatory department of Beloit College. This was a great opportunity, and I grasped it eagerly, though I had not yet lost my old timidity about venturing alone among the white people.

On the eve of departure, I received word from Flandreau that my father was dead, after only two days' illness. He was still in the prime of life and a tireless worker. This was a severe shock to me, but I felt even more strongly that I must carry out his wishes. It was clear that he who had sought me out among the wild tribes at the risk of his life, and set my feet in the new trail, should be obeyed to the end. I did not go back to my home, but in September, 1876, I started from Santee to Beloit to begin my serious studies.

A Doctor among the Indians

The Pine Ridge Indian agency was a bleak and desolate looking place in those days, more especially in a November dust storm such as that in which I arrived from Boston to take charge of the medical work of the reservation. In 1890 a "white doctor" who was also an Indian was something of a novelty, and I was afterward informed that there were many diverse speculations abroad as to my success or failure in this new rôle, but at the time I was unconscious of an audience. I was thirty-two years of age, but appeared much younger, athletic and vigorous, and alive with energy and enthusiasm.

After reporting to the Indian agent, I was shown to my quarters, which consisted of a bedroom, sitting room, office, and dispensary, all in one continuous barrack with the police quarters and the agent's offices. This barrack was a flimsy one-story affair built of warped cottonwood lumber, and the rude prairie winds whistled musically through the cracks. There was no carpet, no furniture save a plain desk and a couple of hard wooden chairs, and everything was coated with a quarter of an inch or so of fine Dakota dust. This did not disconcert me, however, as I myself was originally Dakota dust! An old-fashioned box stove was the only cheerful thing on the premises, and the first duty I performed was to myself. I built a roaring fire in the stove, and sat down for a few minutes to take a sort of inventory of the situation and my professional prospects.

I had not yet thought seriously of making a life contract with any young woman, and accordingly my place was at the agency mess where the unmarried employees took their meals. I recall that the cook at that time was a German, and the insistent sauerkraut and other German dishes were new to me and not especially appetizing.

After supper, as I sat alone in my dismal quarters fighting the first pangs of homesickness, an Indian softly opened the door and stepped in without knocking, in characteristic Indian fashion. My first caller was old Blue Horse, chief emeritus of the Loafer band, of which American Horse was the active chief. After greeting me in Sioux, he promptly produced his credentials, which consisted of well-worn papers that had been given him by various high military officers, from General Harney to General Crook, and were dated 1854 to 1877. Blue Horse had been, as he claimed, a friend to the white man, for he was one of the first Sioux army scouts, and also one of the first to cross the ocean with Buffalo Bill. The old man wanted nothing so much as an audience, and the tale of his exploits served to pass the evening. Some one had brought in a cot and an armful of blankets, and I was soon asleep.

Next morning I hunted up an Indian woman to assist in a general cleaning and overhauling of the premises. My first official act was to close up the "hole in the wall," like a ticket seller's window, through which my predecessors had been wont to deal out pills and potions to a crowd of patients standing in line, and put a sign outside the door telling them to come in.

It so happened that this was the day of the "Big Issue," on which thousands of Indians scattered over a reservation a hundred miles long by fifty wide, came to the agency for a weekly or fortnightly supply of rations, and it was a veritable "Wild West" array that greeted my astonished eyes. The streets and stores were alive with a motley crowd in picturesque garb, for all wore their best on these occasions. Every road leading to the agency was filled with white-topped lumber wagons, with here and there a more primitive travois, and young men and women on ponies' backs were gaily curvetting over the hills. The Sioux belle of that period was arrayed in grass-green or bright purple calico, loaded down with beads and bangles, and sat astride a spotted pony, holding over her glossy uncovered braids and vermilion-tinted cheeks a gaily colored silk parasol.

Toward noon, the whole population moved out two or three miles to a large corral in the midst of a broad prairie, where a herd of beef cattle was held in readiness by the agency cowboys. An Indian with stentorian voice, mounted on a post, announced the names of the group whose steer was to be turned loose. Next moment the flying animal was pursued by two or three swift riders with rifles across their saddles. As the cattle were turned out in quick succession, we soon had a good imitation of the old time buffalo hunt. The galloping, long-horned steers were chased madly in every direction, amid yells and whoops, the firing of guns and clouds of yellow dust, with here and there a puff of smoke and a dull report as one stumbled and fell.

The excitement was soon over, and men of each group were busy skinning the animals, dressing the meat and dividing it among the families interested. Meanwhile the older women, sack in hand, approached the commissary, where they received their regular dole of flour, bacon, coffee, and sugar. Fires were soon blazing merrily in the various temporary camps scattered over the prairie and in the creek bottoms, and after dinner, horse races and dancing were features of the day. Many white sight-seers from adjoining towns were usually on hand. Before night, most of the people had set off in a cloud of dust for their distant homes.

It is no wonder that I was kept on my feet giving out medicine throughout that day, as if from a lemonade stand at a fair. It was evident that many were merely seeking an excuse to have a look at the "Indian white doctor." Most of them diagnosed their own cases and called for some particular drug or ointment; a mixture of cod liver oil and alcohol was a favorite. It surprised them that I insisted upon examining each patient and questioning him in plain Sioux—no interpreter needed! I made a record of the interesting cases and took note of the place where they were encamped, planning to visit as many as possible in their teepees before they took again to the road.

The children of the large Government boarding school were allowed to visit their parents on issue day, and when the parting moment came, there were some pathetic scenes. It was one of my routine duties to give written excuses from school when necessary on the ground of illness, and these excuses were in much demand from lonely mothers and homesick little ones. As a last resort, the mother herself would sometimes plead illness and the need of her boy or girl for a few days at home. I was of course wholly in sympathy with the policy of education for the Indian children, yet by no means hardened to the exhibition of natural feeling. I would argue the matter with the parents as tactfully as I could; but if nothing else could win the coveted paper, the grandmother was apt to be pressed into the service, and her verbal ammunition seemed inexhaustible.

Captain Sword, the dignified and intelligent head of the Indian police force, was very friendly, and soon found time to give me a great deal of information about the place and the people. He said finally:

"Kola (my friend), the people are very glad that you have come. You have begun well; we Indians are all your friends. But I fear that we are going to have trouble. I must tell you that a new religion has been proclaimed by some Indians in the Rocky Mountain region, and some time ago, Sitting Bull sent several of his men to investigate. We hear that they have come back, saying that they saw the prophet, or Messiah, who told them that he is God's Son whom He has sent into the world a second time. He told them that He had waited nearly two thousand years for the white men to carry out His teachings, but instead they had destroyed helpless small nations to satisfy their own selfish greed. Therefore He had come again, this time as a Savior to the red people. If they would follow His instructions exactly, in a little while He would cause the earth to shake and destroy all the cities of the white man, when famine and pestilence would come to finish the work. The Indians must live entirely by themselves in their teepees so that the earthquake would not harm them. They must fast and pray and keep up a holy or spirit dance that He taught them. He also ordered them to give up the white man's clothing and make shirts and dresses in the old style.

"My friend," Sword went on, "our reservation has been free from this new teaching until the last few weeks. Quite lately this ghost dance was introduced by Slow Bull and Kicking Bear from Rosebud"—a neighboring agency. "It has been rapidly gaining converts in many of the camps. This is what the council to-day was about. The agent says that the Great Father at Washington wishes it stopped. I fear the people will not stop. I fear trouble, kola."

I listened in silence, for I was taken entirely by surprise. Shortly afterward, the agent himself, a new man and a political appointee, approached me on the same matter. "I tell you, doctor," he began, after an exchange of greetings, "I am mighty glad you came here at just this time. We have a most difficult situation to handle, but those men down in Washington don't seem to realize the facts. If I had my way, I would have had troops here before this," he declared with emphasis. "This Ghost dance craze is the worst thing that has ever taken hold of the Indian race. It is going like wild fire among the tribes, and right here and now the people are beginning to defy my authority, and my Indian police seem to be powerless. I expect every employee on the agency to do his or her best to avert an outbreak." I assured him that he might count on me. "I shall talk to you more fully on the subject as soon as you are settled," he concluded.

I began to think the situation must be serious, and decided to consult some of the educated and Christian Indians. At this juncture a policeman appeared with a note, and handed me my orders, as I supposed. But when I opened it, I read a gracefully worded welcome and invitation to a tea party at the rectory, "to celebrate," the writer said, "my birthday, and your coming to Pine Ridge." I was caught up by the wind of destiny, but at the moment my only thought was of plea-sure in the prospect of soon meeting the Reverend Charles Smith Cook, the Episcopal missionary. He was a Yankton Sioux, a graduate of Trinity College and Seabury Divinity School, and I felt sure that I should find in him a congenial friend.

I looked forward to the evening with a peculiar interest. Mr. Cook was delightful, and so was his gracious young wife, who had been a New York girl. She had a sweet voice and was a trained musician. They had a little boy three or four years old. Then I met several young ladies, teachers in the boarding school, and a young man or two, and finally Miss Elaine Goodale, who was not entirely a stranger, as I had read her "Apple Blossoms" in Boston, and some of her later articles on Indian education in the *Independent* and elsewhere. Miss Goodale was supervisor of Indian schools in the Dakotas and Nebraska, and she was then at Pine Ridge on a tour of inspection. She was young for such a responsible position, but appeared equal to it in mentality and experience. I thought her very dignified and reserved, but this first evening's acquaintance showed me that she was thoroughly in ear-nest and absolutely sincere in her work for the Indians. I might as well admit that her personality impressed me deeply. I had laid my plans carefully, and purposed to serve my race for a few years in my profession, after which I would go to some city to practice, and I had decided that it would be wise not to think of marriage for the present. I had not given due weight to the possibility of love.

Events now crowded fast upon one another. It would seem enough that I had at last realized the dream of my life—to be of some service to my people—an ambition implanted by my earlier Indian teachers and fostered by my missionary training. I was really happy in devot-ing myself mind and body to my hundreds of patients who left me but few leisure moments. I soon found it absolutely necessary to have some help in the dispensary, and I enlisted the aid of George Gra-ham, a Scotch half-breed, and a simple, friendly fellow. I soon taught him to put up the common salves and ointments, the cough syrups and other mixtures which were in most frequent demand. Together we scoured the shelves from top to bottom and prepared as best we could for the issue day crowds.

After the second "Big Issue," I had another call from Captain Sword. He began, I believe, by complimenting me upon a very busy day. "Your reputation," he declared, "has already travelled the length and breadth of the reservation. You treat everybody alike, and your directions are understood by the people. No Government doctor has ever gone freely among them before. It is a new order of things.

Charles Alexander Eastman with guide and bark canoe, on Rainy Lake, Ontario.

But I fear you have come at a bad time," he added seriously. "The Ghost dancers have not heeded the agent's advice and warning. They pay no attention to us policemen. The craze is spreading like a prairie fire, and the chiefs who are encouraging it do not even come to the agency. They send after their rations and remain at home. It looks bad."

"Do they really mean mischief?" I asked incredulously, for Mr. Cook and I had discussed the matter and agreed in thinking that if the attempt was not made to stop it by force, the craze would die out of itself before long.

"They say not, and that all they ask is to be let alone. They say the white man is not disturbed when he goes to church," Sword replied. "I must tell you, however, that the agent has just ordered the police to call in all Government employees with their families to the agency. This means that something is going to happen. I have heard that he will send for soldiers to come here to stop the Ghost dance. If so, there will be trouble."

As I was still too new to the situation to grasp it fully, I concluded that in my case the only thing for me to do was to apply myself diligently to my special work, and await the issue. I had arranged to give a course of simple talks on physiology and hygiene at the Government boarding school, and on the evening of my first talk, I came back to my quarters rather late, for I had been invited to join the teachers afterward in their reading circle, and had then seen Miss Goodale safe to the rectory.

I had given up two of my rooms to Colonel Lee, the census taker, and his wife, who could find no other shelter in the crowded state of the agency, and found them awaiting me.

"Well, doc," said the jolly Colonel, "I suppose you have fixed your eye on the prettiest of the school teachers by this time!"

"I should be a callous man if I hadn't," I laughed.

"That's the right spirit. And now, here's a big bundle the stage left for you. Open it up, doc; it may be some pies or Boston baked beans from your folks!"

The parcel contained a riding suit of corduroy lined with leather, and reversible, also a pair of laced riding-boots reaching to the thigh, a present from an old friend in Boston. Nothing could have been more timely, for I now spent a good part of my days and not a few nights in the saddle. I was called to the most distant parts of the reservation, and had bought a fine white horse, part Arabian, which I named "Jack Frost." When I called for George to saddle him the next morning, I was surprised to have him hesitate.

"Don't you think, doctor, you had better keep pretty close to the agency until things are a little more settled?" he asked.

"Why, George, what do you mean?"

"Well, this news that the troops have been sent for, whether it is true or not, is making a good deal of talk. No telling what some fool Indian may take it into his head to do next. Some of the white employees are not stopping at the agency, they are going right on to the railroad. I heard one man say there is going to be an Injin outbreak and he intends to get out while he can."

16
Impressions of an Indian Childhood

GERTRUDE BONNIN (ZITKALA ŠA)

A Dakota Sioux of the Yankton band, Gertrude Simmons Bonnin was born in 1876 and lived in a fairly traditional manner on the Yankton reservation for the first eight years of her life, at which point she decided to attend a Quaker school in Indiana. Renaming herself Zitkala Ša, "Red Bird," in her teens, she continued her education at Earlham College in Indiana, demonstrating a talent for oratory and the violin, while trying her hand at a variety of written forms of expression. After graduation from Earlham in 1897, she taught for two years at Captain Pratt's Carlisle Indian School, accompanying the Carlisle band to Paris in 1900, the year she enrolled at the Boston Conservatory of Music. This was also an important year for her literary career. Bonnin published three autobiographical essays in the January, February, and March issues of the Atlantic Monthly *that attracted sufficient attention for* Harper's Bazaar *to include her that April in a column called "Persons Who Interest Us."*

In 1901, her first book, Old Indian Legends, *was released by a Boston publisher, and, in that same year, Bonnin met Dr. Carlos Montezuma, a Yavapai, a graduate of Carlisle, and a well-known "Red Progressive." Although the two were sufficiently attracted to one another to become engaged for a time, they were too far apart in their beliefs—and, apparently, too stubborn—to stay together. Montezuma always considered Pratt his friend and mentor, for example, while Bonnin found Pratt pig-headed. Most divisive perhaps was the difference in their feelings about their Native heritage, feelings that ran very deep. Bonnin, for all her successes in the wider American world, wanted to be near and with Indian people; Montezuma, for all his commitment to the rights and advancement of Indians, was committed to his urban practice in Chicago.*

In 1902, Zitkala Ša married Raymond Bonnin, a Lakota, and an employee of the Indian Service. Although in 1913 she collaborated with William Hanson on the composition of an opera called Sun Dance *that premiered in Vernal, Utah,* the *rest of her life was largely spent as a public figure in various Indian rights organizations, from the Society of American Indians, whose secretary she became in 1916, to her founding of the National Council of American Indians in 1926, an organization dedicated to creating "increased interest in behalf of the Indians, and secur[ing] for them added recognition of their personal and property rights." She was the Council's only president until her death in 1938.*

It is important to note that Zitkala Ša's autobiographical work was over by the time she was twenty-five, and to note as well that those twenty-five years span a period of time from Custer through Wounded Knee and the Dawes era. I am suggesting—much more work needs to be done on Bonnin—that what we now call her feminism (she didn't call it that), her commitment to a personal independence and autonomy that would not be antithetical to community with her Indian brothers and sisters, is very unusual for Native intellectuals of that time. She was a success as an Indian woman in the white man's world, overcoming a double debility, and yet she would remain a "pagan": her essay of 1902, "Why I am a Pagan," was a shock to the Carlisle progressives and in every way an extraordinary document for the period.

The selections included here, from the Atlantic Monthly *of 1900, are Bonnin's chapters One and Seven, "My Mother," and "The Big Red Apples," from "Impressions of an Indian Childhood"; chapters One and Two, "The Land of Red Apples," and "The Cutting of My Long Hair," from "The School Days of an Indian Girl"; and chapters One to Four of "An Indian Teacher Among Indians."*[1]

My Mother

A wigwam of weather-stained canvas stood at the base of some irregularly ascending hills. A footpath wound its way gently down the sloping land till it reached the broad river bottom; creeping through the long swamp grasses that bent over it on either side, it came out on the edge of the Missouri.

Here, morning, noon, and evening, my mother came to draw water from the muddy stream for our household use. Always, when my mother started for the river, I stopped my play to run along with her. She was only of medium height. Often she was sad and silent, at which times her full arched lips were compressed into hard and bitter lines, and shadows fell under her black eyes. Then I clung to her hand and begged to know what made the tears fall.

"Hush; my little daughter must never talk about my tears"; and smiling through them, she patted my head and said, "Now let me

1. These are all currently available in Zitkala Ša, *American Indian Stories* (Glorieta, NM: Rio Grande Press, 1976).

Gertrude Bonnin, Zitkala-Śa. Yankton Sioux writer, musician, activist.

see how fast you can run today." Whereupon I tore away at my highest possible speed, with my long black hair blowing in the breeze.

I was a wild little girl of seven. Loosely clad in a slip of brown buckskin, and lightfooted with a pair of soft moccasins on my feet, I was as free as the wind that blew my hair, and no less spirited than a bounding deer. These were my mother's pride—my wild freedom and overflowing spirits. She taught me no fear save that of intruding myself upon others.

Having gone many paces ahead I stopped, panting for breath, and laughing with glee as my mother watched my every movement. I was not wholly conscious of myself, but was more keenly alive to the fire within. It was as if I were the activity, and my hands and feet were only experiments for my spirit to work upon.

Returning from the river, I tugged beside my mother, with my hand upon the bucket I believed I was carrying. One time, on such a return, I remember a bit of conversation we had. My grown-up cousin, Warca-Ziwin (Sunflower), who was then seventeen, always went to the river alone for water for her mother. Their wigwam was not far from ours; and I saw her daily going to and from the river. I admired my cousin greatly. So I said: "Mother, when I am tall as my cousin Warca-Ziwin, you shall not have to come for water. I will do it for you."

With a strange tremor in her voice which I could not understand, she answered, "If the paleface does not take away from us the river we drink."

"Mother, who is this bad paleface?" I asked.

"My little daughter, he is a sham—a sickly sham! The bronzed Dakota is the only real man."

I looked up into my mother's face while she spoke; and seeing her bite her lips, I knew she was unhappy. This aroused revenge in my small soul. Stamping my foot on the earth, I cried aloud, "I hate the paleface that makes my mother cry!"

Setting the pail of water on the ground, my mother stooped, and stretching her left hand out on the level with my eyes, she placed her other arm about me; she pointed to the hill where my uncle and my only sister lay buried.

"There is what the paleface has done! Since then your father too has been buried in a hill nearer the rising sun. We were once very happy. But the paleface has stolen our lands and driven us hither. Having defrauded us of our land, the paleface forced us away.

"Well, it happened on the day we moved camp that your sister and uncle were both very sick. Many others were ailing, but there seemed to be no help. We traveled many days and nights; not in the grand, happy way that we moved camp when I was a little girl, but we were driven, my child, driven like a herd of buffalo. With every step, your sister, who was not as large as you are now, shrieked with the painful jar until she was hoarse with crying. She grew more and more feverish. Her little hands and cheeks were burning hot. Her little lips were parched and dry, but she would not drink the water I gave her. Then I discovered that her throat was swollen and red. My poor child, how I cried with her because the Great Spirit had forgotten us!

"At last, when we reached this western country, on the first weary night your sister died. And soon your uncle died also, leaving a widow and an orphan daughter, your cousin Warca-Ziwin. Both your sister and uncle might have been happy with us today, had it not been for the heartless paleface."

My mother was silent the rest of the way to our wigwam. Though I saw no tears in her eyes, I knew that was because I was with her. She seldom wept before me.

The Big Red Apples

The first turning away from the easy, natural flow of my life occurred in an early spring. It was in my eighth year; in the month of March, I afterward learned. At this age I knew but one language, and that was my mother's native tongue.

From some of my playmates I heard that two paleface missionaries were in our village. They were from that class of white men who wore big hats and carried large hearts, they said. Running direct to my mother, I began to question her why these two strangers were among us. She told me, after I had teased much, that they had come to take away Indian boys and girls to the East. My mother did not seem to want me to talk about them. But in a day or two, I gleaned many wonderful stories from my playfellows concerning the strangers.

"Mother, my friend Judéwin is going home with the missionaries. She is going to a more beautiful country than ours; the palefaces told her so!" I said wistfully, wishing in my heart that I too might go.

Mother sat in a chair, and I was hanging on her knee. Within the last two seasons my big brother Dawée had returned from a three years' education in the East, and his coming back influenced my mother to take a farther step from her native way of living. First it was a change from the buffalo skin to the white man's canvas that covered our wigwam. Now she had given up her wigwam of slender poles, to live, a foreigner, in a home of clumsy logs.

"Yes, my child, several others besides Judéwin are going away with the palefaces. Your brother said the missionaries had inquired about his little sister," she said, watching my face very closely.

My heart thumped so hard against my breast, I wondered if she could hear it.

"Did he tell them to take me, mother?" I asked, fearing lest Dawée had forbidden the palefaces to see me, and that my hope of going to the Wonderland would be entirely blighted.

With a sad, slow smile, she answered: "There! I knew you were wishing to go, because Judéwin has filled your ears with the white man's lies. Don't believe a word they say! Their words are sweet, but, my child, their deeds are bitter. You will cry for me, but they will not

284

even soothe you. Stay with me, my little one! Your brother Dawée says that going East, away from your mother, is too hard an experience for his baby sister."

Thus my mother discouraged my curiosity about the lands beyond our eastern horizon; for it was not yet an ambition for Letters that was stirring me. But on the following day the missionaries did come to our very house. I spied them coming up the footpath leading to our cottage. A third man was with them, but he was not my brother Dawée. It was another, a young interpreter, a paleface who had a smattering of the Indian language. I was ready to run out to meet them, but I did not dare to displease my mother. With great glee, I jumped up and down on our ground floor. I begged my mother to open the door, that they would be sure to come to us. Alas! They came, they saw, and they conquered!

Judéwin had told me of the great tree where grew red, red apples; and how we could reach out our hands and pick all the red apples we could eat. I had never seen apple trees. I had never tasted more than a dozen red apples in my life; and when I heard of the orchards of the East, I was eager to roam among them. The missionaries smiled into my eyes and patted my head. I wondered how mother could say such hard words against him.

"Mother, ask them if little girls may have all the red apples they want, when they go East," I whispered aloud, in my excitement.

The interpreter heard me, and answered: "Yes, little girl, the nice red apples are for those who pick them; and you will have a ride on the iron horse if you go with these good people."

I had never seen a train, and he knew it.

"Mother, I am going East! I like big red apples, and I want to ride on the iron horse! Mother, say yes!" I pleaded.

My mother said nothing. The missionaries waited in silence; and my eyes began to blur with tears, though I struggled to choke them back. The corners of my mouth twitched, and my mother saw me.

"I am not ready to give you any word," she said to them. "Tomorrow I shall send you my answer by my son."

With this they left us. Alone with my mother, I yielded to my tears, and cried aloud, shaking my head so as not to hear what she was saying to me. This was the first time I had ever been so unwilling to give up my own desire that I refused to hearken to my mother's voice.

There was a solemn silence in our home that night. Before I went to bed I begged the Great Spirit to make my mother willing I should go with the missionaries.

The next morning came, and my mother called me to her side. "My daughter, do you still persist in wishing to leave your mother?" she asked.

"Oh, mother, it is not that I wish to leave you, but I want to see the wonderful Eastern land," I answered.

My dear old aunt came to our house that morning, and I heard her say, "Let her try it."

I hoped that, as usual, my aunt was pleading on my side. My brother Dawée came for mother's decision. I dropped my play, and crept close to my aunt.

"Yes, Dawée, my daughter, though she does not understand what it all means, is anxious to go. She will need an education when she is grown, for then there will be fewer real Dakotas, and many more palefaces. This tearing her away, so young, from her mother is necessary, if I would have her an educated woman. The palefaces, who owe us a large debt for stolen lands, have begun to pay a tardy justice in offering some education to our children. But I know my daughter must suffer keenly in this experiment. For her sake, I dread to tell you my reply to the missionaries. Go, tell them that they may take my little daughter, and that the Great Spirit shall not fail to reward them according to their hearts."

Wrapped in my heavy blanket, I walked with my mother to the carriage that was soon to take us to the iron horse. I was happy. I met my playmates, who were also wearing their best thick blankets. We showed one another our new beaded moccasins, and the width of the belts that girdled our new dresses. Soon we were being drawn rapidly away by the white man's horses. When I saw the lonely figure of my mother vanish in the distance, a sense of regret settled heavily upon me. I felt suddenly weak, as if I might fall limp to the ground. I was in the hands of strangers whom my mother did not fully trust. I no longer felt free to be myself, or to voice my own feelings. The tears trickled down my cheeks, and I buried my face in the folds of my blanket. Now the first step, parting me from my mother, was taken, and all my belated tears availed nothing.

Having driven thirty miles to the ferryboat, we crossed the Missouri in the evening. Then riding again a few miles eastward, we stopped before a massive brick building. I looked at it in amazement, and with a vague misgiving, for in our village I had never seen so large a house. Trembling with fear and distrust of the palefaces, my teeth chattering from the chilly ride, I crept noiselessly in my soft moccasins along the narrow hall, keeping very close to the bare wall. I was as frightened and bewildered as the captured young of a wild creature.

The Land of the Red Apples

There were eight in our party of bronzed children who were going East with the missionaries. Among us were three young braves, two tall girls, and we three little ones, Judéwin, Thowin, and I.

We had been very impatient to start on our journey to the Red Apple Country, which, we were told, lay a little beyond the great circular horizon of the Western prairie. Under a sky of rosy apples we dreamt of roaming as freely and happily as we had chased the cloud shadows on the Dakota plains. We had anticipated much pleasure from a ride on the iron horse, but the throngs of staring palefaces disturbed and troubled us.

On the train, fair women, with tottering babies on each arm, stopped their haste and scrutinized the children of absent mothers. Large men, with heavy bundles in their hands, halted near by, and riveted their glassy blue eyes upon us.

I sank deep into the corner of my seat, for I resented being watched. Directly in front of me, children who were no larger than I hung themselves upon the backs of their seats, with their bold white faces toward me. Sometimes they took their forefingers out of their mouths and pointed at my moccasined feet. Their mothers, instead of reproving such rude curiosity, looked closely at me, and attracted their children's further notice to my blanket. This embarrassed me, and kept me constantly on the verge of tears.

I sat perfectly still, with my eyes downcast, daring only now and then to shoot long glances around me. Chancing to turn to the window at my side, I was quite breathless upon seeing one familiar object. It was the telegraph pole which strode by at short paces. Very near my mother's dwelling, along the edge of a road thickly bordered with wild sunflowers, some poles like these had been planted by white men. Often I had stopped, on my way down the road, to hold my ear against the pole, and, hearing its low moaning, I used to wonder what the paleface had done to hurt it. Now I sat watching for each pole that glided by to be the last one.

In this way I had forgotten my uncomfortable surroundings, when I heard one of my comrades call out my name. I saw the missionary standing very near, tossing candies and gums into our midst. This amused us all, and we tried to see who could catch the most of the sweetmeats. The missionary's generous distribution of candies was impressed upon my memory by a disastrous result which followed. I had caught more than my share of candies and gums, and soon after our arrival at the school I had a chance to disgrace myself, which, I am ashamed to say, I did.

Though we rode several days inside of the iron horse, I do not recall a single thing about our luncheons.

It was night when we reached the school grounds. The lights from the windows of the large buildings fell upon some of the icicled trees that stood beneath them. We were led toward an open door, where the brightness of the lights within flooded out over the heads of the excited palefaces who blocked our way. My body trembled more from fear than from the snow I trod upon.

Entering the house, I stood close against the wall. The strong glaring light in the large whitewashed room dazzled my eyes. The noisy hurrying of hard shoes upon a bare wooden floor increased the whirring in my ears. My only safety seemed to be in keeping next to the wall. As I was wondering in which direction to escape from all this confusion, two warm hands grasped me firmly, and in the same moment I was tossed high in midair. A rosy-cheeked paleface woman caught me in her arms. I was both frightened and insulted by such trifling. I stared into her eyes, wishing her to let me stand on my own feet, but she jumped me up and down with increasing enthusiasm. My mother had never made a plaything of her wee daughter. Remembering this I began to cry aloud.

They misunderstood the cause of my tears, and placed me at a white table loaded with food. There our party were united again. As I did not hush my crying, one of the older ones whispered to me, "Wait until you are alone in the night."

It was very little I could swallow besides my sobs, that evening.

"Oh, I want my mother and my brother Dawée! I want to go to my aunt!" I pleaded; but the ears of the palefaces could not hear me.

From the table we were taken along an upward incline of wooden boxes, which I learned afterward to call a stairway. At the top was a quiet hall, dimly lighted. Many narrow beds were in one straight line down the entire length of the wall. In them lay sleeping brown faces, which peeped just out of the coverings. I was tucked into bed with one of the tall girls, because she talked to me in my mother tongue and seemed to soothe me.

I had arrived in the wonderful land of rosy skies, but I was not happy, as I had thought I should be. My long travel and the bewildering sights had exhausted me. I fell asleep, heaving deep, tired sobs. My tears were left to dry themselves in streaks, because neither my aunt nor my mother was near to wipe them away.

The Cutting of My Long Hair

The first day in the land of apples was a bitter-cold one; for the snow still covered the ground, and the trees were bare. A large bell rang for breakfast, its loud metallic voice crashing through the belfry overhead and into our sensitive ears. The annoying clatter of shoes on bare floors gave us no peace. The constant clash of harsh noises, with an undercurrent of many voices murmuring an unknown tongue, made a bedlam within which I was securely tied. And though my spirit tore itself in struggling for its lost freedom, all was useless.

A paleface woman, with white hair, came up after us. We were placed in a line of girls who were marching into the dining room. These were Indian girls, in stiff shoes and closely clinging dresses. The small girls wore sleeved aprons and shingled hair. As I walked noiselessly in my soft moccasins, I felt like sinking to the floor, for my blanket had been stripped from my shoulders. I looked hard at the Indian girls, who seemed not to care that they were even more immodestly dressed than I, in their tightly fitting clothes. While we marched in, the boys entered at an opposite door. I watched for the three young braves who came in our party. I spied them in the rear ranks, looking as uncomfortable as I felt.

A small bell was tapped, and each of the pupils drew a chair from under the table. Supposing this act meant they were to be seated, I pulled out mine and at once slipped into it from one side. But when I turned my head, I saw that I was the only one seated, and all the rest at our table remained standing. Just as I began to rise, looking shyly around to see how chairs were to be used, a second bell was sounded. All were seated at last, and I had to crawl back into my chair again. I heard a man's voice at one end of the hall, and I looked around to see him. But all the others hung their heads over their plates. As I glanced at the long chain of tables, I caught the eyes of a paleface woman upon me. Immediately I dropped my eyes, wondering why I was so keenly watched by the strange woman. The man ceased his mutterings, and then a third bell was tapped. Every one picked up his knife and fork and began eating. I began crying instead, for by this time I was afraid to venture anything more.

But this eating by formula was not the hardest trial in that first day. Late in the morning, my friend Judéwin gave me a terrible warning. Judéwin knew a few words of English; and she had overheard the paleface woman talk about cutting our long, heavy hair. Our mothers had taught us that only unskilled warriors who were captured had their hair shingled by the enemy. Among our people, short hair was worn by mourners, and shingled hair by cowards!

We discussed our fate some moments, and when Judéwin said, "We have to submit, because they are strong," I rebelled.

"No, I will not submit! I will struggle first!" I answered.

I watched my chance, and when no one noticed I disappeared. I crept up the stairs as quietly as I could in my squeaking shoes,—my moccasins had been exchanged for shoes. Along the hall I passed, without knowing whither I was going. Turning aside to an open door, I found a large room with three white beds in it. The windows were covered with dark green curtains, which made the room very dim. Thankful that no one was there, I directed my steps toward the corner farthest from the door. On my hands and knees I crawled under the bed, and cuddled myself in the dark corner.

From my hiding place I peered out, shuddering with fear whenever I heard footsteps near by. Though in the hall loud voices were calling my name, and I knew that even Judéwin was searching for me, I did not open my mouth to answer. Then the steps were quickened and the voices became excited. The sounds came nearer and nearer. Women and girls entered the room. I held my breath and watched them open closet doors and peep behind large trunks. Some one threw up the curtains, and the room was filled with sudden light. What caused them to stoop and look under the bed I do not know. I remember being dragged out, though I resisted by kicking and scratching wildly. In spite of myself, I was carried downstairs and tied fast in a chair.

I cried aloud, shaking my head all the while until I felt the cold blades of the scissors against my neck, and heard them gnaw off one of my thick braids. Then I lost my spirit. Since the day I was taken from my mother I had suffered extreme indignities. People had stared at me. I had been tossed about in the air like a wooden puppet. And now my long hair was shingled like a coward's! In my anguish I moaned for my mother, but no one came to comfort me. Not a soul reasoned quietly with me, as my own mother used to do; for now I was only one of many little animals driven by a herder.

My First Day

Though an illness left me unable to continue my college course, my pride kept me from returning to my mother. Had she known of my worn condition, she would have said the white man's papers were not worth the freedom and health I had lost by them. Such a rebuke from my mother would have been unbearable, and as I felt then it would be far too true to be comfortable.

Since the winter when I had my first dreams about red apples I had been traveling slowly toward the morning horizon. There had been no doubt about the direction in which I wished to go to spend my energies in a work for the Indian race. Thus I had written my mother briefly, saying my plan for the year was to teach in an Eastern Indian school. Sending this message to her in the West, I started at once eastward.

Thus I found myself, tired and hot, in a black veiling of car smoke, as I stood wearily on a street corner of an old-fashioned town, waiting for a car. In a few moments more I should be on the school grounds, where a new work was ready for my inexperienced hands.

Upon entering the school campus, I was surprised at the thickly clustered buildings which made it a quaint little village, much more interesting than the town itself. The large trees among the house gave the place a cool, refreshing shade, and the grass a deeper green. Within this large court of grass and trees stood a low green pump. The queer boxlike case had a revolving handle on its side, which clanked and creaked constantly.

I made myself known, and was shown to my room—a small, carpeted room, with ghastly walls and ceiling. The two windows, both on the same side, were curtained with heavy muslin yellowed with age. A clean white bed was in one corner of the room, and opposite it was a square pine table covered with a black woolen blanket.

Without removing my hat from my head, I seated myself in one of the two stiff-backed chairs that were placed beside the table. For several heart throbs I sat still looking from ceiling to floor, from wall to wall, trying hard to imagine years of contentment there. Even while I was wondering if my exhausted strength would sustain me through this undertaking, I heard a heavy tread stop at my door. Opening it, I met the imposing figure of a stately gray-haired man. With a light straw hat in one hand, and the right hand extended for greeting, he smiled kindly upon me. For some reason I was awed by his wondrous height and his strong square shoulders, which I felt were a finger's length above my head.

I was always slight, and my serious illness in the early spring had made me look rather frail and languid. His quick eye measured my height and breadth. Then he looked into my face. I imagined that a visible shadow flitted across his countenance as he let my hand fall. I knew he was no other than my employer.

"Ah ha! so you are the little Indian girl who created the excitement among the college orators!" he said, more to himself than to me. I thought I heard a subtle note of disappointment in his voice. Looking in from where he stood, with one sweeping glance, he asked if I lacked anything for my room.

After he turned to go, I listened to his step until it grew faint and was lost in the distance. I was aware that my car-smoked appearance had not concealed the lines of pain on my face.

For a short moment my spirit laughed at my ill fortune, and I entertained the idea of exerting myself to make an improvement. But as I tossed my hat off a leaden weakness came over me, and I felt as if years of weariness lay like water-soaked logs upon me. I threw myself upon the bed, and, closing my eyes, forgot my good intention.

A Trip Westward

One sultry month I sat at a desk heaped up with work. Now, as I recall it, I wonder how I could have dared to disregard nature's warning with such recklessness. Fortunately, my inheritance of a marvelous endurance enabled me to bend without breaking.

Though I had gone to and fro, from my room to the office, in an unhappy silence, I was watched by those around me. On an early morning I was summoned to the superintendent's office. For a half-hour I listened to his words, and when I returned to my room I remembered one sentence above the rest. It was this: "I am going to turn you loose to pasture!" He was sending me West to gather Indian pupils for the school, and this was his way of expressing it.

I needed nourishment, but the midsummer's travel across the continent to search the hot prairies for overconfident parents who would intrust their children to strangers was a lean pasturage. However, I dwelt on the hope of seeing my mother. I tried to reason that a change was a rest. Within a couple of days I started toward my mother's home.

The intense heat and the sticky car smoke that followed my homeward trail did not noticeably restore my vitality. Hour after hour I gazed upon the country which was receding rapidly from me. I noticed the gradual expansion of the horizon as we emerged out of the forests into the plains. The great high buildings, whose towers overlooked the dense woodlands, and whose gigantic clusters formed large cities, diminished, together with the groves, until only little log cabins lay snugly in the bosom of the vast prairie. The cloud shadows which drifted about on the waving yellow of long-dried grasses thrilled me like the meeting of old friends.

At a small station, consisting of a single frame house with a rickety board walk around it, I alighted from the iron horse, just thirty miles from my mother and my brother Dawée. A strong hot wind seemed determined to blow my hat off, and return me to olden days when I roamed bareheaded over the hills. After the puffing engine of my train was gone, I stood on the platform in deep solitude. In the distance I saw the gently rolling land leap up into bare hills. At their bases a broad gray road was winding itself round about them until it came by the station. Among these hills I rode in a light conveyance, with a trusty driver, whose unkempt flaxen hair hung shaggy about his ears and his leather neck of reddish tan. From accident or decay he had lost one of his long front teeth.

Though I call him a paleface, his cheeks were of a brick red. His moist blue eyes, blurred and bloodshot, twitched involuntarily. For a long time he had driven through grass and snow from this solitary station to the Indian village. His weather-stained clothes fitted badly his warped shoulders. He was stooped, and his protruding chin, with its tuft of dry flax, nodded as monotonously as did the head of his faithful beast.

All the morning I looked about me, recognizing old familiar sky lines of rugged bluffs and round-topped hills. By the roadside I caught glimpses of various plants whose sweet roots were delicacies among my people. When I saw the first cone-shaped wigwam, I could not help uttering an exclamation which caused my driver a sudden jump out of his drowsy nodding.

At noon, as we drove through the eastern edge of the reservation, I grew very impatient and restless. Constantly I wondered what my mother would say upon seeing her little daughter grown tall. I had not written her the day of my arrival, thinking I would surprise her. Crossing a ravine thicketed with low shrubs and plum bushes, we approached a large yellow acre of wild sunflowers. Just beyond this nature's garden we drew near to my mother's cottage. Close by the log cabin stood a little canvas-covered wigwam. The driver stopped in front of the open door, and in a long moment my mother appeared at the threshold.

I had expected her to run out to greet me, but she stood still, all the while staring at the weather-beaten man at my side. At length, when her loftiness became unbearable, I called to her, "Mother, why do you stop?"

This seemed to break the evil moment, and she hastened out to hold my head against her cheek.

"My daughter, what madness possessed you to bring home such a fellow?" she asked, pointing at the driver, who was fumbling in his pockets for change while he held the bill I gave him between his jagged teeth.

"Bring him! Why, no, mother, he has brought me! He is a driver!" I exclaimed.

Upon this revelation, my mother threw her arms about me and apologized for her mistaken inference. We laughed away the momentary hurt. Then she built a brisk fire on the ground in the tepee, and hung a blackened coffeepot on one of the prongs of a forked pole which leaned over the flames. Placing a pan on a heap of red embers, she baked some unleavened bread. This light luncheon she brought into the cabin, and arranged on a table covered with a checkered oilcloth.

My mother had never gone to school, and though she meant always to give up her own customs for such of the white man's ways as pleased her, she made only compromises. Her two windows, directly opposite each other, she curtained with a pink-flowered print. The naked logs were unstained, and rudely carved with the axe so as to fit into one another. The sod roof was trying to boast of tiny sunflowers, the seeds of which had probably been planted by the constant wind. As I leaned my head against the logs, I discovered the peculiar odor that I could not forget. The rains had soaked the earth and roof so that the smell of damp clay was but the natural breath of such a dwelling.

"Mother, why is not your house cemented? Do you have no interest in a more comfortable shelter?" I asked, when the apparent inconveniences of her home seemed to suggest indifference on her part.

"You forget, my child, that I am now old, and I do not work with beads any more. Your brother Dawée, too, has lost his position, and we are left without means to buy even a morsel of food," she replied.

Dawée was a government clerk in our reservation when I last heard from him. I was surprised upon hearing what my mother said concerning his lack of employment. Seeing the puzzled expression on my face, she continued: "Dawée! Oh, has he not told you that the Great Father at Washington sent a white son to take your brother's pen from him? Since then Dawée has not been able to make use of the education the Eastern school has given him."

I found no words with which to answer satisfactorily. I found no reason with which to cool my inflamed feelings.

Dawée was a whole day's journey off on the prairie, and my mother did not expect him until the next day. We were silent.

When, at length, I raised my head to hear more clearly the moaning of the wind in the corner logs, I noticed the daylight streaming into the dingy room through several places where the logs fitted unevenly. Turning to my mother, I urged her to tell me more about Dawée's trouble, but she only said: "Well, my daughter, this village has been these many winters a refuge for white robbers. The Indian cannot complain to the Great Father in Washington without suffering outrage for it here. Dawée tried to secure justice for our tribe in a small matter, and today you see the folly of it."

Again, though she stopped to hear what I might say, I was silent.

"My child, there is only one source of justice, and I have been praying steadfastly to the Great Spirit to avenge our wrongs," she said, seeing I did not move my lips.

My shattered energy was unable to hold longer any faith, and I cried out desperately: "Mother, don't pray again! The Great Spirit does not care if we live or die! Let us not look for good or justice: then we shall not be disappointed!"

"Sh! my child, do not talk so madly. There is Taku Iyotan Wasaka, to which I pray," she answered, as she stroked my head again as she used to do when I was a smaller child.

Retrospection

Leaving my mother, I returned to the school in the East. As months passed over me, I slowly comprehended that the large army of white teachers in Indian schools had a larger missionary creed than I had suspected.

It was one which included self-preservation quite as much as Indian education. When I saw an opium-eater holding a position as teacher of Indians, I did not understand what good was expected, until a Christian in power replied that this pumpkin-colored creature had a feeble mother to support. An inebriate paleface sat stupid in a doctor's chair, while Indian patients carried their ailments to untimely graves, because his fair wife was dependent upon him for her daily food.

I find it hard to count that white man a teacher who tortured an ambitious Indian youth by frequently reminding the brave changeling that he was nothing but a "government pauper."

Though I burned with indignation upon discovering on every side instances no less shameful than those I have mentioned, there was no present help. Even the few rare ones who have worked nobly for my race were powerless to choose workmen like themselves. To be sure, a man was sent from the Great Father to inspect Indian schools, but what he saw was usually the students' sample work *made* for exhibition. I was nettled by this sly cunning of the workmen who hoodwinked the Indian's pale Father at Washington.

My illness, which prevented the conclusion of my college course, together with my mother's stories of the encroaching frontier settlers, left me in no mood to strain my eyes in searching for latent good in my white co-workers.

At this stage of my own evolution, I was ready to curse men of small capacity for being the dwarfs their God had made them. In the process of my education I had lost all consciousness of the nature world about me. Thus, when a hidden rage took me to the small white-walled prison which I then called my room, I unknowingly turned away from my one salvation.

Alone in my room, I sat like the petrified Indian woman of whom my mother used to tell me. I wished my heart's burdens would turn me to unfeeling stone. But alive, in my tomb, I was destitute!

For the white man's papers I had given up my faith in the Great Spirit. For these same papers I had forgotten the healing in trees and brooks. On account of my mother's simple view of life, and my lack of any, I gave her up, also. I made no friends among the race of people I loathed. Like a slender tree, I had been uprooted from my mother, nature, and God. I was shorn of my branches, which had waved in sympathy and love for home and friends. The natural coat of bark which had protected my oversensitive nature was scraped off to the very quick.

296

Now a cold bare pole I seemed to be, planted in a strange earth. Still, I seemed to hope a day would come when my mute aching head, reared upward to the sky, would flash a zig-zag lightning across the heavens. With this dream of vent for a long-pent consciousness, I walked again amid the crowds.

At last, one weary day in the schoolroom, a new idea presented itself to me. It was a new way of solving the problem of my inner self. I liked it. Thus I resigned my position as teacher; and now I am in an Eastern city, following the long course of study I have set for myself. Now, as I look back upon the recent past, I see it from a distance, as a whole. I remember how, from morning till evening, many specimens of civilized peoples visited the Indian school. The city folks with canes and eyeglasses, the countrymen with sunburnt cheeks and clumsy feet, forgot their relative social ranks in an ignorant curiosity. Both sorts of these Christian palefaces were alike astounded at seeing the children of savage warriors so docile and industrious.

As answers to their shallow inquiries they received the students' sample work to look upon. Examining the neatly figured pages, and gazing upon the Indian girls and boys bending over their books, the white visitors walked out of the schoolhouse well satisfied: they were educating the children of the red man! They were paying a liberal fee to the government employees in whose able hands lay the small forest of Indian timber.

In this fashion many have passed idly through the Indian schools during the last decade, afterward to boast of their charity to the North American Indian. But few there are who have paused to question whether real life or long-lasting death lies beneath this semblance of civilization.

17

My People, the Sioux

LUTHER STANDING BEAR

As H. David Brumble has noted, Luther Standing Bear, whose boyhood name was "Plenty Kill," was "precisely of an age to allow [him] the traditional Oglala education, but none of its application."[1] Standing Bear gave his birth as 1868, although government records give the date as 1863. Like Ohiyesa, Standing Bear volunteered for the white man's school as an opportunity to show his bravery; he chose his name, as the reader will see, from a list chalked on the blackboard, touching that name with a pointer, as if he were counting coup. A member of the first class at the Carlisle Indian School, and, like many Carlisle Indians, generally an admirer of Richard Pratt, Standing Bear found himself able to get by in the world of the whites fairly well. Nonetheless, his experience increasingly made him critical of the hypocrisies of the dominant culture.

My People, the Sioux,[2] *from which our selections are taken, appeared in 1928, the year of the Meriam Report's extremely critical review of government Indian policy. Standing Bear's book, as Lynne O'Brien remarks, is not only an autobiography, but a "request for whites to recognize the Native American's intelligence, to grant him citizenship, and to allow him to take his rightful place in building the country's future."[3] Citizenship had in fact been granted in 1924, but Standing Bear continued to make this "request" in this and his subsequent volumes,* My Indian Boyhood *(1931) and* Land of the Spotted Eagle *(1933).*

Although William Powers has claimed that most of the book was written by a New York editor, rather than by Standing Bear himself, and although a great many of the details of the book are not confirmed by public documents (e.g., the record does not confirm Standing Bear's father's role at Wounded Knee as presented), I believe a case can be made for the ongoing usefulness, if not literal truthfulness of My People, the Sioux. *In this, as in so many areas of Native American literature, a good deal of work remains to be done.*

1. H. David Brumble, *American Indian Autobiography* (Berkeley: Univ. of California Press, 1988), p. 162.
2. Luther Standing Bear, *My People, the Sioux*, ed. E. A. Brinninstool (Lincoln: Univ. of Nebraska Press, 1975).
3. Lynne Woods O'Brien, *Plains Indian Autobiographies* (Boise, ID: Western Writers Series, 1973), p. 23.

I have chosen selections from Chapter 5, "My First Buffalo," Chapter 12, "The Sun Dance," and the concluding section of Chapter 26, "American Citizenship." It must be said again that Standing Bear is probably not the most reliable informant concerning buffalo hunting on the Plains, nor on the details of the Sun Dance; for the reader aware of this, however, his accounts may still be read with pleasure.

My First Buffalo

Once we were camped between the White River and a place known as Crow Butte. As usual, every one in camp seemed to be having a good time. One day I observed a great many horses near our camp. They were such beautiful animals, sleek and fat. I asked my stepmother where the horses came from. She told me the Great Father at Washington had sent them to be given to us. I was very happy, thinking I should get one, as I was now regarded as a young man.

A chief from each band was chosen to distribute the horses to his own people. As the name of each chief was called, he was given as many small sticks as there were horses allotted to his band. My father was called, and he received his bunch of sticks. Then he told all the young men who wanted horses to come to his tipi. As each man came in, he was given a stick, which signified that he was to receive a horse from my father when the animals had been turned over to the camp.

After he had given out all the sticks, there were still two young men without horses. But Father did not let them go away disappointed. He picked up two sticks and gave one to each man. He then said he would give them each a horse from his own herd, as he had already allotted all the animals which the Government was to present them.

Although we had nice ponies in our band, they were nothing as compared to the horses the Government sent. My father would have liked one of them himself, but he was a chief, and was obliged to look out for his people first. How different from the methods of the "big man" among the whites of this day and age! Before he gets in office he is ready to promise anything and everything to those who can put him there by their votes. But do they keep their promises? Well, I should say not! After they are elected, the first thing they do is to feather their own nests and that of their own families.

But the Indian chief, without any education, was at least honest.

When anything was sent to his band, they got it. His family did not come first. He received no salary. In case of war he was always found at the front, but when it came to receiving gifts, his place was in the rear. There was no hand-shaking, smiling, and "glad-handing" which meant nothing. The chief was dignified and sincere.

One day we boys heard some of the men talking about going to the agency. They said the Government had sent some spotted buffalo for the Indians. This was the name the Indians gave to the cows, there being no word in the Sioux tongue for the white man's cattle. Our own wild buffalo had been disappearing very rapidly, as the white people had been killing them as fast as possible. We were very happy to learn that we were to receive more meat, this being our main diet. We had heard about these spotted buffalo, but had never seen them.

So we got on our ponies and rode over to the agency with some of the men. What a terrible odor met us! It was awful! We had to hold our noses. Then I asked my father what was the matter around there, as the stench was more than I could stand. He told me it was the odor of the spotted buffalo. Then I asked him if we were going to be obliged to eat those terrible animals. "The white people eat them," was his reply.

Now we had several white people around us, but they were all bald-headed. I began to wonder if they got that way from eating those vile-smelling cattle. I then recalled that buzzards were bald-headed, and they lived on carrion, and I began to feel sorry for the white people who had to live on such stuff.

Each man was called to receive his cattle, and as they were driven out of the corral they were shot down. Here and there, all about, one could see cows lying where they had been shot down, as they did not care to drive them near their homes. They skinned the cow, cutting out the tenderest parts, and roasted it right there. This roasting killed most of the odor. Then they took the skin and traded it off for calicoes and paints. If they happened to cut the tail off while skinning the animal, and brought it to the trader later, he exchanged some candy for it, to give to the children. The Indians soon "wised up" to this, and thereafter demanded something for the tail, whether it was on the hide or off it.

Did you ever stop to think of the difference there is in meat that is killed while in a contented state, and meat that is carried in trains day after day on the hoof? Some of these poor animals stand so closely together in box cars that they have no room even to lie down and get rested, and if they do, they are poked in the ribs by men on the cars just for the purpose of keeping the animals on their feet. We knew the difference—which was the reason we could not eat this sort of meat when we first began to receive it.

In spite of the fact that we received plenty of beef and rations from the Government, we were hungry for buffalo meat, and we wanted the skins. So one day we left the agency without a permit. We were very independent in those days. We started for the northern part of Nebraska, as we knew that section to be good hunting-grounds.

I had been out with my father and grandfather many times on buffalo-hunts, but they had always attended to the killing, and I had only assisted in the eating afterward. But this time I was going as a hunter. I was determined to try to kill a buffalo all by myself if possible. My father had made me a special bow and some steel-pointed arrows with which to kill big game, and this was to be my first chance to see what sort of hunter I was.

A scout had been sent out, and one morning, very early, he reported that there were some buffalo near. Everybody, including myself, began to get ready. While one of my stepmothers was helping me, she said, "Son, when you kill a buffalo, save me the kidney and the skin." I didn't know whether she was trying to poke fun at me or to give me encouragement. But it made me feel proud to have her talk like that to me.

But my father always talked to me as if I were a man. Of course I now felt that I was big enough to do a man's work. The night before the hunt, my father instructed me as follows:

"My son, the land on which these buffalo have been found is reported not to be rough, and you will not have to chase the buffalo into dangerous places, as the land is very level. Whatever you do, watch the buffalo closely. If the one you are after is running straight ahead and not turning, then you can get in very close, and you will stand a good chance to shoot it in the heart. But if you observe the buffalo to be looking at you from the corner of its eye, then look out! They are very quick and powerful. They can get their horns under your horse and toss him high in the air, and you might get killed.

"If you hit in the right spot, you may kill the buffalo with only one arrow, but if not, you will have to use more. If your pony is not fast enough to catch up with the buffalo, the best thing you can do is to shoot an arrow right behind the small ribs. Perhaps it will reach the heart. If the buffalo runs down a hill or into a bank, then you have another chance. Shoot at the joint of the hips, then your buffalo will sit down and you can take your time to kill it.

"Keep your eyes open! In the beginning there will be lots of dust, but after you pass through that, it will be clear, and you will be able to see where you are going."

This was the first time I was to go on a hunt after such large animals. I had killed several small animals, but a buffalo is far from being a small creature, and you can imagine that I was greatly excited.

Early the next morning every one was ready for the start. I carried my bow in my hand, as there was not room for it in my quiver where I kept my arrows. I rode a little black mare, a very fine runner that could cover the ground like a deer.

Two men on beautiful horses rode in front of us. This was for the purpose of keeping order in the party. There was no chance of one man getting ahead of the others and scaring the game. We all had to keep together and stay behind these men.

They rode to the top of a hill where they could get a good look at the herd and figure if there was any better place from which to approach it. We always got as close to the buffalo as possible, because it makes the meat tough to run an animal any farther than necessary.

After looking at the herd from various positions, they chose what was considered the most advantageous spot. Here they cautioned the hunters to change to their running-horses and be all ready. I did not have to make any change, as the little black mare was all the animal I had. I saw some of the men tying their two braids of hair back, and others, who wore shirts, began rolling up their sleeves. They wanted their arms free once they began shooting. They fixed their quivers on the side instead of carrying them on the back. Nobody wore any feathers or carried any spears or lances.

The extra horses were hobbled and left in the charge of an old man. When the two riders gave the command, everybody started right up. Of course I was right at the front with them. I wanted to do something brave. I depended a great deal on my pony, as I knew she was sure-footed and could run as I wanted her to.

At the top of the hill, all the hunters turned their horses loose, and the animals started in running like the wind! I whipped up my little black mare and nearly got ahead of the others. Soon I was mixed up in the dust and could see nothing ahead of me. All I could hear was the roar and rattle of the hoofs of the buffalo as they thundered along. My pony shied this way and that, and I had to hold on for dear life.

For a time I did not even try to pull an arrow from my quiver, as I had all I could do to take care of myself. I knew if my pony went down and one of those big animals stepped on me, it would be my last day on earth. I then realized how helpless I was there in all that dust and confusion, with those ponderous buffalo all around me. The sound of their hoofs was frightening. My pony ran like the wind, while I just clung to her mane; but presently we came out of the dust.

Then I observed what my father had told me previously. I was quite a bit ahead of the buffalo now, and when they caught sight of me, they started running in two different directions. When I looked at those big animals and thought of trying to kill one of them, I realized how small I was. I was really afraid of them. Then I thought about what my stepmother had said to me about bringing her a kidney and a skin, and the feeling that I was a man, after all, came back to me; so I turned my pony toward the bunch which was running north. There was no dust now, and I knew where I was going.

I was all alone, and I was determined to chase them, whether I killed one or not. By this time I could hear shots fired by some of the hunters who carried guns, and I knew they were killing some. So I rode on after this small bunch, and when I dashed behind them, I pulled out one of my arrows and shot into the middle of them. I did not even know where my arrow went, and was just thinking of quitting when I observed a young heifer running slower than the others.

This encouraged me, so I whipped up my pony again and took after her. As I came close, she stopped and turned. Then she started running in another direction, but I saw she was losing fast. She was not as big as the others, so I was not afraid. I made up my mind I was going to kill that buffalo if it took all the arrows in my quiver.

I rode right up alongside the buffalo, just as my father had instructed me. Drawing an arrow from my quiver, and holding to my pony with all the strength of my legs, I fitted the arrow and let drive with all my strength. I had expected to kill the buffalo right quick, but the arrow went into the neck—and I thought I had taken such good aim! But the buffalo only shook her head and kept on running. I again caught up with her, and let another arrow loose, which struck near the heart. Although it was not fired with sufficient strength to kill at once, I saw that she was fast weakening and running much slower. Then I pulled my third arrow and fired again. This went into the heart. I began to think that buffalo had all the nine lives of a cat, and was going to prove about as hard as a cat to kill, when I saw blood running from her nose. Then I knew she would have to drop pretty soon. I shot my fourth arrow into her, and she staggered and dropped over on her side, and was soon dead. So I had killed my first buffalo.

When I examined the fallen animal and noted that I had shot five arrows into her, I felt that this was too many arrows for just one buffalo. Then I recalled that my father had once killed two buffalo with only a single arrow. He knew he had hit the first one in the right spot, as the arrow penetrated very deeply and he simply rode up alongside, drew the arrow through, pulled it out again and used it to kill the second one.

As I stood there thinking of this, it made me feel ashamed of my marksmanship. I began to think of pulling all the arrows out but one. In fact, I had started to do this, when a remark that my father had once made to me came into my head. It was, "Son, always remember that a man who tells lies is never liked by anybody." So, instead of trying to cheat, I told the truth; and it made me feel happier.

I took all the arrows out and started in to skin the buffalo. I was doing splendidly until I tried to turn the animal over. Then I discovered that it was too heavy a task for me. As I had but one side skinned I began to think of removing the kidney and cutting out a nice piece of meat for my stepmother. Just then I heard some one call me. I got on my pony and rode to the top of the hill. There I saw my father, who had been looking for me. He called to me, but I just rode back to my buffalo. He knew something had happened, so [he] came over, and then I pointed to the dead buffalo, lying there half-skinned.

He was so pleased that I had tried to do my best. Then I told him about the number of arrows I had had to use, and where each one had struck. I even told him how I had shot my first arrow into the whole bunch, not knowing where it had landed. He laughed, but he was proud of me. I guess it was because I had told the truth, and not tried to cheat or lie, even though I was just a youngster.

Then Father started in on my buffalo. He soon had it all skinned and butchered. He said he had been all ready to go home when he discovered I was missing. He had thought I was with my grandfather, while Grandfather thought I was with him. All that time I was having a hard job all by myself. When we reached home it made me very proud to be able to give my stepmother the skin and kidney. And she was pleased that I had done so well.

My father called the old man of the camp, who always acted as herald, to announce that "Ota Kte" (or "Plenty Kill") had shot his first buffalo, and that "Standing Bear," his father, was giving away a horse.

This was the first and last buffalo I ever killed, and it took five arrows to complete the job.

The Sun Dance

It was about the middle of the summer of 1879 that I saw the last great Sun Dance of the Sioux. The Brules were holding the dance about six miles southwest of Rosebud Agency, on the place where old Chief Two Strikes's band now have their allotments. As I started for Carlisle Indian School in the fall of 1879, I cannot say whether this was the last dance held or not.

I have read many descriptions of this dance, and I have been to different tribes which claimed they did the "real thing," but there is a great difference in their dances from the Sun Dance of the Sioux.

The Sun Dance started many years before Christopher Columbus drifted to these shores. We then knew that there was a God above us all. We called God "Wakan Tanka," or the "Big Holy," or sometimes "Grandfather." You call God Father. I bring this before you because I want you to know that this dance was our religious belief. According to our legend, the red man was to have this dance every summer, to fulfill our religious duty. It was a sacrificial dance.

During the winter if any member of the tribe became ill, perhaps a brother or a cousin would be brave enough to go to the medicine man and say, "I will sacrifice my body to the Wakan Tanka, or Big Holy, for the one who is sick." Or if the buffalo were beginning to get scarce, some one would sacrifice himself so that the tribe might have something to eat.

The medicine man would then take this brave up to the mountain alone, and announce to the Great Spirit that the young man was ready to be sacrificed. When the parents of this young man heard that he was to go through the Sun Dance, some of his brothers or cousins would sacrifice themselves with him as an honor.

If some young man of another band had the desire to go through the Sun Dance, some of his friends or relatives might offer to dance with him. Sometimes as many as thirty or forty braves went into the dance.

As soon as the women heard that there was to be a Sun Dance in their band, they began making all the things which were necessary for the ceremony. They placed beautiful porcupine-quill-work on the eagle-bone whistles which the men carried in their mouths during the dance, as well as beautiful head-dresses for the dancers. These were made from porcupine-quill-work. The dancer wore a piece of buckskin around the waist, hanging down like a skirt. This also had pretty quill-work decorations. Soon all the things were ready for the dance.

When the chiefs learned this dance was coming, they called a meeting and selected a place they thought as best suited to hold it. They then sent word to the other bands to get ready.

The main band would move to the place selected, and the other bands would come in one at a time, the boys and warriors mounted on ponies. They would all keep together until they were very near, when they would make an imitation charge on the camp, just as if it were an enemy camp.

After this "attack" they would all go up to a hill near by. Four men were then chosen who were to lead the parade. The warriors would now have a chance to show their beautiful war-ponies and good clothes. Then they would all parade into the village. Just about the time the parade was over, the rest of the camp would be moving in. The women would then be very busy erecting the tipis.

After the various bands had all arrived, there were some special tipis put up for those who were going to dance. These tipis were not erected in one place, but were sometimes considerably scattered. I have seen a camp of this sort which was a mile and a quarter in diameter. There were from four to six of these special tipis for the dancers. Everybody was allowed to go, and there was always plenty to eat in these tipis.

The first day all the people collected at the center of the camp and some scouts were selected to go out and look for the cottonwood pole which was to be used in the dance. After being chosen, these scouts retired to their tipis and dressed in their best clothes, mounted their war-ponies, and rode into the circle. Their parents gave away ponies and other pretty things as a token of respect that their sons had been chosen to act as scouts.

Among these scouts were one or two of the old-timers, who were to act as leaders. A fire was now built in the center of the circle, and the scouts rode their ponies around this fire three times, and, after the fourth time, they were off! They rode their ponies at full speed. All those on horseback rode as fast as they could and encircled the scouts as they went on.

The scouts would be gone about a half-hour. On their return they would come to the top of a hill and stop. The others in the camp would once more mount their ponies and ride out to meet the scouts. Then they would turn about and race back to the center of the circle, where they would wait for the scouts to ride in.

One of the old-timers would then relate how they had found a pole which was considered good enough to be used in the dance. Then everybody got ready to go to the place where the pole had been found.

All the various lodges of the tribe now gathered in the timber near the place where the pole was located. There was the White Horse, Bull, Fox, and Short Hair lodges. As each separate tribe had its form of ceremonies, each selected some of its people to go to the tree and "chop it." They did not really chop the tree, but just simply touched it. As they touched the tree, they gave away ponies or anything they wanted. They stayed here a long time, as they had plenty to eat all the time they were in the timber. If they knew a man who had plenty of ponies, they would select one of his children to come forward and touch the tree, and then he would give away a pony.

After all had finished their ceremonies, some one cut the tree down. There were about twenty men to carry this pole. They had long sticks which they put under it, and two men to a stick to carry it. Everybody was carrying something. Some carried forked branches, others limbs of the tree, etc. They had no one to order them around, but every one did his share toward this religious dance.

As the twenty men lifted the pole, they walked slowly toward the camp. The rest of the tribe trailed along behind. They stopped three times, and each time a medicine man howled like a wolf. The fourth time they stopped, all the men and boys raced their ponies as fast as they would go, trying to see who would be first to reach the center of the camp. Here they found the effigy of a man made from the limbs of trees. Each tried to be first to touch this. There would be plenty of dust as these men and boys rode in to attack this wooden man. Sometimes two ponies would run together, and then some one was likely to be hurt.

At last the men came in with the pole. Then the lodges had some more ceremonies to be gone through with, while some of the men started to dig the hole in which to set the pole. Others would get busy arranging forked poles in a circle. This circle was to serve as our hall.

When the hole was ready, all the men from the different lodges got together to help erect the pole, which was sometimes sixty or seventy feet long. They tied two braided rawhide ropes about the middle of the pole, on which some brave was to hang. Other ropes were to be used to hoist the pole into place. These hoisting ropes were tied in such a way as to be easily removed, after the pole was in the right position. We had no stepladders nor any men with climbers on to go up and untie any ropes that might be left up when the pole was in place.

When all was ready, some of the men used forked poles, some held on to the ropes, and others got hold of the pole. It required about forty men to do this work properly. The pole must be raised and dropped in the hole at one operation, and with no second lifting. Some pushed, others pulled, while the men with the forked sticks lifted. As the pole dropped into the hole, everybody cheered.

There was a strong superstition regarding this pole. It was believed that if the pole dropped before it was set into the hole, all our wishes and hopes would be shattered. There would be great thunder-storms and high winds; our shade or council hall would be blown away, and there would be no Sun Dance. On top of this, it was believed that the whole tribe would have a run of bad luck.

Consequently, when this pole was being erected, every man used all his strength to ward off any accident or mishap. We were taught to believe that if all minds worked together, it helped a great deal. We were taught this by our parents, and we had strong faith in it.

The pole was always a cottonwood tree, as I have previously stated. No other tree would do. It was not always a straight tree, but there was always a branch which extended out from the main trunk. This would be about thirty or forty feet up. This branch would be cut off about four feet from the trunk. On the top of the pole, branches with leaves on would be left.

They made a bundle of branches from the tree which were wrapped in bark and tied together. This bundle was placed in the branch which had been cut off about four feet from the trunk. When this bundle was in place, it looked not unlike a huge cross, when viewed from a distance.

From this cross-piece hung something which resembled a buffalo and a man. These effigies were cut from rawhide and were tied up with a rawhide rope. They were suspended about ten feet down from the bundle of wood or the cross-piece. Both were painted black, the paint being made from burned cottonwood mixed with buffalo fat.

Sometimes there was a small bundle of sticks painted in a variety of colors. At the end of each, a small bag made of buckskin and filled with tobacco was hung. All this was suspended to the cross-piece. Under the pole were many little bags of tobacco, tied on little sticks, as a prayer offering to the spirit.

About ten feet to the west of this cross lay the skull of a buffalo on a bed made of sagebrush. The horns were attached to this skull and it was laid facing the east. Behind the skull, about two feet, were two forked sticks stuck in the ground, with another stick across them. Against this the pipe of peace rested, with the stem pointing toward the east.

The real meaning of having the effigy of the buffalo hanging from the cross was a prayer to the Wakan-Tanka, or Big Holy, for more "pte," or buffalo meat. The effigy of the man meant that in case of war we were to have victory over our enemies.

When the main big pole was all completed, the men bent their energies toward the dancing-hall, or shade, as it should rightfully be called. All the forked poles were placed in a double circle, about fifteen feet apart, with an opening left toward the east. Long sticks were laid from one forked pole to another in the inner circle as well as the outside circle. We used no nails in those days, and anything that was to be fastened must be bound with rawhide or tied with bark. In this case, we peeled off the bark of the willow trees and used that to fasten the poles together. Then the longest tipi poles would be brought in, and laid from the inner to the outer circle. The outside wall was made from entwined branches, and on top would be laid the largest tipi coverings, which made a fine shade. This "shade" was about one hundred and fifty feet in diameter, with a depth of about fifteen feet. It was considered a great honor to have one's tipi covering chosen for this purpose.

After the shade was completed, if any one wanted to give a piece of buckskin, or some red or blue cloth, as an offering to the Great Spirit, he took a long stick and put a cross-piece on it, from which was suspended his offering. These pennants were hung all around the dance-shade. It quite resembled a great convention hall. Several beds of sagebrush were made for the dancers. Sometimes a big dance would precede the Sun Dance. This dance was known as "owanka ona sto wacipi," or "smoothing the floor." It was, in fact, a sort of "house-warming" affair, and was for the braves and young men only. Each carried a weapon and wore his best clothes. The crowd came in from all the different bands in the camp, forming in lines like soldiers as they appeared. Sometimes there were as many as fifteen abreast.

Then an old chief came forward with a scalp-lock tied to a pole. He danced before the others, facing them. When he danced backward, the others danced forward, and *vice versa*. When the old chief led them toward the pole, those carrying guns shot at the buffalo and the effigy of the man, hanging from the pole.

While this dance was in progress, different medicine men were in the tipis with the young men who were to do the Sun Dance. From each tipi came six, eight, and sometimes ten from a band to dance. There was a leader, who carried a pipe of peace; the others followed one by one. They wore buffalo robes with the hair outside, and quite resembled a band of buffalo coming to a stream to drink.

After these Sun Dance candidates reached the shade from their tipis, they did not go in immediately, but marched around the outside three times. After the fourth time, they went in and took their places. Then the medicine man came forward and took charge of four or eight of the dancers. Four of them must be painted alike. They put on beautiful head-dresses richly ornamented with porcupine quills. Their wrists were wound around with sagebrush, and the eagle-bone whistles they used were likewise decorated.

This was a very solemn affair. These men were to dance for three or four days, without food or water. Some of their relatives cried; others sang to praise them and make them feel courageous.

The singers were now in their places. They used no tom-tom, but sat around a large buffalo hide which lay flat on the ground, using large sticks to beat upon the dried skin.

The braves started dancing as soon as the sun started to rise. They stood facing the sun with both hands raised above their heads, the eagle-bone whistles in their mouths, and they blew on these every time the singers hit the skin with their sticks. All day long they stood in one position, facing the sun, until it set.

The sunflower was used by the Sioux in this dance. They cut out a piece of rawhide the shape of a sunflower, which they wore on a piece of braided buckskin suspended around the neck, with the flower resting on the breast. At that time I did not realize the significance of the sunflower, but now I know it is the only flower that follows the sun as it moves on its orbit, always facing it.

The dance would be kept up until one of the participants fainted, then he was laid out on one of the sagebrush beds. On the second day of the dance a young man who had started it would come into the shade. First he would walk all around the hall so that all could see him. Then he went straight to the pole. He was giving himself for a living sacrifice. Two medicine men would lift the young man and lay him down under the pole. An old man would then come forward with a very sharp-pointed knife. He would take hold of the breast of the young brave, pull the skin forward, and pierce it through with his knife. Then he would insert a wooden pin (made from the plum tree), through the slit and tie a strong buckskin thong to this pin.

From the pole two rawhide ropes were suspended. The candidate would now be lifted up and the buckskin string tied to the rawhide rope. The candidate was now hanging from his breasts, but the rope was long enough for him to remain on the ground. Although the blood would be running down from the knife incision, the candidate would smile, although every one knew he must be suffering intense pain.

At this point the friends or relatives of the young brave would sing and praise him for his courage. Then they would give away ponies or make other presents. The singers now began to sing and the young brave to dance. The other dancers were behind him, four in a line, and they accompanied his dancing. These dancers always stood in one spot while they danced, but the candidate danced and at the same time pulled at the rope, trying to tear out the wooden pin fastened through his breasts.

If he tried very hard and was unsuccessful, his friends and relatives possibly could not bear to see him suffer any longer; so they would give away a pony to some one who would help him tear loose. This party would stand behind the dancer and seize him around the waist, while the candidate at the same time would throw himself backward, both pulling with all their strength. If they could not yet tear the candidate loose, an old man with a sharp knife would cut the skin off, and the dancer would fall beneath the pole. Then he would be picked up and carried to a sagebrush bed. Occasionally a man with a very strong constitution, after tearing loose, would get off his bed and resume the dancing. I have often seen these braves with their own blood dried to their bodies, yet going on with the dance.

This brave candidate fasted three or four days; taking no food or water during that time, instead of the forty days the Saviour did. The candidate had his body pierced beneath the cross. I learned all about this religion in the natural way, but after learning how to read the white man's books I compared your religion with ours; but religion, with us Indians, is stronger.

Many things were done during this dance which were similar to what I have read about Christ. We had one living sacrifice, and he fasted three or four days instead of forty. This religious ceremony was not always held in the same place. We did not commercialize our belief. Our medicine men received no salary. Hell was unknown to us. We trusted one another, and our word was as good as the white man's gold of to-day. We were then true Christians.

After the dance was over, everybody moved away, going where he pleased. It was a free country then. But afterward, if we ever returned to that sacred spot where the pole was yet standing, with the crosspiece attached, we stood for a long time in reverent attitude, because it was a sacred place to us.

But things have changed, even among the white people. They tear down their churches and let playhouses be built on the spot. What can be your feeling of reverence when you think of the house of God, in which you worshiped, being used to make fun in?

As I have many times related in my story, I always wanted to be brave, but I do not think I could ever have finished one of these Sun Dances.

American Citizenship

. . . I had heard a great deal about the wonderful climate of Southern California, and concluded to go there. I wrote to Thomas Ince, then one of the big moving-picture magnates. He had some Sioux Indians with him, and I thought I would like to be with them. He wrote me a nice reply and sent me transportation for Los Angeles. . . .

Mr. Ince's moving-picture studio was located at Inceville, five miles above Santa Monica, the beach city, and when I reached the Indian camp it certainly looked good to me.

That was in 1912. Up to that time I had never worked in the "movies," but this was to be my start in an entirely different line of work from any I had ever before engaged in.

As I look back to my early-day experiences in the making of pictures, I cannot help noting how we real Indians were held back, while white "imitators" were pushed to the front. One of these was Ann Little, who afterward became a star. There was also a white girl named Elenore Ulrick, who played the part of an Indian girl represented as my daughter. There was also the wife of a famous Japanese star, Sessue Hayakawa, who also played as my daughter. All these people have risen in the ranks, but we Indians have been held back.

In those early days I worked with Douglas Fairbanks, William S. Hart, Charles Ray, and several others who are now top-notchers in the moving-picture game.

One day Tom Ince was talking with me about the making of Indian pictures. He told me it was through making that sort of pictures that he got his start. Then I told him that none of the Indian pictures were made right. He seemed quite surprised at this and began asking me questions. I explained to him in what way his Indian pictures were wrong. We talked for a long time, and when I arose to leave, he said, "Standing Bear, some day you and I are going to make some real Indian pictures."

Ince had a man in his employ who conceived the idea that, if he could get some more Indians from the reservation who could tell the stories I told, they could direct them. The Sioux who had been with the camp wanted to return home, as their six months' contract had expired. So Ince got sixty more Sioux to take their places.

The new bunch of Sioux had had no experience in moving pictures, and they knew nothing of stage work or about writing a story. They were simply "up against it" and at a loss to know what to do. The moving-picture managers tried to get these people to relate some stories, but the Indians refused to do so. So Mr. Ince asked me to tackle the job at sixty dollars a week.

I wrote Mr. Ince that I was willing to work for my people and to help him, if he would accept my ideas and my stories. I waited for a reply, but none came. Then, as they could get nothing out of the new bunch of Sioux, and they had nobody who could talk their language and direct them, they had to return them to the reservation.

I have seen probably all of the pictures which are supposed to depict Indian life, and not one of them is correctly made. There is not an Indian play on the stage that is put on as it should be. I have gone personally to directors and stage managers and playwrights and explained this to them, telling them that their actors do not play the part as it should be played, and do not even know how to put on an Indian costume and get it right; but the answer is always the same, "The public don't know the difference, and we should worry!"

Bert La Monte, a manager in New York, wired me to come on to take a part in a play he was producing, called "The Race of Man." This was during the World War, and it caught the public fancy and took well. But it was hard work keeping a company together. Just when we would be getting along splendidly, one of the actors would be drafted to go to war. The play finally had to close down for lack of men.

During my travels on the stage my people at home kept in touch with me. When they started to draft the Indian boys, who were not even American citizens, I wrote a strong letter to the old chiefs, advising that the boys demand their citizenship if they were to be expected to go abroad and fight for Uncle Sam. Even my own brother, Ellis Standing Bear, wrote me that he had to go in the next draft. He was greatly worried as to who would care for the children he had adopted, as he and his wife were childless.

One of my own sons was rejected in the draft because he was tubercular. He has since passed away. Our tribe, the Sioux, is the largest in the United States to-day, and during the World War more than *eight thousand* of our boys went across. We certainly feel that we have done our duty to the land that really belonged to our fathers, and is the land of our birth. It is ours, and we are always ready to protect it against any enemy.

I went to Florida with my company to make a picture, and then came back to California, that State that I love so well. I went down to

Venice-by-the-Sea, an hour's ride from Los Angeles, and started in business for myself. While there I was elected president of the American Indian Progressive Association, holding the office two years. I tried to help my own race whenever I could, either in getting work for them or introducing them where they could receive aid. I lectured in high schools, churches, and grammar schools to show the white race what the Indian was capable of doing.

A few months after opening my concession at Venice, a man called on me to say that the Mission Indians of California were holding a council, and as I was a chief who had been to Washington they wanted to meet me in council. I accepted the invitation, and the pow-wow was held in Riverside, lasting three days.

There are about six different tribes of these California Indians, each one of which required an interpreter. None of these Indians understand the sign language, like the plains tribes, so all the talk had to be spoken. If it had been a council of the plains Indians, one of them would have got up and talked in the sign language, which is a universal language among all plains tribes, and, if there had been eight or ten different tribes there in council, all would have understood it perfectly.

I spoke to these California Indians regarding affairs at Washington, and they seemed pleased to hear from me. One day of the council had been set apart for white people to be present. I gave a talk on that day, and after I had finished, a lady sitting at the back of the room arose and said, 'I wonder if Standing Bear remembers me?" I arose and looked at the lady, but could not recall her. I asked one of my nieces who was with me if she knew who the lady was, but she said no. There seemed to be something familiar about her, and finally it dawned upon me that it was my first school teacher at Carlisle, Miss M. Burgess; and such it proved to be.

How glad we were to see each other again! We had not met since 1883, but she had recognized me from my resemblance to my father. To the Indians who were present, it was a great surprise, but no more so than to myself, as I had never expected to see her again.

During 1924 I was chosen to go to Oklahoma as a representative of the city of Los Angeles to invite the Indians of that State to have their next council in California. I went to Tulsa, and the day of the parade I hired an automobile, dressed myself carefully in full Indian regalia and represented the city of Los Angeles.

I was now getting along in years, and my family advised me to give up hard work, and some of my friends suggested I write a book detailing my experiences "from the cradle up." Two of my personal friends in Los Angeles, Mr. Clyde Champion, to whom I am indebted for the photographic work in this volume, and Mr. E. A. Brininstool, a writer of true Western history, and both greatly interested in the Indian question, were especially urgent; so in July, 1925, I gave up my place of business and began the writing of this book. And what you have been reading between these covers is the true history of my own people as I have lived my life among them.

It has taken many weary months to prepare this book, but I trust as you read these pages you will voice my plea to help my people, the Sioux, by giving them full citizenship. They are willing to fight for you and to die for you, if necessary.

The old saying that "the only good Indian is a dead Indian" is no longer a popular expression. The Indian has just as many ounces of brains as his white brother, and with education and learning he will make a real American citizen of whom the white race will be justly proud.

As I am writing these last lines, on July 25, 1927, I am starting an Indian Employment Agency, which I trust will be for the betterment of the whole race. The Indian is bright, and he is capable of holding good, responsible positions if he is only given a chance.

And why not give the Indian that chance?

Part 5
The Anthropologists' Indians, 1900–

No longer able, after Wounded Knee, to alter the course of American history by military action, the Indian became the privileged subject of American science, specifically, of the social science called anthropology. If amateurs and enthusiasts like McWhorter, Marquis, or Linderman into the 1930s (and after) still sought to interview the famous chiefs whose names and extraordinary deeds might be known to the general public, the new, university-trained, professional anthropologists were more interested in people who were not in the least publicly known. To the contrary, they sought to interview men and women who could be thought of as more or less ordinary people generally representative of their cultural formation. The anthropologist was interested not in the history-maker, but in the culture-bearer.

After the Dawes Act—which was, as we have noted, concerned with "civilizing" the Indian—there was a particular sense of urgency to record the Native legacy of America, an urgency that, broadly speaking, was expressed in the phrase "salvage anthropology." If the Indian was soon to "vanish" as an Indian, as was generally assumed, then it was important to *salvage* as much as possible of Native culture as quickly as possible. On the one hand, the early anthropologists brought a respect for and some detailed knowledge of Indian cultures to their work. On the other, they seemed also to have brought what might be called an antiquarian or archivist mentality to their work. That is to say, lives and stories were to be textualized and published in books, in very much the same way as sculptures, head-dresses, and every other item of Native material culture were to be catalogued and displayed in museums, as records of the past. That traditional lifeways might be maintained, however much adapted to present conditions, or that traditional arts might continue to flourish with whatever modifications, seems not very often to have occurred to the anthropologists.

None of this, it should be said, is to discredit the enormous value of these varied anthropological collections. Under the influence of Franz Boas of Columbia University, the major force in American anthropology for over forty years, the professional, university-trained anthropologists who went out into the "field" in the first decades of the twentieth century gathered information about language, ritual, and ceremony, about cosmology, mythology, healing practices, kinship systems, and so on. If they were somewhat insensitive to the fact that Native people had a future *as* Indians (and in this period it was not so easy to see that; even the "Red Progressives," as we have noted, did not necessarily see that), they were very sensitive to what Indians thought about themselves and their culture in the present and in the past.

Where an earlier generation of anthropologists had always measured Native American culture comparatively against the pinnacle of European "civilization," the Boasian anthropologists abandoned this comparative perspective and tried to understand, so far as possible, cultural facts on their own terms: to understand them, in other words, not only from the point of view of the observer, but from the point of view of the participant. Concerned as they were to get an "inside" view of the culture, it could not be long before they would turn to recording life histories. Alfred Kroeber, the first person to take a doctoral degree in anthropology at Columbia under Boas, published a brief autobiographical fragment from a Yurok Indian in 1908, and Paul Radin, another of the first generation of Boas's students, was the first to devote a substantial part of his work to Indian autobiographies.

By the time Radin published his classic *Crashing Thunder: The Autobiography of an American Indian* in 1926, many other anthropologists were trying their hand at "the life history method" — so many, in fact, that Clyde Kluckhohn could survey the field comprehensively by 1945.[1] L. L. Langness, in *The Life History in Anthropological Science*, and Langness and Gelya Frank in *Lives: An Anthropological Approach to Biography*, have continued to document the ongoing attention to life history materials.[2]

One of the results of the anthropologists's turn away from the "world-historical" chiefs was the documentation of the lives of women; two of the four selections in this fifth part of the anthology are women's autobiographies. We begin with Radin's work with the Winnebago Sam Blowsnake, and then proceed to an unnamed Arapaho woman who worked with Truman Michelson. Ruth Underhill's account of Maria Chona's life, a text that has received a great deal of attention of late, comes next, and we conclude with a selection from *Son of Old Man Hat*, a Navajo autobiography.

1. Louis Gottschalk, Clyde Kluckhohn, and Robert Angell, *The Use of Personal Documents in History, Anthropology, and Sociology.* Social Sciences Research Bulletin no. 53 (New York, 1945).
2. L. L. Langness, *The Life History in Anthropological Science* (New York: Holt, Rinehart, 1965); L. L. Langness and Gelya Frank, *Lives: An Anthropological Approach to Biography* (Novato, CA: Chandler and Sharp, 1981).

I believe it is worth mentioning here that, for all the anthropologists' interest in finding the "representative" Papago (currently called Tohono O'odham), Arapaho, Navajo, or Winnebago, the Natives who actually did offer their stories showed themselves, by their very willingness to engage at length in projects of this sort, to be unusual people. They stood apart, for this very reason, from most others of their culture, who typically chose not to engage with the anthropologists. We will later mention (in Part Seven) Albert Yava's criticism of Left-Handed's individualism and personal appeal in this regard; Maria Chona, too, has been noted for her more than ordinary independence.

Finally, it should be said that while Radin's work appeared during the Dawes period of "civilizing" the Indian, all the other texts I have included here were published shortly before (Michelson) or just after (Underhill, Dyk) the passage of the Wheeler-Howard or Indian Reorganization Act of 1934. Short of a comprehensive account of the effect of this change in federal Indian policy (there are many excellent discussions of these policies; one particularly worth consulting is *American Indians, American Justice*, by Vine Deloria, Jr., and Clifford M. Lytle[3]), we can say that, generally, the intention if not always the effect of Wheeler-Howard was to respect, not destroy, Native cultures, and to return to the tribes some measure of autonomy and self-government. For our purposes, it is to be noted that, as we approach the 1930s, the climate improves for texts that unapologetically convey an ongoing Native "way."

The four texts given in this part of the anthology, as noted above, represent only a small percentage of the available anthropologically-initiated life histories of Native Americans. I urge the interested reader to consult Brumble's bibliography and the other general studies (Krupat, Wong, Brumble) for further material.

3. Vine DeLoria, Jr., and Clifford M. Lytle, *American Indians, American Justice* (Austin: Univ. of Texas Press, 1983).

18

The Autobiography of a Winnebago Indian

Edited by

PAUL RADIN

Sam Blowsnake, whose Winnebago name was Hágaga, "Big Winnebago," came from a family that contributed much to Native American autobiography. Along with his autobiography, "The Autobiography of a Winnebago Indian,"[1] from which our selections are taken, there is also the story of Sam's older brother Jasper and of his sister Mountain Wolf Woman.[2]

Born in 1875, Sam Blowsnake narrated his story to the anthropologist Paul Radin in 1917 or thereabouts. He begins with childhood and includes many traditional elements of Winnebago life, e.g., his fasting experiences and his initiation into the Medicine Dance, and goes on to talk about the rather untraditional experiences of drinking, dissipation, and wandering that, if untraditional, were unfortunately becoming all too common for Native Americans early in the century. His story reaches a climax with his conversion to the Peyote religion, an amalgam of various Native and Christian beliefs that would eventually take institutional form in the Native American Church.

Although it was his older brother Jasper's name that might be translated as Crashing Thunder, the full-length autobiographical text that Radin published under that name in 1926 is not Jasper's story, but instead, a very much augmented version of Sam's 1920 account. Sam's Winnebago name, Hágaga, as noted, translated roughly to "Big Winnebago," and Radin, fearing this might unintentionally sound comic (e.g., something like "heap big Indian"), therefore appropriated Jasper Blowsnake's Indian name for Sam Blowsnake's story, something that has caused a good deal of confusion.

Crashing Thunder *is, indeed, the better known text, but I have chosen to publish selections from the earlier version instead because it is closer to what Sam Blowsnake actually produced in response to the request for the story of his life.*

Radin's turn to the life history method was consistent with the Boasian turn

1. "The Autobiography of a Winnebago Indian," ed. Paul Radin, *University of California Publications in American Archeology and Ethnology* 16 (1920): 381–473.
2. Jasper Blowsnake, "The Personal Reminiscences of a Winnebago Indian," *Journal of American Folklore* 26 (1913): 293–318, and Mountain Wolf Woman, *Mountain Wolf Woman: Sister of Crashing Thunder: The Autobiography of a Winnebago Indian*, ed. Nancy O. Lurie (Ann Arbor: Univ. of Michigan Press, 1961).

away from the general to the particular. What Radin wanted, as he wrote, was the "real" Indian, the "representative" Indian, one who could give some human texture to what he referred to as " 'dry-as-bones' memoirs." Although Radin's methods, as I have tried to show (in For Those Who Come After, *and in my foreword and appendix to the Nebraska University Press edition of* Crashing Thunder*) raise many questions, still, his achievement with the Blowsnake brothers is substantial.*

Our selections attempt to cover the entirety of Sam Blowsnake's life, from his childhood to his wanderings and dissipation, and, finally, to his conversion to peyotism.

Early Childhood

Father and mother had four children and after that I was born, it is said. An uncle of mother's who was named White-Cloud, said to her, "You are to give birth to a child who will not be an ordinary person." Thus he spoke to her. It was then my mother gave birth to me. As soon as I was born and was being washed—as my neck was being washed—I laughed out loudly.

I was a good-tempered boy, it is said. At boyhood my father told me to fast and I obeyed. In the winter every morning I would crush charcoal and blacken my face with it. I would arise very early and do it. As soon as the sun rose I would go outside and sit looking at the sun and I would cry to the spirits.

Thus I acted until I became conscious.

Then there were not as many white people around as there are now. My father always hunted. Our lodge was covered with rush mattings and we had reed mattings spread over the floor. After my father had hunted for a considerable time in one place we would move away. My father, mother, older sisters, and older brothers all carried packs on their backs, in which they carried many things. Thus we would pass the time until the spring of the year, and then in the spring we used to move away to live near some stream where father could hunt muskrats, mink, otter, and beaver.

In the summer we would go back to Black River Falls, Wisconsin.

The Indians all returned to that place after they had given their feasts. We then picked berries. When we picked berries my father used to buy me gum, so that I would not eat many berries when I was picking. However, I soon managed to eat berries and chew gum at the same time. After a while I learned to chew tobacco and then I did not eat any berries (while picking them). Later on I got to like tobacco very much and I probably used up more value (in tobacco) than I would have done had I eaten the berries.

In the fall of the year we would pick cranberries and after that, when the hunting season was open, I would begin to fast again.

I did this every year for a number of years.

After a while we got a pony on which we used to pack all our belongings when we moved camp. And in addition about three of us would ride on top of the pack. Sometimes my mother rode and father drove the pony when we moved from one place to another.

After I had grown a little older and taller and was about the size of one of my older brothers, all of us would fast together. My father used repeatedly to urge us to fast. "Do not be afraid of the burnt remains of the lodge center-pole," he would say to us. "Those which are the true possessions of men, the apparel of men and also the gift of doctoring—these powers that are spread out before you—do try and obtain one of them," he was accustomed to say to us.

I would then take a piece of charcoal, crush it, and blacken my face, and he would express his gratitude to me.

At first I broke my fast at noon and then, after a while, I fasted all night. From the fall of the year until spring I fasted throughout the day until nightfall, when I would eat. After a while I was able to pass the night without eating and after a while I was able to go through two nights (and days) without eating any food. Then my mother went out in the wilderness and built a small lodge. This, she told me, she built for me to fast in, for my elder brother and myself, whenever we had to fast through the night.

There we used to play around. However, before we were able to spend a night at that particular place, we moved away.

Fasting

When the girls with whom I used to play moved away I became very lonesome. In the evenings I used to cry. I longed for them greatly, and they had moved far away!

After a while we got fairly well started on our way back. I fasted all the time. We moved back to a place where all the leaders used to give their feasts. Near the place where we lived there were three lakes and a black hawk's nest. Right near the tree where the nest was located they built a lodge and the war-bundle that we possessed was placed in the lodge. We were to pass the night there, my older brother and myself. It was said that if anyone fasted at such a place for four nights he would always be blessed with victory and the power to cure the sick. All the spirits would bless him.

"The first night spent there one imagined oneself surrounded by spirits whose whisperings were heard outside of the lodge," they said. The spirits would even whistle. I would be frightened and nervous, and if I remained there I would be molested by large monsters, fearful to look upon. Even (the bravest) might be frightened, I was told. Should I, however, get through that night, I would on the following night be molested by ghosts whom I would hear speaking outside. They would say things that might cause me to run away. Towards morning they would even take my blanket away from me. They would grab hold of me and drive me out of the lodge, and they would not stop until the sun rose. If I was able to endure the third night, on the fourth night I would really be addressed by spirits, it was said, who would bless me, saying, "I bless you. We had turned you over to the (monsters, etc.) and that is why they approached you, but you overcame them and now they will not be able to take you away. Now you may go home, for with victory and long life we bless you and also with the power of healing the sick. Nor shall you lack wealth (literally, 'people's possessions'). So go home and eat, for a large war-party is soon to fall upon you who, as soon as the sun rises in the morning, will give the war whoop and if you do not go home now, they will kill you."

Thus the spirits would speak to me. However if I did not do the bidding of this particular spirit, then another one would address me and say very much the same sort of thing. So they would speak until the break of day, and just before sunrise a man in warrior's regalia would come and peep in. He would be a scout. Then I would surely think a war-party had come upon me, I was told.

Then another spirit would come and say, "Well, grandson, I have taken pity upon you and I bless you with all the good things that the earth holds. Go home now for the war-party is about to rush upon you." And if I then went home, as soon as the sun rose the war whoop would be given. The members of the war party would give the war whoop all at the same time. They would rush upon me and capture me and after the fourth one had counted coup, then they would say, "Now then, grandson, this we did to teach you. Thus you shall act. You have completed your fasting." Thus they would talk to me, I was told. This war party was composed entirely of spirits, I was told, spirits from the heavens and from the earth; indeed all the spirits that exist would all be there. These would all bless me. They also told me that it would be a very difficult thing to accomplish this particular fasting.

So there I fasted, at the black hawk's nest where a lodge had been built for me. The first night I stayed there I wondered when things would happen; but nothing took place. The second night, rather late in the night, my father came and opened the war-bundle and taking a gourd out began to sing. I stood beside him without any clothing on me except the breech-clout, and holding tobacco in each hand I uttered my cry to the spirits as my father sang. He sang war bundle songs and he wept as he sang. I also wept as I uttered my cry to the spirits. When he was finished he told me some sacred stories, and then went home.

When I found myself alone I began to think that something ought to happen to me soon, yet nothing occurred so I had to pass another day there. On the third night I was still there. My father visited me again and we repeated what we had done the night before. In the morning, just before sunrise, I uttered my cry to the spirits. The fourth night found me still there. Again my father came and we did the same things, but in spite of it all, I experienced nothing unusual. Soon another day dawned upon us. That morning I told my elder brother that I had been blessed by spirits and that I was going home to eat. However I was not telling the truth. I was hungry and I also knew that on the following night we were going to have a feast and that I would have to utter my cry to the spirits again. I dreaded that. So I went home. When I got there I told my people the story I had told my brother; that I had been blessed and that the spirits had told me to eat. I was not speaking the truth, yet they gave me the food that is carefully prepared for those who have been blessed. Just then my older brother came home and they objected to his return for he had not been blessed. However, he took some food and ate it.

That night we gave our feast. There, however, our pride received a fall, for although it was supposedly given in our honor, we were placed on one side (of the main participants). After the kettles of food had been put on twice, it became daylight.

The following spring we moved to the Mississippi in order to trap. I was still fasting and ate only at night. My brothers used to flatter me, telling me I was the cleverest of them all. In consequence I used to continue to fast although I was often very hungry. However, (in spite of my desire to fast) I could not resist the temptation to be around girls. I wanted always to be near them and was forever looking for them, although I had been strictly forbidden to go near them, for they were generally in their menstrual lodges when I sought them out. My parents most emphatically did not wish me to go near them, but I did nevertheless.

My parents told me that only those boys who had had no connection with women, would be blessed by the spirits. However, all that I desired was to appear great in the sight of the people. To be praised by my fellow-men was all that I desired. And I certainly received all I sought. I stood high in their estimation. That the women might like me was another of the reasons why I wanted to fast. However, as to being blessed, I learned nothing about it, although I went around with the air of one who had received many blessings and talked as such a one would talk.

Courting

It was at this time that I desired to court women and I tried it. However, I did not know the proper thing to say. The young men always went around at night courting. I used to mix with the women in the daytime but when I went to them at night I did not know what to say. A brother of mine, the oldest, seemed to know how to do it. He was a handsome man and he offered to show me how. Then I went with him at night. We went to a girl who was having her menses at that time. She was a young girl. When girls get their menses they always have to live apart. It was to such a one that we went. We were very cautious about the matter for the girls were always carefully watched as their relatives knew that it was customary to court them at such a time. (One of the precautions they used) was to pile sticks and branches about the lodge so that it would be difficult to enter. If a person tried to enter he was likely to make a noise moving the branches and this would awaken the people living in the larger lodge nearby and they might run out to see what was the matter.

It was to such a place that we went. After working at the obstacles placed near the entrance for some time, my brother entered the lodge. I went as close as possible and lay down to listen. He spoke in an audible whisper so that I might hear him. Sure enough I heard him. However after lying there for some time I fell asleep. When I snored my brother would wake me up. Afterwards the girl found out and she sent us both away. Thus we acted every now and then.

After a while I entered the lodges myself. We always had blankets wrapped around us and we took care to have our heads well covered (on such occasions).

Sometimes a girl was acquainted with quite a large number of men and then these would gather around her lodge at night and annoy her parents a good deal. We would keep them awake all night. Some of these people owned vicious dogs.

There was one old woman who had a daughter and when this daughter had her menses, she stayed in an oblong lodge with just room enough for two persons. She watched her daughter very carefully. Finally she slept with her. We nevertheless bothered her all the time just out of meanness. One night we went there and kept her awake almost all night. However, just about dawn she fell asleep, so we—there were several of us—pulled up the whole lodge, poles and everything, and threw the poles in the thicket. The next morning the two were found sleeping in the open, it was rumored, and the mother was criticised for being over careful.

The reason why some of the (older) people were so careful at that time was because it had been reported that some young men had forced themselves into lodges where they had not been received willingly.

Once I went to see a young girl and arrived there before the people had retired, so I waited near the lodge until they would go to sleep. As I lay there waiting, listening to them, I fell asleep. When I woke up it was morning and as the people got up they found me sleeping there. I felt very much ashamed of myself and they laughed at me. I was not long in getting away.

We always did these things secretly for it was considered a disgrace to be caught or discovered.

On another occasion, in another place, I was crawling into a lodge when someone woke up as I was about halfway in. I immediately stopped and remained quiet and waited for the people to fall asleep again. However in waiting I, myself, fell asleep. When they woke me up in the morning I was lying halfway inside the lodge, asleep. After waking me up they asked me whether I would not stay for breakfast, but I immediately ran away.

After a while I began going around with some particular girl and I liked it so much that I would never go to sleep at night. My older brothers were very much the same. We used to sleep during the day.

While we were acting in this manner, our parents saw to it that we had food to eat and clothes to wear. We never helped, for we did nothing but court girls. In the fall the Indians used to pick berries after they all came together. We used to help on such occasions. However, we were generally out all night and were not able to do much in the morning. I used to go out courting and be among the lodges all night, and yet, most of the time, I did not succeed in speaking to any of the girls. However, I did not mind that for I was doing it in order to be among the girls and I enjoyed it. I would even go around telling people that I was really keeping company with some of the girls. I used to say this to some of my men associates. In reality, however, I did not get much more than a smile from one or two of the girls, but even that I prized as a great thing.

Initiation into the Medicine Dance

The person who had died and whose place I was to take was an uncle of my father. I was glad of this opportunity for I had always liked the Medicine Dances when I saw them. I had always enjoyed watching from the outside what was going on inside and was always filled with envy. I used to wonder if I would ever be able to be one of them. So, naturally, I was very glad (to join) and anxious as to what (would happen).

We proceeded to the place where the ceremony was to be held, traveling from Tomah to Wittenberg. Sometimes we would have to walk, but I enjoyed it nevertheless. I was very happy.

Finally we arrived at the place and my father explained to the people there that he had turned over his right (to membership) to me and that that was why he had taken me along. They were quite satisfied.

We were to build the lodge immediately, so we went and cut the poles for it, after measuring the length required. Of course we hunted around and got the kind of poles always used for that purpose. Then we made the lodge. We stuck the poles in the earth. We worked together with three old men, brothers of the man who had died. They told me that this ceremony was a holy affair, that it was Earthmaker's play. We always made an offering of tobacco before everything we did. I, of course, thought that it must indeed be a marvelous thing and I was very happy about it. What I was most eager to see was myself killed and then brought to life again, in the lodge. I also realized that a member of the Medicine Lodge, whether man or woman, was different from a person not belonging to it, and I was quite anxious not to be an ordinary person any longer but to be a medicine man.

As soon as we finished building the lodge (the ceremony began) and the first thing the people did was to sing. That first time they kept me up all night and I heard a good deal about sacred affairs. I was not sleepy at any time during the night and I remained this way until morning. I enjoyed it all so much that I did not even go to sleep the next day. The next night they kept me up again, but as before I did not get sleepy. On that night they told me even more things. The third night was the same. Throughout these three nights I did not sleep at all. On the fourth night they sang until morning. On the fifth night they were to have the practice (trial). During the day the people began to come. In the afternoon they went into the sweat lodge. Those (who went in) were all old men. They were the people who had been especially invited with bundles of tobacco. When we came out it was sundown. Then those in the east stopped singing and those especially invited entered.

Then they took me in charge for the whole night and whenever they talked they would say, "In the morning when he for whom we desire life becomes like us." They meant me and that I would be like them in the morning. So I was indeed extremely anxious for the morning to come. They danced most of the night. They were giving their trial performance.

The next morning just before day, even while the dance was still going on, the one (the leader) in the first and second seat and those at the east end, together with some others, took me out in the wilderness. When we got there, we found a place where the ground had been cleared in the outline of the dance lodge. There they preached to me and they told me that the most fearful things imaginable would happen to me if I made public any of this affair. The world would come to an end, they said. Then again they told me to keep everything secret, and that if I told anyone, I would surely die. After that they showed me how to fall down and lie quivering (on the ground) and how to appear dead. I was very much disappointed for I had had a far more exalted idea of it (the shooting). "Why, it amounts to nothing," I thought. "I have been deceived," I thought. "They only do this to make money," I thought. I also thought then that probably many of the sacred things of which they told me were not true either. However, I kept on and did as I was told to do, for I had been taught to deceive in the ceremony in the wilderness. As soon as I was proficient in the act (of feigning death), we started back.

They told me that I would become just like them in body, but I did not have the sensation of any change in me. All that I felt was that I had become a deceiver in one of Earthmaker's creations.

During the day, at the regular meeting, I did as I had been taught to

329

do. We were simply deceiving the spectators. When we were through, those of my band told me that in two years I would be able to imitate the sounds of animals as much as I wanted to, for I had taken the place of a great medicine man. Those who have the privilege of dancing, obtain it by making gifts to the older members and thus get permission. Those who do not buy or get permission, are not allowed to dance. Similarly in shooting: they are not privileged to extend their arms when they shoot (unless they buy that privilege), but must hold their shooting skins close up to their breasts. The right to drum as well as the right to shake the gourd rattles must be bought before it can be exercised. In fact almost every act is bought before it can be exercised. However I was told that I did not have to do all that, but that I would be a great medicine man immediately. That pleased me. I was given a grey squirrel skin for my medicine bag and they told me that it was alive and that I could make it cry out loud. I had heard them do it and had always envied them in this regard. This was another of the things I was anxious to do. Indeed I wondered greatly how this could be done.

The dance was soon over and my father went away and left me there alone; he left me at the home of the deceased man's wife. I did not go back to school but was asked to stay there and do odd jobs for the old woman. So I stayed there all spring.

I had been told that if a person initiated into the Medicine Dance did not regard the affair as sacred, that this was a sign that he was going to die soon. This frightened me a great deal, for I had been thinking of the whole matter in a light manner and I felt that this was an indication that I was really going to die soon. I therefore did my best to consider it a sacred ceremony but, in spite of it all, I did not succeed.

About this time I left for Tomah. It was about the middle of summer (July fourth). I returned and stayed with my grandfather and from that time on was taught by him (details) of the Medicine Dance. (For instance), when I prepared a sweat bath for him, he would teach me some songs. I therefore did this for him frequently. Whenever I prepared such a bath for him, he would be very grateful to me and that is why I did it. Before long I learnt all the songs he knew, so that when I was invited to a medicine dance I would do all the singing and he would only have to do the talking. From that time on I said that it was a sacred affair and I took part in the ceremony for the greatness it possessed. (I boasted of its greatness) in the presence of women in order to make a good impression on them.

About this time I went away with a show to dance. I was fond of dancing and now I had a chance to go around and dance all the time and even get paid for it. I had money all the time. The people with whom I went around never saved anything and were always without funds, for they spent all their money on drink. I never drank. After a while I went with these shows every fall, when the fairs start.

Marriage

One fall I did not go and instead I stayed with my grandfather. He told me to get married. I was about twenty-three years old then. I had courted women ever since I was old enough. Every time I did anything I always thought of women in connection with it. I tried to court as many women as I could. I wanted badly to be a beau for I considered it a great thing. I wanted to be a ladies' man.

My grandfather had asked me to marry a certain girl, so I went over to the place where she was staying. When I arrived there I tried to meet the girl secretly, which I succeeded in doing. I told her of my intention and asked her to go home with me. Then she went home for I had met her some distance from her home.

After a while she came back all dressed up and ready. She had on a waist covered with silver buckles and a beautifully colored hair ornament and she wore many strings of beads around her neck, and bracelets around her wrists. Her fingers were covered with rings and she wore a pair of ornamented leggings. She wore a wide-flap ornamented moccasin and in each ear she had about half a dozen ear holes and they were full of small silver pieces made into ear ornaments. She was painted also. She had painted her cheeks red and the parting of her hair red. She was all dressed up.

I went there on horseback. We rode the horse together. We were not going that night to the place from which I had come, because I had previously been asked to sing at a medicine feast by my band (at a place) which was on our way home. I would therefore not go home until the next morning. So on my way there I had the girl hide near the place where we were to have the feast, for we were eloping and that was the custom.

The girl had a red blanket which she was wearing so I had her hide under a small oak bush. It rained all night and the next day. When we were through in the morning, I went to the place (where I had put her) and she was still there, but she was soaked through and through from the rain and her paint was smeared over her face in such a way that one could hardly recognize her. Then we went home. When we arrived home, my grandfather's wife came out to meet us and she helped the girl down from the horse and led her into the lodge. Then we ate. When we were through, the girl took off her clothing and gave it to them and they gave her other clothing to wear. After the girl had stayed there three nights, she had her menses, so she had to camp by herself, and there she had to sleep at night. Then a horse was given to this girl that I had married.

After a while my grandfather had a private talk with me, and he said: "Grandson, it is said that this girl you have married is not a maiden but really a widow, and I am not pleased with it, as this is your first marriage and you are a young man. I suppose you know whether it is true or not, whether she is a maiden or not?" "Yes," I answered. "You can stop living with her, if you wish," he said. So I went away on a visit and from there I went away for good. After some time I learned that the woman had gone home. Then I went home. He (my grandfather) was glad that I had not stayed with her. "You can marry another and a better one," said he to me, "one that I shall choose for you, you shall marry." Thus he spoke to me. However I said to him, "Grandfather, you have begged women for me often enough. Don't ever ask for anyone for me again, as I do not care to marry a woman that is begged for." Thus I spoke to him. He was not at all pleased at this for he said I was not allowing him to command me.

Boasting and Blessings

At the time I began to drink heavily, I began to boast about being a holy man. I claimed that I had been blessed by spirits and I kept on claiming this again and again. I was, of course, not telling the truth, for I had never felt the stirring of anything of that kind within me; I claimed it because I had heard others speak of it. Generally when I was just about drunk and on the verge of getting boisterous, yet still conscious of what I am saying, I would make this claim. Then I would say that I was blessed by a Grizzly-Bear spirit, that it had blessed me with the power of being uncontrollable; that I had been taught certain songs and these I would sing at the top of my voice. I used to imitate a grizzly bear and begin to exert my power. Then the people (around) would (try to) hold me. It generally required a large number of people to control me. Now I thought this (exhibition of mine) an act worthy of praise.

After a while I began to claim that I was blessed by many spiritual beings. Some time after I said that I was one of the giant beings called *Good-Giants*, that I was the second-born one of these and that my name was *Good-Heart*; that I had become reincarnate among human beings, dwelling with them. All this I would claim and they would believe me.

I Count Coup on a Pottawattomie

I never married any woman permanently. I would live with one woman for a while and then with another. Sometimes while I was living with a woman, I would return after a short absence to find her living with another man. Thus I acted.

My father brought me up and encouraged me to fast that I might be blessed by the various spirits and (thus) live in comfort. So he said. That I might obtain war honors, that I might not be like one who wears skirts (effeminate), thus my father raised me. For that reason he had me join the Medicine Dance, lest in life I be ridiculed by people. To lead a sober and sane life (my father taught me), and when I lived with my grandfather, he said the same. They encouraged me to give feasts and ask the (spirits) for war honors.

At that time I had a comrade and one day he said to me, "We have been thinking of something (of late, haven't we?) We sought to try and obtain some external emblem of our bravery. Do we not always try to wear feathers at a warrior dance? Well, let us then try to obtain war honors, so that we can wear head ornaments." Thus both of us said. We both liked the idea. We decided to go (in search of war honors). We meant to kill an individual of another tribe, we meant to perform an act of bravery. Finally we started out. There were four of us and we went to a place frequented by other tribes. We took the train, carrying some baggage. We had ropes along, too, for we intended to steal some horses as well as kill a man, if we met one. Horse stealing was regarded as a praiseworthy feat and I had always admired the people who recounted the number of times they had stolen horses, at one of the Brave dances. That was why I did these things.

We proceeded to a place where horses belonging to men of other tribes used to abound. Just as we got there we saw the owner of these horses and we killed him. My friend killed him. Then we went home and when we got there I told my father about it secretly. I said to him, "Father, you said it was good to be a warrior and you encouraged me to fast, and I did. You encouraged me to give feasts, and I did. Now we have just returned from a trip. We were looking for war honors and the young people (who accompanied me) decided that I should lead them. I told them that it was a difficult thing to lead warriors, my father had always told me; that I had always understood that one led a band of warriors only in consequence of a specific blessing; that I was not conscious of having received such authority." Thus I spoke. "However, they made me an offering of tobacco as they asked me, and I accepted the tobacco saying that I would at least make an offering of tobacco (for them). Then I offered tobacco to the Thunder-birds and asked them for rain, that we might walk in the power (protection) of rain. This offering we made in the morning and it rained all that day. Then we went to the place where we knew we could find horses. When we got there, we met the owner of the horses and spoke to him. We went with him to a carpenter shop nearby and there we killed him. I counted coup first and I announced my name as I gave a war whoop. I shouted '*Big-Winnebago* has counted coup upon his man.' Then the others counted coup. Then we searched his pockets and found some medicine and money in them. The money we divided among ourselves. After that we cut out his heart, for we had heard that hearts were used for medicine. For that reason we cut out his heart. He had a gun too, and this is it, one of them said. Hide it away, said I to him."

Then my father said to me, "My son, it is good. Your life is no longer an effeminate one. It is this way that our ancestors encouraged us to live. It is the will of those (spirits) in control of war that has led you to do this. On your own initiative you could not possibly have done it." Thus he spoke. "However we had better not have a victory dance. We have the honor nevertheless. We have to be careful about the whites," he said. "In the old time we were at liberty to live in our own way, and when such a deed as yours became known, your sisters would rejoice and dance, it has been said. However now the law (of the whites) is to be feared. In due time you will get a chance to announce your feat, and then you may wear a head ornament, for you have earned one for yourself," he said.

My First Acquaintance with the Peyote

Then my father and mother asked me to come to the Missouri River (Nebraska) but I had been told that my father and mother had eaten peyote and I did not like it. I had been told that these peyote eaters were doing wrong, and therefore I disliked them; I had heard that they were doing everything that was wicked. For these reasons we did not like them. About this time they sent me money for my ticket and since my brothers and sisters told me to go, I went. Just as I was about to start, my youngest sister, the one to whom we always listened most attentively, said to me, "Older brother, do not you indulge in this medicine eating (Peyote) of which so much is said." I promised. Then I started out.

As soon as I arrived (in Nebraska) I met some people who had not joined the peyote eaters and who said to me, "Your relatives are eating the peyote and they sent for you that you also might eat it. Your mother, your father, and your younger sister, they are all eating it." Thus they spoke to me. Then they told me of some of the bad things it was reported that these people had done. I felt ashamed and I wished I had not come in the first place. Then I said that I was going to eat the medicine.

After that I saw my father, mother, and sister. They were glad. Then we all went to where they were staying. My father and I walked (alone). Then he told me about the peyote eating. "It does not amount to anything, all this that they are doing, although they do stop drinking. It is also said that sick people get well. We were told about this and so we joined, and, sure enough, we are practically well, your mother as well as I. It is said that they offer prayers to Earthmaker," he said. He kept on talking. "They are rather foolish. They cry when they feel very happy about anything. They throw away all of the medicines that they possess and know. They give up all the blessings they received while fasting and they give up all the spirits that blessed them in their fasts. They also stop smoking and chewing tobacco. They stop giving feasts, and they stop making offerings of tobacco. Indeed they burn up their holy things. They burn up their war-bundles. They are bad people. They give up the Medicine Dance. They burn up their medicine bags and even cut up their otter-skin bags. They say they are praying to Earthmaker and they do so standing and crying. They claim that they hold nothing holy except Earthmaker. They claim that all the things that they are stopping are those of the bad spirit (the devil), and that the bad spirit (the devil) has deceived them; that there are no spirits who can bless; that there is no other spirit except Earthmaker." Then I said, "Say, they certainly speak foolishly." I felt very angry towards them. "You will hear them for they are going to have a meeting tonight. Their songs are very strange. They use a very small drum," said he. Then I felt a very strong desire to see them.

After a while we arrived. At night they had their ceremony. At first I sat outside and listened to them. I was rather fond of them. I stayed in that country and the young peyote eaters were exceedingly friendly to me. They would give me a little money now and then and they treated me with tender regard. They did everything that they thought would make me feel good, and in consequence I used to speak as though I liked their ceremony. However I was only deceiving them. I only said it, because they were so good to me. I thought they acted in this way because (the peyote) was deceiving them.

Soon after that my parents returned to Wisconsin, but when they left they said they would come back in a little while. So I was left there with my relatives who were all peyote followers. For that reason they left me there. Whenever I went among the non-peyote people I used to say all sorts of things about the peyote people and when I returned to the peyote people, I used to say all sorts of things about the others.

I had a friend who was a peyote man and he said to me, "My friend, I wish very much that you should eat the peyote." Thus he spoke and I answered him, "My friend, I will do it, but not until I get accustomed to the people of this country. Then I will do it. The only thing that worries me is the fact that they are making fun of you. And in addition, I am not quite used to them." I spoke dishonestly.

I was staying at the place where my sister lived. She had gone to Oklahoma; she was a peyote follower. After a while she returned. I was then living with a number of women. This was the second time (there) and from them I obtained some money. Once I got drunk there and was locked up for six days. After my sister returned she and the others paid more attention than ever to me. Especially was this true of my brother-in-law. They gave me horses and a vehicle. They really treated me very tenderly. I knew that they did all this because they wished me to eat the peyote. I, in my turn, was very kind to them. I thought that I was fooling them and they thought that they were converting me. I told them that I believed in the peyote because they were treating me so nicely.

After a while we moved to a certain place where they were to have a large peyote meeting. I knew they were doing this in order to get me to join. Then I said to my younger sister, "I would be quite willing to eat this peyote (ordinarily), but I don't like the woman with whom I am living just now and I think I will leave her. That is why I do not want to join now, for I understand that when married people eat medicine (peyote) they will always have to stay together. Therefore I will join when I am married to some woman permanently." Then my brother-in-law came and she told him what I had said, and he said to me, "You are right in what you say. The woman with whom you are staying is a married woman and you can not continue living with her. It is null and void (this marriage) and we know it. You had better join now. It will be the same as if you were single. We will pray for you as though you were single. After you have joined this ceremony, then you can marry any woman whom you have a right to marry (legally). So, do join tonight. It is best. For some time we have been desirous of your joining but we have not said anything to you. It is Earthmaker's blessing to you that you have been thinking of this," said he.

I Eat Peyote

Therefore I sat inside the meeting-place with them. One man acted as leader. We were to do whatever he ordered. The regalia were placed before him. I wanted to sit in some place on the side, because I thought I might get to crying like the others. I felt ashamed of myself.

Then the leader arose and talked. He said that this was an affair of Earthmaker's, and that he (the leader) could do nothing on his own initiative; that Earthmaker was going to conduct the ceremony. Then he said that the medicine (peyote) was holy and that he would turn us all over to it, that he had turned himself over to it and wished now to turn all of us over to it. He said further, "I am a very pitiable (figure) in this ceremony, so when you pray to Earthmaker, pray also for me. Now let us all rise and pray to Earthmaker." We all rose. Then he prayed. He prayed for the sick, and he prayed for those who did not yet know Earthmaker. He said that they were to be pitied. When he had finished we sat down. Then the peyote was passed around. They gave me five. My brother-in-law said to me, "If you speak to this medicine (peyote), it will give you whatever you ask of it. Then you must pray to Earthmaker, and then you must eat the medicine." However I ate them (the peyote) immediately for I did not know what to ask for and I did not know what to say in a prayer to Earthmaker. So I ate the peyote just as they were. They were very bitter and had a taste difficult to describe. I wondered what would happen to me. After a while I was given five more and I also ate them. They tasted rather bitter. Now I was very quiet. The peyote rather weakened me. Then I listened very attentively to the singing. I liked it very much. I felt as though I were partly asleep. I felt different from (my normal self), but when I (looked around) and examined myself, I saw nothing wrong about myself. However I felt different from (my normal self).

337

Before this I used to dislike the songs. Now I liked the leader's singing very much. I liked to listen to him.

They were all sitting very quietly. They were doing nothing except singing. Each man sang four songs and then passed the regalia to the next one. (Each one) held a stick and an eagle's tail feather in one hand and a small gourd rattle, which they used to shake while singing, in the other. One of (those) present used to do the drumming. Thus objects would pass around until they came back to the leader, who would then sing four songs. When these were finished, he would place the various (things) on the ground, rise, and pray to Earthmaker (God). Then he called upon one or two to speak. They said that Earthmaker was good and that the peyote was good, and that whosoever ate this medicine (peyote) would be able to free himself from the bad spirit (the devil); for they said that Earthmaker forbids us to commit sins. When this was over they sang again.

After midnight, every once in a while, (I heard) someone cry. In some cases they would go up to the leader and talk with him. He would stand up and pray with them. They told me what they were saying. They said that they were asking (people) to pray for them, as they were sorry for their sins and that they might be prevented from committing them again. That is what they were saying. They cried very loudly. I was rather frightened. (I noticed also) that when I closed my eyes and sat still, I began to see strange things. I did not get sleepy in the least. Thus the light (of morning) came upon me. In the morning, as the sun rose, they stopped. They all got up and prayed to Earthmaker and then they stopped.

During the daytime, I did not get sleepy in the least. My actions were a little different (from my usual ones). Then they said, "tonight they are going to have another meeting. Let us go over. They say that is the best (thing) to do and thus you can learn it (the ceremony) right away. It is said that their spirits wander over all the earth and the heavens also. All this you will learn and see," they said. "At times they die and remain dead all night and all day. When in this condition they sometimes see Earthmaker, it is said." One would also be able to see where the bad spirit lived, it was said.

So we went there again. I doubted all this. I thought that what they were saying was untrue. However I went along anyhow. When we got there I had already eaten some peyote, for I had taken three during the day. Now near the peyote meeting an (Indian) feast was being given and I went there instead. When I reached the place, I saw a long lodge. The noise was terrific. They were beating an enormous drum. The sound almost raised me in the air, so (pleasurably) loud did it sound to me. Not so (pleasurable) had things appeared at those affairs (peyote meetings) that I had lately been attending. There I danced all night and I flirted with the women. About day I left and when I got back the peyote meeting was still going on. When I got back they told me to sit down at a certain place. They treated me very kindly. There I again ate peyote. I heard that they were going to have another meeting nearby on the evening of the same day. We continued eating peyote the whole day at the place where we were staying. We were staying at the house of one of my relatives. Some of the boys there taught me a few songs. "Say, when you learn how to sing, you will be the best singer, for you are a good singer as it is. You have a good voice," they said to me. I thought so myself. . . .

I Am Converted

On one occasion we were to have a meeting of men and I went to the meeting with a woman, with whom I thought of going around the next day. That was (the only) reason I went with her. When we arrived, the one who was to lead, asked me to sit near him. There he placed me. He urged me to eat a lot of peyote, so I did. The leaders (of the ceremony) always place the regalia in front of themselves; they also had a peyote placed there. The one this leader placed in front of himself this time, was a very small one. "Why does he have a very small one there?" I thought to myself. I did not think much about it.

It was now late at night and I had eaten a lot of peyote and felt rather tired. I suffered considerably. After a while I looked at the peyote and there stood an eagle with outspread wings. It was as beautiful a sight as one could behold. Each of the feathers seemed to have a mark. The eagle stood looking at me. I looked around thinking that perhaps there was something the matter with my sight. Then I looked again and it was really there. I then looked in a different direction and it disappeared. Only the small peyote remained. I looked around at the other people but they all had their heads bowed and were singing. I was very much surprised.

Some time after this (I saw) a lion lying in the same place (where I had seen the eagle). I watched it very closely. It was alive and looking at me. I looked at it very closely and when I turned my eyes away just the least little bit, it disappeared. "I suppose they all know this and I am just beginning to know of it, " I thought. Then I saw a small person (at the same place). He wore blue clothes and a shining brimmed cap. He had on a soldier's uniform. He was sitting on the arm of the person who was drumming, and he looked at every one. He was a little man, perfect (in all proportions). Finally I lost sight of him. I was very much surprised indeed. I sat very quietly. "This is what it is," I thought, "this is what they all probably see and I am just beginning to find out."

Then I prayed to Earthmaker: *"This, your ceremony, let me hereafter perform."*

I Have a Strange Experience

Many things are said under the influence of the peyote. The members (would) get into a kind of trance and speak of many things. On one occasion they had a peyote-meeting which lasted two nights. I ate a good deal of peyote. The next morning I tried to sleep. I suffered a great deal. I lay down in a very comfortable position. After a while a (nameless) fear arose in me. I could not remain in that place, so I went out into the prairie, but here again I was seized with this fear. Finally I returned to a lodge near the lodge in which the peyote meeting was being held and lay down alone. I feared that I might do something foolish to myself (if I remained there alone), and I hoped that some-one would come and talk to me. Then someone did come and talk to me, but I did not feel better, so I thought I would go inside where the meeting was going on. "I am going inside," I said to him. He laughed. "All right, do so," said he. I went in and sat down. It was very hot and I felt as though I were going to die. I was very thirsty but I feared to ask for water. I thought that I was certainly going to die. I began to totter over.

I died, and my body was moved by another life. It began to move about; to move about and make signs. It was not I and I could not see it. At last it stood up. The regalia—eagle feathers and gourds—these were holy, they said. They also had a large book there (Bible). These my body took and what is contained in that (book) my body saw. It was a Bible. The regalia were not holy, but they were good orna-ments. My body told them that; and that if any person paid attention to Earthmaker's ceremony, he would be hearkening to what the Bible said; that likewise my body told them. Earthmaker's son said that he was the only Way. This means that one can only get life from the Word. (My) body spoke of many things and it spoke of what was true. Indeed it spoke of many things. It spoke of all the things that were being done (by the pagan Indians) and which were evil. A long time it spoke. At last it stopped. Not I, but my body standing there, had done the talking. Earthmaker (God) had done his own talking. I would be confessing myself a fool if I were to think that I had said all this, it (my body) told me.

After a while I returned to my normal human condition. Some of those there had been frightened, thinking that I had gone crazy. Others had liked it. It was discussed a good deal. They called it the "shaking" state. It was said that the condition in which I was, was not part of Earthmaker's religion. I was told that whoever ate a lot of peyote would, through the peyote, be taught the teachings of Earthmaker. Earthmaker's ways and man's ways are different. Whoever therefore wished to help this religion must give himself up (to it). If you ate a good deal of this peyote and believed that it could teach you something then it assuredly would do so. That at least is the way in which I understand this matter.

Once we had a meeting at the home of a member who was sick. The sick would always get well when a meeting was held in their home, and that is why we did it. At that meeting I got into the "shaking" condition again. My body told (us) how our religion (peyote) was an affair of Earthmaker's, and even if one knew only a portion of it, one could still see (partake of) Earthmaker's religion.

Thus it went on talking. "Earthmaker, His Son (Christ), and His Holiness (the Holy Ghost), these are the three ways of saying it. Even if you know one (of these three), it means all. Everyone of you has the means of opening (the road) to Earthmaker. It is given to you. With that (your belief) you can open (the door to God). You can not open it with knowledge (alone). How many letters are there to the key (the road to God)? Three. What are they?" There were many educated people (there) but none of them said anything. "The first (letter) must be a *K*, so if a person said *K*, that would be the whole of it. But let me look in the book (Bible) and see what that means," said the body. Then it (the body) took the Bible and began to turn the leaves. The body did not know where it was itself, for it was not learned in books. Finally in Matthew, chapter 16, it stopped. There it speaks about it. "Peter did not give himself up" (it says). "For a long time he could not give up his own knowledge. There (in that passage) it says *Key*." That is the work of Earthmaker. At least so I understand it. He made use of my body and acted in this manner, in the case of the peyote.

Thus I go about telling (everyone) that this religion is good. Many other people at home said the same thing. Many, likewise, have joined this religion and are getting along nicely.

On one occasion, after I had eaten a good deal of peyote, I learned the following from it; that all I had done in the past, that it had all been evil. This was plainly revealed to me. What I thought was holy, and (by thus thinking) was lost, that I now know was false. (It is false), this giving of (pagan) feasts, of holding (the old) things holy, the Medicine Dance, and all the Indian customs.

Finale

I have written of some of these matters and I have spoken out clearly. I talked about this to the older people but they refused to do it. I thought I would write it down so that those who came after me, would not be deceived. Then my brother had us do this work, (aided by) my older brother and my younger brother.

Before (my conversion) I went about in a pitiable condition, but now I am living happily, and my wife has a fine baby.

This is the work that was assigned to me.

This is the end of it.

19
Narrative of an Arapaho Woman

Edited by

TRUMAN MICHELSON

The unnamed Arapaho woman whose autobiography appears here was inter-viewed by an (also unnamed) interpreter/intermediary for Truman Michelson in 1932. Michelson seems to have published the English text he received with very few changes.

The Arapaho are an Algonquian speaking people whose northern branch oc-cupied the present state of Wyoming, and whose southern branch dwelled in present-day Arkansas. They share many of the traits of the Plains tribes and were particularly close to the Cheyenne. Unlike the Cheyenne, however, the Arapaho maintained generally friendly relations toward the whites, in this more like the distant Crow.

The anonymous woman whose life story we shall read was born about 1855, and raised in a traditional manner. She has nothing to say of the whites, al-though the Arapaho certainly knew of them early in her lifetime. She also has nothing to say of the most important ceremony of the Arapaho, the Sun Dance. This may be because, although women most certainly had an impor-tant part to play in the Sun Dance, it was essentially a ritual for the men. It is probable that Michelson, typical of the practice of Leo Simmons (Sun Chief), Walter Dyk (Son of Old Man Hat), and Ruth Underhill (Autobi-ography of a Papago Woman),[1] among others working in the thirties, pressed her (or had his interpreter press her) for intimate details about sex and marriage. We learn of many marriages, and, in general, of her good fortune with her several husbands (with the possible exception of one, whose behavior moves her to a strong show of independence). In comparison to the apparent ease with which some Plains males like Two Leggings and Crows Heart dis-cuss their sacrifices of flesh, it is interesting to note this Arapaho woman's concern about whether or not it would be appropriate for her to speak of her decision to sacrifice her finger in the interest of her sister's health.

Born in 1879, Truman Michelson studied at Harvard and did postgraduate work at the Universities of Leipzig and Bonn. He worked both as a govern-

1. Excerpts from *Son of Old Man Hat* and *Autobiography of a Papago Woman* make up the following two chapters. The Leo Simmons edited text is *Sun Chief: The Autobiography of a Hopi Indian* (New Haven: Yale Univ. Press, 1974).

ment ethnologist for the Bureau of American Ethnology and as a university anthropologist at George Washington University. He was considered the first to classify the Algonquian tribes accurately on a linguistic basis. Although he worked not only with the Arapaho but also with the Eskimo of James Bay and Hudson Bay, his major publications deal with the Fox Indians. His other autobiographical contributions include "The Autobiography of a Fox Indian Woman" and "The Narrative of a Southern Cheyenne Woman."[2] "Narrative of an Arapaho Woman," given here in its entirety, was first published in the American Anthropologist, the source of the present selection.[3]

I tell this story of my experiences as I remember them since my girlhood.

My father had one wife who was my mother. She had seven children. I had five sisters and two brothers. I was the second oldest child, one brother being older than I.

As was the custom then, the Arapaho made frequent moves from place to place by means of ponies. The old women and children often rode in the travois, and sometimes the heavier things were hauled.

I had a saddle of my own, and always had several ponies.

Whenever a camp was made the girls and boys would get out together and enjoy themselves with various games until sundown when we would all retreat to our tepees for the night.

Up to the time I was ten years old my mother allowed me to play unrestricted with boys of my own age. I was very active in most of our sports, especially in swimming and riding ponies.

When I became older my mother equipped my bedding which was always on the west side of our lodge. Up to the time of my marriage I always slept with a girl chum who was also my cousin (my mother's sister's daughter).

I said that we always played games that were common among the tribes associated with the Arapaho, such as packing one another upside down, swimming across rivers on the back with one foot sticking above the water with a ball of mud on the big toe which represented

2. "The Autobiography of a Fox Indian Woman" appeared in the 40th Annual Report of the Bureau of American Ethnology . . . , 1918–19 (Washington, D.C., 1925); "The Narrative of a Southern Cheyenne Woman" appeared in the *Smithsonian Miscellaneous Collections* 77.5 (1932).

3. "Narrative of an Arapaho Woman," ed. Truman Michelson, *American Anthropologist* 35 (1933): 595–610. Reprinted by permission of the Bureau of American Ethnology, Smithsonian Institute.

a grandchild. We had to swim feet first, and swim straight across regardless of the speed or current of the stream. Then we would line up and see who could dive and swim under the water the longest and farthest without a breath, or coming above the water level. This was usually downstream. We did this ordinarily in the spring and summer. We also played with rag dolls about the camp. We would use forked poles that were usually used about the tepees for our ponies. Some girls would have small squaw-saddles for play like real ones with cruppers. My chum and I each had doll cradles which were beaded and also beaded saddle bags. Mother made us buffalo-calf hide robes to play with. These were tanned with the hair on, just like real robes. Some were decorated with porcupine quills and some were painted. We also had play-tepees and poles. Whenever the camp broke for a move we were made to take care of our playthings, that is, to bundle them up and to see that they were properly packed on the travois; and when camp was pitched it was also our duty to unpack them and to place them in our tepees where they ought to be.

I learned to ride alone on my own pet pony when I was quite small. My mother used to tell me that when I was still a baby in the cradle, she would strap my cradle to her saddle and drive a herd of ponies across the prairies, sometimes all day long.

Whenever my father or my maternal uncles would bring deer or buffalo meat, we would get some small pieces of the meat, slice it, dry it, and put it away in our toy rawhide parfleches. These were made to be playthings but were painted and fixed like real ones.

My mother also taught us girls to braid our own lariats that we used to pack our belongings. Sometimes a hide-rope about one inch wide was used. This was also used to pack firewood. Sometimes women, whose duty it was, would pack wood and carry it on their backs for large distances. I remember when I was quite small that I helped my mother pack wood for a long distance. When I became a young woman I was not permitted to pack wood on my back, as that was the duty of older women.

By the time I was fourteen years old, I learned to do good beadwork, tan hides, and make almost anything. I also learned to do porcupine quill work.

When I became mature a young man, who was known as a brave young warrior, gave me a nice finger ring, which had an inlaid red metal. I thought much of him for this.

The custom of Arapaho mothers was to watch their daughters strictly at all times. They would even accompany us girls to the brush when we went there to attend to nature's demands, for fear some

345

young men might be ambushed, watching their chance to have even an opportunity to talk to us girls. At nights my mother would go out with my chum and myself to see that no young man would molest us.

Sometimes young men would regulate the smoke-draughts of tepees to make them smoky, thinking the girl of the tepee would come out to regulate the draughts by the outside poles that supported the weather-strips; but they were mostly fooled as that would be a mother's duty. But it was commonly known that whenever a medicine bag was kept in a tepee, the tepee would not be molested; and the same respect was shown a tepee in which a medicine man dwelt.

When I became old enough to have my own things I usually had two beaded hidebags for my clothes that were set nicely along my bed next to the tepee-wall, and my beaded saddle-packetbag hung on the head props of my willow bed.

I was always well-supplied with sweet smelling leaves for my clothing. I would pack these among my clothing, some in my pillows, and a bunch was even tied in a small gay-colored calico cloth on to my necklace-beads. We would also gather from weeds some black seeds which we collected in swampy places. We would pound or grind these seeds until they were very fine; we then sopped them and used them to perfume our clothes and hair. We would also use this preparation on the manes and tails of our favorite ponies.

My toilet-case was made out of hide which was nicely beaded; and I would keep in it the paints, mostly red and yellow, to paint my face, a hair-parter (a stick) also used to paint the part yellow or red, a porcupine-tail brush, earrings, bracelets, and rings.

My mother would talk to me for quite a while regarding my behavior. She would tell me not to glance around in public places, not to laugh out loud, not to peep at young men whenever they were near our tepee, and not to respond to the flashes of mirrors held by young men at a distance, as these indications would govern young men's opinions of the character of a girl.

You see that I wear these ear-bobs. My ears were pierced by a Sioux Indian at a Sun Dance when I was a small girl. My father gave his best riding pony, a pack of several robes, goods, and a silver bridle to this Sioux for piercing my ears. This Sioux told of his brave war-deeds.

As my mother was a doctor I learned through her the use of many herbs, roots, bark, leaves, and seeds of certain plants for the treatment of various ailments, before I was married.

This is how my married life was. Since I was not acquainted with the young man who became my husband, he sent his mother, two of his own sisters, and his paternal aunt to ask my brother, and my maternal uncles for permission to marry me. My brother had given his consent before I was aware of it, as I happened to be away at the time. When I came to our tepee my brother came to me, which was unusual, sat near me and started to tell me what he had done, and that he had done so for the good of our father and mother. My father had expressed his willingness also. So when my mother started to talk to me, asking me to say what I thought, I told her that if my brother said it was all right, it would be all right with me, as I didn't want to hurt his feelings by refusing.

My brother had told the women who asked for me that he didn't want the young man to work or care for our ponies for a long time as was the usual custom, before actually living with me, but had told them to bring over the ponies at once, which was done. Eight of the prettiest ponies of my future husband's male relatives were led over. My brother then invited our male relatives, including several maternal uncles, and (male) cousins who, after their meal, made their selections of the ponies brought.

A nice decorated tepee was then erected by my paternal aunts with the necessary equipment that goes with a tepee. Around this tent the ponies were staked which my male relatives had brought in exchange for the ponies they selected.

My female relatives then brought together the food they had prepared in their tepees, mostly buffalo meat with much fat, to my new tepee where my future husband and his folks were then invited to come and eat the food prepared by my people, after which they were told which pony was theirs in return for the one they had brought. Some ponies (not the ones received) were given with robes, blankets (Mexican zarapas), quivers of otter and leopard (panther, jaguar?), bows and arrows, guns, and saddles.

Thus my married life began. I went to my husband in the tepee put up for us, and sat down by him as my mother had instructed me. His brothers and (male) cousins (both sides) came in; and they started to tease me, and joke with me, and I with them; so we sat up almost all night.

My mother had prepared a nice supper that I took to my tepee and served my husband, his brothers, and cousins.

It was, and still is, the practice to dash cold water on one's brother-in-law if he was caught asleep, and vice versa, no matter how cold the weather, which was a great joke. I always got up very early in the morning so that joke was never played on me.

Sometimes a younger brother-in-law or sister-in-law who usually slept in his (her) mother's tepee where the food was prepared or the cooking done, would rub his or her fingers on some sooty pot or kettle, and steal into his sister-in-law's tepee, and while she lay asleep, would black her nose and eyebrows; and a sister-in-law would do the same to her brother-in-law.

It was four years after my marriage before I had my first child. My husband was good and kind to me. He never scolded nor hit me.

After my first child, a boy, was a year old, I became ill, and my mother took me to an Indian doctor at another camp, in accordance with the request of my husband. After I had been away from my husband a few days, word came to me by a messenger that my husband had suddenly become sick and had died. Owing to my serious illness at the time of my husband's death, my father pleaded with me not to cut my hair, nor cause any cutting on my flesh; so while I obeyed my father, I cut my hair just a little.

After the death of my first husband, I was single for two years, caring for my baby son, who was then about two years old. One day my parents told me a young man had asked to marry me. After thinking the matter over a day or two, I told my parents that I preferred to remain single for my boy's sake; so my father accordingly sent word of objection to the young man. In some way, a male relative of mine heard of it, and after telling me of my situation and that of my aged parents, advised me of his consent for me to marry. I agreed to do this; so according to Arapaho custom the young man proceeded to work for my parents, herding our ponies, hunting for us, getting wood, etc. He would always come to our camp for his meals that my mother would prepare and I would talk to him and sit with him in the tepee of my family. Of course my mother would leave and not be in sight of her future son-in-law. For more than a year this young man attended to his duties towards us before I was finally given to him. Three ponies were then brought to my male relatives who took their pick, and each gave one in place of the one received, together with other gifts, to the young man's male relatives. The wife of my male relative who had given his consent erected a large tepee of buffalo hide and set up the full equipments of willow head-props, and then the young man was directed with his relatives to eat the food which my people had prepared.

I was by this time very used to this man, so I immediately began to make our living as happy as I could for him. He was very loving to my boy by my first husband.

In about two years after our marriage we had a baby girl; then about two years later another girl was born, and again two later another girl was born.

In those days I was taught to nurse my children until two years old, or thereabouts. My mother used to tell me to keep my husband from having sexual intercourse with me while I was nursing my children; but to tell him to go to some other woman, for it would make my milk unhealthy for my nursing baby.

Whenever any of my children became sickly my mother would get an older person, either a man or a woman, to suckle my breasts to clean out all the bad milk that made my child sick; and in addition she would make some tea of some weeds for me to drink.

My second husband became sick all at once, and after a very long illness, though many Indian doctors attended him, he finally died. One of my children died while very young which I think made my husband sick, as he could not get over the sorrow for a long time. He was a very kind and loving man to me and to our children. At his death my mother cut my hair off just below my ears, and all of my husband's relatives did the same. As was the custom then, my husband's favorite pony, a nice black gelding, was led to his grave and shot. A pole was staked at the head of his grave to which his warshield was hung.

I again lived with my family, this time with a bigger number of well grown-up children. I was then determined to live single, which I did for many years when I again married in accordance with the advice of my cousin.

After I had been married for about two years, one day my husband told me I was to have a companion to help me with my home work. He said he was going to marry another woman. When I asked who it was, and learned that it was my maternal grandmother's daughter I told him that I would rather that he marry her and leave me as I did not wish to be a plural wife with her. He did leave me and took this young woman to his people. My cousins, the mother, and mother's sisters of this young woman invited me to their camp, and told me I should be a co-wife with her. I told them no, and that since my husband did wrong by such an entangling relationship I preferred to sever my relationship entirely from him; and in that way there would be no hard feelings towards my cousins and this woman. So I again was a widow.

I recite to you the series of my marriages in a brief way. Of course aside from the death of my two former husbands, and my baby boy, over whom I mourned a period of two years each, I was happy, having the confidence of my husbands. I had unlimited liberty with my relatives and former chums when I visited them. I was always at liberty to attend anything that was going on in the tribe, such as handgames at night. These would last all night sometimes. And there were stick-dart games among the young women. I was one of the few who were known as one who threw the darts farthest. Once at a large Cheyenne and Arapaho camp, we were approached with a challenge by a party of young Cheyenne women to throw darts for keeps. After we agreed to accept the challenge we bet our brass bracelets, silver rings, earbobs, sashes, and even our shawls. It was a one-sided game, as two of us Arapaho girls were always far ahead making first and second for our side. On my dart was a nice polished tip of a buffalo-calf horn that my paternal aunt had given me when a young girl, and which she also had used when she was young. There were four on each side. We always made a mound a little higher than the mound beside a prairie-dog's hole; and we would step back from this and make a running start till within a few steps of it, and then we would throw our darts so as to glance ahead quite a way before again touching the ground after which the dart would slide a long distance. This game was mostly played along paths or bare ground or on ice or hard-packed snow. The darts had at all times to be kept very straight, like arrows. As soon as we picked them up after every throw, we had to examine them to see that they did not bow. If no horn was used at the ends they would soon split, or would fly awry. Some had nice darts, painted, and some carved. If they were the right weight they were better to throw. My darts were always plain, but had good weight, and were very straight.

The foot-bouncing ball game of girls was another game played very much. This was played by standing on one foot and bouncing a soft stuffed ball on the instep of the other foot. The game was the highest count with the ball not touching the ground. I was not so good at this, but some of my girl friends were good kickers. Some of them would never miss, but quit kicking of their own accord. Here and there in the camp the girls would gather and play the foot-bouncing ball game.

And there was the arm muscle and palm ball game. This was usually played by bouncing a smaller ball from the arm muscle to the palm of the hand by bending and straightening either arm; the highest count won.

Now I shall tell you of my last marriage; but this time I was a well matured woman. My father and mother were still living. As usual I was married by the consent of my relatives, to which I agreed, knowing the need of a man companion in many ways, not only for my own reasons but for the good of my aged parents. After this marriage I again lived a happy life independent, as usual, to do as I liked through the best years of my life. By my last husband, who died eight years ago, I had four children, three boys and one girl. One of the boys is still living, and he now has several children. For thirty-five years my husband and I lived a contented life. I do not recall that he ever scolded or mistreated me. He was one of the tribal chiefs, and also a brother leader of one of the young men societies. They were very fond of him because of his good nature and joking disposition. He was also noted as one of the Indian doctors; and I am still respected because of him.

My son by my first husband is also living; he also has several grandchildren. My daughter by my second husband is also living, and she also has a grandchild.

I have always been a very early riser, and bathe often. I have never taken any of the white man's medicine, except salves and cough syrup. I have always eaten mostly meat, either dried or fresh, which was the principal diet of my parents and the rest of the tribe. At present I still enjoy good health; only my eyesight is now somewhat dim.

I have refrained from mentioning private personal experiences both during the time I was single and also married, solely out of respect to my brothers and male cousins.

As I said, I wanted to be positive that it was permissible for me to tell of the sacrifice of my finger, and since it is, I will tell of it. It was this way. After my sister had been married several years and had had several children, she became sickly. Realizing the responsibility I was facing in the custody of her children in the event of her death which seemed evident by the failure of two of the best Arapaho doctors after periodical gifts for their services, I unhesitatingly made a vow to sacrifice my left little finger, so that my sister's life might be spared, so that her small children, who were a pitiful sight to me as they were about their helpless mother, might again enjoy happiness with their mother, and so the rest of us would be relieved from the impending sorrow, especially my father and mother who thought so much more of this daughter, as she always was somewhat frail. The next morning an Arapaho woman was called to remove my finger in the usual way. She told me that since I was slender this wound would heal rapidly, which it did. My sister commenced to get better, improving very quickly. She became hungry for deer meat. The young men went out and brought deer that they had killed; they brought turkey and beaver, which my sister ate, getting back her strength very rapidly. After a short time she was again well and happy with her children, which made us all happy again. At the time I made the vow my father expressed his gratitude very forcibly, and praised me for my thought-fulness. I had just one thought, and that was that my sister was going to recover.

This sister, who was several years younger than I was, died six years ago. I am now the only one of the family living, although my brothers and sisters were younger than I. I have many grandchildren and several great-grandchildren. I have gone through all of the age-societies of the tribe, in accordance with the ranks of my husband. I am now very old and live with my youngest son, and have given his several children some of my lands so that they may have places to live upon and have the means to live by reason of the value of the land. I visit my female cousins here and there. Sometimes I stay with my daughter.

If I had a longer time to think of the past I would tell you more, but without previous notice, and in two or three days, this is all and the best I can tell.

In the days when we were moving about as I mentioned in my story there were no briar weeds, or stickers, or burrs; so the children as well as their parents were nearly always barefooted. All that one could see on the prairies was grass, buffalo grass, and blue stem. When camps were pitched we would make our beds on the ground with grass for under-cushions. The air was always fresh. We wore no head-shade; in fact we didn't mind the weather in those days.

20

Autobiography of a Papago Woman

Edited by

R U T H   U N D E R H I L L

*Maria Chona was born in 1845 or 1846. A Papago, or, as they are called to-
day, Tohono O'odham (people of the sun or sunlight, desert people), she grew
up in a village to the west of Tucson, learning to work and to weave baskets,
and, in general, to perform the traditional duties of a "Papago woman." (Although, as her editor, Ruth Underhill, notes, Chona tended to be somewhat
more independent than the ideal Papago woman, early in her life making
songs and claiming visions, things that were more usually left to the men.)
Residing today in their old homelands on the southern edge of Arizona, and in
adjacent Sonora, Mexico, the Papago, closely related to the Pima or River people, were contacted by the Spanish in the late seventeenth century, and more
or less missionized by the eighteenth century—though in a fashion much less
violent and destructive to the Native culture than was the case in California.
Nominally Christian, predominantly Catholic, Papago people still practice elements of an older faith along with Church rituals; indeed, many of the rituals
they perform are a creative synthesis of Native and Christian materials.*

*Ruth Underhill, an anthropology student at Columbia University under
Franz Boas and Ruth Benedict, was sent by her teachers to Arizona in the
early thirties. Although she eventually learned some Papago and Chona knew
a few words of Spanish, the interviews that would become* Papago Woman
*were conducted through Ella Lopez Antone. Recently, Gretchen Bataille and
Kathleen Sands have praised Chona's "style" and "literary" ability, claiming
as well that "white influence [on the text] is minimal." But what "style" we
have is heavily dependent on Underhill's editing; indeed, Underhill herself
wrote that Chona's autobiography was "an Indian story told to satisfy whites
rather than Indians."*

*None of the above is meant to suggest that Chona's story is somehow
"false" or inauthentic. Rather, like all composite Indian autobiographies, it is
a composite, collaborative production, made up of the words spoken by Chona,
of the words of Antone's translation, and, finally, of the words Underhill
chose for the final text.*

*In this autobiography, we learn how houses were built and food cooked, of
war with the Papago's traditional Apache enemies, and of the purification of*

warriors; we are told of the importance of a young woman's first menstruation; of cactus fruit gathering, and of the brewing of cactus wine for the achievement of a culturally controlled drunken spell, among many other matters of interest.

The Autobiography of a Papago Woman *was first published as number* 46 *of the* Memoirs of the American Anthropological Association *in* 1936. *It was reprinted in 1979, preceded by a preface and a section called "Chona: Her Land and Time," which is as much about Underhill's impressions of her first visit to Papago country as it is about Chona. All of this (and more) appears in the most recent edition of the text (Waveland Press, 1985), so that the reader of this edition today learns a good deal about Ruth Underhill before encountering the life of Maria Chona. Our selections are taken from chapters 1, 5, 8, and 11 of the recent edition.*[1]

I

We lived at Mesquite Root and my father was chief there. That was a good place, high up among the hills, but flat, with a little wash where you could plant corn. Prickly pear grew there so thick that in summer, when you picked the fruit, it was only four steps from one bush to the next. And cholla cactus grew and there were ironwood trees. Good nuts they have! There were birds flying around, doves and woodpeckers, and a big rabbit sometimes in the early morning, and quails running across the flat land. Right above us was Quijotoa Mountain, the one where the cloud stands up high and white when we sing for rain.

We lived in a grass house and our relatives, all around us on the smooth flat land, had houses that were the same. Round our houses were, with no smoke hole and just a little door where you crawled in on hands and knees. That was good. The smoke could go out anywhere through the thatch and the air could come in. All our family slept on cactus fibre mats against the wall, pushed tight against it so centipedes and scorpions could not crawl in. There was a mat for each two children, but no, nothing over us. When we were cold, we put wood on the fire.

Early in the morning, in the month of Pleasant Cold, when we had

1. Excerpts from *Papago Woman*, by Ruth M. Underhill, copyright © 1979 by Holt, Rinehart and Winston, Inc., are reprinted by permission of the publisher.

all slept in the house to keep warm, we would wake in the dark to hear my father speaking.

"Open your ears, for I am telling you a good thing. Wake up and listen. Open your ears. Let my words enter them." He spoke in a low voice, so quiet in the dark. Always our fathers spoke to us like that, so low that you thought you were dreaming.

"Wake up and listen. You boys, you should go out and run. So you will be swift in time of war. You girls, you should grind the corn. So you will feed the men and they will fight the enemy. You should prac- tise running. So, in time of war, you may save your lives."

For a long time my father talked to us like that, for he began when it was black dark. I went to sleep, and then he pinched my ear. "Wake up! Do not be idle!"

Then we got up. It was the time we call morning-stands-up, when it is dark but there are white lines in the east. Those are the white hairs of Elder Brother who made us. He put them there so we can know when day is coming and we can go out to look for food.

We crawled out the little door. I remember that door so well. I al- ways crawled out of doors till long after I was a married woman and we stopped being afraid of enemies. Then we made houses with white men's doors. But this one was little and when we came out we could see the houses of my relatives nearby among the cactus, and the girls coming out of them, too, to get water.

Those girls had nothing on above the waist. We did not wear clothes then. They had strips of hand woven cloth in front and be- hind, tied around their waists with a string, for we did not know how to sew them together. Only deerskins the men knew how to sew, but our people had traded this cloth from Mexico and we thought we were very fine. And with good red paint above the waist, it *was* fine. And warm too. But the girls did not put on their paint in the early cold morning. Then they had to work.

There was no water at Mesquite Root; no water at all except what fell from the clouds, and I am telling about the month of Pleasant Cold when the rains were long over. Then our pond had dried up. If we wanted to stay in our houses, the girls had to run for water far, far up the hills and across the flat land to a place called Where the Water Whirls Around. That was a low flat place, a good place for corn, and the water ran down to it from all the hills. A big water hole was there full of red mud. Oh yes, our water was always red. It made the corn gruel red. I liked that earth taste in my food. Yes, I liked it.

The girls used to crawl laughing out of the houses, with their long black hair hanging to their waists, and they would pick up their carrying

Maria Chona gathering yucca. Photo by Ruth Underhill. All rights reserved, Photo Archives, Denver Museum of Natural History.

nets. Fine nets we used to have in those days, all dyed with red and blue. Shaped like a cone they were, with tall red sticks to keep them in shape. When the net was on a girl's back those red sticks would stand up on either side of her face. We used to think a pretty young girl looked best that way. That was how the men liked to see her.

I was too little to have a net then, or even clothes. But I used to help my cousins put the jars in their nets and to put little sticks between them so they would not break. The boys would stand laughing around and if there was one who was not a relative the girls would joke with him. They would throw gravel at him and run away, and once a girl said to one of my cousins: "Give me that male thing you have and I will put it between my water jars instead of a stick." So we called that man Between-the-Jars. Yes, that is how we joked in the old days.

Then the girls put the nets on their backs and if one was married and had a baby, she put that on top in its cradle board. Some men went with them with their war arrows because there were Apaches in the land then. They all went running, running. If they saw dust in the distance that they thought was Apaches, they went dodging behind the giant cactus. You see, women had to run in those days. That was what saved their lives. Many hours they had to run, and when they came back every family had two little jars of water to last for the day. But we did not mind. We knew how to use water. We have a word that means thirst-enduring and that is what we were taught to be. Why, our men, when they went off hunting, never drank at all. They thought it was womanish to carry water with them.

My brother went running off, too. Ah, how we could run, we Desert People; all the morning until the sun was high, without once stopping! My brothers took their bows and arrows and went far off over the flat land.

"Run," my father said to them. "Run until you are exhausted. So you will be a strong man. If you fall down tired, far out in the waste land, perhaps a vision will come to you. Perhaps a hawk will visit you and teach you to be swift. Perhaps you will get a piece of the rainbow to carry on your shoulder so that no one can get near to you, any more than to the rainbow itself. Or maybe Coyote himself will sing you a song that has magic in it."

So they went off in their breechclouts and bare feet, running in the dark when they could hardly see the cactus joints on the ground and the horned toads—rattlesnakes there were not in that cool weather. One of my brothers did really have visions. The others used to come back without him, bringing jackrabbits for our dinner. The little boy would come in much later and never tell where he had been. But we found out long, long after, when he became a medicine man, that he had been lying dead out on the desert all those hours and that Coyote had come and talked to him.

When they were gone my mother would come crawling out. She went to the little enclosure beside our house, made of greasewood bushes piled up in a circle and she got the pot of gruel. We always kept gruel in our house. It was in a big clay pot that my mother had made. She ground up seeds into flour. Not wheat flour—we had no wheat. But all the wild seeds, the good pigweed and the wild grasses. And corn, too! Some summers we could grow corn. All those things my mother kept in beautiful jars in our storehouse. Every day she ground some more and added fresh flour to the gruel and some boiling water. That pot stood always ready so that whoever came in from running could have some. Oh, good that gruel was! I have never tasted anything like it. Wheat flour makes me sick! I think it has no strength. But when I am weak, when I am tired, my grandchildren make me gruel out of the wild seeds. That is *food*.

I used to help my mother. When I was very little I began to grind the seeds, just for a short time. When I was ten years old I did it all, for then a daughter should be able to take over the work and let her mother sit down to baskets. But I am telling you about the early days when I could only grind a little. Then we pulled the grinding slab inside the house by the fire and my mother knelt behind it. I picked the dirt out of the seeds and handed them to her, and the pot boiled on the hearth on the three stones that we kept there.

My father was very busy, for he was the chief of our village. People used to bring their quarrels to him, and I remember him sitting crosslegged under the arbor we had to keep off the sun, listening with his head bent and his arms folded, while people talked.

"My daughter disappeared with a man on the last night of the maiden's dance. I want her beaten." "How many stripes?" "Twenty." "Fifteen," said my father. He was a gay man who liked to war and to gamble. He did not like to beat women.

Some days nobody would come, and then he would gamble with the other men, throwing the sticks that we use for dice, and then moving stones around a circle as many moves as there were marks on the stick. We used to hear the men singing in a low tone, before they threw, to give them luck:

> Down I shall throw
> The smooth stone I shall move
> Move it to the corner.

They smoked, too, and I can smell their tobacco yet, the strong wild tobacco that we do not have any more. It was tied in a long corn husk, so white, so nice, and when one man passed it to another he said: "Friend!" and the other said, "Friend."

When the sun was high, high, my brothers and my sister came home, and as each one came my mother gave them food. She dipped the gruel out of the pot into a bowl, for my mother was a good potter. We all had bowls in our house. Only my father and my mother ate out of the same one laughing together, because they liked each other. When my mother dipped out our food she said: "Do not eat it hot. You will have wrinkles." She set mine on the grinding slab to cool. "It will make you industrious," my mother said. My father said to the boys: "Do not eat it hot, no matter how hungry you are. Wait till it has scum on it. So you will be a runner and not a fat man."

When we had finished we did not wash the dishes. How could we, with no water! We scooped food out with our knuckles. The boys used two knuckles because men have time to eat. We girls used three because women must hurry and work. When we were through it was only my father who could wipe his fingers between his toes. That was because he was a warrior and had killed enemies. The rest of us wiped them on the ground and rubbed our hands together. I do not like water on my dishes even now. They feel so smooth.

Then we made our toilet. We washed our faces in a little cold water, but we did not bathe. Rubbing yourself with earth does just as well. Then the older girls painted themselves with beautiful red paint, all in dots and splashes. I went out to play.

I played with the boys and girls who were children of my uncles. Brothers and sisters, we call them. We had no clothes, any of us, but we were not cold. We went to a sunny place and made ourselves dolls of mesquite leaves tied with strings of corn husk for arms and legs and head. We had a little stone for the grinding slab and some sand for the corn. The boys had men dolls and they would take them away and say: "We go hunting." "Well, go," said the wives. Then the boys would hunt all around the village and find a deer bone. "Here is a deer for you."

Sometimes the boys went to get rats. They poked them out of the holes and hit them with sticks. Then we roasted them on sticks with the skins on. Good food, that used to be!

Sometimes we went to run races. We had a good racetrack in our village. Our men had cleared a road that ran across the flat land as far as you could see, and every day they swept it with greasewood branches to keep off the thorns. They had a song:

> The hawk made the race-track
> And on it we won
> A-a-ah!
>
> We ran with the hawk
> And won a Hawk's heart
> A-a-ah!

All our young men and girls practiced on that racetrack so they could run fast against the other villages. We children ran, too. Every day I ran until I was ten years old and had to be doing the house work.

But we did not stay at Mesquite Root all the time. We were hungry people, we and my father's brothers and his cousins who lived around us. In those winter days my father went to hunt deer and sometimes we all went with him down over the Mexican border to pick the century plant and roast it or to get stalks for our basketry or clay for our pots.

All the year round we were watching where the wild things grew so we could pick them. Elder Brother planted those things for us. He told us where they are and how to cook them. You would not know if it had not been Given. You would not know you could eat cactus stems and shake the seeds out of the weeds. Elder Brother did not tell the Whites that. To them he gave peaches and grapes and wheat, but to us he gave the wild seeds and the cactus. Those are the good foods.

There was a kind of cactus called cholla, and when its buds were green we all went and stayed for many days picking them, up in the hills. We pulled the tops of some palo verde trees together and piled greasewood bushes over them to make a shelter and there we lived. My uncles made shelters, too, and my mother and my uncles' wives all went together to pick the cactus. They broke off the new stems with tongs and rolled them around on the ground to get the thorns off, and then baked them all night into a big pit. They smelled fresh and fine when they came out. When the big pit was roasting slowly in the night, the women threw green cholla stems on the campfire ashes to cook. We pulled them out, knocked off the thorns, and ate them hot. Ah, good, good food! We ate nothing else for those three weeks. Green things!

At last the giant cactus grew ripe on all the hills. It made us laugh to see the fruit on top of all the stalks, so many, and the men would point to it and say: "See the liquor growing." We went to pick it, to the same place where we always camped, and every day my mother and all the women went out with baskets. They knocked the fruit down with cactus poles. It fell on the ground and all the red pulp came out. Then I picked it up, and dug it out of the shell with my fingers, and put it in my mother's basket. She told me always to throw down the skins with the red inside uppermost, because that would bring the rain.

It was good at cactus camp. When my father lay down to sleep at night he would sing songs about the cactus liquor. And we could hear songs in my uncle's camp across the hill. Everybody sang. We felt as if a beautiful thing was coming. Because the rain was coming and the dancing and the songs.

> Where on Quijotoa Mountain a cloud stands
> There my heart stands with it.
> Where the mountain trembles with the thunder
> My heart trembles with it.

That was what they sang. When I sing that song yet it makes me dance.

Then the little rains began to come. We had jugs of the juice that my mother had boiled, and all the women carried them in their nets as we came running down the mountain back to our village. Much, much liquor we made, and we drank it to pull down the clouds, for that is what we call it. I was too little to drink. They put me on the house top with my older sister. Our jars of liquor were up there, too. The house top was the only safe place.

We heard the people singing over by the council house:

> There sits the magician of the east
> Holding the rain by the hand
> The wind holding by the hand
> He sits.

Then they began to drink. Making themselves beautifully drunk, for that is how our words have it. People must all make themselves drunk like plants in the rain and they must sing for happiness. We heard them singing all day all over the village. Then my father and mother came and stood by the house where we were on the roof, with many relatives. Oh, they were very happy. "Reach us down a new jar from the roof," they said. So my sister handed it down. Then they gave it to drink to all the relatives whom they loved. And each, when he had drunk, sang a song.

The next day a relative came and said: "Your father and mother are out by the arroyo sleeping. Let a child go and stay with them until they wake." So my sister went. My brothers were drunk, too, but we did not know where. At last my father and mother awoke and came home very happy. For many days they sang.

V

When I was nearly as tall as my mother, that thing happened to me which happens to all our women though I do not know if it does to the Whites; I never saw any signs. It is called menses.

Girls are very dangerous at that time. If they touch a man's bow, or even look at it, that bow will not shoot any more. If they drink out of a man's bowl, it will make him sick. If they touch the man himself, he might fall down dead. My mother had told us this long ago and we knew what had happened in our village.

There was a girl once who became dangerous and she did not tell.

They were having a good time that day. All the village was planting in her father's field, and he had given them a meal of succotash. They were eating out in the field, her mother was cooking over a campfire. My mother was there and she said this girl was standing with a bowl in the crook of her arm, laughing and eating. It began to rain. The girl and her sisters ran home to take in the bedding, because we sleep out of doors in the summer and it was on the ground.

There was a crash of thunder. All the eating people stood still and then, from the house of that girl they heard a long sigh. They ran there. All the family were lying stunned on the floor, one sister was blind, and that girl was dead. The men dragged the people out into the rain and the house began to burn. "See," said those people, "what has happened to us." Her relatives buried that girl all alone and no one would go near.

Then there was a girl who was going to build a fire, and it seemed that it reached out, and took her, and burned her up. And there was another whose mother was struck by lightning. For it is not always you who are hurt if you commit this sacrilege; it may be any one in your family.

That is why, when the lightning strikes a village, they send for the medicine man to see what woman was dangerous. He summons all the girls and looks at his crystals to see who did it. They do not punish that woman. It is enough to know that she has killed her friends.

Our mothers watch us, and so mine knew when it came to me. We always had the Little House ready, over behind our own house. It was made of some branches stuck in the ground and tied together at the top, with greasewood thrown over them to make it shady. There was no rain then, for it was winter, but it was cold in that little house. The door was just big enough to crawl through, like our house door, and there was room for you to lie down inside, but not to stand up. My mother made me a new bowl and drinking cup out of clay, and put them in that house. When my mother cooked food at the big house, she would come over and pour some in my bowl, but no meat and nothing with salt in it. My father sharpened a little stick for me to scratch my hair with, because if I touched it, it would fall out. I was so afraid to lose my nice long hair that I kept that stick in my mouth all the time. Even when I was asleep, I had it there.

It is a hard time for us girls, such as the men have when they are being purified. Only they give us more to eat, because we are women. And they do not let us sit still and wait for dreams. That is because we are women, too. Women must work.

They chose my father's cousin to take care of me. She was the most industrious woman we had, always running with the carrying basket. That old woman would come for me in the dark when morning-stands-up. "Come," she said. "Let's go for water over across the mountain. Let's go for firewood."

So we would run, far, far across the flat land and up the mountain and bring the water back before daylight. I would leave it outside my father's house and not go in. Then that old woman would talk to me.

"Work hard. If you do not work hard now, you will be lazy all your life. Then no one will want to marry you. You will have to take some good for nothing man for a husband. But if you are industrious, we shall find you a good old man."

That is what we call our husbands: old man. But this woman did it out of modesty, too, so that I should not have young men in my mind. "When you have an old man," she said, "you will grind the corn for him and you will always have water there for him to drink. Never let him go without water. Never let him go without food. He will go to the house of some one else to eat and you will be disgraced."

I listened to her. Do you say that some girls might think of other things and not listen? But I wanted to be a good woman! And I have been. Ask anyone in our village if they ever saw me with idle hands. Or legs, either, when I was younger.

All the girls came around the Little House while that woman talked. They did not come near, because that would not be safe, and she would call to them: "Go away." But they sat and listened and when she was tired of talking, they laughed and sang with me. And we played a game with little stones and a ball. We pick up the stones in different ways with one hand while we catch the ball in the other. Oh, we have good times at the Little House, especially when that first month is over. But other women who were dangerous did not come; that would be too much.

I had to stay four days and then I was not dangerous any more. Everything goes by fours with our people, and Elder Brother arranged it that even this thing should be the same. No woman has trouble for more than four days. Then they gave me a bath just as they did to my father. Oh, it was cold in the winter time! I tell the girls who come of age in the summer they do not know what hardship is. The water even feels nice in summer.

My mother came in the dark of the morning with the water in a big new jar. The women had to run all day to get that water ready for me. I tried to get away, but my mother caught me and made me kneel down. Then she dipped a gourd in the jar and poured that cold water down over my forehead.

Hail!
I shall pour this over you.
You will be one who endures cold.
You will think nothing of it.

It is true, I have never felt cold.

Then my mother washed my hair with soapweed fibres. That is the way women should always wash their hair and it will never grow gray. She cut it so it came just to my shoulders, for we women cannot have hair as long as the men; it would get in our way when we work. But we like to have it thick and shiny, and we know that everybody is noticing. There was quite a lapful that my mother cut off, and she saved it to make hair ropes for our carrying baskets. She had new clothes for me; two pieces of unbleached muslin, tied around my waist with a string. We did not know how to sew in those days. We pinned them together over our hips with bought pins, but it was very modest.

Then I could go back to our house, only still I had to use the stick for four days and I could not eat salt. And then they danced me. All that month they danced me, until the moon got back to the place where it had been at first. It is a big time when a girl comes of age; a happy time. All the people in the village knew that I had been to the Little House for the first time, so they come to our house and the singer for the maidens came first of all.

That singer was the Chief's Leg, the man I told you about. He knew all the songs, the ones that Elder Brother first sang when he used to go over the country, dancing all the maidens. That Leg was the man who danced every maiden in our village when she came of age. His wife danced opposite him. She was the one who was to get the hair that my mother had cut off. He had another wife, too, but not such a good dancer.

"Come out," said my father on that first night. "Now you must dance or the Leg will drag you out. He's mean."

I did not want to dance; I was sleepy and I had run so far. Always when I had heard the others singing those maiden songs, from far away, I had been wild to go. But now it was my turn and all I wanted to do was sleep. But Luis, the Leg, came into the house and took me by the arm. He always danced next to the maiden, with his arm over her shoulders and the rattle in his other hand. He and I were at one end of a long line of people and his wife at the end of a line opposite. There was first a boy and then a girl, all down the line, with their arms over each other's shoulder and the blankets held along at the back. I told you the boys always like that dance.

The lines went to and fro, toward each other, and they kept wheeling a little, till at last they had made a circle.

> On top of Baboquiviri Peak
> here is a fire burning.So near I came.
> I saw it blow all over the ground
> Shining.
>
> On the flat land
> There is a house of clouds.
> There stand white butterfly wings (of clouds).
> It pleased me. That was what I saw.

Those were the songs they sang, with the rattle going in the night. We had no fire; we kept warm dancing. After every four songs Luis stopped, because his voice was hoarse. Then he let me go, and we girls went and sat together while the men smoked. How dark and cold it was then, with only one ember to light their cigarettes!

There were girls who did not come to sit with us and boys who did not sit with the men. How dark it was! Some mothers went looking for their girls in the night and some did not.

At midnight my mother brought jars of succotash. She had been cooking all day for this dance, and every day after that she cooked and ground corn and baked bread in the ashes. Every morning we gave gifts to Luis and his wife. My cut-off hair and dried beans and cooked food and the hand woven cotton that I wore for a dress. And to the girl friends who danced beside me, I gave my beads and my baskets because these people had suffered and endured sleeplessness with us.

We stopped dancing in the dark of the morning and then my mother said: "Come and get firewood. Do you want to grow up a lazy woman?" So then I went out in the dark to pick up the dead branches and bring them back before I slept. It seemed I slept only an hour before they were saying: "Get up! Get water. Get wood. Grind the corn. If you sleep at this time you will be sleepy all your life."

Oh, I got thin in that time! We girls are like strips of yucca fibre after our coming of age is over. Always running, and mostly gruel and ash bread to eat, with no salt. And dancing every night from the time the sun sets until morning-stands-up. I used to go to sleep on Luis' arm and he pinched my nose to wake me.

Every night they came, the people who were not too sleepy from the night before. And always the young people came. Even Luis did not know songs enough for all that month and other men sang, too. It is a nice thing for a man to know maidens' songs. Every man likes to dance next to the maiden and to hold her on his arm. But Luis was an old man and his wife danced opposite. The wife always does.

At last the moon had come around again and they gave me a bath. It was over. I looked like half of myself. All my clothes were gone. All our dried corn and beans were eaten up. But I was grown up. Now the medicine man could cleanse me and give me a name.

You have to be cleansed as soon as the month is over; you must not wait. A cousin of mine did that once. She meant to be cleansed but she just waited. I think, perhaps, she did not have anything to pay the medicine man. But while she waited, one of her brothers was chopping wood. Something fell on him like a hot coal and killed him. So I went the day after my bath.

My mother and I went to the house of the medicine man early in the morning, with a big basket my mother had made, to pay him. He drew a circle on the ground and made me sit in it, crosslegged, with my back to the rising sun. In front of me he put a little dish. Then he walked away where we could not see him and took something out of a little deerskin bag. It was the clay that he carries to charm the evil away from women. No one ever sees the medicine man dig up that clay and no one knows how he mixes it. But I know, because my brother was a medicine man and because I myself have seen things. He grinds up the bone of a dead man and some owl feathers so that they are fine dust.

He put that clay in a tiny bowl before me, mixed with a little water. Then he walked up and down four times, facing the sun that was behind me. Every time he came up to me he blew over my head and dusted me off with this eagle feathers to brush away the evil. And every time he turned, he made a noise like an owl: hm. The fifth time, he took up the bowl of clay and stirred it around with a little owl feather that was standing in the center of it. Then he put the clay to my mouth. "Drink this up!" So I drank it all.

Then he marked me, the sacred marks that are put on the men who have got salt from the magic ocean; the marks that take away bad luck and bring you a good life. On my breast, on my shoulders, my back, and my belly.

"Your name shall be cha-veela." I did not know before what name he was going to give me; neither did my parents. The medicine man names one from his dreams. Some of my friends had names that could be understood like Leaf Buds, Rustling Leaves, Windy Rainbow, Dawn Murmur. But I have never understood my name and he did not tell me.

After all that work, I did not menstruate again for a year!

VIII

My husband was a Coyote-Meeter. That is, when he had his medicine man's dreams, it was our comrade, Coyote, who came to him and sang him songs. It began when he went with the other men to the ocean to get salt, for that is where all our young men go when they want to meet some spirit. They gather the salt, and then they run along that great sandy place where the water is and where there are white birds flying over head. It was those white birds that had sung to my father, but with my husband it was different.

Running along alone, he saw a dead coyote on the sand. He stopped. That coyote rose up and said: "Do you want to see something?" "Yes." My husband died right there and the coyote carried him away.

The other men wanted to go home and they said: "Where is he?" But the leader knew about these things. "He must have Met something. Let him alone."

Next morning my husband awoke and found himself lying by that dead coyote. He went back to the others but he never told them what he had seen.

Only after that he used to go out at night and Meet the coyotes. He would leave early in the evening and come back looking sick or drunk. The coyotes had killed him and taught him while he was dead. He did not tell us this in the house, but we all understood. The same thing was happening to his two brothers and had happened to his father before him. It was coyote who Met them all.

After a while the people began to know that he had something. They would ask him to come and find their sicknesses for them, because people have great faith in a young medicine man. They think he has more power than an old one; he has not used it up. My husband had got himself a gourd rattle and some eagle feathers. We get our gourds down in Mexico where they grow them large and beautiful. He glued a handle on one with some mesquite gum and put some pebbles inside; nice little pebbles that you find the wash among the ants. He got eagle feathers from an old man and tied them on a handle, four of them, tied two and two, beautifully wound about with string. He went to the houses and sat all night, rattling the gourd and singing, and they gave him clothes and food. We got rich.

Six children I had by my husband, for he was a strong man. I never had any trouble in childbirth. And I could tell what sex they would be before they were born. If the movements in my womb were strong, it would be a boy. I had five boys. I was unlucky with them, though. As soon as a new one came, the one before it died. I know a great deal about children, now that I am old, and I think it was the milk. We nurse our children till long after they can walk and talk. We must. We have no cow's milk. What would they eat? But my husband was such a strong man. The children came so fast. I was always nursing one while another was coming, and then the nursing one died.

Perhaps, though, it was only diseases that came by bad luck. That is what my husband said. He treated our children, they were among the first he sang for. One had jackrabbit sickness, which is a sort of coughing and choking that comes to a child so it cannot breathe. Another had dog sickness. I suppose a dog must have breathed on me with its hot breath before the child was born, because the baby had hot breath for days and days before it died.

I always knew when my children were to die. I am one who knows things, because, even though they took my crystals out, there was always something in me. Once, when my baby was sick, I dreamed that I was passing through a wash. A woman sat there with a child, and its hair was blowing back as though it was in the water, only the wash was dry. I said: "What are you doing here?" "We live here." I knew that meant something strange was coming.

Another time I dreamed that someone who seemed a medicine man again led me to a wash. It was full of babies and children, big and little, all crawling around over each other, like worms. "What does it mean?" I asked that man who took me. "It means all your children are going to die. You will have no children at your house."

But I saved one child, a girl. I gave her to my mother to nurse, because an old woman can nurse with us, as well as young ones. That girl grew up. She used to sit on my head when I was running along with the carrying basket, sometimes with another baby on top of it. I took her out to the hills with me when I was gathering fruit and cactus.

"Never step over a snake," I told her, "nor even the trail of a snake, for you will have the vomiting sickness. Don't step on a horned toad, it will make your foot sore. And you must learn the difference between the big ants who are the medicine men and who sting and the little kind ants that will not hurt you."

When all our family camped for days and days, to bake the cholla buds, we made a little enclosure of boughs for our children. "Stay there and do not play hard. You will be thirsty and drink up our water." So they made dolls out of leaves and played at grinding corn with sand and little flat stones. Sometimes the children brought us something to eat. In the Month of Rain, when the birds got their feathers wet in the thunder storms so they hopped along the ground and could not fly, then our children would chase them and catch them in their hands. Doves and woodpeckers they brought in to us, and we roasted them on a spit with the feathers on.

We like children, you know. We talk to them quietly and tell them what to do, but we do not scold. When our children are running about the house, in and around everything, we let them run. If they break something, then that thing is just broken. We do not say anything. Sometimes they run across the circle when we are dancing. Or when the medicine man is going about with his branch of thorns, removing sickness, they might try to grab it. No one would speak about that. We like them to be happy.

I took my little girl with me when we went to dance and sing for the River People. Every year or two we went, we three or four villages that were relatives.

Once we went to The Spring, and Begging for Yucca Fruit made the songs. Then we went to Sacaton and my father made them. The River People came to us, too, and we all went and camped at the village where they were to sing. They sang at Mesquite Root, my father's village, and he put into the singer's hands cow manure and horse manure. That meant he would give them a cow and a horse. Then we went to the Narrow Place and held a great harvest festival, and my husband was one of the singers. A good time we had, roaming over the land.

Once, when my husband and I were away working, word came that my father was sick. All the family came back to Mesquite Root, but the medicine man could not help him. We all began to cry, right then: "Haya, my father!" "Haya, my elder brother!" "Haya, my husband!" It is a sort of tune. We cried all night, but he died.

We did not bury him in a cave in the rocks as our people used to do. We had been up and down to Mexico, and had seen the priests and learned many things. We laid him down and dug a grave. We dressed him in clothes, a good shirt and trousers and sandals and a red headband around his hair. We gave him a blanket and pillow, too, for the grave. Because he was an Enemy Slayer his face was painted, black to the nose and white below. His younger brother did that, for he was an Enemy Slayer, too, and had the right.

All the men of our family dug the grave, and then carried him out and put him there. They put in his blanket and pillow, because we did not sleep on mats any more. And his leather pouch, they put in, and the sticks he had for games and his bow and arrows and his good quiver of wild cat skin. Then his brother spoke: "We put you here. Stay and don't come back to frighten us." My mother said: "Make yourself at home. Be happy. Don't come back to break up my good dreams." She was crying. Then we called him again. "Haya, my father!" "Haya, my elder brother!" "Haya, my husband!"

All the relatives called him. After that, we never said his name, José María. When we talked about him we said my father-gone, my elder brother-gone, my husband-gone. To hear the name would make us feel too bad. And nobody ever said that name to us because my brothers would get angry.

We divided his horses, and my sister and I each got two. My brothers and my mother got more. My brothers took the house down and moved it. Then they put it up again in another place but still at Mesquite Root where they had always lived. There my mother lived and they with her. She said to them: "I didn't bring you up to have you go off with some woman. If you were girls, I would let you go. But since you are men, this is where you should stay. If some woman loves you and falls against you, bring her home. She can cook for me." So they married and brought their wives home. I have many grandchildren from those brothers.

I went back to Where the Water Whirls Around. We lived better there because we had more horses and my husband went often to sing for the sick. People gave him clothes for that singing, and we all had clothes then, not just something tied around our waists. And all the men had trousers instead of breech clouts. My husband and I built a house next door to his family. Shining Evening built one, too, and lived there alone. She used to cook beans and tortillas and have good food there. When my father-in-law died, my mother-in-law lived in that house with Shining Evening, and he was both a son and a daughter, only he was often away, drunk.

There were white men here and there on our land by that time, as there never had been. So our men began to learn to drink that whiskey. It was not a thing that you must drink only once a year like our cactus cider. You could drink it any time, with no singing and no speeches, and it did not bring rain. Men grew crazy when they drank that whiskey and they had visions. My husband did not drink. He had his visions. He said that a good man must get them as he and my father had, by suffering. But Shining Evening got very crazy. She would flirt and laugh with the men more than ever, throw gravel at them and slap their faces. Many names the men got from Shining Evening, for that is how our men got most of their nicknames.

She gave to her brother, Thundering Wings, the nickname of Skirt-string. Shining Evening was the first of us women to make a skirt that was sewed up and had a draw string. Her brother pulled it out and said: "Hey! What's this!" She giggled and said in her funny high voice: "Skirt-string! Skirt-string!" So everybody called him that. Some men wanted to buy the name, it was so funny.

I was much with Shining Evening and the women in those days because my husband was away. People would send for him from far across the desert, and he would go and sing for many nights. Then on other nights he would come to me looking strange and say: "I am going to hunt rabbits." I knew it was not rabbits, but no woman questions her husband among our people. So I lay alone on my mat, thinking that, perhaps, just now my husband was with Coyote. I wonders what the Comrade would say to him, and if he would sing any songs like those I had heard from my father. Then, once, Coyote came to me, too.

I was at Mesquite Root, gathering giant cactus with my family. I always went there in the Cactus month because Mesquite Root was in the hills, near the cactus groves, and Where the Water Whirls Around was down in the hot plain. Once I had picked my basket full of cactus fruit and I was resting. I looked down by my bare toe and there lay a crystal.

I have told you how medicine men find these crystals by magic, after a dream. Those shining stones have power and they can make rain. No one finds them by chance. So when I saw that, I was afraid. It was a big crystal, thick as my finger and as long as two joints of it. I took it home, but I had no use for a crystal then; my heart was cool. I gave it to my brother who was now a medicine man, and he whirled it around and tried to make rain. But he could not: the stone was not for him.

So I took it home. But I could not keep it, I, a woman, who was not meeting any spirit. I was afraid of it, and I gave it to my younger brother-in-law. He is an old medicine man now, at Where the Water Whirls Around, and he has it yet.

But that night Coyote came to me. He did not speak. He looked at me a minute and then he turned away. As he went, he sang:

A frog medicine man
With spotted back
Lies somewhere on the ground
Looking for rain.
Where, where is the rain?

Sick people came often to my husband and his brothers because they were all medicine men, and their father, too. We women, if we had wanted to, could have learned many lovely magic songs and could have looked in their medicine bags and seen the crystals and the feathers and other powerful things. Of course we did not, for those things can make you sick. We knew where the gourds were kept in the thatch of the roof and the long eagle feathers with them, but we never even looked that way. We thought we might begin to menstruate and take away their power.

But sometimes when babies were brought to my husband I could not help looking on, because I had had babies myself, and they had died. There is one thing that happens to babies that is very dangerous. They have a soft spot on the top of their heads. It is there when they are born and then it closes up. But sometimes it does not close. One who is wise will put a finger in the baby's mouth, far back and will push up. That pushes up the whole head and closes that soft spot which really comes because the head has fallen in.

My husband knew this and I have heard him tell mothers about it. But the mothers could not do the pushing. It must be a person with power.

I do not think it was crystals, for I was too old to have them grow within me any longer. Yet once, when I was at cactus camp, I was sick. We did not have a medicine man; my husband and his brothers were far away. I lay there, and my head spun round, and I was hot and cold. Then, out of the desert, a furry, gray coyote came trotting to me. He blew on me as the medicine man blows and I felt cool. I began to sing:

Coyote, my comrade
Hither ran.
To the end of his tail
A cloud was tied.

I felt that cool beautiful cloud, and I saw how funny Coyote looked, waving it over me and running away. I got well.

Then one day, when my daughter was twelve years old, my husband took another wife.

XI

My sons grew up. The first one we called Vincenzo but he bought the name Two Bits from another man because he liked it. We say that name in our language, of course. It sounds good.

We married Two Bits when he was seventeen. Some people came to us and said: "We have a daughter. She was married to a man, but that man went away to the White school, and when he came back he did not take her." "She is older than your son," they said, "but she is industrious. She may be some help to him." We said: "It is true she is older, but we have seen her work. She may be a help."

So we told our son and he said nothing. Her mother brought us that girl, and ever since she has stayed with us and behaved herself like a woman. Some wives are like this; when their husbands are away, they run out to visit. She never does. She is always home working. Many children she and my son had, so that I have grandchildren and great-grandchildren. They live still in that flat place at Standing Rock, and when I go there, they have cactus seed for me to eat.

I went there last year before the husband of my granddaughter died. That man was sick and I could do nothing for him. I sat in their house making baskets, and a little blackbird came and drank out of the water I use to wet the fibres. I told one of my grandchildren to chase the bird away, and it went into the corner of the room. That night the bird came to me. It said: "Why did you chase me from your water? Don't you know I will need it?" I knew that man would die. So that day he did. The next night he came again, with black feathers and a cow tail. "See," he said, "how pitiful I look." I knew the devil took him.

My second son was a medicine man. Ah, that one would have been great! When he was small, he acted strange; his heart was feeling something coming. He would run out in the night, and his father would run after him and find him lying face down in the greasewood. Maybe something had come after him and taken him away.

Once, when a rattlesnake bit me, he cured me. I was picking beans among the weeds in our garden and, along with a handful of beans, I grabbed the snake. I had hold of him near the head but he turned his head back and bit my wrist. My son killed the snake. Then he chewed some greasewood leaves and put them on the little hole where it had bit me. He made a mark with a buzzard's feather all around my wrist, tight, and the poison never went beyond it. Two nights it hurt me and my hand swelled, but not beyond where my son had made the mark.

He used to bring birds home to the house and keep them; he could speak with birds. Once he kept a hawk in our house and killed jack-rabbits for it. Once I saw him coming home in the evening after he had been after the horses, and there was something shining on his shoulder. It was the eyes of an owl. "What will you do with it?" I said. So he let it fly away. But I think he spoke with it after that, behind the mountain.

He had crystals growing in him, and I know he had dreams but he had not told them yet. People only tell their dreams when they begin to cure.

When he was seventeen he went to the drinking ceremony, and he met one of those wild women who run about without husbands and sleep in the arroyos. He put her on his horse and brought her home to Standing Rock. That was a bad thing. I did not like that, but we said nothing. Then she wanted money to buy things. She did not want him to stay and plant our corn with Two Bits. They went to the white man's town of Many Cottonwoods and had two children there. But that woman killed him.

She was a woman who would not wait and do things at the right time. She lay with my son in the house when she should have been at the Little House. That kills the power of a medicine man. It rots his crystals and after a while it kills him, too. So he came back to stay with my daughter and left that woman. She would not come back with him, out of the town.

I went there to my poor son and took him to a medicine man, but that one said: "His crystals are all dead and dried. They build combs like bees and those combs are empty and blue. His power is dead." So he died. "My mother," he said to me, "I will come to you like an owl. You will know me." And it is true. The other day I was passing by a giant cactus, and there sat an owl in the fork and called to me. It does not happen often. I would like to hear my son call again.

That wild woman who was his wife took another husband the next year at the drinking ceremony. The man's name was Jackrabbit Chief and he was an old man, but it was dark and she did not know it. She got on his horse with him and she said: "Where do you live?" "At the place of the Dead Dog," he said. The sun was coming up just then and she saw his face. "Oh, that's too far." She jumped off the horse and we have never seen her again.

My daughter never lived with us very much. She lived with my mother and my brother, so when it came for her to marry, it was my brother who offered her. There was a man named Crooked Lightning whose sister was married to my brother. Crooked Lightning was as old as my brother. He was a singer and a good man. He had a wife who scolded him but he did not scold her. Only one day he went away from her and came to my brother, and said he needed another wife. So my brother gave him my daughter, Crescenza. She is a big fat woman, now, a good woman.

It has been a long time since my children were married. My old husband and I lived with them, and then we lived with our grandchildren. Thirty years my husband and I were together. He grew blind. He lay on his mattress all day long, and I had to pull it round the house to keep it in the shade. All the time he sang. He knew every song in the world, and he lay there singing in a low voice. Sometimes he slept in the day when it was warm and he sang in the night. We would wake up in the night and hear him singing.

Seven years ago he died. He said: "Now I'm going to rest and you shall rest, too." He meant I need not work for him any more, pulling that mattress around the house.

"But I won't come when I am dead to frighten you," he said. "Only when it's time for you to go. Then I'll come to call you. But not yet, I will not call you yet. First you'll hear some man say: 'I want to marry you'."

The next year I did. I had great grandchildren then, but still a man came and asked me to go to his house. But I was tired. I said: "No, I am too old. I cannot cook for you."

So I stay now with my grandchildren. Don't you think my baskets are good? I make them all day—all day long, and the young women do the cooking. While I work I hear voices: "Put a turtle there! Put a Gila monster here! Here put a zigzag." Then I seem to see a woman holding up the finished basket and I know how it will be.

I like to work at my daughter's house, at the Burnt Seeds. She has corn meal there and cactus seeds. I can eat when I live there, and every year I go with her to the drinking ceremony. They want me, for I can sing. But when I go to someone's house I have to stay a long time before I can walk back. It is not good to be old. Not beautiful. When you come again, I will not be here.

21

Son of Old Man Hat

Edited by

WALTER DYK

An Athabascan people whose language is closely related to that of Canadian and Alaskan tribes, the Navajo came to the Southwest from what is considered to be a much more northerly point of origin at a relatively recent date, perhaps around 1000–1300 C.E. Once settled in the Southwest, the Navajo learned farming and weaving from the long-settled pueblo people, acquired livestock from the Spanish in the seventeenth century, and developed fine silver-working skills from contact with Mexicans in the nineteenth century. Numbering some 140,000 persons in 1977, the Navajo today are the most populous tribe in the United States.

When the American government took possession of the southwestern territories from Mexico in 1848, it inherited not only the problem of raiding Apache, as we have noted, but of raiding Navajo as well. In 1863, the government enlisted the aid of the well-known scout Kit Carson, allowing him to pursue a scorched earth policy of destroying Navajo crops and livestock. It took only a year before starving Indians began to make their way into the American Fort Defiance. And it was in that year, 1864, that some eight thousand Navajo were forced to make the "long walk" of three hundred miles from Fort Defiance to incarceration at Fort Sumner, a culturally traumatic event remembered by the Navajo in much the same way as the "trail of tears" is remembered by the Cherokee, Sand Creek is remembered by the Cheyenne, and Wounded Knee is remembered by the Sioux.

In 1868—the year, coincidentally, of Left-Handed's birth—a new treaty with the Navajo established a three million acre reservation for them in New Mexico and Arizona—and the people began to return to their homes. Despite short rations, drought, and further land cessions, the Navajo gradually began to increase in numbers. Today, the Navajo are mostly threatened by corporate desire for access to the oil, uranium, and other commercially valuable minerals on their lands. The Navajo are also embroiled in a land dispute with their Hopi neighbors, onto whose lands they have for long encroached, a dispute that as of September, 1992, has been resolved in favor of the Navajo, although appeals are pending. In this decision, the Court denied the right of Native people to claim land on the basis of religious usage; this is an extremely threatening decision not only to the Hopi but to all of the tribes.

Left-Handed was sixty-six years old when he was interviewed by Walter Dyk in 1934. He spoke little or no English and Dyk worked through a Navajo interpreter, Philip Davis. According to Dyk's own commentary, his editing consisted mostly of the excision of what he felt to be extraneous or repetitive details, and, at least up until the time of Left-Handed's fourteenth year (when, apparently, Left-Handed himself adopted this principle of narration), the chronological organization of the material. Son of Old Man Hat gives us the first twenty years of Left-Handed's life, up until the time of his first marriage. A sequel to this volume, Left-Handed: A Navajo Autobiography,[1] was completed by Dyk's wife Ruth after his death, based on his notes and papers. Although it deals with just three years of Left-Handed's life in the late 1880s, the book runs to nearly six hundred pages! The two volumes together make Left-Handed's life story one of the most densely detailed of all Indian autobiographies.

Born in Germany, but educated at Berkeley, Walter Dyk went on to do graduate work in anthropology at the University of Chicago under the great Edward Sapir. When Sapir went to Yale University, Dyk followed his teacher, earning his Ph.D. from Yale in 1933, with a thesis on Wishram (Northwest coast) grammar. Dyk eventually held a fellowship at the Harvard Psychological Clinic, and it may be the combination of his psychological and anthropological interests, a familiar combination in the thirties, that led him to prod Left-Handed about sexual matters—a subject on which the autobiography is quite outspoken. Our selections, from Chapters 1, 5, and 18, reflect this dimension of Son of Old Man Hat,[2] *although they also record many of the details of the ordinary workaday life of a Navajo of this period. It should be noted that Old Man Hat is not Left-Handed's biological father, but the older clan brother of his "real" father. And Left-Handed, in typical Navajo fashion, uses the words "father" and "mother" in extended kinship terms, rather in our own strictly biological sense.*

1

I was born when the cottonwood leaves were about the size of my thumb nail, but the date was not due yet for my birth. It should have been another month. Something had happened to my mother, she'd

1. *Left-Handed: A Navajo Autobiography* (New York: Columbia Univ. Press, 1980).
2. *Son of Old Man Hat: A Navajo Autobiography*, ed. Walter Dyk (Lincoln: Univ. of Nebraska Press, 1967). The selections included below are reprinted by permission of the University of Nebraska Press. Copyright © 1938 by Walter Dyk. Renewal Copyright © 1966 by Walter Dyk.

hurt herself, that was why I was born before my time. I was just a tiny little baby, and my feet and fingers weren't strong, they were like water. My mother thought I wasn't going to live.

She was very sick when I was born and had no milk, so her older sister picked me up and started to take care of me. She didn't have any milk either, but she went among the women who had babies and begged them for some. She had many necklaces of different-colored beads, and when she brought the women and their babies home with her she'd divide a necklace and give each one a string. Then she'd pick me up and hand me over to one of them. That's where I got my milk. After a while she didn't have to go around among the women anymore, because four of them lived right close by. All four had babies, and every day they came to our place. Whenever they wanted to nurse me one of them would come and give me my feed. They helped me out until I was able to eat. All four were still feeding me while we were moving back to the reservation from Fort Sumner, as far as Chinlee. There they quit, and I was able to eat anything from there on. My mother and her husband were the only ones who took care of me.

When we returned from Fort Sumner we settled at Chinlee. My mother's husband had another wife in a hogan close by, and he left to visit her. While he was gone my mother's former husband came. She had been married to him before the Indians went to Fort Sumner, but he'd stayed behind on the reservation by himself for four years. When he heard we were back he started to hunt for my mother, and at Chinlee he found her. From then on he lived with his wife again. His clan was Many Goats, his name was Old Man Hat.

My mother decided to go with him to Black Mountain where some of his relatives were living. She took me to a hogan where an older clan sister of mine lived and said, "I'm going away, and I'm leaving my baby here with you. Please be sure and take good care of my baby, your younger brother, just as though he were your own child." My sister said, "You can go. Don't worry, I'll surely take good care of him."

This was a year after we returned from Fort Sumner. There were no sheep, and we had nothing to live on. My mother had gone to Black Mountain, but when she got there it was the same. At that time her husband had a slave, a Paiute woman. He took his slave to a man who owned many sheep and traded her. He got seven head and brought them back to where he lived.

A year after she left me my mother came back. She looked all around, outside and inside the hogan, but she couldn't find me. She looked all over and asked, "Where's the baby?" but no one said any-thing. She asked again, "Where's the baby?" Someone said, "The baby was around outside; he must be outside somewhere." I'd been outside, playing where the ashes were piled, and while playing in the ashes I fell asleep. There she found me, lying in the ashes, fast asleep. She grabbed me and picked me up and began to weep and cry as she held me to her breast. She had a broken heart. She took me to where her horse was standing, and as I stood under the horse she reached down and lifted me up. She didn't say a word. We just started off for Black Mountain and got home where my father, Old Man Hat, was living.

All at once, quite a few days later, I took sick. My bowels became loose, and I got worse and worse every day. Soon I was hardly able to walk or play or do anything. I was so weak I just lay in bed. My mother and her husband wondered what had happened. My father said, "He must be hungry for mutton." My mother said, "That must be it." So he saddled his horse and rode to where the sheep were and killed one of the seven he got for his slave. When he brought the meat home I was lying in bed and saw the horse stop in front of the hogan, right at the doorway, with the mutton tied on the saddle. I said to my mother, "I saw meat outside on the horse. I'd like to have some meat." Then they both hurried and built a fire, and when the meat was done they gave it to me, and I ate some mutton and broth. Sure enough, I'd been hungry for meat, and I got well.

In winter we lived on Black Mountain, but in the summer we moved down to the foot of the mountain, to a place called Another Canyon. In this canyon, where there were many lakes, my father, Old Man Hat, and my uncle, Bitahni, planted corn. One day, in a summer when we planted there, it started to rain. It rained hard, I remember that. Outside our hogan stood two cedar trees, right close together, and the one closest to the door the lightning struck. Three times, one after another, it struck the same tree. When it struck the third time my father ran out with his pouch. As soon as he got under it the lightning struck again; my mother and I could see it twisting all around him. She thought, "The old man is gone. He's struck by light-ning." She told me not to look at him, so I turned and looked the other way. But he came in; nothing had happened to him. He said he had mixed beads and corn pollen out there with him to give to the thunder. As soon as he placed the beads and pollen there it never struck any more, not on the ground anywhere close. Lightning flashed, but it was in the air, and the sound of thunder was way off and low. From there on it just rained heavy and slow.

I had a little puppy, and I played with him in the sunshine every day when it was nice and warm. I used to talk and play with him as though I were with another boy. One day we were playing on the top of a little rocky hill. I ran around a rock, and he ran after me, but he wasn't running fast enough, and I ran down the hill. All at once I saw a coyote running towards me. As soon as I saw him I screamed and ran towards home. My mother came out of the hogan, and at that moment the coyote caught the puppy and carried him off. Then I cried more than ever, and my mother was going after the coyote as hard as she could, screaming and hollering and running. She was gone quite a while. When she came back she said, "I couldn't find the puppy anywhere. The coyote has carried him away." I was about to quiet down, but when I saw her coming without my puppy I started again, crying as hard as I could, and I remember I was dancing as I cried. She said, "It's your own fault. I told you not to go far from the hogan. You've given the coyote your puppy. If you'd minded me you'd have your little dog with you right now. If it hadn't been for the puppy the coyote would have gotten you and carried you away. You mustn't go far away; you must stay close to the hogan all the time, because you know coyotes are around here. If you go far from the hogan he'll get you and carry you away."

At lambing time they always separated the lambs from their mothers every morning when they took out the herd, and as soon as the herd left I went among the lambs and played. One day I was chasing the lambs and running after them when, all at once, I fell flat on my belly. It was a sloping place, and I slid to the foot of the corral into the mud. I had on a new muslin shirt, and it was full of sheep manure. When I looked at my shirt I began to cry. I didn't know what to do. I was afraid to go back in the hogan. However, I gave myself up and went over. As soon as I got inside my mother looked up, and as soon as she saw me she scolded me for that. "You dirty little thing. Look at yourself," she said to me. "Now you can just go like that. You don't want your shirt to be clean." She picked up a stick and cleaned a little off my shirt and let me go. She said, "I told you not to go in the sheep corral. You mustn't play with the lambs. You'll kill them. You might run over one, or fall on one. So you stay around here." And my clean white shirt was all black with manure.

In the evening my father returned with the sheep. "Well," he said, "what's happened to you?" As soon as he said this I began weeping again. My mother said, "He was out chasing the lambs and fell in the sheep manure. I've told him many times not to go in the corral and chase the lambs, but he doesn't mind me at all." My father said, "That's all right. You mustn't stop him. Let him play all he wants to. While he's out there chasing the lambs he's making all kinds of noise. In that way the coyotes won't get them. If it's quiet the coyotes will surely get them. So let him play."

About this time I began to herd around the hogan in the morning and evening when the sheep came home. But I was so small. I went out with the sheep like a dog. I just walked along with them and stayed right in the middle of the herd. I was afraid to go around them, but while I was in the middle of the sheep I wasn't afraid of anything.

They used to tell me to race early in the morning, and so every morning while it was still dark they woke me, and I'd start to run. I'd run for a little way, and then I'd start to walk. I'd walk a little way from the hogan, and there I'd stop and sit. I'd sit for a long time, until I could see a long way. I was afraid of something—I don't know what—I was afraid to go away from the hogan. That was why I hid myself. Then, when I could see things way off, I'd get up and start running as hard as I could back to my home. And I'd be standing, or lying, or sitting around, making believe I'd run a long way, making believe I was almost out of breath. I'd been doing this for a long time, but in that I was mistaken; they grew suspicious of me and found me out. They said, "You don't run, you walk from here and sit and hide yourself, and when it's almost daylight you come out and start running back."

But soon I ran a little way, and soon I was getting not to be afraid in the morning while it was still dark. They always told me to run every morning. "If you do that you'll be lively all the time, even when you get to be old you'll be lively. That's what running a race early in the morning is for. It's good exercise for you and your lungs."

In the winter, when they both went out, my mother used to tell me to grind up corn. So while I stayed at home, watching the place, I used to grind corn for our food, but I never ground enough. Once she told me to grind some, but it was a little too hard for me; I wasn't strong enough to break up all the kernels. All at once, as I was grinding, a man came in. His name was Red Wife Beater. He said, "Are you grinding corn?" I said, "Yes, I'm grinding some corn." "Do you have to grind corn?" he asked. I said, "Yes." "Why do you have to grind up corn?" "Because we want to eat it," and I said, "My mother told me to grind it." "Why doesn't she grind it? You can't grind all that corn. You're not strong enough." I had a dishful of corn sitting beside me. He said, "Get up." I got up, and he began to grind the corn. While he was grinding he said, "Look, and watch how I'm holding this rock. Watch how I'm working it." I did, and I learned how to hold the grinding-stone and how to work it. My mother never did show me how to hold the rock, and how to use it. She'd just say, "Go ahead and grind up the corn," that was all, and then she'd go out with the herd. After he'd ground it all up he said, "Now I've made it easier for you. Go ahead now, and grind it a little finer." Then he went away.

One summer, just as the corn was getting ripe, a woman and her daughter came to our place to help us. She was a relative of my mother's. A lot of crows were getting after our corn, and I used to go to the cornfield and watch and scare the crows away. The girl's mother said, "Go with the boy, so that he won't hurry home. You can stay with him until you get hungry, and then you can both come back." The girl and I were the same size. She was half Navaho and half Mexican.

So we stayed where the crows always went, way in the end of the cornfield. We made a little brush hogan, and she made a knife out of a tin can and got some corn and cut it up and started grinding it. But we had no fire with us, so she ground the corn for nothing. She said she was going to make corn bread, but we didn't have a fire, we weren't allowed to carry fire around. When she sat in this little brush hogan I'd be lying right close beside her, "because," I thought, "she's my wife, and I'm her husband." I remembered what my mother had said when I asked her about men and women. She'd said, "The man who goes around with a woman is husband to the woman, and she's wife to the man." So I thought, "I'm a husband to this girl, and she's a wife to me."

Mostly Paiutes lived along the foot of Black Mountain, and in the summer at Another Canyon we lived with them. These Paiutes were poor. They had only an old rag around their hips and camped under the trees in brush hogans. But they used to help us a great deal; they were always willing to do something in order to get clothing or food. We were not much better off, but we had enough to eat and enough clothing.

There were many Paiute girls, and once I went among them and began to play. They said to me, "We'll be goats, all of us girls will be goats, and you be the billy-goat." That's how we started, and they said, "Do to us as the billy-goat does to the goats. Get on top of us." I did that. Just like a billy-goat I jumped on the girls and laid over them. Some had on only one dress, and when I'd get on them they'd scream, and I'd bend over and throw myself back, just like a billy-goat. They sure did like it. After we became acquainted we liked each other, and so we played that way every day.

A Paiute girl came to our place, and my mother told her to herd for us. "Go out with my boy, so that later on he'll know how to herd." She was a big girl. While we were out herding she'd lie down in the shade and go to sleep and tell me to watch the sheep. One day, as she lay all stretched out and sound asleep, I went up to her and lifted her dress. There I saw something. I thought it was a black sheep pelt, and I wondered why she had a pelt on her like that. I tried to see something besides, but all I could see was a great, big thing that looked like something between her legs. Twice I did that to her. I always thought she might have a c—k.

One day we were out of salt. The Paiute Indians got a kind of salt out of the rocks, and this girl, with whom I used to herd, knew just where it was. They said to her, "Go and get some salt, because we haven't any." My mother told me to go with her. We went a long way up in the canyon, and then we started climbing. It was way up, half way to the top of the canyon, where they got the rock salt. In places where the rocks were high she picked me up and lifted me on to them. About half way she said, "Stay here and wait for me." She climbed on, and there I was, sitting all alone for a long time, and I began to cry. I thought, "She's left me here. She's gone away, back to her place." I got up and stood around and walked a little back and forth, and then sat down again, crying as hard as I could. And in the canyon all the wall around me helped me cry. I thought it was some kind of people making fun of me. She must have heard me and came down. When she got up to me she grabbed me and held me to her breast and started crying too. She told me not to cry. I thought she was awfully kind. She had a little salt, and we started back. She carried me all the way down to the foot of the canyon.

Once I was out herding with four Paiute children, three girls and a boy, and we took the herd up in the canyon. There were lots of lakes up in this canyon, and around them were all different kinds of brushes and weeds and lots of flag. Something sweet grows on the end of this flag, and we got into the brush for these sweet things. We took them off and ate them. After a while the girls went away, and the boy too, and I was all alone there in the brush at the edge of the lake. When I started to go, there was a snake lying in front of me. I started back, I went back a little way trying to get out of the brush, and there was another. Then I called the Paiute children. The boy came, and I said, "There's a snake." There was nothing around, no sticks or stones, and when we'd try to get out one way a snake would be lying there. Soon they were all around us. We called for the girls, but they were away, and we started crying. We were afraid of the snakes.

We were standing there, crying, and at last the girls came. The boy spoke to them—I don't know what he said, but I guess he called for some rocks and sticks—and they began throwing them to us. But the rocks didn't reach us; they dropped into the water, and so did the sticks. They couldn't throw them far enough. He must have wanted them to come for us, but they shook their heads and said, "No." One of us would start crying and then the other, and soon we were out of voice. We'd been standing in the water all afternoon until the sun was pretty well down, when, as we started toward one place, nothing was there. We kept on moving along, holding each other, until at last we were out of the brush and water. We were so hungry, and we were voiceless too, from crying.

One morning I went out with the herd again in the canyon. I was wishing for more of those sweet things up by the lakes, but I was afraid to get in the brush. Finally I got three of them. While I was there looking for more I peeked all around in the brush to see if there were any snakes, and I saw what I thought was a sheep pelt. I went close and looked at this thing, and it was tied with a rope. I took it out of the brush and thought, "What a nice soft kid's skin it is." But in the middle there was something on it. Then I broke off a willow and put it between my legs for my horse with the skin for a saddle and started to run.

When I got home with the sheep my mother was walking around outside. I ran up to her and said, "I found a nice, soft kid's skin." As soon as she saw it she was afraid of it. She said, "Throw it down! Throw it on the ground! That's a dangerous thing to have. It'll kill you. It'll break you all in pieces. That thing will set on all your joints; it will get on every joint of yours. That's what's called menstrual." It was what the women used at that time for their monthlies, and there was blood on it.

She picked it up with a stick and took it away and told me not to leave. "Stay there and stand there." She ran up to the cliff, half-way to the top of the canyon, and from there she brought weeds and roots and leaves of various things and different brushes. She mashed it up with rocks and put it in a big pan of water and mixed it and told me to drink some. And she took off my clothes and washed me all over with it. Then she put my clothes in it and washed them. That was a medicine for this thing.

Then she told me to go inside. I went in and put a robe around me, and after she'd washed my clothes and spread them out to dry she came into the hogan and talked to me again. "Those things, they use them when they're passing blood. All women, every month, pass blood. That's a dangerous thing to handle." I asked her again, "What will it do to you?" She said, "I told you before. If you handle those things it'll break your foot, or your legs. It'll get on any of your joints, around your fingers and your back, around your ribs. It'll get on every joint and twist your feet and fingers to all directions. It'll break you, break all your joints, and at last it'll kill you, if you don't get medicine for it." She scared me again. From there on I used to be afraid to touch anything that lay in the brush.

One day, while I was herding quite a way from home, a Paiute girl came to me. I had chewing gum in my mouth, a gum that I got from piñon trees, and she wanted me to give her the gum. I said, "No." She was after me for it, and pretty soon she grabbed me and tried to take it out of my mouth. She jerked me around and said, "Give me the gum." I started fighting her, but I was so small, and I wasn't strong enough. I thought, "I'll get hold of her legs and throw her down." As soon as I grabbed her around the knees she stretched her legs so that my hands slipped, and I got hold of her c—. That made her madder than ever, and she began to beat me. At last I fell on the ground. She got on me and said, "Give me the gum. If you give it to me I'll let you go." She was beating me, and I began to cry. At last I gave up and let her have it. Then she let me go and walked away, chewing the gum. I was almost killed for it. They were cruel, those Paiutes.

One morning when I went out with the herd I picked up my buckskin rope and took it with me after the sheep. We had a little goat that we'd raised, giving her milk when she was small, and she was awfully tame. While I was out with the herd I roped this little goat. After a time I began to play with something else and let the rope and the goat go. I must have gone quite a distance with the sheep when I heard the goat crying. I ran back, and there she was in the willows, almost choked to death. The rope was around a willow, and she was caught. I tried to drag her, but she was too heavy for me. I did my best to loosen her, but I didn't move her at all. In a few minutes the goat was dead. Then I untangled the rope; I had a hard time getting it off the willow, but finally I got it loose and took it off the little goat. I thought she'd get up. I tried to make her get up, but she wouldn't. Then I knew she was dead, and I started to cry and went over to the herd and drove them back to the hogan.

When I got home I told my mother about the goat. I said, "My little goat" — Gray-goat, I used to call her — I said, "Gray-goat is dead. One of the goats ran against this little goat and knocked her down, and my little goat fell over and never moved again. I tried to make her get up, but I found that she was dead, and I started to cry. It's one of the goats that killed her." But they didn't believe me. They began asking me questions, and I must have missed telling something; they must have got me in a corner, and I must have said something about the rope. There they caught me. "You roped the goat, and you choked it to death, that's what you did, didn't you?" they said to me. I didn't go another way; I said, "Yes, I roped the goat, and I let her go with the rope, and she got caught in the willows. She must have gone around the willows, and that's how she choked herself." They said, "What have you been doing?" I forget what I said, but they didn't give me a scolding, they just let it go.

Bitahni's Sister went over and brought it back, and they butchered it. It was good and fat. My mother said, "We shouldn't let him go out with the herd alone. That was a young goat; perhaps after it began getting little ones there'd soon have been ten or twenty goats, or maybe we could have got more than that out of it. And now he's killed it." She said to me, "You think you killed just one. You've killed a lot." From there on I could herd only close around the hogan, where they could see me, and I wasn't allowed to take the rope. "If he carries a rope after the herd pretty soon he'll kill them all by choking them to death."

At that time my father was also married to Bitahni's Sister. She was a clan mother of mine and my mother's clan sister. We were all living together in one hogan. I don't know how he came to be married to her. Maybe my mother told him to marry her, or it may be my father asked my mother, saying he wanted to marry her. Anyway my father had two wives, but it wasn't long before my mother and her sister quarreled.

One afternoon my father and mother began fighting. I was sitting outside watching them. Finally my father threw my mother down and sat on her. Then my uncle's sister dragged Old Man Hat off my mother, and my mother got up and went after my father again. My uncle's sister let them go; she was standing there, watching them too. My mother was just like a man; she was a strong woman. They were fighting for a long time, and then the old man was thrown, and my mother was on top of him. He got up with her, and they wrestled around, fighting and cussing. They fought and fought for a long time. At last they stopped, they must have tired, and just cussed each other. My mother sure did swear and cuss my father and her sister. It was all due to jealousy.

It was evening by the time they quit. My father went inside the hogan and packed his stuff and started to go away. He was going to leave my mother. As he tried to go she cried out and grabbed him and began begging him not to leave her. My father said, "I can't stand this trouble any longer, so I must go and leave you and the whole place." He was standing in the middle of the hogan with a big pack on his back, and she was crying and begging him not to go. They talked for a long time. Then he put down his pack, and for a long time after that they talked. At last they all apologized to one another, and my uncle's sister built a fire.

Sometime after this my mother and father got into a quarrel again over her sister. They quarreled and swore and cussed each other for a long time, and my mother was crying. Then she went out and separated her sheep and goats from my father's herd and saddled her horse and put all her stuff on it. She had only one horse. She got on it and told me to come. I went up to her, and she reached down and lifted me up and sat me behind her. Then we started off and left my father. We went on, driving the herd, and soon we got to Flowing From Rocks. We passed there and went on and got to Anything Falls In that evening where we camped that night.

The next morning she packed all the stuff on the horse again and said, "We'll go back, my son, to your father. We left your poor father yesterday, and he's all alone now. We'd better go back to him." So we turned around and drove back the sheep. When we got home my father was sitting in the hogan smoking. As soon as we got inside she walked up to him and put her arms around his neck and held him against her breast. She was crying and talking, saying, "I'll be with you all the time. I'm not going to treat you like this any more. Forgive me, my husband. I'm sorry for what I've said and done to you. I'm very sorry. Forgive me, right now." And she said again, "I'm not going to treat you like this any more in my life. I'll be with you always." She talked for a long time while she cried and held him. When we returned they all apologized to one another again, and we lived with Bitahni and his sister all that year. I remember we planted corn at Another Canyon that summer, while they were still with us. In the fall they left. . . .

5

That winter, while we lived on Black Mountain at Willows Coming Out, Who Has Mules came to our place. I was out herding. When I returned with the sheep towards evening he came out of the hogan and rode away. He'd been with my father all day; they must have been talking about something. The next day he came again, and when the sun was pretty well down he began gathering up some wood. He gathered together a big pile and then went back to his home. In the evening he came again. My father was lying in the middle of the hogan. He put out a sheep pelt for his nephew, and Who Has Mules sat down at his right side. My place was always on the south side, my mother's place was always on the north, and my father's on the west.

Old Man Hat said, "I'll tell the stories first, then you'll know and remember. You can easily learn if you hear the stories first. If you want to learn about the horses, sheep, cattle and properties, if you want to have all these things, you don't want to be lazy, you don't want to go to bed early at night and get up late in the morning. You have to work hard for all these things. You have to fight everything, the heat in summer and the cold. Everything is hard to get, even little things. If you're lazy you can't get anything. If you do nothing but sleep and lie around you won't get anything, you'll starve to death. You must be lively all the time. When you've acquired stocks you have to work on them day and night. Especially during lambing season will you get only a little sleep. If you fight and resist it you'll soon be accustomed to everything. So you mustn't sleep too long, and you must not be lazy. If you wish to learn something about the stocks and properties, especially after you have learned something about them, you don't want to sleep too long. It will be no use. Even though you learn and know something about it, if you're lazy it will be just no use. You won't get anything."

Then he said, "When you learn about the stocks and properties you'll surely get them. If you go ahead and overcome all these hardships you'll soon have a big herd and property, and you'll have lots to eat. After you get all these things you won't have to go around and beg for them. You'll have everything for yourself. A lot of Indians may say you're stingy. You don't have to mind them, pay no attention to them, just keep on working. That's the way to become a rich man.

"Then, when you learn about all these things, there's a song for each one. Even though you know only one song for each of them everything of yours will be strong. Even if you have only one song for the sheep you'll raise them, nothing will bother them, nothing will happen to them, you'll have them for a long time, the rest of your life. You may live for a long time, you may die of old age, even though you're old you'll still have lots of sheep, horses and cattle. When you haven't a song for the sheep you may raise them for two or three years, maybe longer than that, and you may have a lot, but those sheep will not be strong. Something will bother them all the time. Something will happen to them. They'll get lost every day. Sickness will bother them, and they'll be dying off. Soon you'll have no more sheep. You'll raise them all right, for two or three years, but once it begins they'll go back and disappear, and you won't know what's happened to them. That is, when you haven't a song for them."

While they were talking I was sitting up listening to what they were saying. My father said to me, "Sit up and watch the fire. Keep the fire going." So I was sitting there listening, and I was glad he'd told me to sit up. I wanted to sit up and listen anyhow. Everything my father said I was kind of picking up. So I was glad to be keeping the fire going for I was anxious to hear what my father was saying. I always liked to listen when a man was talking. When the men started talking I always liked to hear them.

He said, "Where there's good grazing and good water, good streams of water and good springs, around those places you'll find good sheep, horses and cattle. When you get one sheep or a horse or a cow and start to take care of it, taking it around where there's good grazing and good water, you'll start raising them, and soon you'll have lots of stock. For there's a million in one. So you don't want to kill a young ewe or young mare or young cow, for there's a million in one of those.

"After you've raised everything, sheep, horses and cattle, and have gotten lots of property you shouldn't cuss and swear at your properties and stock. You shouldn't say, 'Horse of an evil spirit,' or, 'May the bear eat you!' or, 'Let the snake bite you.' If you cuss them in this way it will surely come to pass. If you say, 'Horse of an evil spirit,' they'll soon be dying off, and when you say, 'May the bear eat you,' it will happen. Perhaps a bear will get into your herd and kill them all.

The same with the snake, one will be bitten by a snake and poison the whole herd. So you mustn't say anything like that. These things are like your children. You've got to go easy with them, then you'll have something all the time. Now remember all I've said to you. You want to be stingy. Even though they say you're stingy, be stingy. You don't want to give everything you have to the people. If you do that soon you'll have nothing. Remember what I've told you, you must not lose, kill or give away young ewes, young mares and cows, because, as I told you, there's a million in one of those. Keep them all for yourself, be stingy with them. The others, the steers and wethers, you can do whatever you want to with them.

"Well, my nephew, my little one, you said you wanted to learn something about the stocks and properties. If you want to learn, learn it right now. You're young. While you're a young man you've got to learn. Learn about these things and get them. If you learn about it you'll surely get them. You'll get everything, and soon you won't know what to do with it all. So it's up to you. You'll have everything, that is if you're not lazy. But you've got to go through hard summers and winters. If you fight against it, then you'll soon have all these things."

That was all he said to his nephew, and then he started singing. He started a song from here, from the earth, and went along up to the sun and around and back and came to earth again. There were four long songs. My father said, "You need learn only these four songs. If you learn these four, fix them well in your mind, the rest will be easy." Towards midnight, or a little after, while they were working on the songs I fell over and went to sleep. From there on I don't know what they said, nor how long they sang. Early in the morning my mother woke me and told me to go out and get some wood and build up the fire. She had the fire started. They were still sitting up. They said, "It's morning now," and Who Has Mules said, "I'd better be going back." My father said, "All right," and he went home.

That day I went out with the herd and was herding all day, but he didn't come. The next day my father and I were herding. When we came back in the evening there was a big pile of wood, but he wasn't there, he'd gone back home. After we had supper he came, and as soon as he arrived they started in. My father said, "Now, I guess, you remember all you learned the night before last. You should ask questions on anything you want to ask about. If you want to learn you don't have to be afraid to ask questions. So, if you want to ask a question, go ahead, because you want to learn all about these things, and I'm willing to teach you. I want you to learn all about them. This is a good chance, so you'd better stick to it, until you learn all that I know."

Then he said, "Now you can go ahead and repeat all the songs. Start from where we started and repeat every one. I'll just listen to see if you get it all." So he repeated all the songs; he started from here and went up to the sun and around until he came to earth again, to the middle of his hogan. My father said, "That's right. I know you've got them all now. Every song you repeated is right. You didn't miss anything. I think you got everything the first time. Once you learn it it won't go away from you. You'll remember them always. I know you won't forget them."

While they were working on the songs again that night I fell asleep. In the morning when my mother woke me they were still up, they'd been up all night again. From there on he came every two or three days. That winter we didn't do anything, nor go any place. Those two were working on the songs, prayers and stories all that winter. All that I did was herd, sometimes by myself, sometimes I'd go out with my father or mother, sometimes my mother went out with the herd by herself.

Late in the spring, after he'd been gone again for two days, when I came back with the herd in the evening, there was a big pile of wood. That night he came, and they started on the songs. After Who Has Mules was through repeating all the songs and all the prayers that go with them and all the stories about them, the stories about the sheep, horses, properties and other things, my father said, "Now you've learned everything. You remember everything from where we started to where we stopped. Now I know you remember things, and I think you're a smart man. There are lots of people who can't learn these songs, and now you've learned a few of them. When you start using them on your stocks and properties, if you do it right, you'll soon have everything. Now you can go ahead. You wanted to learn, and I told you you could. I promised you, and I've given it to you." He cupped his hands and spread them out before him and said, "You see, you think there's nothing in my hands, but my hands are full. Everything is overflowing, things are falling out of my hands. That's the way you'll be later on. So just stick to it and learn some more if you want to.

"You must remember everything I've said to you. I told you that I had a handful of things, and that you'd be that way sometime, but you'll have to have a hard time first. You won't get this way just as soon as you learn all the songs about them. You have to work for all these things, you have to go through many dangerous places, down in the arroyos, in the canyons, and climb up and down mountains. You have to kick sticks and rocks and get splinters in your feet and hands and be cut. You may think you'll get them all as soon as you learn the songs, but you must suffer a great deal before you get them. After you've suffered, then, for all your knowing you'll have a handful of things, and you'll look at them and won't know what to do with them. But you'll use them all the time. After you get all this stuff your children will have everything. They won't starve, they won't be ragged, they won't hunger for meat and other things. They'll have everything, if you have it on hand for them. And you can help the poor and others with it all the time. That's after you get all these things, but before that you must be stingy."

They were up all night. Early in the morning my father said, "Now you've learned all that I know, all the songs, prayers and stories. I wanted you to learn, for you are my only nephew. I know you wish to have lots of stock and property, and I know you need them, I know you have children. I don't want your children to go starving. So, now, you can go ahead, tend to your stocks and properties, and do it right. And don't talk roughly, because you've learned many songs and prayers. If you know the songs and prayers you don't want to talk roughly. If you do you won't get these things, because all the stocks and properties will know that you'll be rough with them. They'll be afraid and won't want to come to you. If you think kindly and talk in the kindest manner then they'll know you're a kind man, and then everything will go to you. So, now, just go ahead, this is all I want to say to you. This will be the end." That's what my father said, and Who Has Mules went home. . . .

18

. . . I rode over the hill and turned around towards Cottonwood Standing. As I was riding along near that place, north of Lots Of Wool, I saw a boy herding sheep. I asked him, "Are any horses around here?" "No," he said, "there are no horses around here." I told him what kind I was looking for, the colors and what they were like, and he said, "My father saw three fellows riding across the flat toward Black Mountain, and on the way back, he said, they were riding three good horses and chasing the ones they'd been on. That's what my father was telling about the other day, but he didn't mention the color. You might find out from him yourself. That's all I know."

I stayed there, thinking about the horses, wondering if they'd turned them loose. I thought, "If they turned them loose they ought to have been home long ago. Maybe they're still using them. Maybe they've gone some place. Or maybe they've got them somewhere in a pasture. Or maybe they sold them to someone." The boy said, "My father said the three fellows were from the other side of Narrow Canyon. He said, 'I only know one of them. I recognized him. I'm sure it's he. His clan is Many Goats. The two others may have been his sons-in-law, or maybe some of his boys. But,' he said, 'I know this one very well.' "

I asked the boy, "Where are you living?" He said, "I'm living on that hill." I looked at the sun; it was pretty well down. I asked him, "Where's your father?" "My father isn't home. He went over on the other side of Black Mountain about two days ago, and I don't think he'll be back for several days. He went to visit his children. He's got another family over there." I thought, "I'll go over to his place anyway, and besides I know his wife. I'll go and stay overnight." That was Woman Who Flips Her Cards. The boy was her son.

When I got to the hogan two families were living there, two women, the woman I knew and another one. The other one was the wife of Woman Who Flips Her Cards' husband's uncle. That's why they were living together. Her husband was an old man, and she didn't like him, because she was young. I sat there quietly by the doorway for a time; I didn't speak first. Then Woman Who Flips Her Cards said, "Where have you come from? From where did you drop? We've never seen you around here before." I said, "Oh, I'm just riding around. I've been riding for several days. I missed three of my horses. Maybe somebody's taken them away from me. I was away from home for a few days, and when I came back I missed them. That's what I'm looking for. Whenever I see anyone I ask about them. I ask all the herders, and when I come to a place like this I ask the people, because, I thought, Somebody's likely to see them some place.' "

They said, "We don't know anything about horses. Only the men are always going around, doing the same as you are, looking for horses. Maybe some of them saw your horses somewhere." "Where are the men?" I asked them. "What men?" "The men who are on top of you." "We haven't anyone on top of us. You're the only one who has somebody under you." I said, "Sure, I've got somebody under me." I meant her, but it seemed as though she didn't notice what I meant. I was talking with them that way for quite a while, and they were both laughing and saying to me, "You must be crazy."

I asked them again, "Where are the men? I know from his son that he saw my horses." Then she said, "He went away from here two days ago to Spring On Sunny Side. I don't know when he's coming back. When he left he said, 'Maybe I'll be back in five or six days.' So maybe he'll be back in five days or six. And that was right. He said he saw three fellows riding across the flat; I think it was seven days ago." One horse was white, one blue and the other was a bay." I said, "That's it." "He said he knew them well. It was the man we call White Hair and his sons-in-law. So I guess that's where your horses are." "Thanks very much," I said, "for telling me about it. That's what I want to know. Now I can take my time, because I know now where they are."

I'd been sitting on my heels all this time, but then I sat down on the ground. I said, "I'm glad I know where they are." Woman Who Flips Her Cards got up and laid a sheep pelt by my side and said, "I've known this man a long time, but I haven't seen him lately." She came up and shook hands with me and was holding my hand as tightly as she could. I knew just what she wanted, and I thought to myself, "I'll stay here tonight."

She started cooking, and I said, "I'd like to stay overnight, because it's about evening now. I've got a long way to go to where my horses are, and it's a long way back home. Tomorrow I can start from here early in the morning. Is there any grass around here?" "Yes, there's plenty on the other side of the hill. We don't turn our herds out that way, because we're using it for the horses." I went out then, and took the saddle off my horse and led him away and hobbled him. Everything was ready when I got back, the boy was in with his herd, and we started eating. The two women were sitting there and laughing all during the meal. After supper they said to me, "Tell us about your trip. You say you've been to the dance. Tell us about that." I said, "Yes, I went with my father, Slim Man." She knew Slim Man. She'd been with him too. I told them all about the trip we'd made over to the dance and back.

When we were through talking they spread out their pelts and went to bed. The boy was already sleeping. I lay down too, but I didn't have a robe with me. After a while I got up and said to them, "I haven't any blankets. I'll lie down between you two." They just laughed, and so I went over and lay down between them. They were lying close beside each other, and it was kind of crowded, but they didn't move at all. They said, "What are you trying to do? You're always wanting to do something funny." "Yes," I said, "because I haven't anybody under me."

I pulled the blankets over me, and we lay there together talking, and I began to touch them. They both liked it, and Woman Who Flips Her Cards put her arms around my neck and kissed me. The other woman started doing the same, but when she found the other one already had her arms around me she turned her back. I tried to put an arm around her, but she pushed it away. She was jealous, and so I let her go, and after a while she went to sleep. Then this other woman said to me, "We'll go outside." I got up and went out, and she came after me with the sheep pelts and laid them on the ground, and there I had somebody under me again.

I said, "Now I'll go back inside. I'd like to get after the other woman." She said, "No." She held me there, saying, "She must be your wife too, because I noticed she put her arms around you." I said, "No, she's not my wife. I never touched her before. This is the first time I ever got close to her." But she didn't believe me. I said, "I wonder if she'll tell on us." "No," she said, "I don't think so. I know she won't." "How about the boy?" "No, he won't tell either, because he's my boy. He won't say anything. You must be afraid." "Yes, I'm afraid of your husband." "You don't want to be afraid. He won't know. He isn't around, and nobody will tell him anything about it."

We lay there all night talking about different things. She asked me, "Have you got a wife now?" I said, "No, I haven't." "Oh," she said, "I often wish for you. I wish I were with you. I wish about you like that all the time. I try to forget you, but I can't. I'm always thinking about you day and night." Then she said, "I heard you had a wife. Where's she now?" I said, "Yes, I had a woman, but she's left me already, and I just let her go. I didn't like her anyway. I don't care to have a wife. I think it's too much trouble. That's why I'm not thinking of getting one." Those were the things we were talking about, and towards morning we fell asleep.

We slept a little while, and then I got up and put on my moccasins and went after my horse. He was close by. I brought him back and put the saddle and bridle on him, and she already had a fire going in the hogan and was starting to cook. The other woman and the boy were up too. She went out to the herd and caught a great big sheep and called for a rope and a knife and a pan. The boy took the rope out, and after she'd tied it up she came inside and said to the other woman, "Go out and butcher that sheep," and she said to me, "You go and help her."

While the two of us were out there butchering the sheep and cutting up the meat I started teasing her. She said, "Why didn't you tease me last night?" I said, "I was going to, but you turned your back on me." "Yes, I did that, because you had a wife." "I haven't got a wife," I said to her. "Yes, I know you have. That woman inside's your wife. I know." "No, she's not." We kept saying this to each other while we were butchering, and when the meat was cut up we took it inside, and they roasted some on charcoal. We were laughing and talking. Every time I said something they laughed about it. It was just as though I belonged there.

After we'd eaten the other woman and the boy went out to the sheep. While they were out there she came up and put her arms around my neck and kissed me again, and I gave her three dollars. She was very much pleased with it. "Come around any time you want to. Don't forget me, please. I hate to have you leave. I wish you'd stay longer." "Oh," I said, "I'd like to go right now, because I want to find my horses. I'm worrying about them very much, so I've got to go right now. I'll be around some time. I won't forget you. You're always in my mind too. So don't think I'll forget you." "Thanks," she said, and gave me another kiss and let me go.

A long distance from that place I saw some horses way far ahead of me just going over a hill. When I got on top of that hill, sure enough, there were my horses. They were going to the water. I drove them down to the wash, and they had some water, and so did I, and the horse I was riding. They were looking fine. They'd been used all right, but still they were in good shape. From there I started chasing them straight across the flat for home. By the time the sun was pretty well down we got to Anything Falls In. My home was a little way from there.

My mother was so glad I'd found the horses. She asked me, "Where did you find them?" I said, "Down at Narrow Canyon." "That's a long way from here. I wonder why they went to that place." I told her some fellows had ridden them down there, and she was mad about it. After that she said, "Some people camped here last night. They're trading. They gave me a saddle and two good-sized horses. One's white and the other's blue. They want eighty head of sheep for the two horses and twenty for the saddle. So that's a hundred head of sheep I gave them. But I haven't given it to them yet. They took the blue horse along with them this morning, but they'll be coming back and passing here again tomorrow." I said, "It's too much. We don't want to lose that many sheep, and besides we've got lots of horses. What do you want another two horses for?" "Well, they're both good-sized, and I thought you'd like them. And the saddle's yours. My son also came yesterday." She meant Slim Man. She called him her son. "He was here and said, 'The corn's ripe, and I want you to go and get some for yourself.' I was so thankful. I'm glad we have some corn now for this winter. I want you to go over and see it tomorrow." I was glad too. I went over where she'd hobbled the white horse, and it was kind of poor. I tried to turn her down, but she said, "I like this horse. That's why I'm willing to give forty head of sheep for it."

I stayed at home that night, and in the morning I brought the horse in for her. She put her saddle on it and went out with the herd, and I went out to round up the horses and drive them to water. About noon I came home and started a fire and cooked a meal for myself. Quite a while after my mother came in with the sheep, and we cooked some more, and she ate lunch. Then I went with the herd, and she stayed home. In the evening, when I got back, there were those people. They had quite a number of sheep. The man rode up and asked me, "Where's a good place to camp?" I said, "Any place around here." He rode back to the others, and I put my sheep in the corral and went in the hogan. My mother said, "Don't worry about the sheep, my son. We'll have more this spring. So don't worry about it. We'll get the two horses and give them eighty head. Don't be sorry for them. You shouldn't be sorry for the sheep." She told me a lot about sheep that night, but I didn't say a word.

The people came to our place the next morning and told us about their trips. They said, "Everybody wanted this blue horse." The man said to me, "This horse will be yours, and that saddle, and the white one we're giving to your mother. She can use it for herding, because we know she's old; she can't stand herding on foot." My mother said, "Yes, I'm so pleased with that horse, because he's gentle. I rode him all day yesterday, and I liked him so well." She liked the horse all right, but I didn't. I was sorry for the sheep. I thought twenty head would be enough, but she wanted to give forty. She came inside the hogan and asked me again, "What do you think about the horses?" I said, "It's up to you, mother. You like them very well, so you go ahead and pay for them." She said, "I've been using one horse all the time, and I've turned him loose, so I'll use the white one to herd with." I said, "All right."

I got my bridle and put it on the blue horse they gave me. I thought, "I'll try him. See how he is." I rode around and over the hill, and he was lively. There was a good level place out in the flat for about a hundred yards, and I let him run there. As soon as I wanted him to go he gave a quick jump, and he sure did go swiftly and make the dust fly. I was glad to get him, because he was a good-sized horse and quick too, so that I didn't have to use a whip on him. I'd just give a little kick, and he'd start off quickly.

When I came back the man asked me, "Well, how do you like the horse?" I said, "I like him very well, but I don't know exactly what he's like yet, not until I've used him for a while." He said, "That's a good horse. It's a racehorse. I've been using him only when I've wanted to go to the dances. And it's a strong horse. You can ride him all day and all night and the next day, and he'll be just the same. He won't get tired. And it's a young horse too. He's only four years old."

We stayed with them all day, and he asked me, "Have you got a wife?" "My nephew," he called me. "No," I said, "I haven't." "Why, you ought to have one. A man like you without a wife. You ought to have a wife and children by now. There are some fellows who have children even when they're younger than you are. And you ought to have a wife too." I said, "I guess it's all right to have a wife, but, I don't know why, I don't care to get married. I don't like having a wife." "Well, anyway," he said, "you'd better get yourself a woman. You can get one easily, because you've got lots of property and stocks. If you want a woman I can get you one. Lots of girls haven't got a husband. A lot of them at my place aren't married yet. You ought to come over; we've got lots of pretty girls. And you've got brothers and sisters over there too. You ought to come and visit them. Only your mother, your real mother, is dead now. She died a year ago." While he was saying this my mother started crying. "Oh," she said, "I never did get to see my sister. I've been wanting to go and see her lots of times, but I didn't have any way to go, because I can't leave my place alone. That's why I never got to see her again." That's where I heard that my mother had died. That was my real mother.

Part 6
"Native American Renaissance," 1968–

What has been called the "Native American Renaissance" is usually said to begin with the publication of N. Scott Momaday's novel *House Made of Dawn* in 1968, and with its reception of the Pulitzer Prize the following year. The phrase comes from the title of a book by Kenneth Lincoln (University of California Press, 1983), and it has been widely used, for all that there are a great many more differences between the European Renaissance and the "Native American Renaissance" than there are similarities.

It is important to note that 1968 is also the year in which Congress passed the Indian Civil Rights Act, a major step on the way to President Nixon's announcement, in 1970, of a formal close to the government's "termination" policy instituted in 1953 and pursued vigorously until 1958 (after which the policy remained nominally in effect but was no longer implemented). The termination policy, to state the matter simply, had set out to sever the federal government's relationships, i.e., its treaty responsibilities, to the tribes, often with disastrous results to the peoples affected, most notoriously in the cases of the Klamath and Menominee. The parallel between a more politically favorable and a more critically favorable climate, with respect to Indian culture, is one I think worth noting.

And it is surely the case that, from 1968 to the present, a very substantial body of fine poetry and fiction has been published by Native American writers, gaining considerable notice both here and abroad. Several of these writers have also turned their attention to autobiographical writing; so it is with the personal narratives of Indian artists that the present section of the anthology is concerned.

While it is true that contemporary Native American writers use many of the techniques of Euramerican fiction, poetry, and autobiography, it is important to remember that most if not all of them have highly self-conscious attachments to aspects of the oral tradition. In the same way, although they take some of their themes from the general concerns of the dominant culture, they also treat issues specific to Indian communities. Furthermore, for all that they are worldly and sophisticated, well-educated and well-traveled, many of them continue to have a place-determined sense of self more nearly akin to that of tribal people than to that of Euramericans.

Our selections begin with N. Scott Momaday's *The Way to Rainy Mountain*, a text that very specifically links the author's sense of self to his sense of the traditions, travels, and stories of his Kiowa people. We had intended selections from Leslie Marmon Silko's *Storyteller* to come next, but Silko's publisher insisted on fees that were very high and entirely out of line with those charged by other publishers to reprint. It is with great regret that we cannot include her in this volume. The selection from Wendy Rose is not strictly autobiography. Rather, I've chosen what I take to be intensely autobiographical *poems* from Rose's volume *The Halfbreed Chronicles*. There are, to be sure, autobiographical poems as well by Momaday and Silko, and by Linda Hogan also, whose work concludes this section. Similarly, Rose has written a moving autobiographical essay called "Neon Scars" for the anthology *I Tell You Now: Autobiographical Essays by Native American Writers*,[1] and I would certainly recommend it to the reader interested in her work. Nevertheless, and if only for a certain change of mode, it may be valuable to look to Rose's poetry as autobiography.

Gerald Vizenor comes next, again with a piece from *I Tell You Now*. As I shall describe in greater detail below, Vizenor's essay is one that is very typical of his quite untypical manner. We conclude this section with Linda Hogan's "The Two Lives," which is also included in *I Tell You Now*. Of course, I recommend all of the autobiographical essays by Native American writers in that volume, and I also note, for anyone interested in the lives of contemporary Native American writers, the collections of interviews edited by Joseph Bruchac, *Survival This Way: Interviews with American Indian Poets*, and Laura Coltelli, *Winged Words: American Indian Writers Speak*, among others.[2] At least one other important autobiography by a contemporary Native American poet deserves mention (although I have not found space to include it here), and this is Ray Young Bear's *Black Eagle Child: The Facepaint Narratives*.[3] Young Bear, a Mesquakie poet, has lightly fictionalized himself as Edgar Bearchild in this highly innovative autobiographical text.

1. *I Tell You Now: Autobiographical Essays by Native American Writers*, ed. Brian Swann and Arnold Krupat (Lincoln: Univ. of Nebraska Press, 1987).
2. Joseph Bruchac, *Survival This Way: Interviews with American Indian Poets* (Tucson: Sun Tracks; Univ. of Arizona Press, 1987); Laura Coltelli, *Winged Words: American Indian Writers Speak* (Lincoln: Univ. of Nebraska Press, 1990).
3. Ray Young Bear, *Black Eagle Child: The Facepaint Narratives* (Iowa City, IA: Univ. of Iowa Press, 1992).

22

The Way to Rainy Mountain

N. SCOTT MOMADAY

The awarding of the Pulitzer Prize to Momaday's novel House Made of Dawn *in 1969, as noted above, is generally considered to have inaugurated the "Native American Renaissance," and Momaday has been the most influential of Native American artists for more than two decades. Born in 1934 at the Kiowa and Comanche Indian Hospital at Lawton, Oklahoma, Momaday spent most of his early life in the Southwest, in Navajo country between 1936 and 1943, moving, in 1946, to Jemez Pueblo in New Mexico where his parents had obtained teaching jobs. He eventually enrolled at the University of New Mexico, before going on to graduate school at Stanford University, where he studied with and developed a close relation to the poet and critic Yvor Winters.*

After receiving his doctorate from Stanford in 1963, Momaday went to teach at the University of California at Santa Barbara. It was there that he completed House Made of Dawn, *a project he had begun while at Stanford. In 1969, the year that his book won the Pulitzer Prize, he published* The Way to Rainy Mountain, *the autobiographical text from which our selections below are taken. Momaday has published a second autobiography,* The Names: A Memoir *(1976), a volume of poems entitled* Angle of Geese *(1974), and a second novel,* The Ancient Child *(1989), among many other works. He is also a painter and illustrator whose work has frequently been exhibited.*

Consistent with the orientation of other Native American autobiographers, Momaday writes the story of his life as a search for his relation to his people — his ancestors, his family, their culture, and the places with which their identity is intimately connected. The Way to Rainy Mountain *is framed by a prologue, an introduction, and an epilogue, and is divided into three sections, "The Setting Out," "The Going On," and "The Closing In." The material within each of these sections also has three divisions, distinguished typographically, which sections Alan Velie characterizes as "a legend or story, a historical anecdote or observation, and a personal reminiscence,"[1] although the lines between these categories occasionally blur.* The Way to Rainy Mountain *also contains drawings by Momaday's father, Al (which are not included here).*

1. Alan Velie, *Four American Indian Literary Masters: N. Scott Momaday, James Welch, Leslie Marmon Silko, and Gerald Vizenor* (Norman: Univ. of Oklahoma Press, 1982), p. 24.

Momaday has surely been the most studied of Native American writers (although today a great deal of attention is being paid to Louise Erdrich and Gerald Vizenor). Matthias Schubnell's book-length critical volume N. Scott Momaday: The Cultural and Literary Background[2] *is more a celebration of all things Momaday than a study; nonetheless, it is a goldmine of information for those who wish to know more about the most eminent Native American writer today. Our selections from* The Way to Rainy Mountain *include the Prologue, parts 3–6, 10, and 11 of "The Setting Out," and parts 21–24 of "The Closing In."*[3] *Aho is Momaday's grandmother, whose funeral he goes to attend; she died shortly after taking him to see the sacred Tai-Me or Sun Dance bundle of the Kiowa.*

Prologue

The journey began one day long ago on the edge of the northern Plains. It was carried on over a course of many generations and many hundreds of miles. In the end there were many things to remember, to dwell upon and talk about.

"You know, everything had to begin. . . ." For the Kiowas the beginning was a struggle for existence in the bleak northern mountains. It was there, they say, that they entered the world through a hollow log. The end, too, was a struggle, and it was lost. The young Plains culture of the Kiowas withered and died like grass that is burned in the prairie wind. There came a day like destiny; in every direction, as far as the eye could see, carrion lay out in the land. The buffalo was the animal representation of the sun, the essential and sacrificial victim of the Sun Dance. When the wild herds were destroyed, so too was the will of the Kiowa people; there was nothing to sustain them in spirit. But these are idle recollections, the mean and ordinary agonies of human history. The interim was a time of great adventure and nobility and fulfillment.

Tai-me came to the Kiowas in a vision born of suffering and despair. "Take me with you," Tai-me said, "and I will give you what-

2. Matthias Schubnell, *N. Scott Momaday: The Cultural and Literary Background* (Norman: Univ. of Oklahoma Press, 1985).

3. N. Scott Momaday, *The Way to Rainy Mountain* (New York: Ballantine, 1974). Reprinted from *The Way to Rainy Mountain*, N. Scott Momaday, © 1969, The University of New Mexico Press.

ever you want." And it was so. The great adventure of the Kiowas was a going forth into the heart of the continent. They began a long migration from the headwaters of the Yellowstone River eastward to the Black Hills and south to the Wichita Mountains. Along the way they acquired horses, the religion of the Plains, a love and possession of the open land. Their nomadic soul was set free. In alliance with the Comanches they held dominion in the southern Plains for a hundred years. In the course of that long migration they had come of age as a people. They had conceived a good idea of themselves; they had dared to imagine and determine who they were.

In one sense, then, the way to Rainy Mountain is preeminently the history of an idea, man's idea of himself, and it has old and essential being in language. The verbal tradition by which it has been preserved has suffered a deterioration in time. What remains is fragmentary; mythology, legend, lore, and hearsay—and of course the idea itself, as crucial and complete as it ever was. That is the miracle.

The journey herein recalled continues to be made anew each time the miracle comes to mind, for that is peculiarly the right and responsibility of the imagination. It is a whole journey, intricate with motion and meaning; and it is made with the whole memory, that experience of the mind which is legendary as well as historical, personal as well as cultural. And the journey is an evocation of three things in particular: landscape that is incomparable, a time that is gone forever, and the human spirit, which endures. The imaginative experience and the historical express equally the traditions of man's reality. Finally, then, the journey recalled is among other things the revelation of one way in which these traditions are conceived, developed, and interfused in the human mind. There are on the way to Rainy Mountain many landmarks, many journeys in the one. From the beginning the migration of the Kiowas was an expression of the human spirit, and that expression is most truly made in terms of wonder and delight: "There were many people, and oh, it was beautiful. That was the beginning of the Sun Dance. It was all for Tai-me, you know, and it was a long time ago."

III

Before there were horses the Kiowas had need of dogs. That was a long time ago, when dogs could talk. There was a man who lived alone; he had been thrown away, and he made his camp here and

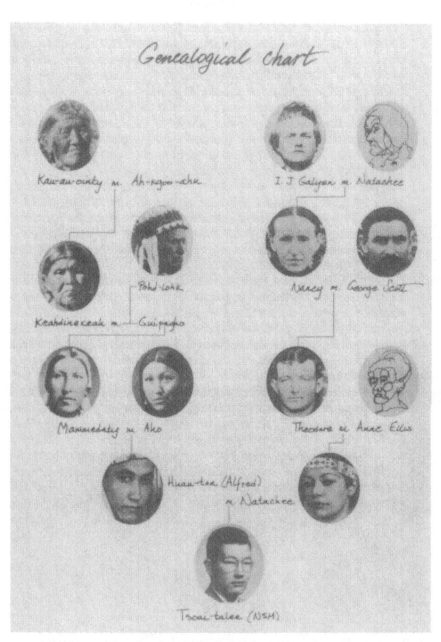

Genealogical chart. Courtesy of N. Scott Momaday.

404

there on the high ground. Now it was dangerous to be alone, for there were enemies all around. The man spent his arrows hunting food. He had one arrow left, and he shot a bear; but the bear was only wounded and it ran away. The man wondered what to do. Then a dog came up to him and said that many enemies were coming; they were close by and all around. The man could think of no way to save himself. But the dog said: "You know, I have puppies. They are young and weak and they have nothing to eat. If you will take care of my puppies, I will show you how to get away." The dog led the man here and there, around and around, and they came to safety.

A hundred years ago the Comanche Ten Bears remarked upon the great number of horses which the Kiowas owned. "When we first knew you," he said, "you had nothing but dogs and sleds." It was so; the dog is primordial. Perhaps it was dreamed into being.

The principal warrior society of the Kiowas was the Ka-itsenko, "Real Dogs," and it was made up of ten men only, the ten most brave. Each of these men wore a long ceremonial sash and carried a sacred arrow. In time of battle he must by means of this arrow impale the end of his sash to the earth and stand his ground to the death. Tradition has it that the founder of the Ka-itsenko had a dream in which he saw a band of warriors, outfitted after the fashion of the society, being led by a dog. The dog sang the song of the Ka-itsenko, then said to the dreamer: "You are a dog; make a noise like a dog and sing a dog song."

There were always dogs about my grandmother's house. Some of them were nameless and lived a life of their own. They belonged there in a sense that the word "ownership" does not include. The old people paid them scarcely any attention, but they should have been sad, I think, to see them go.

IV

They lived at first in the mountains. They did not yet know of Tai-me, but this is what they knew: There was a man and his wife. They had a beautiful child, a little girl whom they would not allow to go out of their sight. But one day a friend of the family came and asked if she might take the child outside to play. The mother guessed that would be all right, but she told the friend to leave the child in its cradle and to place the cradle in a tree. While the child was in the tree, a redbird came among the branches. It was not like any bird that you have seen; it was very beautiful, and it did not fly away. It kept still upon a limb, close to the child. After a while the child got out of its cradle and began to climb after the redbird. And at the same time the tree began to grow taller, and the child was borne up into the sky. She was then a woman, and she found herself in a strange place. Instead of a redbird, there was a young man standing before her. The man spoke to her and said: "I have been watching you for a long time, and I knew that I would find a way to bring you here. I have brought you here to be my wife." The woman looked all around; she saw that he was the only living man there. She saw that he was the sun.

There the land itself ascends into the sky. These mountains lie at the top of the continent, and they cast a long rain shadow on the sea of grasses to the east. They arise out of the last North American wilderness, and they have wilderness names: Wasatch, Bitterroot, Bighorn, Wind River.

I have walked in a mountain meadow bright with Indian paintbrush, lupine, and wild buckwheat, and I have seen high in the branches of a lodgepole pine the male pine grosbeak, round and rose-colored, its dark, striped wings nearly invisible in the soft, mottled light. And the uppermost branches of the tree seemed very slowly to ride across the blue sky.

V

After that the woman grew lonely. She thought about her people, and she wondered how they were getting on. One day she had a quarrel with the sun, and the sun went away. In her anger she dug up the root of a bush which the sun had warned here never to go near. A piece of earth fell from the root, and she could see her people far below. By that time she had given birth; she had a child—a boy by the sun. She made a rope out of sinew and took her child upon her back; she climbed down upon the rope, but when she came to the end, her people were still a long way off, and there she waited with her child on her back. It was evening; the sun came home and found his woman gone. At once he thought of the bush and went to the place where it had grown. There he saw the woman and the child, hanging by the rope half way down to the earth. He was very angry, and he took up a ring, a gaming wheel, in his hand. He told the ring to follow the rope and strike the woman dead. Then he threw the ring and it did what he told it to do; it struck the woman and killed her, and then the sun's child was all alone.

The plant is said to have been the pomme blanche, *or* pomme de prairie, *of the voyageurs, whose chronicles refer time and again to its use by the Indians. It grows on the high plains and has a farinaceous root that is turnip-like in taste and in shape. This root is a healthful food, and attempts have been made to cultivate the plant as a substitute for the potato.*

The anthropologist Mooney wrote in 1896: "Unlike the neighboring Cheyenne and Arapaho, who yet remember that they once lived east of the Missouri and cultivated corn, the Kiowa have no tradition of ever having been an agricultural people or anything but a tribe of hunters."

Even now they are meateaters; I think it is not in them to be farmers. My grandfather, Mammedaty, worked hard to make wheat and cotton grow on his land, but it came to very little in the end. Once when I was a small boy I went across the creek to the house where the old woman Keahdinekeah lived. Some men and boys came in from the pasture, where a calf had just been killed and butchered. One of the boys held the calf's liver—still warm and wet with life—in his hand, eating of it with great relish. I have heard that the old hunters of the Plains prized the raw liver and tongue of the buffalo above all other delicacies.

VI

The sun's child was big enough to walk around on the earth, and he saw a camp nearby. He made his way to it and saw that a great spider—that which is called a grandmother—lived there. The spider spoke to the sun's child, and the child was afraid. The grandmother was full of resentment; she was jealous, you see, for the child had not yet been weaned from its mother's breasts. She wondered whether the child were a boy or a girl, and therefore she made two things, a pretty ball and a bow and arrows. These things she left alone with the child all the next day. When she returned, she saw that the ball was full of arrows, and she knew then that the child was a boy and that he would be hard to raise. Time and again the grandmother tried to capture the boy, but he always ran away. Then one day she made a snare out of rope. The boy was caught up in the snare, and he cried and cried, but the grandmother sang to him and at last he fell asleep.

> Go to sleep and do not cry.
> Your mother is dead, and still you feed
>   upon her breasts.
> Oo-oo-la-la-la-la, oo-oo.

In the autumn of 1874, the Kiowas were driven southward towards the Staked Plains. Columns of troops were converging upon them from all sides, and they were bone-weary and afraid. They camped on Elk Creek, and the next day it began to rain. It rained hard all that day, and the Kiowas waited on horseback for the weather to clear. Then, as evening came on, the earth was suddenly crawling with spiders, great black tarantulas, swarming on the flood.

I know of spiders. There are dirt roads in the Plains. You see them, and you wonder where and how far they go. They seem very old and untraveled, as if they all led away to deserted houses. But creatures cross these roads: dung beetles and grasshoppers, sidewinders and tortoises. Now and then there comes a tarantula, at evening, always larger than you imagine, dull and dark brown, covered with long, dusty hairs. There is something crochety about them; they stop and go and angle away.

When he was a boy, my father went with his grandmother, Keahdinekeah, to the shrine of one of the talyi-da-i. The old woman made an offering of bright cloth, and she prayed. The shrine was a small, specially-made tipi; inside, suspended from the lashing of the poles, was the medicine itself. My father knew that it was very powerful, and the very sight of it filled him with wonder and regard. The holiness of such a thing can be imparted to the human spirit, I believe, for I remember that it shone in the sightless eyes of Keahdinekeah. Once I was taken to see her at the old house on the other side of Rainy Mountain Creek. The room was dark, and her old age filled it like a substance. She was white-haired and blind, and, in that strange reversion that comes upon the very old, her skin was as soft as the skin of a baby. I remember the sound of her glad weeping and the water-like touch of her hand.

X

Long ago there were bad times. The Kiowas were hungry and there was no food. There was a man who heard his children cry from hunger, and he went out to look for food. He walked four days and became very weak. On the fourth day he came to a great canyon. Suddenly there was thunder and lightning. A voice spoke to him and said, "Why are you following me? What do you want?" The man was afraid. The thing standing before him had the feet of a deer, and its body was covered with feathers. The man answered that the Kiowas were hungry. "Take me with you," the voice said, "and I will give you whatever you want." From that day Tai-me has belonged to the Kiowas.

The great central figure of the kado, *or Sun Dance, ceremony is the* tai-me. *This is a small image, less than 2 feet in length, representing a human figure dressed in a robe of white feathers, with a headdress consisting of a single upright feather and pendants of ermine skin, with numerous strands of blue beads around its neck, and painted upon the face, breast, and back with designs symbolic of the sun and moon. The image itself is of dark-green stone, in form rudely resembling a human head and bust, probably shaped by art like the stone fetishes of the Pueblo tribes. It is preserved in a rawhide box in charge of the hereditary keeper, and is never under any circumstances exposed to view except at the annual Sun Dance, when it is fastened to a short upright stick planted within the medicine lodge, near the western side. It was last exposed in 1888.* —Mooney

Once I went with my father and grandmother to see the Tai-me bundle. It was suspended by means of a strip of ticking from the fork of a small ceremonial tree. I made an offering of bright red cloth, and my grandmother prayed aloud. It seemed a long time that we were there. I had never come into the presence of Tai-me before—nor have I since. There was a great holiness all about in the room, as if an older person had died there or a child had been born.

XI

A long time ago there were two brothers. It was winter, and the buffalo had wandered far away. Food was very scarce. The two brothers
were hungry, and they wondered what to do. One of them got up in
the early morning and went out, and he found a lot of fresh meat
there on the ground in front of the tipi. He was very happy, and he
called his brother outside. "Look," he said. "Something very good
has happened, and we have plenty of food." But his brother was
afraid and said: "This is too strange a thing. I believe that we better
not eat that meat." But the first brother scolded him and said that he
was foolish. Then he went ahead and ate of the meat all by himself. In
a little while something awful happened to him; he began to change.
When it was all over, he was no longer a man; he was some kind of
water beast with little short legs and a long, heavy tail. Then he spoke
to his brother and said: "You were right, and you must not eat of that
meat. Now I must go and live in the water, but we are brothers, and
you ought to come and see me now and then." After that the man
went down to the water's edge, sometimes, and called his brother
out. He told him how things were with the Kiowas.

*During the peyote ritual a fire is kept burning in the center of the tipi, in-
closed within a crescent-shaped altar. On top of the altar there is a single,
sacred peyote. After the chief priest utters the opening prayer, four peyotes are
given to each celebrant, who eats them one after another. Then, in turn, each
man sings four sacred songs, and all the while there is the sound of the rattle
and the drum—and the fitful, many-colored glare of the fire. The songs go on
all through the night, broken only by intervals of prayer, additional distribu-
tions of peyote, and, at midnight, a peculiar baptismal ceremony.*

Mammedaty was a peyote man, and he was therefore distinguished
by these things: a necklace of beans, a beaded staff and rattle, an
eagle-bone whistle, and a fan made from the feathers of a water bird.
He saw things that other men do not see. Once a heavy rain caused
the Washita River to overflow and Rainy Mountain Creek to swell
and "back up." Mammedaty went to the creek, near the crossing, to
swim. And while he was there, the water began strangely to move
against him, slowly at first, then fast, in high, hard waves. There was
some awful commotion beneath the surface, and Mammedaty got out

of the water and ran away. Later he went back to that place. There was a wide swath in the brush of the bank and the tracks of a huge animal, leading down to the water's edge.

I like to think of old man Gaapiatan and his horse. I think I know how much he loved that animal; I think I know what was going on in his mind: If you will give me my life and the lives of my family, I will give you the life of this black-eared horse.

XXI

Mammedaty was the grandson of Guipahgo, and he was well-known on that account. Now and then Mammedaty drove a team and wagon out over the plain. Once, in the early morning, he was on the way to Rainy Mountain. It was summer and the grass was high and meadowlarks were calling all around. You know, the top of the plain is smooth and you can see a long way. There was nothing but the early morning and the land around. Then Mammedaty heard something. Someone whistled to him. He looked up and saw the head of a little boy nearby above the grass. He stopped the horses and got down from the wagon and went to see who was there. There was no one; there was nothing there. He looked for a long time, but there was nothing there.

There is a single photograph of Mammedaty. He is looking past the camera and a little to one side. In his face there is calm and good will, strength and intelligence. His hair is drawn close to the scalp, and his braids are long and wrapped with fur. He wears a kilt, fringed leggings, and beaded moccasins. In his right hand there is a peyote fan. A family characteristic: the veins stand out in his hands, and his hands are small and rather long.

Mammedaty saw four things that were truly remarkable. This head of the child was one, and the tracks of the water beast another. Once, when he walked near the pecan grove, he saw three small alligators on a log. No one had ever seen them before and no one ever saw them again. Finally, there was this: something had always bothered Mammedaty, a small aggravation that was never quite out of mind,

411

like a name on the tip of the tongue. He had always wondered how it is that the mound of earth which a mole makes around the opening of its burrow is so fine. It is nearly as fine as powder, and it seems almost to have been sifted. One day Mammedaty was sitting quietly when a mole came out of the earth. Its cheeks were puffed out as if it had been a squirrel packing nuts. It looked all around for a moment, then blew the fine dark earth out of its mouth. And this it did again and again, until there was a ring of black, powdery earth on the ground. That was a strange and meaningful thing to see. It meant that Mammedaty had got possession of a powerful medicine.

XXII

Mammedaty was the grandson of Guipahgo, and he got on well most of the time. But, you know, one time he lost his temper. This is how it was: There were several horses in a pasture, and Mammedaty wanted to get them out. A fence ran all the way around and there was just one gate. There was a lot of ground inside. He could not get those horses out. One of them led the others; every time they were driven up to the gate, that one wheeled and ran as fast as it could to the other side. Well, that went on for a long time, and Mammedaty burned up. He ran to the house and got his bow and arrows. The horses were running in single file, and he shot at the one that was causing all that trouble. He missed, though, and the arrow went deep into the neck of the second horse.

In the winter of 1852–53, a Pawnee boy who had been held as a captive among the Kiowas succeeded in running away. He took with him an especially fine hunting horse, known far and wide as Guadal-tseyu, *"Little Red." That was the most important event of the winter. The loss of that horse was a hard thing to bear.*

Years ago there was a box of bones in the barn, and I used to go there to look at them. Later someone stole them, I believe. They were the bones of a horse Mammedaty called by the name "Little Red." It was a small bay, nothing much to look at, I have heard, but it was the fastest runner in that whole corner of the world. White men and Indians alike came from far and near to match their best animals against it, but it never lost a race. I have often thought about that red horse. There have been times when I thought I understood how it was that a man might be moved to preserve the bones of a horse—and another to steal them away.

XXIII

Aho remembered something, a strange thing. This is how it was: You know, the Tai-me bundle is not very big, but it is full of power. Once Aho went to see the Tai-me keeper's wife. The two of them were sitting together, passing the time of day, when they heard an awful noise, as if a tree or some other very heavy object had fallen down. It frightened them, and they went to see what on earth it was. It was Tai-me—Tai-me had fallen to the floor. No one knows how it was that Tai-me fell; nothing caused it, as far as anyone could see.

For a time Mammedaty wore one of the grandmother bundles. This he did for his mother Keahdinekeah; he wore it on a string tied around his neck. Aho remembered this: that if anyone who wore a medicine bundle failed to show it the proper respect, it grew extremely heavy around his neck.

There was a great iron kettle which stood outside of my grandmother's house next to the south porch. It was huge and immovable, or so I thought when I was a child; I could not imagine that anyone had strength enough to lift it up. I don't know where it came from; it was always there. It rang like a bell when you struck it, and with the tips of your fingers you could feel the black metal sing for a long time afterwards. It was used to catch the rainwater with which we washed our hair.

XXIV

East of my grandmother's house, south of the pecan grove, there is buried a woman in a beautiful dress. Mammedaty used to know where she is buried, but now no one knows. If you stand on the front porch of the house and look eastward towards Carnegie, you know that the woman is buried somewhere within the range of your vision.

But her grave is unmarked. She was buried in a cabinet, and she wore a beautiful dress. How beautiful it was! It was one of those fine buckskin dresses, and it was decorated with elk's teeth and beadwork. That dress is still there, under the ground.

Aho's high moccasins are made of softest, cream-colored skins. On each instep there is a bright disc of beadwork—an eight-pointed star, red and pale blue on a white field—and there are bands of beadwork at the soles and ankles. The flaps of the leggings are wide and richly ornamented with blue and red and green and white and lavender beads.

East of my grandmother's house the sun rises out of the plain. Once in his life a man ought to concentrate his mind upon the remembered earth, I believe. He ought to give himself up to a particular landscape in his experience, to look at it from as many angles as he can, to wonder about it, to dwell upon it. He ought to imagine that he touches it with his hands at every season and listens to the sounds that are made upon it. He ought to imagine the creatures there and all the faintest motions of the wind. He ought to recollect the glare of noon and all the colors of the dawn and dusk.

23
The Halfbreed Chronicles

W E N D Y   R O S E

Wendy Rose is of mixed Anglo, Hopi, and Miwok background. Born in 1948, she has taken a degree in anthropology, taught, and served as program coordinator for the American Indian Studies Program at Fresno City College in California, while also publishing some ten books of poetry. Widely anthologized, her work is remarkable for its intensity and passion; ranging out from her own deeply felt experience as a Native American woman, it connects with the oppressed, and, most particularly, oppressed women everywhere.

Although she has written a moving autobiographical sketch called "Neon Scars" for the volume I Tell You Now,[1] *I have chosen to represent Wendy Rose's life as it is reflected through some of her poems. Our selections are from* The Halfbreed Chronicles, *published in 1985.*[2]

The Building of the Trophy

Well, you caught me unprepared
beached like driftwood
on some city street
pink against brown
in the late evening sun
bleached ivory
after all the bluster
of your storm.

I am counting
all my fingers and toes,
taking stock
of what you took.

1. *I Tell You Now: Autobiographical Essays by Native American Writers*, ed. Brian Swann and Arnold Krupat (Lincoln: Univ. of Nebraska Press, 1987).
2. Wendy Rose, *The Halfbreed Chronicles* (San Raphael, CA: West End Press, 1985). Reprinted by permission of Wendy Rose and West End Press.

Can it be pushed back
together with glue,
tied up with a thread
leaving only the memory
of thin seams, a scar
where your kiss
was blown away?

I turn each bone
carefully this way
and this way,
measure the hope or the lie
all the gods gave us
that pain is a vitamin
to make us grow.

I am sure you had it
precisely figured
these latest of nights
in your ghost books.
You must have surveyed
everything, compiled long lists,
nightmares of ritual
each one a history
or a trophy or both.

But even the strongest crows
can't fly so far west
and anyway, Crow,
you are just a bird.

Join the ranks
of the formerly employed,
the fathers, the lovers, the friends;
remember with me the egg,
the infant, my preliterate self,
the toddler pushed underwater
by her green-eyed brother.

Now she is six—see her
point off the years

on one hand and a finger
expanding her immensity
against the chair legs,
against spaniel pups
older than the small pile
of her years.

Now she is twelve
bleeding between the legs;
and thirteen
bleeding from everywhere
with blood-caked hair,
welts on her thighs, her feet,
bullet holes beginning
between her eyes.

Sixteen she sleeps
in the sound of sirens,
in jail, at salvation army;
she is hungry enough
to bite the hand that would feed her
or deny her food;
she curls about herself
like a cold serpent.

Eighteen at last
in the arms of a doctor,
waiting for the singe
of shock treatments,
tranquilizers coated
in blue sugar;
she grins. At nineteen
can't remember
she was chained for a time
to the glamor of speed.

Twenty years it took
to ask if it mattered
how dark her skin,
how slanted her eyes,
how hung in beadwork

the lobes of her ears,
how set in silver
the coral of her mouth.

Twenty-one
she surrounds him
on his Honda in the mountains;
through Nevada, Utah, Arizona
and on; country roads, slippery
streets of the cities then
home and gone and home again.

Twenty-five she travels
on hands and knees,
bandages trailing loose
in the sage, her bones
sticking out
from years of famine
and she is leaving him again.

The arctic turned tropic
when at thirty she found
not roses but mangos,
not redwoods but palm trees
and city dances
on uneven pavement;
books and readings and cocktails
corner her at sea
then attack
so gently.

Thirty-four: she counts
the storm-wrack washed up
on her knees and she writes,
writes these words
to test elbow and fingers,
toes and lips, pull
strands of hair silver
against black against gold
from her mouth
where the wind has strung them

like seaweed or just
like the sea.

Halfbreed Cry

My people cry ashes,
bleed fire from their eyes
like amber from polished wood
(the newly carved crucifix,
the twisted torso) as dying,
the tree searches it roots
for water
       and I feel it
       as a separation
       across which I stretch
       to almost touch them
turning
in the small space
of my life so distant oh
so very distant.

As natural as ants in a mound,
as geese in a cloud,
as seeds in a melon
they have each other
and here I come
like I could place
my own two hands
where my father laced up
the stones of his house,
       like I could sit
       at the tip of the mesa
       and greet everyone home
       by their most secret names.
I am over the canyon in one step,
down the highway, smelling the sea
and hearing distant thunder; I am leaving

my uselessness behind
for the people to use as they will

or to sell like a pot to a tourist
who would not know

the difference.

Decide What To Do with Her

she's no good to her people this way:
tie her jaws shut and her teeth
grinding together will not succeed
in her release; stand off a ways
and howl at her the namelessness
she approached us with,
the emptiness she brought,
the weapons she hid
in her clay-colored hands.

She'll twist to get free,
bite the binding around her,
melt the glue with her tongue
til, yellowed aspen leaf
that she is, she'll use her feet
to pry loose from the tree
and let go alone

but nourished by her enemies
she waits, muscles flexing,
feet gripping the rock;
you are warned, my sisters,
she will stay,
for she has survived
even if she
has survived
alone.

Comparison of Hands One Day Late Summer

My hand held
between leaf

and bud
is white clay
unshaped,
the earth
parched,
the empty
ravine;
horizontal cracks
trace
the bone and fat
of me
reluctantly
it doesn't matter
as I dodge
the droughts,
configuration of colors
mixed up and unsettled,
oil upon
the puddle.

Solid on mine
and strong,
your hand
contains
summer thunder,
the moist dark belly
in which
seeds sprout,
the beginning
of laughter,
a little boy's voice,
the promise perhaps
of tomorrow.

The wash deepens
east into night,
sculpted by blood
and tumbling
there comes
end over end
everyone's names.

And myself jealous
of the bones you hold
so well, their proper
shapes, precision
of length;
those old songs
whirling from your throat
easy and hot
for the dancers
and the sweat.
You and your memories
of berries picked ripe,
late summer
days like this
with tongue turning black
and teeth blue,
a loosely-made basket
bouncing from your hip.
Your people stretched you
til one day you woke up
and you just knew
who you were.

I would mention
my memories now
but who would
want to hear
of afternoons alone
and cold nights
on Eagle Hill,
of being a wild horse
among oats, bamboo,
eucalyptus
and sunset-colored women
with braided bridles
in their hands.
Or would you want to know
that I
who sing so much
of kin
grew alone and cold
in places so silent

the dragonflies
thunder.
Would you
want to hear
the sound of being tough,
or the hollow high winds
in my mother's heart.
Would you want to count
the handfuls of pills
or touch the fingers
that tighten on my thigh
even now

for what is a ghost after all
but dry, years or apples,
buckeye or sage, dry
memories, dry berries, dry earth,
dry corn, clocks, eyes,
woman-place, words,
not enough crows
to quarrel for the seeds . . .

If I Am Too Brown or Too White For You

remember I am a garnet woman
whirling into precision
as a crystal arithmetic
or a cluster and so

why the dream
in my mouth,
the flutter of blackbirds
at my wrists?

In the morning
there you are
at the edge of the river
on one knee

and you are selecting me
from among polished stones

more definitely red or white
between which tiny serpents swim

and you see
that my body is blood
frozen into giving birth
over and over, a single motion,

and you touch the matrix
shattered in winter
and begin to piece together
the shape of me

wanting the curl in your palm
to be perfect
and the image less clouded,
less mixed,

but you always see
just in time
working me around
the last hour of the day

there is a small light
in the smoke, a tiny sun
in the blood, so deep
it is there and not there,

so pure
it is singing.

24
Crows Written on the Poplars:
Autocritical Autobiographies

GERALD VIZENOR

Born in 1934, Gerald Vizenor, a mixed blood White Earth Chippewa from Minnesota, is one of the most interesting and most prolific of Native American writers. A poet, a film-maker, and a fiction writer of wild energy and imagination, Vizenor has also been a journalist, book reviewer, and critical theorist, as well as a professor of literature at the University of Minnesota, the University of California at Berkeley and Santa Cruz, the University of Oklahoma, and, briefly, at Tianjin University, People's Republic of China.

Among his many novels are Darkness in St. Louis Bearheart *(1978)*, The Trickster of Liberty *(1988), and* Griever: An American Monkey King in China *(1987), which won an American Book Award. His novel* The Heirs of Columbus *(1991) is a Native American narrative response to the quincentennial of the "discovery" of America. His most recent novel is* Dead Voices *(1992).*

Vizenor's Interior Landscapes: Autobiographical Myths and Metaphors *(1990) is his most extended autobiographical work to date. Our selection, however, is taken from an earlier autobiographical piece called "Crows Written on the Poplars: Autocritical Autobiographies."[1] In its frequent citation of a variety of writers, in its highly distinctive vocabulary and syntax, its enthusiasm for Japanese culture, and its reference to the horrifying circumstances of his father's death, Vizenor's account is typical of a good deal of his work. The ironic distancing achieved by the use of the third person is an especially interesting feature of Vizenor's work.*

---

1. Gerald Vizenor, "Crows Written on the Poplars: Autocritical Autobiographies," in *I Tell You Now: Autobiographical Essays by Native American Writers,* ed. Brian Swann and Arnold Krupat (Lincoln: Univ. of Nebraska Press, 1987). Reprinted by permission of the University of Nebraska Press. Copyright © 1987 by the University of Nebraska Press.

One can say anything to language. This is why it is a listener, closer to us
than any silence or any god.
    John Berger, *And Our Faces, My Heart, Brief as Photos*

Each autobiographical utterance embalms the author in his own prose,
marking his passage into a form that both surrenders him to death and yet
preserves his name, acts, and words.
    Avrom Fleishman, *Figures of Autobiography*

This is a mixedblood autobiographical causerie and a narrative on the
slow death of a common red squirrel. The first and third personas are me.

Gerald Vizenor believes that autobiographies are imaginative histories; a remembrance past the barriers; wild pastimes over the pronouns. Outside the benchmarks the ones to be in written memoirs are
neither sentimental nor ideological; mixedbloods loosen the seams in
the shrouds of identities. Institutional time, he contends, belies our
personal memories, imagination, and consciousness.

Language is a listener, imagination is a mythic listener, he pleaded
and then waited for the light to turn green at the intersection. Imagination is a presence, our being in a sound, a word; noise, ownership,
and delusions remain, the material realm reduced to scenes on color
television in the back seat of a white limousine.

"Myth makes truth," wrote Avrom Fleishman, "in historical as well
as in literary autobiography." Myth makes noise, war, blue chicken,
and mixedbloods too, mocked the mixedblood writer. The mixedblood is a new metaphor, he proposed, a transitive contradancer between communal tribal cultures and those material and urban preten-
sions that counter conservative traditions. The mixedblood wavers in
autobiographies; he moves between mythic reservations where tricksters roamed and the cities where his father was murdered.

The Minneapolis *Journal* reported that "police sought a giant negro
to compare his fingerprints with those on the rifled purse of Clement
Vizenor, a twenty-six-year-old half-breed Indian . . . found slain yesterday with his head nearly cut off by an eight-inch throat slash. . . .
He was the second member of his family to die under mysterious circumstances within a month.

"Three half-breed Indians were being held by police for questioning as part of the investigation. . . . Seven negroes were questioned
and then given the option of getting out of town. . . . Captain Pa-
radeau said he was convinced Clement had been murdered but that
robbery was not the motive. The slain youth was reported to have been
mild tempered and not in the habit of picking fights. Police learned that
he had no debts, and, as far as they could ascertain, no enemies."

Clement William Vizenor was born on the White Earth Reservation. He moved to Minneapolis and became a painter and paperhanger in the new suburbs; he was survived by his mother Alice Beaulieu, his wife La-Verne, three brothers, two sisters, and his son Gerald Robert Vizenor, one year and eight months old.

Bound with mixedblood memories, urban and reservation disharmonies, imagination cruises with the verbs and adverbs now, overturns calendar nouns in wild histories where there are no toeholds in material time, no ribbons on the polished line. The compassionate trickster battens on transitions and listens to squirrels, windlestrat patois, word blossoms on the barbed wire, androgynous rumors in college chapels; the seasons are too short down to the mother sea. The end comes in a pronoun, he roared on an elevator to the basement, birth to death, decided over-night in a given name.

"When we settle into the theater of autobiography," wrote Paul John Eakin in *Fictions in Autobiography*, "what we are ready to believe—and what most autobiographers encourage us to expect—is that the play we witness is a historical one, a largely faithful and unmediated reconstruction of events that took place long ago, whereas in reality the play is that of the autobiographical act itself, in which the materials of the past are shaped by memory and imagination to serve the needs of present consciousness." Here we are once more at the seams with pronouns and imagination in an autumn thunderstorm.

"A good hunter is never competitive," Vizenor repeated, a scene from his autobiographical stories published in *Growing Up in Minnesota: Ten Writers Remember Their Childhoods*. "The instincts of a survival hunter are measured best when he is alone in the woods. In groups, people depend on each other for identity and security, but alone the hunter must depend on his own instincts of survival and must move with the energy of the woodland."

Survival is imagination, a verbal noun, a transitive word in mixed-blood autobiographies; genealogies, the measured lines in time, place, and dioramas, are never the same in personal memories. Remembrance is a natural current that breaks with the spring tides; the curious imagine a sensual undine on the wash.

Ten years ago he wrote about what he chose to remember from an experience twenty years before that, when he shot and killed a red squirrel. He was alone then, the autumn of his second year of college, his first year at the University of Minnesota; he was single, an army veteran with two volumes of photographs to prove that he had driven a tank, directed theater productions, survived a typhoon, and walked with the bears in the Imperial National Forest on Hokkaido. When he faced the camera he wore a pensive smile, and at nineteen he had captured two dreams to be a writer.

Clement Vizenor and his son Gerald, in Minneapolis, 1936. Courtesy of Gerald Vizenor and the University of Minnesota Press. From *Interior Landscapes: Autobiographical Myths and Metaphors* by Gerald Vizenor, published by The University of Minnesota Press. Copyright © 1990 by Gerald Vizenor.

The sun was warm, the wind was cold, and the oak leaves were hard on the mound behind an abandoned house north of the cities; the ponds where the whole moon had crashed overnight were calm. In the loose seams of his memories he pictured Aiko Okada at Matsushima in Japan; he remembered his lover there, the loneliness that winter, the old women with their cloth bundles on the train back to Sendai. The squirrels whipped their tails and waited four trees back from the mixedblood.

He folded his cold ears and remembered a scene from a movie: Barbara Stanwyck climbed the stairs, opened a door, and shot a man in his bed; and a soldier in the audience at the army theater shouted, "Cease fire, police your brass and move back to the fifty-yard line." The audience roared, he roared with them; now the audience roars in his head and he smiles in the woods.

He praised Kahlil Gibran then, on the train with chickens and maimed warriors, and later in the leaves; he mentioned Lillian Smith in the barracks and repeated a line from her memoir *Killers of the Dream*, "The heart dares not stay away too long from that which hurt it most." He had been accepted at Sophia University in Tokyo, but at the last minute he decided to return home. Who would he be now in his autobiographies, he wondered, if he had stayed in Japan?

He has never been able to tame the interior landscapes of his memories: the back stoop of a tavern where he fed the squirrels, while his grandfather drank in the dark, breaks into the exotic literature of Lafcadio Hearn. Tribal women in sueded shoes mince over the threshold in the translated novels of Yasunari Kawabata and Osamu Dazai. Alice Beaulieu, in her sixties, married a blind man because, she snickered, he said she looked beautiful; and now, in the white birch, their adventures in the suburbs to peddle brooms and brushes overturn the wisdom of modern families—the blind man and his old stunner soothed lonesome women in pastel houses, and no one bought a broom.

Matsuo Basho came to mind on the mound with the squirrels that afternoon. Basho wrote, in his *haibun* travel prose, that the island at Matsushima "look exactly like parents caressing their children or walking with them arm in arm. . . . the beauty of the entire scene can only be compared to the most divinely endowed of feminine countenances," and at the same time Vizenor remembered a woman who told him that his haiku were too short; she dismissed those poems that were "less than seventeen proper syllables." She would never understand mixedblood autobiographies.

In the distance he heard laughter and smelled cigarette smoke: a hunter in a duck blind in a marsh behind the mound. Silent crows were on the trees. He pinched the side of his nose, abraded the oil with his thumbnail, and rubbed it into the dark grain of the rifle stock. He remembered laughter on a porch, through an open window, at the river, and snickers deep in the weeds behind the cabins at Silver Lake, a Salvation Army camp for welfare mothers. He had taught their children how to paddle canoes that summer, how to cook on an open fire, and how to name seven birds in flight.

He ordered a laminated miniature of his honorable discharge, bought a used car, a new suit, three shirts, a winter coat, and drove east to visit friends from the army. Two months later he was a college student, by chance, and inspired by the novel *Look Homeward Angel*; his two dreams, and much later his grammars, blossomed when his stories were praised by Eda Lou Walton, his first teacher of writing at New York University.

Professor Walton turned her rings, fingered the chains and beads at her thin neck when he lingered in her office; touched, he must remember that she was touched, even amused by his mixedblood meditations. His manuscripts were scented with her lavender water when she returned them with three unpunctuated phrases: the first a comment on imagination, the second on narrative, and at last a note on usage. "Wild imagination," she wrote on his third manuscript, "the boxelder sap stuck to my fingers . . . person and number, horrid grammar." This, the praise and criticism, was a marvelous association because she once shared an office with Thomas Wolfe.

I walked into the woods alone and found a place in the sun against a tree. The animals and birds were waiting in silence for me to pass. . . . When I opened my eyes, after a short rest, the birds were singing and the squirrels were eating without fear and jumping from tree to tree. I was jumping with them but against them as the hunter.

Here, in the last sentence, he pretends to be an arboreal animal, a romantic weakness; he was neither a hunter nor a tribal witness to the hunt. He was there as a mixedblood writer in a transitive confessional, then and now, in his imaginative autobiographies.

He has been the hunted, to be sure, cornered in wild dreams, and he has pretended to be a hunter in his stories, but he has never lived from the hunt; he has feasted on the bitter thighs of squirrel but he has never had to track an animal to the end, as he would to the last pronoun in his stories, to feed his families and friends.

He understands the instincts of the survival hunter, enough to mimic them, but the compassion he expresses for the lives of animals arises from imagination and literature; his endurance has never been measured in heart muscles, livers, hides, horns, shared on the trail. His survival is mythic, an imaginative transition, an intellectual predation, deconstructed now in masks and metaphors at the water holes in autobiographies.

"Language is the main instrument of man's refusal to accept the world as it is," wrote George Steiner in *After Babel*. "Ours is the ability, the need, to gainsay or 'un-say' the world, to image and speak it otherwise. . . . To misinform, to utter less than the truth was to gain a vital edge of space or subsistence. Natural selection would favour the contriver. Folk tales and mythology retain a blurred memory of the evolutionary advantage of mask and misdirection."

I raised my rifle, took aim, and fired at a large red squirrel running across an oak bough. He fell to the ground near the trunk of the tree, bounced once, and started to climb the tree again. The bullet passed through his shoulder, shattering the bone. His right front leg hung limp from torn skin. He fell to the ground and tried to climb the tree again. He instinctively reached up with his shattered paw, but it was not there to hold him. Blood was spreading across his body. He tried to climb the tree again and again to escape from me.

The slow death of the squirrel burned in his memories; he sold his rifles and never hunted animals. Instead, he told stories about squirrels and compassionate tricksters. Once, he leaped over a fence to block a man who raised his rifle to shoot two squirrels. Later, a few months before he wrote the autobiographical scene repeated here, he witnessed an accident: an automobile had crushed the lower spine and pelvis of a red squirrel. He watched the animal scratch the cold asphalt with her front paws; she hauled her limp body to the wet maple leaves at the low curb. Closer, he cried and the squirrel shivered; then he warmed her with his hands and hummed with her down to the mother sea.

He was a survivor. He knew when and where to hide from the hunters who came in groups to kill—their harsh energies were burned in the memories of his animal tribe. I was alone. My presence and my intention to kill squirrels were disguised by sleep and camouflaged by my gentle movements in the woods. I did not then know the secret language of squirrels. I did not know their suffering in the brutal world of hunters.

The overbearing hunter learns not to let an animal suffer. As if the hunter were living up to some moral code of tribal warfare, wounded animals must be put out of their miseries.

The squirrels in his autobiographies are mythic redemptions; he remembers their death and absolves an instance of his own separation in the world. The transitive realism is a mask, the blood and broken bones rehearsed in metaphors to dishearten the pretend hunter. He refused to accept the world as a hunter; rather than contrive stories or misinform, he fashioned a blood-soaked mask that he dared the hunter to wear in his autobiographies.

Three decades later he read *And Our Faces, My Heart, Brief as Photos* by John Berger, who wrote that the "opposite of to love is not to hate but to separate. If love and hate have something in common it is because, in both cases, their energy is that of bringing and holding together—the lover with the loved, the one who hates with the hated. Both passions are tested by separation." He learned that hunters and squirrels were never opposites; the opposite of both is separation. Both the hunter and the hunted are tested by their separation from the same landscapes. Gainsay the sentimental and decadent hunter to forbear the squirrels in trees and autobiographies.

"I write for myself and strangers," said Gertrude Stein, a secular oblation that would become the isolation of imaginative writers. The mixedblood autobiographer is a word hunter in transitive memories, not an academic chauffeur in the right lane to opposition; those mixedbloods at the treelines, he warned, are wild word hunters with new metaphors on separation.

When the squirrel started to climb the tree again, I fired one shot at his head. The bullet tore the flesh and fur away from the top of his skull. He fell to the ground still looking at me. In his eyes he wanted to live more than anthing I have ever known. I fired a second time at his head. The bullet tore his lower jaw away, exposing his teeth. He looked at me and moved toward the tree again. Blood bubbled from his nostrils when he breathed. I fired again. The bullet shattered his forehead and burst through his left eye. He fell from the tree and watched me with one eye. His breath was slower. In his last eye he wanted to live again, to run free, to hide from me. I knelt beside him, my face next to his bloody head, my eye close to his eye, and begged him to forgive me before he died. I looked around the woods. I felt strange. I was alone. The blood bubbles from his nose grew smaller and disappeared. I moved closer to his eye. Please forgive me, I pleaded in tears. Please live again, I begged him again and again.

"The man who takes delight in thus drawing his own images believes himself worthy of a special interest," wrote Georges Gusdorf in his article "Conditions and Limits of Autobiography," translated by James Olney and published in his book *Autobiography: Essays Theoretical and Critical*. "Each of us tends to think of himself as the center of a living space: I count, my existence is significant to the world, and my death will leave the world incomplete. . . .

"This conscious awareness of the singularity of each individual life is the late product of a specific civilization. Through most of human history, the individual does not oppose himself to all others; he does not feel himself to exist outside of others, and still less against others, but very much *with* others in an interdependent existence that asserts its rhythms everywhere in the community.

"It is obvious that autobiography is not possible in a cultural landscape where consciousness of self does not . . . exist," wrote Gusdorf. "Autobiography becomes possible only under certain metaphysical pre-conditions. To begin with, at the cost of a cultural revolution, humanity must have emerged from the mythic framework of traditional teachers and must have entered into the perilous domain of history. The man who takes the trouble to tell of himself knows that the present differs from the past and that it will not be repeated in the future; he has become more aware of differences than similarities."

He blinked at me. His eye was still alive. Did his blinking eye mean that he had forgiven me? Please forgive me, I moaned again and again, until my self-pity fell silent in the woods. Not a bird was singing. The leaves were silent. He blinked again. I moved closer to him, stretching my body out on the ground next to him, and ran my hand across his back. The blood was still warm. I wept and watched the last of his good life pass through me in his one remaining eye. I sang a slow death song in a low voice without words until it was dark.

"Artistic creation is a struggle with an angel, in which the creator is the more certain of being vanquished since the opponent is still himself," continued Gusdorf. "He wrestles with his shadow, certain only of never laying hold of it."

Chester Anderson smoked too much when he edited the ten autobiographies that were published in *Growing Up in Minnesota*. Borrowed books and sprouted markers, notes in his winter coat, and the thin manuscript of my thirteen autobiographical stories returned in a manila envelope smelled of sweet pipe tobacco. The professor lowers one shoulder, as he does when he rides in the wind with a genial smile, and leans closer to listen; no one has been a more sensitive listener.

The crows were written on the poplars that winter when the autobiographies were published by the University of Minnesota Press. The shadows between metaphors vanished in scheduled seminars; personal memories shivered in the buckram and perished on neap tide phrases; memories were measured and compared in a tournament of pronouns.

A teacher at Macalester College in Saint Paul, an *agent provocateur* in reflexive literature, said that my stories were not true. "These are not believable experiences," she announced in the chapel where several authors had gathered to read. Her haughtiness and peevish leer, broadened behind enormous spectacles, reminded me of a high school teacher who refused to honor one of my stories because, she ruled, an adolescent would not have such experiences.

"Mature speech begins in shared secrecy, in centripetal storage or inventory, in the mutual cognizance of a very few. In the beginning the word was largely a pass-word, granting admission to a nucleus of like speakers. 'Linguistic exogamy' comes later, under compulsion of hostile or collaborative contact with other small groups. We speak first to ourselves, then to those nearest us in kinship and locale. We turn only gradually to the outsider, and we do so with every safeguard of obliqueness, of reservation, of conventional flatness or outright misguidance," wrote George Steiner in *After Babel*. "At its intimate centre, in the zone of familial or totemic immediacy, our language is most economic of explanation, most dense with intentionality and compacted implication. Streaming outward it thins, losing energy and pressure as it reaches an alien speaker."

The two dreams to be a writer remain the same as when they were captured in a photograph on a train near Matsushima in northern Japan. The islands there are endowed with "feminine countenances" and mixedbloods must hold back some secrets from the alien speakers in the academies.

25
The Two Lives

LINDA HOGAN

A novelist and short story writer as well as a poet, Linda Hogan is of mixed Chickasaw background. Born in Denver in 1947, she taught American Studies and American Indian Studies at the University of Minnesota before settling in Colorado to engage in ecological work as well as to write. Her recent novels, Mean Spirit *(1990), and* The Book of Medicines *(1993) have been highly praised.*

Our selection is from "The Two Lives," written for the anthology I Tell You Now: Autobiographical Essays by Native American Writers[1] *and a moving account of Hogan's coming to understand how her personal life was affected by social and cultural forces larger than any single person. For all the pointed political analysis, this essay is also marked by the vision and lyricism of the poet.*

November 13, 1984. Today the newspaper contains the usual stories: two countries negotiating money and peace, a space shuttle penetrating the sky, the U.S. government preparing to invade Nicaragua, thousands of Minneapolis teenagers in line to purchase tickets for a Prince concert, an infant girl rejecting the transplanted heart of a baboon. Children are being abused and raped in their families and schools, and by their protectors. There has been a sniper shooting. Two large scorpions guard jewels in Bavaria. Coal miners and other worker struggles are in resistance against governments and police. Microwaves and diamonds are on sale.

In the face of this history that goes on minute by minute, the oppression recorded in the papers, human pain and joy, it is a difficult thing to think of autobiography, that telling of our selves or our lives or innerness.

I tell parts of my stories here because I have often searched out other

1. Linda Hogan, "The Two Lives," in *I Tell You Now: Autobiographical Essays by Native American Writers*, ed. Brian Swann and Arnold Krupat (Lincoln: Univ. of Nebraska Press, 1987). Reprinted by permission of the University of Nebraska Press. Copyright © 1987 by the University of Nebraska Press.

lives similar to my own. They would have sustained me. Telling our lives is important, for those who come after us, for those who will see our experience as part of their own historical struggle. I think of my work as part of the history of our tribe and as part of the history of colonization everywhere. I tell this carefully, and with omissions, so as not to cause any divisions between myself and others. I want it to be understood that the opening paragraph, the news of November 13, 1984, is directly connected to this history, to our stories, to the continuing destruction of Third World and tribal people, and the exploitation of our earth.

I come from two different people, from white pioneers who crossed into Nebraska plains and from Chickasaw Indian people from south central Oklahoma.

Of the pioneers I know very little except for a journal I have that was written by my maternal great-grandfather during the Depression, in 1934. It is a spare book, though it spans the years from 1848 to 1934. His words cover a great movement across the American continent.

The journal describes pre–Civil War 1861 when my maternal great-grandfather, W. E. Bower, hoed broom corn, working from dawn to night before he walked home three miles. In 1862 he moved to where a railroad was being constructed, near the Wisconsin River, for hauling wheat. They used wood as fuel for the engines. He cut and hauled wood. At night he worked with his father making shoes until an accident occurred in which the elder Bower was dragged by horses and injured. The younger man then went to work full time for the lumber industry. In three years (1872) he went to Nebraska to homestead. The crops and trees were all eaten by grasshoppers. I have seen this in my own life, so I know it is true. My father tells of seeing plagues of grasshoppers that ate everything made of wood, even shovel handles.

Desperate after crop failures, Bower began hunting buffalo in order to sell the meat. The settlers were starving, according to his journal, and the government was sending soldiers out to shoot the buffalo. They also hunted beaver and antelope. He was followed once by hundreds of coyotes and was afraid at night.

I see from these words how closely destruction of the land and animal life are linked to the beginning American economy. This continues to be true. I see also how desperate the struggle for survival was for the new white Americans in those days. Their lack of regard for the land and life came out of that desperation. It continues today out of that tradition, but does not work in the service of life.

Bower writes about a Railroad section boss who refused to give him and his cohunters water from a well and refused them water for their horses, and how the hunters went for their revolvers before they were allowed to drink.

I believe he commented upon this cruelty because it surprised him. Historically, the incident took place at a time when major acts of genocide were being committed against tribal people across the country, when Mission Indians were being moved and moved again as settlers began to take over the California lands, when southern tribes were just removed to Indian Territory (Oklahoma), and when numerous other tribes from the North were being forced into the South, many in resistance. It was a continuing time of great and common acts of cruelty and violence.

Bower commented that he saw Indians and they looked friendly. I made this into a poem:

OLD MEN AT WAR, OLD WOMEN

Be silent
old men who live inside me,
dark grandfather that was silent
though I was his blood
and wore his black eyes.
He's living in my breath
when it's quiet,
all his people are walking
through my veins without speech.

And blonde grandfather
fishing the river for Chubs,
many hunts
to sell buffalo who stood quiet
trusting the settlers
starving in Nebraska.
His words:
    We saw Indians but they seemed peaceful.

Red River,
I'm at the red river
and it's going dry,

all of us,
we are here,
and I'm drinking your wine for you,
the color of dawn
heading for light
heading for one light.
I'm wearing your love and hate
like silver
and blue stone.

This face
this body
this hair
is not mine.
This war inside me
is not mine.

I've been waiting,
where are the women?
Are they listening to this
beneath all the soft layers of my skin.
Are they listening.
Are they loving each other?

(from *Eclipse*)

During the time Bower traveled the continent, my Chickasaw people were trying to make a life in Oklahoma after having been moved forcibly over the Trail of Tears, that trail they began unwillingly and with great sorrow, from our homeland in Mississippi in order that settlers there could have the rich southern lands. That was the trail where soldiers killed children in order to make the journey quick, where women were brutalized, men murdered, where the bodies of living people were left to die as markers along a trail of history, pointing the direction back to our homeland.

After Removal, Chickasaws, many of whom had cooperated with whites and been slaveholders in the South before the Removal Act, were told to fight for the South in the Civil War. It is surprising that anyone thought Indian people might want to take up white wars after Removal, which politicized tribes, which Geary Hobson once said was a travesty that turned any white blood running in our veins red.

In a November blizzard those Indians who refused to fight were sent into Kansas without rations, horses, shoes, or clothing. Most died, and it was planned that way. As Joy Harjo has said, there are those of us who have survived who were never meant to survive.

This was followed by the Dawes Act, by other wars, by one tragedy laid down upon another, by land loss and swindles during the oil boom and the Depression, by continuing struggle, poverty, and loss.

My great-grandmother Addie was the granddaughter of Winchester Colbert, head of the Chickasaw Nation. She married Granville Walker Young, a rancher and politician of French-Indian (*métis*) ancestry and as such, in Indian Territory, was considered to be white. As a white intermarried citizen of the Chickasaw Nation, he was given land, and later a place on the Chickasaw legislature, and they built a large home. It is said that as a commissioner of lands, he managed to accumulate money from the tribal holdings. I would like to think this is not true and that I've been misinformed, but historically, it sounds correct. It is not that different today with some Indian leaders.

Their daughter, Lucy Young, was my grandmother. When she married a Chickasaw named Charles Colbert Henderson, her father disowned her, as he did another daughter.

My grandmother graduated from the Bloomfield Academy for Chickasaw girls in 1904. In school, she learned to play the violin and the piano. She learned the manners of white upper-class southern women, for this was what the teachers valued in Indian girls, yet when I was a child, she and my grandfather lived in southern poverty, without water or lights, with horse and wagon.

That is the history of most of the southern tribes. I believe that when I say the truth, many of my family will feel defensive, as if I am saying that there was something wrong with my grandparents or family that we did not have money. But it is a shared experience. Some Indians built ranches, farms, or nearly comfortable lives only to lose them and return to poverty. We are landless Indians. Most of us continue to live below the poverty level defined by the U.S. government. We often dislike ourselves. We are made to believe that poverty is created by ourselves and not that it is an economic problem existing within the history of the American way of exploiting the colonized.

I come from people who have not had privilege. This is because of our histories. Those who are privileged would like for us to believe that we are in some way defective, that we are not smart enough, not good enough. In fact, it may seem that way because we speak separate languages and live a separate way of life. Some of us learn their language, the voice and ways of the educated, and we are then bilingual or trilingual and able to enter their country in order to earn a better living. But seldom do any of them understand our language, and our language goes deeper than words. It goes all the way to meaning and heart.

We have not valued the things that are desired by the privileged. We do not assume that we will go to college, or that there are places for us out in the dominant and dominating world, or that if we do certain things we will be taken care of. We generally do not know these "skills," and we often settle for very little because it seems like so much to us. We do not often fight for our rights, nor do we know what they are. We assume we are lucky to be doing so well. Plus, we are accustomed to a "system" that removes small liberties from us when we ask for what we deserve. My ex-husband's father, a non-Indian, worked in Oregon for a grocery firm for less than standard wages. He tried to organize his fellow workers to strike for decent pay and the company threatened to close down. The men, who had no other source of income and lacked also the means to move, had no choice left but to work for substandard wages. And it has been even harder for minority people.

For me, when I was a child, two lives lived me. In Gene Autry, Oklahoma, where my grandparents lived, they still went to town in a horse and wagon. They had no water. I wrote a poem about my sister and me in the 1950s in Indian Territory, Oklahoma:

> Already you have a woman's hip bones,
> long muscles
> you slide your dress over
> and we brush each other's hair
> then step out into the blue morning.
> Good daughters,
> we are quiet
> lifting empty milk cans,
> silver cans into the wagon.
> They rattle together
> going to town.

> (from "Going to Town," *Calling Myself Home*)

There was no water, electricity, or plumbing but when we were there we did have Coke, orange soda, and spoonfuls of white sugar. We bathed outside in a galvanized steel tub with Lava soap and water our grandmother heated on the woodstove. Our water came from the pump in town, over the few miles by wagon. My grandmother cooked dozens of eggs in the morning. She raised chickens. She rose from bed before daylight in order to brush her floor-length hair. When I was there, I got up early to help brush out her hair. I have felt this life deeply to be mine; though I lived in many other places and was born in Denver.

Outside of Denver, Colorado, in what was then a rapidly changing rural area called Lakewood, my father worked as a carpenter. That place is now city suburbs, but then we lived near a turkey farm. My mother took me a few times on a bus into the city to Woolworth's, and there was a legless man outside on a cart selling red paper poppies. My mother bought me ice cream. Here is an excerpt from around this time. It is from a short story called "Ain't No Indians in Hell" (*13th Moon*) and is about our first move into a neighborhood at the time our father was gone to the Korean war:

> We were going to talk to my father and we were having a television delivered, all in one day. One of my father's checks had come through and mom's ironing money went for a down payment on the console and the rabbit ear antenna.
>
> The television arrived first and we watched the Fred and Fay show with the clown and just heard Fred say, "You know, boys and girls," when mom shut off the picture.
>
> We all walked together toward the church by the park.
>
> A man with only one leg passed us. I turned to watch him. "Quit staring," Marnie said. "It isn't nice."
>
> In the basement of the church was a large radio with a brown speaker. There were funny sounds coming through it and we waited while a voice took shape in there. The voices were stale and static. A woman standing in front of my mom spoke to the voice and left, crying. Then it was our turn and my mother spoke to a voice she said was my father. "I love you, honey," the voice said. And she told him we had seen grandma, that we had gotten one of the checks, and that the tomatoes were fine but the worms were eating us out of house and home. Marnie told him about the elephant she rode, and said also, "Gracie wouldn't ride him. She was plum afraid." I stared at the box and couldn't speak to it except to say, "Hello" and "Fine."
>
> We walked back home, silent. Mom changed back into her large blue dress and went outside with the rusted rake and began to rake the place where there wasn't even any garden or dry grass.
>
> She raked until it was dark and then she stayed outdoors. Marnie and I had stared at her through the window, raking at nothing, and then we saw her lie down on the grass to watch the stars begin to emerge.
>
> Marnie tucked me in. "Okay," she said. "On the floor is the King-

dom of the Alligators. If you put a foot down there or get out of bed, they will eat you."

When I woke up later, the light in the corner was still lit and there was a small circle of gold on the wall. Marnie was asleep, her arms neatly and perfectly on top of the sheet. Mom was in the living room watching television and ironing. She lifted the iron and placed it back down again and moved rhythmically.

I turned around in my bed so that my head was at the bottom and watched the television. The room was doorless so no one could close me in or out. I heard a sound, a chirping in the bedroom, and followed it. I stood on the bed, careful to not fall into the Kingdom of the Alligators. It was a small green cricket up on the doll shelf. It was rubbing together a wing and leg, over its head. In this way it started a jungle or a fire, and I stood, forgetting the heat and watched it sing with its body, hearing the song of the night.

After the Korean War, when my father returned to us and I was eight, my parents moved to Colorado Springs to live in a housing project called Stratton Meadows, a name that signified that the land there was once beautiful. It was near the Fort Carson army base. This was a mixed-race area, and working class. There were a lot of "Spanish" as Mexican-Americans used to call themselves out of their own sense of self-dislike. I wrote a story called "Friends and Fortunes" about Stratton Meadows. One time a woman from National Public Radio read this story and said, I always knew there must be people like this, but I have never read about them. By "them" she meant the Others, those she had never been. She did not understand that I was one of them, alive and breathing, standing before her.

Where I live, people do things outdoors. Out in the open air, they do what wealthier and more private people hide inside their homes. Young couples neck beside the broken lilac bushes or in old cars parked along the street. Women knead bread on their steps, and sometimes collapse in a fury of weeping on the sidewalk. Boys breaking windows do not hide in the darkness of night.

We are accustomed to displays, so when Mr. Wrenn across the street has the DTs in front of his house, conversations continue. *What will be will be, and life goes on,* as my mother is fond of saying. The men who are at home go over to convince Mr. Wrenn that the frogs are not really there. If that tack fails, they kill off the frogs or snakes with imaginary machetes or guns. While they are destroying the terrors that crawl out of the mind, the rest of us talk. We visit while the men lift their arms and swing, aiming at the earth, saying there are no more alligators anywhere. "Lovely day, isn't it?" someone says.

I am grateful that I have learned how to analyze what happens to us on a daily basis in the form of classism and racism. Otherwise, like many others, I would have destroyed myself out of frustration, pain, and rage. Several times, like so many others, I have bordered on that destruction. We do it with alcohol, suicide, insanity, or other forms of self-hatred: ways of failing in our good, strong living.

It is sometimes easier to stay where we are, where we know our place, can breathe, know the language, but for the fact that we are largely powerless there to make any change for ourselves, for others, for our children. It is difficult for us to gather our human forces together because our circumstances force us into divisions and anger and self-destruction.

From childhood I believed that oppression (I had no word for it then) was wrong; that the racism I heard daily—all sorts from without and from within my own family—was wrong; that cruelty, all forms of violence and destruction of earth and life, was wrong. I learned every single thing that I know in order to fight these wrongs, and I have not often bothered to learn other things. I began fighting against brutality and oppression when I was still only half-formed in my ideas and language, and sometimes at great risk to my own self. With great courage I began a fight toward growth and integrity, and I am very proud of that young woman I was who believed so strongly in life and had so much hope of change that she found energy and courage and was politicized rather than paralyzed by the struggles.

When I began to write, I wrote partly to put this life in order, partly because I was too shy to speak. I was silent and the poems spoke first. I was ignorant and the poems educated me. When I realized that people were going to read the poems, I thought of the best ways to use words, how great was my responsibility to transmit words, ideas, and acts by which we could live with liberation, love, self-respect, good humor, and joy. In learning that, I also had to offer up our pain and grief and sorrow, because I know that denial and repression are the greatest hindrances to liberation and growth. Simon Ortiz has said that denial is the largest single factor working against us in this country.

My life has been a constant effort at self-education, a constant searching and re-searching what was important for me to learn. I went to college as an older student. I had years of work experience behind me. I started work at fifteen as a nurse's aide in Hill Haven Nursing Home, where there were rats and where we aides laundered the sheets and diapers of the patients at 4:00 A.M. I felt fortunate to have this 75-cents-an-hour job. I did not know how many other girls prepared for college at that age, did not work full time. It was never mentioned to me that I might go to college, although my mother did try to convince me not to quit high school. I was engaged young and I wanted to get married. I didn't know anyone who went to college, or even what it was.

I worked many jobs like this. I worked for a dentist at $1.05 an hour. When he praised me for learning to mount X-rays after only one lesson, it made a great difference in my life that he thought I was intelligent and mentioned it to me on several occasions; but in spite of that encouragement, I worked at many other low-paying jobs, in nursing homes, in dental offices, and filing for a collection agency where I occasionally threw away the files of people who called to tell how hard their lives were. I believed them, although the owner said they would manipulate the collectors with their lies about death, poverty, or illness.

The poor tell terrible stories, it is true.

The last job I had before I went to college was working for an orthodontist who believed Ayn Rand's philosophy, received her *Objectivist Newsletter*, believed I was inferior because I worked for less than his wife's clothing budget or their liquor bill (I paid their bills at the office), and who, when I received money to attend night school and was proud, accused me of being a welfare leech and said, during the first space flight which cost lives in money, that I should be ashamed of myself. He fired me shortly after that for missing a day of work. I yelled at him as I left the office. It was the first time I fought back for myself.

That fighting back was an act of strength and self-respect, though I felt badly about it at first. Again, I look back through the years with great love for who I was, for knowing something was wrong, even though it was years before I had words for what it was:

> Tell them all
> we won't put up with your hard words
> and low wages one more day.
> Those meek who were blessed
> are nothing
> but meat and potato eaters,
> never salsa or any spice.
> Those timid are sagging in the soul
> and those poor who will inherit the earth
> already work it
> so take shelter

take shelter you
because we are thundering and beating on floors
and this is how walls have fallen in other cities.

(from "Those Who Thunder")

When I say that I spent my life in self-education, I want people to know that part of this was done even when I went to college. I was a commuter student, attending night classes until my last year or two. There were no classes that made any connection to my own life experience or perception of the world. The closest I came to learning what I needed was in a course on labor literature, and the lesson there was in knowing that there were writers who lived similar lives to ours.

This is one of the ways that higher education perpetuates racism and classism. By ignoring our lives and our work, by creating standards for only their own work.

Education can be a hard process for minority and women students who have already learned too much of what we don't need to know. As an educator now I use books that are significant for us and are not often found in the university.

I find this especially necessary because I am aware of the fact that as a light-skinned Indian person I am seen as a person of betweens, as a person of divided directions. Non-Indians are more comfortable with me than they are with my darker sisters and brothers, for they assume that I am similar to them, or somehow not as real as other Indian people. This preference for light skin is true of other minorities also; the light ones, the mixed ones, are seen as closer, in many ways, to the dominant culture. But I want to point out how exclusion works in a divided society and how color affects us all. To be darker means to experience more pain, more racism, less hope, less self-esteem, less advantage. It means to be vulnerable to attack by police, to be left untreated more often by physicians, to be more vulnerable to rape and other forms of violence and abuse, and to have less of resources or assistance. I know women who have been raped by police (the protectors of life and property). A young boy I know was stripped naked by the police in Denver and let out of their car to walk home across town with no clothing. He had not committed a crime. He looked suspicious because of his dark skin. These are not isolated or unusual incidents. They happen most often to darker people.

My teachers have been those who before me found the first ways to speak of these things. Writers like the women in *This Bridge Called My Back*, Audre Lorde, Meridel Le Sueur, Tillie Olsen, and D'Arcy Mc-Nickle, a Flathead Indian writer who documented the truth, as did Gertrude Simmons Bonnin, Zitkala Ṡa. I have been deeply interested in the work of many writers of the 1930s, and of writers from other countries who are engaged in struggles for survival. I continue to read books from contemporary radical and alternative presses, for those are the books that talk about our lives. I wonder why it is that to be working class or a woman of color in America and to write a book about it is a radical action and one that must be published by the alternative presses. Why is it that telling our lives is a subversive thing to do? Perhaps it is again that burden of denial and of repression. Still, it seems that the covering-up of the truth is the real act of subversion.

I read books of feminist theory and often relate that to culture and class. The experience of being a woman has the same elements as being Indian, black, and poor, even though some of the strongest divisions seem to be cultural ones, and some of the most difficult forms of exclusion and misuse that I have felt have come from white women in the women's movement and in the academy where some women have, by necessity and for their own survival, perfected the language of dominance and entered into competition with one another. I believe in the women's movement as another resistance struggle, not as an entering into the ways of the bosses. For many women, their movement is not resistance as much as infiltration. As Audre Lorde has said, "The Master's tools will not dismantle his house." My own efforts have gone into new tools, the dismantling, the rebuilding. Writing is my primary crowbar, saw, and hammer. It is a way of not allowing ourselves to be depowered by disappearance.

When I was a child, I knew that my journey through life was going to be a spiritual one.

I mention this here because I have met many people on this journey and I know there are those who will find this useful. I am hesitant, however, to go too deeply into it because of the misuse of Indian spiritual beliefs and traditions by those non-Indians who are in spiritual crises, and who hope to gain from the ways of other cultures because they do not find their own ways to be valuable. Searching out "ways" may be a problem in itself, since we are all part of the same motion of life, our work being to serve the planet and its people and creatures, whether we show respect to the life energy through ceremonies or through other kinds of services or through the saying of mass. It seems like people search for ways instead of integrating meaning. North Americans emphasize what they call "method" and "analysis" but do not often get into the center core of living.

Also, many spiritual traditions would have us believe so completely in a caste system that we may come to see the paths of others as superior or inferior to our own. Again, it is because we learn to measure the weight of our accomplishments without learning to love our inner lives. We must learn to see those measurements as meaningless, and to honor that innerness as real and as sacred. Here is a poem I wrote about traveling to Chicago:

EVOLUTION IN LIGHT AND WATER

Above gold dragons of rivers
the plane turns.
We are flying in gravity's teeth.
Below us the earth is broken
by red tributaries
flowing like melted steel,
splitting the continent apart
and fusing it
in the same touch.

It is easier to fall
than to move through the suspended air,
easier to reel toward the pull of earth
and let thoughts drown in the physical rivers of light.
And falling, our bodies reveal their inner fire,
red trees in the lungs,
liquids building themselves
light in the dark organs
the way gold-eyed frogs grow legs
in the shallows.

Dark amphibians
live in my skin.
I am their country.
They swim in the old quiet seas
of this woman.
Salamander and toad

waiting to emerge and fall again
from the radiant vault of myself,
this full and broken continent of living.

(first published in *Denver Quarterly*, Winter 1985)

That amphibious woman, the light and dark of myself, the ancient woman I am, comes to be viewed in another way in a later poem that realizes the essential value and strength of humor as one of the tools the masters have not used in the building of their houses: to every living thing that graces my eyes or whose sound fills my ears. It is best if I return some of my richness to the spirit world and to the earth, if I feed the birds and carry love into the world. This is all that is required, not elaborate rites and ceremonies, just the need to *be* and to live fully. The healing ceremonies only return us to our being when the busy life and fast world have broken down our inner ways. They return us to our love and connection with the rest of creation. That is their purpose. They remind us of where we are within the framework of all life.

Other means that are consciously and actively used for this return to creation are the labor of service, basic and daily work, a strong consciousness of our moment-by-moment living. It is with great meaning that we live, every minute of our lives, but too seldom do we consider that meaning and the significance of our actions and words.

The stories of my life are many. I have omitted the small stories here in favor of the larger story that lays itself down with those of others. The stories of my life:

I have loved the songs of the first frogs in springtime, the red light of morning, the red earth, the heartbeat of trees and waters. I have been comforted by human and animal closeness and I have given comfort to the living and to the dying. I have taken care of the bodies and hearts of the sick. I have cooked meals, laid linoleum, cut wood, fixed roofs. I have bathed children, woven wool, made jewelry, painted pictures, and made music. I have lived with old people and with children, with no one too easily. I have worked as a fry cook, a waitress, a nurse's aide, a teacher's aide, a secretary, a dental assistant, and in numerous other jobs. I have protested cruelty and other wars. I have not been afraid to offend the offensive, disturb the disturbed, nor to be kind and loving to the gentle. I have fought and I've given up easily and wondered if I could live one more day, and lived. I have been careless and made separations through my words and actions. I have made healing unions in the same ways. I've listened to the songs of night. I have hated death and taxes and I still do. I never once believed, not for a minute, that there are any two things you can't avoid:

I am the big woman with black eyes and a quiet face. I have a slow walk except when the breeze whistles at me like a cop after loiterers. I wear my white skirt wrapped over my big hips and walk through town laughing. I have a sailor in every port. I'm greedy, I drink all the coconut soda, and eat plum jam I never offer to guests, even to you whom I like.

Every day about this time when the world is coming to life, I think about death and I weep, laugh, and am silent. Once silent, I remember the smell of whiskey so I go to the water with my blue bucket and taunt the fishermen who have drunk too much the night before and who are baiting for something under the surface of the world. I say, "You don't even know what you might pull up from the water; an old shoe, a tire, or a snapping turtle. And you call yourselves fishermen." Then I wade out by the rocks and reach in with my bare hands. When I am through, my catch is the best, silver fish the size of my pan. I don't give them away. It pays a woman to be greedy. It is a heavy price we pay for what we give too easily.

Sit still now, the miners are passing by and we will wave at them from the window. Sometimes they are small men, but it is big work they do. When we women wave, it reminds them to be large. See their poor faces, dark with the coal in their lungs? Their souls have vacated the premises so they won't have an inner revolution when they listen to their own voices say, "Hey, the bosses are getting rich and my family is still hungry, my back hurts, and my lungs are half gone, and the president of this country has cut my pay, so the hell with this place *and* the war tax."

(from "The Big Woman")

Part 7
Traditional Lives Today

The Native American artists whose highly sophisticated and "literary" autobiographies were included in the previous section are undoubtedly the best-known Indian autobiographers today. But it is important to remember that there are a number of Native people, who, although they may not be known to a wide audience, have also recorded their lives in a variety of interesting ways. These are also extremely sophisticated people, quite able to negotiate the ways of the dominant Euramerican society, for all that they remain firmly rooted in the traditional values of their tribal peoples. Although some of them have been educated in the whiteman's schools, they generally tend to be not so much writers (excepting Peter Kalifornsky) as healers, political and cultural negotiators, storytellers, and, to an important degree, self-conscious and proud preservers of their languages and traditions. Recognizing that some textual record of their knowledge would be useful to future generations, all of these autobiographers chose to work either with a professional writer on Indian subjects (as in the case of Fools Crow) or with anthropologists (in the cases of Albert Yava and Angela Sidney). Even Peter Kalifornsky worked with academic linguists. Although a certain amount of stubborn refusal to see the worth of indigenous cultures still exists, since the 1960s the climate for these efforts has in general been favorable.

In addition to the texts represented in this part of the anthology, we should mention at least some of the other contemporary life histories which could not be included here. Among the best known of these is Lame Deer's collaboration with Richard Erdoes, *Lame Deer: Seeker of Visions*,[1] though it should be noted that a forthcoming study by Julian Rice demonstrates how much Erdoes and Lame Deer took from, and to what degree they altered, earlier Lakota texts, for the most part without acknowledgement. Erdoes has also worked with Mary Crow Dog to produce two autobiographies, *Lakota Woman*,[2] and (she using the name Mary Brave Bird) *Ohitika Woman*.[3] Less known, but quite

1. John Fire/Lame Deer and Richard Erdoes, *Lame Deer: Seeker of Visions* (New York: Simon and Schuster, 1972).
2. Mary Crow Dog, *Lakota Woman* (New York: G. Weidenfeld, 1990).
3. Mary Brave Bird, *Ohitika Woman* (New York: Grove-Atlantic, 1993).

moving is Kay Bennett's *Kaibah: Recollections of a Navajo Girlhood;*[4] a rather odd, but nonetheless interesting recent collaboration has resulted in *Yellowtail: Crow Medicine Man and Sun Dance Chief: An Autobiography by Thomas Yellowtail "as told to" Michael Oren Fizgerald.*[5]

4. Kay Bennett, *Kaibah: Recollections of a Navajo Girlhood* (Los Angeles: Westernlore Press, 1974).

5. Thomas Yellowtail, *Yellowtail: Crow Medicine Man and Sun Dance Chief: An Autobiography,* as told to Michael Oren Fizgerald, introduction by Fred Voget (Norman: Univ. of Oklahoma Press, 1991).

26
Fools Crow

Edited by

THOMAS E. MAILS

A Teton Sioux born in 1891, Frank Fools Crow began his collaboration with Thomas E. Mails in 1974. From his early days as a runner, a dancer, and a performer in shows to his later days as ceremonial chief of his people and shrewd negotiator with the government for Lakota rights, Frank Fools Crow tells of a life lived in accord with traditional values, but also of a life in which these values were applied to the modern world. I have chosen only two chapters of his fascinating autobiography, Fools Crow:[1] *Chapter 9, "Stirrup and Fannie," which tells of some of his travels, his friendship with Black Elk, and his first marriage, and Chapter 19, which, for the most part, deals with his own recovery from health problems, and his many successes in healing others by traditional means.*

Thomas E. Mails is a California writer and artist long interested in Indian subjects. In Fools Crow *he has produced what I find a somewhat annoying book about an extraordinary man. I mean to say that Mails is intrusive, and his intrusions are as often as not pretentious; he clearly sees himself, as David Brumble has noted, in the role of John Neihardt to Black Elk. He presses Fools Crow to speak of things the old chief was reluctant to discuss—things which, indeed, Black Elk had warned him against discussing—and he writes general histories and ethnographic notes that are less than trustworthy. Nonetheless, it is certainly true that, if not for his initiative, Fools Crow's story—however heavily edited and even badly written—might not have been preserved. Yuwipi is a curing ritual. Wakan-Tanka is The Great or Holy Spirit.*

Stirrup and Fannie

In 1911 I saw my first automobile. I was visiting the agency at Pine Ridge when a man named Hegel, from Rushville, Nebraska, drove up. He was hauling mail for the government.

1. *Fools Crow*, ed. Thomas E. Mails (New York: Doubleday, 1979). Reprinted by permission of the University of Nebraska Press. Copyright © 1979 by Thomas E. Mails.

I remember the occasion well, because the thing he was riding in was so strange-looking. It wasn't very big, and it had solid rubber tires. Yet Mr. Hegel claimed it could go as fast as a horse, even thirty miles per hour.

At that time we Indians didn't know what miles per hour meant, but we weren't in the least ready to find out either. He offered to give all of us there a ride, but no Indian would even touch that thing. Everyone was afraid. I know that I for one wouldn't get off my horse because I couldn't tell what exactly it was, or whether it might suddenly lunge toward me if I did.

It was 1913 before I went on my first long trip off of the reservation. John Apple and Emil Afraid of Hawk made the arrangements, and fifteen of us went to Salt Lake City for a dancing contest. There were ten men and five women. We went on a train, and I enjoyed it so much that I still prefer to travel that way. The meals were very good. There was plenty of meat. And that was fortunate for us, because all we had with us were gingersnaps and cheese. Since our funds were limited, we rode in coaches, and sat up all the time. Usually the cars were cool, and the windows could be opened for air. The only time we were bothered by soot and smoke was when the train was coming to a tunnel or making a turn. So whenever we were coming to a tunnel, the conductor always warned us to close the windows.

While we were at Salt Lake City, Emil took all of us out to the famous Salt Lake. I urged him to ask a white man there if I could go out in the lake to swim. The man said, "Sure, go on out there and swim if you want to." So I took all of my clothes off except my underwear and walked out into the water. But the deeper I got the more it felt like some bad spirit beneath the water was pulling at me and trying to drag me under. Finally, I was really scared. The people on the shore could see this and were laughing at me. So I knew that something was haywire. But I was not going to take a chance, and I just got out of there as fast as I could. Only then was I told that you can't swim in such salty water in the usual way, but that you can float easily. So later on I went back in the water and found this out for myself.

I won first prize at that dancing contest in Salt Lake City. I did a traditional dance, and my prize was fifty dollars.

During the years from 1910 to 1920, I competed in many dance contests like this, and also in many horse races. A certain trader friend bought a one-year-old bay horse for one hundred dollars, and I rode that horse more times than I can count. He was a big horse, and no one knew whether he was a thoroughbred or not, but he outran every horse in the area. My riding partner was Robert Iron Cloud, and between us we won several races at Martin, South Dakota. Then we went down to the Rosebud Reservation and were victorious in all our races there. We took the horse to different places in Nebraska and won there, and after that to Rapid City, where we did the same. That horse could win races ranging anywhere from 300 yards to 2 1/2 miles in length. I always tied a special Indian medicine on his mane and tail to give him added stamina and speed. As soon as I did so he would flare his nostrils and stamp his hooves. He was ready to go.

In 1913, a lot of Sioux men went to a meeting at the agency that was chaired by Charles Red Cloud, Flying Hawk, and several other district leaders. A white man named Miles was there from the Defense Department in Washington, D.C. Speaking through an interpreter, he explained that the government had decided that our leaders should approve a request from the Great White Father concerning our participation in the armed services. If there was a war between the United States and another country, our men would agree to either volunteer or to be drafted into the Army, so as to defend our country. Miles said that we should sign it, because it was our country, and in any event we had no way of turning the request down.

As everyone there recognized, all of the elderly Sioux men had proven themselves to be great fighters in the wars against the United States Army. So we knew well what war was like, and we had always defended our land in a powerful way. Ignoring for the moment the political and moral questions that were plain to us all, Charles Red Cloud and Flying Hawk put their thumbprints on the paper that Miles had brought. But then we began to ask aloud why the white men, who had defeated and humiliated us, felt we should join them in a war against their own kind. They had done their best to put an end to our ability to make war, and had put us on reservations without weapons. Now they wanted us to agree to fight by their side against the very countries where they came from originally! Their answers did little to satisfy us. But what could we do? We were helpless and dependent upon them. All of the district leaders made their thumbmark on the paper. Yet it brought chills to everyone, for we sensed that things were about to change again, and just when everything seemed to be going so well.

In 1914, Stirrup came to visit my father. Stirrup's purpose was to obtain Eagle Bear's approval of Stirrup's choice of me to carry on his work as a holy man, and especially a Yuwipi man. He knew it was Eagle Bear's wish that I become a holy man. Nevertheless, Eagle Bear still wanted to know why he had chosen me for this great honor. Stirrup answered that he had considered several young men in the dif-

ferent districts, but had always been led by *Wakan-Tanka* back to me.
So my father wanted to know how I felt about it, and whether I would
accept the challenge and holy calling. I told him I wanted to do it, although I knew that the first step demanded of me would be another
vision quest, and that not everyone was successful at this — my earlier
experience with Stirrup near Allen notwithstanding. Sometimes men
quest and don't see or experience a thing. In fact, not many people do
manage it successfully, let alone going on to become a Yuwipi man
and a holy man. But I was pleased with Stirrup's offer and not afraid.
I knew that Stirrup had helped and healed many people. His life had
proven to be a happy one, which he clearly accepted and loved. Indeed, it was the highest possible calling for any Sioux, and I knew
that I would strive to live just as Stirrup had lived.

Shortly thereafter I traveled on horseback the long hundred-mile
trip to Bear Butte, the most awesome vision-questing place in the
Black Hills of South Dakota. The greatest Indian leaders had made
their vision quests on this mountain for several centuries, and it was
the questing place to which Grandfather called me. Sonny Larvie
went with me, and waited at a base camp while I fasted and prayed
on top of the butte for four days and nights. On the third night I had
a vision in which I learned many secret things about being a medicine
man, and was given a special herb to use in a special sweatlodge ceremony, but I remained on Bear Butte until the traditional four days
and nights were finished.

I left some tobacco for an offering to the spirits, and took about an
hour to descend to where Sonny was waiting for me. We returned to
Porcupine, where Stirrup spent a full week showing me the medicines he used for different kinds of sicknesses, and explained how he
performed his Sun Dance, Yuwipi, and sweatlodge ceremonies. He
also described the ways in which other medicine men had helped
him.

Stirrup included several warnings about the kind of life I would be
expected to lead. He said that while Indian people usually had to pay
when they went to a white doctor, there would be many instances
when I would be called upon to cure people without pay. It was a sacrifice I should expect to make many times. He also said I could never
argue openly with any Indian about political issues or laws — either
from the government's side or from the people's side. Even if I was
strongly against something, I could not stand up and debate with my
own people. I could never engage in war or in a personal fight, and I
could never hate anyone or indulge in jealousy or revenge. It was a
challenging life I was confronted with, but I accepted it, and I have

kept faith with the sacred life-way entrusted to me. For the first time, I felt well settled. The pattern of my life was beginning to be established, and the shape of my future could be seen in at least a hazy way. But my life as a healer would not begin for some years. I was still a young man, and I cherished my freedom as young men do.

In 1916, there was a well-publicized foot race in Gordon, Nebraska. It was advertised as a fifty-yard contest, and all of the best white and Indian runners in the area were invited to compete. The prize was fifty dollars, and that was a lot of money for just running. All of the best sprinters came, and I laugh now as I remember that Dallas Fire Place and I ran barefooted, outran the rest, and tied for first place. We had to split the first and second prize money, which totaled ninety dollars, and came home with the huge sum of forty-five dollars apiece. We were rich men for a while! Dallas is still alive and lives in the town of Batesland. I am sure he could tell people a lot of exciting stories about those early days.

This same year I went to Cheyenne, Wyoming, and while I was there I was selected by the Indian dancers to lead them in the Frontier Days grand parade. That was a great honor, because large groups had come to Cheyenne from many Indian reservations. We had a large group there too. Fifty-two Oglala from Pine Ridge had made the journey. There were thirty-two men, fifteen women, and five children. We went by train, and the group was really a special one. Besides my uncle, Black Elk, it included such men as Flying Hawk, Little Horn, Looks Twice, White Bull, Holy Bear, Little Soldier, Long Soldier, Jim Grass, Jim Braveheart, Tommy Grass, Tommy Little Elk, Brown Eyes, Little Committee, Hand Soldier, Black Horn, Charley Whistle, and others. Charley Whistle had a huge herd of beautiful horses at that time, easily the greatest number owned by anyone on the reservation.

While we were riding the train toward Cheyenne, Black Elk took me aside and talked with me. After we had talked for a while, he told me that as a medicine man I would learn many sacred secrets and perform countless ceremonies for people. He said that over the years, Grandfather would show me wondrous things, that I would receive valuable messages and signs, and that solutions to reservation and healing problems would come to me during my vision quests and rituals.

Black Elk went on to say that, as I traveled to competitions and toured with Wild West shows, word of my healing and prophetic power would spread. Then people who were doubters would ask me to prove what I could do by telling my visions and performing my ceremonies for them. Black Elk also said, "Even then they won't believe you unless you perform your most powerful ceremony. One of these days doubters will come to the reservation and ask you to do it. They will do their best to discover why and how you heal. And they will want to know who helps you perform your healing and prophetic work. In fact, they will attempt to learn everything about you, but you must not tell them about your 405 Stone White Men helpers, which the Great Spirit had made available to you." Black Elk was right. This very thing has happened to me many times, but I have not until now revealed any of the most important things.

During that same conversation we had on the train, Black Elk predicted that annual trade fairs would soon come to our people. And he was happy about this, because he knew it would bring about a spirit of co-operation in a time when it was badly needed.

I have always thanked Grandfather for this wise and holy man. In a way, his prediction about people wanting to know my secrets began to come true while we were still in Cheyenne. I used my prize earnings to purchase my first automobile, a much-used and battered Model T Ford touring car. A fine young white man taught me how to drive it. I had a terrible time learning, and while the many lessons required were under way the young man told me he had a deep interest in what I did and in the Sioux culture. As a result, while I did not say too much about myself, I did teach him more about life on the reservation than he taught me about driving. I had an exciting trip home, and from then on I always owned a car; but never a new one.

That same year, 1916, Black Elk gave me my first eagle feather headdress. It was a beautiful head bonnet, and it had thirty or more tail feathers in it. The headdress was made especially for me as a reward for my success in relay horse races at the Cheyenne Frontier Days, at Colorado Springs, at Salt Lake City, at Chicago, and at Cedar Rapids, Iowa. I came in first in all of these, and so was given the bonnet.

During the depression, and sometime after 1930, I sold it for one hundred and fifty dollars, which was a lot of money in those days. I have many times regretted its sale, and whenever I do I remember a story. Knife Chief told me to emphasize the importance of the eagle feather headdress. He said that in his time the warrior's trail bonnet, one with an eagle-feather tail hanging clear to the ground, was highly respected. In fact, the people were in great awe of anyone who was able, because of his successful war deeds, to wear an eagle-feather bonnet with such a tail. Then he told me a story about Eagle Shield, a leader who, while mounted on horseback and wearing his trail bonnet, performed heroically to save his people. Once, while his camp was under attack by Indian enemies, Eagle Shield rode everywhere in a desperate attempt to keep his people together and fighting. If anyone panicked and ran, he went after them on his horse and brought them back, including women and children.

Eagle Shield also carried a long lance, and when all else had failed, he drove it through the tail of his headdress and pinned it like a soldier sash to the ground. The tail was so long that he was still mounted on his horse when he did this. Then he drew his bow and arrows and remained there fighting until he was shot from his horse and killed. But the camp was saved. This shows, Knife Chief said, how brave and worthy the trail-bonnet wearers were, and why they were held in such great respect.

In those happy days I was in excellent physical condition and I could do well at anything I put my mind to. I was a jockey, ran foot races, and I danced. I suppose I did most of the things any ambitious young man does to build his confidence and make his place in his own world.

The year 1916 turned out to be an eventful one for me. On July 4, a big four-day celebration got under way at Kyle. I was there with a few racehorses and a relay team. The evening of the first day, just as I was sitting down to dinner with my family, a friend of ours named Fannie, the youngest daughter of Emil Afraid of Hawk, came to our camp and told me her parents wanted to see me. So I went along with her without eating my supper, and all the way there I was wondering what it could be about.

When we arrived at her camp, her parents fed me supper, and when I was finished, Emil came over and shook my hand. Then he told me that Fannie had fallen in love with me. He and his wife approved, and wanted very much to have me for a son-in-law. I was really shocked by this, and was speechless for a moment, because I really hadn't thought much about marriage; I thoroughly enjoyed my freedom to travel and enter contests. Finally, I said I would need to return to my camp and ask my father what he thought about it. When I did so, my father smiled and said they had already discussed it with him, and that he whole-heartedly approved. In fact, he was the one who had suggested they ask me that day.

So I thought about it for a while, and said I would marry her. Right then I went to her camp and we collected what few belongings she had and moved them to my camp. As simply as that we were wed. I feel it was one of the best decisions of my life, for we had a wonderful marriage, even though we lost most of our children while they were very young. Our firstborn was Mattie, in 1923. She died at the age of three—from pneumonia, I think. She was terribly sick, and just died. In 1925, we had twin girls, named Grace and Marie. Grace passed away from pneumonia at the age of three. Marie is still living and has a family of her own. In 1930, Fannie and I had twin sons, named James and Andrew. Both of them cried continually, and they lived only six months. It was common for reservation people to lose their children like this in those days. The weather was a factor, and the kind of medical care we now have at hospitals was not available. The medicine men also did their best, but had no success whatsoever in treating pneumonia.

I knew that, as a married man, things would be better for us if we had either a regular food source or an income, so in 1916 I took my first job. The telephone had come to Pine Ridge in 1914 or 1915, and in the winter of 1916 the agency people offered me a job as a lineman. I was to service the line from Porcupine to Kyle, a distance of about twenty miles. This line ran from the main agency office to the farm agent's branch offices. The farm agents were the white men who now served as middlemen between the head agent and the Indian district leaders. So I traveled each day in a wagon between Porcupine and Kyle to check the condition of the wires and the poles. If a wire was down, I put it back up. If a pole needed replacing, I would get one and replace it. The poles were not as big as they are now. I received no money for the job, just rations, and worked at it for about eighteen months.

Until now, neither the telegraph nor the telephone had been popular with the Sioux, since in the last part of the nineteenth century there was a big battle that the Sioux almost had won. Then the Army used the telegraph to summon help, and the Sioux were driven away. For a long time we thought of it as bad medicine.

Time was passing swiftly, and world-shaking events were taking place. Without my realizing it, since few of us Sioux could read English and thus understand much of what that paper really meant that Miles had brought from Washington, my marriage was to save me from going to war. As soon as the United States entered World War I in 1917, we were told that all of the men must go to the agency to fulfill the commitment to fight that the leaders had made. So I went, and together with the others put my thumbprint on a government paper that said they could take us as they needed us. I was very unhappy, because Stirrup had told me I should not fight. But as it turned out, only single men were taken, and I never had to go.

I hardly regret this, because so many who went to war came home wounded and crippled. Others were physically well, yet never mentally the same again. A person cannot return easily to normal life once he has been in that kind of a war. The elderly people of those days understood this. They knew very well what it was like to return home after fighting other Indian tribes and the whites. So as the veterans arrived back at Pine Ridge the elders and the older religious leaders did what they could to restore and renew them. They gave the veterans sweatbaths, which cleansed and purified their bodies and souls; they gave them the best food available; and they talked with them for days on end.

Then when the time was right, the parents and relatives of the veterans put on huge feasts to thank *Wakan-Tanka* for bringing their young men home, and these feasts were always followed by the traditional giveaway. From that time on it became the custom for many traditional parents to select only those who had served their country honorably in war to be the ones to bestow upon their children, in a naming ceremony, an Indian name.

The Pipe and Power

During the winter of 1974–75, I was very ill, and in bed either at home or at the hospital for 42 days. Before this happened, I weighed 212 pounds, and when it was over I was down to 162. My illness started before Christmas, and although I was still quite sick, just before Christmas Day I walked out of the government hospital. I was uneasy and uncomfortable because they had moved me into the section where people are put when they expect them to die. Someone was dying there nearly every day, and people were wailing and weeping constantly. I didn't like it a bit, and despite the doctor's protests, I got up and left. I went home, and on January 3, I had a major heart attack. By January 5, I was back in the hospital, and was unconscious for 2 days and 2 nights. After a few more days I was released and went home to continue my recovery.

By February 15, I was considerably improved, and I was receiving visitors according to my usual schedule. Kate protested about this because family members had to pick me up off the floor twice and she was very worried. But I was able to get around, and I did. By the end of February, my interpreter, Matthew King, and I were traveling to Chicago, New York, and Washington, D.C., for meetings and appearances. Since this kind of activity places me so often in the midst of whites, you want to know whether I regret not having an education in the white man's school, and as a result not being able to speak, read, or write English. I do not regret any of it. God has guided my steps to where I am today, and what might appear to be a handicap to others is actually a source of strength to me. God communicates with me personally, and I am wealthy in spiritual information and discipline. I practice these disciplines regularly, and I live a simple life. These free my energies for the more important things I know I must do for my people. Despite my recent physical illness, which, actually, is not unusual for a man of my age, I have remained mentally well. I give God and my simple way of life credit for this.

Simple living is less wasteful and more in harmony with nature because it permits us to share our resources with all other life. Therefore I use earth's gifts sparingly and with gratitude, attempting wherever possible to replace what I consume, and I try to preserve the natural beauty of the earth. My people only need the basic necessities of life, not the luxuries. The problem is that in these modern times under white domination we are so poor we are without even the necessities. Still, despite our painful and humiliating poverty, most Sioux accept their lot and take the sorrows and the sufferings as they come. So when I visit them in their homes and see how patient they are it only fills me with resolve to try harder and harder to help them.

No, I do not regret my lack of white schooling. Spiritually, I am far richer for not having left my people in any way, and I am one with them. I share fully their lives, conditions, needs, hopes, dreams, and anguish. I have made this commitment to *Wakan-Tanka* and to them, and I will die here in their midst because it is the role I have been given. Now this part of the story is told. I have done what *Wakan-Tanka* and Grandfather commanded me to do. The tapes and the papers have not crumbled. Black Elk will be happy. I am happy. This is *waste hcá* (very good).

The year 1976 was an eventful one. Once I was well again I went on with the practice of my medicine. So I will tell you now about some of the people I healed, and also something wonderful about the Sacred Pipe at Green Grass.

In March of 1976, a large man from Devil's Lake in North Dakota came to my house. He drove up in a car, and got out with a filled pipe in his hands. He brought it into the house, lit it, and without saying a word offered it to me.

I smoked the pipe with him, and when it was finished asked him what he wanted. He was about forty years old, and quite uncomfortable when he spoke. I think it was because he was not Sioux and didn't know how I would react to that. His father was paralyzed from the lower chest down, and sitting out in the car. "Will you heal him?" the man asked.

I told him to bring his father in, and the man carried him into the house and placed him on my bed. I had Kate wrap the black cloth around my head, I prayed, did my ceremony, and gave the paralyzed man an herb medicine to drink. The man and his son stayed at my house for four days, and we repeated the ceremony four times. Each day a little of the medicine was left over, and after the treatments there was still enough for an additional four days of treatment.

The man and his son went back to Devil's Lake and continued the use of the medicine. Three weeks later they returned to my house with a large supply of food, and the father, who was well now, carried it into the house himself and gave it to me.

In the spring of 1976, my long and passionate desire to see the Sacred Pipe was realized. It was the fourth time I had gone to Green Grass, and while I was there, the bundle was opened by the Keeper, and I saw the pipe. Until now I have told no one about this except my wife, Kate. There were many people in the vicinity of the building at the time, including Kate and Everett Lone Hill, but I was taken inside, I prayed with my hand on the bundle, and then it was opened for me.

When I saw the pipe I really crumbled inside. I felt completely humble, pathetic, pitiful. I don't know how long I looked at the exposed pipe, and I don't like to talk about it. I am still afraid of its sacred power, and I am thinking again about what just happened to one of our medicine man who spoke of things he shouldn't.

I will not describe the pipe, except to say that it was a very good-looking pipe. I will tell you one more thing, and it will be the last thing I have to say about the pipe. When this lady (Calf Pipe Woman) came and gave the Sioux the pipe, she told them to go and kill four warrior members of another tribe. They were to remove a little hair from each man's head and to tie it to the pipe. Also an ear was to be removed from one victim and attached to the pipe. Then they were to get two tail feathers from a golden eagle and tie these to the stem. They followed her orders completely, and those things are there. When I saw the pipe, the hair, brittle from age, was breaking in places, and the two feathers were so worn away that only the quills remained. The ear was still in perfect condition, although it was as white as tanned deer skin.

After I looked at the pipe, the Keeper placed it back in its wrappings, and the bundle was brought outside to be seen by the other Sioux assembled there. Four flags with the four sacred colors were set up to mark the corners of a medium-sized square, inside of which a bed of sage was laid. On the bed in a circle there was a string of 405 tiny tobacco bags to invite the presence of the 405 good spirits who serve *Wakan-Tanka*. The bundle itself was laid on the sage in the middle of the entire arrangement, so that the people could walk around it and still be on the sage. As they did so they walked in a clockwise direction. They also prayed, and those who were bold enough bent down to touch the holy bundle. The people left gifts there inside the string circle, gifts of money, feathers, quilts, blankets, and clothing. When all of them had done this, I collected the gifts and presented them to the Keeper, Orvall Looking Horse.

Then the Sacred Pipe bundle was picked up and returned to its building, where it was laid on its platform and covered with the buffalo robe. I placed my right hand one last time upon the robe, and after a few minutes, I left. This day marked the crowning event of my life, and I could not have been happier.

In June of 1976, while I was the intercessor for the Sun Dance at Greenwood on the Yankton Reservation, I saw in the audience a boy about eight years old who was on crutches. His right leg was sharply bent so that the knee and leg were up in the air, and he looked very sad. The dance was already in progress, but I felt so sorry for him that I went over to him and brought him out to the Sun Dance pole in the center of the mystery circle.

By now everyone was watching us; even the dancers were looking to see what was going to happen. First I walked with the boy in a circle around the pole, then I stared twice at the crutches, prayed, and took the crutches away from him. I bent down and grabbed his right leg and straightened it out until he could touch the ground with it. Then I straightened his left leg, which was bent a little from favoring the right leg, and I told him to stand up and to walk over to his parents. He did. He walked over to them and sat down between them, and everyone was overjoyed. The sound of approval and thanksgiving ran through the crowd, and it became so loud that it could be heard above the noise of the singers and the drum. If the dance had not been going on, I think the people would have shouted for joy and pounded on the drum themselves!

The boy's father rushed over to me, his face beaming with gratitude, and asked me what he could give me. The mother came to shake my hand and also asked what they could do. But I told them I did not want anything, that I was pleased to have this opportunity to perform the healing where so many people could see it and know about *Wakan-Tanka*'s power. They insisted they had to do something, though, and several weeks later they came to my house with food and other gifts.

Patients and their families often come back in later years to express their gratitude. Sometimes they come and bring me things such as coffee and sugar. They tell me it is in thanksgiving for what I have done. At other times families ask Kate and me over to their house for a big feed, serving us good meat and cake. Whenever something like that is brought or served to me, I take a small part of it outside and offer it to *Wakan-Tanka*. I make a small excavation in the earth, and after holding the food out to the west, north, east, south, up to *Wakan-Tanka* and *Tunkshila*, and finally down to Grandmother Earth, I bury it in the hole. Then I return to the house and eat the rest.

I want you to know that I am very happy and that I appreciate your interest in these things. I am going to tell you about another recent healing. Ida Two Dog is about fifty-two years old and has had serious heart trouble. In fact, at times her body literally shook from it.

When I treated her there was time to do a full ceremony. So I took singers with me and went to her house in the evening. Enough of the living room was cleared of furniture to make a space for an altar in the center of it. I made the altar with four pieces of cloth in my sacred colors. Each cloth was four by six inches, and was laid flat on the floor so as to mark the corners of a three-foot square. The square itself was covered with sage, and on the south side four eagle feathers were laid side by side with their tips toward the west.

The spirits used the feathers to fan and purify all of the air inside the room. Then I told Ida to remove her shoes and to stand barefooted on the sage in the middle of the altar. I stood to one side of her, and the usual black-cloth wrapping was used to cover my head. Then I prayed, and as the singers sang the rain song, I could see that the woman was telling the truth about her heart. I could see that it was beating irregularly. So I removed the cloth, boiled an herb medicine for her, and had her drink a glassful. Then I told her to take the remainder home and finish it. Today there is nothing wrong with her. She is well.

Only a short time ago I had a patient, forty-two years of age, who had an ugly birthmark that began at his eyes and covered the entire lower part of his face. He had gone to doctors in Denver, Omaha, Rapid City, Sioux Falls, and Hot Springs to see if they could remove it. None could, and finally he came to me. I boiled an herb, and using a cotton swab dipped in it—I wiped the birthmark area. Then I told the man to repeat this procedure every evening, just before he went to bed, for the next three days. He did as he was told, and when he woke up on the morning of the fifth day, the birthmark was gone!

I am singing to you now my healing song, each part of which ends with a soft "whoo, whoo." In this song I pray to God to help me cure the person. Then I ask Grandmother Earth to help. Following this I appeal to the directions, to the day and the night, and to the four seasons. I tell them I want this person to be able to walk with straight limbs and body again, to be healthy and to have a good heart, with love for other people. In the song, I describe the patient as a friend, because all people are my friends. I finish the song by again asking the spirits to help the patient and to return him to good health, walking in a straight path. The "whoo, whoo" is my special sound to the spirits. It is an ending remark just between us, one that is gentle and affectionate.

In the fall of 1976, a lady was brought to me from the Cheyenne River Reservation. It was about noon when they arrived. She was suffering from terrible headaches and a continual nosebleed. Doctors had burned (cauterized) her nose in an attempt to stop the bleeding, but hadn't been successful. She had not stopped bleeding for four days when they brought her to me.

To treat her I built a small fire outside, near where the sweatlodge is, and set out my flags. Then I took a hollowed-out buffalo horn and with a knife scraped some shavings into the red-hot ashes to make smoke and incense. We stood together by the fire and I put a blanket over both of us—to capture the smoke and so that we were in darkness. I prayed, and soon the spirits helped me see that the swelling in her nose was receding, and that the drops of blood were slowing down. Pretty soon they stopped completely.

When she left for home I gave her the rest of the buffalo horn to take with her. As of now she has had no more headaches and no more bleeding.

You want to know why, since I have made such broad and positive claims, everyone does not come to me for healing. One reason is that I do not advertise for or encourage patients to come. So only a modest number of people here and there know what I can do. And those who are healed do not talk about it among themselves and spread the news. That is not the Sioux way. If a thing is holy and sacred, if it is a miracle, it is not talked about. It is too special for that. Visions we receive are in the same category. They are something personal between *Wakan-Tanka* and the seeker that affects the whole of his life. Even the person's family will not discuss it or tell their friends.

There are other reasons. Many people are cured in other ways.

Some go to the hospitals. Some are cured by other medicine men, and by their own praying and singing of sacred songs. Some of the Christian Indians have been taught to have no regard for our medicine men, and will not go to them. More than a few have been told by their priests or pastors that medicine men are witch doctors.

You have also mentioned that at the time of our last talk together in Rapid City, Kate was a patient at the Indian hospital. She was being treated for pneumonia and had been in bed for ten days or so before we visited her. She was doing quite well though, and was expecting to go home in another week. You want to know why I had not healed her if I can indeed heal any illness? The answer is that I often know when people are becoming ill, and I knew it was happening to Kate. But she didn't bring me a filled pipe or tobacco of any kind and ask for my help, so I just couldn't help her! I must remain true to my rules. I cannot, even for those I dearly love, violate procedures that *Wakan-Tanka* has directed me to follow as a holy man.

You ask me whether I can lose my medicine power? Any medicine man can lose it by failing to do a ceremony properly, or by not doing something *Wakan-Tanka, Tunkashila,* or the spirits tell him to do, or by bad conduct or bad-mouthing someone. However, he can regain the power by making things right again. He has to right the wrong. He must do more than apologize and say he is sorry. The Indian way is to show sincerity by doing things over a long period of time for those who are offended. One must show his remorse and continue to show it until his power returns and he can heal again.

You have to demonstrate your change of heart by thinking good thoughts and doing good works over a long period of time, and when God wants you to do something a certain way, you must do it just like that, or the gifts and powers will be taken away from you. Then to get them restored by *Wakan-Tanka* you are required to treat him like you would an offended person. There must be continual meditation, prayer, and sweatlodge purification, until at last your change of heart and desire are again proven. You know when you have your power back by your ability to cure again and by your inner feeling.

But all of these years I have tried to be a good man, and I have never lost my power. I am an old man now, and I am not even concerned about this. I don't even feel the threat of losing my power.

When a person is right with God he always has a special feeling. When I am curing I feel a charge of power and I am excited! I know about these things because they are going on inside of me. When people come to me for help, for an ailment or curing or whatever, as I do my ceremony I feel the strength, the energy, building up. And I know

I can cure them. The spirits let me know it. They even come inside of me and give me confidence and strength. And I feel good about this as it builds up inside of me.

But that is enough about my healing and medicine powers. We should talk now about the problems that exist between the Sioux and the United States Government. Much of my time in recent years has been given over to this, and *Wakan-Tanka* wants the world to know the more important things I have done and said.

As you know, the Teton Sioux have attempted for many years now to get the government to return the Black Hills to us. We believe the Black Hills belong to us, and that the government does not have legal title to them. They have offered us money to settle the claim, but we do not really want the money, we want the Black Hills. That would give us jobs and incomes and a chance to live like human beings again. So I have gone several times to Washington, D.C., to talk about this, but it is only now that the government people have begun to listen. Therefore I am able to say more, and I want you to know what I say.

27
Big Falling Snow

Edited by

HAROLD COURLANDER

Albert Yava (1888–1990) was given the name Nuvayoiyava, "Big Falling Snow," by his paternal aunts, with reference to his Hopi father's membership in the Water Clan. The name was shortened by Anglos to Yava, and, in the white schools he attended, he was assigned the name Albert. Yava's mother was a Tewa, and, because descent was reckoned from the mother's side, he considered himself a Tewa quite as much as a Hopi.

He grew up in Tewa Village, called Hano by the Hopi, on First Mesa in northern Arizona. As Yava's editor, Harold Courlander, writes, the First Mesa Tewas "speak Hopi as well as Tewa, intermingle and marry with Hopis, and share Hopi ceremonies and life in general, while as best they can they tenaciously hold on to their Tewa identity."[1] These western Pueblo people are cultivators of the arid desert, growing corn, beans, and squash and sustaining a highly elaborated ceremonial life that is very much alive today. Catholics began the conversion of the pueblos in the seventeenth century, only to be set back, in 1680, by the pan-Pueblo rebellion, which largely ended the process of christianization until the late nineteenth century, at which time not only Catholics but missionaries from various Protestant denominations went actively to work.

If Native Americans in general tend to subordinate the individual to the community, the people of the pueblos do so more than most. In an extraordinary comment in 1943, the respected anthropologist Leslie White wrote, in regard to his own work producing the autobiography of an Acoma pueblo Indian, "the autobiography of a pueblo Indian is about as personal as the life story of an automobile tire."[2] We are, today, tempted to raise our eyebrows at such a narrowly culture-bound notion of what it means to be "personal." But White's observation does point to something important, for it seems to be the

---

1. *Big Falling Snow: A Tewa-Hopi Indian's Life and the History and Traditions of His People,* ed. Harold Courlander (New York: Crown, 1978), p. ix. The text below is reprinted by permission of the University of New Mexico Press, copyright 1992.

2. Leslie White, "Autobiography of an Acoma Indian," in White, *New Material from Acoma,* Smithsonian Institution, Bureau of American Ethnology, Bulletin 136, *Anthropological Papers* no. 32 (1942), p. 326.

case still that pueblo people, as already noted, strongly resist the sorts of individualism, and self-preoccupation of most Western autobiography.

Yava says, for example, of the autobiography of Don Talayesva[3] (whom he knew at the Keam's Canyon School), that "If there's any fault to find with the book it's that [Don] talked about a lot of personal things" (in particular, it should be said, his sex life). He adds that "another book that gave me that feeling was Son of Old Man Hat," *the Navajo autobiography edited by Walter Dyk, included above, which is also quite outspoken about sexual matters.*

Harold Courlander, born in Indiana in 1908, has worked as an editor, press officer, and political analyst as well as an ethnographer. Books to his credit range from studies of West Indian and African American folk music, to an account of how the United Nations works, to fiction. For all the wide range of his interests, his specific focus on Albert Yava, the Hopis, and the Tewas has produced a book that is particularly solid, sensitive, and careful.

Our selections are from Big Falling Snow: A Tewa-Hopi Indian's Life and the History and Traditions of His People, *edited and annotated by Harold Courlander. The book was originally published in 1978, and has been reissued in paperback by the University of New Mexico Press (1992). I have included pages 1–10, which offer some reminiscences of childhood, and pages 71–79, which tell of Yava's initiation into the One Horn Society.*

This is a true story of events that happened in my lifetime, things I learned through living, and things that were taught to me by the old ones who were here before I arrived. If I have set down anything wrongly or incompletely, it is only because what a person recalls from the past is a combination of what he remembers and what he forgets. To the best of my recollection, this book tells things truly. As for those things I know but cannot speak about, I am sure I will be forgiven.

Albert Yava
Tewa Village, First Mesa
July 10, 1977

My people were Tewas from the Rio Grande Valley who came here to live with the Hopis on First Mesa some time around the year 1700. They settled near the Hopi village of Walpi, close to the southern edge of the mesa-top gap from which Walpi took its name. Hopis and whites often refer to our settlement as Hano. That is because we were thought to be Tanos, or T'hanos, but we were true Tewas and the

3. *Sun Chief: The Autobiography of a Hopi Indian*, ed. Leo Simmons (New Haven: Yale Univ. Press, 1942).

proper name for our settlement is Tewa Village. In the old days, if a group came from a distant place and made a village, other people gave that village a name indicating what tribe or clan settled at that place. There were Kawaikas (now they are called Lagunas) who settled on Antelope Mesa, and their village was called Kawaika. Some people called Payupkis from the Rio Grande came and made a settlement on Second Mesa, and their place was known as Payupki. After a while they went back, according to what we were told, to the Rio Grande to live in the Pueblo of Sandia. Quite a few other eastern Pueblo groups came here at different times. Some of them merged with the Hopis, but most of them only stayed for a few years and then left. We First Mesa Tewas are the only ones who came and remained without losing our own culture and our own traditions. We still speak the Tewa language, and we speak it in a more pure form than the Rio Grande Tewas do. Over there in New Mexico the Tewa language has been corrupted by the other Pueblo languages and Spanish. We also speak Hopi fluently, though there are very few Hopis who can converse in Tewa.

My father was actually a Hopi, but we count descent on the mother's side, and as my mother was a Tewa, I am a Tewa. My mother, Iechawe, which means Blue Smoke in Tewa, belonged to the Peh-towa, or Wood [Stick], Clan, so that is my clan also. Hopis call it the Spruce Clan. Though I am full-fledged Tewa, I am also a Hopi—not because of my father being a Hopi, but because I was initiated into the Kwakwanteu, or One Horn kiva society. It is one of the four major kiva fraternities among the Hopis. A member of any one of those fraternities is considered to be a Hopi. On First Mesa, the One Horn fraternity is regarded as the most important of the four. They tell us that you can be born in a Hopi village of Hopi parents and speak the Hopi language, but still you aren't a complete Hopi unless you go through the initiations and become a member of one of the four kiva groups. That's because it's only within these societies that you can get all the important teachings that have been handed down mouth to ear from one generation to another. Only by having a place in the kiva can you possibly understand all the ceremonial relationships within the village—who the important figures within the clans are, how the clans relate to one another, which of them has ultimate authority in particular matters, who has the right to be the kikmongwi, or village chief, what the different kiva groups stand for, where the responsibility lies for things that have to be done, what the traditions of the different clans are and how they are shared, and the special rights claimed by this clan or that clan.

471

Albert Yava and his half sister, Pinini. Courtesy of Harold Courlander.

Our traditional Hopi society is a complex tangle of relationships. When two people meet for the first time they try to figure out what their relationship is, because it's important to the way they act toward each other. As a Tewa, I have ceremonial ties with many Hopis through my kiva society. As a member of the Spruce, or Wood, Clan, I have a tie with anyone from that clan, whether he's a Tewa, a Hopi, a Zuni, a Supai, a Navajo or a Paiute. Certain clans are linked together. My clan is affiliated with the Bear, Strap, Grease Cavity, Bluebird, Spider and Gopher clans, so people of those clans are, you might say, my relatives. But certain particular clans are especially close. The Spruce and Spider clans go together. The Bear and Strap clans go together. And the Gopher, Grease Cavity and Bluebird are-

Albert Yava with his son-in-law, Dewey Healing. Courtesy of Harold
Courlander.

close together. People of those closely related clans can't intermarry. At least it was that way in former times, but I think that young people are ignoring clan relationships these days, not bothering to follow the old restrictions.

Whenever we men sit together in the kiva to smoke, one person passes the pipe to another saying "my uncle," "my father," "my younger brother" or "my older brother" to indicate a relationship. "Brother" isn't literal. It means a person with whom you are in harmony, and whom you respect. If he is older than you, you say "na-vaypaday" or "navaypipi," meaning "ahead of me" in age. Everybody in the kiva has a particular relationship with the others. You have to know a man's clan or you won't know your appropriate relationship with him or how to behave toward him. If someone offers tobacco to you you may not feel like smoking, but if that man is a member of the Tobacco Clan you never refuse, because tobacco is sacred and it is a special kind of gift coming from a Tobacco clan member. We are never allowed to forget how our society fits together, and only if you are exposed to the teachings of the kiva societies can you fully understand these things.

The name that was given to me when I was born was Nuvayoiyava, meaning Big Falling Snow. You can also translate that as Big Falling Snowflake. I received this name because my father belonged to the Rain-Cloud, or Water, Clan. It was traditional for aunts on the father's side to name a child, and they usually selected a name that revealed the father's clan affiliations. Snow is an aspect of rain, so Nuvay-oiyava indicated my father's clan. If you meet a man named Hontoe-chi, meaning Bear Moccasins, you know that his father was a Bear Clan person. If a man's name is Chucka, meaning mud, you know that his father was Sand Clan, because earth and sand together cover the breast of Mother Earth. If a name has tawa in it, meaning sun, that means the father belonged to the Sun Clan, which claims a special affiliation with the sun. However, a person's name doesn't reveal his own clan, which is the same as his mother's. Nuvayoiyava was the only name I had till I went to school. Because my teachers couldn't pronounce it very well they shortened it to Yava. But that wasn't enough for them. They didn't like it that the children had no family names. So they sort of turned our individual names into family names and then gave us personal names like John, Mary, Henry, Peter and so on. One teacher wanted to call me Oliver, but another one who took a personal interest in me said, "No, I like the name Albert, and that's what we're going to call him." This explains how I came to be Albert Yava. Later on in life when I was initiated into the One Horn

Society they gave me a ceremonial name, Eutawisa, meaning Close In the Antelopes. It was supposed to drown out my original name, but people still call me Yava.

What we people are like has been studied by lots of anthropologists, but they were able to find out only so much about us and quite a bit of their information has been wrong. A lot of it has been right, of course, we don't deny it, and some anthropologists in particular have had a great gift of learning about our ways, even learning some things that should have been private to our kivas. But I am one of the old men here now, and if I tell something about my life and what I recall of our traditions, maybe a little bit will be added to what is publicly known, and maybe certain errors will be corrected. Maybe, also, our own people will want to know these things.

I was born in 1888 and I probably remember some events and traditions that will be forgotten soon if they are not set down. Quite a few of our traditions have already slipped out of memory because so many knowledgeable old people have been called by the Great Spirit. The children spend days and years away at school, and I think most of them speak better English than Hopi or Tewa. Also, there isn't much mouth-to-ear teaching in the kivas any more. So I am going to recall some of the things I know, the way I saw them or heard them, or the way they were taught to me. Maybe our young people will get an inkling of what life was like on this mesa when I was a boy, or how it was in the time of our fathers and grandfathers. If I seem to say a lot about myself, it is really my times that I am thinking about. I am merely the person who happened to be there at a particular time. It is hard to put down something with myself as a center of interest—that is, to say I did this or that. It makes me out as important, which isn't the way I see it. We Tewas and Hopis don't think of ourselves that way. In our histories and traditions we don't have individual heroes with names to remember. It is the village, the group, the clan that did this or that, not a man or woman. If an individual happens to stand out, we probably don't remember his real name, and if a name is required we probably have to make it up. Anyway, I am going to tell about some of the things that I know or remember, and you will understand that I am really talking about my people, the Tewas and the Hopis, and their experiences and recollections.

These villages up here on First Mesa looked quite different when I was just a boy and growing up. If you ever happen to see any old pictures of Walpi and Tewa Village at that time, you'll notice that quite a few of the houses had second stories up above. They were terraced buildings. I myself was born in an upper level house. But all those upper stories decayed and were never replaced. Some of the lower stories have also disappeared, and here and there you can see walls still falling apart. Probably some walls were already coming apart back in the 1880s and 1890s when I was growing up. But the fields that the people kept in those days were in good shape. We used to get more rain than now. There was a lot of grass and all kinds of growing things that you don't see any more. Some of those growing things were higher than your head. Sunflowers were everywhere. When the plants were in bloom there were hummingbirds all around. Nowadays you don't often see them. If we were out in the fields when it rained, the washes would quickly fill with water and we couldn't cross, so it was hard to get home.

Even though there was more rain in those times, life was a struggle for everybody. I don't think the Hopi people ever had an easy time of it from the beginning. It seems that they were living up to a prophecy that was made when the people first came out of the underworld. That is the basic Hopi creation story, that humans emerged into this land from a world beneath the earth. When the people came out, the mockingbird arranged them according to tribes, the tribes they were going to be. He said to one group, "Sit over there. You will be the Comanches." To another, "Sit over there. You will be Hopis." Another, "Sit over there. You will be Bahanas, or white people." After that, the mockingbird set out the corn. He put out different kinds of ears, all the varieties of corn that we know. He told all these tribes to take whichever ears they wanted, and he told them what each ear meant. He said, "Now, this yellow corn will bring prosperity and enjoyment, but life will be short for whoever chooses it." And when he came to the short blue ear he said, "This one, the blue corn, means a life of hardship and hard work, but the people who choose it will have peaceful times and live to a ripe old age." He described all the different ears, and the leaders of the tribes sat looking at the corn trying to make up their minds.

Then one big tall fellow, a Navajo, said, "All right. You people can't decide." So he reached out and grabbed the long yellow corn that meant a short life but much enjoyment. The others said, "Ayih! He's always grabbing!" Then everybody began to grab. The Supais took the yellow speckled corn. The Comanches took the red corn. The Utes took the flint corn. Every tribe got its corn, but the leader of the Hopis sat there without taking anything until only one ear was left, the short blue corn. He picked up the short blue ear and said, "Well, this ear is mine. It means we will have to work hard to live, but we will have long, full lives." And all through their migrations after that there were prophecies that the Hopis would make their final home at an austere place where life would be difficult, but their guiding spirit promised to watch over them if they led decent lives. The Hopis were not supposed to accumulate wealth, but to be generous with everything. And when they settled here in this country they said, "Life will be hard in this place, but no one will envy us. No one will try to take our land away. This is the place where we will stay."

Whenever life was difficult in the Hopi villages, the old people would explain that the Hopis were destined for this kind of living. In the time of my boyhood the thing that people had to strive for was to raise enough food to tide them over the year. They'd go out early in the day to cultivate their fields of corn, beans and melons. They were always trying to produce better crops. In the summertime, the men were always in the fields. You'd hardly ever see them in the villages until evening. At other times of the year, of course, they did things like weaving blankets, kilts and sashes. They didn't know how to waste time. The women worked just as hard. Even getting water wasn't easy. There were several springs down at the foot of the mesa, but the water didn't flow very fast. The early risers were the ones who got their water right away. Women who came later had to wait for the springs to fill up again. If a woman came late and couldn't fill her water jar, she set it by the spring to stake out her turn. The next woman would set her jar behind, indicating that her turn would follow. Sometimes they had to make several trips a day to get as much water as they needed. Nowadays the young people don't have an inkling of this. Since those old days the Government has drilled wells for us, improved the springs and even piped water to the top of the mesa. Now there is a tank with a standpipe on the mesa, waiting for the people to come and get their water.

We young boys were expected to get up early and help with the fields or other chores. We generally did what we were expected to do. But if a boy became careless about getting up on time and doing his work, his mother called on her side of the family—her clan relatives—to do something about it. They'd take you from one house to another where your relatives lived, and they'd pour cold water on you. When a boy went through this experience he was embarrassed and ashamed, and after that he did what he was supposed to do.

One of our responsibilities was to keep the field rats from eating the corn seeds. If we found a little mound where a rat had made a fresh hole, we would dig down till we found the rat, and we'd kill it if we could. But sometimes that rathole had a second entrance and the rat would run out there, maybe right behind you. So one boy would dig and another would be watching for the rat to come out somewhere else. To keep us alert to the right way to dig for rats, some of the older people told us, "Watch what you're doing. If the rat escapes behind your back while you are digging you will get a hunchback." In order not to get a hunchback you kept your eyes open.

There were lots of crows to contend with too. We young ones were sent out to keep the crows away from the corn and melons. Everybody would have a particular place where he was supposed to stay to either shoot the crows with bows and arrows or scare them away. (We used the bows and arrows given to us on ceremonial occasions, such as the Home Dance. They weren't very good and we never hit any crows with them.) The job they gave me was to roll up a sheep pelt and hit it with a stick. It made a sound like a gunshot, and when the crows heard that they just took off. We had one boy, his name was Cheeda, he'd stick something up his nose to make it bleed. Then he'd smear a little of the blood on a cornhusk and put it somewhere to attract the crows so he could shoot at them. Sometimes when we were in the fields we'd pretend to be warriors fighting each other—Hopis against Comanches or Utes or some other tribe—throwing corncobs. After the game was over we'd go back to guarding the corn and melons from the crows.

Another thing we did when we had time was to go after prairie dogs. They were good to eat. We would strip down and crawl along the ground as quietly as possible. Whenever a prairie dog came out of its hole and barked, we would try to shoot him. If we were lucky enough to get one we would clean it out, burn off the hair, put salt on it, wrap it in corn leaves and roast it in hot ashes. That was always a great treat for us young ones.

Another responsibility we had was to watch over those long-legged goats and sheep that some families owned. If a family had only one or two ewes they'd bunch them up with other people's animals, and we boys would stay with them and keep them together. If we were a good distance away from the village we might have to stay out all night, and we younger ones would be scared but we tried not to let on to the others. We also had the responsibility of taking care of the melons in the fields. We had to build windbreaks to protect the plants from wind and drifting sand. If a windstorm came up at night we would have to go out in the morning and uncover the plants. I learned about all these things from my stepfather. He would take me out to the fields with him and show me just the right way to do things. If a melon vine was covered with dust, he would show me how to gently clear it off, how to tap the soil firmly around the stem where it came out of the ground. We'd take snake brush, the root part, and set it in front of the plants for wind protection. We would build up brush for shade to keep the ground cool. If the young watermelon plants weren't kept cool their roots would rot away.

I also learned a lot about corn from my stepfather. Our Hopi corn has to be planted deep, maybe six or eight inches, so that it gets some moisture. You can't plant Iowa corn that deep because it won't grow. Of course we couldn't fertilize our corn like the white man did, and like some eastern Indians are supposed to have done. Our best rains would come in June or July, and we would expect the floodwaters to flow over the fields and bring something along to fertilize them. The water must have washed down minerals of some kind. And of course we left the cornstalks in the fields where the blowing sand would cover them up, and this helped fertilize the ground.

My stepfather was very patient about teaching me all these things. His name was Peki, meaning Turned Over, and he belonged to the Corn Clan. He took care of me just as if I were his own son. He tried hard to keep me well clothed. He really cared for me and was always wondering what I might need. One time he even bought me a saddle, and I know he had to give up something else for that. He was respected by everybody in the village, both for his character and the way he conducted himself. He knew what was right or wrong, but generally he was gentle and softspoken. Nobody ever knew him to avoid work. If he wasn't working the fields he'd be out trading with the Navajos for sheep. Then of course he had to give a lot of time to kiva affairs. In important ceremonies he was the one that laid out the sacred path with cornmeal. I was the only boy in the family for a while, and so I was the only one to work with my stepfather. Later on I had two half brothers and a half sister. But I always had a special role in working with my stepfather, and even after I was older and went away to school, whenever I came home I'd help him in the fields, or take his turn when he was supposed to be out herding the sheep.

When I was very young I never saw very much of my real father, Sitaiema. He belonged to the Water Clan and to the Kwakwanteu, or One Horn kiva fraternity. He left me and my mother, as they say, while I was still in the cradle. However, in later years, after I was initiated into the Kwakwanteu, I saw a lot more of him and he told me many things about Water Clan traditions that I would never have heard anywhere else. The One Horn rituals were brought here by the Water Clan (we Tewas call it the Cloud, or Mist, Clan) and its related clans when they came from a place in the south called Palatkwa. The real meaning of the clan name in Hopi is Dwelling On Water, or Houseboat, alluding to the tradition that they once crossed a great body of water in their migrations. My father was the headman of the One Horn fraternity and he wanted me to be in it. Eventually when I was old enough I was made a member. So as it turned out, I learned about rituals, ceremonies and traditions from my father, and from my stepfather I learned how to make the land fruitful. Today the young people aren't getting any of this. Initiations into the main kiva societies seem to have come to an end on First Mesa, and you hardly ever see young children working in the fields the way we did. There is a big break between the old ways and the new ways.

Of course, it wasn't all work and no fun for the children in the old days. We had lots of games. Some of them were pretty simple, but they were great sport for us and I guess you could say they kept us out of mischief. One game was pretty much like shinny. The ball was made out of buckskin stuffed with deer hair, and the players all had specially shaped sticks to knock it around with. Hopis call that game nahoydadatsia, Tewas call it huntamaylay. There was a sloping piece of clear ground, and we used to play over there. This game is the one the two warrior gods, Pokanghoya and Palengahoya, are supposed to be playing all the time. You hear about it in the old stories.

We also had a dart-throwing game. We made the darts out of corncobs, with feathers at one end and a sharp greasewood point at the other. We had teams. We would throw at a target made out of corn leaves, or something like that, or throw at hoops. Another game we had that was great fun for the boys was a sort of throwing race with corncobs. You'd have a corncob, or a ball as a substitute, tied to a string, and the other end of the string was tied to a little crosspiece made of wood. A boy would put the crosspiece between his toes, lie down on his back, and flip the corncob with his foot as far as he could over his head. Then another boy would flip it. The last boy down the line would start the corncob going back the other way. Whichever side got its corncob back to the starting place was the winner. We also had another corncob game, but we played it a little differently. The objective was to throw the corncob down into the kiva.

Most of us young children in the village didn't have decent clothes to wear. Up to a certain age we ran around naked, but at some point we wanted to have something on us. There weren't many nearby trading posts where clothes could be bought even if people had the money, which a great many of them didn't. A few kids had overalls, which gave them distinction. I had an uncle that used to go out trading to different places, and sometimes he would bring back a twenty-pound sack of flour for my mother. She used to mix the white flour with our own blue corn flour to make it last longer. When the white flour was gone my mother converted the sack into a kind of tunic for me by ripping out the bottom. One time my uncle brought some white muslin, and my mother made it into something like pajama pants. It was the first pants I ever wore.

Another thing about those days, the children weren't allowed to wander around like they do now from one end of the village to the other. Unless they were down in the fields with their parents they were expected to stick pretty close to their homes. They were warned to stay away from the kivas, couldn't go near them. People used to tell them that if they got too near to a kiva one of those man-eating monster kachinas would come out and get them. Kids were really scared of those monster kachinas, who used to go around the village on certain occasions to see if the youngsters were behaving themselves.

I was five or six when I first went to the day school below the mesa at Polacca. It was a small stone building that belonged to an uncle of mine, of the Tobacco Clan, and it was used as a temporary school until they finished building the new day school. The old building is still there, and now it has gone back to the Tobacco Clan. On our first day at school they gave us all new clothes, white man's style. We didn't like those clothes very much because they made us feel ridiculous. Altogether, we felt pretty strange, getting educated in a language we didn't understand. When the teacher sent us outside for recess we took off the clothes and hid them under some bushes, then we ran naked back to the village up on the mesa. We tried to be invisible up there because the truant officer, a Hopi uncle of mine, Chakwaiena, was coming after us. He had to chase us all through the village and over the roofs to catch us. When he did, he took us down to the school and we had to put those clothes on again and listen to the teacher, a tall white man name Mr. Spink, trying to teach us things in English. We ran away several times before we gave up.

One of the things Mr. Spink taught us was how to count, "One, two, three, four, five," but we couldn't get it because we didn't know what he was talking about, and we just sat there dumb. Chakwaiena, the truant officer, was sitting in the room, and one time he jumped up and said, in Hopi of course, "What's the matter with you kids? Don't you understand anything? Just say like I do, 'One and two and hai hai hai.'" It sure made us laugh. Even later, remembering it made us laugh. We'd say to each other, "What's the matter with you? One and two and hai hai hai." When the new day school opened we were transferred over there. We had a teacher named Miss Cunningham. It was still hard for us to understand English and to pronounce English words. Our mothers told us, "Watch your teacher's tongue, then you'll know how to say the words." I had a girl cousin in that class, and she went home and told her mother, "Oh, that teacher's tongue is so loose! She says, 'A-atah, o-cha-tah!' " My cousin must have thought that was English.

You have to remember that this school business was new not only to the children but also to most of the people in the villages. There had been a big commotion when the Government gave the order that all the children would have to attend school. There was a lot of resistance. Over on the other mesas—in Oraibi, Shongopovi and Mishongnovi—the reaction was even stronger than on First Mesa. The conservatives—you can call them that or Hostiles—felt very strongly that the white man was cramming his ways down our throats. Many people felt that the Government was trying to obliterate our culture by making the children attend school. And if you want to be honest about it, the schooling the children have been getting over the past seventy-five or eighty years has educated them to the white man's ways but made them less knowledgeable about the traditional ways of their own people. A lot of what they have been taught is good. It makes them able to understand the way the white man thinks, and to compete in the outside world. But at the same time, they aren't getting as much of their own traditions as they should. Something important is being gained, but something important is being lost. . . .

The things I have been telling about the clans, I didn't really know much about them when I was growing up. You might say that there were different levels of knowledge in the villages. There were people like me who had picked up a little knowledge of traditions here and there, but who didn't know too much about the inner workings of things. Then there were the ones who'd been educated in the kiva societies. As I mentioned before, the individuals who had been initiated into the kiva groups, particularly the four main fraternities, were the "real" Hopis, and the rest of us were unfulfilled, like unripened corn. At least that's the way it was seen by the ones who knew the history and traditions of the clans and the mysteries of the kiva ceremonies.

If it hadn't been for my work as an interpreter at the Keam's Canyon Indian Agency I might never have become a member of the Kwakwanteu, or One Horn Lodge. Whenever Hopis came with problems, I interpreted for them and the Agency people, Hopi into English and English into Hopi. If a Hopi spokesman said something about a certain matter, I had to understand what was back of what he said and all the things that were implied but not spoken. I had to know something about the situation in his village, and how his clan stood in his village. My job was not only to translate words but to translate culture. After a while I began to feel that some of the village or clan spokesmen were holding back a little, not saying everything that was on their minds. If I asked them directly about this they were a little evasive and didn't give me good answers. But little by little I gathered that they didn't trust me to interpret faithfully for them because I didn't belong to one of the important kiva groups. Because of that, they felt I did not have an adequate understanding of a lot of things they were talking about. Because I didn't know the claims and traditions of the kiva societies, or how various persons fitted into the scheme of things, they felt I would not know what their point of view was based on or what their authority was. Once in a while one of those men told me confidentially, "If you join one of the important kiva groups and get to really know what persons and clans are significant to these questions, people will have more confidence in you."

As I said before, my father, Sitaiema, was a Water Clan man, and he was one of the top-ranking members of the Kwakwanteu, or One Horn Fraternity. He had some very important responsibilities. Among other things, he was the official Sun Watcher for the village. By his readings of the position of the sun, the village would know when all the various ceremonies were to take place. His observatory was out at the point of the mesa, at the south end. He had a notched stick, with the notches in groups of four, and he'd hold this notched stick in such a way as to measure the horizon and see exactly where the sun was coming up. There was a natural bowl in the rock, a kind of smoothed-out pothole, and he would record his readings inside that bowl. His sun readings set the calendar for all important events and indicated to the different clans when they were supposed to do various things. He'd begin in January with Pameuya. They would have these free-for-all dances for a good time. Even the high mucka-mucks got involved, playing gambling games or doing other things to celebrate. Next the Sun Watcher would announce the date of the Bean Dance to the man in charge of the Bean Ceremony. Next, the planting season. He announced the time for planting corn in the fields from which the Niman dancers would later bring in the first corn. He announced everything through the year, and the whole cycle of ceremonial events was set by his sun readings.

Well, my father had always wanted me to be initiated into the One Horn Fraternity. (In translation, we call the kiva groups fraternities, societies or lodges.) Even before I was out of school he had called on a man named Nitioma to invite me to join and to sponsor me. There are different reasons why a certain person becomes a sponsor of a young man and sees him through an initiation. One circumstance is this: Let us say that a boy or young man had some kind of sickness. His parents would go to some elderly person with curative powers, a knowledge of "medicine," as that word is used by Indians. They would ask this man to do something for their son. The man would treat the sick boy and cure him. After that, of course, the boy owed something to the man who had made him well, but in curing the sick boy the man had assumed an obligation to him. That obligation was to sponsor the boy's initiation. The man would go to the parents and say, "I'd like to take your son into my lodge." If the parents agreed to that, and they usually did because they also had incurred an obligation, the man would become the boy's sponsor. In this kind of situation you can see another one of the invisible relationships that exist in a village. In my own case, I hadn't been sick, but my father, whom I hadn't seen much of when I was small, had it in his mind that he wanted to share his ceremonial knowledge with me and make me a true Hopi. He gave ceremonial cornmeal to Nitioma and asked him to take me in charge. The first time Nitioma approached me, I was still going to school in Keam's Canyon. He asked me if I was ready to be initiated, because the winter initiations were coming up soon. I was a little vague about it. I wasn't sure I wanted it. I told him I'd see if I could get my parents' permission.

Next time I was home in the village I let my mother and stepfather know about the invitation. But my uncles—my mother's brothers— heard about it and they were against it. They told my mother, "No, let things remain the way they are. Some of the things going on in those lodges could be dangerous to Albert. Let him just be a Tewa and stay out of those lodges. Even if his father is pushing for it, Albert shouldn't get involved. If Sitaiema comes around to talk about it, tell him we don't agree." In our Hopi and Tewa way, a boy's uncles have a lot of authority in such things, and so my mother told my father and Nitioma that I couldn't be initiated. But my father didn't let the matter die.

Now that I was finished with school and back at First Mesa, Nitioma came to me again. He said, "Son." I said, "Yes." He said, "Do you want to enter my lodge?" By this time I had already decided to go ahead with it despite the opposition of my uncles. I realized that as translator for the Keam's Canyon Agency I had to know much more about the inner workings of Hopi life, how the people were ceremonially related, who were the moving forces. So I told Nitioma, "Yes, I'm ready now." He said, "Good, then it's settled. I'll prepare for it." By that he meant he'd start weaving a ceremonial sash and kilt for me. A person's sponsor was supposed to do that. He'd weave those complicated designs into the kilt and sash to represent elements in our present life and the life to come. Those weavings aren't just to look artistic, they are symbolic.

The initiations into the four important societies take place in November in connection with the New Fire Ceremony. The four fraternities are these: the Kwakwanteu, usually called the One Horn after the horned water snake of Palatkwa; the Aalteu, which simply means Horn, but usually called Two Horn to distinguish it from the One Horn. It's based on clans having names of animals with two horns, such as deer and antelope. Any of those clans can use the Aal kiva. The other two are the Wuwuchimteu and the Tataukyameu. On the day of Lalakon, the Women's Basket Dance, in September, our chakmongwi, or crier chief, made the announcement that initiations were going to be held. He said, "Everyone who has someone to be initiated, get ready."

The families that had young men who were going into one or another of the lodges made preparations. One of the things to be done was to provide for a jackrabbit feast that would be given when the first stage of the initiation was finished. There was a kind of ceremonial jackrabbit hunt in honor of each of the boys to be initiated. The boy's sponsor was usually present at the hunt, but if he couldn't be there a member of the Rabbit Clan took his place. And when they'd caught enough jackrabbits for the feast they'd bring them to the initiate's mother. The boy himself participated in the hunt, dressed up something like a kachina, and he had a rabbit stick made for him by his sponsor. All of this was what you might call a preliminary festival.

The day that Nahtna—our initiation ritual—was to take place, the boys—really young men—didn't go anywhere, just stayed home waiting for their sponsors to come and get them and take them to the kiva. It was around five in the afternoon when the sponsors started to call for their initiates. My sponsor, Nitioma, couldn't see very well and it was hard for him to get around, so he sent his nephew for me with a blanket. I had to take off all my clothes except my briefs. All I wore was the blanket, and it was the same with the other fellows who were being initiated. We went to the Wuwuchim kiva in Walpi, and Nitioma was waiting for me at the kiva entrance.

Before we went down he gave me some sacred meal and said, "Now, Albert, do you want to reconsider? This is your last chance. Are you serious about going through with it? If not, you can still turn away from it. It's up to you."

I said, "No, I don't want to turn back. I've made up my mind." He said, "All right. Sprinkle your cornmeal into the kiva." After I'd sprinkled my cornmeal into the kiva opening he took me down.

All four of the societies were gathered inside. But as I said before, the One Horn separates its rituals from those of the other three fraternities. From the top of the ladder down, a blanket hung across the kiva to divide the One Horn people off from the Two Horn, the Tataukyameu and the Wuwuchimteu. There were two men standing at the base of the ladder. If a boy belonged to the One Horn group, one of the men took him to that side, behind the blanket. If a boy belonged to one of the other groups, a man would guide him over there. Our part of the activities was completely curtained off from the other fraternities.

The first phase of the rituals was bringing the sacred fire out of the wood. That is where the New Fire Ceremony got its name. Everyone sang the sacred fire chant. Each group had its own fire stick or drill. The points were set against tinder that would catch fire when the friction generated enough heat. There were four men at each stick. One man would rotate the stick swiftly between his palms, his hands gradually moving downward. Then another man would take over at the top of the stick, keeping it rotating. When his hands had moved toward the bottom, another man would take hold. One after another they took turns, always keeping the stick in motion. When the wood underneath smouldered and sparks were visible, someone called, "The fire has come out!" Each group generated its own sacred fire this way.

The Two Horn, Tataukyam and Wuwuchim, groups took their new fire and went out, to their own kiva. We One Horn stayed where we were. After that those other three groups conducted their ceremonies separately from us. We stayed in the chief kiva till quite late. Then someone went up and looked around. He said, "Well, it looks safe. There doesn't seem to be anybody up here. Let's go." We all went from there to the One Horn Kiva with our new fire. Everyone was chanting. When we got to our own kiva my sponsor rubbed me with ice-cold water from an earthen jar. He said, "Now, Albert, I want you to drink some water, as much as you can. It's the last water you'll have for a long time. Drink slowly, don't hurry." I drank the whole jar of water. Nitioma had told me the truth. It was the last water I tasted for four days. That was part of the test they were putting us to, making us endure thirst.

There were four of us One Horn initiates, and for four days we sat in the kiva with blankets around us, mostly in one position, with hardly any breaks. They gave us white piki to eat once in a while, but no water. We couldn't eat the piki because our mouths were too dry. Some of those old-timers would bring drinking water into the kiva, but not for us. After a while we got so that we could *smell* water on the far side of the kiva. I never knew it was possible to smell water. The fellow sitting next to me said, "Albert, that man coming down the ladder is bringing water with him. Don't you smell it?" I said, "Yes, I smell it." And I really did. Another thing, those old-timers would always be talking about water, how it flowed down the Little Colorado, and what such and such a lake looked like. It was for our benefit, of course. Old man Charlie was always talking about Grand Canyon and all the water that went through there, and how he used to swim in it when he was young. It made us pretty mad.

Once a day, in the evening, we were allowed to stand up and stretch ourselves. Usually it was when the men of the other lodges arrived up above our kiva with their initiates and chanted sacred songs. After they'd gone and when there weren't many people around, our sponsors took us out of the kiva and walked us to the end of the village with blankets over our heads so that we couldn't be recognized. Then at a certain place where we couldn't be seen from the village, they took the blankets off us and rubbed us down to loosen our muscles. Now, as I said, this was in November, and it was pretty cold to be standing there without any clothes on. We felt a little better when we got back to the kiva because there was a fire down there, but then we had to get into those cramped sitting positions again. Once in a while they let us put our heads on the floor and get a little sleep, but it wasn't long before we heard someone thumping on the kiva roof and calling, "All right, time to wake up." So then we sat up again. There was always something going on. From time to time the One Horn members would gather and sing sacred chants.

The other three lodges also had something going all the time for their initiates. They had their own tests, and the Two Horn Society was in charge. Often they took the initiates here and there, made them run to distant places or do unpleasant things. The boys had to do whatever they were told, even if it was nonsensical. They were supposed to be learning discipline and how to endure hardship, like you hear about U.S. Marine training.

Of course, most of the things that happened in their initiation ceremonies were kept secret from us, just as our doings were kept secret from them. But later I learned that one of the things their initiates had to do was to run all the way to Huckyatwi, Badger Butte, about four miles from Walpi. You can see that butte from the west side of Walpi where the Alosoka shrine is. There was an Alosoka shrine at Huckyatwi, too, and rituals were carried out at that place. Alosoka is closely connected with the New Fire Ceremony activities of those three lodges. Well, in the evening they'd make the initiates race back from Huckyatwi, and this would take place in the dark. People would be watching from the top of the mesa for fires and other signals from the valley, and they would call down into our kiva, "They're moving this way. . . . We see their light at such and such a place."

In the kiva, we One Horn people would be chanting for the welfare of the Alosoka initiates. When our watcher up above announced, "Now they're at the foot of the village," we stopped chanting. The initiate who won the race back to Walpi was met by his sponsor, who escorted him back to their kiva while chanting, "My mother is very fertile. Why is my mother fertile? Because of my father." Where the chant says "my mother" it refers to the earth, and "my father" means sun and rain, the forces that make things grow. That is what Alosoka is all about, bringing things to fruition.

We One Horn initiates had our own running ordeal. They took us northeast to that place where the Tewa inscription is on the cliff wall, telling about the battle with the Utes. A little beyond there at a place not far from the spring, they said, "Now, boys, line up. We are going to test you. Start running. Run as fast as you can. Don't stop. We older men will follow you and catch you." Well, we tried to run but we couldn't. Our legs were weak. How could we run after we'd been sitting in that cramped position so long, and without any water? We could hardly hobble. But we tried. They caught us before we'd gone very far. I don't know what the purpose of that test could have been. Maybe it was just to put us in our place and teach us young ones a little humility, I don't know. I heard a story about one of those tests that took place in the old days. There was a good strong boy, or young man, among the initiates, and when they were told to run he just took off. They couldn't catch him. He got further and further away from the village, and the men couldn't even get close to him. At last he disappeared out there in the distance somewhere, and it was the last they ever saw of him. He never came back.

When we returned to the kiva we brought lots of firewood with us to keep the main kiva fire going. It kept the kiva warm, of course, but it was also the only thing we had for light. There weren't any lamps of any kind. The person who fed the fire and kept it going was called the fire chief. The sacred fire that had been brought out of the wood in the New Fire Ceremony could not be used for any utilitarian purpose. If someone wanted to light a pipe, it had to be from the main kiva fire. A Tobacco Clan man was in charge of filling the pipes. As for the New Fire, it had to be extinguished when the ceremonies ended.

Eventually the fourth day came and we initiates were liberated from our sitting position. Our sponsors said, "All right, boys, now you can get up and stretch yourselves." Well, we rolled around, rubbed our legs to get the circulation going, and looked a little more alive. However, we didn't get any water yet. Before we could drink anything they took us into the plaza, washed our bodies down with cold water and scrubbed our heads with yucca suds. You might say it was a kind of christening, because we received our new names. That was when I got the name Eutawisa, meaning Close In the Antelopes. Afterwards they took us back into the kiva and rubbed us all over with cornmeal. When that was done they offered us our first water. But they saw to it that we'd drink properly and not gulp. My sponsor said, "First thing, just rinse your mouth and spit the water out. Now let just a little trickle down your throat. All right, now take a small swallow. Take it easy. Rest for a while, then take a little more." After not having had any water for four days, it was hard to swallow. My throat didn't want to accept the water. But by taking it in easy stages I was able to drink. I don't remember any time in my whole life when water tasted so good.

The next morning our One Horn Society put on its last dance of the New Fire Ceremony in the Walpi plaza with the whole village watching. As we initiates came up from the kiva we imitated the emergence from the underworld. We had our arms locked going up the ladder (they say that's the way it was when the people came up to the Fourth World inside the bamboo), and an older man was calling, "Be careful! Be careful!" He was imitating the mockingbird who guided the people upward in the emergence. After the public dance we returned to the kiva, and in the evening they brought us all that jackrabbit food that our families had prepared for us. We had a feast.

About that name they gave me, Eutawisa—it came from my sponsor. He belonged to the Deer Clan, related to the Antelope, that came to Walpi from Tokonave or Navajo Mountain. Deer and Antelope belong to the Horn Clan group, they're affiliated. So the name that Nitioma gave me referred to his clan. But the meaning of the name can be explained another way. Nitioma told me, "When we arrived here from Tokonave, the Bear and Snake clans closed off the village to us at first, barred the path. We Deer Clan people and our relatives, the Horn, Antelope and Grass, were, you might say, closed in. So the name refers to how we were barred when we first arrived at First Mesa."

Now, that four-day ordeal I went through during Nahtna was really only the first stage of my initiation. There are four degrees you have to go through. The second stage is Soyalana, or Winter Solstice Ceremony, in December. After that, in February, comes Invaya, the Bean Planting Ceremony. On the other mesas they call it Pachaveu. Then, finally, in July, the Niman Ceremony, when the kachinas are supposed to be departing for their home over at San Francisco Peaks. All through those ceremonies your sponsor will be teaching you, as they say, mouth to ear. After the New Fire Ceremony is over he talks to you in the kiva. He explains things to you. Tells you that you must be disciplined in your behavior. "Remember that you are a Hopi. Treat everybody equally, and with respect, just the way you yourself want to be treated. If somebody comes to your home, feed him, give him something to drink. Remember that there's someone watching you, the Great Spirit. He's here with you. Conduct yourself as you should. When you get up in the morning, look towards the east where the light comes from. Pray that you'll live like a decent person and have a long life. You're a Hopi now."

What they mean when they say "You're a Hopi now" is that you're obligated to try to conduct yourself without any flaws. Of course we all have flaws, but we're supposed to make every effort to be models of decent behavior. When you've gone through all four of the ceremonies you're regarded as a full-fledged Hopi. But the teaching goes on. Your sponsor continues through the years teaching you traditions and stressing good behavior. Without going through these initiations with a "godfather," or sponsor, informing and teaching a young person, how can the generation coming up now learn standards of good living and be educated in the traditions? The prospects don't look very good, because the initiations into the main kiva societies here on First Mesa have ended. They still have initiations in Shongopovi, but they came to an end in Oraibi in 1906, when the village broke in two. The Oraibis are trying to revive the ceremonies and the initiations, but they really can't do it. . . .

28
My Stories Are My Wealth

Edited by

JULIE CRUIKSHANK

Angela Sidney was a Tagish and Tlingit woman of the southern Yukon. Born in 1902 in the village of Carcross, she got her English name (in addition to names in Tagish and Tlingit), when a prospector came in to warm himself at her parents' fire, and, seeing the newborn baby, said she looked like an angel. Her people are hunters and fishers, salmon fishing in the summer, and hunting large, solitary game animals when possible in the winter. Born just after the disruption in Yukon life caused by the Klondike gold rush of 1896–98, Sidney also experienced the disruptions of the second "rush," the building of the Alaska Highway by the American Army during World War Two.

Very much concerned with adapting the old ways to modern conditions, Angela Sidney was active in working with linguists (she was the last fluent speaker of Tagish, an Athabaskan language) and anthropologists to preserve her cultural knowledge for future generations. Because the first language of Yukon children is now often English, for all her fluency in Tagish and Tlingit, she recorded her life and her stories in the English with which they would be most familiar.

Julie Cruikshank, an anthropologist, began work with Angela Sidney in 1974, eventually including Sidney's life history along with those of two other Yukon Native elders, Annie Ned and Kitty Smith, in a superb book called Life Lived Like a Story: Life Stories of Three Yukon Native Elders *(1990), from which the selections included below are taken.*[1] *Sidney's autobiography is a mixture of traditional stories and more or less factual recollections. But, as Cruikshank makes clear in her fine general introduction and introductory notes, the stories are as much autobiographical as the factual material, inasmuch as Native elders use narrative as a means of explaining, commenting on, understanding, and resolving issues of every sort. As Sidney says, in the quotation Cruikshank has used as a title for the autobiography, "My stories are my wealth." Mrs. Sidney died in 1991. Bracketed words are Cruikshank's additions.*

1. The selections included here are reprinted from *Life Lived Like a Story: Life Stories of Three Yukon Native Elders*, by Julie Cruikshank, by permission of the University of Nebraska Press. Copyright © 1990 by the University of Nebraska Press.

Cruikshank's collaboration with these Yukon women to produce their life stories seems to me one of the finest examples of its kind. At every point, Cruikshank's explanations of her editing procedures, of the anthropological use of life history material, of the function of story telling among traditional people, and, indeed, of the warm relations that she developed with Angela Sidney, Annie Ned, and Kitty Smith, exemplary for recording traditional lives today.

My Parents

*"We're pretty smart, we're doing this.
This is long before my time and yet I know it."*

My Mother

My mother was named K̲aax̲'anshee; her white-man name is Maria. She's *Deisheetaan sháa* — that means she is a woman of *Deisheetaan* Nation. Now I'll talk more about my mother's people.

That *Deisheetaan sháa* who came inland had daughters, and *they* had daughters. One of those daughters was *Sa.éek'*. She was my grandma on my mother's side; and also on my daddy's side because her brother was my daddy's father, *Tl'úku*. I heard my mother and my daddy talk about their grandmother.

I never saw *Sa.éek'*, but I knew two of her daughters, Grandma Hammond, *Aandaax̲'w*, and Annie Atlin, *Sakinyáa*. I never saw my mother's mother, either: her Tagish name was *Kashadandá*; her Tlingit name, *Keikandagán*.

She died when my mother was six or seven. My mother had no sisters after that. She died going through that pass from Millhaven, going through to West Arm. There's a little creek comes down — they call it Rosebud Creek — that's where they climbed up right on top of the mountain. She was carrying her baby, my mother's sister. Here that baby died five days after her mother — that baby must have starved herself, my mother said. Well, of course, they burned people that time I'm talking about, and they brought her ashes back to Carcross. This is my mother's time I'm talking about.

That fall that her mother died, my mother went down Taku River with her aunt, *Sakinyáa*. She went down in falltime. My mother was raised by her aunt that one year. In springtime they came back, and here, her father was staying with *Stóow* already. That *Stóow* was Tagish Charlie's sister, my mother's mother's half-sister. *Stóow*—her husband had died, too—and people said, "You fellows just go with each other. Who's going to guide you fellows? You fellows just help yourself, enjoy yourself together. Your husband died, and his wife died, and they're your people."

And they talked to my Grandpa *Shaakóon*: "This is your people's wife, too. And you're her people's husband. Might as well be you people stay together." That's what they told them. That's why they stayed together. So *Shaakóon* married a Tagish lady, *Deisheetaan*. So that's all my mother stayed with her aunt, just that part of one year. My mother said she was only one year without a mother. From then on, she called *Stóow* "Mother": *Stóow* is the one that died at Indian Point, *Ta Tígi*.

My Father

My father was *Ḵaajinéek'*: his name in English is Tagish John. Later they gave him his second name—*Haandeyéiɫ*, "come on crow" [or "hither, crow"]. He was a *Daḵl'aweidí* [that is, Wolf] and *Deisheetaan yádi*: that means "child of *Deisheetaan*" [or "child of Crow"]. Now I'll talk about my father's people.

My daddy's mother, *Guná*, was sister to *Shaakóon*, my mother's daddy.

My daddy's daddy, *Tl'úku*, died at Quiet Lake. *Tl'úku* was a brother to *Sa.éek'*, my mother's mother—that's why my father took the news to *Sa.éek'* when his father, her brother, died. People burned the body in those days—they would bring the ashes and bones back in a blanket or whatever they've got. Then they put them away in the spirit house, and then they had a party in the springtime. People came together to pay the people who've been handling him. Wolf people carried back my father's father, because he is Crow. After *Tl'úku* died, *Guná* married *Dzagwáa*.

Aandaax'w—Mary—was the daughter of *Sa.éek'* and was my daddy's cousin. When they were kids, they traveled around together all the time. Whenever my daddy used to tell a story, he always said, "*Aandaax'w* was with us." They grew up together like partners because my daddy's daddy traveled with his sister, *Sa.éek'*, and her hus-

493

band: those brothers-in-law were partners. They were all together when that animal came to them.

My daddy's mother, *Guná*, died in 1898 or '99. They were in Skagway and my daddy was freighting—that's the time his mother died at Bennett. The old people can't go over the pass so they stayed at Bennett. She was never well for six years, never walked for six years. In those days people lived in brush camp, and people packed [carried] her when they moved; in wintertime they used a sleigh.

Well, my father was in Skagway when they brought the news his mother died. So Tagish John and Tagish Jim and other *Dakl'aweidí* went over to Bennett. They [*Deisheetaan*] burned her—those were the days they burned people—and they had a cup of tea. They never really had a good party for her till they came back from Skagway, falltime. Then they brought the bones back to the spirit house in Tagish—they brought them back in a trunk: they gathered up the bones and ashes and brought them back to Tagish. That's all my mother told me about her.

My daddy had a twin sister, and they both grew up. After their mother, *Guná*, died, his twin sister married *Dzagwáa*. She was Bill Bone's mother.

My daddy's other sister married *Yéiɬ'aagí*. When he died, and when *Gunaaták'*'s wife died, she "took over" because it was their people—*Gunaaták'* was Marsh Lake Chief. They never had kids together. That auntie, *Tashooch Tláa*, had a son, though—*Tashooch*. They claim that she was single, too, long after her husband died—that's why she never had another child. But *Gunaaták'* [already] had a daughter: she's the one my auntie raised—Mrs. Whitehorse Billy—my aunt raised her since she was two years old.

Tagish women married to all parts of the Yukon—I think that's why now they want Tagish people at that elders' meeting, because we went everywhere: my father's sister *Tashooch Tláa* married *Gunaaták'*, Marsh Lake Chief; Jimmy Kane's mother married to Champagne; *Tatl-'èrma*, Kitty Smith's mother, married to Dalton Post; Jenny Dickson married to Ross River; Tagish Jim's mother's sister married to Mandasaa, Laberge Chief. I remember my mother said, "How come you people call yourselves like that [use Tagish names]? Go back to your country, Marsh Lake! You just like to use our names but you don't want to go back to your country," she told them. But I guess that's why they want us at that meeting.

My daddy was maybe thirty when he married: my mother had just become woman. Old-timers got kids married right away. They tell them, "You're ready for marrying now. You've got to get married."

In 1898 Mother was in Skagway. Mother lost four kids—all at one time: one was six years old, next were two girl twins, then one other girl. They are buried at Dyea, under one house in Dyea. My mother got that 1898 sickness, too—measles—and it made her blind. The doctor and the bishop told her not to sew because she would damage her eyes more.

After that, they came over the Summit and found Atlin. Johnny was born that year, 10th of July, 1898. After Johnny, there was one girl died between Johnny and me, and then me, Angela—I was born in 1902. My Indian name is *Stóow*. After me came a girl named Dora, who died later, then David, who died 1929, then Dora, born July 29, 1916—her real name is Alice Dora, but we call her Dora.

Stories from My Parents' Time

"My father died in 1920,
But he told me all these stories before he died."

Dzagwáa

My father told us this story.

He said when they were kids—ten or twelve years old—he and my
  mother's aunt, Mrs. Dyea John, *Aandaax'w*, were pals.
They used to run along and get water—play around all the time.

And here, all of a sudden, dogs begin to bark in the night always.
People never used to have a lot of dogs—
Maybe one family got just one dog—they never used to have big
  bunch of dogs.
They miss salmon, too, when dogs bark.

So finally, Tagish Jim's father, *Yéiɬhaan*, told my daddy's stepfather,
  Dzagwáa
"What's your doctor [shamanic power] for?
Go find out. Find out what's doing that.
Is that a person, or what is it?
Is it an animal stealing fish?"

495

He said, all right, he's going to try to find out.
So he made doctor one night, and he sees that it's an animal doing
    that.
"It's not a human being," he said.
So he watched for it, watched for it.

The next night he said,
"It's going to come . . . huh, huh . . .
Its mind comes here already . . .
It's going to come again . . . "
So he told those people exactly where to sit down and watch for it.
"It's going to come over there, right there.
You fellows watch that all the time."
And in the meantime, he made that arrow—the head of that arrow is
    bone.
He put his paint on it and he told *Yéikshaan* to watch for it.
He gave that bow and arrow to him for him to shoot it.
He knows just when it's going to come. He said,
"His mind comes here already."
That's the time he told them to watch for it.
Him, he's at the camp—he's sleeping all the time.
After those people went to watch, he lay down again—
He sleeps—put his blanket over his head.
"Kids have to keep still," he said.

My father said they put the kids to bed while the sun is still up yet.
Those kids got to go to bed—never run around.
Nobody runs around—just lay still one place.
But he's making doctor.

Pretty soon, all at once, it started to get dusk but you could still see
    good yet.
All of a sudden it just came out of a kind of valley between the moun-
    tains where an old water bed came out—
Little creek down at the bottom—
But it's got shoulder on it—it's steep, too.
Here that thing just came out and he's just watching the camp, just
    looking at the camp.
All of a sudden that *Yéikshaan* took a shot at it with his bow and arrow.
And it's just gone, like that.
Just gone.
Disappeared.

Well, they watched for a while, I guess.
That Indian doctor said,
"He shot it all right, but it took off with the arrow.
There's a little arrow sticking into him yet" —
It's just the spear of the arrow, you know:
They put the arrow somehow on a stick
And when the arrow goes through, the stick just falls off but the bone
    stays inside.

He watched all the time, that Indian doctor, *Dzagwáa*.
Never eats — never eats anything.
Other people ate early in the morning and late in the evening.
But that Indian doctor is just sleeping all the time —
Watching . . .

Pretty soon . . . "Aha," he said.
"It's coming back to its mother.
And oh, his mother feels sorry — that animal died after it came back to
    its mother.
Now his mother is going to come here, she's starting to come."

It's going to come, so everybody keeps quiet, keeps still.
Here, the next night, it's going to come.
"You fellows watch between the mountains."
I wonder what in the world that could be?
Couldn't be that big . . .
I would like to see that place at Quiet Lake where they looked, at Big
    Salmon.
They said it was between the valley, like that.
Here it comes out.
Something just like toward Tagish, I guess, between mountains.

Here all of a sudden in the evening he said,
"Here it's coming, it's coming.
Watch that place up there, you fellows — [pointing]
Watch up there. It's going to come out."

So people watch it.
The kids are all in bed.
The women are all in bed, too, with the kids.
Just that Indian doctor — that *Dzagawáa*, his name — my father's
    stepfather —

497

And her, that animal's mother.

Pretty soon . . . "I'm going to meet it,"
He said that when it came out.
There was a light just like a moon, they say—
Just like the moon, her eyes between those mountains—
Two lights there, it seemed just like two moons.
And he said he's going to meet it.
So he went.
He's gone.
My father's stepfather, whole thing, gone—just like he's flying!
And he told those people,
"When I'm coming back, you fellows stand like a **V**,
Like a *shal*, like head of a *shal* [fishtrap]," he said.

And *Yéiłshaan*, oh, he's the one!
He don't believe in Indian doctor, don't believe him.
He [*Dzagwáa*] said to him:
"You stand right there and try to catch me."
And his feet are that far off the ground! [two feet]
He's flying, they said.
"If you don't catch me, I'm going to go round the camp and come
    back the same way again.
Then you try a second time.
You try with your bare hands first."
He gave them willows and a little tree top and his mitts.

He said, "You switch me with this one.
Switch me with it if you can't catch me."
That's what he told them.

The first time, he went dressed just like he was, and that thing said to
    him:
"Why are you coming to me with dirty clothes?"
So he came back to camp and he wants clean clothes.
And nobody had clean clothes, I guess—only his wife, that's my fa-
    ther's mother—
She had a brand-new dress.
Well, they thought she [the spirit] wouldn't mind it.

So he used that dress—it's homemade, you know—sewed by hand.
He put that on and he went to meet it again.

It just stayed there in one place right there—
I guess his doctor tied her up there, too.
He went again.

You could hear, they said, from the camp.
Just like something roaring—You know . . . "RRRRRRRRR"—
That's when she's talking to him, I guess.
And here he's coming with that dress.
And again, she didn't like it.

"Why are you coming to me with a dress?" she said.
"I want a man, not a woman."
So she did that to him: [indicating tearing]—
Here that dress just ripped right from the neck right down to the bottom.
That's what happened to him the second time.

Well, he went right back again—he went home.
"I'm going to lead her the other way," he said.
"Lead her past the camp, lead her farther on."
And soon he's gone again.

Well, he's coming back—it's just like he's flying in the air.
And that *Yéilshaan* couldn't catch him—
He tried to grab him, I guess, but he couldn't catch him.
And here he went around the camp.
And he came back the same way, second time.
That's the time *Yéilshaan* switched him with those willows—
The little tree top and his gloves, that Indian doctor's gloves.
And he just dropped right there.
That's the way they catch him again.

And the third time he went.
That's the time he led her down the other way.
Everything quieted down after that, after he led her past the camp.
She took off the other way.

This happened at Quiet Lake, head of the Big Salmon River.

That Indian doctor stayed in bed for pretty near a whole week
To get straightened out again.
His name was *Dzagwáa*, Billy Bone's father, my father's stepfather.

Childhood

"I know what I know because my mother taught me . . .
After company goes, I asked her questions.
That's how come she told me all that."

I was born on January 4, 1902. My mother says it was four days after New Year's Eve, and we think it is 1902 because that's what it says on my baptism card.

This prospector, George Dale, was mining down at Coal Creek— *T'ooch' Lutú* —below Carcross town in wintertime. Here, New Year's Eve he wants to go to Carcross, I guess. So after he got through working, he walked there on the ice. About two o'clock in the morning, he started to make Carcross—he saw lights. It was a *cold*, cold night, he said. And here the only light there was in my father's house, my father's place—my father Tagish John's place. And he knocked on the door, and here my father answered.

He turned to the heater and he got warmed up. And my father said, "Well, my wife got a little baby girl. That's why I was keeping the fire burning." Them days there were no houses yet: they were living in tent frame. He's got tent frame—boards on it, bed, and everything. There is curtain between: one side they [use] as a kitchen; other side they use as bedroom.

So he asked George Dale, "Would you like to see the baby?" And George said okay. So he brought me out—I guess it was me—and he showed me to George Dale. George Dale looked at the baby: "Oh," he said, "that baby looks so sweet. Just like a little angel."

And that's how come I got my name Angela. He told my father, "Call her Angela. She looks like a little angel. And when she is going to be baptized, let me know. I want to be her godfather because I'm the first person she saw." That's why he claimed me.

Year 1917, that's the time I was already living with my husband. Well, we just got married in July and this was in August. He was working on section. One time he was coming home from work and there was a party going on where that George Dale rented a house. The boys called him in—so he went in, and then they introduced him around and told George [Dale], "This is George Sidney, Angela's husband."

"Angela who?" George Dale inquired.

"Angela John, used to be."

"Oh, my," he said, "that's my godchild." So anyway, he shook hands with George, and he told George that he was supposed to be my godfather and everything.

After a while, George came back and I asked him, "How come you're so late?"

"The boys up there invited me in for a drink. And you know what? I met your godfather."

"My godfather? Who's that?"

"George Dale," he said.

"Aw, go on. How in the world you know he's my godfather?"

"He told me himself."

I didn't believe it, so I asked my mother about it. And my mother said, "That's right, that's right. About two weeks later, we took you to the church. Somebody took you off my arm and held you. So it must have been George Dale. White man, anyway." So he's the one that gave me this name, Angela.

When I was born my mother must have had a nurse, but she didn't tell me who was with her. I told you they partitioned that tent frame off—my dad wouldn't have been in the same room. Somebody must have been with her, but she didn't tell me who was her nurse.

You've got to give kids a name as soon as they're born. Otherwise they get lost—their spirit gets lost—that's what they claim. I've got two names: *Stóow* for my grandmother—my mother's stepmother— and *Ch'óonehte' Má*. My mother gave me a little dog: *Ch'óonehte'*, they call it—that's how I got that name, *Ch'óonehte' Má*, "mother of *Ch'óonehte'*." That *Ch'óonehte'* means "deadfall" tree: "Deadfall Mother," they say. And *Stóow*, my grandmother, had the same name—she had a dog named *Ch'óonehte'*, too.

Some women have two Indian names. They get one when they're a baby, and another one when they make a potlatch for her brother. When you give a child a name, you can only use a name of someone related to you. Every nation [clan] has its own names, and you have to use the right name. Sometimes a baby is given the wrong name, and that causes fights.

My mother had *lots* of babies: four died before Johnny, including those two twins. Let's see . . . she had my oldest brother Willie. Then she had three girls—all buried at Dyea. Then she lost one at *Dasgwaanga Áayi*—Squanga Lake—that's after they came back, that's after Johnny. . . . Johnny was born 1898, then one died at *Dasgwaanga*. They started burying people before that, I guess; they brought her back where the graveyard is at Tagish, anyway. Then me, I'm the next girl to this one they brought back from *Dasgwaanga*. Then I had another sister—Dora—we lost her 1912, her. Then my brother David

501

was born 1905 or '06. And Pete was 1908 . . . I remember I was in school then, and one afternoon my aunt Mrs. Austin came. She got us out of school for the weekend, and she told me, "You've got a new brother. You got another brother." Here it was Peter. I was really happy to see that baby anyway!

Then six years after Peter, she had another baby, a girl—she lost that one, too, when she was four months old. I've got a picture of that baby, too. And then no babies after that until six years after, my sister Dora, the one that's living. Her first name is Alice and her second name is Dora. But I missed my sister—the one next to me that died in 1912—I missed her so much I started calling the new baby Dora. Pretty soon *everyone* started calling her Dora. That's her second name: Alice Dora is the way she was baptized.

I guess my mother took it hard to lose those babies—she must have taken it hard, but what can they do? Nothing! She never talked about it, not in front of me. She just told me about it.

But I remember when my sister Dora died—the first Dora—*Kaneegweik*. My mother used to cry every now and then, summertime. And I missed my sister so much I used to cry myself. I used to wander off some afternoon when I see two girls playing together, dolls and stuff like that, and me I've got nobody to play with. I used to cry quietly to myself. When I came home, though, it used to be nobody knew when I was crying . . . Boy, when I found out my mother was going to have a baby, I used to pray, "Let it be a girl, let it be a girl." And here she happened to be a girl! But I didn't play dolls with her anymore! I played babies with her!

In my mother's time, Indian way they say, if they put wolf droppings around your waist when you become woman, then you won't get babies. But some people get babies just the same—they say they did that to *Nadagáat'*, but she had babies just the same. They did that because her mother used to have a hard time. They also throw a puppy down your dress so you could have your babies quick like nothing—I remember my auntie, my father's sister, did that for me. My mother's dog had puppies, and when those puppies were first born—their eyes closed yet—she called me and my sister and she threw those puppies through our dress down to the bottom. That's so I wouldn't have hard time when my babies started to come. Year 1910 she did that.

They used to nurse babies all the time. Then, after a while they gave them rabbit's brain or gopher brain to eat—anything soft. They boil it and soften it and feed the babies. They begin that even younger than one year old—until the next baby.

When a baby is born, he sleeps with his mother and father until the next one. My mother sure used to get surprised when she sees baby sleeping alone in a crib. She said, *"Tlaagóo!* Surprise!" Claps her hands like that. "Is that what they do? Nowadays people let their babies sleep alone? My days it never was like that. People always sleep with their babies!"

My mother used to tell me that my aunt used to tease me after the first Dora was born. "Did you get kicked out? Did your sister kick you out?" And I was supposed to make a sad face and say, "Yes!"

They used to teach kids to behave themselves. Girls—they had little jobs to do, too—they try to teach them to sew. I don't know how old I was when my mother told me to make moccasins, told me to sew my own moccasins. She gave me a new pair of moccasins and told me to sew it, told me how to start it. And here I started gathering it. I guess I gathered too much, or not enough, and here my moccasin was just crooked, like that. And I showed it to my mother. "Look! It looks funny!" I told her. One side had hardly any gathering. She told me to undo it, then start all over. Then finally, I got it right. That's when I was eight or nine years old.

I don't remember ever getting spanked. Of course, my mother gets after me, gets mad at me once in a while. But my father *never* did.

I know what I know because my mother taught me—I was alone with her, don't know how long. I was ten years old that time my sister Dora died—she was eight years old. When we're in the bush, well, I'm alone with my mother. Sometimes I could hear them talking—I listened to what they're talking about; I always know it. After company goes, I asked her questions. That's how come she told me all that.

They spoke Tagish language all the time. Us kids, we talk Tlingit—don't know how come. Mom and Dad spoke Tagish lots of times, to each other, and my mother said when I was really small I used to talk like that, too. But as soon as we got a little older—four or five years old—we started talking Tlingit. Our cousins—David and Willie and Sophie and Isabel Hammond—they're Tlingit: they don't talk Tagish language. Every once in a while they would come up to Carcross and we got all mixed up with them, and we talked Tlingit. In the first place, we are Tlingit, you see: our ancestors got married into Tagish.

They used to teach us with stories: they taught us what is good, what is bad, things like that. I remember they always told us this story: There's supposed to be an old lady—or an old man—sitting at the water hole. And you tell kids, "Go and knock the old lady down, or the old man down." Early in the morning, they give you a bucket, and if you knock that one over, well, then, that's your money, your future. But there's no old lady or old man there, of course. Those kids go every morning to get water, look for it. It's never there. Gee, I sure laugh. "I run down to the water, never see an old lady," they say.

Well, it's supposed to be like that, you see; knock that old lady down and your money comes in easy. If you're lazy, then your money is lazy, too; you won't get it. That's why lazy people don't have money.

The old people thought the earth was all flat—my father used to argue with my brother about it. My brother used to tell him: "No! The earth is round. It's like a ball."

"Nah!" my father said, "it can't be. Those two ladies down below are supposed to be watching the world. They're the ones looking after the world. If it's round, going round, how come the water stays one place all the time? Shouldn't the water leak out some way?"

My brother said, "You fill a bucket of water and make it go round. See if it comes out!" He won't believe it—they argue with each other. My brother put water in a bucket, made it go round, and found it never comes out. "That's the way it is," he tells him.

When I was a kid, we traveled lots. I went to Chooutla school twice before I stayed there for good. Even then, we didn't stay there for very long, because my father took us out of school when I was ten. That was because my sister died there, so my father blamed the school because they didn't get help soon enough. He took me and Johnny out of school—Johnny was in the fourth grade then, and I was in the first. I was just going to pass that spring! After that, my father never allowed me to have pencil and paper. He thought I would write to boys, I guess.

But I learned reading from books. I used to babysit Lilly Henderson, and she had a storybook. I used to just study and practice the words—the first word I learned myself was "SUPERINTENDENT." Here I just spelled it out, spelled it out, and finally I figured out what it meant! So I can read even big words. But I don't write.

I must be seven years old when we went to school first. I remember we used to go just to morning class—that's the time we only went to school four hours a day. Before grade 4, you go to school in the morning; after grade 4, you go to school in the afternoon. There was me, and there was Daisy (Smith), and one boy Tony—Ginny Thomas's son—used to go to school in the morning. We learned some little writing, some reading. I don't know that part of it much. All I know is we used to play in the yard in the afternoon, the three of us. The rest of the time, we packed wood, packed water, sewed patches, darned socks—things like that.

The school used to be in Bishop Bompas's house: they used half the house for classroom. Then, year 1911, that's the time they started building that school, Chooutla school, and they finished that fall.

When they were building it, we went there for a picnic one time. They were working there, and we went down to the river—digging bear roots. And one girl called, "Oh, Dora fell in!" I started looking to see what happened—and here they were fooling me! And me, I missed a step and then *I* was the one that fell in. The kids grabbed me and pulled me out, and they said, "What did you see when you fell in the river?"

"Well, I saw the heavens open." How quick I think! "I saw the heavens open but they pushed me back. You pulled me out, I guess!" They laughed, those kids, thought it was lots of fun. They knew I was joking, I guess, that's all.

In the falltime, when the school opened, we went over in October. When we first went over to that Chooutla school, all those kids got off the cars, horse teams—we all started running around the Chooutla school first. Oh, boy, lots of fun! We thought it was a good place we're going to stay. But that's the time we found out we couldn't even talk even to our brothers! We got punished if we did. And we weren't supposed to talk Indian, Tlingit. There were three of us: my cousin Sophie and my sister Dora and me. Daisy [Jim] she never went back to school again; one year was good enough for her! She never went back. She told them about the school, I guess, and her father and mother didn't want to take her back anyway. Anyway, this was about year 1911.

I just went to second reader—I came out in May. That's when I remember my daddy was building a house, and they were putting a roof on it. Daisy and I were down there—and we climbed up that house and lay on top of the roof, and we were singing songs up there. That's the time Tagish Jim [Daisy's father] and my daddy went to West Arm, Millhaven, hunting, falltime, mid-October.

The earliest time I'm talking about is 1910—I can't remember when I was much younger. I remember we were staying across Ten Mile on that island—they used to call that island "Tagish John Island," and later they started to call it "Old Scotty Island"—it's right straight across Ten Mile. I remember that time—that's year 1910. I remember my father was fishing and we were staying on that island. I remember we used to play getting married. I don't know how in the world we ever thought of that! We made mud-pie wedding cake—how in the world I knew those things I'll never know!

Brother David was there . . . brother Peter was walking around by then . . . my auntie Mrs. Austin's two boys were there—Pete and Edward. We were fishing for my aunt Mrs. Austin's husband—Arthur was his name, but they used to call him "Shorty." And I remember we got a visitor—my father's nephew—my father's sister's son and his wife. They were coming back from Marsh Lake. They came—they landed. Well, I guess they knew that my father was living there and they wanted to see him.

We were staying at Scotty Island—across from Ten Mile. I was just a little girl—I must have been smart . . . well, I heard my mother talking and I remember her asking, "How is Mrs. Tagish Jim?"

"She's okay."

And I remember my mother asking, "She never get her baby yet?"

And she [Mrs. Bill Bone] said, "Yes, she never get her baby yet. She's just about falling over backwards now, bent backwards." I didn't even know what they were talking about. How could she be bent backwards and never get her baby yet? I used to wonder about it . . . After a while, I found out, of course; when I got grown up, I knew.

Stories from Childhood

> *"They used to teach us with stories.*
> *They teach us what is good, what is bad, things like that . . .*
> *Those days they told stories mouth to mouth.*
> *That's how they educate people."*

How People Got Flint

Bear was the only one that had flint one time.
There was no flint, they say.
People were having a hard time—sometimes fire would go out, you know.
Mice are the ones that really got it.
They say Bear tied it under his tail where he had long hair under there.

So one time, mice tried to get fur from him.

"What are you doing?"

"My kids all froze up on me," Mouse said.
"I want some of your fur."

Well, get it from under my tail. There's lots."

So he did. In the meantime, he chewed that flint off.
The bear noticed it right away, but Mouse threw it to the animals.

First, Fox ran with it.
Oh, he crossed two valleys and here Bear couldn't catch him.
Finally, Bear gave up.
Fox threw it down to a big rock and here that flint broke up.
He threw the pieces around, and said,
"Go all over the world.
People need you.
Make lots of flint for people."

And it did fly all over the world.

Oh, Fox waited to see if Bear would come.
No, he never came.

So Fox started to backtrack.
Here he came to a little lake and he got dry rhubarb—
Hollow in the middle.
Then he went down to the lake and shoved that rhubarb stick in
    the lake
And it came up.

"I wish that when people are dead, they come back like this,"
    Fox said.

But that Bear was sleeping pretty close to him, and he heard it.
Here he picked up a rock and threw it in the water.

"I wish that when people die they would be like that.
Let them die like a stone," Bear said.

He was mad.

"Oh, Grandpa, I didn't know you were there.
I guess you're right."

If he didn't do that, I guess people would come back.
That's why when they die, they die for good.

The Old Woman under the World

There are two old ladies down below who look after the world.
One is supposed to be sleeping;
The other one holds up the earth with a pole.
When she shakes it, that's when there's supposed to be an earthquake.
That old lady there with the pole is supposed to be Death.
She always argues—she's the one who always says,
"Let people sleep for good when they go to sleep.
Let them die."

That Death Woman wants to kill people before their time.

But Sleep Woman says,
"No!
Can't you see how my boss put a good pillow for me to sleep on?
And you want me to let her go to sleep for good?
No. No—I won't do that."
Those two old ladies—
One is Sleep Woman, the other is Death Woman.

Moldy Head—Shaatláax̱

One time there was a little boy who lived with his mother and father.
People dry fish—that's how they rustle for food.
If they do that, they don't have much hard time in winter when it's
    hard to rustle for game.

And so this little boy always cried for food in the evening,
Before he goes to bed his mother always gives him dry salmon,
    head part.

Here he tells his mother,
"How come it's always moldy?"
He gets disappointed, throws it away.
"It's moldy."
Anyway, his mother gave him another one again, always.
Every now and then, like that, it's moldy.

But he said something wrong against the fish spirit.

So the next year, they go to the same place—
That's where they dry fish.
They were there again.
Here, his mother was cutting fish.
And you know how seagulls want fishguts all the time?
Here he set out a snare for that seagull.
Set out a snare to catch him.

Anyway, that toggle wasn't very strong or very big or very heavy.
And seagull started to drag it out.
That little boy started running after it.
He ran in the water to try to catch it.
Pretty soon, he fell in a hole.
He caught it, I guess, but they couldn't save him.

And here right away the fish spirit grabbed him—they saved him.
And when the fish went back to the ocean, they took him.
But for that boy, it seemed like right away he was amongst people.
They got a big boat, and they took him with them down to the fish
    country.
They came to a big city, big town—
Oh, lots of people run around, kids playing around.

One time they're playing outside and the little boys see fish eggs.
He starts to eat some.
He doesn't know what those people eat—he never sees them eat
    anything.
Here, he starts to eat fish eggs.

Here, someone called out *Shaatláax*, "Moldy Head."
They call him that because he used to call fish moldy.
"Moldy Head eats someone's poop," they said.
Here it was fish eggs.

Oh, by gosh, right away he gets shamed!
When the kids come home, they tell older people about it:
"Moldy Head eats people's poop."

Next morning, adults tell them,
"Why don't you kids go play around that point, play ball.
While you play, you catch fish.
But when you eat it and when you cook it
Don't let anything fall in the hole, that cooking stick hole, where they
    put the stick in to roast fish."

So they make fire and one lady sees fish and clubs it and cooks it for him.
Now and then when he gets hungry, they do that for him.
In the evening when they come home,
Here that boy never came home until last.

They told him,
"Throw the bone and skin and everything into the water,
But don't let anything fall in the cooking stick hole."
He threw everything in the water except that one eye.
It fell in the cooking stick hole.
They didn't see it—the lost eye.
So when they came home, that boy has got one eye missing.
He came back to life again, and he's missing one eye.

The parents tell him to go back—look in that cooking stick hole,
See if there's anything there.

So they went to the playground,
And sure enough there is fish eye there.
He picked it up and he threw it in the water.
And when he came back, all of a sudden
That boy has got both of his eyes back.

Finally, springtime started to come.
Everybody started to get ready to go up the river again.
That boy stays with those people that adopted him first and they all
    go up the river again.

They come to that same place—"Hee hut, hee hut," they pole
    upriver.
That's how come they know where to go:

They say when the fish go up the river
Their great-great-grandmother is at the head of the creek.
And that's why they go up to visit the great-great-grandmother,
    that fish —
They come back to the same place.

Here he sees his human mother —
His mother is cutting fish.
He goes close to his mother.
Just the same, his mother never paid any attention to him —
It was just a fish to her.
I don't know how many times she tried to club that fish
But it always takes off.

So finally, she tells her husband about it.
"How come that one fish always comes to me and just stays right
    there all the time?
But after when I go back to see him, that fish is always gone.
Why is that?"

"I don't know why that is.
Let's try to kill it," he said.
"You know we lost our son last year.
Could be something. Must be something.
Let's try to catch it, okay?"
So they did. Anyway, they got it.

And here she started to cut that fish.
And here that fish had copper around his neck
Just like the one that boy used to wear all the time.
And that's the one when that lady started to cut his head off,

She couldn't cut the head off.
So she looked at it good.
Here she saw this copper ring on his head.
So she told her husband right away,
"Look at that. What's this here?"

And her husband said,
"Well, you know, our son used to wear a copper ring all the time
    around his neck."
Yes, they remembered that.

So they washed it good.

And then they took it home.
There's an Indian doctor there, too.
And the Indian doctor said,
"Put it in a nice clean white skin."
Old people used to have lots of that.
They put it in a nice clean skin,
Covered it with down feathers.

Then they tie it way up to where the smoke goes up,
Smokehole.
That Indian doctor told them to go fast for eight days.

So people fasted for eight days.
That Indian doctor said,
"If you see feathers blow up,
Then you take it down quick."

So they put the body up there,
Fasted for eight days.
That Indian doctor sang all the time.
They were singing, too, I guess—
Got to help the doctor sing.

Finally, on the eighth day, here they see the feathers blow up.
They take it down quick.
Here that little boy comes to life again, in human's body.
They brought him back to life.

That's how they know about fish.
That's why kids are told not to insult fish.
And kids are not to play with seagull because that happened.

29

My Life Story and Recent Events: A Dena'ina Legacy

Edited by

JAMES KARI AND ALAN BORAAS

A Kenai Dena'ina, Peter Kalifornsky was born in 1911 at Kalifornsky Village, founded by his great-great-grandfather at Cook Inlet Bluff, Alaska. His language is of the large Athabaskan group; Dena'ina *roughly means "the people," as does the Navajo* diné. *As one may guess from Peter's name (and the names of his relatives, e.g., his sister Fedosia Sacaloff), this part of Alaska was originally colonized by the Russians, so that Native people converted to Russian Orthodoxy when they became Christians and learned Russian as their second, in some cases even as their first language. The Russians, as Alan Boraas has written in a short biography of Peter Kalifornsky, were "relatively tolerant of indigenous cultural practices." When the Americans arrived, however, things changed, as American teachers pursued a policy of indigenous language extinction; Peter remembers being beaten because his English was clumsy.*

Educated by his mother's brother in the matrilineal Dena'ina society and by a relative by marriage known as Old Man Karp, Peter Kalifornsky lived through periods of rapid, and, indeed, traumatic change. He had a very difficult time of it in the forties and fifties, breaking a hip and suffering from arthritis and tuberculosis. In the early seventies, in response to Alaskan movements toward cultural revival, Kalifornsky began to discover the work that would continue to occupy him for the rest of his life. At that time, he met with other elders to consider how a Kenai Dena'ina potlatch (ritual giveaway ceremony) might be held, and he also met James Kari of the Alaska Native Language Center, who was interested in the language of Kalifornsky's people.

By 1974 he began to write, first to provide linguistic materials, but increasingly to record sukdu, *traditional stories of his people. To date, Peter Kalifornsky's written work is quite substantial, although it is difficult to find. A bibliography of "Kalifornskyana" exists in the volume from which our selections are taken,* A Dena'ina Legacy, K'TL'EGH'I SUKDU: The Collected Writings of Peter Kalifornsky.[1] *Peter Kalifornsky died in 1992.*

1. The selections included here are reprinted from *Peter Kalifornsky, A Dena'ina Legacy, K'TL'EGH'I SUKDU: The Collected Writings of Peter Kalifornsky,* by James Kari and Alan Boraas, by permission of The Alaska Native Language Center, copyright 1991.

It is a particular pleasure to conclude this volume with autobiographical selections that exist in both English and the Native language original. I have included several of the brief accounts of Peter Kalifornsky's life and activities, concluding with his presentation of the 1972 potlatch ceremony. In the brief section "Putting Up Fish," balik *are smoked strips of salmon.*

Peter Kalifornsky writing in Dena'ina, November, 1986. Photo by Roy Shapley, *Peninsula Clarion*, used with permission of the Alaska Native Language Center.

Ginihdi Shi Sukť'a

1Nudgheltant Kalifornsky Qayeh October 12, 1911. Shunkda bequsil janq'u ch'anik'en ełanh. K'ushť'a esh'il. Shbach'a'ina q'u shqigheten. Ts'ełt'an shitih ch'u ki ghel'en.

2Yethdi sez'a Theodore Chickalusion hni'iju ch'u shighetneq. Yadi hey k'ushť'a qzelnik', 1915 k'ushu. Jitq'u h'elnesh tsents'didatl' shlupch' yunch'eh ch'tunani Tikahtnu. Ts'ił k'gheł'an yi Alaska packers sbayles ts'etsali heyiq'.

3Ch'u shihdi q'u quhť'ana usdeth, shi qyan. T'qinalt'ah tik'u'eldush ch'u eshchih ch'u nteldeh, hneltish shtukda shuda ch'u shcheyakda. Sez'a k'ushť'a yuh idul. Tik'teh k'uhul'ih k'ushť'a ghesdne da, hq'u shegh nink'delyish ch'at' tghesht'ił, qgheldihni ts'its'atnaq'. "Hunlk'et' ch'u ghednu, ch'u q'ench' nugh qetnashigu. Nqeł'uda yetq'u tghelgheł, hna ghen dults'eł ch'q'u."

4Ts'iłq'u q'ut'en qanilchit shełni, hq'u k'ushť'a qa'elcheł. Ezhiyi miłni stsindnúlqet'. Ughashť'a qanelnik.

5Ch'u Naqazhegi Cannery qiz'in dighelak. Heyi shu 1919 yethdi quhť'ana ghesh'ih. Ch'u yet nuhtetnish ch'u shiqyan nindelnish heyi daghesediq', hq'u nagh qghedełi shi hnayeh k'u heyiq' daghesediq', hbesukt'a ch'u hbek'elik'a ch'u chiqul'iłch'.

6Ch'u shtukda hni'iju Fedosia bunkda 1921. Yethdi sez'a nushtał'u shtukdach' duhdgheldihni. Shcheyakda ił gheshduh shanteh ch'u heyteh nagheyik.

7Łik'teh'i gheła tik'teh diłaq'adghelnen ch'u shi qyan, ch'u yet guduh nindanlnent hk'uch' sheł ninen'i'u. Dena'inaq' ch'elqadi beqel'ani.

8Ch'u henugh tanshu ghu Libby diqelasht ch'qiluq' ts'ił jan gidaytsi bu.

9Ch'u shtukda be'u qusil 1925 ch'u shcheyakda ch'u Nik'analguk. Yit htl'eghhdi yina qebequsil, ch'u Unhghenesditnu dnaqusil. Ch'u shtukda tininu ch'u łuq'u qil'eh hdaqilchet. Peter Constantine yunich'enh hda'ilchet Tubughnenh. Yin ey shkela.

10Ch'u shihdi tik'teh hdanelchet. Shtukda k'uhu ghel'ih gheshdnuh k'uhu el'ih yadi henu ghetgheshuł. Ki heyda niłtu chik'a estsił ch'u garbasnik yih diqelasht. Nutiha dingi qyigheqit, yethdi ch'qiluq' nidal'eq'.

11Łitl'enteh Kahtnu ht'ana Libby dik'elash qghutnuh. Ch'u łuq'aka'a uhu qul'ih yet May 25 to June 25. Yet tahbił ghelayi chik'a k'ents'esa ts'ah tahbił.

12Yet hey thirties Alex Wilson ił tahbił ch'gheł'an nutiha dingi łu-

This Is My Life Story

1I was born at Kalifornsky village, October 12, 1911. My mother died when I was a baby. I never saw her. My aunts took care of me. One would keep me, and then another.

2Then my maternal uncle, Theodore Chickalusion, got married and took me. I don't remember what year it was, maybe 1915. I barely remember going down to the boat to go across the Inlet [to Polly Creek]. He had a contract with Alaska Packers to cut pilings, year round.

3And here I was, away from people, by myself. Many times I would go out in the woods and cry and go to sleep, lonesome for Dad, and Sister, and Grandpa. My uncle never stayed home. He was in the woods hunting when he was not working, but he would instruct me in what to do every day, training me in the real old-time way. "You exercise and work, and don't answer back, if you're sent to do something; move right at the very word."

4One morning he told me to get up, but I didn't get up. I got cold water over me. I was up fast!

5And Snug Harbor Cannery was canning clams around the year 1919. Then I saw some people. Then, when they left, I was left alone again for all the long winter, but their visit to us was my company for all winter, their stories and their songs, and the games they played.

6Then my father married Fedosia Sacaloff's mother in 1921. Then my uncle sent me back to my father to go to school. I stayed with my grandpa in summer, and in winter he visited us.

7I was wild because I had been raised in the woods by myself, and when I got back on this side [of Cook Inlet], I had to live a different life. I was used to Native food.

8Then I went to work for the Libby Cannery for a dollar a day, for the Chinese crew.

9Then my father's wife died in 1925, and also my grandfather and Nickanorga. After they died, Kalifornsky village died out too. And my father left the house, and everyone took off for elsewhere. Peter Constantine went across the Inlet to Tyonek. He was a younger brother to me.

10But as for me, I went to the woods. I hunted and trapped on my father's trapline and took whatever work I could find. I cut wood for next winter, and trap poles for the cannery. They paid forty cents a pole, and later it went up to one dollar.

11In springtime the Kenai people worked for the Libby Cannery. The king salmon fishing was from May 25 to June 25. In those days the nets they used had wooden floats and linen web.

q'aka'a. Ch'u Granquist niłtu tanalt'eq'i q'aghdeq łuq'u tahbił t'ghe-ł'an. Denłts'ek'i tanalt'eq'i itena nungheshtih. Ch'u dik'elyashh hnugh nuteshjish, niłk'uch' henu ghen k'u nuk'detseden nungheshtih.

131941 hnineshju Agrafena Sacaloff ił hq'u k'usht'a yuh eshdul. 1941 henugh tanshu ghu Portage ch'u Whittier Qeghtinitunt qałnigi ch'qeldedzi. Yet htl'egh hdi Tsani'un yeh Amchitka. Yet htl'egh hdi q'ench' Whittier qeghtinitunt unch' hdanłnen. Yet htl'egh hdi qeliq' 1945 Naknek dik'elash tanshnu yi P.A.F. Yet htl'egh hdi naqeli tunghanshdnik Kahtnu. Ch'u q'iłdu q'u gheshdu.

14Ch'u ch'bala ggats'a ch'aghełak dora ghech niłtu, ch'u dora gheshghun tahbił t'eł'ana niłtu, ch'u burhut ank'dghełak ch'u qenq'ah, yadi henu shlaq'a tul'eh. Yethdi tinitun hnugh Kahtnuh hech' tinitun hqeshqa.

151956–57 hkut' qeł'anh nidanlnen tuberculosis ghu Seattle Laurel Beach Sanitarium k'uych'eni beq'di hqugh. Ch'u tunghanshdnik id-iłdi shqenq'a ghu k'qul: yuleq qul, hdukaq'di qul, belda qyan ez'un. Shlaq'a ghel'eq'i $30.00 ni'iq' yi beł ch'dalnigi.

16Q'uch'a shnunastunen Dan France duhhdeldih q'ank'ułqes. Dnigi k'qatl'na shlaq'a ghełggat, ch'eda bach'k'elqedi gudlik ch'u qadi shlaq'a ghełdatl'. Ch'u dora buzełchin. Qughesht'a qyushiluq.

171960 tahbił ch'eł'ani q'aghanshdnu sheghes egeduyi hnes t'eshjuq, hq'u yeqech' q'u ghegheshdnu ndahduh henu shlaq'al'eh. 1965 Jack Farnsworth bu henugh tanshu yi nutuyu'ułi shgaba bik'eghneltishi łuq'u beqeghyeh hqugh bik'eyeshi yeq'ahdetałtlet. Deghełkegh hqugh 20' x 60' yi bu dnuyełuq, nutiha shani begh k'egh gheshdnu.

18Yethtl'egh hdi kiq'u burhut t'nuch'eł'ani ch'u ki dora ch'eghuni. Ch'u yet qizlan ch'u ki gheshdnuni qil sheghes egeduyi. Ch'u qadi dink'a shlaq'a ghel'eq ch'u yethdi qyeł k'nunetuhi.

19Ch'u yethtl'egh hdi 1972 idashla Jim Kari be'u ił shegh niyu. "Dena'ina hnaga gheniynik'eset," shełni.

20"Ch'du'inaghełt'ey shi'i," bedeshni, hq'u bech' henugh ch'tazdatl'. Ch'u nutastnu ch'u 1973 tunghastnik idiłdi Dena'ina hnaga ch'k'tuchek shełni. Ch'u yek'echek ch'u "Nen k'u k'ichek," shełni. Benanltun hq'u qil egduyi shgguna shq'eya. Ch'u "Ch'hdechedigu," shełni.

21Ch'u yethdi *Kahtnuht' ana Qenaga* niłtut'elyuyi k'yeshchex. Ch'u gin niłtu t'elyuyi yus qayeh California łuhshiniłtan, qayeh ndahdu unhshcheyakda yeghenik'ghadnuy be'izhi: Kalifornsky unhtsah Tahtna ił q'anghudnesh yeh Fort Ross.

12One year in the thirties Alex Wilson and I net-fished for king salmon, for forty cents a fish. And everybody netted for Granquist [the cannery superintendent] between the traps. I helped the owners of small hand traps. And I would go back to work in the cannery and do other kinds of work, like being a blacksmith's helper.

13In 1941 I married Agrafena Sacaloff, but I never stayed at home. In 1941 I went to work on the Portage and Whittier tunnel as a rock driller. After that, I went to the Aleutians, to Amchitka, and after that back to Whittier to work on widening the tunnel. After that, in the spring of 1945, I went to the Naknek Cannery for PAF. After that, in the fall, I came home to Kenai. And I stayed home then.

14And I dug out spruce roots (natural knees) for ribs for dories, and I built some dories for fishermen, and I repaired boats and houses— whatever work I could get. Then I worked on the highway out from Kenai for the Alaska Road Commission.

15In 1956–57 I landed in the hospital with tuberculosis, in the Laurel Beach Sanitarium in Seattle, for sixteen months. When I came home, my house was empty—no windows, no door, only a stove there. What I got was $30 a month from social security.

16The only person who helped me was Dan France, who was driving the school bus. He gave me the hindquarter of a moose, and he gave me some blankets, dishes, and pots, and some groceries. Then I built him a dory, and he paid me well.

17In 1960 I had to give up fishing because my arthritis got bad, but I kept on working wherever I could find work. In 1965 I went to work for Jack Farnsworth on a floating barge on which the freezer's chemicals had rotted everything below the decking. It was 20' x 60', what I repaired for him, and I worked on it for him for two summers.

18After that I repaired more boats and built more dories. Then the time came when I couldn't work anymore because of arthritis. So I went on food stamps, and later on welfare.

19Then after that, in 1972, my friend Jim Kari and his wife came to visit me. "I am interested in learning the Dena'ina language," he told me.

20"It is a hard language," I told him, but we got going on it. Then he came back in 1973 and at that time told me the Dena'ina language could be written. Then he started writing it and told me, "You write something too." I tried, but the pain was bad in my arm and hip. And he told me, "Don't give up on it."

21And finally I wrote the book *The Kenai People's Language* (1977). And (in 1979) this book took me out to the state of California, the state where my great-great-grandfather earned his name: Kalifornsky, who went with the first Russians to Fort Ross.

Łuq'a Ch'k'ezdelghayi

Tahbił tanełkiz. Łuq'a shegh dighelagh,. Dich'anełtan. Ch'u ghest'uts' ch'u nunghestseq'. Balik załchin. Nutin'at nutiha tsiq' tughełu. Yethdi chuq'eya ch'u esni eł bet'uh idghełq'en. Łq'ich'idi jani yethdi nunghełu. Ch'u nanłghal. Ch'u dghaznigi yidgheshchet. Yethdi heyi niłtu.

K'nuy'a Uhuch'el'ani

1Gu dach' qents'ugh'i ben dazdlu. Undadi ben en'at k'enuy'a qan gheneshu.

2K'iłkedi ba tanełu ch'u quggił ba tananłu. Łtaqul'i bidults'i. luq'u q'anik'danełnen.

3Betsen ghenhdi k'q'ush gheshghun. Ch'u yethdi dasgedi yighełu. Qughusht'a dayesh hdi qun, załghal, heyi niłtu.

George Ch'u Shi

1Gin yadi heyi shuq'u 1960s George [Peteroff] ił yach' North tinitunh yuh ts'dalts'i. George ghun yunit beldagh san. Shihdi hdukaq' hch'en yet ghu hdukaq' hyesh quht'ana qwa ch'a'iltlet.

2K'usht'a telgheł. Shi ki shi qyan ghash'an ideshni. Ił George ghun, "Yadi di? Yadi qwa di?" shełni.

3"Hch'ilneshigu," bedeshni. Suk Dena'ina sukdu nuhqulnish. Yuh T'ana Qwa łu qghe'ih yaghaliyi niłtu łu," bedeshni.

4Łuq'u didetl'ich' qwa quqelq' q'u qilt'an.

Putting Up Fish

I set the net in the water. A fish swam in to me. I took it out. And I cut it and made it into strips. I made *balik*. I put it in brine for two hours. Then I kept a fire of birch and cottonwood under it. I did that for nine days, then I took it down, and I bundled it. And I put it in the cache. Then it's for winter.

Beaver Trapping

1Over here there is a series of seven lakes. At the last lake I came upon a beaver lodge.

2I set traps in the water for them and I set snares in the water for them.

3There were eight of them staying inside (the lodge). I caught all of them. I made dried carcasses out of that meat. And I smoked them. When they were nicely wind cured, I bundled them up (keeping them) for winter.

George and I

1One winter in the 1960s George Peteroff and I were staying in a house out on North Road. George was in back, standing by the stove, and I was on the side by the door. Just then a little man appeared.

2I didn't move. I thought I was the only one who had seen it. Then George said to me, "What is that? What is that little man?"

3I told him, "Don't be scared. The Dena'ina used to tell stories about seeing the Little Housekeepers. It is good luck to see them."

4He was all green and he looked like asparagus (small, upright, layered like shingles).

The 1972 Potlatch

Written explanation of the potlatch held on March 4, 1972, by the Kenai Dena'ina. Peter Kalifornsky's first cultural writing, this presages themes in his later work.

The first words of the song are: "Where does everyone scatter on to like the wind, blow dust away." That is to every tribe of people that has a young man going to the Army. Some overseas and out on jobs, and the family moving from one place to the other countries.

The rest of the song mentions the relatives, friends, aunts, and so on. That they may come in with love and cheer, and the second part of the song, the same words are used. That was to everyone. That was at the program that everybody come in with love and cheer and be happy. That's why the song can't be sold, but the song could be used by any tribe under permission. That is, permission for their respected.

And there are four short stories. When the little ones with bearskin, and dance around it before they sit down, and the song that was sung for them.

They were out at their winter camp. There, the head man told his people, we are going to move down to the mouth of the river. Come and move along with me. That was down to their fish camp. They had to do lots of work before they sat down to rest for the night, and the story was told about the other planet had light so the old crow goes over to the other planet and steals the light and brings it back to this planet. Complete the story.

And that crow song is another story. The song *ya-la-oh-he-ye-he*. This story is before anybody thought of singing. At this time, the crow can make work and come there. He was walking along the beach, he came to a small river. On high-water mark, he found an old fish.

He was going to eat on the old fish, and he saw a camp just above him, so he turned himself into a nice-looking young man, and he visited the people and there were no men. He asked where the men folk were and the women told him they were out hunting, and he could see that they didn't have much to eat, but they offered him something to eat. But he had his mind on that old fish he saw on the beach, so he refused the food offered to him.

He asked for the scoop to go fishing and he went down the beach. There was a big cottonwood drift log so he took his one eye out and laid it on the drift log and he told his eye to say "*yo-ho*" if you see someone and he went down to the old fish to eat. By the time he started to eat, the eye said, "*yo-ho*" and he runs to the eye and there was no one. He spanks his old eye and laid it back on the log. You say "*yo-ho*" if you see somebody. The third time he didn't believe the old eye, so he went on eating the fish. He heard people talking. He ran up to the people.

The hunters were coming home without any meat. They asked him where he came from. He said you wouldn't know. I travel all over and seen many people. He came here and was trying to fish, but there were no fish.

The only one was an old one washed up on the beach, and some bird had been picking on it. He had a bandage over his eye. They asked and he said he had sand in his eye. They said let's look at it and he said no.

He told them I doctor myself when I get something like this or get sick. And he was in trouble. He had to think fast and outsmart people and get his eye back, so he told them, let's look farther up the river.

And he walked ahead of them up to where his eye was lying on the log and he picked it up and started to sing. [He] sounded finer. The people wanted to look at it. They said it looks like an eye. He said no you can't touch it. If you do, it will be unlucky to us. He's looking out for us, and he kept throwing it up and singing. [He] sounded finer. And he pulls the bandage off and let the old eye drop down in its socket. And he started to sing *ya-la-oh-he-ha-he*.

So the people learned that everything they do was *do-ya-do-ho*. And soon they had a tone and song with *oh-he-ya-he* added onto it. That is the story of song and the youngsters with the bear skin at potlatch program. That's the kids with the bear skin, it may mean something else to other tribes of Indians.

I don't know, and the game with wooden discs is called *ka-ma-gu* [*qamuga*]. It's the same as horseshoe game.

The people were on the trail to another village for a potlatch to camp on the trail, one poor boy didn't have an axe. He was asking a friend for his axe, and he said it will be fine and will have a big camp-fire, and we'll have games and have fun and the game played to guess the marked one in your hand. That game is called *chanlahe* [*ch'enlahi*] and the songs that were sung are all mixed languages of all the tribes around Cook Inlet. This song was made out in the ocean on the sea otter hunt, and they learned one another's language and made songs. When they got to the mainland, they played a game of *Chanlahe*. The costumes that could have been mixed at the potlatch program, but *noxri* [*nuhzhi*] had red ribbons. *Tolcina* [*Tulchina*] had blue ribbons. *Nalcina* [*Nulchina*] is related to Tolcina with white.

Index

Index

Wisconsin Studies in American Autobiography

William L. Andrews
General Editor

Robert F. Sayre
The Examined Self: Benjamin Franklin, Henry Adams, Henry James

Daniel B. Shea
Spiritual Autobiography in Early America

Lois Mark Stalvey
The Education of a WASP

Margaret Sams
Forbidden Family: A Wartime Memoir of the Philippines, 1941–1945
Edited, with an introduction, by Lynn Z. Bloom

Journeys in New Worlds: Early American Women's Narratives
Edited by William L. Andrews

Mark Twain
Mark Twain's Own Autobiography:
The Chapters from the North American Review
Edited, with an introduction, by Michael J. Kiskis

American Autobiography: Retrospect and Prospect
Edited by Paul John Eakin

Charlotte Perkins Gilman
The Living of Charlotte Perkins Gilman: An Autobiography
Introduction by Ann J. Lane

Caroline Seabury
The Diary of Caroline Seabury: 1854–1863
Edited, with an introduction, by Suzanne L. Bunkers

Cornelia Peak McDonald
*A Woman's Civil War: A Diary, with Reminiscences of the War,
from March 1862*
Edited, with an introduction, by Minrose C. Gwin

Marian Anderson
My Lord, What a Morning
Introduction by Nellie Y. McKay

American Women's Autobiography: Fea(s)ts of Memory
Edited, with an introduction, by Margo Culley

Frank Marshall Davis
Livin' the Blues: Memoirs of a Black Journalist and Poet
Edited, with an introduction, by John Edgar Tidwell

Joanne Jacobson
Authority and Alliance in the Letters of Henry Adams

Kamau Brathwaite
The Zea Mexican Diary
Foreword by Sandra Pouchet Paquet

Genaro M. Padilla
*My History, Not Yours: The Formation of
Mexican American Autobiography*

Frances Smith Foster
*Witnessing Slavery: The Development of Ante-bellum
Slave Narratives*

Native American Autobiography: An Anthology
Edited, with an introduction, by Arnold Krupat

American Lives: An Anthology of Autobiographical Writing
Edited, with an introduction, by Robert F. Sayre

Carol Holly
*Intensely Family: The Inheritance of Family Shame
and the Autobiographies of Henry James*